THE CLASSIC CAR

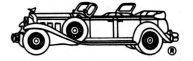

THE
CLASSIC
CAR

THE ULTIMATE BOOK ABOUT THE
WORLD'S GRANDEST AUTOMOBILES

EDITED BY
BEVERLY RAE KIMES

PRODUCED BY THE
CLASSIC CAR CLUB OF AMERICA

book design by Ralph D. Cox

published by the
Classic Car Club of America, Inc.
2300 East Devon Avenue, Suite 126
Des Plaines, Illinois 60018

typesetting and printing by
Stoyles Graphic Services, Inc.
Lake Mills, Iowa 50450

book trade distribution by

Publishers & Wholesalers ®

Library of Congress Catalog Card Number 90-84421
ISBN 0-9627868-0-2

CONTENTS

European Marques 546

Divers Classics 738

Index 749

CCCA: The Club

classic (klas'ik), adj., of the first or highest class or rank . . . n., something noteworthy of its kind and worth remembering. . . .

It was an idea whose time had come. At least this spirited band of enthusiasts thought so. The year was 1951. Owners of Packards, Cadillacs and the like—vintage late 1920's to early 1930's—had been finding to their chagrin upon arriving at old car meets that they were not eligible to participate because the vehicles they were driving were "too modern." The Antique Automobile Club of America, the nation's oldest organization in the hobby, had relegated the enthusiasts' chosen wheels to Class 19, designated "Tow Cars." Since these vehicles were, to their minds, more properly defined by the Latinate word above, a new organization seemed verily cried for.

The Classic Car Club of America was born later that year. In March of 1952, entertainer Herb Shriner invited the fledgling club to exhibit at the International Motor Sport Show held at the Grand Central Palace in New York City. A 1931 Cadillac V-16 All Weather Phaeton was spruced up and set up on the balcony—with a recruiting table alongside. Before the show, CCCA membership stood at twenty. By the end of the show, seventy more enthusiasts had been signed up. And the Club roster more than doubled again in the next six months. On September 17th, 1952 the Classic Car Club of America was incorporated with 212 founding members.

In January of 1953, Volume I Number 1 of *The Classic Car* magazine came off the press. That July the Club's first show—the Grand Classic—was held at Washington's Crossing State Park in New Jersey. In August the first tour—the CARavan—wended its way from the East Coast to Detroit where the Club was the guest of the Packard Motor Car Company, whose hospitality included a trek to Utica where the Classics were exercised on the famous Packard proving ground track.

July 12th, 1953: note the "modern cars" in the foreground in which spectators traveled to the first Grand Classic.

Above right: Ted Kavenagh, who incorporated the CCCA in September of '52, shown shortly thereafter in his 1930 Packard 733 Dual Cowl Phaeton. "I drove it all over New Jersey, New York, Pennsylvania, Vermont, Massachusetts and Connecticut," comments Ted, "visiting members and signing up new members."

Center right: The late Gordon Webber, the first president of the CCCA, addressing members at the first Grand Classic. Page opposite: Among the cars that attended, a Franklin, Duesenberg, Packard and Bentley 3½ Litre.

Below: The magazine's inaugural issue delineated the Classics in the new CCCA logo: Auburn, running boards; Cadillac, headlamps; Cord, horns; Chrysler, fenders; Duesenberg, body; Franklin, trunk; Kissel, front bumper; Lincoln, hood; Locomobile, door handles; Marmon, radiator shell; Nash, front fenders; Packard, windshields; Pierce-Arrow, taillights; Rolls-Royce, wheels; Stutz, rear bumper; Wills Sainte Claire, grey goose mascot. The logo was the idea of member S. Presley Blake, refined by artist member Don Clairmonte The third issue of The Classic Car detailed the first CARavan. Again, note the brand-new Packard among all the Classics.

THE CLASSIC CAR

January 1953

OFFICIAL QUARTERLY OF THE CLASSIC CAR CLUB OF AMERICA

First Issue

THE CLASSIC CAR

Fall 1953

OFFICIAL QUARTERLY OF THE CLASSIC CAR CLUB OF AMERICA

CARavan Issue 50c

Already the AACA had changed its Class 19 designation to "Classic Cars." The nice thing about ideas whose time has come is how quickly the word gets around and is cheerfully accepted. The CCCA proceeded from strength to strength. By 1960 membership passed the 2,500 mark. Today members number more than 5,000 worldwide. The Club is headquartered at O'Hare Lake Office Plaza near Chicago. But, intrinsically, the CCCA is everywhere that Classic cars are celebrated.

Which brings us to the matter of definition. What is a Classic car? This book answers that question. Just a few notes here will suffice. Vintage is the first requisite. The Club defines the Classic Era as 1925 (by which time automobiles had emerged from their own antiquity) through 1948 (or those first years following World War II when the cars produced echoed those built prior to the onset of hostilities in Europe and Pearl Harbor in America). Distinction is the second requisite for a Classic: noteworthy design, refined engineering, superior workmanship. The Classification & Technical Services Committee studies long and hard before recommending that any automobile be accorded Classic status. The Board of Directors ponders the issue further before granting approval. That the Club does its homework well is indicated in the acceptance by hobby organizations worldwide of the parameters for both Classics and the Classic Era as defined by the CCCA.

"To further the restoration and preservation . . . to provide a channel of communication . . . to bring together in good fellowship all who own or admire these finest examples of automotive craftsmanship." That is the credo of the CCCA. The Club is fond of pointing out that, although its cars are elite, its members are not elitist. Camaraderie is as integral to the Club as its Classics. And, oh, what a good time is had.

In the nearly four decades of the CCCA's life, 5,000 trophies have been awarded at 183 Grand Classics. And over 1,700 Classics have toured over 17,000 miles in 28 CARavans. From one show in 1953, the Club has graduated to at least seven Grand Classics each year, on two dates and in locations throughout the United States. Alas, the CCCA can no longer trek to the Packard Motor Car Company as was done in '53 but in the years since CARavans have traveled everywhere—from the Pacific Northwest to Nova Scotia, from California to the Carolinas, from New England to the heart of Dixie, and throughout the Middle West. The Club gets together every January for its Annual Meeting which for many years was held at Buck Hill Falls in Pennsylvania but recently has become a moveable feast traveling to a different area of the country each year. And there's more—for in addition to the big national events, activities are organized throughout the year and throughout America by the twenty-seven chartered Classic Car Club Regions.

Readers of this book who are not already members are invited to join the CCCA. An interest in Classics is the sole requirement for membership. For information, write to CCCA Club Headquarters, 2300 East Devon, Suite 126, Des Plaines, IL 60018. Join us in continuing to celebrate the most glorious motorcars the world has ever known.

CCCA: The Classic Dividend

By Richard G. Gold

A great deal of attention is paid in the media today to the value of Classic cars. Whenever a new high mark is realized at an auction, headlines are everywhere—and people naturally become curious. I would bet that every CCCA member whose Classic appears in this book has been asked, a lot more than once, "how much is it worth?" To the owner who loves his car, there is no ready answer.

How can a tangible value be put on a prized possession that provides so many intangible joys? How can you realistically quantify the worth of an object that has become a vital and integral part of your life?

Well, I will try. I am a businessman and will use a business-like approach. My Classic car "balance sheet" computes like this:

The Golds in their 1931 Pierce-Arrow Model 42 Sport Phaeton, purchased in 1948,
the year they were married. With Dick and Joyce in the front seat is granddaughter Andrea,
aged one-and-a-half. Eleven-year-old Matthew stands on the running board.
In the rear seat are grandchildren Michael, seven; Lisa, six; and Michelle, thirteen.

In an average year, I drive my Classic about a thousand miles around the Minnesota city in which I live. This represents about thirty hours. Driving a Classic is a rewarding experience for me. I feel it's worth at least $25.00 per hour, or a total of $750.00 for the season.

About once a week, during the warm months, I take my Classic to work, which is great fun. I park the car behind our building and talk to customers all day about it. A real ego trip this is. I value it at $50.00 per day; figuring, conservatively, twelve times a year, and the total is $600.00.

Now to cleaning and polishing. Admittedly, hard work is involved here but the admiring looks from the neighbors make it well worth $25.00 per session. I usually clean up my car every week during the summer; sixteen times at $25.00 per totals $400.00.

At least six times a year I drive my Classic to a Classic Car Club function. This experience is worth at least $100.00 per event, for a total of $600.00. Then there is the annual Grand Classic, the ultimate show for a CCCA member—no better place to see lots of other Classics, no better place to have your Classic seen by other Club members. At the Grand Classic you meet old friends, make new ones, have your Classic judged by your peers and hope to take home a trophy. The Grand Classic is without a doubt a $500.00 day.

Next comes the CARavan, the Classic Car Club's famous touring event which takes members and their cars to wonderfully scenic areas from coast to coast. There is at least one CARavan a year. Motoring in Classics with your friends is the greatest time. CARavan driving should be worth at least $50.00 per hour, but there are factors that can cut the rate down. For instance, your wife looking at the gas gauge and saying, "Dick, are we running out of gas?," or glancing at another gauge and commenting, "Dick, I think the car is getting hot because that little needle is wiggling all the time!" Plus such sensory perceptions as "Dick, I smell something!" or "Dick, I hear a funny noise!" And pragmatic pessimism like "Dick, I think you made the wrong turn, we're going to get lost and we'll never catch up with the rest of the CARavan!" All this cuts the rate in half. Only $25.00 per hour. Total six hours a day for five days, and we have $750.00. But . . . driving is not all there is to a CARavan. At the end of each day's tour, there is a cocktail party—the perfect place to brag about how great your Classic is performing. Every day for five days at $50.00 per session equals $250.00.

Family time has to be counted too, like driving around with grandkids in the rumble seat. This is really heavy time. Not much will beat this. At least $100.00 per day about six times a summer for a total of $600.00.

Sunday brunch in a Classic? You bet. Another super opportunity to show off your car and meet a lot of nice people. This is worth at least $50.00 per Sunday a half-dozen times a year for a total of $300.00.

Touring in the autumn makes for fabulous enjoyment as well. Many of our CCCA Regions sponsor Fall Foliage tours. Seeing the colors in your Classic and amidst friends is worth at least $500.00. And each October, there is Hershey, the largest old car meet in the world, with a flea market that goes on for miles and miles. The time spent there looking for parts or accessories for your Classic is the ultimate treasure hunt—three days, eight hours a day, at least $15.00 per hour, for a total of $360.00.

Now, let's add all this up:

1. Normal Driving	30 hours at	$ 25.00	$ 750.00
2. Driving to Work	12 times at	$ 50.00	600.00
3. Cleaning and Polishing	16 times at	$ 25.00	400.00
4. Club Functions	6 times at	$100.00	600.00
5. Grand Classic	1 time at	$500.00	500.00
6. CARavan	5 days at	$150.00	750.00
7. CARavan Cocktail Sessions	5 times at	$ 50.00	250.00
8. Grandkids in Car	6 times at	$100.00	600.00
9. Sunday Brunch	6 times at	$ 50.00	300.00
10. Fall Tour	1 time at	$500.00	500.00
11. Hershey Shopping	24 hours at	$ 15.00	360.00
		TOTAL	$5,610.00

How about that! A $5,610 clear profit on my Classic for one year. Say the "book" value of the car is $30,000; that's an 18.7% return on investment. What other investment can match it? Banks don't even come close. And the stock market has been known to behave erratically. Imagine, a risk-free $5,610 profit! But what about taxes? Won't Uncle Sam want his share? Wondering how much tax I would have to pay on this windfall profit of mine, I called my son-in-law Bill, a tax attorney and C.P.A. He contacted the ultimate authority for an opinion. I couldn't believe my ears. The Internal Revenue Service determined that the profit was not taxable. The I.R.S. doesn't do that sort of thing often.

So you see, the actual market value of any Classic—whether it is $10,000 or $350,000—has little to do with what its value is to the Classic car enthusiast. Every time you display your Classic or just look at it sitting in the garage or in front of your house, it makes a profit for you. And that profit is tax-free! Every time you drive your Classic, it pays you a dividend.

Cynics like to say that romance is dead. Cynics obviously don't own Classic cars. Those who say the age of adventure is over as well have not experienced motoring in a Classic. And for sheer exhilarating pride? Just look at the face of a Classic owner when he gazes at his car.

CCCA: The Museum

by Norman H. Knight

One could begin by saying that what follows is the story of an idea that, like Topsy, "just growed." But what is really fascinating is how fast it "growed." The Classic Car Club of America Museum outdid Topsy. Briefly, this is the chronology.

In the spring of 1981 Dick Gold presented the idea of a Classic car museum to the board of directors of the Classic Car Club of America. The feasibility of the project was explored and rapidly propelled into a reality. As a neophyte museum director, I offered my help and suggested an association with the Gilmore Car Museum. After all, we had ninety acres of lovely landscaped grounds at Hickory Corners, plus thirty Classic cars and an endowment. The following dates reveal the chronology and formation of the Gilmore-Classic Car Club Museums.

• February 9th, 1982: The Classic Car Club of America board of directors approved the creation of an affiliated museum using the Classic Car Club of America name.

• August 15th, 1982: The Gilmore Museum in Kalamazoo, Michigan was proposed as a possible home for the CCCA Museum.

• January 13th, 1983: The CCCA Museum received tax exempt status.

• August 15th, 1984: The CCCA Museum board of trustees approved affiliation with the Gilmore Car Museum in Kalamazoo.

• October 11th, 1984: "Resolved, by the CCCA Museum trustees, that the 'Agreement Respecting Property of Exhibition' with the name changed for the museums to Gilmore-Classic Car Club Museums is hereby approved. . . ."

• June 20th, 1987: Dedication of the Classic Car Club Museum Barn.

• May 21st, 1989: Dedication of the Noel Thompson Library.

Since 1987 the Museum has sponsored four elegant Concours d'Elegance. The first was the Duesenberg Experience which featured fifty-three Duesenbergs, and Sergio Franchi as Grand Marshal. Not to be outdone the 1988 Concours featured Rolls-Royce and Bentleys. The 1989 Experience was dedicated to V-12 and V-16 auto-mobiles—an outstanding show. The Formal Car Experience took the limelight for 1990 with nearly one hundred elegant vehicles for display. Obviously this event was planned from the beginning as an annual one. In 1991 we will celebrate Senior cars, those CCCA Classics which have been perennials at the Grand Classics and

enjoy venerated status. We're already thinking about themes for future Experiences.

The word "experience" was quite deliberately chosen for our concours, incidentally, for at Hickory Corners we believe that historic cars should not merely be seen. By bringing them together in a setting of rolling hills with long, winding "driveways" and a circular "test track," these wonderful automobiles can truly be experienced.

Let me give you a tour of the facilities, with a little background regarding how all this came about.

The Gilmore Car Museum was founded as the result of a restoration project on a 1920 Pierce-Arrow by Donald Gilmore, chairman of the board of The Upjohn Company in Kalamazoo, Michigan. This project was started at his summer home on Gull Lake in 1962 with the help of two friends, Maynard Stimpson and Dr. Prosper Bernard. Like many restorations, this one dragged on and was finally finished in mid-winter under a tent with aid of a kerosene construction heater. Mr. Gilmore found these conditions a bit austere, so he purchased three farms of some 280 acres just to the north of his summer home to provide sufficient space for his new-found antique car hobby. Then he scouted the nearby countryside in search of distinctive old wooden barns to house his growing collection of antique vehicles.

First, two old wooden peg barns were relocated to form an entry way to the museum. One barn serves as the office complex and the other is utilized for storage. The Carriage House was built specifically to house antique cars and provide a respite for weary antique car travellers. It has a small kitchen to serve light refreshments and a waiting room in the form of a silo to provide a view of the inner grounds. The renowned Kleba mascot or hood ornament collection is located on the mezzanine. It is composed of more than 500 examples from Europe, Canada and the United States. The collection was acquired over a period of thirty years and dates from the early 1900's to the present. It could not be duplicated today. Mike Kleba and Henry Peksyk of Toronto chose us as the recipient in return for keeping this fine collection intact. On occasion one might find a collector with a few hood ornaments from a particular make, but nowhere in the world will you find a collection as complete as this one.

In the early days of automotive development, it was not uncommon to seek noted artists and

Aerial view of the Gilmore Car Museum during the 1970's prior to the association with the Classic Car Club of America. Below: The Classic Car Club Museum Barn, with the Noel Thompson Library to the right and the ramp leading to the Museum's second exhibition floor on the left.

Photographed at the Hickory Corners bus depot, two recent acquisitions for the Classic Car Club Barn: the 1930 Packard 734 Speedster Sedan donated by Louis Steinberg, the 1938 Packard 1607 Convertible Victoria, Dietrich, donated by Richard Roach. Just part of the mascot/hood ornament collection is shown here. In the case above, third from the left on the top row, is an Aztec Indian signed by French sculptor Bazin. In the second row is Rudolph Valentino's cobra from his Isotta. The case above left includes a group of ornaments commemorating Lindbergh's flight. The case below left comprises a group of Cadillac hood ornaments, including the herald.

sculptors for the design of hood ornaments. Among them were such masters as Tiffany, Bazin, Lalique and Baccarat. Quite often a coat of arms was incorporated into the design. The Cadillac herald of 1929 wears a coat of arms as a shield. In like manner, the Packard cloisonné crest used on the crankhole cover and radiator is a coat of arms. The Packard pelican is a design motif taken from the crest. Other unique works of art in the collection include an entire case of replicas, twenty in all, commemorating the *Spirit of St. Louis*. They date from 1927 when Charles A. Lindbergh flew across the Atlantic Ocean solo in his small airplane. Another piece is a U-16 Bucciali hood ornament from the only such car ever made. Rudolph Valentino, the early silent movie star, drove an Isotta Fraschini with a serpent-designed radiator cap. We have that cap as well as one given to him by the "Woman in Red" following his production of *The Sheik*.

During the early 1930's, six Bugatti Royales were produced in France. All have survived to this day—some sixty years after their manufacture. The most expensive automobiles ever built, they were made with such precision as never to wear out mechanically. Because of their longevity, Ettore Bugatti chose an elephant standing on its hind legs as a fitting hood ornament for these cars. The symbol continues today as we celebrate white elephant sales for items that haven't worn out. A museum in Mulhouse, France has two Bugatti Royales: one vehicle sports an original hood ornament, the other wears a replica. The Museum is proud to possess an original Bugatti Royale hood ornament.

Other interesting ornaments include a bronze-faced Indian from Pontiac, a chrome-plated hand grenade from World War II, a series of Michelin tiremen, as well as mascots from Chevrolet, Plymouth and Pierce-Arrow. When you become saturated with viewing automobiles, all containing four wheels, a front seat and a radiator, take a few moments to look at the hood ornament collection as an art form.

The impressive two-story Campania Barn was built in 1897 about thirty miles west of the Museum on the Todd Farms, which at the turn of the century supplied peppermint and spearmint oil to an enterprising young gum manufacturer in Chicago named P. K. Wrigley. The barn was dismantled, moved and rebuilt on the Museum grounds. A ramp permits easy access to the second floor, or one may use the ornate cherry staircase rescued from one of the local mansions. A full-sized replica of the *Kitty Hawk* dangles from the ceiling, while Wilbur Wright at the controls glowers at the crowd below. The second floor has hosted many wedding receptions, political rallies and Great Gatsby parties. About twenty-five vehicles can be displayed in the barn. Currently, six of the fourteen different cars manufactured in Kalamazoo are displayed. These include a Michigan, Barley, Roamer, Checker, Jeep and Handley-Knight.

The structure called S Barn is a replica of a horse foaling barn built on the shores of Lake Michigan. The owner refused to sell the building to Donald Gilmore, but did permit him to take a few measurements and to construct a duplicate. It is 110 feet in height to the barn peak. It houses Gilmore's very early antique cars as well as a narrow-gauge Porter locomotive, steam vehicles, the Cadillac and Ford collections (ranging from 1902 to 1965).

G Barn, originally located on the Upjohn Farms at G Avenue, was moved to the museum complex for a special purpose. Within it is a unique movie set from Walt Disney's *The Gnomemobile*. A gift to Gilmore from Disney upon completion of the movie, the set is a doorway and back seat built three times normal size to make people resemble gnomes. Walt Disney came to Kalamazoo in the fall of 1966 to see the Gilmore Car Museum, and together he and Donald Gilmore dedicated the set in its new location.

Other structures include the bus depot, which is a replica of the Marshall, Michigan train station, a machine shop, van barn, fire barn and railroad signal tower. The north ninety acres was landscaped and the grounds accessed by three miles of Class A roads, including a half-mile oval timing track. The museum was opened to the public on July 31st, 1966 with Dr. Prosper Bernard as curator for the sixty cars on display.

Sadly, Donald Gilmore died in December 1979. But he made certain the Museum would be perpetuated, by charging his children and grandchildren with the civic responsibility of administering and maintaining the Museum for all to enjoy, just as he had enjoyed his hobby. To this end, Genevieve and Donald Gilmore endowed the Museum with funds to perpetuate its place of honor as one of the finest transportation museums in the country. Dr. Prosper Bernard died in December 1980, and was replaced by Norman Knight as director, which brings us back to the beginning of this story, for it was shortly thereafter that I suggested the association with the CCCA. It's hard to believe the progress that has been made in less than a decade.

Currently, the Gilmore-Classic Car Club Museums are the repository for one of the largest collections of Packard automobiles anywhere in one location. They range from a 1905 Model L Touring to a 1956 Model 400. The Cadillac display runs the gamut from a 1903 Demi Tonneau to a 1965 Model 75 Limousine. The fifteen-car Rolls-Royce collection ranges from a 1910 Silver Ghost Roi des Belges Touring up to a 1938 P-III Park Ward Limousine. The earliest vehicle in the collection is an 1899 Locomobile originally owned by Dr. W. E. Upjohn, founder of The Upjohn Company. It was the first new car sold in Kalamazoo. About 120 vehicles are currently on display.

On behalf of everyone at Hickory Corners, I wish to express deep indebtedness to a large number of enthusiastic members of the Classic Car Club of America for vision, confidence and gifts in making the Gilmore-Classic Car Club Museums one of the finest institutions on earth.

INTRODUCTION TO THIS BOOK

This is the biggest book ever on a grand subject. Within these pages you will find the history of the companies that built Classics and how the cars evolved through the Classic Era. Facts and figures abound—when engineering refinements were introduced, when body styles changed, how many examples were built, the technical specs, the price tags, what differentiates one model or model year from another.

But there is much more. This book is a Classic potpourri—for, in addition to history and documentation, it has enthusiasm and emotion. Never before has the story of Classic cars been told through the eyes (and hearts) of the people who love them. This book, in essence, has over 600 authors.

Getting together and talking cars is one of the great pleasures of the CCCA. Here club members get together and do just that. Briefly, the logistics were these. An invitation was extended to the entire membership to share their cars with us and the world. The response was super. From coast to coast, and on both sides of the Atlantic, scrapbooks were scoured and shutters clicked furiously as Classics were photographed for this book. Memories were jogged and files were perused as Classic data sheets were prepared for each car.

"Don't be afraid to brag," owners were told—and they weren't. Classic people are fiercely loyal. One of the glories of possession is the visceral subjectivity that it engenders and the spirited good fun one owner has in proclaiming his automobile's superiority over another. A Classic car is a passionate love affair.

Lest passions amongst readers of this book be misdirected, let it be noted that the information and opinions regarding a specific Classic are the owner's own and do not necessarily reflect the thoughts or conclusions of the editor (who has her own Classic favorites) or the Club (which impartially views all Classics with equal favor). Questions regarding a Classic should be posed to its owner who will doubtless relish the opportunity to document and talk further about his or her car.

It should also be noted that Classic ownership is as submitted for this book. Inevitably, in a project of this extended duration, some cars have since changed hands. Lovers of Classic cars are no more fickle than the general population but are just as likely to be occasionally seduced away from a long-time inamorata by more comely and shapely wheels.

More than 100 companies worldwide produced these cars during the Classic Era. Classics run a wide gamut—from production and series custom cars to those one-of-a-kind (or one-off) automobiles especially created for the salons or specifically tailored for an individual customer. Many CCCA members have been able to trace their cars back to the original (sometimes famous, sometimes infamous) owner, others have been able to unearth fascinating details regarding their car's life during the Classic Era, still others have stories to tell of their Classic's latterday career. Before rescue, some of these superb automobiles were used as drag racers, to power sawmills, to store oats.

Many of the cars in this book have been painstakingly restored, others remain quite purposefully original. Some are perennials on the show circuit with trophies aplenty; others are Classics for the open road, tour cars or "drivers," as CCCA members like to say. Many Classics are both—for "show and go," in another phrase popular to the hobby.

What is it about these cars that appeals to their owners? You'll learn this in full measure. The reasons, like the cars themselves, vary: aesthetics, prowess, history, nostalgia. This is a sentimental book sometimes, a funny one sometimes too. As anyone who has ever possessed an historic car knows, adventure is part and parcel of ownership. And the adventure can be alternately poignant and hilarious.

Many of the Classic marques (or makes) that follow are instantly recognizable. Some perhaps the reader will be encountering for the first time. In keeping with the Classic Era, the photographs are black and white. Whenever possible, the cars were shot against a background appropriate to the period. But if salon, coachbuilder and factory photography a half century ago was invariably in black and white, promotional artwork often exploded in a rainbow of colors. Classic catalogues and advertisements were designed to entice; included in this book is a big color portfolio illustrating how lavish the enticement was. This also provides effective counterpoint to the Classics themselves. The cars were works of art; no less so was the promotion that sold them.

For any project the magnitude of this book, the acknowledgements necessarily are many. First, to Richard G. Gold whose idea this project was and whose enthusiasm was contagious—as witness the hundreds of CCCA members who participated and who deserve a round of applause. To the members of the CCCA board of directors who carefully reviewed all of the cars submitted for the book, gratitude is great.

Equally so is the appreciation extended to those CCCA members who meticulously read text sections for Classic marques in which their expertise is considerable, who made sure the cars were designated as they had been by the factory, verified production, horsepower figures and the like, checked the facts and made innumerable suggestions to enhance the text. Grateful thanks to Bill Abbott, Bob Belf, Barry Briskman, Bill Davis, Irv Davis, George Dragone, Dick Greene, Bill Greer, John Holcolm, Tom Hubbard, Jim Hull, C. A. Leslie, Bill Locke, Al McEwan, Pete McManus, Skip Marketti, Duke Marston, Paul O'Malley, Gene Perkins, Jack Rabell, Jerry Remlinger, Dick Roach, Chip Rohr, Bob Rooke, John Sivoveland, Stan Smith, Matt Sonfield, Truman Stockton, Bruce Thomas, Ed Wachs and Karl Zahm.

And a big tip of the hat to Kitty Katzell, Fred Roe, Bill and Jo Snyder and Dale Wells, who graciously proofread the entire text in galley form. Those who helped coordinate the art and divers Classic portfolios are acknowledged in those sections, and are thanked here. The dust jacket to this book effectively acknowledges the talent of Roy Query, as does the title page artwork the deft hand of Walter E. Gosden. Thank you, Roy; thank you, Walt.

Special notes of appreciation are extended to Katie Robbins, CCCA executive administrator, and to Cindy Werner, headquarters secretary, for cheerfully replying only "when do you need it?" whenever asked a favor and then following through even faster. Finally, boundless gratitude to Jim Cox, editorial associate, research consultant, photographer, associate art director, genial go-fer and non-union laborer, my husband and "jim of all trades," without whose support this book would not yet be completed.

"THE BOOK"—that's what this project has been called by CCCA members during the nearly three years from inception to realization. At long last, here it is: THE BOOK—an epic celebration of Classic cars by the people who know them best. All 600+ authors, and their editor, hope you enjoy.

Beverly Rae Kimes

New York, New York
September 1990

ROSTER OF DESIGNATED CLASSICS 1925-1948

A.C.—All
Adler—Please Apply
Alfa Romeo—All
Alvis—Speed 20, Speed 25, and 4.3 litre
Amilcar—Supercharged Sports Model
Armstrong Siddeley—Please Apply
Aston-Martin—All 1927 through 1939
Auburn—All 8- and 12-cylinder
Austro-Daimler—All
Ballot—Please Apply
Bentley—All
Benz—Please Apply
Blackhawk—All
BMW—327, 328, 327/318 and 335
Brewster—All Heart Front Fords
Brough Superior—Please Apply
Bucciali—TAV 8, TAV 30, TAV 12 and Double Huit
Bugatti—All except Type 52
Buick—1931-1942 90 Series
Cadillac—All 1925 through 1935
    All twelves and sixteens
    1936-1948—All 63, 65, 67, 70, 72, 75, 80, 85, 90
    1938-1947—60 Special
    1940-1947—All 62 Series
Chenard-Walcker—Please Apply
Chrysler—1926 through 1930 Imperial 80, 1929 Imperial L,
    1931 through 1937 Imperial Series CG, CH, CL and CW
      Newports and Thunderbolts
    1934 CX
    1935 C-3; 1936 C-11
    1937 through 1948 Custom Imperial, Crown Imperial
      Series C-15, C-20, C-24, C-27, C-33, C-37, C-40
Cord—All
Cunningham—Series V6, V7, V8, V9
Dagmar—6-80
Daimler—All 8- and 12-cylinder
Darracq—8-cylinder and 4-litre 6 cylinder
Delage—Model D-8
Delahaye—Series 135, 145, 165
Delaunay Belleville—6-cylinder
Doble—All
Dorris—All
Duesenberg—All
duPont—All
Excelsior—Please Apply
Farman—Please Apply
Fiat—Please Apply
F.N.—Please Apply
Franklin—All models except 1933-34 Olympic
Frazer Nash—Please Apply
Graham—1930-1931 Series 137
Graham-Paige—1929-1930 Series 837
Hispano-Suiza—All French models
    Spanish models T56, T56BIS, T64
Horch—All
Hotchkiss—Please Apply
Hudson—1929 Series L
Humber—Please Apply
Invicta—All
Isotta Fraschini—All
Itala—All
Jaguar—1946-48 2½ litre, 3½ litre (Mark IV)
Jensen—Please Apply
Jordan—Speedway Series Z
Julian—All
Kissel—1925-26, 1927 8-75, 1928 8-90 and 8-90 White Eagle,
    1929-31 8-126

Lagonda—All models except 1933-40 Rapier
Lanchester—Please Apply
Lancia—Please Apply
LaSalle—1927 through 1933
Lincoln—All L, KA, KB, and K, 1941 168 H and 1942 268 H
Lincoln Continental—All
Locomobile—All models 48 and 90, 1927-29 Model 8-80, 1929 8-88
Marmon—All 16-cylinder, 1925-26 74, 1927 75, 1928 E75,
    1930 Big 8, 1931 88 and Big 8
Maserati—Please Apply
Maybach—All
McFarlan—TV6 and 8
Mercedes—All
Mercedes-Benz—All 230 and up, K, S, SS, SSK, Grosser
    and Mannheim
Mercer—All
M.G.—1935-39 SA, 1938-39 WA
Minerva—All except 4-cylinder
NAG—Please Apply
Nash—1931 Series 8-90, 1932 Series 9-90, Advanced 8, and
    Ambassador 8, 1933-34 Ambassador 8
Packard—All sixes and eights 1925 through 1934; all twelves
    1935 Models 1200 through 1205, 1207 and 1208
    1936 Models 1400 through 1405, 1407 and 1408
    1937 Models 1500 through 1502 and 1506 through 1508
    1938 Models 1603 through 1605, 1607 and 1608
    1939 Models 1703, 1705, 1707 and 1708
    1940 Models 1803, 1804, 1805, 1806, 1807 and 1808
    1941 Models 1903, 1904, 1905, 1906, 1907 and 1908
    1942 Models 2003, 2004, 2005, 2006, 2007 and 2008
    1946-47 Models 2106 and 2126—All Darrin-bodied
Peerless—1925 Series 67, 1926-28 Series 69, 1930-31 Custom 8,
    1932 Deluxe Custom 8
Peugeot—Please Apply
Pierce-Arrow—All
Railton—Please Apply
Raymond Mays—Please Apply
Renault—45 HP
Reo—1931-33 8-31, 8-35, 8-52, Royale Custom 8,
    1934 N1, N2, and 8-52
ReVere—All
Riley—Please Apply
Roamer—1925 8-88, 6-54e, 4-75, and 4-85e, 1926 4-75e, 4-85e,
    and 8-88, 1927-29 8-88, 1929 and 1930 8-120
Rochet-Schneider—Please Apply
Röhr—Please Apply
Rolls-Royce—All
Ruxton—All
Squire—All
S.S. and SS Jaguar—1932 through 1940 S.S. 1, S.S. 90,
    SS Jaguar and SS Jaguar 100
Stearns-Knight—All
Stevens-Duryea—All
Steyr—Please Apply
Studebaker—1929-33 President except Model 82
Stutz—All
Sunbeam—8-cylinder and 3-litre Twin Cam
Talbot—105C and 110C
Talbot Lago—150C
Tatra—Please Apply
Triumph—Dolomite 8 and Gloria 6
Vauxhall—25-70 and 30-98
Voisin—All
Wills Sainte Claire—All
Willys-Knight—Series 66, 66A, 66B—Please Apply

1925-1948 custom-bodied cars not listed above: Please Apply.

AMERICAN MARQUES

The face of Bill Locke's 1931 Mercer Model SR Convertible Coupe by Merrimac.

Prohibition was the law of the land—and cheerfully broken. Prosperity was rampant—and, it was thought, would go on forever. Bobbed hair, bathtub gin, rolled stockings, plus fours, the Charleston, the Black Bottom—probably no decade in American history was more hedonistically raucous than the Roaring Twenties. Much of the noise—and the prosperity—came from cars. In 1925 there were nearly twenty million automobiles in America, more than twice the number from 1920. While Henry Ford was putting the nation on wheels with his Model T for "Every Man," other men (and women) were opting for more luxurious transport. In an era when, for many, desire had supplanted need, only the best was good enough. Classic cars were a reflection of the age of unalloyed optimism. Then the Jazz Age met with the Great Depression—or, as F. Scott Fitzgerald wrote, "somebody had blundered, and the most expensive orgy in history was over." How Classic marques coped with the new exigencies—or were unable to—is reflected herein as well. In the portfolios that follow, American Classics are presented alphabetically, with individual sections for those marques more plentiful on the road during the Classic Era—and in the club today. . . .

In essence, the Black Hawk was to Stutz what the LaSalle was to Cadillac—or, in the Indianapolis company's own words, "a worthy companion, a true blood-brother, smaller, lower in price—but with the same aristocratic parentage." Its designation derived from the Black Hawk Speedster, the high performance Stutz which went racing in 1927 and was hands-down AAA National Stock Champion. Trading on that impressive name for its brand-new car made sense, of course, although apparently the company was not sure precisely how to do it. "The name on the headlamp bar badge reads 'Black-Hawk,' with a hyphen, if you please," comments Alvin Harris, "while the name on the door sill is clearly 'Black Hawk' (two words)." Stutz catalogue references indicate manufacture by "the Black Hawk Division of the Stutz Motor Car Company." For differentiation purposes, advertisements for the new marque, and its own catalogue, spelled the name "Blackhawk" (one word)—usually. It is certainly a conundrum.

One word or two, hyphen or no, this companion car was truly a blood-brother. The radiator ornament was a sundial (the Stutz's was Ra, the sun god). Body styles were as varied as the larger cars (but did not include the boattail that was the Stutz Black Hawk's alone). With eight cylinders (Continental engine), like John Morgan's Speedster, developed horsepower was 88 from 268.5 cubic inches. As an overhead cam six (Stutz's Vertical Eight less two cylinders), the respective figures were 85 and 241.6. Both eight- and six-cylinder Black Hawks were on a 127½-inch-wheelbase chassis. Comparatively, the big Stutzes that year were 322-cubic-inch 113 hp eights on 134½-and 145-inch wheelbases. A price tag of just over $3,500 for the Black Hawk was about half what it cost to buy a Stutz. And it bought a lot of car.

"Sitting behind the slim steering wheel on a heavily-padded leather seat with the right armrest down is like being ensconced in a cockpit," says Alvin Harris. "The instrument cluster is neatly displayed and features indirect lighting for night driving. The overhead cam six-cylinder engine is entirely reliable

1929 Black Hawk Model L-8 Speedster.   *Owner: John E. Morgan of Manalapan, Florida.*

1929 Black Hawk Model L-6 Speedster.   Owner: Alvin J. Harris of Sequim, Washington.

1929 Black Hawk Model L-6 Speedster

Owner: Don Presson of Clovis, California

and performance is brisk in the lower gears. In my view, the Black Hawk was given more graceful fenders and better proportioned body dimensions than the Stutz had. At approximately 4,000 pounds, a low center of gravity and frame rails with the structural rigidity of I-beams, this car has no creaks or rattles.''

''My wife and I restored this car from the chassis back up, which required several years,'' says Don Presson of his Speedster. ''I purchased the car in 1979 in good condition. It had a lizard pattern leather upholstery, and I was fortunate to obtain the exact original. The original top and side curtains were with the car so I could have patterns made. I also matched the paint to the original. Today the car looks just like it did in the Stutz showroom in 1929.''

Black Hawk sales for 1929 totalled 1,310 cars vis-á-vis Stutz sales of approximately 2,000 for the same period. Introduction during the stock market crash year was inopportune for a brand-new car. In 1930, after approximately 280 Black Hawks were built, the marque was quietly discontinued.

B R E W S T E R

In 1934 a Brewster body was among the sublime metaphors Cole Porter used in his song "You're the Top" from the smash Broadway musical *Anything Goes*. The timing couldn't have been better for John Inskip, the president of Rolls-Royce of America and its wholly-owned subsidiary, Brewster & Company. Those firms were now being evolved into Springfield Manufacturing Corporation so that Rolls-Royce might avoid the stigma of bankruptcy of its American branch, which seemed imminent as the Great Depression took hold. Business failure wasn't Inskip's plan, however; he thought he had come up with an idea to avoid bankruptcy altogether. And it was a good one: a custom Brewster built on a Ford V-8 chassis. Body styles would be four: town car, limousine, convertible coupe, convertible sedan, all carrying the same $3,500 price tag. This was about half the price of custom-built creations, which would appeal to a clientele that continued to crave luxury but could no longer easily afford it. And the plebian chassis would appeal to those who had managed to survive the crash financially unscathed but considered it *déclassé* to flaunt their good fortune in an era of soup kitchens and bread-lines. (They could say they were driving a Ford.)

A Brewster car was not itself a new idea. From 1915 until the company's acquisition by Rolls-Royce of America in 1926, a Knight-engined Brewster had been produced in the firm's Long Island City (New York) plant. The new car would, however, also be built in the Rolls-Royce plant in Springfield, Massachusetts. And—another good idea—Inskip said his concept for the Brewster Town Car was "on the principle of a fountain pen: that chassis parts, even the chassis itself, could be renewed or replaced from time to time and still have a beautiful Brewster body which was worth more than the asking price of the car." Some owners—which included the estimable likes of Vincent Astor, Al Jolson, Gertrude Lawrence, Edsel Ford, Fred Waring and (not surprisingly) Cole Porter—did indeed swap chassis later on, and Inskip was of course happy to put his Brewster body on another chassis if the client so chose. A few did opt for Buick, Cadillac, Lincoln, Packard and Rolls-Royce as the basis for their Brewster.

Most chose the Ford V-8 chassis, however, which was lengthened fifteen inches (to 127) and considerably revamped (indeed, improved) to accept the Inskip-designed Brewster coachwork. Production of the cars began in 1934 and ended in 1936. Inskip had been unduly optimistic. A good idea did not necessarily translate to business success in that era. Approximately 135 Brewsters were built, most in Springfield, perhaps a few at the Long Island City plant. The vast majority were town cars.

The production number of Convertible Coupes, like William Lyon's car, is not known. Brewster

1935 Brewster Convertible Coupe.   *Owner: William Lyon of Trabuco Canyon, California.*

1935 Brewster Town Car   Owners: Pete & Joanne McManus of Thornton, Pennsylvania

1934 Brewster Convertible Sedan
Owners: Mr. & Mrs. C. W. Roth, Jr. of Auburn, California

Convertible Sedans numbered approximately twelve. Mr. & Mrs. C. W. Roth, Jr. acquired their car six years ago from the Sage family of Albany, New York: "Mrs. Cornelia Sage had bought this Brewster for $2,000 from its original owner in 1936. Convertible Sedans had been built with either single- or double-belt lines. Our car is one of two known to survive with the latter—and is original. We like its rarity, the reliability of the Ford running gear, and it's fun to drive!"

Pete & Joanne McManus have owned their Town Car since 1975: "It is a curious mixture of Brewster & Company coachwork, Ford chassis and C. M. Hall headlights as on '29 Packards and other Classics. The heart-shaped grille defies description, which overshadows the uniquely-shaped fenders and train 'cow-catcher' style bumpers. This same body—together with interior appointments, door handles and running boards—was used on some Rolls-Royces in the 1930's. Mechanically, the car has a Startix starting system and an oiling system for the springs which I believe was a Brewster innovation. We have put many miles on the Brewster, and it drives effortlessly at 55 mph. The rear-view mirror behind the divider window in the rear compartment, together with the usual one on the windshield frame, does make driving interesting, however; you get reflections from the divider window and you also have to look around the second rear-view mirror to see through the very small rear window. But there are compensations. One of the most common comments that Classic owners hear from interested spectators is that 'my father (or grandfather, uncle, etc.) used to have a car just like that!' We can honestly say no one has ever made that comment to us about our heart-front Brewster."

Nor probably has anyone to the other owner whose Town Car appears here. "Heart-shaped" is the consensus designation for the Brewster's radiator grille but Edward Field prefers "fountain pen point" which, given its creator's overall concept, may have been Inskip's inspiration too: "Luxury features are many in the Brewster Town Car— mahogany running boards accented with German silver mouldings, fine chrome-plated brass hardware, stylish leather front seats with an all-weather metal and fabric folding top, beautiful hand-painted canework that has held up all these years . . . plus a Jaeger eight-day clock still keeping near-perfect time, luxurious rear seats

*1936 Brewster Town Car
Owner: Edward A. Field
of Blackwood, New Jersey*

with lighted vanities on each side panel, and such options as a lamb's wool floor cover and a wicker picnic basket complete with plates, cups, silverware, wine bottle, etc. It has been our good luck to have owned and preserved this beautiful car for over a quarter of a century."

C U N N I N G H A M

James Cunningham, Son & Company of Rochester, New York was world famous years before the first horseless carriages began chuffing American roads. Although builders of sleighs, tally-hos, victorias and carriages of all kinds, the company was best known for its hearses and ambulances. Wrote an admiring reviewer, ''In no other country are the remains of the dead borne to the grave in such costly vehicles as are the departed sovereigns of this 'land of the free and home of the brave'.'' A Cunningham was upper echelon in price from the beginning.

At the turn of the century the third generation of Cunninghams entered the family firm and became enthused about that new-fangled contraption that moved under its own power. Like many carriage makers, Cunningham initially built only the coachwork for its cars, purchasing engines and most drivetrain components from industry suppliers. By 1910, however, a Cunningham had become pure Cunningham. And by 1916 the firm joined the Cadillac bandwagon in offering a V-8, a big 442-cubic-inch unit developing 90 hp at an unruffled 2400 rpm. Ralph De Palma drove a light boattail version 98 mph at Brooklyn's Sheepshead Bay in 1919, and a small series of Cunningham speedsters followed. But most of the Rochester products carried heavier, more formal coachwork during these years when the Cunningham was becoming inalterably identified as a carriage-trade car. ''*The* most prestigious V-8 of the era,'' one historian has written. Commented another, ''It is hard to avoid running out of superlatives.''

With the dawn of the Classic Era, four-wheel mechanical brakes were fitted to the V-8 Cunningham's two (132- and 142-inch) chassis. Prices ranged from $6,000-$8,000. Some 800 craftsmen were producing about 650 vehicles (including hearses and ambulances) annually. The practice of annual model revisions was eschewed in Rochester, however, as was a dealership and authorized repair station network. There were Cunningham dealers, many of them undertakers who were clients for the firm's traditional product; other purchasers ordered their cars direct from Rochester. The factory saw to the Cunningham's continued good health after delivery, the company routinely dispatching a mechanic to ailing cars.

It was in coachwork that the Cunningham star shone most brightly from first to last. Fenders and hoods were sturdy steel. The body was whitewood and ash, iron braced and covered with hand-shaped sheet aluminum. Painting was a painstaking process: a coat of primer, two of lead, five of rough paint stained and rubbed, two of

1928 Cunningham Series V-7 Dual Cowl Phaeton.   *Owner: William S. Abbott of Jerseyville, Illinois.*   *Photo: Jerry Manis*

1928 Cunningham Series V-7 Dual Cowl Phaeton.   *Owner: William S. Abbott of Jerseyville, Illinois.*   *Photo: Jerry Manis*

color, no fewer than three of varnish, followed by enameling. Overkill in attention to detail was a Cunningham byword.

The crash of the stock market on Wall Street was a sound that echoed ominously in the Rochester factory. Within a few years Cunningham had discontinued automobile series production for ambulances and hearses exclusively. Though most people couldn't afford a Cunningham anymore, they still got sick and died. The firm continued in a small way applying custom coachwork to manufactured chassis if a client so requested. The last Cunningham body was built in September 1936—nearly a century after James Cunningham had built his first quality carriage.

Few Cunninghams survive today. William Abbott has owned his '28 Dual Cowl Phaeton for seventeen years. Henry Uihlein's '29 All Weather Cabriolet is a recent addition to his collection, and he is enormously enthusiastic about it: ''Elegance, class and craftsmanship—the Cunningham was the most expensive automobile built in the United States in the late twenties and was rightfully called the American Rolls-Royce. The accessories in my car are either original French Baccarat glass or sterling silver. The woodwork is all hand inlaid walnut in pattern, and fantastically beautiful. This car is a quiet Classic to look at, but it makes a lasting impression. Cunningham is still in business today, manufacturing non-automotive parts. The legacy the company left in the field of fine automobiles is one of excellence in taste and quality of construction—and is tellingly demonstrated in the Cunninghams which have survived. They tell the story better than words.''

Engine and rear compartment in Henry Uihlein's '29 Cunningham.   *Photos: Cindy Lewis*

1929 Cunningham Series V-7 All Weather Cabriolet.   *Owner: Henry Uihlein II of Lake Placid, New York.*   *Photos: Cindy Lewis*

D O B L E

Though the Doble was an engineering masterpiece not improved upon by the few steam cars that were built after it, a commercial success it was not. If, despite its advantages, the steam car was destined for oblivion, it is fitting that the Doble of the Classic Era should retain best-ever honors. It was an incredible car.

An MIT-trained engineer, Abner Doble had begun outsteaming the Stanleys prior to the First World War. The Series E, introduced at the San Francisco Automobile Show in 1923, was his apogee. Most of the car's components were produced in Doble's Emeryville, California factory. Coachwork was designed by W. Everett Miller and built by the Walter M. Murphy Company of Pasadena. The Series E was a huge car, stretching 150 inches between the axles and weighing about three tons. The speedometer read to 100 mph, which was not merely optimism. There wasn't a luxury car anywhere that could better a Doble in performance. Audaciously, Doble guaranteed ''100,000 luxurious, silent and trouble-free miles.''

J. Martin Anderson explains how his Doble works: ''The engine is a four-cylinder cross-compound geared directly to the rear drive with a ratio of two to three. Developing about 65 hp, it turns 900 rpm at touring speed, and at 100 mph only 1500 rpm. Maximum torque is at 0 rpm. Fuel can be anything, gasoline to #2 furnace oil or any mixture with no changes or adjustments. Fuel mileage is about 10 mpg. There are no gears to shift. The throttle is a small wheel in the center of the steering wheel which turns about 45 degrees closed to open. The boiler is monotube, about 640 feet of tubing in pancake coils. From cold, steam is raised to 1000 p.s.i. in fifty seconds. In less than a minute, the car is underway. And quickly.'' Indeed, one contemporary road test report on the Series E advised caution to the first-time Doble driver because of the car's ''exceptional acceleration.''

Possibly the most enthusiastic Doble owner of the Classic Era was Howard Hughes. The Anderson car was originally his, built as a runabout and later converted to a roadster by Hughes. Doble's problem with his Series E was making a profit; he couldn't manage it even with a $10,000 price tag. Finally a shady stock manipulation scheme (of which

Doble wasn't aware until too late) and the stock market crash combined to take the steam out of Doble Steam Motors by 1931. Few more than forty of these magnificent cars had been built.

1925 Doble Series E-22 Roadster, Murphy   *Owner: J. Martin Anderson of Kent, Washington*

D U P O N T

*1928 duPont
Model G
Sport Phaeton,
Merrimac.*

*Owner:
Willis H. duPont
of Palm Beach, Florida*

By 1920 both Pierre S. duPont and E. Paul duPont were in the automobile business. The former was president of General Motors, the latter president of duPont Motors. Neither regarded the other as competition.

Introduced at the Automobile Salon in New York City's Hotel Commodore in 1919 and produced for most of its life in Wilmington, Delaware, the duPont was an automobile low in production, high in price, sometimes unusual and always interesting. After nearly a decade in business, the company had proceeded from Models A through F and manufactured approximately 350 cars. Comparatively, the new duPont Model G, with 200 produced in three-and-a-half years, would be a best seller. There were several reasons.

One was the new duPont dealer in New York City: A. J. Miranda, Jr., whose other wares included Maybach and Delage. Within weeks of the Model G's introduction in late 1929, duPont announced two entries in the 24 Hours of Le Mans the following June, Miranda to co-drive one of the cars with Charles Moran, Jr., sportsman, gentleman driver and American representative to the Fédération Internationale de l'Automobile (FIA). Those credentials, and Miranda's profession, might suggest the Le Mans expedition was something of a lark. Not so. This first all-American entry in the renowned French race was very serious. Alas, one of the cars wasn't completed on time and the other one retired after only three of the twenty-four hours. Moran and Miranda lamented afterwards that the culprit was the compulsory ballast in the rear of the car: it had broken through the floorboards, put a kink in the driveshaft and cracked the gearbox casing.

Still the car's early retirement did not mitigate the sporting prowess of the Model G. Thirteen Four-Passenger Speedsters similar to the Le Mans cars were produced; three survive, among them Bill Lassiter's. The only doors on the car are the two on the passenger side which makes entry and egress something of a chore but not one that bothered Bill much when he drove this car on the Michigan CARavan.

According to serial numbers, Willis duPont's Merrimac Sport Phaeton, which he has owned since 1973, was the first Model G built. It was shipped June 29th, 1928, to Baltimore, Maryland. Approximately thirty Model G's were produced during that calendar year.

1929 duPont Model G Four-Passenger Speedster, Merrimac   Owner: W. G. Lassiter, Jr. of West Palm Beach, Florida

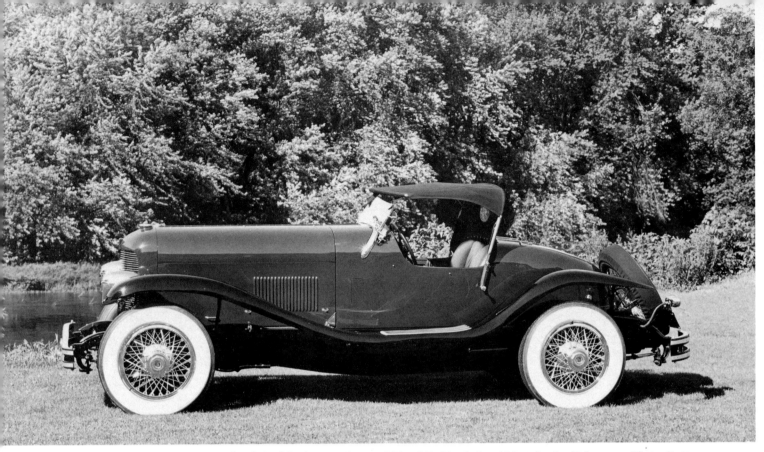

1929 duPont Model G Two-Passenger Speedster, Merrimac.   Owner: Richard E. Riegel, Jr. of Montchanin, Delaware.   Photo: K. Karger

Few things enhance the sales appeal of a new model more than an early purchase by a celebrity. The show car of the Model G Two-Passenger Speedster was bought the moment Mary Pickford spotted it as the perfect birthday present for her husband, Douglas Fairbanks. Veteran duPont designer G. Briggs Weaver couldn't have been more delighted because the Speedster had been planned as a swashbuckling sports car for those who still mourned the demise of the Mercer Raceabout. The car was wonderfully atypical: an aluminum body with one-piece sweeping fender, cast aluminum grille, Woodlite headlights, tachometer and exhaust cutout as standard equipment. Some Speedsters had the spare tire contained within the tail, others had rumble seats. All were guaranteed 100 mph by the factory.

Total Two-Passenger Speedster production was eleven cars, of which six survive. Jerry Riegel's was originally owned by Irving Smith, Jr. of Orange, New Jersey; Bill Lassiter's by W. H. Hodgman of Los Angeles. The first owner of Willis duPont's Speedster was the artist Fred Dana Marsh, who purchased at least three duPonts from 1927 through 1930. At some point during the forties, Marsh gave the Speedster to the police chief of Ormond Beach, Florida.

1930 duPont Model G Two-Passenger Speedster, Merrimac
Owner: Willis H. duPont of Palm Beach, Florida

1930 duPont Model G Two-Passenger Speedster, Merrimac

Owner: W. G. Lassiter, Jr. of West Palm Beach, Florida

Among the further factors that made a success of the Model G was its engine. DuPont had begun life with a four and continued with a six through 1928. The Model G was the company's first straight eight, a 322-cubic-inch Continental delivering 125 hp. With this model, too, duPont expanded its offerings from a mere handful of body styles to a full dozen on a 141-inch wheelbase (five inches longer than the Model F). Elegant and graceful coachwork had been the mark of the duPont since its introduction. The Model G carried these attributes to their zenith.

Many duPont bodies were produced by Merrimac, like Jerry Riegel's Convertible Sedan which was one of eight built. Originally shipped to the E. A. Van Trump, Jr. dealership in Los Angeles, the car remains in essentially original condition.

The Waterhouse Four-Door Sedan has been in the Ryon family since 1939 when Mortimer's father purchased it from a New York City Cadillac dealer to do chores on the family farm: "Because it had been consigned to be cut up as scrap, my father bought the car by the pound, $50.00 or a half-cent per pound. He always claimed it cost more to license the car in New York State than he paid for it, a fact I've not been able to confirm. From first sight I fell in love with the duPont; I was ten years old at the time. Over the next several years, the car performed all the tasks for which it had been purchased: lifting hay into the hay loft, carrying barbed wire and fence posts to the far reaches of the property, hauling feed for the cows and plowing snow in the winter. And I learned to drive on the car when I wasn't old enough to do so legally. On July 15th, 1945, I got my official driver's license and my father, who knew how I felt about the duPont, gave it to me for my birthday. During my college years, the car remained my sole transportation and was still capable of cruising at 70 mph between my home and Lafayette College in Easton, Pennsylvania. This was with the original tires, including the left rear which had been made bald by hauling hay up into the barn. Once I gave a ride home to a fraternity brother over the Pocono mountains during Christmas vacation. He never asked for another ride in my car. It has never had a heater. Finally, after farm work, teenage and college transportation, the duPont was retired from active service. Stored for many years thereafter, restoration began in 1979 and was completed in 1990. The original work order for the car, which

1929 duPont Model G Convertible Sedan, Merrimac
Owner: Richard E. Riegel, Jr. of Montchanin, Delaware   Photo: K. Karger

I obtained from the files of Mrs. E. Paul duPont, was a considerable help in returning the Waterhouse Sedan to the splendor it had when first exhibited at the Philadelphia Automobile Show in 1930. The car certainly deserved it.''

Above and above center: Instrument board and engine compartment in Mort Ryon's '29 duPont Model G Four-Door Sedan, Waterhouse.

Photos: Stan Smith

1929 duPont Model G Four-Door Sedan, Waterhouse   Owner: Mortimer Ryon of Solebury, Pennsylvania   Photos: Stan Smith

This page: 1930 duPont Model SG1
Indianapolis Race Car, Waterhouse

Owner: Willis H. duPont
of Palm Beach, Florida

Although duPont Motors cannot be
said to have had an extensive competition program, the company did race
on two continents. The Le Mans
excursion of '29 was followed by
entry in the Indianapolis 500 in 1930.
The Model G wheelbase was
shortened to 125 inches, the Model G
engine was race tuned to 140 hp. The
race car had its own special axle
ratio, propeller shaft, carburetor and
Rudge-Whitworth wire wheels; the
usual speed-reducing appurtenances
(windshield, fenders, etc.) were
removed. Charles Moran was the
driver, and qualified the car at just
under 90 mph. The Indy 500 was a

crash carnival in '30, and the duPont,
alas, was among the ten racers that
came to grief. On the 22nd lap Moran
slid on an oil patch and into a wall.
Thus ended the duPont's racing
career. Interestingly, although
Speedway officials had changed the
rules to give semi-stock cars a
fighting chance against the purebred
racers, few manufacturers had been
enticed. That duPont Motors tried is
a credit to the marque, and that the
car still exists is super. Willis duPont
has owned the Indy racer since 1979.

Page opposite: 1931 duPont
Model H Sport Phaeton, Merrimac

Owner: Richard E. Riegel, Jr
of Montchanin, Delaware

In May of 1930 Paul duPont
purchased the Indian Motorcycle
Company of Springfield, Massachusetts and moved his engineering
department there to be closer to
Merrimac, producer of many of the
Model G bodies. The Model H was
duPont Motors' last attempt to stay
alive in the custom automobile
market as the Great Depression took
hold. The engine and drivetrain
remained the same but the wheelbase
was lengthened to 146½ inches. Just
three examples were built, two
sedans and the car you see here,
which Jerry Riegel has owned for
nearly three decades. It was shown,
together with several Model G
duPonts, at the 1931 New York Automobile Show. Cummins Catherwood
of Philadelphia was its first owner.
Production of all duPonts ceased in
January 1932. A receiver was
appointed in February 1933.

1929 Graham-Paige Model 837 Dual Cowl Sport Phaeton, LeBaron　　　　　*Owner: John E. Morgan of Manalapan, Florida*

GRAHAM
PAIGE

The Graham-Paige emblem was a stylized profile rendering of the brothers Graham (Joseph, Robert and Ray) in knightly-helmeted splendor; Paige was the Detroit company they bought out in order to enter America's most formidable jousting arena—the automobile industry. It was 1928. Scarcely dilettantes, the Grahams had previously been allied with Dodge Brothers in the truck-producing field. That January Gene Tunney and Knute Rockne were among the celebrities who spoke at the lavish luncheon at New York's Hotel Roosevelt during which the new Graham-Paige was announced to the world.

Sharing the spotlight with the production models at the New York Automobile Show was a quintet of one-off custom cars designed by LeBaron, the coachbuilding house responsible for the styling of the entire Graham-Paige line. This served effective notice that the Graham brothers fully intended to claim a healthy share of the carriage trade market. How serious they were was amplified a month later when the eight-cylinder Model 835 Graham-Paige joined the line of sixes intro-duced at automobile show time. Its 322-cubic-inch Continental-built engine developed 120 hp, a figure matched only by the gargantuan McFarlan TV6 and exceeded by none.

The news was even better in January 1929 when the big straight-eight was provided a chassis longer by two inches (137 inches) in the new Model 837. Standard equipment included a four-speed Warner trans-mission, thermostatically-controlled radiator shutters, Bijur lubrication and adjustable shock absorbers. Among the nine body styles offered were three $5,000-range LeBaron customs which did not, interestingly, include the dual cowl sport phaeton which had been a 1928 Graham-Paige custom offering. It remained available on special order. The number of people who ordered one in '29 is not known but John Morgan's car—whose previous ownership includes the Rothmans of Pall Mall Canada, Ltd.—is one of only two extant.

Custom models continued in the company catalogue in 1930, the year in which the brothers dropped Paige from their car's name though, to their chagrin, the public generally continued referring to the cars as Graham-Paiges. Typically, LeBaron held in reserve complete but un-finished and untrimmed bodies earmarked for Graham whenever an order was received. As the Great Depression deepened, few were.

Because of the Graham brothers' solid contacts overseas, a number of their chassis received coachwork by such renowned European builders as Erdmann & Rossi of Germany, Henri Labourdette and Saoutchik of France, and Van den Plas and Vesters & Neirinck of Belgium. The last custom Graham was produced in 1939. In 1940 Graham-Paige announced the closing of its automobile plant. During World War II controlling interest was acquired by Joseph W. Frazer who, when peace came, allied with Henry Kaiser for manufacture of another car altogether.

Classic Graham-Paiges are a rarity, the tenor of the times no doubt the reason. The brothers Graham were well-positioned and savvy enough to do spirited combat in the automobile industry. Jousting with the Great Depression was another matter.

H U D S O N

1928 Hudson Super Six Town Car, Murphy
Owner: C. A. Leslie, Jr. of Midwest City, Oklahoma

A common joke among automobile historians is the wisdom shown by the Hudson Motor Car Company in naming the car after the man who put up the money (Detroit department store magnate Joseph L. Hudson) rather than the engineer responsible for the design (Howard E. Coffin). There the jokes end, however, for the Hudson was a no-nonsense automobile that commanded respect. From 1910 to 1939, the company pioneered no fewer than fifty-nine industry "firsts"—like the late twenties introduction of an electric gauge on the dashboard which with the push of a button informed the driver of his fuel and oil levels (a clever little device adopted by Packard a few years later and Rolls-Royce after World War II). Hudsons were fast cars too, from the 1911 "Mile a Minute Roadster" (which was guaranteed) to the Super Six which captured the one-mile straightaway (102.5 mph) and twenty-four-hour (75.8 mph) stock car records in 1916. The L-head Super Six remained the mainstay of Hudson production until superseded by a 288.5-cubic-inch 92 hp F-head six in 1927.

For Hudson's 1928 model line, the Murphy Body Company of Pasadena, California was enlisted to design two production body styles—and it followed that Murphy's clientele might find the idea of a custom Hudson attractive. How many Murphy Hudsons were produced that year is not known, but C. A. Leslie's Town Car had to be the most grand: "It's a one-off body and, at $13,500, is purported to be

the most expensive Hudson ever produced. The car was ordered by Frederick William Schumacher of Columbus, Ohio. His fortune had been made in a variety of enterprises from patent medicine to gold and silver mines. He was a man of impeccable taste. The Hudson's frame was stretched from 127 to 136 inches for this town car. The advanced styling belies its 1928 heritage. The rear-mounted spare produced a long, low, sleek appearance that production Hudsons would not achieve until years later. Mahogany running boards with see-through mud scrapers are typical on Murphy-bodied cars, as is the single nickeled beltline trim strip and absence of outside door handles on the chauffeur's compartment. The equilateral Hudson triangle was replaced by an elongated version, and a voluptuous one-off hood ornament graced the taller-than-standard radiator shell the vertical shutters of which could be manually controlled by a ratchetted pull lever on the damascened dash panel. Only the rear compartment was heated, and the chauffeur had to suffer the cold in silence since he was unable to reply to the one-way intercom system. The blind rear quarter and fully curtained windows provided privacy when needed. Buffalo wire wheels, mahogany strips for the gas tank cover, the leather top and landau irons added a touch of class. Family chauffeur James Hartigan drove the town car on trips from the Schumacher Victorian mansion to Mr. Schumacher's offices in the Hartman Hotel, a distance of less than a mile. Occasional jaunts to the board of trade and to the opera, accompanied by his wife, Maribel Hartman Schumacher, did not add many miles to the odometer. The Murphy Town Car registered only slightly more than 22,000 miles when sold by the estate following Frederick Schumacher's death in 1957. In 1974 I became the fourth owner and have used the car for touring, parades, weddings, and to transport visiting dignitaries. Total mileage is 26,682.''

Perhaps it was the Murphy experience which prompted Hudson to offer its own catalogue customs in 1929. Biddle & Smart, which had been producing production bodies for Hudson since 1922 and also built several Murphy-designed cars for the company, was the logical source. A long 139-inch-wheelbase chassis was introduced for the purpose. Just about the only unpopular move Hudson made that year was to abandon its traditional ''Super'' designation for ''Greater.''

C. A. Leslie's 1928 Hudson Town Car by Murphy. The voluptuous one-off radiator ornament must be removed for access to the filler plug below. Three dancing nymphs grace the Lalique courtesy lights above each of the flush-mounted opera seats.

1929 Hudson Greater Six Model L Club Sedan, Biddle & Smart
Owner: John Soneff of Denver, Colorado

"During the fifties I sold Hudsons alongside my father," comments John Soneff. "He is the one who started me in collecting the marque. Classic Hudsons are rare, and I very much wanted one. I acquired mine in 1978. I am very proud to show off my 1929 Hudson. At Classic Car Club meets it stands right up there with Packards, Duesenbergs, Cadillacs, Cords, Auburns, etc. I have a 1932 Cadillac V-12 Town Coupe, but I love my Hudson more."

Paul Loree goes John two better: "Of my three Classics ('28 Packard 526 Dual Cowl Phaeton, '38 Lincoln K Brunn Touring Cabriolet), the Hudson is my first and favorite. Just thirteen Biddle & Smart Dual Cowl Phaetons were built in 1929; six remain extant. Mine was ordered by a family in Quebec City; I acquired it in 1973 in Toronto. The large Hudsons of the late twenties were fast (82 mph) and durable machines. My two spare engines were obtained from saw mills where they functioned as stationary units for years. The coachwork on my car is especially graceful and well-proportioned, I think. I drive the car a lot—weddings, picnics, parades and tours."

There were some LeBaron designs built on the Hudson chassis as well but after 1929 Classic cars from the company would be few. Following the stock market crash, Biddle & Smart closed its doors and Hudson elected, doubtless with typical wisdom, to focus on production cars to keep its doors open. Carriage trade Hudsons had never paid the rent on the company factory.

1929 Hudson Greater Six Model L Dual Cowl Phaeton, Biddle & Smart
Owner: Paul J. Loree, M.D. of Grand Island, New York

1925 Julian Sport Coupe, Fleetwood   Owner: William F. Harrah Foundation National Automobile Museum, Reno, Nevada

J U L I A N

Julian S. Brown was the son of millionaire Alexander T. Brown, whose automotive affiliations included the Brown-Lipe Gear and H. H. Franklin companies. His home was in Syracuse but his image as a playboy cut a wide swath throughout Upstate New York. Julian Brown was also an eccentric. He not only marched to his own drummer, he positively cantered. But nothing of the aforementioned derogates the man's engineering acumen and inventive flair.

The Julian automobile is a super paradigm—in some aspects a contradiction in terms, in others wildly progressive for the era. Like a Cecil B. DeMille epic, it had been years in the making. Although never profitably, Brown had been manufacturing engines since before the First World War and had also built his first automobile shortly after the Armistice. The heart of his new Julian was its engine: an air-cooled rear-mounted radial of six cylinders, 268 cubic inches and 60 hp. Unlike earlier rotaries which literally revolved, the Julian's engine was fixed, a rigid

eight-inch crankshaft supported by two massive main bearings carrying fork-and-blade connecting rod assemblies in near-perfect balance. The Julian's frame weighed but ninety-seven pounds (one-third the industry norm) and was a platform-backbone type anticipating Dr. Ferdinand Porsche's Volkswagen by almost a generation. The Julian's two-wheel brakes were adjustable from the driver's seat, even with the car in motion. The wheelbase was 125 inches. Road-ready weight of the car complete was a comely 2,400 pounds. Julian Brown decided on $2,500 for the price tag.

Fleetwood of Pennsylvania was responsible for the Julian's body, but Julian himself was responsible for its design. The flat floor pan was a mere sixteen inches from the ground, yet road clearances of 11.5 inches was two inches the better of most contemporary cars. The obtuse Brewster-type windshield, the vast expanse of glass and the curious position of the spare tire might occasion comment from an onlooker twenty feet away. Up close, the observer would be

astonished to find the driver's seat centrally located in front, with a two-passenger seat behind him and accommodation for two more passengers on flanking jumpseats, sort of a reverse cloverleaf. Even more curious in such a radical car, the upholstery was Victorian, which most of the industry regarded as passé.

Establishment of the Julian Brown Motor Car Company was Julian's next order of business, but that alas is where the business ended. He was unable to raise more than a fraction of the capital necessary to get his car into production. Thereafter, Julian Brown turned his back on the automobile industry. The $4,000,000 he inherited upon his father's death sustained his flamboyant lifestyle for a time, but his further business adventures ended as dismally as his automobile. Four ex-wives and a passel of creditors kept Brown's attorneys busy for years.

Among the assets left in his estate when Julian Brown died in Daytona Beach, Florida in 1964 was his automobile. Today, in the Harrah Foundation museum, the Julian serves as testimony to the pragmatic inadvisability of being too far ahead of one's time—and to the creative genius of the man who conceived it.

1926 Kissel 8-75 Speedster   Owner: George A. Newhall of Sausalito, California

K I S S E L

Produced in Hartford, Wisconsin for a quarter of a century, the Kissel was well finished and highly respected—a mainstream Americana kind of car. The brothers Kissel, George and Will, were conservative to a fault, but this did not prevent them from kicking up their automotive heels on occasion. As early as 1913 they had offered the novelty of an "All Year" body with easily removable hardtop. And, although adopting automatic chassis lubrication and balloon tires about the same time as other manufacturers, the Kissels were early to market with Lockheed hydraulic brakes in 1925. But the Kissel heels were kicked up most spectacularly in their Speedster model, which was among the snazziest cars on the road in the mid-twenties. George Newhall's 1926 Speedster is a splendid example. With its Lycoming-derived 287-cubic-inch straight-eight engine generating 75 hp, the car was capable of 85 mph. George acquired his Speedster from its original owner, Adelheid DeRose, in 1973 and declares it "extremely fun to drive and also

much easier to drive than many later Classics." Although the Hartford-built Speedster was fetchingly racy, this particular car presents an even more glamorous appearance—and authentically so. Because Kissel had a strong following among Hollywood celebrities, the California distributor in Los Angeles was given the okay to incorporate special touches not seen

on Kissels sold in other parts of the country. Woodlites were a favorite of this distributor. Further, the loose fasteners for the top of this car allow the entire assembly to be removed for a more thoroughly sporting look. Unfortunately, the Kissel did not survive long into the Classic Era. In 1931, the Kissel brothers formed an alliance with Archie Andrews for production of the Ruxton in the Hartford factory. The deal went awry. Shortly thereafter the Kissel Motor Car Company requested receivership from a friendly creditor.

1925 McFarlan Twin Valve Six Model 154 Knickerbocker Berline Limousine
Owner: Craig Karr of Santa Monica, California   Photo: Rick Lenz

Prior to the First World War, the McFarlan Carriage Company of Connersville, Indiana evolved into the McFarlan Motor Car Company. Probably few paid much attention; the McFarlan of that period was a good if prosaic automobile. By the twenties, however, it was impossible not to notice the McFarlan. Consider the specification of Craig Karr's

Knickerbocker Limousine: six cylinders, triple ignition, 24 valves, 18 spark plugs, 572.5 cubic inches, 120 hp. The Twin Valve Six McFarlan was the most powerful production automobile in America at the dawn of the Classic Era. With its 140-inch wheelbase ("will turn easy in average street," the catalogue insisted) and two-plus tons with closed coachwork,

it was one of the biggest. And, with prices for production models ranging up to $9,000, among the most expensive.

Hollywood flocked to Connersville. Movie star purchasers included Wallace Reid and Fatty Arbuckle. Boxing champ Jack Dempsey was an owner; band leader Paul Whiteman owned two. Craig Karr's McFarlan was ordered in Connersville by a member of the Romanoff family who had fled Russia following the Bolshevik revolution with enough gold bullion to pay for two: a touring and this limousine, one of a pair built, individually styled and reputedly the most expensive vehicles ever produced by the company. Romanoffs always traveled in style and insisted on having their caviar in comfort so this McFarlan was ordered with some special picnic equipment, as Craig explains: "A silver-trimmed trunk was originally fitted on the teakwood platform at the rear, into which was placed not only small suitcases but collapsible brass poles with eagles on top. Once assembled, the poles permitted a tent to be hooked to the rear leading edge of the leather top and positioned so the Romanoffs might enjoy a sun-shaded lunch seated on two canvas pillows which fastened to the teak-wood platform once the trunk was removed."

At some point during its checkered career, the trunk was removed permanently from the McFarlan (and remains to be re-created). Craig has owned the car since 1977 and has researched the history. Just twenty-one McFarlans remain extant of the 2,087 produced during the company's eighteen years of life. Of these, just eight are Classic Era cars. Following the death of Harry McFarlan in 1928, the company itself became history, a young empire builder named Errett Lobban Cord purchasing the McFarlan real estate for the produc-tion of his own cars. The Romanoffs remained in the United States until wiped out in the crash of '29, where-upon Mr. R (his first name is known, but discretion dictates it not be revealed) dropped the two McFarlans off in a California junkyard and took off himself for Switzerland where he still had some money stashed. The limousine was salvaged from the junkyard by an Oldsmobile dealer to use as an attention-getter on his car lot. The McFarlan caught the attention of a Palos Verdes resident who purchased the car in 1932 and kept it until the mid-seventies when Craig, pleading that the car deserved to be restored, convinced him to sell.

"The sheer size of this vehicle and its massive powerplant attracted me to it," says Craig. "Weighing in excess of 7,000 pounds, it handles like a Mack truck. Due to its rear end ratio, it's not a fast car but can climb hills effortlessly. With its heavy insulated roof, the passenger compartment remains cool on the hottest of days, windows open, of course. With its construction and appointments, the McFarlan is more like a royal carriage than an automobile. In fact, it is the most ostentatious vehicle in my collection and, being a collector of giant autos, that says a lot."

1925 McFarlan Twin Valve Six Model 154 Knickerbocker Berline Limousine
Owner: Craig Karr of Santa Monica, California   Photos: Rick Lenz

M E R C E R

1931 Mercer Model SR Convertible Coupe, Merrimac
Owner: William S. Locke of West Lafayette, Indiana
Photos: Roy Query, Special Interest Autos

Mercer. To old car enthusiasts, the name calls to mind a single word. Raceabout: monocle windshield in front, round gasoline tank in the rear, two bucket seats in between, coachwork totalling hood and fenders in a yellow vivid enough to blind. The car was blindingly fast too. With numerous race victories, the Race-about made Mercer famous. Only the Stutz Bearcat was in its league. Production in the Trenton (Mercer County, New Jersey) factory seldom exceeded 500 cars a year in all body styles, but in the Mercer price class, that was enough for a profit. Advertisements from 1914 boldly declared that ''the Mercer is the Steinway of the automobile world.''

But by the twenties the Mercer Automobile Company was playing offkey. A Wall Street-inspired merger with Simplex and Locomobile proved disastrous. By 1926 Mercer Motors (as the firm had been retitled during reorganization) was performing only service work. In 1928 Harry M. Wahl, a former associate of Billy Durant's, decided to revive the marque. Wahl was no starry-eyed dreamer. Legends die hard; the very mention of Mercer was magic. But the name and a few parts were all Wahl bought. Outbid on the Trenton factory, he turned to the Elcar Motor Company of Elkhart, Indiana. Chief engineer Mike Graffis was enthusiastic.

The Mercer's straight-eight engine, modified from the Continental 12K, delivered 140 hp, squarely in the upper power echelon among American cars. The 135-inch-wheelbase chassis featured a Belflex suspension system providing a satin-smooth ride. Merrimac provided striking convertible coupe coachwork. Just one car was completed for exhibit at the Hotel Montclair during New York Automobile Show week in January 1931. Meanwhile, everything that could have gone wrong had—the stock market crashed, ill health felled Wahl, Graffis was grappling with the failure of Elcar. Even as spectators were admiring the new Mercer, Mercer Motors was being sued into receivership. From the Hotel Montclair, the show car and its companion exhibit chassis were taken to the Cutter Automobile Agency in Dover, New Jersey. Frank Cutter and Mike Graffis thought a new Mercer remained a possibility. But by now that had become a starry-eyed dream.

Ask Bill Locke how long he has owned the '31 Mercer and his reply is "since it was new." That is, wittily, correct. In 1950 Bill discovered the car in the old Cutter dealership and, finally, in 1964 was able to buy it. The odometer read 00004. Driven sparingly since, the Mercer's now less than 100 miles were accumulated principally on the Indianapolis Motor Speedway. The car remains as it was acquired—totally original and history's final evocation of the magic that was Mercer.

1931 Mercer Model SR Convertible Coupe, Merrimac
Owner: William S. Locke of West Lafayette, Indiana
Photos: Roy Query, Special Interest Autos

N A S H

The cars in this portfolio boast more cylinders than Charles W. Nash had ever offered before and as many as he would ever consider. The number of cylinders is eight. Charlie Nash was the conservative sort. But his life out-Algered Horatio. Abandoned by his parents at the age of six and bound out by the district court to work for a Michigan farmer until twenty-one, Charlie ran away at the age of twelve to seek his fortune. He did rather well. By 1912 he was president of General Motors. By 1917 he had his own automobile company in Kenosha, Wisconsin. Because he chose not to run wild during the Roaring Twenties, Charlie Nash was better prepared for the Great Depression and made $4.8 million in 1931, while other automobile manufacturers lost a lot more.

The billboards announcing the Twin-Ignition Eight read ''80 Miles an Hour in 3 Blocks,'' which perhaps was as conservative a claim for the car as the man who built it. The engine was a nine-main-bearing overhead-valve straight eight of 298.6 cubic inches and 100 hp at 3200 rpm. Exceptionally quiet and smooth, it has been acclaimed as one of the finest in-line eights ever built. The chassis featured Bijur lubrication, automatic thermostatically-controlled radiator shutters, dash button

1931 Nash Series 890 Sedan
Owner: Thomas J. Lester of Deerfield Beach, Florida

starting control and shock absorbers adjustable from the instrument panel. *Motor West* praised the new Nash's styling as possessing ''the long, low, powerful profile characteristics of the smartest hand-built custom cars.'' *Automobile Topics* called the new line ''another fulfillment of Charles W. Nash's undeviating ambition to supply at moderate cost automobiles which possess everything in appearance, performance, comfort

and quality offered by the country's most costly cars.'' A Twin-Ignition Eight could be bought, fully optioned, in the $2,000 range.

Those assessments from the thirties are echoed by Twin-Ignition Eight owners today. ''Probably the all-time 'under-dog' Classic,'' says Bob Cosgrove. ''The cars were virtually hand-built in small numbers (3,900); the quality of workmanship and materials is equal to its Classic

1932 Nash Series 999 Victoria   *Owner: Robert J. Cosgrove of Islip, New York*   *Photo: K. Karger*

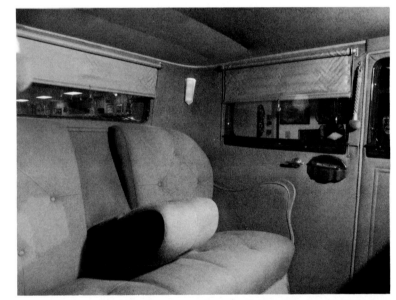

contemporaries. Thirty-six of them were used in Chicago by the police to chase gangsters. This was a powerful car the government could afford. Only six of the 990 series are known to exist; mine is the only Victoria.'' And it is an original car.

Ray Miller's '32 Advanced 1099 Victoria has been restored but retains its original upholstery, and its odometer shows an original 11,400 miles. This car's more sweeping fender line and its quasi beaver-tail rear, together with the lack of a sun visor among other details, identify it as a second series model introduced in March of 1932. Introduced with the second series was a new 142-inch chassis (the longest ever offered by Nash) to augment the Twin-Ignition Eight's usual 133-inch wheelbase.

Tom Lester's Ambassador 1193 Convertible Sedan is one of only two known extant and is, he says, ''often mistaken for a Duesenberg.'' Appearances deceive, but Tom is not the only enthusiast today who refers to the big Classic Nash as ''Kenosha's Duesie.'' One suspects Charlie Nash would have liked that.

Above and page opposite:
1932 Nash Series 1099 Advanced Victoria
Owner: S. Ray Miller, Jr. of Elkhart, Indiana

1933 Nash Series 1193 Ambassador Convertible Sedan
Owner: Thomas J. Lester of Deerfield Beach, Florida

O L D S M O B I L E

The Redfern Saloon Tourer body by Maltby's Ltd. of Folkestone, Kent was fitted to a variety of British chassis in the mid to late thirties. Among its charms was the fully hydraulic power top which, as Maltby's catalogue commented with piquant sexism (and grammar), could be operated ''by the driver (even a young lady) when sitting in his seat.'' The Redfern on an American chassis is rare, although fortuitiously there are two of them in this book: a Buick and the Oldsmobile which Jerry Remlinger has owned for nearly two decades.

Records indicate that three Oldsmobile Series L37 (257-cubic-inch straight eight, 124-inch wheelbase) chassis were shipped to England in 1937. What became of the other two is anyone's guess. So is the identity of the original owner of Jerry's car: ''Whoever he was, he liked convenience. Four hydraulic jacks were fitted that lift the whole car off the ground for tire changing. This was not included with the usual Redfern Saloon Tourer. The car is all Oldsmobile from the cowl forward and aluminum from the cowl back. And, of course, it's right-hand drive. A few years ago I received a letter from England with some aged photos showing the car when it was owned by the Yorkshire postmaster, was in poor repair and for sale, and stored in a garage so small the bumpers had to be taken off. After owning the car myself for twelve years, I decided to restore it. Being the only one, the Maltby Oldsmobile deserved that.''

1937 Oldsmobile Series L37 Redfern Saloon Tourer, Maltby
Owner: Jerry L. Remlinger of Massillon, Ohio

P E E R L E S S

Prior to the First World War, Peerless was one of the celebrated "Three P's" (with Packard and Pierce-Arrow), marques the very mention of whose names connoted unabashed luxury. "All that the name implies" was the Peerless slogan. By the dawn of the Classic Era, however, the Cleveland, Ohio company's star had begun to dim. Entry into the popular-priced field diluted the marque's prestige image, and managerial changes were so frequent that the company might have been well advised to install a revolving door to the executive suite. Matters took a turn for the better when Alexis de Sakhnoffsky (the Russian-born designer later responsible for Packard styling innovations among others) was hired to design the 1930 line. But the new Peerless was introduced as Wall Street crashed. The company that had not been able to capitalize during the boom years was ill-equipped to cope in an economy gone bust.

To the everlasting credit of the marque, Peerless exited with bravura. Project XD had begun in 1927, when rumors spread of multi-cylinder development by Cadillac and Marmon. Anxious not to be left behind, Peerless began experimenting with a V-16; the Aluminum Company of America (Alcoa), which earlier had collaborated on all-aluminum coachwork development, asked to join the effort. Early in 1929 former Marmon vice president James A. Bohannon became the new Peerless president. Work on Project XD accelerated. The 464.6-cubic-inch V-16 engine was bench tested at 170+ hp. Aluminum was also used extensively in the 145-inch chassis. Enlisted to design the coachwork was Franklin Q. Hershey, the twenty-two-year-old designer of the Walter M. Murphy Company of Pasadena, California. The magnificent car on these pages was the result.

Taken to Muroc Dry Lake, the Peerless V-16 tested at over 100 mph. At little more than 4,000 pounds, the new car promised to be a svelte challenger to the new sixteen-cylinder models from Marmon (5,360 pounds) and Cadillac (nearly three tons). But in Cleveland a cold look at reality had been taken. Peerless sales were less than a quarter of pre-crash

1932 Peerless Touring Sedan Prototype, Murphy
Owner: Crawford Auto-Aviation Museum of the Western Reserve
Historical Society, Cleveland, Ohio   Photo: Strother MacMinn

The Peerless V-16 engine; Peerless prototype photo by Strother MacMinn

levels. Going on seemed futile. Most of the company office furniture was sold, and the assembly line was shut down. Following the repeal of Prohibition in 1933, Peerless bought out Carlings of Canada and went into the beer business. ''From motors to malt and from hubcaps to hops,'' James Bohannon would say.

In 1946 James Bohannon donated the 1932 Peerless V-16 Prototype to the then Thompson Products Museum, forerunner of the Crawford Auto-Aviation Museum. Its mileage at the time was 4,775; at this writing it registers a bit less than 5,000 miles. This unique and original Classic deserves a velvet glove. In addition to its inherent place in history, the V-16 Peerless was the last passenger car produced in Cleveland. It is, the Crawford people proudly state, the ''flagship'' of their collection.

P H A N T O M   C O R S A I R

Twenty-four thousand dollars was an enormous price to pay for a new automobile in 1938, though not for Rust Heinz, the twenty-three-year-old scion of the H. J. Heinz (''57 Varieties,'' at that time) family. He designed the car himself, although Maurice Schwartz of the famed Bohman & Schwartz coachbuilding house lent a valuable hand. The chassis was a Cord front-drive 810. Its 288.6-cubic-inch Lycoming V-8 engine would be given a hefty boost via a semi-racing camshaft designed postwar by Andy Granatelli of Indy 500 renown, bringing horsepower to 190, top speed to 115 mph. When first seen in *Esquire* magazine in '37, the Phantom Corsair had been called ''a conception of the car of tomorrow.'' When completed in 1938, the car appeared in the movie *The Young in Heart,* where it was less flatteringly referred to as the ''Flying Wombat.'' Rust Heinz planned to produce the Phantom Corsair in small numbers, with a price tag half what this prototype cost him. His death during the summer of 1939 brought a swift halt to the project. The Phantom Corsair passed through a number of owners thereafter, including entertainer and talk show host Herb Shriner, before finding a permanent home in the Harrah collection in the mid-seventies.

1938 Phantom Corsair Six-Passenger Coupe   *Owner: William F. Harrah Foundation National Automobile Museum, Reno, Nevada*

Total production of the Rauch &
Lang Gas-Electric was four cars. This
was considerably less than had been
hoped. Instigator of the project was
Col. E. H. R. (Ned) Green, son of the
late Hetty Green who had enjoyed
being proclaimed the world's richest
woman (though probably not also
being called ''The Witch of Wall
Street''). Because the Colonel was
handicapped, he had long used
electric cars to tour his estate in
South Dartmouth, Massachusetts.
But by the Classic Era, the electric
was almost extinct in America. Ergo
this hybrid—gasoline engine, electric
drive—seemed an ideal solution, both
to Col. Green and to the electric-
producing Rauch & Lang, Inc. of
Chicopee Falls, Massachusetts. Basis
for the new car was the Stearns-
Knight M-6-80 of Cleveland's
F. B. Stearns Company, whose straits
were even more dire (imminent
liquidation) than Rauch & Lang's.
Undoubtedly the price negotiated for
inventoried cars was attractive, and
their quiet sleeve-valve engines
seemed perfect for the project.

The Rauch & Lang Gas-Electric had
problems. The electric drive
developed by General Electric
engineers was a modified commercial
transmission originally designed for
heavy-duty application and, as such,
inordinately heavy. A more powerful
engine than the Stearns-Knight was
needed. Although sluggish, the
Rauch & Lang Gas-Electric did have
the advantage of no gears to shift,
which was not an ineffective selling
point. The car's problems were not
insuperable. But then destiny inter-
vened. The stock market crashed,
and Col. Green withdrew the
financial support upon which Rauch
& Lang depended. The production
project was over virtually before it
began.

Bobbie Crump has owned his
Rauch & Lang Gas-Electric since
1976. It was the fourth car built,
intended as a pre-production or pilot
model. Col. Green housed the car at
his estate in South Dartmouth until
his death in 1936. Overall weight is
5,240 pounds, mileage to date is
26,210, the only pedals are for
acceleration and braking, the
speedometer reads 0-80 indicating a
performance potential far in excess of
the electric's norm. Bobbie has a very
rare piece of history that-might-have-
been.

1930 Rauch & Lang Gas-Electric Sedan
Owner: Bobbie B. Crump, Sr. of Baton Rouge, Louisiana

R I C K E N B A C K E R

The week before, Edward Vernon Rickenbacker recorded a mile in thirty-eight seconds flat during road testing of the new Super Sport. "Frankly, it is a costly toy," Captain Eddie told New York Automobile Show reporters in recommending that most motorists *not* consider purchase of the $5,000 model which had been designed for "the expert driver who has space and opportunity to open her up on occasion and who wants the fastest stock car on wheels." What Rickenbacker did not say was that the Super Sport had also been designed to give a much-needed boost to the firm. One year later the Rickenbacker Motor Company of Detroit was dead, its lifespan a mere six years. There were many reasons for the failure of the venture named for World War I's "ace of aces." The Super Sport was not among them.

Its dual-carbureted 315-cubic-inch straight-eight engine delivered 107 bhp at 3000 rpm, but puissance alone had not been responsible for the car's widely publicized 95 mph. At a time when aerodynamics was seldom even thought about in the American industry, Rickenbacker

promoted "scientific streamlining" —a full chassis underpan, low-slung bullet headlamps, curved visors, laminated "aerofoil" bumpers, torpedo lines, front cycle fenders (which, incidentally, turned with the wheels), and lightweight construction (aluminum everywhere save cowl and doors). Absent were running boards; present was safety glass. "None other would be suitable," Rickenbacker said, "or safe in a car capable of such tremendous speeds." The dashboard resembled an airplane cockpit, upholstery was lush Spanish grain leather and teakwood trim surrounded all windows.

How many Super Sports were produced before the Rickenbacker company failed is not known. Thirty bodies were painted but possibly not all were mated with chassis. This Super Sport was number seven and the New York Automobile Show car. Originally owned by a Rickenbacker dealer, it was acquired by Harrah's Automobile Collection in 1975. Tom Lester purchased the Super Sport in 1983: "Prior to Bill Harrah's death, I often visited in Reno. Walking the collection, Bill and I would always stop at the Rickenbacker because of

its unique styling. The Roaring Twenties didn't roar much in automotive design. This car, we both agreed, had character." In spades.

1926 Rickenbacker Super Sport
Owner: Thomas J. Lester
of Deerfield Beach, Florida

R E O

"A gorgeous new creation whose style is exclusive and whose behavior leaves nothing proper to be desired" was the verdict of *Automobile Topics* when the Royale was introduced. Since 1904 when, following a dispute with his board of directors, Ransom Eli Olds left the company bearing his name and chose his initials for his next automotive venture, the Reo had enjoyed a splendid reputation as a medium-priced car. The Royale, introduced for 1931, was the company's first (and last) attempt to challenge Packard and Chrysler in the luxury field.

In charge of Reo's engineering department was Horace T. Thomas. The Royale chassis was rugged and sturdy, with lever-action one-shot lubrication, thermostatically-controlled radiator shutters and huge fifteen-inch Lockheed hydraulic brakes. Statistically and dynamically balanced, the nine-main-bearing engine displaced 358 cubic inches. Ninety miles an hour was assured, courtesy partly of the 125 hp straight eight, partly because of the car's aerodynamics. The Royale was one of the first American production cars to be wind-tunnel tested. Responsible for its wind-cheating form was Amos Northup, chief designer of the Murray Corporation of America. By previous coachbuilding standards, the Royale lines were smooth, soft and gently flowing, with rolled edge fenders, a double curvature rear panel sweeping down to conceal the fuel tank and the roof panel curving back from the top of the fixed, sloping, narrow-pillared windshield.

1932 Reo Royale 8-35 Convertible Coupe (engine above)   *Owner: S. Ray Miller, Jr. of Elkhart, Indiana*

1931 Reo Royale 8-35 Convertible Coupe   *Owner: Gregg Whitney of Orangevale, California*

Six million dollars had been budgeted for the Royale's development—money well spent in the view of the Royale owners in this portfolio. "The finely detailed engine compartment is a joy in itself," says Ray Miller. "The long hood, sculptured fenders, the streamlined design . . . a beautiful Classic," comments Jim Callahan. Jim's 1933 Sedan is the only Classic Royale to feature the "Self-Shifter," which Reo introduced that year as America's first production automatic transmission of the Classic Era. The system was entirely workable, if not especially fast in doing its job.

With price tags in the $2,500 range, the Royale should have been a runaway best seller. But at Reo red ink was everywhere, and the company was torn by internal strife. In a few years, automobile production would be discontinued to focus all energy on truck manufacture. Royale production had been limited. Just forty-nine convertibles were built: Gregg Whitney's '31, which was once owned by Universal Studios, is one of only a handful extant; Ray Miller's '32 likewise.

1933 Reo Royale N-1 Sedan   *Owner: Jim Callahan of Oakland, California*

1931 Reo Royale 8-35 Sport Sedan, Dietrich   *Owner: Alden Peach Thomas of Northport, Michigan*

Records from 1931 indicate the production of three Royales with Dietrich bodies. Alden Thomas' is the only one remaining: "I watched it being built. At the time I was in my junior year at the University of Michigan. I had been a member of the Reo family since birth because of my good fortune to have the vice president of engineering as my father. There just can't be a better car than my Royale. Being able to acquire it eight years ago was 'the impossible dream' come true."

Walter Sprague's '31 Sedan has a sentimental history as well. Reacquired by the company in the fifties and with the Diamond Reo emblem added to the hubcaps, the car was used for display at the Lansing plant and for V.I.P. chauffeuring until 1975 and the Diamond Reo bankruptcy auction. Walter was high bidder—and thus, in addition to owning a coveted Royale, has the distinction of possessing the last Reo passenger car ever sold by the factory.

1931 Reo Royale 8-35 Sedan   *Owner: Walter Sprague of Portland, Michigan*

1929 Ruxton Roadster　　　　　　　*Owner: S. Ray Miller, Jr. of Elkhart, Indiana*

The Ruxton story began in the late twenties when self-made engineer William J. Muller was given permission by his employer, the automotive body-building Edward G. Budd Company of Philadelphia, to develop a front wheel drive prototype. Muller impishly used a question mark for the car's radiator emblem. Answering his query was self-made entrepreneur Archie M. Andrews, a board member of both Budd and the Hupp Motor Car Corporation. Budd providing bodies and Hupp building the car made wonderful sense.

So did the Ruxton. Front wheel drive would allow for an automobile discernibly lower than rear-drive American cars, which was sure to get the Ruxton noticed. And Muller's ingenuity was impressive. Designing his own transaxle, he split the transmission with first and reverse ahead of the differential and second and high between differential and clutch, and he replaced conventional ring and pinion final drive with a worm gear and wheel unit. His aim was to shorten the driveline, which he managed by a foot.

Meanwhile, the first snag developed. Hupp said no to the project. Undaunted, Andrews organized his own company—New Era Motors, Inc.—with corporate offices in New York City and a

1930 Ruxton Roadster

Owner: W. G. Lassiter, Jr. of West Palm Beach, Florida

promise from Fred Gardner that his automobile factory would manufacture the Ruxton under contract. Scarcely had Muller shipped the first load of tooling when Gardner reneged. Searching for another factory, Andrews struck out on his first three tries: Stutz, Jordan and Peerless. But his next time at bat looked to be a home run: the Moon Motor Car Company in St. Louis was interested. Enough intrigue followed for a daytime soap opera. Deftly, Andrews acquired a controlling interest in Moon in exchange for rights to the Ruxton design. When

the people in St. Louis realized what had happened, they barricaded themselves in the plant. Armed with a court order, Andrews, Muller and company climbed in through a back window. Moon sued. In the meantime, Muller, dissatisfied with the antiquated equipment in St. Louis, suggested a back-up plant would be a good idea. So Andrews also negotiated a deal with Kissel in Hartford, Wisconsin. When the Kissel brothers awoke to reality, they requested receivership.

His questionable tactics notwithstanding, Andrews was genuinely

enthusiastic about the potential of Muller's design. And he announced the new Ruxton before Errett Lobban Cord did his L-29. But amid the contretemps, Cord was first to market with a front wheel drive car, and that hurt. The aftermath of the stock market crash was the Ruxton's coup de grâce.

Still, in between shenanigans, 298 Ruxtons were built from June to September of 1930, the vast majority at Moon, with twenty-seven at Kissel, eleven at Budd. Powering the cars were 268.6-cubic-inch 100 hp Continental engines. The cars' overall

1930 Ruxton Phaeton
Owner: Richard Slobodien of South Orange, New Jersey

1930 Ruxton Sedan
Owner: Blackhawk Classic Auto Collection, Danville, California

height was just 63 inches on 130-inch wheelbase chassis. The price was $3,195. Replacing Muller's question mark radiator emblem was a beautifully styled rendering of a griffin, the half-eagle/half-lion monster of classic mythology. Most cars wore seductive cat's-eye Woodlites.

Fewer than twenty Ruxtons remain extant. Roadsters—like the Adler and Lassiter cars shown here—carried bodies by Baker-Raulang. Closed bodies by Budd included the Black-hawk Classic Auto Collection Sedan which sports the theatrical eight-band color scheme created for the Ruxton by New York stage designer and interior decorator Josef Urban. Just two Ruxton Phaetons like Dick Slobodien's were produced, with Baker-Raulang bodies, in Hartford for the Kissel brothers. Ray Miller's Roadster is one of the handful of Ruxtons built by Budd in 1929 to take to the automobile shows. Archie Andrews later sold this particular car to his dentist.

In December 1930 New Era Motors filed for bankruptcy with liabilities of $855,000 and assets less than half that. Andrews said he personally lost over $70,000 in the project.

There had been a Ruxton in the Ruxton saga, incidentally. He was an influential stock broker whom Andrews hoped would invest in the venture. This William V. C. Ruxton did not do, though typically he had to take Archie Andrews to court to prove it.

1930 Ruxton Roadster
Owner: Andrew Adler of Millbury, Ohio   *Photos: Torque*

S T E A R N S
K N I G H T

In 1904 the noisy valve gear in the Knox he was driving so irritated Charles Yale Knight that he was moved to invent an engine in which sleeves did the work of valves. A printer and publisher by profession, Knight was hard pressed to find anyone in the U.S. interested in his idea at first but after traveling to Europe and selling licenses to a variety of manufacturers there—among them, Minerva of Belgium—he returned home to a considerably more receptive audience.

First to sign on for a Knight sleeve-valve license was the F. B. Stearns Company, producer of luxury cars in Cleveland. Earlier Frank Stearns had applied for a patent to protect his car's most distinctive feature—the "white line radiator"—and now he looked forward to the distinctiveness of producing America's only sleeve valve. Alas, Stearns wasn't the only manufacturer enamoured of the quiet, smooth performance of Charles Knight's engine. Undeterred as well by the increased expense of its construction over poppet-valve engines and the copious quantities of oil it required was John North Willys of Toledo. Others would jump on Knight's bandwagon, though their efforts would be short-lived. Only

Willys would continue vociferously to champion sleeve valves in America into the Classic Era—with his own Willys-Knights and Stearns-Knights too.

Citing ill health Frank Stearns had retired from active participation in his company during World War I. In December of 1925 Stearns' company belonged to John North Willys. Willys made it clear that he had no intention of integrating the firm into his Willys-Overland empire. His purchase of Stearns was to acquire a Knight-engined luxury car as companion to his medium-range Willys.

Stearns-Knights were big cars, produced in both six- and eight-cylinder models, with wheelbases stretching to as much as 145 inches and prices stretching up to $5,800. The three examples shown here have six-cylinder engines.

Frank Stearns himself was the first owner of Al Ferrara's 1926 S-95 Roadster: "The Stearns factory in Cleveland is still standing, and the Stearns-Knight cars were tested on the same road on which I live in Gates Mills. I know Frank Stearns' granddaughter, Ann Barnes. The sleek body style, power-assist brakes and quietly smooth engine make the Stearns-Knight a fine Classic, in addition to an unusual one."

The 1926 S-95 Seven-Passenger Touring has been in the Minden Automotive Museum for over two decades. Comments Milton Bacon: "The original owner was Don C. Foote of Billings, Montana. Total mileage is 21,260. The originality is remarkable. Years ago this Stearns-Knight was saved from total destruction by being pushed out of a flaming hay barn by the blacksmith whose sparks from the forge started the blaze. The car still bears the paint-singe scars."

The Classic Car Club of America Museum's 1927 F-6-85 Four-Passenger Coupe was donated to the collection by Phil Kersh in 1985. The figures in the designation seemingly should represent cylinders and horsepower, but the latter is illusory. The six developed 70 hp in 1926, 82 in 1927. However, Stearns-Knight purchasers weren't attracted to the car for its performance—the eight's 100 hp offered just 75 mph—but to its silken smooth luxury. Unfortunately, after 1929, there would be no Stearns-Knights to be attracted to. The company had not been healthy when John North Willys bought it and began losing money heavily in 1926. Shortly after the Wall Street crash in October of '29, Stearns stockholders voted for dissolution.

1926 Stearns-Knight Series S-95 Seven-Passenger Touring
Owner: Minden Automotive Museum, Minden, Nevada

1926 Stearns-Knight Series S-95 Roadster
Owner: Alfred Ferrara of Gates Mills, Ohio

1927 Stearns-Knight Series F-6-85 Four-Passenger Coupe   Owner: Classic Car Club of America Museum, Hickory Corners, Michigan

In 1926 Albert Russel Erskine scanned the figures and noticed that Studebaker was selling proportionately more of its higher-priced than moderately-ranged six-cylinder cars. Supplementation at the top of the Studebaker lines was suggested— and eight cylinders in a prestige car seemed just the ticket. Erskine pondered all this from a position of strength. In 1911, when the wagon-building empire of the Studebaker brothers was transformed into Studebaker Corporation, he was treasurer. Appointed president four years later, he became a virtual meteor, tripling sales in less than a decade, which made Studebaker stockholders very happy. Now his two top engineers balked at Erskine's prestige car idea. He solved that by firing them and hiring Delmar G. "Barney" Roos, whose resumé included top engineer-

ing posts at Locomobile, Pierce-Arrow and Marmon, and whose usual rejoinder to "why" was "why not." Erskine had his man. He asked the peripatetic Ray Dietrich to "consult on body matters." In two years Studebaker had a straight-eight President at the top of its model line-up. Meanwhile, Studebaker's president was doing some engineering of his own—which resulted in a merger with Pierce-Arrow during the summer of '28. A marriage made in heaven, Erskine thought, affiliation with the top-drawer Buffalo company would allow for mutual support and cooperation beneficial to both, and would provide him an extensive

eastern plant particularly well suited for Studebaker's export trade.

Portugal was the original destination of Whitney M. Kerr's '30 President Seven-Passenger Sedan where it resided in the garage of Marshal Carmona who had taken over the country in a 1926 coup d'état and was elected president in '28. At some point during the turbulent Salazar era, the car was put into storage. Brought to this country in 1980, it was acquired by Whitney in 1985: "The odometer read 34,300 kilometers (21,000 miles) at the time. Since then I've driven the car over 12,000 miles. There's a wonderful flow of smooth power, and the three-shoe Bendix brakes are excellent. The President performs nicely at 60 mph. It's fun to drive in heavy, fast city traffic and keep up with modern cars."

This page and page opposite:
1930 Studebaker President Series FE Seven-Passenger Sedan
Owner: Whitney M. Kerr of Overland Park, Kansas   Photos: Carder Photography

In July of 1928 four Presidents were driven 25,000 miles around the board track at Atlantic City, the two sedans averaging 64 mph, the two roadsters over 68 mph. If the Studebaker stock car could perform that well, test track supervisor George Hunt reasoned, just think what a Studebaker race car might do. Corporation executives looked the other way as Hunt raided the parts shelves and enlisted the on-company-time assistance of Studebaker mechanics to build a President-based race car. Herman Rigling of Indianapolis provided the coachwork. In 1931 the Hunt Special won Pikes Peak and was leading the Indianapolis 500 late in the race when an encounter with a patch of oil sent it into the wall. South Bend was ecstatic at the car's potential. The Studebaker President, Albert Erskine concluded, deserved a full factory-sponsored team. The Hunt Special was repaired and served as proto-type, Herman Rigling again provided the coachwork, the cars' drivetrains and engines were 85% stock President. Although the checkered flag would not be waved for the South Bend company, the Indy performance of the Studebaker Specials was terrific: three of the five cars entered in '32 finished, in '33 seven of the first twelve finishers were Studebakers. Bob Valpey's car is the original Hunt Special: ''It finished 6th in the 1932 Indy 500, 12th in '33. Ab Jenkins owned it for many years. It's been mine for three. The car appeals to me for many reasons: the style of the open two-man Indy-type racer, the stamina and durability of

1931 Studebaker President Indianapolis Race Car
Owner: Robert W. Valpey of Center Harbor, New Hampshire

the Studebaker President engine. No other Classic using stock components came close to equalling Studebaker's racing achievements of this era. This is a very exciting car to drive. It's not highway legal, of course, but I've driven it numerous times in vintage events, both road racing and hill climbing.''

Studebaker Presidents became even finer cars in 1931. The original 337-cubic-inch straight eight had five main bearings. Now it had nine, plus seven more horses for 122 hp at 3200 rpm. Freewheeling (controlled by a button on the shift knob) was new and so was the styling, with the vee of the radiator grille complemented by a deeper version of same in the single-bar front bumper. The Presi-dent's double-drop chassis remained rugged. Lubrication was provided by ''high pressure lubricators which enable the driver to forget the grease rack for 2,500-mile intervals.'' The clutch was automatic, the steering wheel adjustable, the shock absorbers double-acting Houdailles, the trans-mission a three-speed Warner. Sales of the new Series 80 President totaled 6,340 cars.

The ''Presidential'' styling speaks to Ray Miller: ''With chrome radiator stoneguard, twin salon horns and sidemount spares, this car radiates elegance. Visitors to our museum are always commenting on this car's appearance.''

Whitney E. Kerr has owned his Four-Season Convertible Roadster since 1983: ''This very handsome car will outperform most Classics of 1931. That the straight-eight engine is rugged was demonstrated by the 25,000 miles over the old board track at Atlantic City. And few stock car engines in the history of the Indian-apolis 500 have ever competed as well as the Presidents. Many design features and parts were shared by Studebaker and Pierce-Arrow during this period. Barney Roos designed the straight eights for both companies. Some people have called the President the 'baby Pierce.' Collectors who own Presidents, Cadillacs and Packards of the same era will attest to the superior

1931 Studebaker President Series 80 Four-Season Convertible Roadster
Owner: S. Ray Miller, Jr. of Elkhart, Indiana

1931 Studebaker President Series 80 Four-Season Convertible Roadster   *Owner: Whitney E. Kerr of Kansas City, Missouri*

1931 Studebaker President Series 80 Four-Season Convertible Roadster   *Owner: John E. Morgan of Manalapan, Florida   Photo: K. Karger*

handling and performance of the big Studebakers. Unfortunately, the high production volume of the lower-priced Studebaker sixes and Dictator and Commander eights have overshadowed the much-lower-production President models.''

''I like high performance cars and this is one,'' says Tom Lester. ''And the 'convertibility' of this body style from roadster to convertible is super.''

Comments John Morgan: ''When I was a young man I felt this was one of the finest cars made and hoped to own one some day. Now I do. A car similar to this model set eleven stock car speed records at Muroc Dry Lake in California in November of 1931. George Hunt both tuned and drove it and took the flying mile at 91.79 mph and the hour at 90.35.''

Fewer than 2,400 Studebaker Presidents were sold in 1932. Previous model years had seen both a short and a long wheelbase for the President, now just the longer (135 inches) was used. The French-style windshield visor introduced in 1930—what Studebaker called its ''jaunty polo cap''—was eliminated but further changes were few. Tom Sparks bought his '32 Series 91 Coupe from singer Phil Everly nearly three decades ago and considers it ''one of the best driving Classics I have ever owned.''

If the declining sales figures might seem to have preordained discontinuation of the prestige President line, that was only part of a story which took a tragic turn as the Great Depression raged. In late March of 1933 Studebaker Corporation was in receivership. In early July a devastated Albert Erskine took his own life. Survival was the sole Studebaker priority now. The big President died with the man whose idea it had been.

1931 Studebaker President Series 80 Four-Season Convertible Roadster
Owner: Thomas J. Lester of Deerfield Beach, Florida

1932 Studebaker President Series 91 Coupe
Owner: Tom Sparks of North Hollywood, California

Because his mother was fond of Byron, Childe Harold Wills was his full name, which he hated and never used. Still, there was a sense of the poet in the man. For the radiator of his new car, he chose the Gray Goose, in his words, ''the wisest, freest traveler in the skies.'' For his car's name he joined his own with that of the Saint Clair River along which his new factory in Marysville, Michigan was built—but he added an ''e'' to both words because it looked more elegant.

Only 14,000 Wills Sainte Claires were produced, which was partially C.H.'s doing. That the car was produced at all was pretty much Henry Ford's. Because of the verbal agreement made between the two men when Wills joined Ford during his experimental days, C.H. left Ford Motor Company in 1919 with a check for $1.5 million in his pocket. He had earned it. Much of the engineering thought in the Model T Ford had been his, including its use of vanadium steel. Now Wills had discovered a metal even stronger than vanadium: molybdenum. With the million plus and molybdenum, he could develop an automobile that would set the industry on its ear.

The Wills Sainte Claire was

planned as a car short in wheelbase, light in weight, and abundant in advancements. The longest chassis was 127 inches, the heftiest weight 3,400 pounds, the advancements could fill a book. Wills' overhead cam V-8 engine, alas, was too sophisticated for the average garage mechanic to fathom so he developed a 273-cubic-inch 65 hp straight six (which powers both cars shown here). A single overhead cam shaft-driven by bevel gears, the head and crankshaft were fully machined, 35%

of the latter supported in seven main bearings lubricated by a forced-feed oil system. Wills' ingenuity was also revealed in such details as automatic spark advance, de-clutching fan, back-up light activated by shifting into reverse, single-key ignition/locking system, single-unit starter/generator, and headlights with magnetic mirror reflectors that with a touch of a button give a high and low beam effect. And his fitting of Lockheed hydraulic brakes as early as 1924 was avant-garde. Wills' problem was that

1926 Wills Sainte Claire Model T-6 Gray Goose Traveler Roadster
Owner: Henry Ford Museum & Greenfield Village, Dearborn, Michigan

whenever he got a new idea for his car, he would stop the assembly line to incorporate it. Such perfectionism, while admirable, was bad business. With his car priced in the $3,500 range, Wills couldn't afford the luxury of being himself. He chose not to change. The Wills Sainte Claire Motor Company simply ceased to exist in 1927.

Production of 2,085 Wills Sainte Claires in 1926 represented one of the company's better years. The CCCA Museum Phaeton was the donation of William J. Greer, who had purchased the car from original owner August G. Maross in 1982. Only two other T-6 Phaetons like it are known to exist, one of them fittingly displayed in the board room of Amax, the American molybdenum company.

The T-6 Roadster has been in the Ford Museum since 1946. Its original owner was Ray Dahlinger, the friend of Henry Ford's who was the "father" of a boy named John who, evidence suggests, was the illegitimate son of Henry Ford himself. The paternal arrangement had been agreed to by the two men. One wonders if Dahlinger paid for this Wills Sainte Claire.

1926 Wills Sainte Claire Model T-6 Gray Goose Traveler Phaeton
Owner: Classic Car Club of America Museum, Hickory Corners, Michigan
Page opposite: side curtained, and not.

77

1931 Willys-Knight Great Six Series 66B Phaeton
Owner: Al Copsetta of Lindenwood, New Jersey

Granted, John North Willys had overextended himself badly and retrenchment was certainly in order, but he was mortified nonetheless in 1920 when Chase National Bank called in Walter Percy Chrysler to set matters right in his Toledo, Ohio company. Chrysler's first action—cutting Willys' annual salary in half, to $75,000—was clearly a power play since Chrysler himself was being paid a cool million dollars for his annual efforts by Chase. But John North Willys kept his cool as Chrysler called the shots in Toledo until the bankers offered Walter P. another salvage operation with Maxwell in Detroit that seemed more promising. Certainly Chrysler had helped Willys-Overland but whether he regarded his job there or the Toledo company itself as finished is moot. Willys-Overland was undead, so to speak, but still mighty sick.

John North Willys was delighted to see Chrysler depart and relieved that the only Willys car he was interested in was an experimental poppet-valve six engineered by the Zeder-Skelton-Breer triumvirate (it would ultimately see production as the first Chrysler). Walter Chrysler was as uninterested in Knight sleeve-valve engines as Willys was enthusiastic. With Chrysler gone, John North got to work. From 50,000 cars sold in 1921, Willys worked sales up to over 200,000 by 1925. From an indebtedness of over $20 million, he worked up to a profit almost equalling that figure during the same period. In 1925, too, Willys bought out Stearns-Knight of Cleveland. With the subsequent introduction of the Falcon-Knight, Willys had sleeve-valve models in all price ranges from high (Stearns) to low (Falcon). ''The Day of the Knight'' is here, company advertisements burbled.

Although the Willys-Knight was middle-market range, John North couldn't resist giving his namesake car an upscale edition. Introduced at the 1929 New York Automobile Show, the 87 hp Great Six Series 66B Plaidside Roadster was styled by the talented Amos Northup, with Griswold of Detroit building the coachwork. Short and sassy (120-inch wheelbase), the Plaidside was a perfect accompaniment to the Jazz Age. Flappers with bobbed hair and rolled stockings, raccoon-coated gents with hip-pocket flasks went wild at the New York show. The Willys-Knight Plaidside Roadster was the most talked-about new car there.

Al Copsetta enjoys talking about these Willys-Knights today: ''A great combination, in my view, sleeve-

valve engine and Amos Northup
design. It appears the Plaidsides were
displayed at the automobile shows
for three years as my Phaeton was
shown in '31. Only the Roadsters
were catalogued by Willys. The
Plaidside Phaetons were never
advertised and apparently were built
only for the automobile shows in the
U.S. or for export. I know that three
were produced for the 1931 shows,
one for Chicago, one for San Francisco, and my car which was
purchased by a Michael Collins from
the Willys exhibit at the New York
Automobile Show.

"The Baker-Raulang Phaeton body
was purchased by Cliff Cornell,
president of the Cleveland Flux
Company, to replace the coupe body
on his recently-purchased 66-B
Willys-Knight. Baker-Raulang was the
coachbuilding arm of the former
Baker and Rauch & Lang electric-
producing companies. Only three
bodies like my phaeton were made;
the other two went on Ruxton
chassis.''

Plaidside Willys-Knights are seldom
seen today. They weren't produced
long. In March 1930, with his factory
humming and believing (as most did)
that the Wall Street crash would have
only short-term effect, John North
Willys became America's first
ambassador to Poland. Two years
later, at the request of President
Hoover, he returned to manage his
now-troubled company. The Jazz Age
was over. So was the jazzy Willys-
Knight Plaidside.

1931 Willys-Knight Great Six Series 66B Phaeton, Baker-Raulang
Owner: Al Copsetta of Lindenwood, New Jersey

1930 Willys-Knight Great Six Series 66B Roadster
Owner: Al Copsetta of Lindenwood, New Jersey

Above—Al Copsetta's 1931 Willys-Knight 66B Phaeton by Baker-Raulang and his Plaidside Roadster; below—the Roadster

A U B U R N

The Auburn-Cord-Duesenberg Museum's 1935 Auburn 851 Speedster in front of the Museum

At the turn of the century, carriage and wagon makers by the hundreds tried their hand at producing automobiles. Frank and Morris Eckhart of Auburn, Indiana were typical. Modest capitalization of $2,500 for their Auburn Automobile Company was followed by modest production. Most firms similarly begun in small towns throughout America were overwhelmed as the automobile business turned into a big-time industry. But the Auburn motored on. During World War I the Eckharts boasted that their secret of success was the fact that there had been "no change in ownership or officers" in their company since its inception, but the truth was they were not very successful. That secret was out in 1919 when the brothers sold controlling interest in Auburn to a Chicago consortium including officers of the Harris Trust and First National banks and William Wrigley of chewing gum fame, all of whom were quickly chagrined to find that what they bought wasn't making money. The new Beauty-Six, that designation a thinly-veiled comment on the plain-jane Auburns the Eckharts had produced, didn't boost sales much. Finally in 1924 Ralph Austin Bard, who had put together the disgruntled consortium, approached the hotshot Moon salesman of the Quinlan Motor Company in Chicago. Go to Auburn, Errett Lobban Cord was told, find out what's wrong. At the factory Cord discovered a dismal production of six units a day, a parking lot full of unsold cars—and a dazzling opportunity. The nest egg of $100,000 Cord had saved from his commissions and investment in the Quinlan dealership was burning a hole in his pocket. Back in Chicago he wheeled a deal. For a modest salary, he would become Auburn's general manager provided he was given the option of buying control if he could save the company. To this, all parties readily agreed. Very quickly, the Auburn became a very different car. . . .

A little chic nickel plating and some flashy repainting and those formerly black and green Auburns in the factory parking lot began to sell, a carload of 100 of them to a single dealer in Brooklyn bringing in some needed cash to move on. The automobile was a "style vehicle," Errett Cord said about this time, which was really more in the nature of a prediction because almost everyone else in the industry talked about engineering a vehicle not styling it. Even before General Motors recognized the wisdom of creating a design department, E. L. Cord was his own Art and Colour Section. He knew what sold cars—and who bought them. His comment that it was the woman "who passes final judgement" on a family car purchase was rather avant-garde as well because it had been only a half-decade since she had been given the right to vote.

E. L. Cord and designer Alan Leamy spent many a late evening together in Cord's kitchen in Auburn sketching ideas. At that kitchen table was begun the conscious policy of body-design changes every few years as a major sales tool.

Equally aware was Cord of the sales potential of performance. With improving roads, America had become interested in speed. A marque that did well on the track drew a lot of showroom attention, so Cord set out to capitalize on this growing fetish for bigger and faster cars. Eight cylinders in a Lycoming engine promised pizazz—and delivered. In 1929 two Auburn 8-88 Roadsters averaged better than 60 mph for 15,000 miles on the board track at Atlantic City, breaking all records for fully equipped stock cars from 5 to 5,000 miles. On Independence Day at the Rockingham Speedway in Salem, New Hampshire, factory driver Wade Morton took the checkered flag at an impressive 89.9 mph average. Admittedly, Stutz was not on hand. In the other races entered during '27, Auburn trailed the Black Hawk Speedster across the finish line. The difference in power—Stutz's 125 and Auburn's 90—was considerable. But in the marketplace, the difference between the two cars was even more pronounced—in price.

What Errett Cord provided in the Auburn was more car than anyone had a reasonable right to expect. And he continually was offering more. The two 8-88's on display in the Auburn-Cord-Duesenberg Museum (which is housed in the company's former administration building, now

1926 Auburn Model 8-88 Roadster
Owner: Auburn-Cord-Duesenberg Museum, Auburn, Indiana

1928 Auburn Model 8-88 Sport Sedan
Owner: Auburn-Cord-Duesenberg Museum, Auburn, Indiana

on the National Register of Historic Places) are a perfect example. The 1926 model offered 298.6 cubic inches, a stiff "twist-proof" pressed steel frame and a three-speed "racing crash box." For the second series 8-88 introduced in 1928, hydraulic four-wheel brakes replaced the former mechanicals and Bijur lubrication was added. All this for a car selling in the $2,000 range. The 8-115 followed in 1928—promoted in full-page advertisements depicting 115 white horses stampeding off the page. This left no room for a photograph of the car, but perhaps it would have been superfluous anyway.

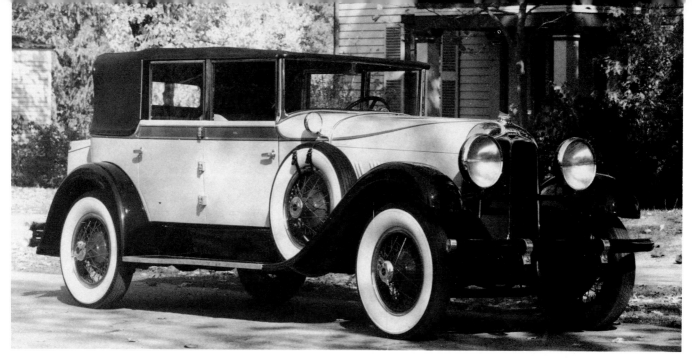

1930 Auburn Model 8-95 Phaeton Sedan   Owner: *Henry Ford Museum & Greenfield Village, Dearborn, Michigan*

The over 22,000 Auburns sold in 1929 represented a 1000% increase over sales figures of scant five years previous. And by now Errett Cord's empire included two more automobiles: the Model J Duesenberg and a front-wheel-drive car bearing his own name. The man's rise in the automobile industry had been meteoric. The stock market crash was a nuisance that saw Auburn sales decrease to 13,700 cars in 1930. Errett Cord was sure he could handle it.

The smaller straight-eight Auburn for 1930 was the 8-95: 246.7 cubic inches, 100 hp, a 125-inch-wheelbase chassis. "Low price, high style," says Randy Mason of the Ford Museum's 8-95. "This is a marvelous early example of the convertible sedan body style with low, very narrow pillars, thin-top profile and a superb two-tone paint combination."

Styling also attracted Tom Lester to his 8-95 Cabriolet: "At $1,495 new, this was not an expensive car although its roadability would suggest otherwise. The Lycoming engine and hydraulic brakes are great. The car had 11,000 original miles when I bought it about thirty years ago. The odometer is closing in on 20,000 miles now."

1930 Auburn Model 8-95 Cabriolet   Owner: *Thomas J. Lester of Deerfield Beach, Florida*

The Model 125 of 1930 was the final rendering of Auburn's largest-ever straight eight. The only concessions to the prevailing economy were the elimination of a couple of previously low-selling body styles and the overall lowering of the price range by several hundred dollars. This paid off. Automobile showrooms were often lonely places in America in 1930. Comparatively, Auburn sales remained brisk.

The Speedster owned by Al Copsetta is an example of Auburn's retaliation to Stutz's Black Hawk. A record-breaking 84.7 mph for twenty-four hours at Atlantic City in '28 and a Penrose Trophy-winning assault on Pikes Peak later that year were the Auburn Speedster's finest performances. The Black Hawk remained a slightly faster car, but an Auburn Speedster could be driven out of a showroom for several thousand dollars less.

And the Auburns with less racy coachwork than the boattail Speedster were plenty quick too. Just ask Bob Daryman about his 125 Cabriolet: "This is one of the few muscle cars of that era. With 125 hp, it can get to 105 mph. Just looking at it, you can tell the car can go. When Errett Cord took control at Duesenberg, one of his first moves was to have his Auburn stylists redesign the Auburn radiator to look like a Duesenberg and add those large headlamps and classy round-type bumpers. I bought this 125 Cabriolet four years ago from a junkyard owner who had stored it since 1953 and who seemed to have no interest in it. I sure do. Adding the accessories to this car has been fun. We have it dressed up like a dapper young man of the time might have done it."

1930 Auburn Model 125 Speedster
Owner: Al Copsetta of Lindenwood, New Jersey

1930 Auburn Model 125 Cabriolet.

Owner: Robert S. Daryman of York, Pennsylvania

1930 Auburn Model 125 Phaeton Sedan
Owner: Ken Kenewell
of Fenton, Michigan   Photos: Torque

Interesting to Ken Kenewell is the first owner of his 125 Convertible Sedan: ''Peter Nessor was a bootlegger who operated a speakeasy in Racine, Wisconsin. Auburn history shows the 125 was made one year only and was the company's most powerful straight eight ever. I'm sure the original owner appreciated the pep of the engine. I've owned the car for over two decades. This particular body style has it all: roll-up windows, nice low-profile top when up and also stored nice and low when down. The back window section is removable for partial open touring.''

In two years Jim Cox has driven his 125 Sport Sedan over 5,000 miles: "The car is very comfortable for touring. When it's cool, there's ample heat; when it's hot, there's ample cooling with the windshield cranked out. I love the close-coupled look of this Auburn, particularly in side profile with the Brewster windshield and trunk. Sitting behind the wheel, I also enjoy the view over the stout hood toward those huge Indiana headlamps. The fact that this car was a finale intrigues me. This was the last year the Brewster-style windshield appeared on any production automobile, and also the last year for the tubular Balcrank bumpers. And most important historically, 1930 was the last year for the big eight engine which had set so many speed records and made the name Auburn famous far beyond the small town in Indiana that was the headquarters of the company."

For 1931 Auburn dropped its 125 and 8-95 as well as its non-Classic six-cylinder models to focus production on a single new eight: a 268-cubic-inch unit delivering 98 hp at 3400 rpm. At 127 inches, the wheelbase was three inches shorter

1930 Auburn Model 125 Sport Sedan
Owner: James H. Cox of Matamoras, Pennsylvania

than the Model 125, but the new body design made the car appear just as big or bigger. *Fortune* magazine used the superlative in proclaiming the 8-98 "the biggest package in the world for the price." And the price: an incredible $945-$1,195 in the standard line, $1,195-$1,395 in the custom line which included the perk of an L. G. S. Free Wheeling unit. Auburn enjoyed a record year: 29,536 cars sold and a $3.5 million profit. Meanwhile most automakers were wondering how they could hold on to their shirts.

Nineteen thirty-two brought another new twist: "Dual Ratio," produced by the Cord-owned Columbia Axle Company. By turning a lever on the dash, a driver could preselect the desired axle ratio (4.55:1 or 3.04:1) for best performance under prevailing load, speed and road conditions. This was an effective selling point, and in a year which saw sales of most manufacturers plunge into a veritable abyss, Auburns sold numbered 11,646 which was a big decrease but not as drastic as most.

Jim & Carol Beauchamp have owned their Model 8-100A for six years: "This was our first Classic. The all-original state of the car is rare and educational and its less-than-show-quality condition makes it easy to enjoy and hard to worry about. In Auburn tradition, this is definitely a performance-oriented automobile with exhaust cutout, two-speed differential and free wheeling. And the body design was an outstanding achievement of Auburn's Al Leamy. The absence of sidemounts on our sedan accentuates the sweeping lines of the belt moulding and graceful fenders. In tough times, this car sold well. The '32 Auburn was a very affordable Classic, advertised as such then, and it remains so today."

1932 Auburn Model 8-100A Four-Door Sedan
Owners: Jim & Carol Beauchamp of Austin, Texas

87

Ray & Carol Kroll echo the Beauchamps' sentiments: ''The overall design of the 1932 Auburn resulted from the talent of Auburn's Al Leamy. Continued was the gathering of the paint trim at the center of the hood which had been a distinctive feature of Auburns since E. L. Cord's early years with the company. We particularly appreciate the opportunity to drive this Classic sedan and view the narrowed long hood crowned by the winged Mercury ornament and flanked by the two freestanding headlamps. In addition to the unique headlamp design and matching cowl lights with their split-appearance design tastefully achieved with chromium mouldings, the front appearance of the car with its radiator grille unobstructed by a headlight bar set the Auburn apart from its contemporaries of the early thirties. The two-speed Columbia rear axle was a plus; a debit was the fitting of mechanical rather than hydraulic brakes. The historical mystery that surrounds our 1932 Custom Touring Sedan is the fact that it was first titled on August 9th, 1939 by the Auburn-Cord-Duesenberg Company (as Dallas Winslow renamed the firm following his acquisition). The original title shows a delivered purchase price of $175.00 and an Ohio sales or use tax paid of $5.25. This Certificate of Title No. 630007580 was issued in the county of Paulding in Ohio. This is a mystery we would like to solve.''

1932 Auburn Model 8-100A Custom Touring Sedan
Owners: Raymond F. & Carol T. Kroll of Brooklyn Center, Minnesota

1932 Auburn Model 12-160A Cabriolet

Owner: Behring Museum, Danville, California

The mystery in 1932 was how Auburn could do it: a V-12 for $975-$1,275, the most economical twelve-cylinder car ever placed on the market anywhere. The bargain-basement price for multi-cylinder luxury was partially possible by using the same bodies as the eights and making components of like, if not interchangeable, design. The brakes on the twelve were hydraulic. The

wheelbase, at 133 inches, was a half-foot longer. Since the late twenties Lycoming had been part of the Cord Corporation empire and produced the 391-cubic-inch 160 hp V-12 to Auburn specification.

"A fabulous V-12 engine with twin carbs and a fast 90-95 mph performance," enthuses Dick Gold regarding his Speedster. "The only luggage space is behind the seat, so

there's not much room, but who cares?"

For fifty dollars less than the Speedster, or $1,225, one could have purchased a Cabriolet in '32 like the car in the Behring Museum. Auburn prices always strained credulity during the Classic Era; the literary willing suspension of disbelief is necessary to conjure the Auburn V-12.

1932 Auburn Model 12-160A Speedster

Owner: Richard G. Gold of Deephaven, Minnesota

1932 Auburn Model 12-160A Four-Door Sedan   *Owner: Auburn-Cord-Duesenberg Museum, Auburn, Indiana*

The '32 V-12 Sedan in the Auburn-Cord-Duesenberg Museum is a remarkable car for yet another reason. In the past half-century-plus it has travelled a total of 8,800 miles and is completely original even to its double-white Firestone tires. Museum curator Skip Marketti says it will stay that way.

During the first quarter of 1932, the Auburn Automobile Company made a net profit of $7,959—or less than one-fortieth that of the previous year. That summer in an attempt to improve this situation, a fully-equipped V-12 Auburn Speedster was taken to Muroc Dry Lake where in a series of speed tests it covered a standing mile at 67.03 mph, a flying mile at 100.77, completed a one-hour run at 92.2 mph average and 500 miles at 88.95. All figures—many of which would stand until after World War II—were extravagantly publicized but to no avail. On November 30th, Auburn reported a net loss of $974,751 for the fiscal year. Red ink was everywhere in the automobile industry, of course, and Auburn's

money-losing year was not as dismal as that suffered by most manufacturers. In 1933 the company tried with a larger model line-up, including the V-12 Salon series higher priced in the $1,800 range. But overall sales fell—to 5,040 units. The good news remained the cars themselves.

"The body style is gorgeous and exciting. The V-12 performance is smooth and powerful," comments Bill DiCiurcio about his '33 Salon Speedster. "The two-speed Columbia rear enables this car to cruise at highway speeds all day. With an Auburn of this era there is no need for the hobbyist who likes to drive his car to worry about having high-speed gears fabricated, which is the case with other Classics. And the braking system of the Auburn, which accommodates various weather and road conditions, works and is basically a rudimentary A. B. S. system—this in 1933."

1933 Auburn Model 12-165 Salon Speedster   *Owner: William T. DiCiurcio of Mt. Laurel, New Jersey*

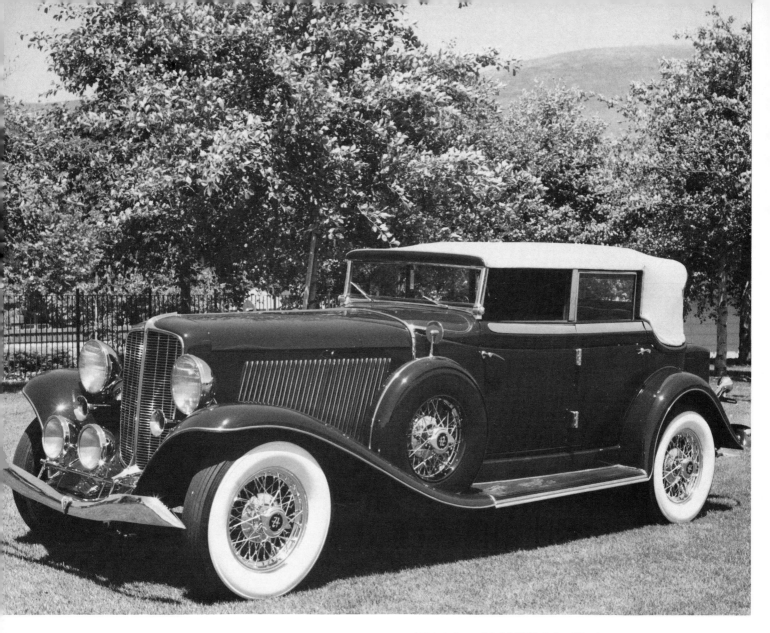

1934 Auburn Model 1250 Salon Phaeton
Owner: Blackhawk Classic Auto Collection, Danville, California

As Auburn sales continued on a downward spiral, the decision was made early in 1934 to complete the V-12 chassis remaining on hand and then discontinue the line. In introducing the twelve, Auburn had dropped its smaller and lower priced six—a miscalculation, it was now believed. Two lines of Auburn sixes were reinstated for '34 to generate volume sales. When the figures were totalled, approximately 2,500 V-12's had been produced in three years, about 250 of them in '34, approximately 27 of those Salon Phaetons like Knox Kershaw's and the car in the Blackhawk Classic Auto Collection.

David Engel's 850Y Convertible Sedan exemplifies Auburn's efforts to create a moneymaker out of its straight eight in '34: "The styling was changed. The front fenders had teardrop panels, the side panels had sweeping horizontal vents, the radiator cap was moved under the

1934 Auburn Model 1250 Salon Phaeton
Owner: Knox Kershaw of Montgomery, Alabama

hood. The cars are now generally considered among the best styles of mid-thirties Auburns, but back in '34 they were not popular, possibly too advanced for public taste. They were made for only six months. The return of hydraulic brakes to Auburn's eight was a definite plus. I've owned my 850Y Convertible Sedan since 1969; in 1972 it joined my wife and me on our honeymoon on the Empire State Region CARavan.''

1934 Auburn Model 850Y Convertible Sedan

Owner: David C. Engel of Greenland, New Hampshire

1935 Auburn Model 851 Coupe   Owners: Bud & Judie Hicks of Marshall, Michigan

A half-million dollars had been spent to design the 1934 line; $50,000 was budgeted for revisions for '35 to make the car more acceptable to the public. Duesenberg president Harold Ames, among those in the Cord empire who had been critical of the earlier design, was dispatched to Auburn to oversee the operation. He took Gordon Buehrig and Augie Duesenberg with him. They got to work immediately.

"With a $50,000 budget, we couldn't do much," Gordon said later. "The decision was made to do nothing to the chassis or body and to concentrate on the front end sheet metal and fenders." The latter were more deeply skirted, the side panels received new louvers, the Auburn signature "streamer stripe" was eliminated, the radiator grille was made bolder. The cars were introduced in June of '34 as 1935 models.

Bud and Judie Hicks have owned their '35 851 Coupe for fifteen years

during which time it has been gently driven.

The Osbornes' 851 Convertible Sedan was anything but initially. Bruce explains why: "As a purveyor of cars for movies and television, I've owned literally hundreds of old cars. This was my first Classic, bought expressly to be the lead car in the movie *Shanghai Express*, given partial mechanical restoration, a quick paint job (as the villain's car, it had to be black), and shipped to Hong Kong. This Auburn was a revelation. Over fifty years old when I got it and disused much of that time, the body was still firm and sturdy; the doors didn't need rehanging but shut easily and smoothly with a quiet click and no effort. And the performance was remarkable. The car has such unexpectedly powerful acceleration. During the filming of the movie the Auburn was chased by two motorcycles with sidecars, and the director had to keep reminding its driver not to take off so fast since he

was unable to keep both the car and cycles in the same shot. After returning from Hong Kong, we gave the Auburn a proper restoration. It is beautiful with a graceful top and possibly the best-proportioned side windows of any four-door convertible I've ever seen."

The mid-'34 introduction of the 1935 Auburns had been a boon for the company but for automobile show time, when the rest of the industry would be introducing its new 1935's, Auburn needed what Gordon Buehrig called a "bomb"—a sensational car that would guarantee headlines amidst the welter of other new cars competing for same. Augie Duesenberg worked with Lycoming and Switzer-Cummins on a supercharger that would boost the Auburn straight eight's 115 hp to 150. Gordon Buehrig was sent back to the drawing board to come up with the car's design. Aware that Union City Body—another Cord Corporation subsidiary—had about a

1935 Auburn Model 851 Convertible Sedan.   *Owners: Bruce & Norma Osborne of Bloomington, California*   *Photos: Rick Lenz*

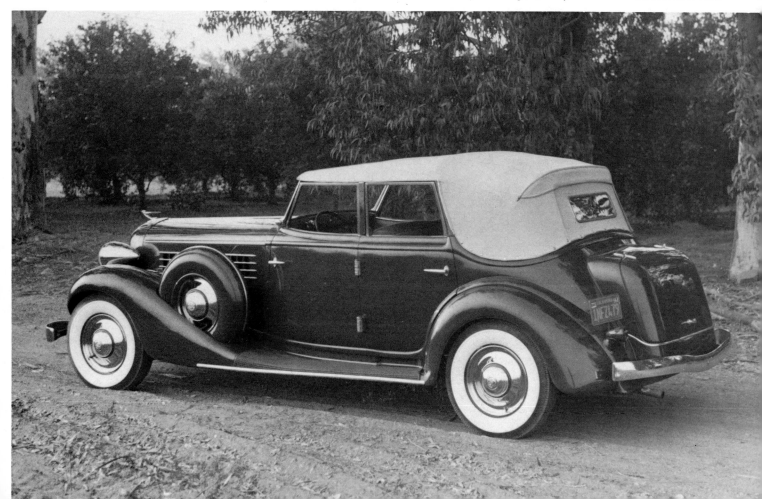

hundred former Auburn Speedster bodies remaining in stock, Harold Ames suggested a boattail speedster might be perfect for the attention-getting show model Auburn needed. Given an assignment markedly less than carte blanche, Buehrig turned sorcerer. The result is seen here. *The* most flamboyant U. S. car design," says Dave Holls. "My 851 Speedster was originally owned by Mr. D'Iteren of the Belgian custom body building house. I bought it about two decades ago and drove it in Europe from 1970-1974 while working there for General Motors. Needless to say, the car came back home with me."

1935 Auburn Model 851 Speedster

Owner: David Holls of Bloomfield Hills, Michigan

Auburns for 1936 were designated 852. ''That was our total facelift for the new model year,'' Gordon Buehrig said.

''Beautiful styling, a lovely interior,'' comments Bob Pierson about his 852 Sedan. ''Just a great and beautiful car,'' says Al Ferrara of his Speedster, ''which I would say even if it hadn't been designed by my good friend Gordon Buehrig.''

Auburn sales rose 20% in 1936—not enough for a profit, however. But Auburn's troubles extended beyond the factory to the turmoil within Cord Corporation. With Ab Jenkins driving, the 851 and 852 Speedsters set up more than seventy new speed marks. For awhile all U. S. stock car records up to twenty-four hours and 15,000 miles belonged to Auburn. The Speedster was the first fully-equipped American production car to exceed 100 mph for a twelve-hour period. All this produced headlines in 1935 and 1936. The sad headline from Auburn shortly thereafter announced the company's obituary.

1936 Auburn Model 852 Speedster   *Owner: Alfred Ferrara of Gates Mills, Ohio*

1936 Auburn Model 852 Four-Door Sedan
Owner: Bob Pierson of Bloomington, Indiana

The face of Alvin Zamba's 1932 Buick Series 90 Sport Phaeton, photo by Charles Vatter

Neither the fellow who founded Buick nor the man responsible for its early success were with the company when the Classic Era began. Genesis for the marque had been 1903 when David Dunbar Buick—who had previously invented a method of affixing porcelain to cast iron, thus giving America the white bathtub—became bored with plumbing fixtures and built an automobile. An inveterate tinkerer, Buick was a consummately bad businessman. Enter William Crapo Durant, an entrepreneur and super salesman who enjoyed tinkering in big business. Under Durant, Buick fortunes soared and in 1908 Billy parlayed the Buick Motor Car Company into a brand-new corporation called General Motors. The pace in Flint was too fast for David Buick, who left the company that year. The pace Billy Durant set for General Motors was too fast, and reckless, for the banking community—and Durant was booted out of the corporation by 1912. Billy got General Motors back, spectacularly, by organizing another firm (Chevrolet) and quietly buying up GM stock, but by late 1920 was forced out of the corporation for the second, and final, time. Alfred P. Sloan, Jr. picked up the GM pieces and recognized Buick as the "vital link" in the empire Durant had built. Billy himself had always referred to the Buick as "my number one baby." Except for the lamentable styling decision that made the 1929 models appear enceinte—the cars would ever after be known as the "pregnant Buicks"—the company seemed not to do anything wrong during the twenties. In 1931 Buick bragged in advertisements that it was the "First Large Producer to Adopt Eight Cylinder Engines Exclusively." Among the new Buick straight eights was an exciting series numbered 90. . . .

Prior to production of its 1931 line, Buick tested its front axles for over 900,000 miles, the rear axles for nearly as much, with testing miles in the hundreds of thousands as well for the three-speed synchromesh transmission, clutches, steering gears, frames and bodies. The company wanted to make certain that the rest of the car was worthy of its new engine. Like all units from David Buick's first twin in 1903, the straight eights were overhead valve, or "valve in head," as the company preferred. Powering the top-of-the-line Series 90 was the largest, displacing 344 cubic inches and developing 104 hp at 2800 rpm. An oil temperature regulator to cool the engine at high speeds and warm it in cold weather was featured, as were thermostatically-controlled radiator shutters.

Buick's caution paid off. "It's a big well-built car, you might say over-built like most Classics," says Bud Hicks of the 1931 Convertible Coupe he and Judie have owned for eight years. This particular body style was a mid-season addition to the Series 90 line; 1,066 were sold by the end of the model year.

1931 Buick Series 90 Model 96C Convertible Coupe
Owners: Bud & Judie Hicks of Marshall, Michigan

1932 Buick Series 90 Model 91 Club Sedan
Owner: Paul F. Richardson, M.D. of Baltimore, Maryland

The Series 90 increased in wheelbase from 132 to 134 inches in 1932. An adjustable shock absorber system was new (used this year only). The amusingly-named Wizard Control was a vacuum-operated clutch which enabled the driver to shift from second to third by pushing a button on the floor.

A brand-new body style offering for '32 was the close-coupled Club Sedan. "Only 2,237 were built and apparently less than 25 exist," comments Paul Richardson. "I like the smooth power of the valve-in-head straight-eight engine. My Buick, which I've owned since 1972, requires very little gearshifting and climbs hills with ease. It also cruises effortlessly at legal speeds."

"This car can keep up with traffic anywhere," echoes Alvin Zamba regarding his '32 Sport Phaeton which he's owned since 1982. With just 146 built (15 of those for export), the Sport Phaeton was Buick's lowest-production Series 90 model. The wooden spoke wheels on Al's car were an option, and '32 was the last year they would be available on any production Buick. The dual sidemounts on both the Zamba and Richardson cars were a standard equipment perk for all Series 90 buyers.

1932 Buick Series 90 Model 95 Sport Phaeton   Owner: Alvin Zamba of Pittsburgh, Pennsylvania.   Photos: Charles Vatter

1933 Buick Series 90 Model 90 Seven-Passenger Sedan   *Owner: Onofrio Imbasciani of Kings Park, New York*

All-new styling throughout the Buick lines and, for the Series 90, enhanced prestige with all body styles placed on a long 138-inch wheelbase distinguished the marque for '33. Less fortuitous was a sales decrease overall, shared with most manufacturers, which resulted in Buick's worst year since 1915. Just 890 (versus 1,368 in '32) Seven-Passenger Sedans like Onofrio Imbasciani's were produced: "Growing up in a very large family, we needed a large car. My Dad owned a 1933 Buick Series 90 Model 90 that disappeared in 1967. My love of that car left me determined to find another one. After a ten-year cross-country search, my dream came true in 1982. Appropriately, I think, this Buick remains an all-original car."

Nineteen thirty-four was a better year for Buick overall and for the Series 90. With the discontinuation of the Series 80, the top-of-the-line Buick (now on a 136-inch wheelbase) received three new body styles—Convertible Coupe, Sport Coupe and Convertible Phaeton with built-in trunk. Production of cars like Knox Kershaw's totaled 138, nineteen of those for export.

1934 Buick Series 90 Model 98C Convertible Phaeton
Owner: Knox Kershaw of Montgomery, Alabama

1937 Buick Series 80 Limousine, Brewster

Owner: Russ Jackson of Phoenix, Arizona

Late in 1933 Harlow Herbert "Red" Curtice had been appointed Buick president. Formerly the dynamo at AC, Curtice now became the spark plug that pulled Buick out of its Depression doldrums. Nineteen thirty-six was the landmark year for winsome new Buick styling courtesy of Harley Earl and evocative names for the various Buick series: Special for the 40, Century for the 60, Roadmaster for the 80, Limited for the 90. While turning Buick into a solid moneymaker, Curtice did not neglect the carriage trade. That a clientele able to afford any chassis upon which to have custom coachwork applied often chose the Buick is a tribute both to the marque and the acumen of its leader.

The Series 80 131-inch Roadmaster chassis was selected by the original owner of the 1937 Brewster Limousine now owned by Russ Jackson: "I have always been partial to Buicks. I drove a Super throughout World War II from Army Air Force base to base. This '37 Brewster Buick is very special, the only one built. Hypoid gears make the car easy to shift, and this was the first year for the steering wheel horn-ring."

103

The 140-inch long wheelbase of the Series 90 Limited was the choice of Howard "Dutch" Darrin for the very theatrical Opera Brougham owned by Jim Robbins. Banker Fernandez, the liaison Dutch made following Tom Hibbard's return to the States, was largely a silent partner on styling matters. The Darrin touch is evident in the car's elongated fenders sweeping from the front of the grille to the back door, the sloping windshield that makes the body appear more compact and the hood a lot longer, as well as the oversized front opening "suicide" doors which Dutch subsequently carried even into the Packard Darrins. Buick identification is readily discernible in the car's cowl, bumpers and lights (though Marchal lenses are in the headlamps and there is an additional Marchal taillight). After completing the design, Dutch returned to the States, and it is believed the car was finished by Franay. Following display at the 1938 Paris Automobile Salon, the Opera Brougham was acquired by the Countess Max de Palaska, a.k.a. Sandra Plankinton, who used it primarily for round trips between her summer *pied-à-terre* on Long Island and her winter home in Palm Beach, Florida. Jim Robbins' belief that Buick had the best running and performing automobile on the market in 1938 enticed him to acquire the Opera Brougham in 1972 from its second owner. "This Buick is the kind of car you either think is gorgeous and love, or think is ugly and hate," comments Katie Robbins. "Needless to say, Jim thought it was gorgeous.

It took a little time for the car to become a favorite of mine." This Buick is also the kind of car people crowd around, and the Robbins have provided ample opportunity for that. Everybody in the CCCA who has been on a CARavan knows the Fernandez & Darrin Buick, because it's been on twelve of them.

1938 Buick Series 90 Opera Brougham, Fernandez & Darrin
Owner: Jim Robbins of Dearborn, Michigan

General Motors itself commissioned the Series 60 Dual Cowl Phaeton from Maltby's Motor Works & Garage, Ltd., a coachbuilding establishment in the English seaside resort of Folkestone, Kent. Since 1936, when the Redfern Saloon Tourer with hydro-electric top was first shown on a Buick chassis at the Olympia Motor Show, GM had apparently become quite interested in Maltby's work. Putting the sporty Saloon Tourer on the 126-inch Series 60 chassis was a natural since the 320-cubic-inch 140+ hp Buick Century was arguably the hottest car in America at the time. The result was dynamite. Among those ogling the Maltby Buick at the 1939 International Automobile Show in Copenhagen was Carl Jensen, who was on a reconnaissance mission to find something ''both modern and distinctive'' for his employer, Danish furniture manufacturer James Lǿve. Since the Lǿve garage already housed three Buicks, chauffeur Jensen knew he had found just the car for his boss. General Motors' reluctance to sell did not deter James Lǿve, and ultimately he prevailed. During World War II, the car was hidden for the duration of the German occupation of Denmark. Following the

*1939 Buick Series 60 Redfern Saloon Tourer, Maltby
Owner: Russell L. Creason of Franklin, Michigan*

liberation, the Maltby Buick was back on the road. Because its owner was a personal friend of the Danish royal family, the car was used on ceremonial occasions by visiting heads of state. Both General Eisenhower and Winston Churchill are believed to have paraded in it. In 1966 James

Lǿve died and bequeathed the Buick to his chauffeur. That same year Russ Creason, on a visit to Copenhagen, saw it for the first time, and three years later had himself a wonderful Christmas present. In December 1969 Carl Jensen agreed to sell him the car.

The Series 90 Limited for 1940 was a big Buick with the same engine as the Century mounted in a 140-inch chassis and cloaked with roomy bodies providing accommodations for eight. Academic matters were no doubt discussed in the back seat of the car Larry Sciortino has owned for eight years: "My Buick was originally bought by Arthur Cutts Willard, president of the University of Illinois. It remained in the state until 1980, then went to Colorado and in 1982 came back home. The Limited was truly limited in 1940. Out of 310,995 Buicks built that year, only 796 were the Series 90 Eight-Passenger Touring Sedan."

Total Series 90 Limousine production was 526 cars. Sonny Abagnale has owned his since 1961: "It was purchased at an estate sale. I paid $35.00. There were no other bids. The sidemount spares have never been used, and the tires on the road wheels are original. I've driven this Buick 10,000 miles and at times at speeds up to 100 mph. But the car's most spectacular performance was in the movie *The Godfather.* That sensational U-turn on the George Washington Bridge? This was the car!" And the photograph shown here is a still from the film.

Noel Thompson's custom Series 90 Town Car was built for Mrs. Richard Whitney, whose husband was president of the New York Stock Exchange. Noel has owned the car since 1962: "The distinctive Brewster radiator shell, the P-100 headlights, the very unusual vee windshield and custom aluminum body attracted me. But most important at the time was the town car configuration, providing the parents of four children the opportunity to sit up front and put the kids in the back. The subsequent full restoration, right down to the bud vases, took three years."

1940 Buick Series 90 Model 90 Eight-Passenger Touring Sedan
Owner: Larry Sciortino of Elmhurst, Illinois

1940 Buick Series 90 Model 90L Limousine   Owner: Sonny Abagnale of Cedar Grove, New Jersey

1940 Buick Series 90 Town Car, Brewster   Owner: Noel Thompson of New Vernon, New Jersey   Photo: K. Karger

1940 Buick Series 70 Townmaster, Brunn

Owner: Daniel J. Slowik of Berwyn, Illinois

Had Cadillac not cried foul, possibly more collectors would enjoy ownership of a Buick like Daniel Slowik's. His was the prototype for an ambitious custom program which died aborning. Dan tells the story: "As good as this era was for Buick, characteristically, it was not quite good enough for Buick's Harlow 'Red' Curtice. For the 1940 model year he decided to go custom. First he approached Cadillac and Fleetwood/Fisher asking for cooperation in the supplying of bodies. The answer was a resounding 'no'—which might have been expected. Buick Limiteds were already making inroads into the luxury-class territory which Cadillac regarded as its private preserve in General Motors. So Brunn & Company of Buffalo, New York was contacted. Brunn chose to work with the 126-inch-wheelbase Roadmaster chassis, which was a Series 70 this year because of Buick's division of the Limited into two individual model lines. To revise the Roadmaster Four-Door Sedan into a town car, Brunn sectioned the roof just behind the driver, with provision for roof panels over the driving compartment (to be stored in the header

behind the driver's seat) and a two-piece sliding divider window separating the driver and passenger compartments. This sectioning made necessary the relocation of the radio antenna to the rear of the left front fender. Stock 1940 Buick fender skirts were used. However, a very luxurious passenger compartment

was created featuring amenities from hidden radios to overstuffed cushions. The finished car was exhibited at the Waldorf Astoria during the New York Automobile Show at the old Palace. It enjoyed an enthusiastic reception, but the price of $3,750 proved a deterrent to sales. Buick officially named the Brunn the

The instrument panel in Dan Slowik's 1940 Buick Series 70 Townmaster, Brunn

1941 Buick Series 90 Model 90L Limousine

Owner: Robert Stork of Grand Blanc, Michigan

Townmaster and officially introduced it on February 18th. But my prototype was the only one built. After being used to pick up Buick VIP's at the Flint airport, the Townmaster was sold and lived on a Connecticut estate until 1975 when it was traded on a Jaguar. The Jaguar dealer put it on the collector car market simply as an old car. I acquired the Brunn in 1980. To me, it is the ultimate 1940 Buick—a Roadmaster, a convertible, a town car, a very special piece of General Motors history.'' Dan is exactly right. Four custom Brunns were specially ordered on either Roadmaster or Limited chassis. None exist today. Dan's car is the only tangible reminder of the ambitious custom program that Harlow Curtice planned and which might have worked had not Cadillac complained to GM corporate management that Buick was treading into sanctified custom territory and with coachwork that, heaven forbid, wasn't even built by General Motors. Harlow Curtice knew when to quit.

Unlike 1940 when the Limited was offered on two wheelbases, the 1941 version was a 139-inch-chassis Series 90 only. Dual sidemounts were no more; two-tone color schemes were available at no extra charge. Compound carburetion was new which, Robert Stork says, improved performance measurably: ''My 1941 Buick, one of 605 built, is a big comfortable automobile to drive and always dependable, even in the hottest weather. The car has an unusual five-band radio. Owning a hometown product of the Classic Era has a special significance for me.''

Following Pearl Harbor in 1941, Buick went to war. In the early fifties, when GM president Charles Wilson left to become U.S. Secretary of Defense, his successor was no surprise: Harlow Curtice.

Rear passenger compartment in Dan Slowik's 1940 Buick Townmaster, Brunn

109

CADILLAC

Hub and wooden spokes from Henry Lewis' 1927 Cadillac Series 314 Sedan, photo by Charles L. Smith

In 1908 the Cadillac Motor Car Company won Britain's Dewar Trophy—the first time ever for an American manufacturer—for its successful demonstration of standardized parts. In 1913 this coveted trophy for automotive advancement was won by Cadillac again, in part for the self-starter and electric lights. September 1914 saw Cadillac introduce its new V-8, an epochal refining of that configuration into an engine of supreme sophistication. Small wonder the marque was referred to pridefully by the slogan, "Standard of the World." Two years later wordsmith Theodore MacManus wrote "The Penalty of Leadership," one of the greatest advertisements ever created. But by 1917 Cadillac's creator and leader, the patriarchal Henry Martyn Leland, was gone from the company. The usual turmoil followed for awhile—then a new problem. Although there was no denying the marque's eminence in engineering, styling had clearly been an afterthought to Henry Leland. And America was becoming style conscious. Packard roared into the twenties first with an in-line six, then a handsome straight eight—and took over leadership in the $2,500+ price class. But in 1925, with Ernest Seaholm already comfortably ensconced as chief engineer (a position he would hold until World War II), Lawrence P. Fisher of the coachbuilding Fisher brothers arrived as Cadillac president and general manager. Internal affairs were put in order, the magnificent V-8 remained, and Larry Fisher would soon talk a West Coast stylist named Harley Earl into coming aboard. . . .

1925 Cadillac Type V-63 Coach   Owner: Auburn-Cord-Duesenberg Museum, Auburn, Indiana

Though designations differ, Cadillacs for 1925 and 1926 carried the same dimensional 314-cubic-inch L-head V-8 descended from the historic 1915 original. Extensive re-engineering reduced weight by 130 pounds and raised hp from 80 to 85.5 in 1926. Crankcase ventilation was improved and an oil filter added. The pressurized fuel system was charged by an engine-mounted compressor with a hand pump on the dash for starting. The narrower and taller radiator was fitted with thermostatically-controlled radiator shutters. Most important aesthetically was the introduction of Duco finishes which provided a rainbow of available colors. The A-C-D Museum's 1925 Type V-63 reflects Cadillac's traditional Leland-like look.

1926 Cadillac Series 314 Custom Four-Door Phaeton.   *Owner: Eugene G. Bond of Lake Ariel, Pennsylvania.*

Eugene Bond's 1926 Series 314 indicates the stylish difference softer hues as well as the larger 138-inch wheelbase (versus 132) of the "Custom" line made.

"When I was a child of eight years, I saw my first 1926 Cadillac phaeton," says Eugene. "I can remember everyone saying that the owner of that car had achieved success. For a long time I dreamed of owning one. It took until the age of fifty-nine (in 1985) to realize my dream, but it did come true. To this day I am impressed with this car and for the same reasons as at age eight: the powerful V-8 engine, the shutters over the radiator, the lines and looks, the wind wafting over your body as you drive, making you feel you are going ever so fast."

1927 Cadillac Series 314 Five-Passenger Sedan   *Owner: Henry H. Lewis of Owings Mills, Maryland*   *Photos: Charles L. Smith*

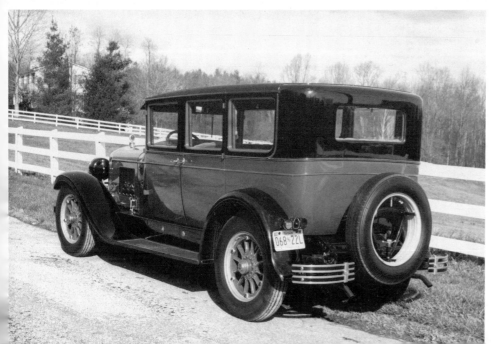

A new round emblem above a sharp point in the radiator shell distinguished the 1927 Series 314 outside, a new walnut instrument panel with silver inlay effect elegantly beckoned inside, and repositioning just about everything under the hood gave a new appearance to the 314 engine. Sales of 36,369 Cadillacs for 1927 represented a fine increase over the two years previous. One of those sales went to Henry Lewis' grandfather: "This car has been in my family since it was new, which lends significant attachment to me and is most unusual among Classic collectors. I bought the car from my grandmother in 1953. The Cadillac still drives great but remains hard to stop when you get up steam due to the mechanical brakes."

1928 Cadillac Series 341-A Sport Phaeton   *Owner: Henry H. Lewis of Owings Mills, Maryland   Photo: K. Karger*

A smaller bore and longer stroke for 1928 resulted in 341 cubic inches for the first displacement change in Cadillac's V-8 since 1915. Horsepower was up to 90. A longer 140-inch wheelbase and underslung rear springs allowed Harley Earl to design his first Cadillac as a long, low car. The strong moulding treatment was an accentuating complement, the wicker motif a delicate touch. Mounted on a hefty cross bar were new twelve-inch bullet headlamps, with a monogram rod between. Parking lights were mounted on the cowl. The new Cadillac, which bore a familial resemblance to Earl's smashing 1927 LaSalle, made a bold statement, and nowhere more dramatically than in the dual cowl Sport Phaeton. "Advertisements pictured stylish women leisurely driving this model with the top down and the windshield folded," says Alvin Zamba. "All of this added to the sex appeal of the vehicle." Comments Henry Lewis: "This car is an eye-catcher and a conversation piece—much flashier than my other Classics."

1928 Cadillac Series 341-A Sport Phaeton   *Owner: Alvin Zamba of Pittsburgh, Pennsylvania   Photo: Roger Nehrer*

Synchromesh transmission, dual acting shock absorbers, chrome plating and safety glass were four advancements on 1929 Cadillacs. Most obvious of the styling refinements was the relocation of the parking lights to the fenders. Sales totalled 18,004 cars, a decrease partly attributable to the burgeoning popularity of the LaSalle, which passed Cadillac in sales in '29.

The dual cowl Sport Phaeton continued as a most rakish and popular Cadillac model, then as now. "When I saw this one, I just had to have it," says Joel Gougeon. "It has a Hollywood 'roaring twenties' flair with lots of chrome."

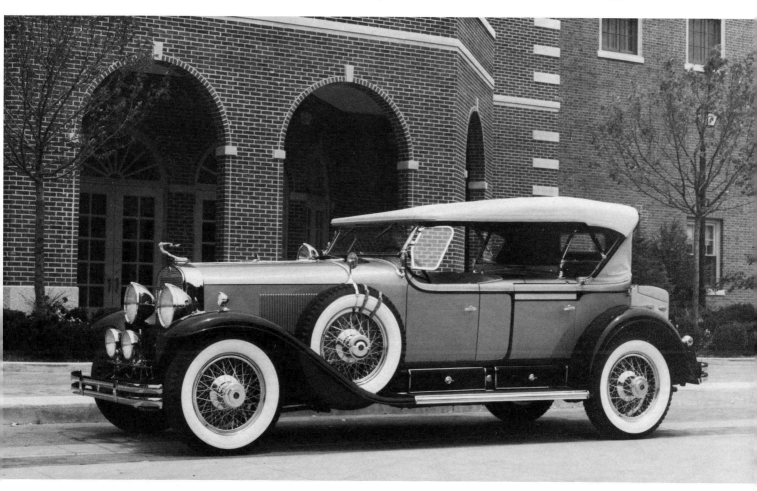

1929 Cadillac Series 341-B Sport Phaeton   *Owners: Joel & Kaye Gougeon of Bay City, Michigan*   Photos: Torque

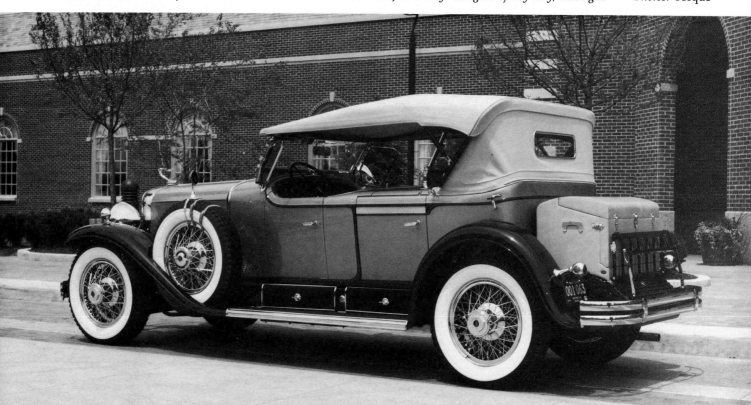

1929 Cadillac Series 341-B Sport Phaeton   Owner: George F. Mano of St. Petersburg Beach, Florida   Photos: Media Productions

The location of battery and tool compartments at the side of the body attracted George Mano to his Sport Phaeton, as well as such nice touches as the counterbalanced rear cowl and windshield with its large mirror (10 by 22 inches) for ladies underneath—plus "the way the car drives and behaves on the road . . . it is both heavy and powerful."

In 1929 the Fleetwood Metal Body Company (previously acquired by Fisher which by now was wholly owned by General Motors) was in the process of being moved from Pennsylvania to a new plant in Detroit. The Schilds' custom Transformable Town Cabriolet—the only Fleetwood style no. 3512 believed extant—is a working Cadillac, used in Jim and Myrna's Classic limousine service . . . "about 8,000 miles per year with a still untouched original engine."

1929 Cadillac Series 341-B Transformable Town Cabriolet, Fleetwood
Owners: Jim & Myrna Schild of St. Louis, Missouri

116

Complete originality was the major factor that drew Steve Babinsky to the acquisition of his 1930 Series 353 Town Coupe: "The car was purchased from its original owner—Arthur Bopf, the man who discovered and developed lanolin for commercial use—by long-time CCCA member Harry Dunn. I purchased it from Harry last year. All original with only 29,000 miles, the car drives beautifully. And I really like the body style."

Total V-8 Cadillac production for 1930 was 11,005 cars. Among other popular body styles was the Town Sedan like Marc Ohm's. This year all V-8 Cadillacs featured a wider radiator, larger headlights, a shorter cadet-type visor and a longer set of louvers extending now almost to the front of the hood. Boring out of the engine to 353 cubic inches had resulted in the model designation change—and 96 hp. Front tread was increased from 56 to 59 inches, the rear from 58 to 59½ inches, among other chassis revisions so that parts would be interchangeable with a brand-new Cadillac of twice the cylinders.

1930 Cadillac Series 353 Town Coupe
Owner: J. Stephen Babinsky of Bernardsville, New Jersey

1930 Cadillac Series 353 Town Sedan.

Owner: Marc S. Ohm of St. Louis, Missouri

Everything seemed possible in the twenties. As the decade roared on, the luxury car buyer became very demanding. Larger bodies, lavish accoutrements, more power was the cry from those who didn't look at the price tag before making a purchase. While enlarging its V-8 might partly answer the demand, Cadillac engineers determined that thermal and drivetrain problems would result. Better to multiply the cylinders. The 452 of the new V-16's series designation, as previous Cadillac practice, translated to cubic inches. Advertised horsepower was 175. This impressive new overhead valve engine was essentially two straight eights tilted at a narrow 45° angle to use a common crankshaft. A technical mini-coup was the engine's "automatic valve silencers," hydrau-lically-controlled zero-lash mechanisms which eliminated noise, well before the era of modern hydraulic lifters. In addition to dual exhausts, there were dual fuel feed and ignition systems. To the engineering excellence of the new unit was added a lavish aesthetic factor. Wiring was concealed, and covers hid the plumbing. The engine compartment was a polished, plated and enameled jewel. Despite the massive 148-inch-wheelbase chassis in which Cadillac placed its V-16, a top speed of 95 mph was possible. And Cadillac catalogued fully fifty body styles from which a purchaser might choose. Cadillac's magnificent new V-16 was introduced in January 1930, less than three months after the stock market crash. With price tags starting at well over $5,000 (or approximately two thousand dollars more than the V-8 line), V-16 sales totaled 3,251 cars for 1930 and 1931.

Of these, 105 were the Roadster. Stephen Brauer's car is unusual in carrying a Fisher body. Most V-16's had Fleetwood coachwork, like John Mozart's Roadster, which is a totally original 22,000-mile car: "As such, it presents one of the very few opportunities to drive a great American Classic that has not had the body off, the suspension apart, etc. The car is rattle free, cruises at 75 mph and is a pure joy to own, drive and enjoy."

The Sport Phaeton remained popular among Cadillac body styles, although by now it was no longer a dual cowl because some owners had complained about difficulty in entry and egress. Cadillac solved the problem by encompassing a lower-

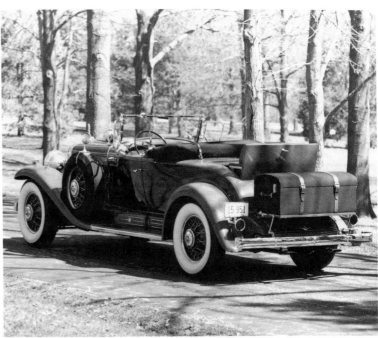

1930 Cadillac V-16 Series 452 Roadster

Owner: Stephen F. Brauer of Bridgeton, Missouri

1930 Cadillac V-16 Series 452 Roadster, Fleetwood
Owner: John Mozart of Palo Alto, California

1930 Cadillac V-16 Series 452 Sport Phaeton, Fleetwood
Owner: Charlie Harper of Meredith, New Hampshire

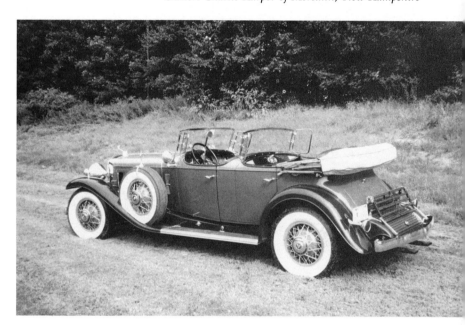

able windshield behind the front seat. Only seventeen 1930 Sport Phaetons are known to exist of eighty-five built. Fred Weber's is a recent acquisition.

Charlie Harper has owned his for twenty-five years. "The car has good looks, good ride and lots of power," comments Charlie, ". . . what more can you ask?" Possibly for a heater. Charlie's Sport Phaeton was an habitué when the CCCA Annual Meeting was held at Buck Hill Falls in the Poconos, and he remembers one very cold January well: "The car has no heater and never had anti-freeze in the radiator. We warmed it up, covered the lower part of the radiator and ourselves, and drove the 300 miles from New England to Pennsylvania to a heated garage. We froze more than the car did!"

1930 Cadillac V-16 Series 452 Sport Phaeton, Fleetwood

Owner: Fred Weber of St. Louis, Missouri

1930 Cadillac V-16 Series 452 All Weather Phaeton, Fleetwood   *Owner: Richard G. Gold of Deephaven, Minnesota*

Andrew Darling's Sport Phaeton does have a heater in both front and rear seats. It was an option selling for about $50.00, little more than the optional windwings cost. The Darling Sport Phaeton is driven 500 miles a year, always with warm feet front and rear, and passengers in the latter enjoying Cadillac's "stopwatch" (chronometer, clock and speedometer mounted in the front seat back).

At list price $6,650, the All Weather Phaeton was $150 more costly than the Sport Phaeton but offered better climatic protection. Over 250 of these cars were produced. Andrew Darling has driven his 10,000 miles in twenty years and enjoys "how effectively it runs in today's traffic, especially with the high-speed rear end."

Dick Gold's All Weather Phaeton is a veteran of seven CARavans and "steady driving since purchase thirty years ago."

"The V-16 All Weather Phaeton is especially appealing as it offers the best of open and closed car driving comfort," comments Al Waters. "High commodious seats, lots of rear seat passenger space and a trunk with fitted luggage make it ideal for touring." This particular Cadillac, which was used in the California citrus groves during World War II, was originally delivered in San Francisco on March 26th, 1930 carrying a reduced factory price of $4,251, which indicates that already Cadillac was having a problem selling its ultra-expensive new car.

1930 Cadillac V-16 Series 452 Sport Phaeton, Fleetwood
Owner: Andrew D. Darling of Edina, Minnesota

1930 Cadillac V-16 Series 452 All Weather Phaeton, Fleetwood
Owner: Andrew D. Darling of Edina, Minnesota

1930 Cadillac V-16 Series 452 All Weather Phaeton, Fleetwood   Owner: Dr. Al Waters of Bloomington, Minnesota

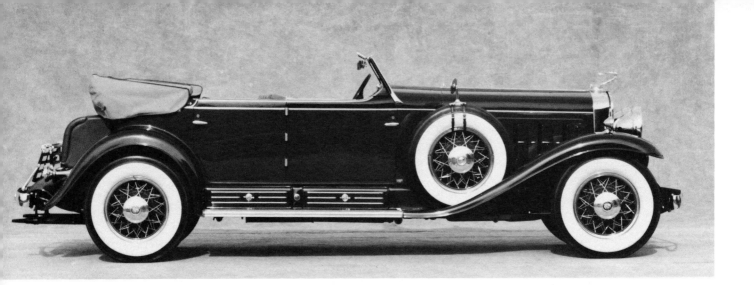

Charlie Harper's V-16 Club Sedan further elucidates the difficulty: "My car was shipped in August of 1930 but did not sell and was returned to the factory for credit (try that today!). Then it was sent to Ottawa, Canada where it ultimately was sold"—though perhaps not at its list price of $5,950. Charlie describes his Club Sedan as "a good rainy day car."

"Cadillac put its heart and soul into the engineering of the V-16, the detailing was plentiful, nothing was spared or overlooked," comments Ron De Mieri about his Imperial Seven-Passenger Limousine: "The interior is original and can accommodate seven people comfortably. The rear jump seats fold in and out of the way when not needed. Interior wood is burl and rosewood inlaid. Silk shades are on all windows including the division. The rear compartment has a parcel carrier and a place to store an umbrella. Overhead is a combination rear dome light and vent making it possible for a person to smoke without having to open a window for proper ventilation. The rear compartment also has two beautiful vanities with a silver-plated comb and mirror, a clock, cigarette lighters and a speaker for communication. With just the press of a button behind the smoking vanity, the passenger could signal the driver at any time."

Most custom Cadillacs of this era carried bodies by Fleetwood, the company's "in-house" coachbuilder. Only about one percent of the Series 452 chassis were sold to independent coachmakers, which makes John Mozart's Convertible Sedan by Murphy a singular automobile: "This one-off has traditional Murphy features like the roll-up windows which are concealed in their down position and a very slanted, low-cut windshield. When the top is down, the car appears to be a phaeton."

1930 Cadillac V-16 Series 452 Convertible Sedan, Murphy
Owner: John Mozart of Palo Alto, California

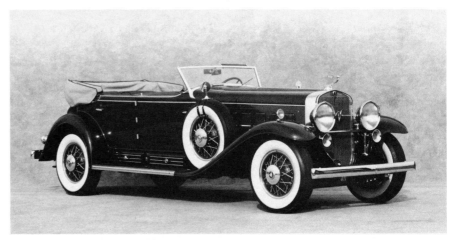

1930 Cadillac V-16 Series 452 Club Sedan, Fleetwood
Owner: Charlie Harper of Meredith, New Hampshire

1930 Cadillac V-16 Series 452 Imperial Seven-Passenger Limousine, Fleetwood
Owner: Ron De Mieri of Bethpage, New York

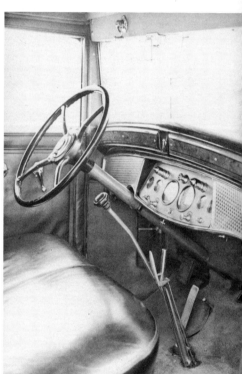

1931 Cadillac V-8 Series 355-A
Roadster, Fleetwood

*Owner: Richard G. Gold
of Deephaven, Minnesota*

The five-point engine suspension introduced on the V-16 was adapted to the V-8 in '31 but, although the numerical designation changed, the engine's displacement remained 353 cubic inches. Adopted too were the five hood ports and a modified version of the coach sill which had debuted as well on the sixteen-cylinder car. Bodies were lower and longer, and windshields were set at a jaunty angle. Sales of 10,709 cars indicated that, for the moment, the V-8 Cadillac was holding its own as the Great Depression began to take hold.

The Schilds' Fisher-bodied Seven-Passenger Sedan, like their '29 Fleetwood Town Cabriolet, is a Classic limousine service car and has logged over 22,000 miles since 1984. To Jim and Myrna, '31 represents the "peak of early Classic styling."

Dick Gold agrees: "Many people think that the '31 Cadillac Roadsters were the best looking of all Classics."

*1931 Cadillac V-8 Series 355-A Seven-Passenger Sedan
Owners: Jim & Myrna Schild of St. Louis, Missouri*

Comments Jack Royston about his Sport Phaeton: ''When my Dad had a Cadillac-LaSalle distributorship in 1931, this is the model he used as a demonstrator. As a youngster, it was my dream to own the same model. I acquired my car twenty-eight years ago. To my daughters, the Sport Phaeton has always been known as 'The Jolly Green Giant.' It went to their proms and averaged about ten weddings a year.''

The sleek lines of the '31 Convertible Coupe ''particularly with its top down, and ending with its quaint rumble seat'' attracted Gil and Diane Ranney to their car in 1980: ''The installation of an overdrive allows us to comfortably cruise at 65 mph or above. We drive the car about 400 miles a year.''

1931 Cadillac V-8 Series 355-A Sport Phaeton, Fleetwood
Owner: Jack Royston of Scottsdale, Arizona

1931 Cadillac V-8 Series 355-A Convertible Coupe, Fleetwood   *Owners: Gil & Diane Ranney of Huntington Beach, California*

Steve Chapman's Convertible Coupe was shipped from the factory on March 24th, 1931 to the Greenlease-Moore dealership in Oklahoma City. Scarcely had it been put on the showroom floor when Wichita Falls (Texas) businessman John Moran brought his Cadillac Sedan in for minor repairs and, although he had not the slightest intention of a new car purchase, fell in love with this one and bought it on the spot. On his way home, he wondered what his wife would think, so he parked the car at his country club and invited some friends and his wife there for dinner that evening. "He thought that after a good meal and visit with friends, he would introduce his purchase," Steve relates; "his wife could not say much in front of company, and it would give her a chance to cool down before they left. It worked fairly well, he reported. John said that he certainly enjoyed the car but soon found that he was not a convertible man. An all-day drive to Hot Springs, Arkansas with the top down resulted in such a bad case of sunburn and windburn that he never lowered the top again and ultimately traded the car in on a 1934 sedan." The '31 Convertible Coupe passed through two more owners prior to 1968 when Steve, just three years out of law school, acquired it: "My father, with whom I practiced law, was very dubious about my spending all my savings, about $4,000, on a nearly forty-year-old car but after giving strong negative advice recognized the inevitable and contributed $500 on the purchase!"

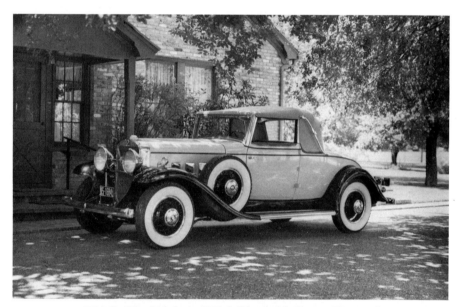

1931 Cadillac V-8 Series 355-A Convertible Coupe, Fleetwood
Owner: Steve Chapman of Waxahachie, Texas

1931 Cadillac V-12 Series 370-A Two/Four-Passenger Coupe   *Owner: Philip H. White of Sulphur Springs, Texas*

It was truly an embarrassment of riches. In addition to the V-8 and the V-16, Cadillac introduced a V-12 in October of 1930. Priced about a thousand dollars more than the Cadillac with four fewer cylinders, the V-12 was considerably better than a thousand dollars less than a V-16. Engine displacement was 368 cubic inches; 135 was the horsepower. Wheelbase was 140 inches except for seven-passenger cars and most Fleetwood semi-custom styles which were mounted on a 143-inch chassis. Although Fisher supplied coachwork, all body interiors were by Fleetwood. The V-12's hood was four inches shorter than the V-16, five inches longer than the V-8. Although seemingly the answer to a question Cadillac enthusiasts hadn't asked, sales of 5,725 Series 370-A V-12's indicated the car did present an attractive alternative to those who found eight cylinders too few and sixteen too many (or too pricey).

Philip White's 370-A rumble-seat Coupe was sold new in Rochester, New York. Among the earliest V-12's built, it was titled as a 1930 car by its new owner who perhaps was unaware (or didn't care) that Cadillac regarded the car as a '31. Phil has owned it for six years: "At the time of restoration, the odometer read 45,000 miles, which appeared to be confirmed by the condition of the engine. The Fleetwood interior was retained as original. An interesting sidelight during restoration was the discovery of a hat feather imprinted 'Win with Landon' behind the back seat! And an interesting feature of this car is a courtesy light mounted on the left rear fender, which seems to be either a factory accessory or a very good aftermarket one because of the quality and the fit. On the personal side, this is the first Classic I have been privileged to own, and it's great fun for a foursome with the rumble seat in use.''

The mileage on Ray and Wanda Eberenz's Five-Passenger Sedan registers a bit over 60,000 and, except for upholstery and tires, this Cadillac is original. A few years ago the FBI requested the car's participation at its A.T.F. (Alcohol, Tax & Firearms) Show in St. Louis, which gave the Eberenzes and friends the opportunity to dress in vintage thirties dress and play the good guys, though Ray suspects the Cadillac had been otherwise used originally: ''I like my car because it hails from Prohibition days, an era of unrest but an important part of history. This car, which is black, was the working tool of the gangster. Both the right and left running boards in front of the main stepping pads are completely bare of rubber, as if some person or persons stood there as a body guard might.'' The car's performance appeals too: ''It will pull away from a stop sign in third gear fully loaded. Among the many advantages of the V-12 was the negative benefit of not having to shift so much. Six miles a gallon is about the best gas mileage you can expect. But the car will move. Former owner Rodger Sprake was clocked on radar doing 85 mph in Minnesota. The trooper let him go. I've had the car up to 85 myself in a test run and believe it is easily capable of 100 mph.''

1931 Cadillac V-12 Series 370-A Five-Passenger Sedan
Owners: Raymond & Wanda Eberenz of St. Louis, Missouri

1931 Cadillac V-12 Series 370-A Town Sedan   *Owner: Roy A. Judd of Hermosa Beach, California*

"In reliability, smoothness and aesthetics, the Cadillac V-12 was unmatched, even by Pierce and Packard," declares Roy Judd, who likes the stately style, engraved side mirrors, roll-up windshield, two-way wipers and other examples of attention to detail in his '31 Town Sedan.

The Rittenhouse Fleetwood Convertible Coupe was one of 237 produced in 1931. The original owner of Dick Gold's similar car, indicated by factory records, was General Motors president Alfred P. Sloan, Jr., who asked for a few personal touches: chrome door saddles, full chrome trunk rack, bolstered and pleated cloth interior, special interior door and windshield reveals, triple silver striping. Of all Dick's Cadillacs, this is the one he drives the most. It is an original car with 58,000 miles.

1931 Cadillac V-12 Series 370-A Convertible Coupe, Fleetwood
Owners: Ed & Pam Rittenhouse of Mercer Island, Washington

1931 Cadillac V-12 Series 370-A Convertible Coupe, Fleetwood   *Owner: Richard G. Gold of Deephaven, Minnesota*

1931 Cadillac V-12 Series 370-A Roadster, Fleetwood
Owner: Richard G. Gold of Deephaven, Minnesota

1931 Cadillac V-12 Series 370-A All Weather Phaeton, Fleetwood
Owner: Jim Robbins of Dearborn, Michigan

"The Cadillac Convertible Coupe had removable window irons that enabled the top to fold down like a roadster," says Dick, who happens to love that body style too, as evidenced by his other '31 V-12 gracing these pages.

Since 1927 it had been Cadillac practice to refer to its four-door convertible sedan as an All Weather Phaeton. With a base price of $4,895, the '31 V-12 version was among the most expensive in the Series 370-A line. And it was weighty, at 5,290 pounds on a 140-inch wheelbase. Cadillac advertising stated that the car "has California appeal." Jim Robbins knows why: "Since owning this Cadillac I have discovered what 'All Weather' means. . . . It means if it rains on the outside, it is raining on the inside. The car drives like a truck but is a crowd pleaser."

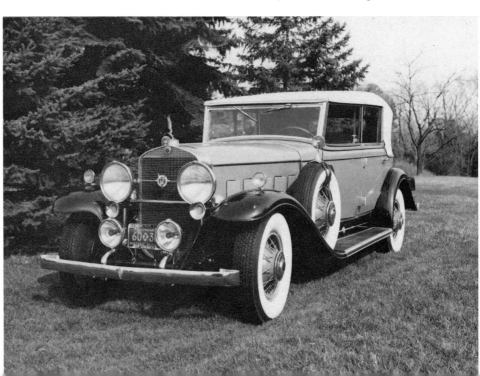

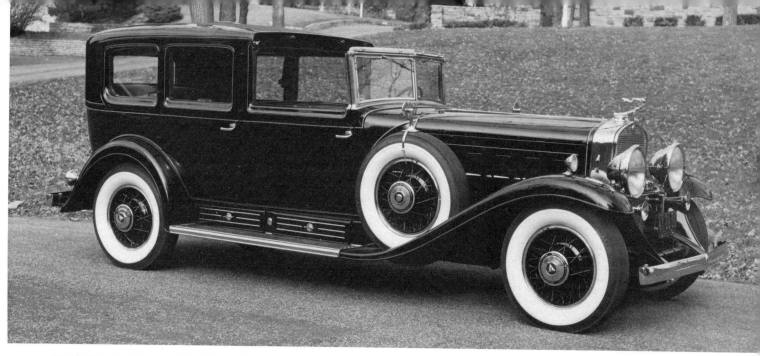

1931 Cadillac V-16 Series 452-A Limousine Brougham, Fleetwood   Owner: *Richard G. Gold of Deephaven, Minnesota*

When introduced in January 1930, the Cadillac V-16 bristled with new styling features: single bar bumpers, dual horns, radiator screen fronted by concave monogram bar, large thirteen-inch Tiltray headlights matched in design by the dual rear taillights, five vent doors in the hood complemented by one in the side of the cowl. Some of these features, as we have seen in the pages preceding, were incorporated in the V-8 and V-12 lines for 1931; others remained uniquely the V-16's.

John O'Sullivan is the third owner of his '31 Imperial Sedan Limousine which was delivered new to a Maurio Luna of Mexico. Total mileage is 17,000 kilometers. "The Cadillac V-16 was magically smooth, uncommonly capable, quiet and powerful," says John. "Every engine component was so rugged that many original engines run as well today as they did over a half-century ago."

Over a half-century ago Dick Gold's '31 Limousine Brougham was owned by Metropolitan Opera star Madame Ernestine Schumann-Heink. One of thirty such Fleetwood town cars built, it is one of only two known extant: "We, of course, affectionately refer to the car as 'The Madame.' She has never been restored. Total mileage to date is 31,000, and it's a kick to drive an original V-16. Madame Schumann-Heink was obviously not the flamboyant type, as the photo indicates. There is an interesting absence of accessories on this car: plain painted wheels, no sidemount covers and no mirrors, no accoutrements whatsoever except double whitewall tires."

1931 Cadillac V-16 Series 452-A Imperial Sedan Limousine, Fleetwood   Owner: *John Patrick O'Sullivan of Grand Blanc, Michigan*

1931 Cadillac V-16 Series 452-A Sport Phaeton, Fleetwood   *Owner: W. G. Lassiter, Jr. of West Palm Beach, Florida*

Owners of less formal cars generally were more adventurous, as Bill Lassiter's '31 Sport Phaeton indicates.

And Charles Gillet's '31 All Weather Phaeton is in the same idiom: "There is a mystique about a sixteen-cylinder car, and this particular body configuration—convertible sedan with divider window—is quite appealing. Moreover, the under-hood design is truly amazing for its clean, uncluttered layout; compare it with a Duesenberg engine compartment, and the difference is startling. To me, this Cadillac is one of the most awesome, mouth-wateringly beautiful vehicles ever to roll on four wheels. The Packards, Pierces, Lincolns and Rollses are great, but 'Carlotta' Cadillac need yield to none!"

1931 Cadillac V-16 Series 452-A All Weather Phaeton, Fleetwood   *Owner: Charles B. Gillet.   Photo: K. Karger*

1932 Cadillac V-8 Series 355-B Convertible Coupe

Owner: David Holls of Bloomfield Hills, Michigan

Extensive reengineering of manifold and carburetor brought over 20% more power—115 hp at 3000 rpm—to Cadillac's V-8 for 1932. The non-mechanical fuel system was discarded and a mechanical fuel pump installed on all models, eliminating the vacuum tanks. Triple-Silent Synchro-Mesh (all three speeds helical) was the new transmission. And 134 inches joined the traditional 140 as a new wheelbase length for some models. Restyling brought clam-shell fenders, curved running boards and headlamps in a more pronounced bullet shape. A flat grille was now incorporated into the radiator shell, the longer hood had six hood doors instead of five, and the outside visor was eliminated. Sales were way down: 2,693 V-8's as the Great Depression took its toll.

David Holls' Convertible Coupe, mounted on the shorter 134-inch wheelbase, sports the wheel discs which were offered (at ten dollars apiece) as an option by Cadillac for the first time. "The most beautiful of the Classic Era Cadillacs" is his verdict on the '32 line.

1932 Cadillac V-8 Series 355-B Town Sedan
Owner: T. E. Wenger of Ferguson, Missouri

On the Town Sedan, the trunk was integrated into the body for the first time. Terry Wenger's car, purchased as a complete basket case in 1982, was owner restored over the next four years: ''Purportedly, the '32 Cadillac was Harley Earl's favorite, and 1932 is thought of generally as the year of the ultimate in Classic styling. I have always liked the close-coupled sedan body style. For '32 the Town Sedan was somewhat more rounded than the two years previous and incorporated a long, flowing fender line.''

Edward Putnam's 1932 Town Sedan, like Steve Chapman's '31 Convertible Coupe, had its first home in the Greenlease-Moore dealership in Oklahoma City. It arrived there in early autumn but was not sold until December of 1932 when Streeter Flynn, a lawyer whose contributions to the state earned him recognition in the Oklahoma Cowboy Hall of Fame, bought it as a Christmas present for his family. The car remained in the Flynn family until 1939 when it was traded in on a new Christmas present: a 1939 Cadillac 60 Special. In the years since, the '32 Town Sedan has been owned by a number of CCCA Oil Belt Region members—including Streeter Flynn, Jr. The car has been in the Putnam garage since 1987.

1932 Cadillac V-8 Series 355-B Town Sedan

Owner: Edward Putnam of Fallbrook, California

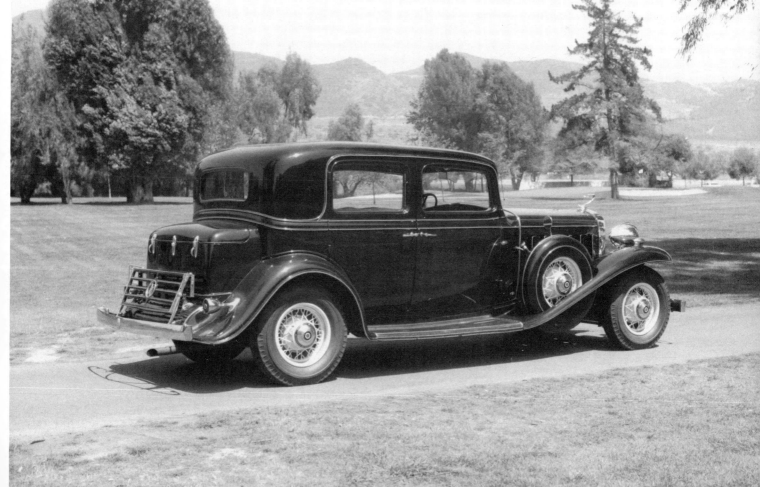

1932 Cadillac V-8 Series 355-B Five-Passenger Coupe   Owners: Berta & Jay Leon of Hubbard, Texas   Photo: Roy Query

The Leons' Five-Passenger Coupe on the 140-inch wheelbase gives an easy 55-65 mph on interstates and with its "comfortable ride and spacious trunk" is a great CARavan car for Berta and Jay. "The 20% added power on the 1932 V-8 was especially helpful on the Rocky Mountain CARavan," comments Jay.

The '32 Sport Phaeton is a recent acquisition of the Blue Suede Shoes Auto Collection as well. Curator Joe Bortz was drawn to it because of its history: "The original owner received this car in 1932 as a high school graduation present. He never parted with it. In 1952 the car was stored in a one-car brick garage, and in the late 1960's the owner promised that if ever he sold the Cadillac it would be to me. Almost twenty years later, to the day, he did. The car is amazing in its originality, every detail of it. I've been adding some to its 27,000 miles since the car has become the favorite of my dog Spuds, who enjoys touring around the North Shore suburbs with me on warm afternoons and evenings."

1932 Cadillac V-8 Series 355-B Sport Phaeton
Owner: Blue Suede Shoes Auto Collection,
Highland Park, Illinois

Introduced throughout the Cadillac lines for '32 was vacuum assist for the clutch which, in Cadillac's phrase, provided ''Controlled Free Wheeling'' (depressing a foot button released the clutch, releasing the button or depressing the accelerator reengaged it.)

''Smooth quiet performance with exciting spirit,'' comments Robert Leich regarding his Special Phaeton, one of 1,709 V-12's built for '32. ''The car handles well and is especially stable on expressways. The top is easy to raise and lower manually. There's a look of elegance with the top up and of sporty classicism with the top down.''

Just 296 V-16 Cadillacs were produced for '32 on two wheelbases of 143 and 149 inches. Stephen Brauer's Special Phaeton on the longer chassis sports a rear windshield and instruments—and is one of only two of that body style extant.

Extremely rare as well is the Indy Museum's Madame X, body number two of four Imperial Cabriolet Sedans built by Fleetwood in 1932. The slender door and windshield pillars, chrome edge window mouldings and sloping windshield readily identify the Madame X, which was produced in very limited numbers in five body styles in 1932 and 1933. This particular car was shown at the Chicago World's Fair in '33 and thereafter purchased by Rudolph Block whose family owned an Indianapolis department store. Two decades ago the Madame X was donated to the museum by the Block family.

1932 Cadillac V-12 Series 370-B Special Phaeton
Owner: Robert A. Leich of Bloomfield Hills, Michigan

1932 Cadillac V-16 Series 452-B Madame X Imperial Cabriolet Sedan, Fleetwood
Owner: Indianapolis Motor Speedway Hall of Fame Museum   Photo: Ron McQueeney

1932 Cadillac V-16 Series 452-B Special Phaeton

Owner: Stephen F. Brauer of Bridgeton, Missouri

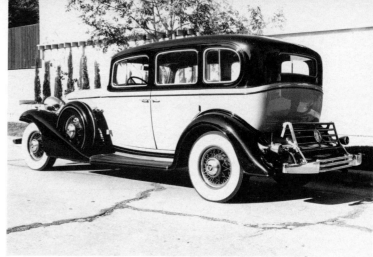

1933 Cadillac V-8 Series 355-C Five-Passenger Sedan
Owner: Leonard Urlik of Beverly Hills, California

Just 3,173 Cadillacs were sold in 1933, the fewest of any year in the Classic Era. Of these, 2,096 were the V-8's. Only the Great Depression was to blame for the plummeting sales since the cars were remarkable and presented a new look. Free wheeling was discontinued, but the brakes on the V-8 were given the vacuum assist previously introduced on the V-12 and V-16. In styling, 1933 represented the emerging transition from functional classicism to the streamlined envelope. Fenders were skirted, radiators were veed, the radiator cap moved under the hood, hood vent doors went horizontal, bumpers went three-bar, and closed models received wing windows which Cadillac advertised as providing "no draft ventilation."

Frank Bramante admires the "art work and craftsmanship" on the Town Sedan he purchased two years ago.

Leonard Urlik has owned his Five-Passenger Sedan since 1962: "I purchased this car as a rolling junk-pile for $75.00. The restoration required twenty-one years."

The Raines' Town Sedan was originally shipped from the factory on December 31st, 1932 directly to Brooklyn for the New York Automobile Show. They purchased the car in 1974. Ted did the restoration himself, save for the interior which remains original. The car's factory-installed radio is unusual for the early thirties. The car also includes foot stools in the back for the additional comfort of passengers—and included among the accessories is an original Moto-Pack (flashlight, tire gauge, whisk broom, lamb's wool dust mitt, full set of light bulbs, and ice blades for the windshield wipers). "We derive a great deal of pleasure and satisfaction from restoration being done at home," says Jo. The Raines call their '33 Cadillac Gregory. He's been driven 8,000 miles since 1975.

1933 Cadillac V-8 Series 355-C Town Sedan
Owners: Ted & Jo Raines of Castro Valley, California

138

1933 Cadillac V-8 Series 355-C Town Sedan　　　　　　　　　　　　*Owner: Frank Bramante of Holmdel, New Jersey*

1933 Cadillac V-12 Series 370-C Seven-Passenger Sedan, Fleetwood   Owner: Malcolm Willits of Los Angeles, California

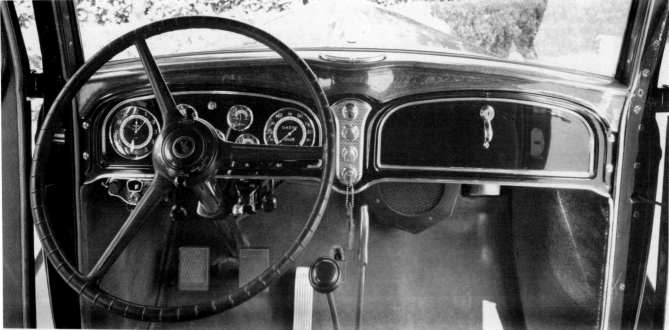

Malcolm Willits' V-12 Fleetwood Seven-Passenger Sedan sports a rear-mounted spare and wooden-spoked wheels, most unusual for 1933—but then so was this car's original owner. "She was Amelia Carson, daughter of the man who had built the world-famous Victorian Carson mansion in 1885 in Eureka, California," relates Malcolm. "It is interesting that Amelia ordered a radio with her 1933 Cadillac but no heater, this considering the damp, cold weather Eureka often has. But Amelia Carson was noted for buying fine things and never using them." This Cadillac was no exception; it has only 5,000 original miles: "The car still smells new. I have always considered Cadillac's styling for '33 to be very flamboyant as opposed to the more traditional design concept of 1932. I love my example. I would term this Cadillac truly swank."

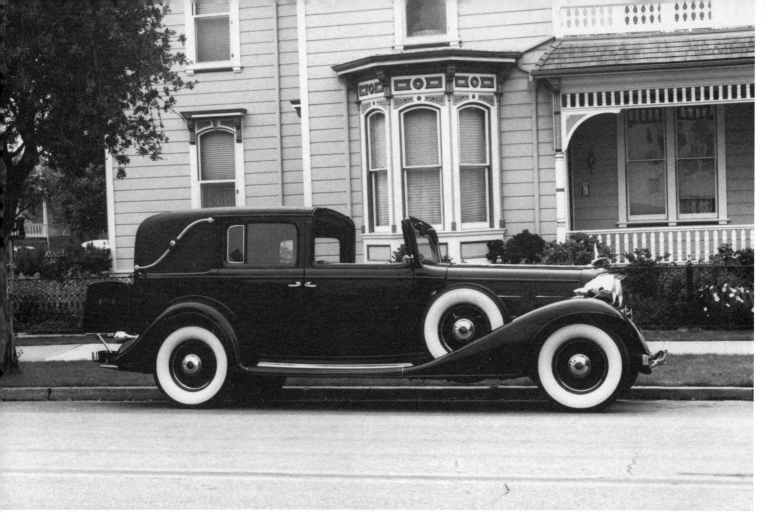

1933 Cadillac V-12 Series 370-C Town Car, Fleetwood   *Owner: Carl L. Steig of San Leandro, California*

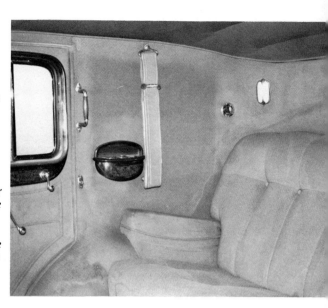

Carl Steig's 1933 V-12 Fleetwood Town Car. The small lower left instrument on the dash is indicator for the ride regulator (the adjustable shocks controlled by the lever below the gauge). In the rear compartment, note the chauffeur call button (by assist strap), microphone (by courtesy light) and vanity cases.

A total of 952 Series 370-C Cadillacs were produced for '33. Eleven Fleetwood Town Cars were built on the V-12 chassis; Carl Steig's is the only one known to exist: ''The car was originally shipped on February 17th, 1933 to Don Lee Cadillac in Los Angeles. It had changed hands several times prior to my purchasing it in 1973. Much of the car remains original. Nineteen seventy-five found it on a 600-mile trip to Harrah's car show with a circuitous return trip via Bodie (a ghost town which, at that time, was thirteen miles from the nearest paved road) and then over Tioga Pass (9,945-feet elevation) into Yosemite National Park. All told, my wife and I have driven the car about 11,000 miles thus far.''

''The Nineteen Thirty-three production of the Cadillac V-Sixteen is Limited to Four Hundred Cars custom built to order,'' the advertisement read. ''Early reservations are sincerely advised.'' Since fewer than 300 V-16's had been sold in 1932, Cadillac wasn't fearful of demand outstripping supply in '33. Instead, the elegant and socially correct typographical style of the ad, the social magic of the number 400 and the exclusivity it represented—it was hoped—would encourage demand for the V-16 in the drastically-diluted ultra-high-priced market.

In '33 one could differentiate a V-8 and V-12 Cadillac only by lifting the hood or looking at the emblems. Harley Earl provided the V-16 a number of styling fillips all its own: the massive four-bar bumper, spinner-type wheel covers, and three horizontal ventilator spears which were repeated on the lower edge of the front fender skirts. Moreover, while the heron hood ornament, which had replaced the herald in 1930, graced the radiator of the V-8 and V-12, the goddess was resurrected for the V-16, redesigned in a much more voluptuous form.

Did it help? Cadillac V-16 sales totalled 125 cars in 1933. Just two Fleetwood Convertible Victorias were built, carrying price tags of $7,500 each, this one for the movie actor Robert Montgomery. William Jahant has owned the Montgomery car for over three decades.

1933 Cadillac V-16 Series 452-C Convertible Victoria, Fleetwood
Owner: William F. Jahant of Claremont, California   Photo: Dennis Adler

Instead of two wheelbases, all V-12 Cadillacs for 1934 were on a brand-new 136-inch X-frame chassis with stabilizer bar at the rear. Independent ''knee action'' front suspension with coil springs and center point steering replaced the former solid front axle with leaf springs. Hotchkiss drive replaced the former torque tube. Outside, the changes were just as dramatic. Two inches lower overall, the new Cadillac styling was highlighted by teardrop headlights with parking lights mounted below, airfoil front fenders and a fixed, sharply sloping windshield. In the back a beaver-tail deck completely covered the chassis; the spare tire was concealed. The car's horns had joined the radiator cap under the hood. Present for this one year only were bi-plane bumpers, handsome in configuration but very fragile in use.

Cadillac V-12 sales totalled 683 cars. The Beauchamps' Fleetwood Limousine Brougham is believed to be the only one of that style built. John acquired the car in 1973: ''Several manufacturers moved into the 'Deco' look and a more enveloped body in 1934, but Cadillac took this styling advance further than the others. The traditional grandeur of the town car body was retained, however. The vee windshield frame on my car is one-piece, solid cast

brass. Under the chauffeur's seat, accessible only when the door is open, is a small, sliding trapdoor that looks like a cartoon mousehole and conceals an umbrella. The original is still with the car. Dan Dailey, the movie actor and dancer, was the

original owner of my car. In 1960 ownership passed to another dancer, José Greco. The third owner was Frank Miller, the family doctor for both those entertainers, who had known the car since it was new. I am the fourth owner.''

1934 Cadillac V-12 Series 370-D Limousine Brougham, Fleetwood
Owners: John & Wilma Beauchamp of Granite Shoals, Texas

"*Again* . . . Cadillac limits the year's production of the V-16 to 400 cars," the advertisement for 1934 read. Alas, sales limited production of the V-16 to just 56 (during a year when V-8 sales climbed to over 5,000). The new 154-inch wheelbase was the industry's longest; further distinguishing the V-16 from Cadillac's V-8 and V-12 was the tall eggcrate grille and the radiator-shell-mounted headlamps with park lights fitted to the fender.

Although reduced in price from over six thousand dollars to under four, just five Fleetwood Seven-Passenger Sedans were produced. Clifford Woodbury has owned his since 1977: "I started driving at age sixteen in 1930, just when the V-16 was launched, so it had tremendous charisma for me. My father owned twelve successive Cadillacs from a 1916 to a 1961 model. I learned to drive with his 1929 Town Sedan. When I purchased my car thirteen years ago, more than seventy parts were missing. Needless to say, I had a lot of work to do. In the winter of 1981 I removed the gas tank, cut about a three-inch-wide strip full length out of the top, and scooped out three-and-a-half gallons of thick gummy rust. After reconditioning and installing the tank, I could finally drive the car more than four miles without fuel filters becoming completely clogged! I continue to admire and enjoy this series Cadillac, combining the magnificent V-16 engine with the new 'knee-action' suspension and power-boosted brakes."

*1934 Cadillac V-16 Series 452-D Seven-Passenger Sedan, Fleetwood
Owner: Clifford A. Woodbury, Jr. of Haverford, Pennsylvania*

1935 Cadillac V-8 Series 355-D Convertible Coupe
Owner: Clifford A. Woodbury, Jr. of Haverford, Pennsylvania

In June of 1934 Nicholas Dreystadt had succeeded Lawrence Fisher as Cadillac's general manager—and did not enjoy a felicitous first year. The 1935 Cadillac V-8 remained on the same three 128-, 136- and 146-inch wheelbases as in '34, but the production of 3,209 cars was a significant decrease. Sales of both the V-12 and V-16 dropped as well, to 377 and 50 respectively. A significant advance was the all-steel Turret Top on Fisher-bodied cars, which would be provided the Fleetwoods in 1936.

Walt Nienaltowski's Convertible Coupe, which he has owned for three decades, was originally a Canadian car, indeed the first one to roll off the assembly line in 1935 at the GM plant in Oshawa, Ontario.

Clifford Woodbury has owned his Convertible Coupe even longer: "I purchased it from first owner Murray Kaskel on October 14th, 1940. When one has owned a Classic car for a half century, obviously a book-full of interesting anecdotes accumulate. The car had 21,750 miles when acquired; today the odometer shows over 60,000 more than that. A few weeks after I bought the car, I drove my wife to the hospital to bear our first child. Likewise in 1943 and 1945 for our other two children. Countless memorable day trips were taken during the first two decades of my ownership, most often with the top down, one child upfront and two in the rumble seat. The Cadillac performed flawlessly to the top of Mt. Washington in New Hampshire, an eight-mile road up, at least half in low gear, four gallons of gas. I call this V-8 a 'carefully' used car—repaired and renovated but never restored. I do try to make it run as well as I possibly can. My wife was and is a very good driver. Also our three children were by nature and training very careful with 'Daddy's car.' My son is a natural mechanic (with a PhD in Mechanical Engineering) and will be enjoying this Cadillac long after my lifetime, God willing."

1935 Cadillac V-8 Series 355-D Convertible Coupe
Owner: Walter Nienaltowski of Walled Lake, Michigan

146

1936 Cadillac V-8 Series 70 Touring Sedan, Fleetwood
Owners: Mr. & Mrs. Max Davis Murray of Huntsville, Alabama

Cadillac had begun revising numerical designations earlier, if haphazardly, finally settling in 1936 on both model year and series (i.e., 36-70, 37-70) which continued through the end of the Classic Era. For the sake of brevity, only series numbers are used here. With the introduction of the smaller 121-inch-wheelbase non-Classic Series 60 Cadillac in '36, the bodies of all Series 70 (131-inch wheelbase) and Series 75 (138-inch) were vee windshield styles by Fleetwood. Respective sales were 2,000 and 3,227 cars.

The V-8 engine for the Series 70/75 was all new: a flathead 346-cubic-inch unit generating 135 hp and featuring block and crankcase cast en bloc with full-length water jackets and hydraulic valve lifters/silencers. Smooth, quiet and powerful, this unit would be continued with refinements through 1948. Widely respected for robustness, the engine was used in pairs to power light tanks during World War II.

Nineteen thirty-six also marked Cadillac's introduction of hydraulic brakes on the V-8. With advanced engine and chassis design, the new cars weighed from 500 to 800 pounds less than their predecessors, and promised enhanced performance.

"Excellent acceleration and low-end torque, effortless hill climbing even in high gear and touring at interstate speeds are wonderful advantages," says Max Murray of his Fleetwood

The "face" and the driver's compartment of the Murray 1936 Cadillac V-8 Fleetwood Touring Sedan

Touring Sedan. "With the narrowed radiator grille incorporating horizontal louvers, the divided vee windshield and all-steel turret top, the 1936 Series 70 was a landmark design for Cadillac. And it's a very stylish automobile with large pontoon front fenders with sidemounts, the ribbed chrome full-wheel covers with large balloon tires, the moderate-length touring sedan body with built-in rear trunk. The long hood provides an especially powerful, impressive and well-proportioned appearance." The original owner of this Cadillac was Williamina Fullerton, a spinster who lived at the Olin Hotel in Denver. The car was always chauffeur driven. Following her death in 1957, the Cadillac passed through several owners prior to the Murrays' acquisition in 1985. Since restoration, the car has been driven over 2,000 miles including "four days of touring through Alabama and Tennessee in 90 to 100 degree weather during which 653 miles of troublefree operation were accumulated."

Driven extensively too (six CARavans to date) is the Clarke Series 70 Sport Coupe which Mary and Tom have owned for two decades. "This car was very original when purchased with the odometer registering 42,000 miles," says Tom. "A complete restoration was done seventeen years ago. Only 200 of this model were built. With full coil-spring padded seats, large powerful brakes and an excellent power-to-weight ratio on a 131-inch wheelbase, this Cadillac is my favorite driver."

1936 Cadillac V-8 Series 70 Sport Coupe, Fleetwood
Owners: Mary & Tom Clarke of Fenton, Michigan

1936 Cadillac V-12 Series 80 Convertible Sedan, Fleetwood
Owner: Andrew D. Darling of Edina, Minnesota

Instead of one 146-inch chassis, the V-12 Cadillac was available in two wheelbase lengths for '36: 131 inches (Series 80) and 138 inches (Series 85). Hydraulic brakes were a significant addition. Power increased to 150 hp at 3600 rpm, and sales increased (250 for Series 80, 651 for Series 85 vis-à-vis the 377 V-12's produced for 1935).

''The Art Deco style has a Clark Gable look,'' enthuses Dick Gold regarding his V-12 Convertible Coupe. ''This car is all original at 14,800 miles, is the best original open car I have ever seen and the best driving Cadillac I have ever had.''

''The steering and handling of this car show great improvement over earlier twelves and sixteens,'' comments Andrew Darling who acquired his V-12 Convertible Sedan two years ago.

The V-16 Series 90 remained on the epic 154-inch chassis, and without hydraulic brakes. The Kughns' V-16 was one of fifty-two built for 1936 and the only seven-passenger Town Cabriolet. Its first owner is known only by the initials A.G.H. on the driver's door. The car is documented to have been donated to the Navy during World War II and was used by Admiral Ernest Joseph King, commander-in-chief of the U.S. Fleet and subsequently chief of naval operations.

1936 Cadillac V-16 Series 90 Town Cabriolet, Fleetwood
Owners: Richard & Linda Kughn of Southfield, Michigan

1936 Cadillac V-12 Series 80 Convertible Coupe, Fleetwood
Owner: Richard G. Gold of Deephaven, Minnesota

1937 Cadillac V-8 Series 70 Convertible Sedan, Fleetwood
Owner: Gilbert A. Mack of Grosse Pointe Woods, Michigan

The die cast eggcrate grille and a new side moulding treatment were introduced on the Cadillac V-8 for '37. Revised bumpers and hubcaps carried the Cadillac crest in their centers. On the V-8 engine, the flywheel was lighter, an oil filter was installed, and the new carburetor boasted full-automatic choke. Series 70 sales totalled 1,001 cars; 3,227 of the long-wheelbase 75 were built.

As traditionally, Streeter Flynn's Sport Coupe includes a rumble seat: "This is strictly a four-passenger capacity vehicle. There's a large luggage area behind 'fold-back' seats but no rear seating inside. Chrome is minimal, and there are no hood vents. Only the horn button reads 'Cadillac'; nowhere on the outside of the car does the name appear."

The base price of Gil Mack's Series 70 Convertible Sedan was $2,960: "The styling on most cars in 1937 was great. I wanted a convertible sedan that was well proportioned and included such modern engineering features as hydraulic brakes, independent suspension, a powerful V-8 and closer-ratio transmission."

1937 Cadillac V-8 Series 70 Sport Coupe, Fleetwood
Owner: Streeter B. Flynn, Jr. of Oklahoma City, Oklahoma

1937 Cadillac V-8 Series 75 Touring Sedan, Fleetwood   Owner: Ronald M. DeWoskin of Madison, Wisconsin.   Photos: Brent Nicastro

''My car recently turned 45,000 miles,'' comments Ron DeWoskin about his Series 75 Touring Sedan which was purchased new in Chicago by John Deere Corporation for use as an executive car, was bought by a John Deere employee just before and donated to a convent in Wisconsin just after World War II. Ron has owned the car four years: ''This was the last year for the floor shifter. My car accelerates in high gear from 5 mph without hesitation and can cruise all day long at highway speeds. It's an elegant Classic that is easy to drive.''

1937 Cadillac V-8 Series 75 Seven-Passenger Touring Sedan, Fleetwood　　　　*Owner: John Robert Kausal of Park Ridge, Illinois*

John Kausal has owned his Series 75 Seven-Passenger Touring Sedan for over two years: ''I think that the sheer austerity of the car's outside appearance reflects the mood of this 'depression within a depression' year among luxury car buyers. This was the first year for the glass-winged 'goddess' mascot and the last for this particular type of wheel covering on the twin sidemounted spares.''

Nineteen thirty-seven was also the last year for the V-12; 474 were built. The V-16, which was given hydraulic brakes, tempted just forty-nine purchasers, among them Lorillard Tobacco's George Hummel whose car is now in Dick Gold's collection: ''At 17,000 original miles, this is probably the lowest mileage V-16 left. The 1937 model was the peak of the overhead-valve sixteen's smoothness. The coupe body on the 154-inch wheelbase makes for an enormous car; still, there is a cozy feeling inside and a fast and fabulous ride. Fold-down opera seats behind individual front seats make this very large automobile convenient for two or four passengers.''

1937 Cadillac V-16 Series 90 Stationary Coupe, Fleetwood　　　　*Owner: Richard G. Gold of Deephaven, Minnesota*

1938 Cadillac V-8 Series 60 Special Five-Passenger Sedan
Owner: Henry Ford Museum & Greenfield Village, Dearborn, Michigan

1938 Cadillac V-8 Series 60 Special Five-Passenger Sedan
Owner: Elmer F. Brown of Grove, Oklahoma

1938 Cadillac V-8 Series 60 Special Five-Passenger Sedan
Owner: C. Douglas Houston of Ortonville, Michigan

The biggest news in the V-8 Cadillac lines for '38 was the 60 Special styled by Harley Earl's protégé, William Mitchell. Set on its own 127-inch-wheelbase chassis, the car was equally notable for what it did not have (running boards or belt mouldings along the side) as what it had (a horizontal grille, a notch back and convertible-type chrome-framed door glass). More than 3,700 people bought 60 Specials in 1938, making it easily the best-selling Cadillac of the year.

"A design classic," says Randy Mason of the Henry Ford Museum. "Bill Mitchell's first car for GM was also the first sedan to feature both a fully-integrated rear deck and hardtop-like styling."

"This innovative Cadillac predicted styling trends for many manufacturers for many years to follow," comments Doug Houston. "Beautifully balanced and handsomely proportioned, it was intended to be owner-driven. The body was a Cadillac-only and remained so through 1941, with minor facelifts and instrument panel changes during each of the years in-between." Doug became the second owner of his 60 Special in 1960, purchasing the car from a Mamaroneck (New York) used car dealer who had acquired it from the estate of original owner Annie R. Cushion of Rye: "The roadworthiness of the 60 Special is frequently expressed in superlatives. There is no exaggeration here. After buying the car, I drove it back home to Detroit via the New York Thruway and Canada. I had not owned the car for twenty-four hours, and it had obviously not been driven much for a couple of years. After overcoming a couple of minor glitches and a rainstorm of hurricane proportions, the trip was a breeze the rest of the way. This was the first model year in which Cadillac installed the radio in a single unit to the dash panel, with the speaker in the dash, and my car is so equipped. Total driving since my ownership has been 14,000 miles. Because of the significance of this model, my car was requested for use in William Mitchell's funeral procession to carry members of his family."

Elmer Brown regards the Bill Mitchell-designed 60 Special as "one of the finest cars Cadillac ever made." Originally sold in San Francisco, this 60 Special had been relegated to a construction yard in El Cerrito prior to Elmer's acquisition fourteen years ago: "Except for the lack of power steering, this car handles better than any I own—by far."

1938 Cadillac V-8 Series 75 Five-Passenger Imperial Sedan, Fleetwood
Owner: Jim Raisbeck of Seattle, Washington   Photo: Sherry Raisbeck

The Series 70 was eliminated for '38, and the 75 was lengthened to 141 inches. The eggcrate grille was more massive, the hood was alligator-type, three sets of horizontal louver bars graced the hood sides, headlamps were mounted between fender and hood, and sidemount covers were hinged to the fenders. Inside, the gearshift moved to the steering column. Sales totalled 1,802 cars.

Dick Haeberle's 7567 Convertible Coupe was one of forty-four built: "This is the only one remaining of six without sidemounts, which makes it rare to say the least. It is also incredibly reliable and starts right up after sitting for a long period of time. If I don't get another car ready for CARavanning, I can always rely on this '38. It has never failed me."

Originally owned by Clinton Barnum Seeley of Bridgeport (Connecticut), Jim Raisbeck's 7519F Imperial Sedan was number thirty-four of thirty-four built: "I like it because it is a five-passenger formal limousine for personal ownership, unlike seven-passenger styles which frequently were bought for livery use. Since my ownership, the car has seen 'livery' service once—in 1989 when Sherry and I were married."

1938 Cadillac V-8 Series 75 Convertible Coupe, Fleetwood
Owner: Dick Haeberle of Summit, New Jersey

154

1938 Cadillac V-16 Series 90 Town Sedan, Fleetwood
Owner: Richard A. Taylor of Philadelphia, Pennsylvania

1938 Cadillac V-16 Series 90 Town Sedan, Fleetwood

Owner: C. Douglas Houston, Jr. of Ortonville, Michigan

Cadillac had no V-12 in '38 but a brand-new V-16: a flathead 135° dual-carbureted unit that was less of a problem and more of an economy to build. In a drastically reduced market, even Cadillac couldn't afford the luxury of two multi-cylinder engines and overkill chassis. The new V-16 shared the V-8's more maneuverable 141-inch wheelbase and all its body styles. For about two-thousand dollars more, a Cadillac purchaser could have twice the cylinders. Differentiating the V-16 outside were a more imposing egg-crate grille, fender-mounted parking lights, and the louvers on hood and fender skirts. The sale of 311 cars represented the best V-16 year since 1931.

Richard Taylor's 9039 Town Sedan was number six of twenty built: ''It's the rarest of the seven basic body shells in terms of surviving examples. The formal roof line flows back to a solid rear quarter and into a seemingly lengthened trunk compartment unique to this model.''

Doug Houston has owned his 9039 Town Sedan since 1963: ''I traded my freshly restored 1940 LaSalle 52 Sedan for it. This car was 'in process'; the owner had run out of time, money and enthusiasm. Not a bad deal, but the Cadillac was a disaster. The interior had been 'fab-

1938 Cadillac V-16 Series 90 Seven-Passenger Formal Sedan, Fleetwood
Owner: Allan E. Jones of Byron, California   Photos: Bud Juneau

1938 Cadillac V-16 Series 90 Seven-Passenger Town Car, Fleetwood   Owner: Katie Robbins of Dearborn, Michigan

sprayed' a bilious brown and had the texture of canvas. The instrument panel had been painted with a can of dime-store chocolate brown enamel. And so forth. The car remains in the process of restoration today. While not Cadillac's greatest achievement, the second generation V-16 is an impressive performer and, as Packard's handsome twelve-cylinder brutes, displays almost overwhelming low-speed torque. Developing 185 hp at 3400 rpm, the engine gives torque converter performance without a torque converter.''

Seventeen 9033F Formal Sedans like Allan Jones' were produced in '38: ''My car had been driven into a salvage yard near Bakersfield (California) in 1957, and the owner just walked away from it. There the car sat for eight years before I found it. In over three decades of ownership, I have driven this Cadillac 40,000 miles, south to the Mexican border and north to Canada. Its smooth, silent, torque-like feel can only be experienced with sixteen cylinders. It had been rumored for awhile that the second-generation V-16 would be

placed in the new 60 Special. This did not happen, and the engine instead was put into the Series 90 to carry on the tradition of the Great Sixteen Era. The brilliant work in designing and marketing a sixteen-cylinder car in less than two years, and using many V-8 parts, was good business strategy. The new V-16 was offered in the price range of the former V-12. There is no question in my mind as to who won the battle of the luxury car market for 1938. Cadillac retained as much individuality as possible in this series with a wide array of leather options, fabrics and inlaid woods. The rear compartment of my car was upholstered in wisteria velvet, complemented with a black broadcloth headliner, side panels and window curtains to match. Black silk accessory pillows and black silk-covered assist straps lined with wisteria velvet complete the ensemble. Garnish mouldings in the rear compartment are of Honduras mahogany with burled walnut veneer insets in the center, one of three wood options offered. The car has radios front and rear, the

console for the latter mounted in the right rear armrest. The hardware—including courtesy lamps, reading lamps and door handles—was the same design as used from the early thirties. Included in the hardware package was a polished aluminum accelerator pedal and a horn button inscribed ''Sixteen'' in Art Deco script. Outside, the car has a leather padded top set off by a metal insert which meets the top above the driver's window and extends above the windshield, this special trim suggesting at first glance that it is a town car.''

Katie Robbins' Fleetwood 9053 V-16 is a true town car, of course: ''This is the best of two worlds—the convertible and the sedan. A handsome car to view, it is a luxurious car to ride in, the rear compartment almost soundproof even from the front chauffeur's compartment. This Cadillac is a good road car as well; just set it on course and it never deviates. The car is a little cumbersome for city driving, however, the blind rear quarter making it difficult to maneuver in town.''

From 1939 the 60 Special carried Fleetwood not Fisher bodies, though the bodies continued to be built in the Fisher plant. New options were a center division and the Sunshine Turret Top, the latter adding fifty dollars to the base $2,195 price.

Jerry Fields' car has one: "What drew me to this 60 Special was that it has four of the biggest features for 1939: the all-leather interior (seats, door panels and headlining), dual sidemounts, two-tone color and the factory's new idea for open air motoring. Of the 5,506 cars sold in 1939, only 225 were fitted with the Sunshine Turret Top. Decades later, this feature would be reintroduced simply as the sunroof."

1939 Cadillac V-8 Series 60 Special Five-Passenger Sedan   *Owner: Jerry Fields of Beverly Hills, California*

1939 Cadillac V-8 Series 60 Special Five-Passenger Sedan   *Owner: Donald V. Mueller of Summit, New Jersey*

Don Mueller purchased his 60 Special a decade ago while a graduate student at Yale and offers this lively "dissertation": "Stylish, youthful and daring, the 60 Special made the competition's offerings look old-fashioned. Many hailed it as the first truly 'modern' car and driving it on the road I find that claim hard to dispute. The steering is light and the large drum brakes require merely a tap to scrub speed off. The 60 Special's road manners belie a car of its size and weight. The V-8 engine is inaudible at idle and provides spirited acceleration as well as more than adequate highway cruising capabilities. I recall taking my 60 Special out onto an interstate several years ago and accelerating to what appeared to be a comfortable cruising speed of 60 mph. I could not understand, however, why I was passing at least ninety percent of my fellow travellers. Later I discovered that my speedometer was reading ten miles an hour less than the actual road speed."

1939 Cadillac V-8 Series 75 Seven-Passenger Sedan, Fleetwood   Owner: Charles W. Kerner of Center Harbor, New Hampshire

Radiator grille styling was new for all Cadillac V-8's in '39. Functional die cast side grilles flanked the pointed center grille, differing in dimension only on the various series. Hood side louvers decreased from three to one. Sales for the largest V-8, the Series 75, increased to 2,065 of which 412 were Seven-Passenger Sedans (base priced at $3,325) like the one that Charlie Kerner has: "My car was delivered new from the Gluck (Hempstead, New York) dealership to Frank R. Smith of Garden City. I have a complete file from the original bill of sale through all repair bills. Since I bought the car in 1974, I've driven it about 12,000 miles. It's good riding, reliable and a pleasure to drive. And, except for paint, it remains original."

Cadillac's V-16 changed little for 1939, the most noticeable styling refinements being the chrome strip along running board edges and the full chroming of hood and fender skirt louvers. Total V-16 sales of 136 cars was less than half that of 1938.

Emil Bayowski's Convertible Sedan was one of four built in 1939: "During my college days in the early thirties I recall seeing many Classics in wrecking yards priced at $100-$180, but my parents discouraged any purchases of these massive, exotic cars because of public resentment to automobiles which represented wealth while others were struggling for food and shelter. Multi-cylinder cars were not very economical for long distances. The mayor of my hometown (Youngstown, Ohio) shipped his V-16 by rail when spending winters in Florida.

1939 Cadillac V-16 Series 90 Convertible Sedan, Fleetwood
Owner: A. Emil Bayowski of Girard, Ohio

My most vivid memory is President Roosevelt arriving in Youngstown in 1939 in his V-16 stretched Cadillac Convertible Sedan both because of the car's graceful appearance and the physical struggle FDR had to make transferring from the train to the car. Many in the crowd shed tears. Seven years later I bought my V-16 Convertible Sedan from the Auto Swap Shop operating behind a gas station. O.P.A. regulated prices and the Red Book National Used Car Market put its value at $725 plus $27.65 for the radio and $9.22 for the heater. The O.P.A./Red Book used value for a 1931 V-12 or V-16 was $90.00 at the time. The V-16 Convertible Sedan projected status as we toured with my dance band; it was good for our public image. In 1950 the car was retired behind my horse barn and used for storage of oats. As old cars began to reappear in the hobby, I saw a convertible sedan, purported to be Arthur Godfrey's, which was an identical model to mine. My initial restoration included parts cars secured from a sand bank in Boston and a vandalized limo formerly owned by Sally Rand, fan dancer of World Fair notoriety. There is a rewarding satisfaction in bringing a Classic back to life, and a lot of fun follows. On one occasion I had the privilege of parading with Governor Lausche and a U.S. Senator from Ohio who were not on speaking terms. . . .''

Five Five-Passenger Coupes were built, and all five survive. Doug Houston has owned his since 1961: ''This is the ideal personal car. The presence of a full bench seat in the rear compartment makes it as useful as a sedan, while maintaining the character of a coupe. And, as coupe bodies go, this one is gigantic, having been fitted to the same chassis as the seven-passenger sedan bodies. Today part of the enjoyment of a car such as this is the disbelief of the masses that such an automobile ever did, in fact, exist. People in general are very willing to believe that the V-16 emblems refer to valves rather than cylinders.''

Most popular of the V-16 Cadillacs in 1939 was the Imperial Seven-Passenger Sedan. Sixty of these limousines were sold, one of them Jack Royston's car: ''Mrs. Elizabeth Flynn of Pittsburgh was the original owner. She willed it to her chauffeur. Jim Campbell and I waited ten years to get this car. It had 21,000 miles on it then; eighteen years later it has 33,000. The car has never been painted or restored, nothing new but tires, plugs and battery.''

1939 Cadillac V-16 Series 90 Five-Passenger Coupe, Fleetwood
Owner: C. Douglas Houston, Jr. of Ortonville, Michigan

1939 Cadillac V-16 Series 90 Imperial Seven-Passenger Sedan, Fleetwood
Owner: Jack Royston of Scottsdale, Arizona

1940 Cadillac V-8 Series 60 Special Five-Passenger Sedan
Owners: Jerry & Temple Thrall of Coon Rapids, Minnesota

A bolder grille and more chrome accentuated Cadillacs for 1940. Sealed beam headlights and turn signals were new additions. This was the final year for optional sidemounts and the transparent-winged goddess hood ornament.

On a per-pound versus price tag basis, the Thralls' 60 Special was a fantastic bargain, 4,032 the former figure, $2,090 the latter: Says Jerry: "This car handles especially well on the road, and rides smoother than a new car, particularly when it comes to railroad tracks! The roomy back seat feels like a limo. Only 4,242 cars like mine were made in 1940."

The Series 72 was a one-year-only addition to the Cadillac line, placed on a 138-inch-wheelbase chassis and, at $2,670, priced midway between the 60 Special and the $2,995 Series 75. Recirculating ball steering, introduced on the Series 72, would be extended to the full Cadillac line in '41. A total of 1,526 Series 72's were produced, 18 of them Formal Sedans like Gene Peltier's: "I've had my car since 1978. Except for paint, it is pretty much original—and is road ready for tours anytime!"

1940 Cadillac V-8 Series 72 Formal Sedan, Fleetwood
Owner: Gene M. Peltier of Lake Elmo, Minnesota

162

Jerry & Temple Thrall's 1940 Cadillac 60S—profile, rear three quarter, driver's compartment, goddess hood ornament views

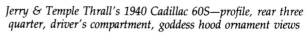

1940 Cadillac V-8 Series 75 Imperial Seven-Passenger Sedan, Fleetwood
Owners: John & Wilma Beauchamp of Granite Shoals, Texas

The total 959 Series 75's sold in 1940 represented less than half the 1939 production of Cadillac's largest V-8. Most popular of the body styles was the Imperial Seven-Passenger Sedan, the Beauchamps' car again unusual because of its original private ownership: "Our car was delivered new on July 10th, 1940 from Don Lee Cadillac to L. G. Kirkoff of Los Angeles, who willed it to his chauffeur. The car still carries its original 'Cadillac Identification Card,' the original hand mirror (with Cadillac crest and tortoise shell handle) stowed in a slip pocket in the rear armrest, and still displays the 'A' gas ration window sticker. Since our purchase of this Cadillac in 1983, we've put over 7,000 miles on the car."

Of the forty-five Series 75 Convertible Sedans produced, eight remain extant, the two in this portfolio having also been traced back to their original owners. The first garage in which the Clarkes' Convertible Sedan resided was one of the duPont families in Wilmington, Delaware: "The car was a Christmas present for Mrs. duPont who liked to wear large floppy hats and had insisted on this rear-door opening arrangement. The car was ordered with special paint and leather upholstery; tinted green glass and the installation of a custom bar in the rear compartment were also specified. This was the last year a convertible sedan was available on the long 141-inch wheelbase. It is an ideal tour car—powerful, quiet and smooth."

1940 Cadillac V-8 Series 75 Convertible Sedan, Fleetwood   *Owners: Mary & Tom Clarke of Fenton, Michigan*

The United States Government was the original owner of Joel Haffner's Convertible Sedan: "The car was soon sold to the City of New York for use as a V.I.P. and/or parade car during the final years of Fiorello LaGuardia's administration. Interestingly, it was delivered new with wool upholstery, not leather as found in most convertibles." In the seven years Joel has owned this Cadillac, he's driven it 30,000 miles.

Two Formal Sedans were offered on the Series 75 chassis in 1940: the 7559 five-passenger and the 7533F seven-passenger. Forty-eight of the former were produced; Joel Haffner has one of the two remaining extant: "The differences from the 7533F seven-passenger are these. The front seat is the same material as the rear, not leather, and there is no frame for the divider window. Instead of coming out from the floor, the jump-seats pull out from the rear of the front seat, the one on the right with the backrest, the one on the left with a backrest perpendicular to the rear seat. With its cloth front seat, this model was designed to be owner or chauffeur driven and to appear to be a large sedan rather than a limousine. Mine started life as a six-window limo and was pulled off the assembly line for the following customizing— plates welded over rear quarter windows, a wood buck inserted into the rear window area to make it smaller, a quarter vent window installed in the rear doors, a leather padded top added, and special gold brocade upholstery fitted."

1940 Cadillac V-8 Series 75 Convertible Sedan, Fleetwood
Owner: Joel Haffner of St. Louis, Missouri

166

1940 Cadillac V-8 Series 75 Five-Passenger Formal Sedan, Fleetwood   Owner: Joel Haffner of St. Louis, Missouri

Forty-two purchasers chose the seven-passenger 7533F Formal Sedan on the Series 75 chassis in 1940. Whitney Otis has owned his car for seven years: ''This was the last year for the Fleetwood custom body program. After 1940 only a three-window sedan or limousine would be offered; gone were the coupes, convertibles, formal sedans and open-front town cars. From this point forward, if you wanted a custom-bodied automobile, you would have to employ the services of Brunn or Derham. Nineteen forty seemed to close the era of opulent custom automobiles. Even Packard had begun to really push its cheaper models at the expense of the large series cars. Basically, the demand for our Classics had disappeared.''

1940 Cadillac V-8 Series 75 Seven-Passenger Formal Sedan, Fleetwood
Owner: Whitney B. Otis of Casper, Wyoming

1940 Cadillac V-8 Series 75 Town Car, Brunn   *Owner: Charles W. Coleman of Boca Raton, Florida*

Exemplifying the lack of demand for custom automobiles is Charles Coleman's Brunn Town Car. In a 1976 letter Hermann C. Brunn told Charles that his Cadillac was the last composite body town car built—and that so poor had business become that the Brunn company had dispensed with a professional photographer and Hermann was now not only designing the cars but photographing them too. For the past three decades

the Brunn Town Car has been the pride of the Coleman family: "Its original owner was E. J. Kulas, who was general sales manager for the Peerless Motor Car Company before World War I and president of Otis Steel Company at the time of his death in 1952. In between he served as adviser to President Hoover. Kulas Auditorium at John Carroll University was built by the family foundation. The Kulas town car weighs over

5,000 pounds and remains largely original, even to the yellow stripe which Mr. Kulas specified because he didn't want the dour look of an all-black formal body. After acquiring the car from the Kulas estate, we found papers inside indicating that it had been prepared for delivery to Mr. Kulas in Lakewood, Ohio by Sanderson Motors, which we visited. The service manager remembered the car well. During World War II it was

The original interior in the rear compartment of Charles W. Coleman's 1940 Cadillac Series 75 Brunn Town Car

garaged there, and then reactivated for Mrs. Kulas' use after the war. The service manager added that, although he meant no disrespect, whenever the car came in for service, he would say, 'Here comes the circus wagon.' To this my wife replied, 'It is in good hands now as it belongs to a couple of clowns.' This Series 75 was one of three 141-inch chassis released by Cadillac to custom coachbuilders in 1939. That fact and its styling for a

conservative town car make it most unusual. This Brunn is one of the best driving cars I own. Original mileage registers just 41,000.''

Nineteen forty was the final year for the Cadillac V-16. Body styles available were eleven; cars sold numbered just sixty-one. Walter Sprague has owned his Formal Sedan for nearly two decades: ''It was body number one of two of this style, and it was the twenty-seventh V-16 built

that year. Fifteen different special compartments were fitted in the Formal Sedan. These include a three-bottle rack under the jumpseat on the right side, a strong box under the left jumpseat, a bar in the front seat back and an umbrella tube in and under the front seat cushion. Front and rear radios and heaters were installed too, as well as an intercom in the right rear armrest to a speaker in the windshield header.''

1940 Cadillac V-16 Series 90 Formal Sedan, Fleetwood　　　　　　　　　　　*Owner: Walter Sprague of Portland, Michigan*

1941 Cadillac Series 60 Special Five-Passenger Sedan   Owner: Robert J. Sauerschell of Schenectady, New York   Photos: Daniel B. Lyons

Nineteen forty-one was the first year since 1926 in which all Cadillacs shared the same engine: the venerable 346-cubic-inch 150 hp V-8. New chassis engineering features included the options of Hydra-Matic transmission, factory-installed air conditioning, electric divisions and power tops. In styling it was an important year for the marque as well because the face of this Cadillac set a pattern for the generation ahead, making a bold statement with a horizontal grille that subtly suggested the power behind it.

"The '41 Cadillac 60 Special is a Classic and a great road car, for the best of two worlds," says Robert Sauerschell. "It was the style setter for the entire GM line after the war. The lengthened front fender extended onto the door only on the 60 Special. This was the first year for the gas cap in the taillight, a feature which would endure through 1958. It was also the first year for the optional automatic heater, which my car has."

John Paulson has owned his '41 for seven years and regards it as "the best of the 60 Special series."

Both the Kerner and the Gold 60 Specials feature Hydra-Matic transmission and the factory sun roof. "This is a somewhat rare combination," says Charlie, "since only 185 were made with the sun roof and only a few of these with Hydra-Matic since this was the introductory year.

Dick Gold especially likes the automatic transmission: "We use the car mostly for family touring. And it's great when I've had a few cocktails. My wife can drive us home!"

Of the 4,100 60 Specials produced in '41, all but six were sedans. Andy Johnson owns one of the exceptions: "The original owner of my Derham Town Car was Mary Byers Lyons of Glen Cove, New York. The Lyons family had founded the Fanny Farmer candy empire. The car was used mainly by Mrs. Lyons to go to the theatre in New York City, but along with the chauffeur it was also sent to Europe five times for extended family vacations. Custom features on this Derham body include an open-front driver's compartment, two-tone paint, padded leather top with small oval rear windows,

1941 Cadillac Series 60 Special Five-Passenger Sedan
Owner: Charles W. Kerner of Center Harbor, New Hampshire

1941 Cadillac Series 60 Special Five-Passenger Sedan (details above)   *Owner: John R. Paulson of Golden Valley, Minnesota*

1941 Cadillac Series 60 Special Town Car, Derham   *Owner: Andrew W. Johnson of Roslyn Heights, New York*

1941 Cadillac Series 60 Special Five-Passenger Sedan
Owner: Richard G. Gold of Deephaven, Minnesota

running boards by the rear doors only, a modified small rear seat with footrests built to the size and specification of Mrs. Lyons, formal division window, modified front windshield and coach lights so Mrs. Lyons could easily sight the car after the theatre. When I purchased the car eighteen years ago from the Lyons estate, however, I discovered the coach lights did not work. In discussing this with the chauffeur, he told me they had been operational when he visited the Derham plant but had not worked since he brought the car to Glen Cove in 1941. In tracing the wiring, it was discovered that the last thing Derham did was screw cover plates over the Fleetwood name on the sills and in doing so shorted out the wiring to the coach lights. So, while Mrs. Lyons was never able to enjoy this feature, I can—and those illuminated coach lights are something to see. I fell in love with this car the moment I laid eyes on it. For a long time I wanted a formal yet sporty Classic with the division window, a close-coupled look and two-tone paint. This one answered all my wishes, and is a fantastic driving car.''

The Series 62 was on the same 126-inch wheelbase as the 60 Special but with a lower price tag: a seven hundred dollar differential in five-passenger sedan form. Of the 24,726 Series 62's produced in '41, the majority were sedans. But the Series 62 was also the only Cadillac series to offer convertible sedans through 1941 and convertible coupes through the end of the Classic Era.

"The Series 62 was a car of Classic stature that more people could afford to own," comments Earl Rosen. "In styling, its horizontal grille, fifteen-inch wheels, sharply raked wind-shield and lowered roofline gave it an exceptionally modern appearance. Optional automatic transmission and a powerful V-8 gave it excellent performance. Smaller points such as a push-button radio, power antenna and turn signals gave it refinement." Earl has owned his 62 Convertible Coupe for three years: "In 1940, when I was sixteen, my father gave me a brand-new Ford. I thought he was being generous but the real truth was that he did not want me to drive his cars, which included Classic Packards and then a 1941 Cadillac. I never did get to use them, but from the way he drove the Series 62 Cadillac, I knew it was a real per-former and exceptionally reliable. One lasted him through the war. The moment the Series 62 became a Classic, I got one."

"It is the familiar 'Dad had one' story for me too," echoes Dick Haeberle. "I remember the car so well. He sold it after the war and made money on it. I think the '41 Cadillac Convertible Coupe is one of the best-looking cars ever made. Mine is unusual in having running boards; I've seen only one more like it. By 1941 manufacturers were moving away from running boards, but they remained an option."

The "styling, engineering and driving comfort" are what attracted Lowell Carlson to his '41 Convertible Coupe, which he has owned since 1979.

Doug Houston has owned his car since 1960: "The original owner, reportedly the president of the Manhattan White Shirt Company, had willed this Cadillac to his chauffeur, which was done a lot in those days. The car is equipped with Hydra-Matic, which became available after March 1st, 1941. While a few minor mechanical and styling changes were made on Cadillacs thereafter, the chassis was virtually unchanged through 1948, the last year of this engine series. Like the other three 1941 Cadillacs in my

1941 Cadillac Series 62 Convertible Coupe
Owner: Earl Rosen, Jr. of St. Louis, Missouri

1941 Cadillac Series 62 Convertible Coupe
Owner: Dick Haeberle of Summit, New Jersey

1941 Cadillac Series 62 Convertible Coupe
Owner: C. Douglas Houston, Jr. of Ortonville, Michigan

1941 Cadillac Series 62 Convertible Coupe   Owner: Lowell H. Carlson of Belleair Bluffs, Florida

1941 Cadillac Series 62 Convertible Sedan   *Owner: C. Douglas Houston, Jr. of Ortonville, Michigan*

possession, this car is excellent on the highway and a ton of fun to drive. Mileage since restoration has been approximately 8,000. I use whatever excuse I can, for this car is one of my favorite toys.''

Series 62 Convertible Coupes produced in 1941 totaled 3,100. Just 400 Convertible Sedans were built. This was the last year for a four-door convertible from Cadillac, which is among the reasons the Smileys and Doug Houston are fond of their cars. Barney & Verma acquired their Series 62 Convertible Sedan in 1983. Doug purchased his in 1970 in what he

describes as ''virtually unrestorable condition''—but obviously that didn't stop him.

The Series 62 Club Coupe has been in Doug Houston's collection since 1969: ''The design of this body is most appealing to me. Proportions of the upper/lower areas were well laid out, and the result is a smooth and sleek impression of graceful motion, consistent with the subtle elegance that became the marque. My car has Hydra-Matic and also the factory-installed air conditioner, one of 300 such installations that year. At this time there are only two of these 300

cars known to exist. The air conditioner makes summer driving pleasurable more because of the dehumidification of the air than the cooling of it. The lack of tinted glass, not available that year, makes the unit's job a great deal harder. The air outlet for the conditioner is behind the rear seat and tends to chill the rear window and cause fogging from the outside of the glass on a humid day. Once on a brief tour, someone pointed out the fogging to me and I immediately assured him there are only two 1941 Cadillacs where this is possible!''

1941 Cadillac Series 62 Coupe   *Owner: C. Douglas Houston, Jr. of Ortonville, Michigan*

1941 Cadillac Series 62 Convertible Sedan   *Owners: Barney & Verma Smiley of Lakeside, California*

1941 Cadillac Series 63 Touring Sedan

Owner: Charles G. Williams of Sturtevant, Wisconsin

The Series 63 was a new offering for 1941 on the 60 Special's 126-inch wheelbase. Available only as a five-passenger sedan, the model would be produced through 1942. Charles Williams has owned his Series 63 for nearly two decades: "The car was sold new through Tallman Cadillac of Decatur, Illinois to Miss Gussie Gorin. She owned it for twelve years. Thereafter it passed through a number of different owners, none of whom apparently drove it much. In 1965 the car was serviced by Morrone Cadillac in Westerly, Rhode Island. The mileage was 19,900. Since I've had the car, I've driven it over 30,000 miles. It handles excellently and is smooth and powerful. Only 5,050 of the Series 63 were produced in the 1941 model year. Mine came equipped with automatic transmission, a Fleetwood interior, fender skirts, locking gas cap, fully automatic heater, radio and trunk light. Cadillac referred to the Series 63 as the 60 Special of its field. The interior in my car is completely original. Only the bumpers and the side spears have been replated. The top of the car was painted in 1971. All accessories are, like the car, in fine working order. This Cadillac drives and looks too nice to give it a ground-up restoration."

178

At 136 inches, the wheelbase of the Series 75 was five inches shorter for 1941. Sales increased to 2,104 cars. Of these, 422 were the Five-Passenger Touring Sedan like Joe Malaney's: "I consider the 1941 Series 75 the high-water mark for Cadillac. My 'Black Beauty' is a delight to drive and I take every appropriate opportunity to do so."

Similarly low in production was the Seven-Passenger Touring Sedan, Mike Evans' car among the 405 that were built in 1941: "I believe the Series 75 has the look of old money. But mostly I like my Cadillac because it's big. Shipping weight was 4,800 pounds. The price f.o.b. Detroit was $3,140."

1941 Cadillac Series 75 Seven-Passenger Touring Sedan, Fleetwood
Owner: Mike Evans   Photo: Dan Evans

1941 Cadillac Series 75 Five-Passenger Touring Sedan, Fleetwood (details above)
Owner: Joseph R. Malaney of Lakewood, Colorado

1942 Cadillac Series 62 Convertible Coupe   Owner: Farrell C. Gay of Springfield, Illinois

Cadillacs for 1942 were provided a bolder grille and the first of the bullet-shaped bumper guards which would mature into the infamous ''Dagmars'' of a generation hence. World War II made '42 an abbreviated model year.

Of the total 4,960 Series 62's built, 308 were the Convertible Coupe. Farrell Gay has owned his car since 1974: ''I have the original receipt which delivered this car to an H. H. Beaumeier at the Bell Telephone Company in St. Louis, Missouri. It is believed to be the only '42 Series 62 Convertible Coupe extant, of which there are only a handful, that has a standard transmission.''

Evidence suggests that possibly Derham built two 60 Special Town Broughams, but the Karel Deibel car is the only one known to date: ''The car was ordered sometime in the fall of 1941, well before the attack on Pearl Harbor, by W. Deering Howe as a wedding present for his second wife, Elizabeth Shevlin Smith (daughter of famous Yale football star Tom Shevlin). The Howes main-tained homes on Long Island, in New York City and at Aiken, South Carolina. With his father, Howe maintained a stable at Belmont race track. He founded Transair, Inc. and was the first mayor of Brookville on Long Island. The car was shipped as a Fleetwood 60 Special Formal Sedan with Imperial division window from the Cadillac plant in Detroit on December 17th, 1941, ten days after the U.S. was drawn into World War II. The selling dealer, Central Cadillac in Newark (New Jersey), arranged for the custom car conversion by Derham in Rosemont, Pennsylvania. In the process, Derham removed all three Fleetwood body emblems, installing two of their own and screwing stainless steel plates over the Fleetwood emblems in all four door sills [presumably without messing up the wiring]. Precisely when the car arrived in Newark and when it went to Rosemont are unknown, but it appears to have been 'frozen' by presidential order, along with other undelivered new cars, on January 2nd, 1942.

Seemingly, Howe, by then a Major in the Army stationed in D.C. and a man of prominence, secured a 'priority.' Nevertheless, it was not until December of 1942 that delivery was made. The car was not built as a 1942 B 'black-out' job, production of which was mandated in November of 1941, effective no later than January 1st, 1942 to conserve copper, nickel and chromium. With black paint, black top, all black trim and red wheels, it would have looked peculiar, to say the least. Major Howe died of a heart attack while swimming near Havana in 1948. His widow used the car until 1951 when her third husband, John P. Rutherford, replaced it with a used powder-blue Rolls-Royce with gold-plated trim, which had recently been repossessed from a less than distinguished 'gentleman' residing at the time in New York's Sing-Sing prison. I've owned the car since 1974. It is a uniquely glamorous as well as dependable car. Mileage is uncertain. It could have about 120,000 miles, or possibly 220,000.''

180

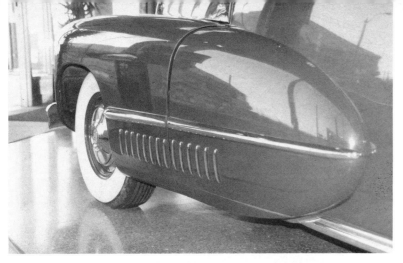

Details on the Deibel Town Brougham. Radio controls in the rear seat armrest, with pushbuttons for center division window. The "hash marks" on the front fender. The plain oval plate screwed over the "Fleetwood" emblem in order to hide it.

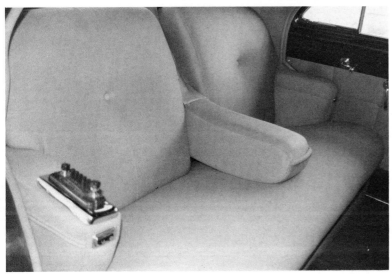

1942 Cadillac Series 60 Special Town Brougham, Fleetwood/Derham   *Owner: Karel Deibel of Seattle, Washington*

1946 Cadillac Series 62 Five-Passenger Sedan   *Owner: Donald F. Ketteman of Williamsville, New York*

During World War II, Cadillac 346-cubic-inch flathead V-8's with Hydra-Matic transmissions were used virtually unmodified, in pairs, in the M-5 and M-24 light tanks, M-8 howitzer carriages and M-13 anti-aircraft vehicles. "On the battlefields of the world, they were improved to meet demands never before made of any units employed in a passenger car," Cadillac advertising for 1946 proudly stated.

To an owner, CCCA members with early postwar Cadillacs point with equal pride to that fact. The shortage of materials and GM's 120-day strike make any 1946 Cadillac a rarity today.

The best seller that year was the Series 62 Five-Passenger Sedan. Donald Ketteman has owned his for over ten years: "It is a real head turner and a great and dependable car to drive. My wife Judy and I have driven it 7,000 miles thus far, including a trip to Lake Placid, New York during which the car performed flawlessly."

Notchback styling characterized all Series 62 bodies except for the fast-back Club Coupe of which Bob

1946 Cadillac Series 75 Five-Passenger Sedan, Fleetwood
Owner: Thomas Conron of Danville, Illinois   Photo: Mike Conron

Messinger's is one of the 2,325 produced for '46: "The fastback on the Series 62's 129-inch wheelbase

gives the car a long, sleek appearance. And it proved immensely popular, outselling the lower-priced

1946 Cadillac Series 62 Club Coupe
Owner: Robert M. Messinger   Photos: Dorothy Olsson Messinger

non-Classic Series 61 coupe by almost three to one. Since a youngster, I had always admired Cadillacs, so when the postwar Series 62 was designated Classic, I began making inquiries. I wanted an 'easy' driving/roomy car for CARavans and one preferably with automatic in case my wife wanted to (or had to) drive it. The '46 has an excellent vent system to provide better fresh air supply than many Classics, for a more comfortable cooling effect while driving in hot weather. The ride and comfort of the seats are like sitting in an easy chair. Even though the car is over four decades old, it has very few rattles and no water leaks. Except for exterior paint and some replating, our 62 Club Coupe is original. When I purchased it in July of 1987, the odometer read 46,381 miles. At this writing, it's closing in on 53,000.''

The long 136-inch wheelbase Series 75 for '46 continued to use the '41 body shell which was not shared with any other GM division. Tom Conron's Five-Passenger Sedan was one of 150 built and, like the Messingers' Cadillac, has been well driven in the three years since acquisition: ''Mileage total thus far is 14,000. Jeanne and I drive this car all the way—no trailering. This is an outstanding Classic road automobile. Its original owner was the opera singer, Lauritz Melchior.''

1947 Cadillac Series 60 Special Five-Passenger Sedan   *Owner: Robert J. Dziewit of Anchorville, Michigan*

In 1942 the Cadillac 60 Special had been extensively restyled on a longer 133-inch-wheelbase chassis, and thus did it enter the postwar era. Sales for the 1947 model year totalled 8,500 cars, all of them five-passenger sedans.

Bob Dziewit has owned his since 1986: "This marked the end of the second-generation Cadillac 60 Special. As with many of the prewar bodies, '47 was its last year. The car's Hydra-Matic transmission, improved during its extensive use in World War II, shifts positively with whipped-cream smoothness. The engine is whisper quiet. When I purchased the car in Milwaukee, the temperature was approximately 98°, which made the trip through the Chicago area most adventurous. A clogged radiator and defective generator regulator made themselves

known, and frantic searches for service parts added to the memorable character of the twenty-five-hour trip home to Michigan. Following arrival, and several corrective and preventive maintenance measures, the car has inspired confidence and has become a carefree pleasure to drive. And, being solid, it will be a relatively easy restoration project. The original Madeira Maroon color is currently obscured by a paint job of a rather depressing 'fence post' green. It is theorized by many that this paint job was applied by some unknown party who was angry with the car. The original maroon will soon replace the bilious hue that now encases this fine 60 Special."

Rod Brewer's 60 Special, which he purchased from its original owner in Salt Lake City over fifteen years ago, needs no such attention: "I consider

this car to be one of the best examples of an original 1947 60 Special left. Other than paint work to repair door dings, etc., the car needs nothing. The interior is like new with the exception of a little fraying in the front carpet where it was necessary to check the transmission oil over the years. The original owner's I.D. card is still in the holder on the right-hand kick panel. Also, the original radiator hoses are still in service, being a little on the hard side! This car had only been used on special occasions and therefore was in well-preserved condition with 47,000 original miles when I purchased it. I was lucky because a 60 Special of this generation was precisely what I wanted. The first car I could remember my mother having was a 60 Special, not surprisingly, that was the first 'old' car I wanted to own."

1947 Cadillac Series 60 Special Five-Passenger Sedan Owner: *Rodney R. Brewer of Golden, Colorado*

1947 Cadillac Series 62 Convertible Coupe (driver's compartment below)   Owners: Gil & Diane Ranney of Huntington Beach, California

With its fastback styling, the Series 62 Club Coupe continued to be the best-selling two-door Cadillac in '47. Elmer Brown's car was one of 7,245 built.

Series 62 Convertible Coupe sales totalled 6,755. Gil & Diane Ranney have owned theirs since New Year's Eve of 1979: ''The car had been purchased new in 1947 by Earl Lewis of Cranbury, New Jersey and had travelled only 18,000 miles when he sold it nearly three decades later. This Cadillac is an interesting combination of prewar styling with modern conveniences and characteristics that make it very enjoyable to drive today. Windows, seat and top are hydraulically operated. The power is ample and the acceleration very smooth. Behind the wheel one can appreciate the quality engineering that produced an extremely comfortable ride, excellent steering and brakes, and a solid rattle-free body.''

History is among the facets that makes the Opps' Series 62 Convertible Coupe special to them. Comments Al: ''During World War II Cadillac's automatic transmission and V-8 engine proved above expectations their workmanship and durability —and the trust that could be placed in their engineering. This helped to bring peace. I am very proud of that, and both my wife and I take good care of the automobile that represents part of that history. To me, this car has class in all aspects—style, looks and driving pleasure.''

1947 Cadillac Series 62 Club Coupe
Owner: Elmer F. Brown of Grove, Oklahoma

186

1947 Cadillac Series 62 Convertible Coupe   Owners: Alfred & Helgard Opp of Richmond, British Columbia

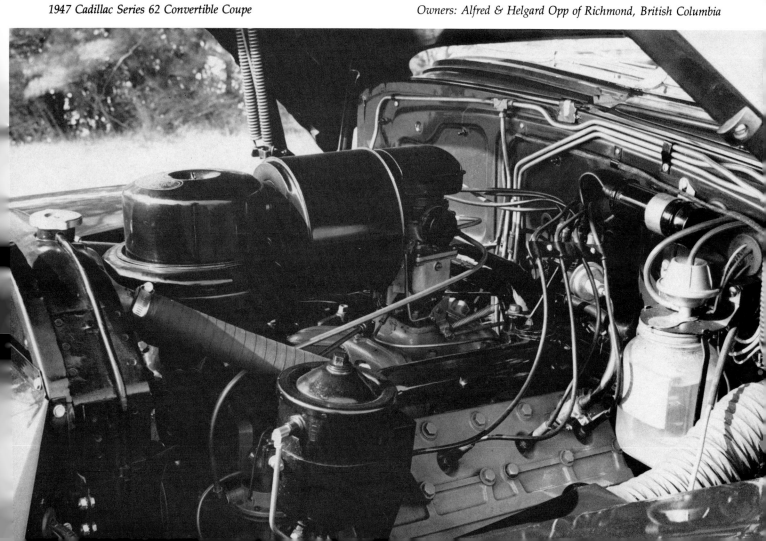

The Blaines' Series 62 Convertible Coupe was purchased four years ago at an unusual auction in Denver, Colorado conducted on behalf of the American Cancer Foundation. Before she died of that ravaging disease, the original owner had bequeathed the car to that organization. "The Cadillac Series 62 Convertible Coupe is among the most beautiful of all postwar U.S. cars," says John. "The grille was redesigned for '47, as were the chrome-plated stainless steel 'sombrero' wheel covers. At $2,902, the Convertible Coupe was the most expensive body style. It's an elegant car with top up or down—and a powerful tour driver which can hold its own in modern-day traffic, city or turnpike. Last year, on the occasion of the introduction of the 1990 GM cars to corporation employees, my wife and I were invited to show our Series 62 at the General Motors Proving Ground in Milford in order to acquaint contemporary workers with what Cadillacs looked like over four decades ago."

1947 Cadillac Series 62 Convertible Coupe
Owners: Lt. Colonel & Mrs. John Blaine of Milford, Michigan

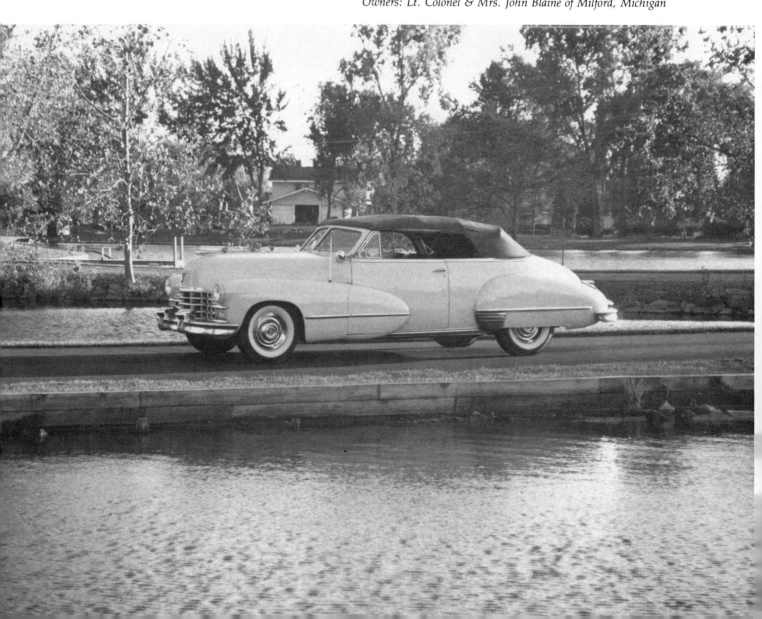

In 1948 Cadillac introduced its first postwar redesign in all series except the 75. Total Series 75 production was 2,067 cars; 382 of them were Imperial Seven-Passenger Sedans like Rod Brewer's: "Sold new by Rickenbaugh Cadillac to the Meyers Drug family in Denver, this car remained in the Meyer family until the late seventies. A grandson sold it to the Rippey Museum, and I bought it soon after. Having been garaged for most of its life—and showing only 44,223 miles—the car is very well preserved. For example, the never-used jack is still in its original cloth cover with the instructions attached! This car represents the finale of Classic Era Cadillac styling. The stainless steel running boards add a lot to the look of the car. The most distinguishing feature of the '48 Cadillac limousine is the dashboard, used only this year, which has a leather look as opposed to the wood-grain finish of all other '48 Cadillacs. Also, exclusive to the limo are gold ring spacers in the door and window handles—for a final touch of Classic Era class."

1948 Cadillac Series 75 Imperial Seven-Passenger Sedan, Fleetwood   *Owner: Rodney R. Brewer of Golden, Colorado*

C H R Y S L E R

Gazelle hood ornament from Charles Montano's 1933 Custom Imperial, photo by Daniel B. Lyons

Walter Percy Chrysler seemed to always be in the right place at the right time. And he seemed never to make mistakes. "The majority of men pay too much attention to the way stations and not enough to the terminals," he once said, using terminology natural to the son of a Kansas Pacific Railroad engineer. Working on the railroad was a natural too; Chrysler began as a roundhouse sweeper for the Union Pacific and by 1910 was Pittsburgh plant manager of the American Locomotive Company when General Motors beckoned with the Buick presidency. Though the job meant a cut in salary by half, Chrysler didn't hesitate. He liked locomotives but he loved automobiles. Less than a decade later, he left Buick with a comfortable kitty of $10 million from GM stock. Another door opened: Willys-Overland's. Chase National Bank offered Chrysler a cool million dollars a year to set that faltering company on the right road. That job done, he took on a similar salvage operation for Maxwell which had recently been merged, none too happily, with Chalmers. The stage had been set. In 1924 the first Chrysler was introduced; by mid-1925 Chrysler Corporation succeeded Maxwell. Walter Chrysler had help, of course, most importantly in the "Three Musketeers"—Fred Zeder, Owen Skelton and Carl Breer who had engineered a marvelous car. A six-cylinder high compression engine, four-wheel hydraulic brakes, aluminum pistons, oil filter, air cleaner, full-pressure lubrication and tubular front axle had never before been combined in a volume-produced automobile. By 1927 Walter Chrysler had moved his company up from the bottom rung of the industry ladder (32nd place) to fourth. And among his recently introduced model lines in 1926 was a Chrysler called Imperial, designed to compete with Lincoln and the like. . . .

1927 Chrysler Imperial Series E-80 Sportif, Locke   *Owner: Henry Ford Museum & Greenfield Village, Dearborn, Michigan*

Part of the Imperial's appeal was its prowess. From 288.7 cubic inches, 92 hp was developed; Chrysler's L-head six had more horses than the engines of some luxury manufacturers boasting two more cylinders. And the top-of-the-line Imperial's look was distinctive—at least to Chrysler— with its famous fluted hood patterned after Lawrence Pomeroy's design for Vauxhall, which pleased everyone except the British company. Chrysler didn't catalogue customs in '27, although some—like the Henry Ford Museum's Locke Sportif—were individually produced.

Nineteen twenty-eight saw major changes. The Chrysler engine was bored out to 309.6 cubic inches. But more dramatic was the new compression ratio, raised from the former 4.7:1 to 6.0:1 and resulting in a power increase to 112 hp. And from three wheelbase lengths in '27 (120, 127 and 133 inches), the Imperial chassis stretched to one of 136 inches. Now Walter Chrysler went catalogue custom with offerings from LeBaron, Locke and Dietrich. Ray Dietrich later recalled the many ''Saturday afternoons in the two-bit lunch room where Walter and I ate frankfurters washed down with beer and discussed new design programs.''

The new Locke offering for '28 happened serendipitously. Working for the New York City custom house at the time was John Tjaarda (later responsible for the pacesetting Lincoln Zephyr). The Dutch-born Tjaarda had designed a jaunty two-door phaeton for his own use; Locke had displayed the car at its stand at the '27 New York Automobile Show; Walter Chrysler liked it. Whimsically, and appropriately, designated the Touralette, the four-passenger phaeton was catalogued in 1928 at $4,485, a thousand-dollars-plus more than the production Imperials and two thousand dollars less than the Dietrich offerings. Conceivably, the car was underpriced. To create its canework rear panel was a time-consuming chore for a steady-handed craftsman using a device similar to that of a cake decorator to squeeze out an even bead of paint top to bottom. Twenty-one Touralettes were thusly caned that year; the Behring Museum's car is one of three extant. The Locke body style was not offered again in 1929.

1928 Chrysler Imperial Series E-80 Touralette, Locke   *Owner: Behring Museum, Danville, California*

But others were, among them Tom Lester's Locke Custom Roadster. Identifying it as a '29 Chrysler is the narrow profile radiator and the arched vertical hood louvers. By now, with their splendid performance and rakish good looks, Chryslers were in the garages of sporting drivers on both sides of the Atlantic. French racing champion Louis Chiron drove the cars exclusively for his personal transportation, found them supple and pleasurable even for his African journeys and pronounced himself "enchanted with them." Tom Lester is similarly enthusiastic: "Believe it or not, old story. My father (honest) had one just like it. My '29 Imperial drives excellently. The steering is a little strong for a little lady, but the car is quite fast for a plain-jane L-head engine. It will really exceed 80 mph." Tom has demonstrated this routinely during the decade he has owned this Chrysler.

1929 Chrysler Imperial Series L-80 Custom Roadster, Locke
Owner: Thomas J. Lester of Deerfield Beach, Florida

1931 Chrysler Imperial Eight Series CG Dual Cowl Phaeton, LeBaron
Owners: Richard & Linda Kughn of Southfield, Michigan   Photo: Torque

By the early thirties, whether he was at the factory in Detroit (where his time card was Number One and invariably the first punched in each morning) or in New York in his top-floor offices at the Chrysler Building (the world's tallest skyscraper until the Empire State took the honors and arguably the world's grandest architectural evocation of Art Deco),

Walter Chrysler was a busy man. Buying Dodge Brothers and introducing the low-priced Plymouth in '28 had both cemented his footing in the industry and positioned him well to withstand the buffeting of the Great Depression.

Ego might have persuaded Walter Chrysler to join with other luxury car manufacturers in succumbing to the

temptation of a twelve- or sixteen-cylinder engine for his Imperial, but Chrysler never did. Needless extravagance, he thought. Indeed, it was only after extensive development by his engineering "Three Musketeers" that Chrysler introduced a straight eight—in 1931. The new 384.8-cubic-inch nine-main-bearing side-valve L-head developed 125 hp at 3200

1931 Chrysler Imperial Eight Series CG Dual Cowl Phaeton, LeBaron
Owner: William Lyon of Trabuco Canyon, California

rpm, only a couple of dozen or so less horses than its many-cylindered competition.

The new Series CG Imperial was quick to accelerate (0 to 60 in 20 seconds, which was splendid for that era), and a top speed of 96 mph meant Chrysler drivers, if they so chose, rarely saw headlights in their rear-view mirror. This was a car that was hard to catch. "A super driver," says Joseph Morgan of the '31 Imperial he has owned for eight years. "The motor runs quietly and there is more than ample power. The four-speed transmission and hydraulic brakes give the car a 'modern' feeling. And the styling is incredible."

Chrysler was very deft at gentle cribbing. Front-drive Cord L-29 influence in the Series CG Imperial is apparent from the deeply set-back grille to the car's proximity to the ground—but the total was put together with a styling identity that was Chrysler's own, and the envy of the industry that year. Especially effective was LeBaron's dual cowl phaeton rendering of the Imperial. "This automobile was truly ahead of its time," comment Dick & Linda Kughn. "In comparing phaetons of this vintage, the '31 Chrysler is much lower slung than any of its rear-drive competition. And the long 145-inch wheelbase makes the car seem even closer to the ground. The vee radiator shell was very advanced. The low roofline, of course, brought the windshield down for styling that subsequently was followed by other manufacturers." The graceful gazelle that was added to Chrysler's winged cap hood ornament was the perfect finishing touch.

1931 Chrysler Imperial Eight Series CG Dual Cowl Phaeton, LeBaron
Owner: Joseph Morgan of Windham, New Hampshire

193

1931 Chrysler Imperial Eight Series CG Roadster, LeBaron
Owner: John M. Elling of Oldwick, New Jersey   Photo: K. Karger

LeBaron supplied all semi-custom bodies for 1931 Chrysler Imperials—a total of 330 in four body styles. Among the eighty-five purchasers of the Dual Cowl Phaeton was actress Myrna Loy, although how much time she had to enjoy it that year is questionable since 20th Century Fox was keeping her occupied in about a half-dozen movies. Since acquiring

the Myrna Loy Chrysler two years ago, Ray and Lou Bowersox have been able to enjoy this "superb driving car" doubtless a lot more than the actress did in '31.

"It handles like a large sports car. The four-speed transmission with a close-ratio third gear gives excellent passing and hill climbing ability," declares John Elling of the LeBaron

Roadster he has owned for two decades, one of just 100 built in '31: "Interesting details include the handsome pleated leather upholstery which continues around inside the cowl edge, over the door tops and rear of the compartment to create a cockpit effect, the rumble-seat latch release hidden in the storage compartment behind the passengers."

1931 Chrysler Imperial Eight Series CG Dual Cowl Phaeton, LeBaron (full profile on the page opposite)
Owners: Ray & Lou Bowersox of Milton, Pennsylvania

1932 Chrysler Imperial Custom Eight Series CL Convertible Sedan, LeBaron
Owner: Joseph Morgan of Windham, New Hampshire

Again in 1932, most semi-custom Imperials carried LeBaron bodies. Under them was a new double-drop "girder truss" chassis with free wheeling, vacuum-operated clutch, power-assisted brakes and drop-center wheels.

Joseph Morgan likes the '32 Series CL Imperial so much he has two: "Although Chrysler had advanced engineering that year, I think the most impressive aspect of the car is its overall styling. From whatever angle, it looks good. Nineteen thirty-two was the first Chrysler and the first Classic to incorporate 'cowl-less' design. The extremely long aluminum hood accentuates the low and lean appearance. The split windshield with its twin opening panels is very smart and, together with the flat-folding top, makes the top-down profile of the Convertible Roadster very smooth. Total production of that body style was just 28 cars; mine is Number 25 and one of only a handful in existence. My LeBaron Convertible Sedan was one of 49 built and one of possibly two with an unusual custom interior featuring 'bucket' seats front and rear upholstered in square and diamond tuft patterns. Further, the car has very ornate black walnut door and seat wood trim, and the custom metal trunk matches the rear body curves. In this car especially, the close-coupled body makes that already long hood seem even longer."

The 1932 Imperial Landau Formal Sedan in the Henry Ford Museum was Walter Chrysler's personal car, acquired from the Chrysler family in 1960 for the museum. "This is a great example of a one-off Classic done by a major corporate design studio," comments curator Randy Mason, "and incorporates early bowl-type headlights and a special fabric-covered top. Updated while in use, the car sports a '37 Custom Imperial Airflow engine and is painted in a favorite Walter Chrysler color, a red that he took from a Ming vase."

1932 Chrysler Imperial Custom Eight Series CL Convertible Roadster, LeBaron
Owner: Joseph Morgan of Windham, New Hampshire

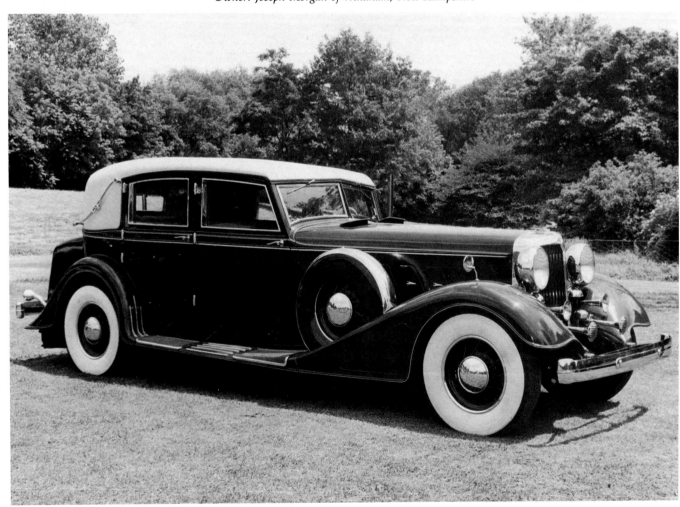

1932 Chrysler Imperial Custom Eight Series CL Landau Formal Sedan
Owner: Henry Ford Museum & Greenfield Village, Dearborn, Michigan

1932 Chrysler Imperial Eight Series CH Cabriolet, Bohman & Schwartz
Owner: J. Martin Anderson of Kent, Washington

Chrysler Imperials were divided into two series for '32. Both carried the 384.8-cubic-inch straight eight but the CH, at 135 inches, was eleven inches shorter in wheelbase than the Imperial Custom CL. Although no catalogue customs were available in the CH series, nine chassis were provided with custom bodies by independent coachbuilders. Two of them are shown here.

J. Martin Anderson's CH Imperial Eight Cabriolet was probably the first car completed following the demise of the Walter M. Murphy Company when Murphy employees Christian Bohman and Maurice Schwartz stayed on and set themselves up in business in the same facility. The original owner of the car was Theodore Lincoln Perry, better known as Stepin Fetchit, the black comedian popular in films of the thirties.

Al Nippert purchased his CH Imperial Eight LeBaron Speedster over twenty-five years ago from its original owner, Walter P. Chrysler,

Jr., and thereby hangs a fascinating tale: "Walter Chrysler, Sr. had driven the car at his summer home in New England for about a year, then gave it to his son. Obviously, this speedster was used to try out a lot of new ideas because many of the mechanical parts are marked 'experimental'—the gas pedal starting, the anti-stall restart system, the generator, the automatic choke with flood gas charge dump button on the dash, the pendulum control valve that disengages the clutch in a panic stop, etc. An original photograph indicates that none other than Barney Oldfield (with engineer Fred Zeder as passenger) road tested the car. Everything about this Chrysler is special. The headlamps are larger and the radiator shell four inches taller than stock. The body is aluminum but the fenders are steel, the fronts made in twelve pieces welded and hand hammered. The bumpers were custom made too. Leather-lined tool boxes were provided with the car. A Philco radio (cathedral dial head) is

mounted on the steering column with its antenna sewn into the leather binding of the top. The disappearing top folds down into a leather-lined compartment that also accepts the side curtains. The spare tire, held in by sidemount brackets on a trolley base, slides out of the trunk compartment on track rails. The LeBaron styling of the car is unsurpassed. So is the Chrysler engineering, with the high compression engine vibration-free on floating power engine mounts. It's a superb riding chassis. When I purchased the car, the WPC monogram was (and is) still on the door and the odometer read 8,600 miles. That was as close to driving a new 1932 Chrysler as one could get. The car remains totally original, now with 12,800 miles. With its high-speed rear end and extra high compression aluminum head, passing other cars on the road is accomplished with great ease. Cruising speed is an easy 70 mph, but this Chrysler is always ready to rip on."

1932 Chrysler Imperial Eight Series CH Speedster, LeBaron
Owner: Albert D. Nippert of Peekskill, New York

Bruce Thomas discovered the Trifon in 1965 in the Chrysler Engineering warehouse. He was there on a mission—to drive retired engineer Carl Breer's personal Airflow to the Society of Automotive Engineers' 60th anniversary show. But what he found under the first canvas shroud he picked up was a dusty and dirty car he was unaware at the time had ever been built. Carl Breer's Airflow was located elsewhere in the warehouse and duly taken to the SAE show. But for days afterwards, Bruce could not get the strange car he had seen out of his mind. Following four months of discussion and negotiation with Chrysler Corporation, the Trifon was moved, for the first time in two decades at least, from the Chrysler warehouse to the Thomas garage, where it has remained ever since.

Meanwhile, Bruce, who today is head of the Chrysler Historical Collection, set about ferreting out the saga of this unique automobile: "As far back as 1927 Chrysler Corporation began work in aerodynamics. The research started after Carl Breer noticed a flock of geese approaching over the horizon near Port Huron one day and marvelled at their effortless smooth flight. To his surprise, the 'geese' turned out to be Army planes returning to nearby Selfridge Field. Mr. Breer's engineering mind took over and he reasoned that his mistake was due to the fact that both a plane and a bird took the best and most natural advantage of air currents. He wondered why an automobile shouldn't be streamlined too. Subsequent research culminated in 1932 in the first road-test car of this concept. Completed that September, the Trifon embodied many advanced engineering ideas, the most pronounced and prophetic being the complete relocation of the passenger compartment forward to permit 'between the axle seating' for all occupants. This in turn required relocation of the engine about twenty inches further forward in the chassis over the front axle which moved the radiator core well ahead of its traditional location. In toto, the concept provided for a much longer passenger compartment than found on anything but seven-passenger limousines of the era. The partially concealed running boards were the result of an unusually wide body which further increased the inside room. Another prophetic feature was the one-piece curved windshield incorporated in the styling mock-up.

"The Trifon name itself is interesting too. To provide security on this unique automobile, Chrysler

Corporation licensed and registered the car in the name of Demitrion Trifon, a mechanic-driver in the road test garage who had worked on it. To further confuse the competition, licensing used only the Trifon Special name, with Chrysler appearing nowhere in the paperwork. Whenever the car was road tested, it was transported from the plant in an unmarked closed trucking van. And whenever corporation personnel, including even Walter P. Chrysler, journeyed to West Branch to drive the car, they made the trip in a competitive vehicle so that no one would connect the Trifon to Chrysler Corporation.

"The Trifon Special was subjected to many road and laboratory tests but by 1933 had been superseded by another series of experimental vehicles. Those, so far as is known, were all destroyed. How the Trifon survived is anyone's guess. Chrysler history is enhanced because it did."

1932 Chrysler Trifon RD 1000 Four-Door Sedan

Owner: Bruce Thomas of Troy, Michigan

1933 Chrysler Custom Imperial Series CL* Roadster-Convertible, LeBaron
Owner: Charles Montano of Gloversville, New York   Photos: Daniel B. Lyons

While Chrysler was experimenting behind the scenes in 1933, the Imperial went to market changed only minimally. The biggest difference during these years was sales. As the Depression deepened, Imperial production had fallen from over 3,000 units in 1931 to less than 2,000 in 1932. Nineteen thirty-three found the CH discontinued and replaced with a downsized line; Custom Series CL*s—and why Chrysler chose to asterisk these cars in '33-'34 defies logic—found just 151 buyers.

Just nine LeBaron Roadster-Convertibles were produced in '33. "Lots of chrome yet not overpowering and exceptionally engineered" is Charlie Montano's verdict on his car which, just three years ago, was "a basket case."

1933 Chrysler Custom Imperial Series CL* Phaeton, LeBaron   *Owner: W. G. Lassiter, Jr. of West Palm Beach, Florida*

Thirty-six was the total production of the $3,395 LeBaron Phaeton, revised in '32 from a dual cowl to the more-easy-to-enter dual windshield. The Blackhawk car was a wedding present from Edward Long of New York City to his daughter and honeymooned with the newly-married couple in Sweden.

"Beautiful car, drives and handles beautifully too," says Bill Lassiter. Comments Andrew Darling: "The body is so well designed that when you look at it, especially from the front, it gives the illusion that the car is moving. Look at the picture. I hope it gives you the same impression of motion as it does me."

1933 Chrysler Custom Imperial Series CL* Phaeton, LeBaron   Owner: Andrew D. Darling of Edina, Minnesota

1933 Chrysler Custom Imperial Series CL* Phaeton, LeBaron   Owner: Blackhawk Classic Auto Collection, Danville, California

"Breathlessly different looking," gushed Carolyn Edmundson of *Harper's Bazaar*. "Splendid just from its appearance," commented Professor Alexander Klemin of the Daniel Guggenheim School of Aeronautics. Look at the car for two or three days, the editors of *MoToR* suggested, and it will look right and all other automobiles will look wrong. The Airflow had arrived. Its look had happened naturally, Chrysler said, with the help of a wind tunnel. Underneath the aerodynamic body, the passengers were cradled between the axles à la the experimental Trifon. Semi-unitary construction was another Airflow idea whose time had not come elsewhere. Headlamps were recessed in front, the trunk was integral in the rear. Top-of-the-line Imperial Custom Airflows had the industry's first-ever curved one-piece windshield. The interior of the car was as Art Deco as the Chrysler Building. Wheelbase of the Series CW was the same 146 inches as the predecessor CL, cubic inches of the engine remained the same 385. But there similarity ended—dramatically.

Bob Joynt is as enthusiastic about his Airflow today as the aforementioned critics were in 1934: "Totally unorthodox and radical, this was the most advanced car available that year and the first modern car in history. It's also the most powerful Classic Chrysler, with high compression aluminum head, overdrive transmission and a top speed of 110 mph. And it's the largest, at 7,000 pounds, fully six feet two inches high and stretching twenty feet. The first owner of my CW was Huntington Hartford, patron of the arts and A&P heir; the third owner was Carl Breer, head of Chrysler Advanced Engineering and father of the Airflow. His son used to say that when he borrowed the Airflow to go out on a double date in the thirties all four of them sat in the front seat. In the nine years I've owned the Airflow, I've driven it 10,000 miles. On the road it feels like the 20th Century Limited. Is this the greatest car ever built? My natural modesty forbids answering this question. But the car speaks for itself!"

Chrysler went all-out with the Airflow. In addition to the rarefied $5,000 CW, the Imperial Custom was offered in the Series CX on a 137.5-inch chassis with 323.5-cubic-inch straight eight delivering 130 hp and a price tag in the $2,300 range. Internal corporation memos reveal Chrysler targeted the CX as a contender in the Packard 1102, Buick

1934 Chrysler Imperial Custom Airflow Series CW Limousine, LeBaron (details page opposite)
Owner: Bob Joynt of Batavia, Illinois

90, Cadillac V-8, Pierce-Arrow and Lincoln twelve market.

Why Charles Goddard chose the CX Town Sedan that Paul Tatman owns today is not known but an interesting story lies behind the car: ''Goddard, one of the founders of Humble Oil, was building a ranch in Oklahoma at the time. One evening his son was involved in an automobile accident near Joe Walker's sawmill; Walker rushed the boy and his companions to the hospital in his Chevrolet flatbed truck. Although the son subsequently died of his injuries, Charlie Goddard bought the Imperial Custom Airflow for Walker in gratitude. Joe kept the car for thirty-five years. I've owned it for seven. With overdrive it has the ability to cruise all day at 65-70 mph.''

The principal problem of the Airflow was that it didn't sell. In the five series offered, just 11,292 cars found purchasers in 1934; the single conventionally styled Chrysler available that year outsold all Airflows by more than two to one. Of the Series CW Airflows like Bob Joynt's, just 47 found buyers. Total CX sales stopped at 128, and Paul Tatman's Town Sedan was the only one built in that body style. Historians generally regard the Airflow as Walter Chrysler's first mistake. A critical success, it was a commercial failure. Chrysler Corporation would spend the next three years trying to undo what had been done, modifying the Airflow's natural waterfall grille into a more usual vee and replacing the functional hood louvers with versions more simply decorative, until finally in 1937 the remedial action was discontinued—and the Airflow was history.

1934 Chrysler Imperial Custom Airflow Series CX Town Sedan, LeBaron
Owner: Paul E. Tatman of Wichita, Kansas

206

Nineteen thirty-eight for the Custom Imperial brought sales of 519 cars and styling that was modish but not radical, courtesy of Ray Dietrich who became Chrysler's new chief body designer following the move of Oliver Clark, the man responsible for the Airflow, up to executive rank. Don & Carol Alexander have owned their LeBaron Imperial Limousine for nearly two decades: "Only five are known to exist of 145 built. The car behaves great on the road and the overdrive makes it ideal for expressways."

1938 Chrysler Custom Imperial Series C-20 Limousine, LeBaron
Owners: Don & Carol Alexander of Riverside, Illinois

1939 Chrysler Custom Imperial Series C-24 Five-Passenger Sedan, LeBaron   *Owner: Gerald B. Talkington of Mineral Wells, Texas*

The 1939 Custom Imperial introduced Fluid Coupling which with the three-speed and overdrive provided a semi-automatic transmission with fine flexibility. Of the 300 Series C-24's produced, 88 were five-passenger sedans like Gerald Talkington's: "The wheelbase is 144 inches, the engine the 323.5-cubic-inch straight eight that would be used until 1950. Sidemounts were an option for the last time in 1939 on the Custom Imperial. My car was base priced at $2,595 and weighs 4,590 pounds. The pontoon-like fenders with the Art Deco lights in contrast to the bold outline of the hood spells Speed—Speed with Grace. Fluid drive with overdrive makes for a wonderful road car with a 'modern' feel."

1939 Chrysler Imperial Series C-23 Station Wagon, Bohman & Schwartz
Owner: Bruce R. Thomas of Troy, Michigan

The most unusual 1939 Imperial has to be the car Bruce Thomas acquired from John Way, Jr., son of the orignal owner, in 1985: ''This one-off Bohman & Schwartz amazes me! As far as I can research, it is the only Imperial Station Wagon built on a 1939 chassis, or any other year for that matter. With this car came total documentation, including the original sketch for customer approval, all correspondence and lots of the bills, etc. The metal-framed windows are rare for a wagon, and the lowered beltline provides better side visibility. The specification called for extra reinforcements everywhere to reduce (or eliminate) squeaks and rattles—and they worked. After 65,000 actual miles the car is still 'silent.' Except for soft trim and chrome plating, I restored this wagon myself. For a long time I didn't have any fingerprints due to the sanding-sanding-sanding. The last bits of 1000 grit were smoother than my fingers.''

A sign of the times . . . the only 1940 Crown Imperial 145.5-inch chassis consigned to an individual coachbuilder for a custom body produced the Parade Phaeton shown here. By now most coachbuilding houses were no more. Still in business—and ultimately the last survivor—was Derham of Rosemont, Pennsylvania. "This very late special-order, special-purpose full custom Derham is really a political history artifact," comments Henry Ford Museum transportation curator Randy Mason. "It was the official New York City parade car from 1940 to 1952. A lot of ticker tape fell on this Chrysler during that period."

The Thunderbolt, named for the car that Captain George Eyston had sped to a new land speed record of 357.5 mph on the salt flats of Bonneville in 1938, was commissioned by Chrysler. Having learned a lesson well with the Airflow, this advanced design was not intended as a car for the marketplace but one for the showroom—to increase traffic and, hopefully, sales of conventionally styled Chryslers of the period. Certainly there was nothing conventional about the Thunderbolt, nor its companion dual-cowl-phaeton Newport. These cars were dreams of the forties presaging full envelope and straight-through fender line styling that wouldn't

become reality until well after the Classic Era ended. Underneath the Thunderbolt's body is a standard 127.5-inch New Yorker chassis with Imperial straight-eight engine. The hardtop is retractable, the doors open by pushbutton inside and out, the windows operate electrically. Total production of these show cars was twelve, six Thunderbolts, six Newports. Crowds thronged Chrysler showrooms to see them until after Pearl Harbor. Then Walter Chrysler, Jr. took one of the Newports (sadly, his father had died in 1940); the other eleven cars were sold. The Thunderbolt in the Blackhawk Classic Auto Collection is one of the few extant.

1940 Chrysler Crown Imperial Series C-27 Parade Phaeton, Derham
Owner: Henry Ford Museum & Greenfield Village, Dearborn, Michigan

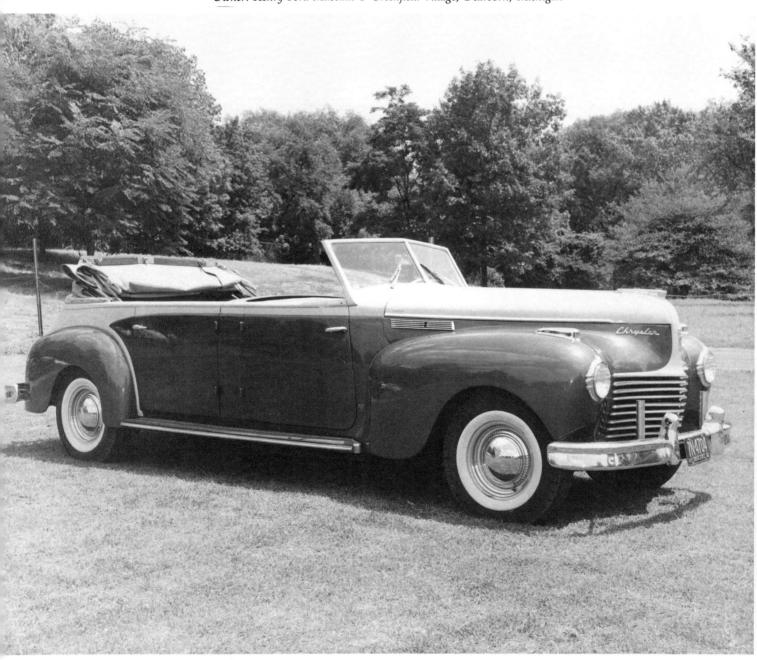

1941 Chrysler Thunderbolt, LeBaron   Owner: Blackhawk Classic Auto Collection, Danville, California

1948 Chrysler Crown Imperial Series C-40 Limousine
Owner: Bob Joynt of Batavia, Illinois

Jumping into production following the war, Chrysler sold every car it could build. Logic dictated the wisdom of focusing on the bread-and-butter models. Total production of the top-of-the-line Crown Imperials for 1946 through 1948 was 1,400 cars, 650 sedans, 750 limousines. Bob Joynt has owned his car for four years: ''The engine is the venerable 323.5-cubic-inch straight eight, the wheelbase is 145½ inches, the transmission is fluid drive. Featured are power windows including divider, jump seats, mouton carpets and leather chauffeur's compartment. This was the last year, of course, of the prewar body style, and the car is a 1940's explosion of jukebox dash, lavish wood trim, jumbo 8:90x15 tires and a smiley face grille. A wonderful road automobile, this Imperial is 100% original.''

Bob Rostecki's Imperial Brougham Limousine is 100% unique: "Marjorie Merriweather Post, the cereal heiress, commissioned Derham to build this car on the '48 Imperial chassis with a design updated from a 1928 Barker body style. The cost for the finished product was $19,000. In 1956 Mrs. Post donated the car to the Mount Vernon School for Girls of which she was a patron, stipulating that when it broke down it was to be junked. The following year the rear axle developed a problem and the body was becoming shabby, so that stipulation was followed. Someone bought it from the junkyard for $125.00; the bad axle made for a lot of grinding and banging as the poor old car motored along so when this fellow entered the Air Force, he gave the Derham to Bill Pettit for his museum in Louisa, Virginia. Initially, Bill considered using the Derham as a parts car but instead kept it intact for twenty-six years. I bought it from him five years ago and am now in the process of restoration. Following a complete bumper-to-bumper mechanical overhaul, this 58,000-original-mile car is pleasant and solid to drive. And it will always intrigue me because of its history. The car is a one-of-a-kind and so, for that matter, was its original owner. But most poignantly, this Brougham Limousine represents the last Classic body built in its entirety by the last of the old-time Classic coachbuilders—Derham of Rosemont, Pennsylvania. This beautiful Classic which escaped destruction twice has an honored place in our garage. She is a lady. We call her 'The Merriweather'."

1948 Chrysler Crown Imperial Series C-40 Brougham Limousine, Derham
Owner: Robert K. Rostecki of Winnipeg, Manitoba

C O R D

Sidemount spare with lock from Len Urlik's 1930 L-29 Phaeton Sedan

Its pedigree was impeccable. Nearly 2,000 orders for the new car were received before the first one had even been seen. Errett Lobban Cord had made a style leader of the Auburn and recently introduced the Model J Duesenberg. Now he was entering the marketplace with a brand-new automobile he felt was worthy of carrying his name. For a full year the industry had gossiped about the forthcoming L-29 Cord. Small wonder. The specification was impressive: Lycoming 298.6-cubic-inch 115 hp straight-eight engine, a chassis incorporating hydaulic brakes, Bijur lubrication, thermostatically-controlled radiator shutters, the industry's first X-braced frame—and, most significant, front wheel drive. The cadre of consultants who had helped make the L-29 happen was top-drawer: Cornelius Van Ranst, Harry Miller, Leo Goossen, Leon Duray. These were names familiar to everyone in America who was a fan of the Indianapolis 500. Mention of them—which the Cord p.r. department did vociferously—guaranteed that the new L-29 Cord would be regarded as a high-performance car. That the car scored equally high in aesthetics was discernible at a glance. The Cord was E.L.'s pet. He missed most of the hoopla concomitant to its debut, choosing to spend the time instead with a mechanic and an L-29 itself on a "10,000-mile buggy ride," as it was described by *World's Work* in an article about the thirty-five-year-old industrialist entitled "Youth at the Top." While a million-and-a-half people flocked to Auburn showrooms to see the new Cord during the first three days of its introduction, Cord himself was talking to gas station attendants, garage hands and toll booth workers on the highways of states from Indiana to Arizona. The success of his new car seemed assured. . . .

The L-29 Cord was introduced shortly before Labor Day of 1929 in four body styles priced from $3,095 to $3,295. Among the early purchasers was one A. U. Snyder, the original owner of Jeff Broderick's Four-Door Sedan: ''Snyder owned the car until 1960 although it had been stored on blocks since '37. When I purchased the L-29 in 1973, it had a total of 36,200 miles. Restoration followed. The greatest thing about the Cord, of course, is its front wheel drive. Due to the low silhouette, the car is a guaranteed eye-catcher. But front wheel drive also offered effortless handling, a different roadability, a sense of security and an absence of fatigue for driver and passengers heretofore unknown. Without the 'hump' down the middle of the car, leg room was greatly increased. Because my car is a closed sedan, the interior is especially luxurious with a two-inch band of embroidery completely surrounding both front and rear passenger areas. The hardware is highly detailed German silver. The dashboard is a marvel to behold: detailed metal accentuated with black and two complete clusters of gauges, each gauge being a circular swivel rather than just round dial with needle. The front windshield raises and there is a baffle openng system in the muffler (creating a 'straight pipe') to increase power. The gearshift lever protrudes from the center of the dash and is handled easily. I thoroughly enjoy driving this car, especially on curving country roads where the front wheel drive allows excellent maneuverability.''

Industry competitors did not take the arrival of the L-29 in stride. Rebuttal was swift. Dealers of conventionally driven cars started a whisper compaign of some proportion regarding the ''risks'' of front wheel drive. True, the L-29 did have mechanical teething problems common to any new design but not

1929 Cord L-29 Four-Door Sedan
Owner: Jeffery P. Broderick of Gap, Pennsylvania

in the front-drive system. Purchasers of the new Cord seem to have been as enthusiastic about the car as collectors are today.

"The L-29 handles well and is not hard to steer despite the usual legend," says Len Urlik regarding his Phaeton Sedan (the designation Cord preferred for its four-door convertible).

The worst driving experience Alexander Cameron has had with his L-29 wasn't the car's fault: "I lost a front wheel on the Pennsylvania Turnpike going at top speed. This was due to the fact that the front hubs had been switched by a mechanic, thereby the right hubcap was on the left wheel and unwound." Both Cord and Cameron survived the mistake.

1930 Cord L-29 Phaeton Sedan
Owner: Leonard Urlik of Beverly Hills, California

1930 Cord L-29 Phaeton Sedan (door handle detail above)

Owner: Alexander Cameron III of Reading, Pennsylvania

1930 Cord L-29 Phaeton Sedan

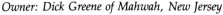Owner: Dick Greene of Mahwah, New Jersey

No collector carries the L-29 gospel with more fervor than Dick Greene, who owns twelve of them: ''The L-29 is the only car in E. L. Cord's empire that he personally conceived, helped design, worked on its development, test drove the prototype, and put his name on. E. L. Cord was *very* proud of the L-29. During its introductory year, the car won thirty-three international first-place awards for design excellence.''

The Phaeton Sedan shown here is one of two of this body style in Dick Greene's collection: ''Designer Alan Leamy is credited with the first convertible sedan on the 1928

Auburn and carried the success into the L-29 low profile. The vee grille was very avant-garde. Geared a bit low, my convertible sedan is an excellent road car up to about 60 mph.''

Dick Greene's L-29 Brougham is, again, one of a pair: ''All told, 618 of this style were produced on the L-29 chassis; eight are known to exist. Alan Leamy and E. L. Cord worked together on this design to produce a closed car with the look of a convertible sedan—a hardtop convertible, in other words. I purchased this car a decade ago. Literally owned by 'a little old lady

from Pasadena,' it had enjoyed warm, dry and salt-free roads its whole life. Original mileage is just 33,000. It's the only car I've ever seen with termites, however. It's also one of the forty odd with the 'deluxe' dashboard; the stoneguard is an original and very rare. With a 53-11 differential, this L-29 is undergeared for the open road but *very* pleasant to drive in town (for which it was designed). During the 1980's, I had the pleasure of chauffeuring Mrs. E. L. Cord in this car during her visits to our home in New Jersey and to Auburn, Indiana. She still refers to it as 'her car'!''

1930 Cord L-29 Brougham   Owner: Dick Greene of Mahwah, New Jersey

L-29 Brougham details. Door hardware and embroidery detail.
Front drive spring suspension. Stoneguard and mascot were
dealer options. Note the air-cooled inboard front brakes.

On Memorial Day of 1930 an L-29 Cabriolet served as pace car for the Indianapolis 500. Appropriately, an example of this body style is in the Indianapolis Motor Speedway Hall of Fame Museum: ''The L-29 is an important addition to our grouping of cars made in Indiana. Harry Miller, famed California racing car engineer had successfully used front wheel drive in Indianapolis 500 competition. Miller, race driver Leon Duray and engineer Leo Goossen served as advisers to Cornelius Van Ranst, project engineer for E. L. Cord, for this vital component. Following the revision of the frame to X-bracing under the direction of Auburn chief engineer Herbert Snow, Van Ranst completed the design and engineering required to mate the Lycoming engine and complete the chassis for both production and custom bodywork. The low profile and beauty of line from E. L. Cord himself, Auburn chief stylist Alan Leamy and associate John Oswald made for a sleek elegance previously unknown.''

1930 Cord L-29 Cabriolet (rear view opposite)   *Owner: Indianapolis Motor Speedway Hall of Fame Museum*   *Photos: Ron McQueeney*

1930 Cord L-29 Cabriolet　　　　　*Owner: Len Weiss of Homosassa, Florida*

"Frank Lloyd Wright bought this car new and had it until he died in 1959," comments Len Weiss about his L-29 Cabriolet. "His emblem is still on the windshield." In conversations for his autobiography, the celebrated architect used the word "heroic" to describe the L-29: "[It] certainly looked becoming to my houses—the best design from my 'streamline' standpoint ever put on the market. . . . The Cord was an innovator along right lines that changed the whole field of body design for the better."

Frank Hayward's L-29 Murphy Dual Cowl Phaeton arrived in South Africa in 1946 (bearing '37 California license number 2-6737) and has been in Frank's garage since 1964: "The only other L-29 known to exist on the continent of Africa is owned by the King of Morocco. Seven examples of my custom Cord were built; only two have survived (the other owned by Dick Greene). The long 144-inch wheelbase (the production L-29's was 137½ inches), the dual cowl and sweep panel of the Murphy custom style designed by Franklin Hershey make this one of the most beautiful and elegant cars on the road. The top gear performance is excellent, the steering light and responsive, the brakes outstanding. This L-29 has won nearly every major rally/reliability trial for vintage cars on the South African sporting calendar. My wife (and navigator) Judy and I have both received the prestigious 'Sports Merit Award' from the State President, which is the highest honor our government can bestow on our old car hobby participants."

1930 Cord L-29 Dual Cowl Phaeton, Murphy
Owner: Dr. Frank Hayward of Johannesburg, South Africa

Note Pilot Ray lamps, which turn with the wheels and which were popular on Classics during this era.

Introduced less than two months before the stock market crash of '29, the Cord did not have the saving grace of time to establish a clientele. Just 2,678 L-29's had been sold by the end of 1930. In 1931 the price was slashed a thousand dollars, but that helped little. Thinking perhaps that more power would, the L-29's engine was bored out to 321.9 cubic inches for 125 hp in 1932.

Bill Locke has owned his '32 Cabriolet for over a quarter of a century: "A landmark car. The engineering innovation of front wheel drive, the styling achievement of lowness and the positioning of the windshield at mid-wheelbase, and the detail of craftsmanship throughout established a standard for the entire industry. The L-29 has it all. Our Cord has raced on dirt roads for movies, climbed the mountains of Pennsylvania, fought flooding rains in Kentucky and plowed through blizzard snows in Indiana. It has pulled heavy floats in 4th of July parades and towed stalled trucks from their distress. And there's more to come. The L-29 has it all."

1932 Cord L-29 Cabriolet
Owner: William S. Locke of West Lafayette, Indiana

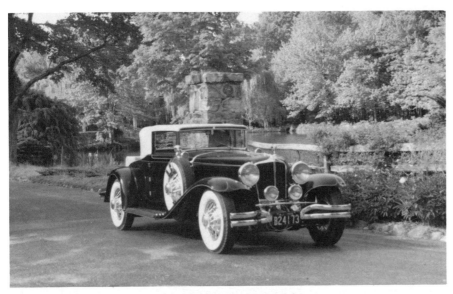

1932 Cord L-29 Cabriolet
Owner: Dick Greene of Mahwah, New Jersey

Dick Greene made two trips to pick up his '32 Cabriolet in 1956: "The car was originally delivered to a well-to-do family in Englewood, New Jersey who sold it in 1949 to a TYDOL service station. A subsequent owner took the car apart and stored it in two places, as it was when I bought it at the age of sixteen. This was my first Classic. It's been restored by me twice. The dual Pilot Ray lamps were a wedding gift from my wife Carol in 1969. Since the last restoration in 1975, I've driven the car about 16,000 miles. For a nearly sixty-year-old automobile, it is a great performer and, with the 53-13 differential, cruises nicely at 65 mph. The L-29 was the lowest Classic produced and set styling trends for the next several years. The Chrysler Imperials of that era were a direct copy."

Imitation was flattering but did not change the L-29's fate. Late in 1931 the car was quietly discontinued after a total production of 5,014 units. Of those, 55 carried custom bodies. The last 335 units produced in 1931 were sold as 1932 models. On January 2nd, 1932, the manufacturing complex in Auburn, Indiana was returned to the production of Auburn automobiles. During the L-29 era, Auburns had been built in the Cord Corporation's plant at Connersville, some 135 miles away. A few years later, Connersville would see production of a new Cord . . .

221

By the mid-thirties the Great Depression had taken a devastating toll in the automobile industry, with obituaries routinely being written for firms which had roared profitably through the twenties. Errett Lobban Cord's automotive companies remained alive, but shaky. Sales of his medium-priced Auburn had plummeted, production of his super-luxury Duesenberg was a trickle. A new car, it was thought, might generate sales interest. But what would it be? Ideas were tossed about among Cord Corporation executives, E. L. himself only peripherally involved since aviation and other interests in his far-flung empire were by now absorbing his time. The ultimate decision was for a V-8 engine, front wheel drive, independent front suspension and revival of the Cord name. Time was short. Eleven cars were literally banged together for the automobile show circuit. ''Radically different'' and ''ultra-modern'' were among the phrases reporters thought described the new Cord well. The British *Autocar* flatly declared it ''the most unorthodox car in the world today.'' It shall ever remain a tribute to the formidable talent of Gordon Buehrig that, as nonconforming as the body design was, it was universally applauded as looking right. And the same fervor which the L-29 enjoys among those who own the first-

1936 Cord 810 Convertible Phaeton Sedan   *Owner: Paul Bodine of Kildeer, Illinois*

generation Cord today is echoed in full measure by those who own an 810 (as introduced for '36) or 812 (as designated in '37).

''Easily the most important car introduced at the New York Automobile Show in late 1935,'' says Paul Bodine. ''I was twelve years old when a family in the next block

bought an 810 Cord. I vowed then that I would have one. It was an absolute styling sensation. Engineering needed some attention due to hasty preparation for the show. Shifter and universals were the major drawbacks. Restored cars today are better than 'factory' in many respects.''

1936 Cord 810 Convertible Phaeton Sedan

Owner: Allen E. Light of Williamsport, Pennsylvania

Comments Al Light about his 810 Phaeton: "Forty years of engineering design work on piston engines for both automotive and general aviation aircraft, and retirement as Vice President of Engineering from Lycoming Division of AVCO, makes driving and maintaining a Lycoming-powered Classic a pleasurable pastime." In five years Al has driven his 810 "over 15,000 enjoyable miles" and he neatly turns one purported drawback to long-distance Cord motoring into an advantage: "Limited luggage space eliminates the unwanted desire to carry unnecessary baggage."

223

"This is a timeless Classic in sleek form," comments Len Weiss. "Pontoon fenders, disappearing headlights, flush taillight and gas cap cover, concealed hinges, the list of its styling innovations could go on and on."

The Art Deco interior and the aircraft-style instrument panel attracted the Bjorklunds to their 812 Beverly Sedan: "Cord offered options of front door window wind wings and an accessory trunk rack. These are now extremely rare items. Our Cord sports a custom trunk with fitted luggage."

The 812 Coupe in the Auburn-Cord-Duesenberg Museum is even more unusual. Possibly the only original Cord of this body style in existence, it was especially built for Robert Stranahan, president of Champion Spark Plug, and includes Auburn headlights, circular louvers and a leather-covered top.

1937 Cord 812 Convertible Phaeton Sedan
Owner: Len Weiss of Homosassa, Florida

1937 Cord 812 Coupe

Owner:
Auburn-Cord-Duesenberg Museum,
Auburn, Indiana

1937 Cord 812 Beverly Sedan

Owners: Russell & Marie Bjorklund of New Brighton, Minnesota

1937 Cord 812 Beverly Sedan   *Owner: John C. Dennis of Mukilteo, Washington*   *Photos: Jim Arrabito*

John Dennis continues the Cord rhapsody. ''The extraordinary styling makes for a car with instant recognition by the public. The electric pre-select transmission with four speeds forward also makes this car unique. It is a joy to drive on the highway and can keep up with traffic all day long. The most important thing to a Cord owner is to have a transmission that will shift. The unit is complex but if understood and well maintained, the Cord can be a very dependable car. I have had no serious problems with mine over three decades of ownership.''

1937 Cord 812
Convertible Phaeton Sedan

Owner: Steve Moore
of Los Altos Hills, California

Like Paul Bodine, Steve Moore coveted a Cord since childhood: "I was about ten when I saw a photograph and at that moment fell in love. I remember checking out any book from the library that contained a photo of the Cord. I told myself that someday and somehow I would own one. Five years ago, at the age of twenty-five, I obtained my Cord. I had been particularly looking for a supercharged convertible. In 1937 a Switzer-Cummins centrifugal blower was an option. Supercharging raised the horsepower of the 288.6-cubic-inch Lycoming V-8 from 125 hp at 3500 rpm to 190 at 4200 rpm and resulted in one of the fastest road cars of the Classic Era. But the futuristic styling of the Cord's all-steel unitized body attracted me equally: the step-down floor eliminating the need for running boards, the wraparound louvered grille that didn't look anything like a radiator, the completely disappearing convertible top, the new idea of full wheel covers. In 1951 my car had been pulled from a creek bed in the Sierra Mountains where it had been sitting in the mud, water and sun for three years. Amazingly, it was in respectable condition. In 1952 Ray De Vault of Walnut Creek, California began a two-year restoration. The car passed through two more hands prior to my acquisition. Much detailing has been done inside and out and I am attending to various other mechanical and cosmetic areas. I bought this car to drive and enjoy."

1937 Cord 812 Sportsman's Convertible Coupe   *Owner: Dr. Frank Hayward of Johannesburg, South Africa*

In 1968 Frank Hayward bought his 1937 Cord 812 as ''scrap'' from a service station near Pietermaritzburg in Natal, South Africa: ''This car is stabled with an L-29 Cord and two Auburns in Johannesburg. Since restoration in 1972 it's been driven 10,000 miles including a number of post-vintage (1931-1941) rallies in South Africa. The car has won on occasion but has generally proved unreliable for rallying due to unexpected mechanical failures. Some problems have been: broken first gear, supercharger seizure, broken pistons, difficulty in starting, annoying and intermittent wheel shimmy at about 55 mph. But when it's running well, the Cord provides a superb ride on open roads in fourth gear at speeds of 80 to 90 mph. The top speed was advertised in excess of 100 mph.''

Any problems the Cord 810/812 had on the road paled in comparison to the vexations Errett Lobban Cord was suffering at the same time. During his empire building, he had made some powerful enemies. In August of 1937, under government investigation of his business activities, E. L. Cord disposed of his automotive holdings. Fewer than 3,000 810/812's had been built. The car's ''coffin nose'' was prophetic.

DUESENBERG

"Duesenbird" from Bill Deibel's 1935 JN Berline

Eight years old when his widowed mother emigrated to the United States from Germany in 1885, Fred Duesenberg grew up on a farm in Rockford, Iowa. Agriculture wasn't his thing. Fortuitously, there were a half-dozen other Duesenberg children to do the chores as he sallied forth to install windmills and repair farm machinery. By the mid-1890's, with his brother August, Fred had opened a bicycle shop in town. On a two-wheeler of his own design, he set a world speed record that was to last for fourteen years. Unfortunately, his bicycle business was kaput long before that. In 1903, with liabilities of some two thousand dollars (twice his assets), Fred declared bankruptcy. By now bicycles bored him anyway. He had been bitten by the automobile bug. In 1904 Fred and Augie opened a garage in Des Moines and designed a car they planned to call the "Marvel" until made rudely aware that getting into the automobile business was more costly than bicycles. Local attorney Edward R. Mason put up the money. By 1910 the Mason became the Maytag when the Iowa senator who made washing machines bought the company. Never again would Fred Duesenberg design a car that did not bear his name but for a long time his automobiles would be built solely for motor sport. In 1920 a Duesenberg scorched the sands of Daytona for 156.04 mph (a record that would stand for over half a decade); in 1921, at Le Mans, a Duesenberg became the first American car to win a European Grand Prix (and remained the only one until Dan Gurney's Eagle of 1967). Duesenbergs won the Indianapolis 500 in 1924, 1925 and 1927. Racing made the Duesenberg name famous. Of course, by now his financial backers had insisted that he also produce automobiles for sale, which would make the Duesenberg name immortal. . . .

"The World's Champion Automobile," early advertisements headlined. "Built to Outclass, Outrun and Outlast Any Car on the Road." These were not idle boasts. The Model A Duesenberg was one of the most significant new cars ever introduced in the United States, its overhead cam straight-eight engine and hydraulically-operated four-wheel brakes firsts for the industry. Typically, although exhibited at New York City's Commodore Hotel in October of 1920, the new Duesenberg did not see production until the 1922 model year. Fred was making changes. Now in Indianapolis (by way of Minnesota and New Jersey whence his post-Iowa ventures had taken him), Duesenberg was financed by a consortium of Hoosier businessmen to whom the automobile industry was a glorious new adventure. In the following half decade, more than 600 Model A's would be built.

"The overhead cam, valves and hemispherical combustion chamber were features I liked," comments Victor Benischek of his '26 Model A Opera Coupe. "I purchased the car in May 1971 and drove it home in pieces from Orlando, Florida in a large Hertz rental truck. The next five years were to be the most challenging I ever experienced in the car hobby. I had to make molds to create original

Climax universal joints, machine hood latches and duplicate the rear taillights since there were none available anywhere. With the same dark green leather for outside top material, interior seats and headliner, the car is truly distinctive. It always generates lots of interest wherever it goes. And the Duesenberg has been on many tours, accumulating over 6,000 miles in the process. The fact that it cruises well at 50-55 mph

makes it an excellent long-distance touring car. We have climbed Pikes Peak in a snowstorm, driven the Black Hills in South Dakota and explored the Smoky Mountains in Gatlinburg, Tennessee—all without problem one. My main interest in the car is keeping it in top mechanical order so that we will always be able to tour trouble-free. It's a wonderful way to see the U.S.A. and preserve some of our history too."

1926 Duesenberg Model A Opera Coupe, McNear
Owner: Victor V. Benischek of Cedar Crest, New Mexico

1927 Duesenberg Model A Rumble-Seat Roadster, Schutte
Owner: Indianapolis Motor Speedway Hall of Fame Museum
Photos: Ron McQueeney

Before his death in the fifties, Augie Duesenberg presented this Model A to the Indianapolis Motor Speedway. Except for seven-passenger bodies, Model A Duesenbergs usually used 134-inch chassis. This car's 141-inch limousine wheelbase made for both a long roadster and a comfortable one. In the ample rumble seat, folding armrests are positioned as the rear panel is opened. Throughout his ownership, Augie Duesenberg modified this car. The wire wheels are not believed to be original and may have been adapted from later Duesenberg models.

The Indianapolis Museum Duesenberg is among the last of the Model A's. Despite the allure of a powerful engine (260 cubic inches, 90 hp), a princely price tag (ranging upwards of $6,000) and sales that were scarcely shameful for a car in the Model A's league, the Duesenberg company had not made a profit. Fred's backers decided the automobile industry wasn't such a glorious adventure after all and began looking for a way out. In 1926 Fred Duesenberg had a new boss: Errett Lobban Cord. The most fabulous automobile America has ever seen, cost no object, was the directive Cord gave Duesenberg. Fred got to work, producing the very limited production Model X as a test pad. The Model J arrived two years later.

1929 Duesenberg Model J Dual Cowl Phaeton, LeBaron   *Owner: William Lyon of Trabuco Canyon, California*

''It's a doozy'' is a convenient phrase to use when other words fail. No need to mention its popular etymology. The Model J Duesenberg was a larger-than-life metaphor for the unrelentingly grand—and remains a legend that transcends time. Everything about the Model J was heroically proportioned. The massive double overhead cam straight-eight engine stretched fully four feet from fan to flywheel, boasting 420 cubic inches and 265 horses, twice the power of any other American car on the road. The epic chassis stretched 142½ inches in short wheelbase form, 153½ in long. The introductory chassis price was $8,500. All Model J's would carry custom coachwork, adding at least half again to the chassis price. But then the Model J Duesenberg was, like Commodore Vanderbilt's yacht, an object which one couldn't afford if the price had to be asked. Probably no car in America

attracted a clientele as wildly diverse as the Model J. Ownership was more effective than a megaphone in announcing that one had arrived. ''He Drives a Duesenberg'' was all advertisements said, and that needed

saying. ''She Drives a Duesenberg'' too, although with three tons of car to manage, it helped if ''she'' was not the swooning sort. Mighty is the adjective universally used for the Model J. No American automobile

1929 Duesenberg Model J Dual Cowl Phaeton, LeBaron
Owners: Richard & Linda Kughn of Southfield, Michigan

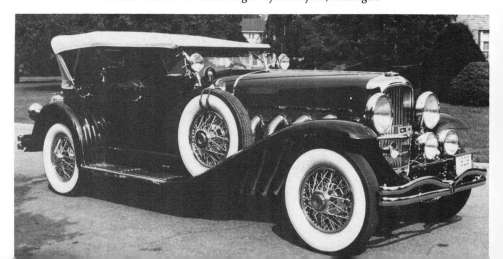

*1929 Duesenberg Model J Sport Sedan, Derham/Bohman & Schwartz
Owner: Mrs. Keith Brown of Fort Wayne, Indiana*

*1929 Duesenberg Model J Sedan, LaGrande
Owner: Fern E. Wilson of Rhinebeck, New York*

produced since has approached its splendid intimidation.

William Lyon's LeBaron Dual Cowl Phaeton was the very first Model J built. Engine serialed J-101, it was displayed at the New York Automobile Salon in December 1928. Apparently the car was used awhile as a demonstrator by the Chicago factory branch of Duesenberg, Inc.

The original owner of J-129, the Kughns' Phaeton, was John Duval Dodge, scion of the Dodge dynasty. While J-101 has certain details that distinguish it as the prototype LeBaron sweep-panel phaeton, J-129 can be said to represent the "production" version as reproduced in 1929 and 1930.

Because of the early Derham number of Mrs. Keith Brown's Sport Sedan, this body is believed to have been built before the J chassis was available, perhaps was mounted on a prototype chassis for exhibition purposes in 1928 and then remounted as J-118 in 1929. Gerri Brown explains the Bohman & Schwartz connection: "During the mid-thirties the car was owned by M. K. Barbee, president of Coca-Cola Bottling in Los Angeles. He is thought to have been the second owner. In unloading the car from the ferry returning from Catalina Island, it was dropped into the water where it remained for several days. This caused so much water damage that, when the car was taken to Bohman & Schwartz in Pasadena for repair, the decision was made to restyle it as well. I've owned the car for nine years. The Bohman & Schwartz interior remains original. The car is of very low mileage (24,473) and drives superbly."

Fern Wilson's J-189 LaGrande Sedan began life with a Weymann fabric body and is believed to have been originally owned by Alice Paddock whose husband, Colonel Paddock, was a Duesenberg owner too. When the car was traded in several years later, the factory had new coachwork fitted. Whether it was rebuilt from the original or an all-new body is not known. Whichever, the updating was effective; the lines of this sedan are very modern for 1933. In 1985 the LaGrande was acquired by the late Everest Wilson. "My husband loved old cars and owned a lot of them through the years," comments Fern. "His feeling was that the ultimate was to own a Duesenberg. Sadly, he didn't have the chance to drive it a lot. Still, once he got the Duesie, Everest felt he had made it. He had realized his ultimate old car dream."

233

Of the approximately 480 Model J Duesenbergs built, over 120 carried coachwork by the Walter M. Murphy Company. Murphy's Pasadena location was among the reasons. Southern California conformed less to tradition than the East Coast, and the Model J was anything but a conformist's car. No faddish pejorative is implied regarding Murphy design, as the cars on these and the following pages attest, nor did Murphy produce exclusively for a West Coast clientele.

The Bowersoxes' J-139 Sport Sedan, for example, was first owned by J. Warden Reid of Kansas City, Missouri. And its most flamboyant moment had happened back home in Indiana when gangsters stole the unbodied chassis while it was en route to the Indianapolis Speedway for the testing every Model J received prior to delivery to the coachbuilder. Comments Ray: ''With its sharp-slanted vee windshield, chrome window framing, narrow aluminum pillar between windows and close-coupled look, this is one of the most attractive sedans ever made.''

John Mozart echoes those sentiments: ''This car combines a great chassis with a very unique and stylish sedan-type body that is not overly formal. A closed car with a real sporting look was achieved, not an easy thing to do.'' The Mozart J-151 was originally owned by the Norris family and spent part of its life in Colorado Springs in the basement

1929 Duesenberg Model J Sport Sedan, Murphy
Owners: Ray & Lou Bowersox of Milton, Pennsylvania

1929 Duesenberg Model J Sport Sedan, Murphy

Owner: John Mozart of Palo Alto, California

of the Broadmoor Hotel.

"It's special because it's super-charged," says Sonny Abagnale of his J-169 Convertible Sedan by Murphy. The SJ, as it is popularly known (though never referred to as such by the factory), was really overkill. It arrived in 1932, four years after introduction of the J and in the time since no American manufacturer had come close to approaching that car's 265 horsepower. Supercharging

the Duesenberg to 320 hp was glorious excess. "In answer to the demand . . . for a fast strictly sport automobile" was the company's official *raison d'être*. Perhaps closer to the truth, Fred Duesenberg had been hankering to supercharge a road car since 1924 when his Indianapolis entry that year became the first blown race car to win the 500. (Sadly, he would die from pneumonia while recuperating from injuries received in

an automobile accident shortly after completing the centrifugal unit which brother Augie would refine.) Preliminary testing at the Indianapolis Speedway revealed 129 mph and, when this figure was revealed to the press, the reaction was amazement. Not surprisingly, some Duesenberg owners then, and enthusiasts since, decided that supercharging their early J's was the *ne plus ultra*. In a way, it was icing on the icing.

1929 Duesenberg Model J Convertible Sedan, Murphy   Owner: Sonny Abagnale of Cedar Grove, New Jersey   Photo: K. Karger

1929 Duesenberg Model J Town Limousine, Murphy Owner: Blackhawk Classic Auto Collection, Danville, California

The Blackhawk Collection J-218 Murphy Town Sedan was one of six Duesenbergs owned by George Whittell, the wealthy financier who had made wild game preserves of his two estates on the West Coast. Records indicate that he paid $15,000 for his formal car designed by Frank Hershey, who deftly extended the doors into the roof for ease of entry. Whittell was a big man with a heavy foot—and he drove his Duesenbergs fast everywhere until doing so during the Great Depression became embarrassing for someone who obviously had suffered not at all in the aftermath of the stock market crash. But, if he chose no longer to flaunt his good fortune in public, this Duesenberg owner still had plenty of room in which to exercise his cars. One of Whittell's estates encompassed most of the Nevada side of Lake Tahoe.

The likelihood is that the good fortune enjoyed by Whittell was not shared by Charles Jackson, the Chicago doctor who was the first owner of Joe Folladori's J-187 Murphy Clear Vision Sedan because he sold it soon after purchase. The car passed through four other hands prior to Joe's acquisition four years ago: "Nearly everyone who views or knows of this Clear Vision Sedan appreciates its graceful lines. The slanted *very thin* post, center divider, rear door upper post and window frames make most other 1929 sedans look old-fashioned by comparison. The polished aluminum belt line enhances the symmetry of the design overall. This is a wonderful driving car too."

Joe Folladori's J-137 Judkins Rumble-Seat Coupe is important historically as the first Duesenberg designed by Gordon Buehrig, who

1929 Duesenberg Model J Clear Vision Sedan, Murphy   *Owner: Joe Folladori of Indianapolis, Indiana*

had been hired shortly after the Model J's introduction as the company's chief designer. And it is interesting as well in being another Duesenberg that was not long in the hands of its original owner. "Joseph P. Wright of New York City purchased the car on June 1st, 1929," explains Joe, "but he sold it shortly thereafter to Shreve Archer of Minnesota who had the Murphy convertible body removed and a rumble-seat coupe designed by Gordon Buehrig installed instead. J. B. Judkins built the Buehrig-designed body and the installation was completed in 1930. Shreve Archer titled the car in 1931. Only two of these bodies were made, the second one never identified by car number. The design included a hidden compartment behind the seat and under the ledge to the rear window where nine bottles could be concealed. Inside the golf club door, there is a roll-out wooden bar for crystal and such. Very handsome —and for that era, very practical."

1929 Duesenberg Model J Rumble-Seat Coupe, Judkins   *Owner: Joe Folladori of Indianapolis, Indiana*

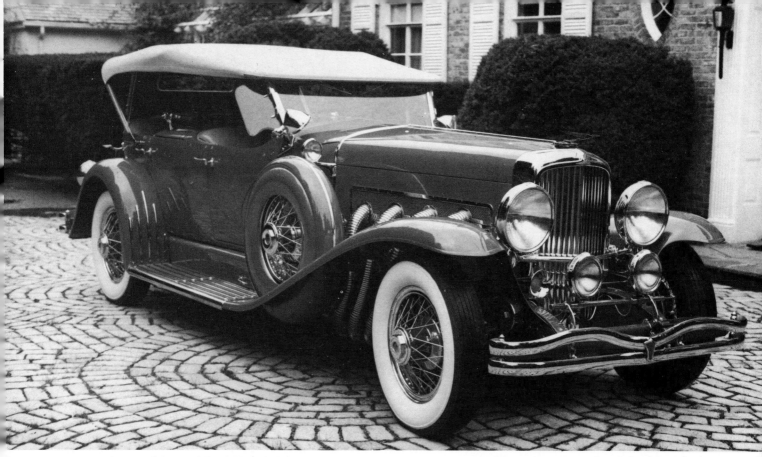

1929 Duesenberg Model J Dual Cowl Phaeton, LeBaron   Owner: Robert C. Rooke of Morristown, New Jersey

Bob Rooke's J-223 LeBaron Dual Cowl Phaeton exemplifies another interesting Duesenberg metamorphosis. Those side pipes say supercharger, but they're fooling. After 1932 the Duesenberg factory offered an external exhaust conversion to early J owners in order to make their cars look *au courant*. The owner who had this sweep-panel LeBaron thusly modified is not known, but Bob's car, which had been barn stored for twenty-two years, was owned at one time by Col. Dave Pennington, a P-51 pilot and member of the Confederate Air Force, an organization of historic plane collectors.

239

The Duesenberg factory manufactured twelve right-hand-drive
Model J chassis of which no more
than three survive. Just five Model J's
are believed to have been sent to
England. The Dougherty J-159 Town
Car was exhibited on the Barker
stand at the 1929 Olympia Motor
Show in London. Following World
War II, the car was purchased from
the stable of Sir Ralph Mallais by one
C. S. Phillips who entrusted its
restoration to Hooper, the renowned
English coachbuilding house. Hooper
closed its doors while this car was
being restored, but a few men stayed
on to finish the job. This Duesenberg
represented the last work done by
Hooper and included fabrication of
the unusual bumpers seen here
which replaced the original bow-knot
bumpers that were missing from the
car. This Duesenberg returned to the
States in the mid-1960's.

1929 Duesenberg Model J Town Car, Barker
Owners: James & Walter Dougherty of Indianapolis, Indiana

1930 Duesenberg Model J Dual Cowl Phaeton, LeBaron   *Owner: Miles C. Collier of Naples, Florida*

Over twenty American coachbuilders dressed the Model J. The
sweep-panel dual cowl phaeton on
the short 142½-inch wheelbase was
both the most popular LeBaron
design and the best-selling open four-
door body style from any
coachbuilder.

The original purchaser of the J-325
LeBaron Dual Cowl Phaeton owned

by Miles Collier and on display in his
Naples, Florida museum was
C. T. Ludington, owner of Ludington
Airlines, an all-Stinson Tri-Motor air
service out of New York, Newark
and Philadelphia. Ludington was a
friend of E. L. Cord's.

Stephen Brauer's J-256 was first
sold from the Los Angeles Duesenberg branch to James Hammond,

publisher of the *Memphis Commercial
Appeal*. But the garage in which this
LeBaron Dual Cowl Phaeton
subsequently found itself made it
more famous. ''Between 1936 and
1964 the car was owned by a colorful
ecdysiast in Montreal,'' explains
Stephen, ''and hence it has come to
be known as 'The Stripper' in
Duesenberg circles.''

1930 Duesenberg Model J Dual Cowl Phaeton, LeBaron   Owner: Stephen F. Brauer of Bridgeton, Missouri

1930 Duesenberg Model J Town Car, Murphy   Owner: William Lyon of Trabuco Canyon, California

William Lyon's J-393 Murphy Town Car typifies yet another Duesenberg transmogrification. Originally a LaGrande dual cowl phaeton graced this chassis, and this Murphy town car body had previously been mounted elsewhere. The reason for this Duesenbergian game of musical chassis was that this car was originally owned or used by Lucius B. Manning, one of the powers-that-be in Errett Lobban Cord's empire, who shifted cars and bodies with great abandon according to the season, his personal whim and/or the factory's need for a particular chassis. After being fitted with a supercharger and the Murphy body, this Duesenberg was sold to movie star Dolores del Rio in 1934. In subsequent years, the car became a movie star itself when owned by Pacific Auto Rental. Were its history not sufficient to make this car special, it is distinguished as well by the center-post door hinging which appears only on this Murphy Town Car.

John Mozart's J-120 Murphy Boattail Speedster on the long 153½-inch wheelbase was a one-off custom built for George Whittell which the sportsman drove among the lions, elephants and giraffes on his West Coast estate during the thirties. John has encountered no wildlife in the decade he has owned the Whittell speedster: "A great design by Murphy, a great car to drive with 31,000 original miles."

1930 Duesenberg Model J Boattail Speedster, Murphy (profile page opposite)

Owner: John Mozart of Palo Alto, California

1930 Duesenberg Model J Convertible Berline, Murphy   *Owner: Richard G. Gold of Deephaven, Minnesota*

The original Chicago area owner of Dick Gold's J-217 Murphy Convertible Coupe is not known but the garage in which his J-259 Murphy Convertible Berline was first housed is. Dick tells the tale: "George McQuerry, the young Murphy designer responsible for the car, delivered it personally and received a fifty-dollar gold piece for his efforts. It was Christmas time, and the new owner was in a giving spirit. He was Arthur K. Bourne, grandson of one of the founders of the Singer Sewing Machine Company. The Bourne home ran one full block from San Pasquale to California Street in Pasadena, California. On hand when George McQuerry delivered the car were the five Bourne chauffeurs: one each for Mr. and Mrs. Bourne and their children, a fourth for the servants for shopping, the fifth for guests. Apparently, A. K. Bourne was something of a dandy. He also served as a courtesy deputy sheriff and fire marshal in Pasadena, which accounts for the red lights, the siren and the blue light on the rear license plate taillamp bracket. A pair of buttons in the front compartment in the middle of the cowl operated the siren: two to blow it, one to stop it. There was also a radio installed in the rear compartment which, according to George McQuerry, was designed by two young electronic engineers who later founded Motorola. Another most unusual feature of this Duesenberg was its steerable headlights. Only a few sets of these were ever fitted to any Model J's, and this instance of their installation was certainly at the request of A. K. Bourne. What debonair fire-engine chaser, after all, would be without them? I've owned this car since 1977. It's never been restored and is, I feel, one of the few remaining Model J's that has the original Duesenberg feel. I've driven it over 20,000 miles and plan to continue doing so forever. But I don't think I will chase any fires."

1930 Duesenberg Model J Convertible Coupe, Murphy   *Owner: Richard G. Gold of Deephaven, Minnesota*

1930 Duesenberg Model J Berline Convertible Sedan, Murphy   Owner: Joe Folladori of Indianapolis, Indiana

"The Murphy Berline Convertible Sedan is a one of a kind," comments Joe Folladori about his long-wheelbase J-391. "Two were built; however, the second one was converted to a fixed top by its owner. The divider window is mounted in the rear of the front seat and cranks up. The ten-inch-wide armrest in the rear seat includes the only handle to open the trunk and, when open, folds out like a tray to hold two decanters and two glasses. Driving this car is an interesting experience. The long wheelbase changes the character of the handling and ride considerably compared to a short-wheelbase Duesenberg." Joe's car is distinguished also by the roster (and that is truly the word) of people who drove J-391 before he did. The original owner of the car was Rear Admiral Gene Markey, who was variously a movie producer and Under-Secretary of the Navy, and who was married to Lucille Whitney whose Calumet Farms in Fayette County, Kentucky bred many Triple Crown winners, Whirlaway in 1941 and Citation in 1948 among them. Roland Rich Wooley, a Hollywood divorce attorney, was the second owner of J-391. During the forties the car passed through a number of hands and in 1949 was sold to James B. Talmadge, son of Buster Keaton and his wife Natalie (whose sisters were Constance and Norma Talmadge). Purportedly, following the Keatons' divorce, Norma Talmadge insisted on the name change of Natalie's two sons. Jim Talmadge restored J-391 and subsequently sold it to Tyrone Power in 1952. Although the movie actor was a latterday owner, this Duesenberg is commonly referred to as the "Tyrone Power car." Subsequent homes included the Nethercutt and Harrah collections on the West Coast prior to Joe's acquisition in 1986. "After more than a half of a century," says Joe, "this one-of-a-kind Duesenberg is 'back home in Indiana'."

1930 Duesenberg Model J Convertible Victoria, Hibbard & Darrin   Owner: *Andrew D. Darling of Edina, Minnesota*

The Marquis Louis Martinez de Rivas of Paris and Madrid was the original owner of the Bowersox J-319 Convertible Town Car. ''The body was made of cast aluminum referred to as 'Sylentlyte' by Hibbard & Darrin,'' says Ray. ''Prior to being shipped to Paris, the chassis was tested on the Indianapolis Speedway on February 4th, 1930 and on the back stretch was clocked at 110 mph at 4000 rpm.''

Andrew D. Darling's J-277 Hibbard & Darrin Convertible Victoria was originally owned by Honore Palmer of Chicago, who happened to be living in Paris at the time and had the chassis shipped there for its coachwork: ''The small swirl on the hood by the radiator and the landau bar make this car distinctive. In later years Dutch Darrin described his personal touches on the car to me. To the best of my knowledge, J-277 remained in Paris until the World War II era when, for fear of commandeering by the Germans, it was shipped back to the United States. For many years prior to my purchase two decades ago, the car sat in a New Jersey warehouse. I rate my driving experience with J-277 very high. The car is exceedingly responsive and the brakes are without equal. There is a brake control on the dash for driving on ice and snow (a feature shared by Stutz). Warning lights indicate when the car is being lubricated and when not.''

1930 Duesenberg Model J Convertible Town Car, Hibbard & Darrin (profile page opposite)
Owners: Ray & Lou Bowersox of Milton, Pennsylvania

1931 Duesenberg Model J Tourster, Derham   *Owners: William & Helen Vaccaro of Bedminster, New Jersey*

1931 Duesenberg Model J Tourster, Derham
Owner: Alfred Ferrara of Gates Mills, Ohio   Photo: Torque

The Duesenberg straight-eight engine in the Vaccaros' Derham Tourster

The Derham Tourster was designed by Gordon Buehrig. Eight were built. Incredibly, seven original bodies of this style still exist.

"I love the beauty that my friend Gordon Buehrig designed into this touring model," says Al Ferrara of J-412, which he has owned for over three decades. "And the power. The Duesenberg was the greatest American car ever built."

"This was said to be Gordon Buehrig's favorite design," comments Bill Vaccaro. "The features I like most are the lowness of the top and the close-coupled body on the long 153½-inch wheelbase. Popular too was the tonneau windshield which cranked down into the rear cowl, which was later copied by Cadillac and Chrysler. The most notable detail about our J-489 Derham Tourster was its original owner: Helen Hay Whitney, daughter of Secretary of State Hay and widow of Payne Whitney, who left $178 million when he died in 1927. Mrs. Whitney was the first lady of American turf at the time. She won the Kentucky Derby with her horse Twenty Grand in 1931, the same year she bought J-489."

1931 Duesenberg Model J Dual Cowl Phaeton, LeBaron Owner: Alfred Ferrara of Gates Mills, Ohio Photo: Torque

This dual cowl phaeton design by LeBaron became popularly known as the "barrel-side." Al Ferrara's J-318 was the only one built on the long-wheelbase chassis and featured a special non-standard hood side design with thirty-six louvers in six groups of six. Al has owned the car for over a decade: "It was originally ordered by William F. Ryan of New York City and was delivered to him in Paris in 1931. He raced J-318 with other high-powered cars in Europe for two years, then came back to the U.S. and traded it in on another Duesenberg."

Ray & Lou Bowersox's J-299 LeBaron barrel-side Phaeton was raced as well in a quite extraordinary contest on Muroc Dry Lake in 1932. Its owner was Phil Berg, attorney to such stars as Clark Gable and Gary Cooper—and neighbor to Errett Lobban Cord, who had recently built

1931 Duesenberg Model J Dual Cowl Phaeton, LeBaron Owners: Ray & Lou Bowersox of Milton, Pennsylvania

1931 Duesenberg Model J Convertible Victoria, Rollston
Owner: Henry Ford Museum & Greenfield Village, Dearborn, Michigan

1931 Duesenberg Model J Convertible Victoria, Rollston
Owner: Blue Suede Shoes Auto Collection, Highland Park, Illinios

1931 Duesenberg Model J Convertible Victoria, Rollston
Owner: W.G. Lassiter, Jr. of West Palm Beach, Florida

his Beverly Hills home. The only other car in the race was Zeppo Marx's SSK Mercedes. The $10,000 wager between Berg and Marx had happened as casually as the Stutz-Hispano encounter (related elsewhere in this book). The difference was that in this case the American car won, J-299 averaging 102.5 mph over a measured fifteen-mile course and the Mercedes nowhere in sight when it crossed the finish line. Of course, the Model J did enjoy some factory support which the SSK did not. But it was all in sporting fun. The glittering spectators included Gable, Cooper, the Marx brothers, Al Jolson, Carole Lombard, Bébé Daniels and Mae West. Not to mention ''race car'' owners Phil Berg and Zeppo Marx who, probably wisely, entrusted the driving to more seasoned professionals. None other than racing's Harry Miller served as official starter. Actually, the two cars were basically glamorous props for an afternoon of mayhem at Muroc, but Phil Berg had to have been pleased with the $25,000 he collected at day's end. The wagering among the stars had been spirited before the starting flag.

In 1930 and '31 the Rollston Company of New York City built about a dozen convertible victorias for Duesenberg to designs developed by Rollston's own Rudolph Creteur. Essentially the same body was mounted on both the long 153½-inch and the short 142½-inch chassis lengths.

The Henry Ford Museum's J-266 was originally owned by John Warren Watson, maker of the Watson ''Stabilator'' shock absorbers, and was donated to the museum by his estate in 1962.

On August 5th, 1931 J-472, now in the Blue Suede Shoes collection, was delivered to Ralph Pulitzer of Manhasset, Long Island. His father, Joseph, publisher of the St. Louis *Post-Dispatch*, had established the renowned Pulitzer prizes, and Ralph Pulitzer had been a newspaper publisher himself, of the New York *World* and *Evening World* until 1930 when he sold out to Scripps-Howard. This Rollston Convertible Victoria is one of only three known short-wheelbase blind-quarter types.

Conversely, Bill Lassiter's J-456 is one of only two long-wheelbase Rollston Convertible Victorias with rear quarter windows which have survived.

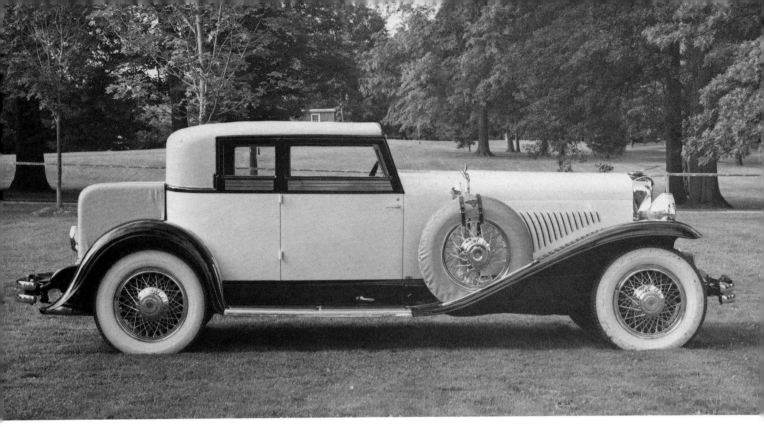

1931 Duesenberg Model J Victoria Coupe, Judkins   Owner: Alfred Ferrara of Gates Mills, Ohio   Photo: Milton Gene Kieft

Seen on the campus of Penn State in the early thirties was J-160, the Judkins Victoria Coupe originally purchased by Prof. E. C. Woodruff. Al Ferrara has owned the car for sixteen years: "This is a very rare body style, one of two built."

Noel Thompson has owned J-437 since 1987: "Gordon Buehrig designed this car and Weymann built it. The Tapertail Speedster is on the short wheelbase and has no windows, step panels or running boards. Sitting still, it gives the impression of going 110 mph."

1931 Duesenberg Model J Tapertail Speedster, Weymann   Owner: Noel Thompson of New Vernon, New Jersey   Photo: K. Karger

1932 Duesenberg Model J Torpedo Convertible Coupe, Murphy
Owner: Auburn-Cord-Duesenberg Museum, Auburn, Indiana

1932 Duesenberg Model J Coupe-Roadster, Murphy
Owner: Bill Murray of Boonton Township, New Jersey

1932 Duesenberg Model J Beverly Sedan, Rollston
Owner: Alfred Ferrara of Gates Mills, Ohio

J-476, the ''disappearing top'' Murphy Torpedo Convertible Coupe in the Auburn-Cord-Duesenberg Museum, enjoyed a host of interesting former owners. The first was Cliff Durant, the race driver and son of General Motors founder William C. Durant. For a Model A Duesenberg (and a certain amount of cash, one presumes), Cliff traded the car to J. Paul Getty later in the thirties. Among subsequent owners was the novelist John O'Hara. In 1954 the late Don Carr acquired J-476 and drove it many miles in many years, sometimes with the body off as the car was being restored. When he was no longer able to drive the Duesenberg, Don donated it to the A-C-D Museum in the mid-eighties.

Just about the same time, Bill Murray acquired J-284: ''Nineteen thirty-two was the first year for the SJ. And with the two-carb supercharger, this car is very fast. I am the sixth owner of J-284 and can document the car all the way back to its original purchaser—J. W. Martin, a New York City real estate magnate.

Adia E. Wrigley was the first owner of Al Ferrara's J-501 Beverly Sedan. The Wrigleys were very good friends of E. L. Cord. ''The body style is by Gordon Buehrig,'' comments Al. ''This car was one of two Rollston Beverlys built and the only one to survive. The other Rollston was destroyed some years ago.''

1932 Duesenberg Model J Convertible Coupe, Murphy   *Owner: Bill Buddig of Frankfort, Illinois*   *Photo: Dottie Gheen*

The original owner of Bill Buddig's J-461 was Siegfried Roebling of the bridge-building (Brooklyn, among others) Roebling family of Trenton, New Jersey. At that time the car carried a LaGrande sweep-panel phaeton body—and was involved in an accident in 1932 which left the car a complete wreck, according to the New York Duesenberg outlet service manager. When the chassis was rebuilt, a Murphy disappearing-top convertible coupe body was mounted. Bill has owned J-461 since 1984: ''It is rather unusual in being one of the few Duesenbergs *without* sidemounts. The rear-mounted spares make the car look extra long and racy. It's a thrill to drive, especially with the dual exhaust cutouts; the sound is really something.'' In addition to bridges, incidentally, the Roebling family was involved with the automobile industry—specifically Mercer.

Surviving coachwork by Willoughby & Company of Utica, New York is rare on the Duesenberg chassis. Ed Perkins has owned his J-343 Willoughby Berline for three years: ''I have always been partial to club sedan styling and fine interior woodwork. This Classic combines the best of both. Even though it is a divider-window seven-passenger body, the car is rather close-coupled and looks like a club sedan. The long-wheelbase chassis allows the room for this deception. Inside, the woodwork is some of the best I have seen—a straight-grain walnut with German silver inlaid around the bird's-eye maple overlay—and is in exceptionally nice original condition. The car was originally ordered in 1932 by Henry J. Merle, owner of the Irving Theatre in Chicago. It passed through about ten more owners prior to my acquisition. This Duesy is a good driver. We use it at least twice a week April through November, and anytime the weather permits in winter months.''

1932 Duesenberg Model J Berline, Willoughby   *Owner: Ed Perkins of Guilford, Connecticut*

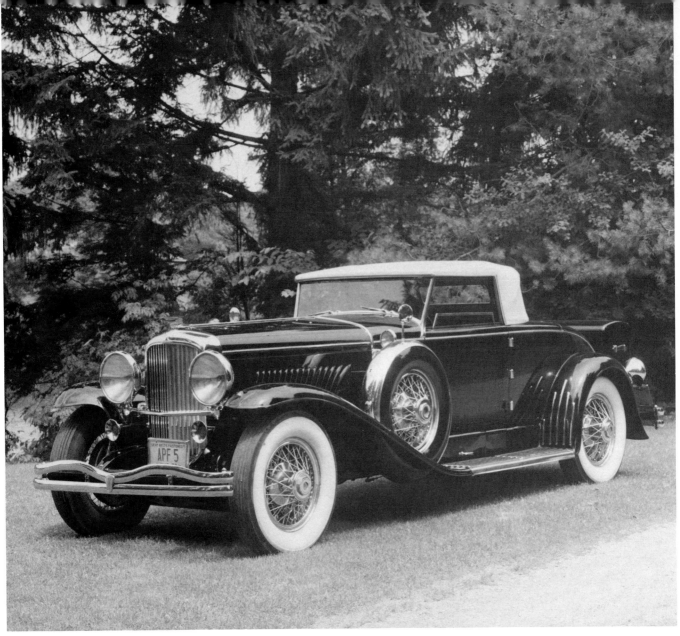

1933 Duesenberg Model J Convertible Coupe, Murphy　　　　　*Owner: Alfred Ferrara of Gates Mills, Ohio*　　　*Photo: Torque*

"The first owner was Cornelius Vanderbilt Whitney of New York," comments Al Ferrara of his J-428 Murphy Convertible Coupe. "I bought the car off a used car lot in 1949 in Minneapolis, Minnesota. Archie Walker Motors had taken it in on trade. In the past four decades, I've driven this Duesenberg all over the eastern and midwestern parts of the U.S. Fine coachwork by Murphy, excellent engineering by Duesenberg, lots of power and great comfort—all a man could want in a motor car."

Gene Perkins has owned his J-399 Murphy Convertible Sedan Berline for over two decades: "On the long 153½-inch wheelbase, this car looks sporty with its rakish windshield and short section of top behind the rear door. It came equipped with a zip-out headliner (which I still have), divider window and external exhausts."

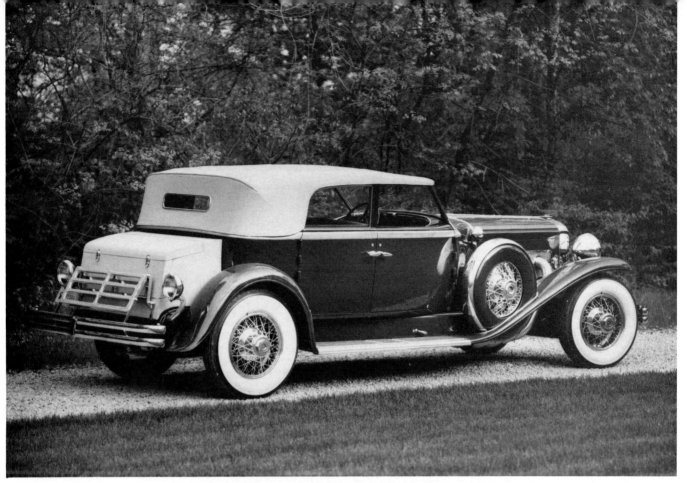

1933 Duesenberg Model J Convertible Sedan Berline, Murphy
Owner: N. Gene Perkins of Greenwood, Indiana   Photo: Nancy Bailey
(three-quarter view on page opposite)

Keith Brown's Derham Convertible Sedan exemplifies how difficult, and often confusing, Duesenberg genealogy can be. As Keith explains: "Harry G. Liebhardt of Denver, Colorado purchased Derham Convertible Sedan J-507/2523, now J-170/2145, in 1933. I use both engine and chassis numbers because this story needs them. Five Derham convertible sedans were built for the Duesenberg chassis; four remain in existence. Shortly after purchasing the car, Harry Liebhardt changed the back window from a small oval to an oblong, switched to blackwall tires and fitted an Hispano-Suiza ornament. He was a racing enthusiast. A friend of the family tells of Harry and his chauffeur driving the J to Indiana for the Indianapolis 500. A full-page Duesenberg ad in the 1933 Indianapolis Speedway program mentions Harry as a Duesenberg owner. The restyling of the convertible sedan body was done on the chassis, and the Derham body was placed in storage. Sometime during the early fifties Arthur Rippey, also of Denver, acquired the Derham convertible sedan body, which he subsequently sold to someone in the Midwest. When I saw it in 1963, I knew what a beauty this car could be. The next thirteen years were spent in returning the Derham convertible body to its original styling. Surprisingly, the interior of the car was intact. The front fenders are off the Duesenberg used in the movie *Giant* (starring Elizabeth Taylor and Rock Hudson) which I purchased from Robert Gates, owner of J-204 Murphy Berline at that time. Engine J-170 was located by my father-in-law Glenn Hughes. He purchased it from Lawrence Ackerman, who planned to use it in a boat. This engine had originally been in chassis 2147, a special long-wheelbase Floyd Derham phaeton built for R. F. McCarthy of Chicago in the thirties. The original chassis with the Walton speedster body eventually was purchased by Bill Harrah, who removed the Walton body and had a new one built for the chassis by Maurice Schwartz of Bohman & Schwartz. J-507/2523 is now a Schwartz reproduction Weymann Speedster. I make reference to the Walton Speedster and Schwartz bodies in order to clarify why the Derham convertible sedan body was a unit alone, why there was a need to find a chassis, engine and fenders, along with other Duesenberg parts in order to have a complete Duesenberg. But finally I had it.''

1933 Duesenberg Model J Convertible Sedan, Derham
Owner: Keith Brown of Fort Wayne, Indiana

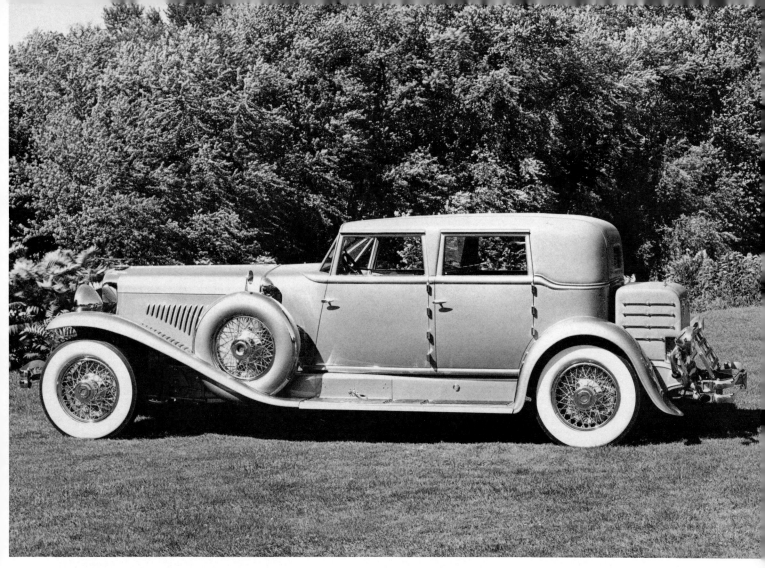

1934 Duesenberg Model J Beverly Sedan, Murphy   Owner: Noel Thompson of New Vernon, New Jersey   Photo: K. Karger

1934 Duesenberg Model J Berline Sedan, Bohman & Schwartz
Owner: John C. Dennis of Mukilteo, Washington

"The Beverly is the best-looking closed body style on the Duesenberg," comments Noel Thompson of the Buehrig-designed Murphy-built J-468 sedan which he acquired in 1987.

John Dennis has owned his J-450 Bohman & Schwartz long-wheelbase Berline Sedan for a quarter of a century and has spent much of that time bringing the car back to life: "This is an ex-George Whittell car. Originally a Murphy sedan, it was restyled for a new owner by Bohman & Schwartz. The original Murphy interior was retained, however. The car is important to me because I was able to essentially make something out of nothing with a lot of help from fellow hobbyists and many skilled craftsmen. I'm happy I was able to 'save' this Model J. I believe I am the ninth owner. A few things still need correcting, which I'll get after in the months ahead. Beautiful coachwork on an 'overbuilt' chassis, that says it all. But I must add I like everything about Duesenbergs."

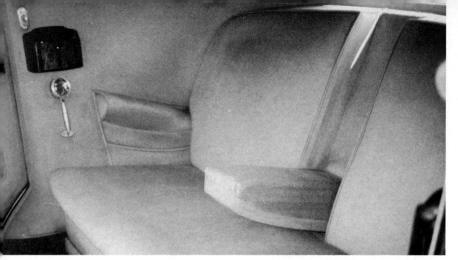

In the mid-thirties John Shaffer of Evanston, Illinois was being chauffeured in the Rollston Berline Sedan but no doubt the adventures under his ownership paled in comparison to those the Snyders have enjoyed in J-374 since their acquisition of the car in 1959. Bill relates: "This was the first, and possibly only, Duesenberg ever driven around the Indianapolis Speedway by a pregnant woman. At four days of age, our son Steve was the youngest passenger ever to ride in a Duesenberg. In the 14,000 miles this car has been driven by us, we chauffeured ex-Duesenberg president Harold Ames on his first visit to the Indianapolis plant since the firm closed and also chauffeured Classic Era designer Phil Wright from Long Beach to Santa Barbara to receive his honorary membership in the Classic Car Club. The car is, if any mechanical thing can be, part of the family. This Duesenberg always appealed to me (I saw it long before we bought it) because it is so original. The leather top, interior, wood paneling, even most of the paint, is as delivered in 1935. The car has the seventeen-inch wheels and skirted fenders that were introduced about that time. In keeping with its formal nature, the radiator shutters are painted body color (black) and the dashboard is covered with black leather. The very elegant touches found only on closed Classics, particularly town cars, also make it a delight. The Duesy drives beautifully and handles easily. The ride greatly improves when there are passengers in the back, which of course was the usual during the Classic Era." John Shaffer was a banker and probably wouldn't have approved of the next owner of J-374: Charles Powers, a professional gambler, to whom the car was sold following Shaffer's death. Excluding dealers, the Snyders are the third owners of Shaffer's J-374.

1934 Duesenberg Model J Berline Sedan, Rollston
Owners: Bill & JoEllen Snyder of Orange, California

1935 Duesenberg Model J Convertible Coupe, Walker-LaGrande

Owner: William Lyon of Trabuco Canyon, California

Yet another Gordon Buehrig-designed Beverly is Andrew Darling's J-512 Murphy Sedan, which is believed to be the only Duesenberg Beverly built on a supercharged Model J chassis.

William Lyon's J-515 Walker-LaGrande Convertible Coupe was one of three built in that body style and, again, the only one super-charged. The hyphenated coach-builder designation translates to

mean that the body was built by the A. H. Walker shop in Indianapolis to a design originated in the Duesenberg styling department which used the LaGrande name to distinguish its work.

1935 Duesenberg Model J Beverly Sedan, Murphy

Owner: Andrew D. Darling of Edina, Minnesota

1935 Duesenberg Model JN Convertible Coupe, Rollston/Bohman & Schwartz
Owner: Blackhawk Classic Auto Collection, Danville, California

Rollston built only two JN-type bodies on the supercharged Duesenberg chassis. So Clark Gable already had a rare automobile in his Convertible Coupe, but he wanted to make it uniquely his own. Bohman & Schwartz certainly did that for him or, more accurately, B & S designer W. Everett Miller did. In later years, Everett enjoyed reminiscing about the many hours he spent at the drawing board, with the movie actor behind him contributing ideas. Panache is perhaps the single word that best describes the result. The top was lowered seductively, a bold sweep was given the fenders, the hood was stretched back to the windshield. It was in J-560, the car now in the Blackhawk Classic Auto Collection, that Clark Gable and Carole Lombard took their clandestine trips—away from the prying eyes, and probable disapproval, of both movie studios and fans—during the several years of

their discreet courtship prior to Gable's second wife granting him a divorce.

The Model JN was designed by J. Herbert Newport, who followed Gordon Buehrig as chief designer at Duesenberg. Just ten were built, all of them by Rollston, three of which were berlines like Bill Deibel's J-500: "Herb Newport's JN's employed bodies integrated with the chassis and distinguished by four features— doors that overlay the frame sills, bullet taillights, an extended rear overhang with apron over fuel tank and skirted fenders. The last named were optional on late J's while all '35-'37 Duesenbergs had seventeen- inch wheels and chrome radiator shells as standard. Wheel covers, tire covers and Packard bullet headlamps were other options on late J's and JN's. The Cadillac bullet headlamps, one-piece bumpers and painted radiator shell on my car were

modifications made by Bohman & Schwartz for first owner Bill 'Bojangles' Robinson. Following Robinson's death in 1949, the JN was acquired by Phil 'New York's Singing Cop' Regan who kept it just three years. The car passed through four more owners before I purchased it in 1955 with money that was to have been my graduation present from college. I consider this a particularly well-balanced handsome automobile. In engine design, the Duesenberg was far ahead. The four-valve head with double overhead cams is revolu- tionary today in some quarters. The car is truly a thing of beauty and power. I have driven it over 10,000 miles and at speeds up to 85 mph. My several long trips are a source of interesting memories. Wouldn't you like to remember throwing a rod on the Pennsylvania Turnpike or having fuel pump problems pulling the Continental Divide?''

1935 Duesenberg Model JN Berline, Rollston

Owner: Bill Deibel of Seattle, Washington

1935 Duesenberg Special/Mormon Meteor   Owner: Knox Kershaw of Montgomery, Alabama

That the Model J Duesenberg was mighty quick is a truism. In 1935 Ab Jenkins, the teetotaling Mormon who frequently engaged in go-fast exercises for E. L. Cord, decided to prove it—with a vengeance. This exercise didn't cost the Duesenberg company a penny. Accessory and oil company sponsorships paid for the car; Ab Jenkins simply guaranteed his sponsors that records would be set. The Duesenberg Special used the short J chassis with redesigned front axle and higher axle ratio—and the supercharged J engine tuned to a fare-thee-well. Apparently most of the development work was done in Auburn, some in Augie Duesenberg's shop in Indianapolis, with the body probably built in Connersville. Duesenberg did benefit from the work, notably in the ram's horn two-carb manifolding which was subsequently installed on a few factory cars. And Jenkins' sponsors were happy in October that year when Ab drove the Duesenberg Special on Bonneville's salt flats for an hour at 153.97 mph and for a full day at 135.57 mph, the twenty-four-

hour record remaining unbroken until 1951. To paint the lily, a Curtiss Conqueror aircraft engine was fitted the following year, the car was re-christened the Mormon Meteor, and still further records were set. The speed work finished in '38, the original Duesenberg supercharged engine was reinstalled—and for the next half decade Ab Jenkins and his son drove the car another 20,000

miles in routine motoring. Some road car this! Virtually everyone knows this record machine as the Mormon Meteor today, despite its return to Duesenberg Special guise. Following Ab Jenkins' sale of the car, it passed through various hands before being acquired by Royce Kershaw in '59. Knox inherited this one-of-a-kind, very "special" Duesenberg from his father.

Like the SJ, the designation SSJ was never used by the Duesenberg factory, but since only two such cars were built, they are popularly known as such. The letters translate to "short, supercharged J." The 125-inch wheelbase was certainly truncated by Duesenberg standards. Increased was the horsepower, with the ram's horn manifolding developed by Augie Duesenberg pushing the already formidable supercharged J's figure to close to 400. Perhaps only one of these cars would have been built, save for the man who bought the first. The original owner of J-563, the car now owned by Miles Collier, was Gary Cooper. Although a friend of Coop's and already the owner of a pretty-quick JN Convertible Coupe, Clark Gable was not about to be upstaged. The year following he was driving what is now Al Ferrara's J-567.

1936 Duesenberg Model J Speedster, LaGrande
Owner: Alfred Ferrara of Gates Mills, Ohio

Superchargers roaring, these two cars were raced through the Hollywood hills during the thirties by Cooper and Gable. In 1987 the cars were brought together in Hickory Corners, Michigan for the Gilmore-Classic Car Club Museums' concours de'elegance —and gave visitors an idea of how film folk amused themselves a half-century ago.

1935 Duesenberg Model J Speedster, LaGrande

Owner: Miles C. Collier of Naples, Florida

1936 Duesenberg Model J Convertible Coupe, Bohman & Schwartz
Owner: John Mozart of Palo Alto, California

Both of the Bohman & Schwartz Model J's shown here are supercharged. Noel Thompson's J-544 was originally owned by Henry J. Topping. "The car has a disappearing top, a folding second windshield and diamond tufted upholstery," comments Noel. "The tonneau windshield and cowl designed for J-544 can be folded compactly and concealed within a paneled compartment in the seat back."

J-572, the Bohman & Schwartz Convertible Coupe owned by John Mozart, was paid for by Princess Barbara Hutton Mdivani and was a gift from the Woolworth heiress to her new royal husband. The car was delivered to the couple in Palm Beach. Among the factors attracting John Mozart to this particular Duesenberg was the "custom-built, one-off very-contemporary-for-the-period styling."

Likewise, J-548, the Walker-LaGrande Dual Cowl Phaeton, was irresistible to John Mozart because of its "very rare, great styling coupled with a tremendous chassis."

1936 Duesenberg Model J Convertible Sedan, Bohman & Schwartz
Owner: Noel Thompson of New Vernon, New Jersey   Photo: K. Karger

1936 Duesenberg Model J Dual Cowl Phaeton, Walker-LaGrande   Owner: John Mozart of Palo Alto, California

1937 Duesenberg Model J Convertible Coupe, Rollston   *Owner: Bob Bahre of Oxford, Maine*   *Photo: K. Karger*

J-529, the Convertible Coupe owned by Bob Bahre, was the last Rollston body built for Duesenberg and one of the last Duesenbergs delivered in 1937, the year the factory closed its doors. Comments Chris Charlton: "This car carries the JN features but was a custom-ordered car so it is not a JN. It has scoop fenders and the flowing rear body section referred to as a fishtail by Rollston. We do not know who ordered J-529 originally but we acquired the car in 1987 from Robert Kelso, a truck driver from Michigan who had regularly passed this Duesie on his daily route. After a month of this, he finally stopped and made a deal with the used car dealer to trade his old '34 Packard plus $1,100, which he financed. This was in 1947."

One suspects the Duesenberg saga had to end this way—with a curtain call as epic as the years the marque held center stage on the American road. Bill Pettit tells the dramatic story: "This was the last new Duesenberg delivered by Duesenberg. The invoice for the coachwork was dated April 25th, 1940. The body design was by its owner, the artist Rudolph Bauer. Originally this super-charged chassis was to have been shipped to Germany for coachwork by Erdmann & Rossi. But war clouds were darkening over Europe. After being rescued from the Nazis by Solomon Guggenheim, Rudolph Bauer took delivery of this car in the United States, where he already housed two other Duesenberg J's at his mansion on the ocean at Deal, New Jersey. Now Rollson—as the firm was redesignated following the '38 bankruptcy of Rollston—was given the job of translating the Bauer design into reality. This would be one of only two Rollson bodies that was not a Packard. That was significant, but more important was the relation of its style to that of the year in which it was delivered as a new car. Bauer was an artist. This Duesenberg is a piece of his sculpture. It is huge but sleek. It is completely outrageous but impressive in style and color. The leather, head-liner and carpet are violet. Fitted into the black leather trunk are three pieces of luggage, one full length to accommodate trousers or dresses without creasing. There is a radio in the rear compartment, with speaker and buzzer for communication to the chauffeur. The three-position top is fully convertible. I discovered this car in 1955 and acquired it from Rudolph Bauer's widow. The odometer read 9,884 miles. The car's complete originality coupled with its unique coachwork make it an eye-popping attraction. I have driven it sparingly, approximately 1,000 miles in the last thirty-five years. Unlike any other J I have driven—and I have owned six—this car behaves like the new car it is."

1940 Duesenberg Model J Convertible Town Car, Rollson
Owner: The Pettit Collection of Virginia   Photos: K. Karger

F R A N K L I N

"Spirit of flight" hood ornament from Al Nippert's 1931 Series 15 Airman Speedster

Perhaps no Classic entered the Classic Era more dramatically than the Franklin. Since 1902, when former newspaper publisher Herbert H. Franklin teamed up with Cornell engineering graduate John Wilkinson in Syracuse, New York, the marque had marched to its own drummer. The company's devotion to air cooling was messianic. Its engineering budget —computed on a percentage of income basis—was among the highest in the industry. High quality with less weight was the Franklin credo. Ash wood was the choice for the chassis for twenty-six years; the engine sported overhead valves from the beginning. Full-elliptic suspension provided such stingy tire wear that it was not until 1922 that the company offered detachable rims as standard equipment. As early as 1913 Franklin had been in the forefront in championing the sedan body style. The cars seemed to be indomitable. By the Classic Era, fully 75% of the Franklins built since 1902 were still on the road—and recognizably so. No other car looked quite like the Franklin. No one in Syracuse regarded that as untoward. . . .

1925 Franklin Series 10C Touring

Owner: Don Presson of Clovis, California

Nineteen twenty-five was Franklin's first year for the lion mascot on an imitation radiator and the last for the "horse collar" front. Franklin dealers, led by Ralph Hamlin (the company's distributor for southern California since 1905), had descended upon Syracuse with an ultimatum: new car or no car. It was becoming increasingly difficult, they said, to sell the unconventional Franklin. Chief engineer John Wilkinson was aghast; to him, the single-piece hinged-at-the-front hood of the air-cooled car was a sublime example of form following function. Probably had he been there, Don Presson would have agreed with Wilkinson. He has owned his Series 10C horse-collar Franklin (a former Harrah Collection car) for over a half decade. On a Nevada tour several years ago in pouring rain, many cars gave up but, Don says, "this Franklin just seemed to enjoy the pull."

Despite Wilkinson's protestations, Herbert H. Franklin, faced with a mass defection of dealers, decided a change was in order. Even if the Franklin didn't need a radiator, it should look like it had one. Wilkinson quit in protest. The new Series 11A, designed by J. Frank de Causse who had gained fame as the creator of the Locomobile Sportif, was introduced in March of 1925.

Randy Still is a de Causse enthusiast. He acquired his Series 11A, another ex-Harrah car, in June of 1986. Among the features that won him over were the unusual triple pinstriping, the canting of the side-window glass and the rare and optional painted (not plated) radiator shell—plus the Masco heater, electric intercom, interior lights that activate when a curb side door is opened and dash-mounted oil level indicator, all of which were rather advanced for 1925: "I've always liked limousines and this one with a rear-mounted trunk with fitted luggage and a center-mounted spare excited me. The Enclosed Drive Limousine was advertised as a chauffeur-driven car made instantly convenient for owner driving by lowering the partition window. The rear compartment is broad enough for three while provision for two extra passengers is made by the auxiliary folding seats." The divided windshield glass and the word "Franklin" on the wheel hubs indicate this car was built early in Series 11A production.

1925 Franklin Series 11A Enclosed Drive Limousine
Owner: E. Randy Still of Kingsport, Tennessee

1926 Franklin Series 11A Four-Door Sedan   *Owners: Jim & Betty Hull of Littleton, Colorado*

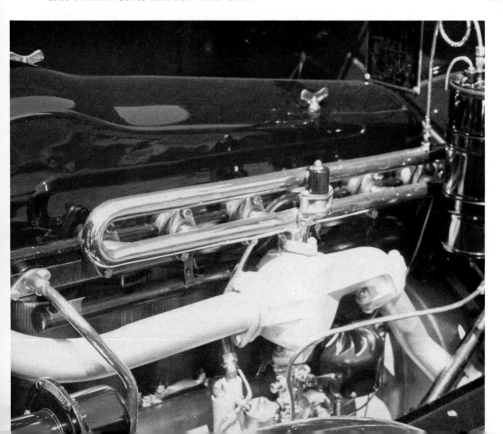

Doubtless it had been the sales decrease from over 10,000 cars in '23 to 6,075 which had resulted in the dealer ultimatum to the Syracuse factory. Franklin sales from '25 through '28 would average about 8,000 cars annually. Among them was the Hulls' 1926 Four-Door Sedan which Jim and Betty have nicknamed Aunt Sophie. She gets around a lot—three CARavans to date and tours on both coasts of Canada. "Aunt Sophie's air cooling eliminates the major problem we encountered in touring Classics—overheating," says Jim. "While underpowered by today's standards (the 199.1-cubic-inch six generates 32 hp), the Franklin was an excellent performer in 1926. Since very few roads were paved at the time, handling and ride were more important than sheer power. With her triple-laminated ash frame (as strong as steel but lighter and more flexible) and the full elliptics, she is very nimble and easy to drive."

"The boattail body hidden by the spare tire epitomizes Franklin's understated style." Brad Hindall's comment about his '27 Sport Runabout is exactly right. From the standpoint of history, it also amuses that the company most famous for its sedans was the first in America (in 1925) to catalogue a boattail, the body style that came to be regarded as the raciest of the Classic Era.

Even today the car excites attention. Bob Knapp's '28 Sport Runabout is one of the major attractions at his Deer Park Auto Museum.

1927 Franklin Series 11B Sport Runabout   *Owners: Brad & Jane Hindall of Sarasota, Florida*

1928 Franklin Series 12A Airman Sport Runabout   *Owner: Robert Knapp of San Diego, California*

For Franklin, 1928 was as radical a year as 1925 had been. Introduced on all Airman models were four-wheel hydraulic brakes and, although the shorter 119-inch-wheelbase models continued with the laminated ash frame, the new 128-inch Series 12A employed Franklin's first steel chassis in twenty-six years. This was less because the Syracuse company had become suddenly enamoured of steel than the expense of having ash shipped acoss the country from the Pacific Northwest and storing it for a half decade or so while it seasoned. By 1929 all Franklins would sport steel chassis. As previously, the use of aluminum in the Series 12A was extensive, including body, crankcase and housings for the transmission and differential. Reportedly, Franklin was the world's largest consumer of the metal.

The Sport Touring that the Olsons have owned for nine years is one of only two known to exist and is a former Harrah car.

Dick and Linda Kughn have owned their Airman Coupe since December of '88.

The Airman designation introduced in '28, of course, was to honor the man who had soloed the Atlantic in '27. Although besieged with offers and gifts after his epic flight, Charles Lindbergh accepted only a Franklin, which he donated in 1940 to the Henry Ford Museum. ''Lucky Lindy'' was an avid enthusiast of the marque. ''The most comfortable mile-a-minute car ever built,'' Franklin advertised its new Airman, ''. . . the automobile's nearest approach to flying.''

1928 Franklin Series 12A Airman Coupe
Owners: Richard & Linda Kughn of Southfield, Michigan

1928 Franklin Series 12A Airman Four-Door Sedan
Owner: Henry Ford Museum & Greenfield Village, Dearborn, Michigan

1928 Franklin Series 12A Airman Sport Touring   *Owners: Richard & Ruth Olson of Florissant, Missouri*

1929 Franklin Series 13 Airman Model 135 Convertible Coupe

Owner: Richard A. Harry of Alma, Wisconsin

Series 13 Franklins for 1929 were offered in three models: the 130 (234-cubic-inch engine, 119-inch wheelbase), and the 135 and 137 (each with 274-cubic-inch engine but on 125- and 132-inch wheelbases respectively). With 14,432 cars built, '29 was Franklin's biggest year ever. Synchromesh transmission was featured throughout the line. This was the last year for vertical copper cooling fins on the cylinders. With the death of Frank de Causse in 1928, Ray Dietrich had become the Franklin's designer. The beautiful Ryan headlamps with matching parking lights were a deft Dietrich touch. The top on Richard Harry's Convertible Coupe folds compactly into a well behind the front seat.

Bob Agle's Sport Touring was Dietrich's first dual cowl for the company, and the first open Franklin sold following the death of Bill Harrah who, as this portfolio indicates, had been an indefatigable collector of the marque. Since 1981 Bob has driven the car extensively and pronounces it an excellent tourer whether open or closed.

Alyce Oberhaus says the same for her Franklin Sedan: "The car cruises well at 50 miles an hour."

Although air cooled for over a quarter of a century, the Franklin continued to confound some people. Perhaps its *faux* radiator had been done too well, complete with bolted-on cap sporting a knurled edge for gaining a better grip. "Among Franklin owners of yore," Richard Harry comments, "there used to be many tales of unknowing filling station boys trying to wrestle the cap off. In one story the station man even used a Stillson wrench."

1929 Franklin Series 13 Airman Model 137 Sport Touring
Owner: Robert Agle of Jefferson, Ohio   Photos: Don Smith

1929 Franklin Series 13 Airman Model 137 Seven-Passenger Sedan
Owner: Alyce R. Oberhaus of Napoleon, Ohio   Photos: Jamie Kuser

1929 Franklin Series 13 Airman Model 137 Speedster, Dietrich

Owner: Art Kenniff of Southold, New York

When introduced in June of 1929, the Speedster was described by Franklin as a closed car providing "a hint of future style development in the quality car class." A half century later, giving a sedan a convertible look began to enjoy a certain vogue again in the United States, but few would argue that Ray Dietrich did it much better. At $3,375 the '29 Franklin Speedster was $890 more costly than the Model 135 Sedan, but significantly less pricey than other Franklin custom models which began at $5,000+. The narrow low-profile body was a hallmark of the Speedster, as was the aerodynamics-enhancing rear-mounted spare tire. A burned-out connecting rod is essentially the reason Art Kenniff was able to purchase this Franklin fifteen years ago. After suffering same on a trip to Florida and being unable to find anyone to fix the car, original owner Sidney Strong decided to sell. The Franklin passed through two dealers before Art acquired it. He is the second registered owner of the car.

A true convertible version of the Speedster was offered by Franklin in 1930. Retained was the four-speed transmission and high-speed rear end gearing (4.25:1); the factory claimed a top speed performance of 80 mph. Donald Reddaway's Convertible Speedster was one of no more than fifty built, and one of only three known to exist today. The sedan's convertible top is a three-position. Base price for the Dietrich Convertible Speedster in 1930 was $3,725, but options on this one raised that figure quite a bit. Among the rare or unusual accessories on the Reddaway car are the stoneguard complete with script and crank cover, the hood mascot styled after the Ryan monoplane flown by Lindbergh, demountable wood wheels and dual-mounted rear spares. A long road was traveled before this car was brought back to life. It had been used as a parts car for eight years before Don's acquisition: "Only four doors, hood, cowl, back section and a bent frame were left." Don spent five years collecting parts, and fourteen in the car's restoration.

*1930 Franklin Series 14 Airman Model 147 Convertible Speedster, Dietrich
Owner: Donald A. Reddaway of Seattle, Washington*

For 1930 Franklin discontinued its smaller engine and focused all effort on the larger unit. Now side-draft, the Franklin six also had larger valves, intake manifold and carburetor and a smaller but more efficient Sirocco fan. All this contributed to a monumental increase in horsepower from 65 to 95 at 3100 rpm—absolutely unprecedented for an air-cooled engine of a mere 274 cubic inches. Still, except perhaps for the Speedster, most Franklins weren't bought for how fast they traveled the roads. Not then, not now. Witness Bobbie'dine Rodda who joined the Franklin fraternity three years ago: "Everyone knows the Franklin is air cooled, but hardly any folks understand that it is more than just a car without a radiator or hoses or coolant or fan belts or any of the other plumbing that causes problems in water-cooled vehicles. What I discovered with my Franklin is that it is the easiest Classic to *drive* of any. The steering is light and direct. The brakes are phenomenal. The car is truly comfortable." Prior to Bobbie'dine, this Franklin hadn't been driven in a couple of decades. She's making up for lost time—to date, two CARavans and over 5,000 miles.

1930 Franklin Series 14 Airman Model 147 Salon Special Sedan   *Owner: Bobbie'dine Rodda of Glendale, California*

No fewer than seven Classic Era Franklins reside in the Gazza garage. The '30 Pursuit Phaeton is a favorite. The car has long been reputed to have been originally owned by Marion Davies, though Gene has not been able to document that to his satisfaction yet. Not that it matters to him who the first owner was, only that he owns it now: ''The beauty of the body style is most important to me; I think the proportioning is all but perfect.''

Ken Johnson's Four-Door Brougham is special to him because of its ''singular engineering—the steadfast reliability of the engine, the unique suspension system and a high ratio of sprung to unsprung weight which together provide a degree of roadability and comfort not to be found in any other car of that vintage.'' Ken bought this Franklin ten years ago as a parts car for the restoration of a four-door sedan in better condition. Its rarity and sportier lines led him to restore it instead. The ''parts car'' has been back on the road for a couple of years now. Says Ken: ''The factory high-speed rear axle allows for comfortable highway speeds.''

Not comfortable for the Franklin company when these cars were built was its financial picture. As the Depression took hold, sales plummeted from 6,036 in 1930 to 2,851 in 1931.

1930 Franklin Series 14 Airman Model 145 Pursuit Phaeton
Owner: Eugene Gazza of Huntington, New York

1930 Franklin Series 14 Airman Model 145 Four-Door Brougham   Owner: Kenneth R. Johnson of Valhalla, New York
(profile view on page opposite)

Both of these Franklins were originally owned by Herbert Cue, a merchandise buyer for F. W. Woolworth in London, England. Depending upon the weather, the Cue chauffeur would deliver his boss from his suburban home to his London office in either the Pirate Phaeton or the Deauville Sedan, spend the day ferrying Mrs. Cue and then return to the city to bring Mr. Cue back home. The Cues' daughter, Edna Crane of Yorkshire who learned to drive on the Pirate and was chauffeured to her wedding in 1933 in the Deauville, has been Tom Hubbard's guest in Tucson on several occasions and joined him in the freshly-restored Pirate for the 1988 Pebble Beach Concours d'Elegance. From Edna, Tom has been able to learn fascinating details about both cars.

Air cooling was a novelty in England, which the family chauffeur enjoyed showing off. Often when the Cues would return to their car following an evening out, the Franklin would be surrounded by other chauffeurs. The odometer on the Pirate, she said, had been over twice, making the mileage total for the twenty years the family owned the car about 250,000. In restoration Tom found evidence of both much use and careful maintenance; the front carpet had been mended, then the mends were mended.

Tom has owned the Deauville Sedan for twenty-seven years, the Pirate for fourteen: "The Deauville has a very elegant, formal look. As part of the custom line in 1930-1931, its $4,100 price tag was about twice that of a standard Franklin sedan. The aluminum skin of this body is unique in that there is no belt moulding around the rear quarter. The skin is one piece from the base of one rear door, around the windshield and back to the base of the other rear door. This made the necessary rebuilding of the wood framing very difficult as the sub-structure had to be exactly right for the sheet metal and doors to fit."

About the Pirate Phaeton, Tom comments: "The running boards on this car are concealed under full-length doors. Further, they have become part of the body in this design, with the A, B and C door posts extending past the main body sill to incorporate the running boards. Thus a truss-like structure results, giving a main sill of unusual depth and strength, especially important on an open touring car. The body is mostly aluminum so while it looks heavy, weight is only 4,200 pounds. The car is also so wide that persons from the rear seat can come and go without making those in the jump seats move."

1930 Franklin Series 14 Airman Model 147 Deauville Sedan, Dietrich
Owner: Tom Hubbard of Tucson, Arizona

1930 Franklin Series 14 Airman Model 147 Pirate Phaeton
Owner: Tom Hubbard of Tucson, Arizona   Photos: Maurice Koonce

The use of "Transcontinental" was Franklin's way of reminding America that one of its cars held the record for the fastest trip from coast to coast—69½ hours for a 46.9 mph average, more than eight hours better than any water-cooled car to date. The man responsible was famed transcontinentalist Cannon Ball Baker. "That old waffle iron was the greatest car I ever drove," said Cannon Ball. "That snub-nosed baby buggy would run forever."

Just thirty-six Transcontinental Sport Salons were produced. The roofline is several inches lower than the standard Franklin for 1931, and its padded top of sport material gives it a convertible look. The original owner—Mary Mott of Portland, Oregon—was less than five feet tall, so she ordered the car with extensions on the brake and clutch pedals and a special hand throttle of extra length so she could accelerate without using her foot. Additional accessories she specified included a silver initial plate on both rear doors, step-plates and a small fog light. The car arrived equipped with a front fresh air heater, wire wheels, sidemounts and a trunk rack. To all this, second owner Julian Eccles added a deluxe hood ornament and "See-Rite" side-view mirrors on the metal

tire covers. Julian has known this car since it was new. He worked part-time in the Franklin dealership where it was sold and recalls when it was delivered; subsequently he was a gas jockey in a local service station and Miss Mott was a regular customer. Because of a family dispute, the car was put up on blocks in 1936. Discovering it again in late 1945, Julian spent sixteen years persuading Miss Mott and her relatives to sell. The car remains original except for tires (the

spares are the unused originals), new carpeting, glass and top cover. Julian has driven it more than Miss Mott ever did. When put up on blocks, the odometer read 7,100 miles. It now reads more than 17,800. Because Franklins were up to 100 hp by 1931, gas mileage was down. Julian averages about 10 mpg: "The transmission is a Warner four-speed with silent third gear. Low gear is only for steep hill starts. The car is comfortable to drive up to 60 mph."

1931 Franklin Series 15 Airman Model 152 Transcontinental Sport Salon
Owner: Julian Eccles of Klamath Falls, Oregon

This Franklin was exhibited on the Derham stand at the custom coachwork salons in Chicago and New York. One of three built (and the only one to survive), it was purchased for $5,800 by William Erdell of Allentown, Pennsylvania, who owned the car until his death in 1941. Since the age of fifteen when he saw its picture in a magazine, Walt Gosden had coveted this Franklin. He finally was able to find and acquire it in 1973: "I have driven the car approximately 25,000 miles without mechanical problems. It is most comfortable in the 55-60 mph range and extremely comfortable to ride in for many hours without driver fatigue. The quality of the coachwork is outstanding; the structural woodwork is substantial and reflects the fact that Derham started out as a quality carriage builder. I particularly like the styling feature of the traditional 'coach lip' at the bottom of the door posts. The short-coupled 'brougham' body styling is complemented by the placing of the spare at the rear.''

1931 Franklin Series 15 Airman Model 153 Sportsman's Coupe, Derham
Owner: Walter E. Gosden of Floral Park, New York

1931 Franklin Series 15 Airman Model 153 Pirate Touring   *Owner: Albert D. Nippert of Peekskill, New York*

Al Nippert has owned both these Franklins for over a quarter of a century. The Pirate is fully restored; the enclosed Speedster is completely original. Because of the monogram on the rear doors of the Pirate, that car is believed to have been originally owned by the Walker Body Company family, builders of Franklin production coachwork and the largest stockholders in the Syracuse firm save for H. H. Franklin himself. Charles Lindbergh, hired by Franklin as an engineering consultant following his New York to Paris flight, owned a 1931 Speedster and claimed it to be one of his best cars ever. Al Nippert regards the car as Dietrich's finest closed body design. The trunk is a permanent mounting at the rear.

Both Speedster and Pirate carry Dietrich's ''spirit of flight'' hood ornament. The front windows on the Pirate roll down and the rear door wind-wings open on a slide-and-lever arrangement, swinging out of the way as the door is opened. When not needed, they can be folded and latched against the rear tonneau windshield. Four mud flaps under the fenders keep the car clean during inclement weather motoring. The walnut-paneled rear-seat compartment accepts side curtains so occupants can be kept likewise.

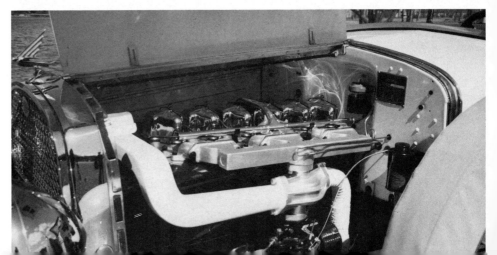

1931 Franklin Series 15 Airman Model 153 Speedster   *Owner: Albert D. Nippert of Peekskill, New York*

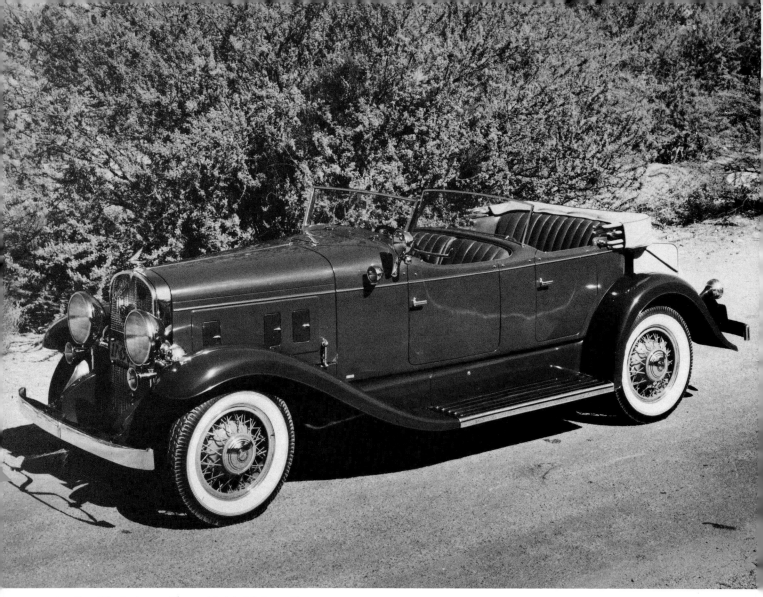

1931 Franklin Series 15 Airman Model 153 Sport Phaeton, Merrimac
Owner: Tom Hubbard of Tucson, Arizona

1931 Franklin Series 15 Airman Model 153 Coupe
Owner: Tom Hubbard of Tucson, Arizona

1931 Franklin Series 15 Airman Model 153 Speedster Owner: *Tom Hubbard of Tucson, Arizona* Photo: *Robert Townsend*

In 1930, following the introduction of a true convertible version of the Speedster, only the open car was part of Franklin's custom line. Although priced just $150 less and actually built by Dietrich, the closed Speedster became a standard model, albeit the most expensive in the Franklin catalogue. ''It is the kind of car that carries with it the strongest kind of appeal to the young society woman or to the up-and-coming type of young businessman,'' Paul Gardner, a Franklin salesman at the Wilkes-Barre (Pennsylvania) agency, was quoted as saying. ''Having a half-dozen Franklin Speedsters running about town is . . . the finest advertisement that the Franklin dealer can have.'' Tom Hubbard has owned his Speedster thirty years.

Likewise the Merrimac Sport Phaeton: ''This was a one-off custom built for Stillman F. Kelley of Lexington, Massachusetts who was

twenty-seven at the time and had grown up with Franklins. He admired a body type offered by Cadillac in which the windshield for the rear seat could be cranked down into the middle cowl when not needed. The nearest type offered by Franklin had the second windshield mounted on a hinged tonneau deck. To get what he wanted, Kelley ordered only a chassis and had the Merrimac Body Company do the rest. Many people think this results in the best-looking Franklin ever made. In my opinion it also produced possibly the most satisfactory car to drive too because the four-passenger aluminum body keeps the total weight to 4,010 pounds and, with a single rear-mounted spare, the weight is almost even on the front and rear axles, making for excellent balance and a splendid 'feel.' I've enjoyed driving this car every year since I bought it, including two transcontinental trips.''

The Model 153 Coupe has been in the Hubbard garage since 1952. Its original owner had turned the car in for a new Packard in 1936 (when, of course, it was no longer possible to buy a new Franklin). Buying the five-year-old car then was Gaylord Hoyt, who had been sales manager for Locomobile in the early 1920's and subsequently became assistant sales manager for Franklin: ''Mr. Hoyt was well acquainted with top people in the Franklin organization including H. H. Franklin, the top engineers, the stylists J. Frank de Causse and Ray Dietrich, and many of the Franklin dealers including Ralph Hamlin of Los Angeles who was a life-long friend. Shortly before World War II, he drove the car from Los Angeles to Syracuse where the engine was rebuilt. He kept the car for sentimental reasons until he was about eighty years old and decided it was time for someone like me to have it.''

Tom's Dietrich Town Car was offered for sale at $800 in the September 1952 issue of *Motor Trend*. The price was far too high, both for the car (Duesenbergs didn't bring much more at the time) and for Tom (who was just twenty-one): "I could do nothing but watch helplessly. The car went to Florida and thence to Mobile, Alabama where I lost track of it. In 1966 a letter to the Mobile police chief offering a reward for information leading to purchase resulted in an immediate response. The car belonged to an officer on the police force! But while pictures showed it in pristine condition when offered on Long Island in 1952, in Mobile the car had come on hard times. Stored outside in a hot, humid climate, it would have been a mercy had kids thrown rocks through the windows so the interior could have been ventilated and allowed to dry out. The result was 4,500 hours of restoration work, most of which would have been unnecessary had I the $800 in 1952. . . . The Dietrich Town Car exemplifies a styling factor singular to Franklin. In 1931 the radiators of most cars sat directly over the front axle, where Franklin placed part of its air-cooled engine. Thus a body of essentially the same dimensions could fit on a Franklin chassis approximately six to eight inches shorter than its competitors. So a similar Dietrich body on a Packard, say, would require a wheelbase of about 140 inches versus this car's 132-inch wheelbase. The shorter wheelbase makes for more efficiency and easier handling in traffic but a less glamorous look since the hood line appears shorter."

1931 Franklin Series 15 Airman Model 153 Town Car, Dietrich
Owner: Tom Hubbard of Tucson, Arizona

Nineteen thirty-two was the last year for the Dietrich Speedster. It had five more horses than the year before, courtesy of the 1/4 p.s.i. boost of the sirocco cooling blower and the cooler intake air from out front. And it retained a faster rear axle ratio (4.25:1 vis-à-vis 4.73:1) than the rest of the Franklin model line.

Bill Deibel purchased his car from its third owner—Robert Carlson of Belmont, Massachusetts—for $75.00 in May of 1953. The financial transaction was followed by an admonishment from the seller: ''Young man, this is a very old, very worn-out car, and I don't want to see you back here complaining about this or that being broken or missing. . . .'' The odometer read 190,000 miles. The following month Bill, who was a junior at M.I.T. at the time, drove the Franklin from Cambridge to his home in Lakewood, Ohio: ''The only problems I recall were a broken hydraulic brake line, a totally blown apart exhaust pipe and muffler, the windshield falling completely out onto the hood due to dry rot where it was hinged at the top, and no less than seven flat tires. Atlantic gasoline was used as much as possible for in those days their slogan was 'Atlantic Keeps Your Car on the Go.' One attendant thought we were going to be the exception.''

Arrival in Lakewood and a look under the hood revealed new horrors —and a restoration story that could fill this entire book. But, as Bill says, unique engineering, a handsome body design for a purchase price of less than a hundred dollars, and thirty-five years of memories do count for a lot. At this writing the Speedster had less than 200 miles to go before turning over 200,000, a momentous occasion that he planned to celebrate on the 1990 Pacific Northwest CARavan.

1932 Franklin Series 16 Supercharged Airman Model 163 Speedster
Owner: Bill Deibel of Seattle, Washington

Since the stock market crash, Franklin sales had more than halved each year through 1931; for '32 the figure was 1,905 cars, for '33, 1,011; just 360 cars would be produced before the factory closed its doors in '34. Despite savagely plummeting production, Franklin had been virtually forced to enter the multi-cylinder race of the thirties in order to retain its luxury image. Franklin's entry was not universally admired in the factory. The banking syndicate in control of H. H. Franklin's company was calling the shots. The new V-12 eschewed the full elliptics and tubular axles of previous Franklins and was considerably heavier, which to the weight-conscious Syracuse engineers was anathema. But the 200 people who were able to afford a V-12 Franklin during the three years it was built loved the car, and doubtless for the same reasons that Franklin collectors do today. The LeBaron-designed coachwork was gorgeous. And the car had gusto. Its supercharged twelve-cylinder engine, with dual throat Stromberg carburetion, developed 150 hp. The dash-board-adjustable ride control, three-speed transmission with free wheeling, and dual ratio rear axle

1932 Franklin Series 17A Model 173 V-12 Club Brougham
Owner: Albert D. Nippert of Peekskill, New York

made for a Franklin that was both comfortable and a fine performer. The two-speed rear end meant that in high range the engine had a piston speed much like any modern V-8 so, with the motor "loafing," the Franklin could cruise easily at 70 mph all day. Moreover, the new V-12 retained the Franklin's traditional dependability.

"CCCA members Ray and Elly Yeck drove this car 14,000 miles on Club tours without a breakdown," says Al Nippert of his '32 V-12. "I have had about 8,000 miles on tours without any mishaps." Al is the third owner of this Franklin, which was delivered new to S. P. Cooper of Grand Rapids, Michigan. "Unsurpassed" is Al's word for the LeBaron styling of his Club Brougham.

Equally enthusiastic about the LeBaron touch is Bob Larrabee who wittily describes the design of his big 6,000-pound sedan as "architecturally very pleasing." This '33 V-12 was once in the collection of D. Cameron Peck, a foremost early collector of Classic Era cars. "It was evident during restoration that V-12 Franklins were of limited production," says Bob, "as each front fender was made from six separate pieces of metal and the fenders were hand-shaped to fit the body." The Larrabee Franklin was a 40,000 mile car when he purchased it in 1973. "Runs with ease at highway speeds," he comments, and Bob runs with his Franklin often in West Coast events.

Bob Agle's 1934 Club Brougham was the fifth from the last V-12 built and the last one known to survive. The original invoice for the car, which Bob has, indicates the dire straits into which the Franklin company had fallen by then. List price was $2,885, a full thousand dollars less than the figure at which the model had been introduced. The car was delivered on April 4th, 1934 to Francisco Gonzalez of Mexico City. Ironically, that was the final day of life for the Franklin company. "This car had an extremely hard life for thirty years in Mexico," says Bob. "Service was very difficult in the U.S. and almost impossible so far from the factory." In the mid-1960's the Franklin was discovered near Mexico City by Edward King, who acquired and shipped it to his home in Michigan. Five years ago Bob Agle added the car to his collection of Classics from Syracuse which, at this writing, numbers eight. Why this particular one? There is something very poignant about a Franklin that represented the end of a memorable line.

1932 Franklin Series 17B Model 174 V-12 Seven-Passenger Sedan
Owner: Robert D. "Bob" Larrabee of Clarkston, Washington

1934 Franklin Series 17B Model 174 V-12 Club Brougham
Owner: Robert Agle of Jeffersonville, Ohio   Photos: Don Smith

L A S A L L E

René Robert Cavalier LaSalle hood ornament from Don Hoelscher's 1929 Series 328 Sedan
Stylized bird hood ornament from Lester Wax's 1931 Series 345-A Five-Passenger Coupe

The symbiotic relationship between the two cars was suggested in their names. The older honored the French explorer who discovered Detroit: Le Sieur Antoine de la Mothe Cadillac. The new car was named for the French adventurer who explored the Mississippi Valley in the 17th century. But the LaSalle was much more than a companion to Cadillac. It created a styling revolution at General Motors. Not that this was planned initially; the car resulted simply from GM president Alfred P. Sloan, Jr. noticing a price gap that needed filling between the Buick and Cadillac. Cadillac president Lawrence Fisher was assigned to fill it. Among those invited by Fisher to compete for the design of the new LaSalle was Harley Earl, the young director of the coachbuilding Don Lee Corporation in California. "Not quite as conservative as the Cadillac" was the instruction given Earl; Harley chose "a car I was deeply in love with"—the Hispano-Suiza—as inspiration. Earl's design was accepted by GM, and the new LaSalle's smashing critical reception—"just about the most beautiful car I ever saw," wrote one reporter—persuaded Alfred Sloan to suggest the creation of a GM design department with Harley Earl as its head. Harley thought the new department's designation, Art and Colour, was a "sissy name." There was nothing effete about the cars that came out of it. . . .

1927 LaSalle Series 303 Roadster   Owner: Henry Ford Museum & Greenfield Village, Dearborn, Michigan

1927 LaSalle Series 303 Sport Phaeton
Owner: Rhodes A. Finley of Trinity Center, California

A smaller package (V-8 engine with eleven less cubic inches at 303, wheelbase seven inches shorter at 125) at a price lower by about $500—that was the new LaSalle. But those figures probably didn't matter as much to the 10,767 people who bought the car in 1927 as the striking figure it cut in styling.

"The Art and Colour Section at GM was the industry's first major styling studio," comments Randy Mason of the Ford Museum. "The LaSalle was a very important car in auto design history." The museum's Series 303 Roadster, one of only a handful extant, was the LaSalle in which the fire chief went to blazes in Montville, Connecticut for years.

Rhodes Finley has owned his Series 303 dual cowl Sport Phaeton for over a decade: "The lack of a side-mounted spare reveals some of the fine styling detail; location of the spare at the rear also makes for a better balanced look."

1928 LaSalle Series 303 Victoria
Owner: Ron Stem of Plymouth, Michigan

The LaSalle for '28 was a many-louvered thing, twenty-eight hood vents matching the model year in number, which was probably a coincidence since the Cadillac had thirty. It was no coincidence, however, that the Cadillac for '28 bore a striking resemblance to its smaller brother. LaSalle sales increased to 16,038 cars this year.

''Very few Classic LaSalles survive,'' says Ron Stem. ''That, more than anything, makes the car special.'' Ron inherited his Series 303 Victoria from his father seven years ago, although he had been using it for a lot longer than that: ''In the early fall of 1970 I deliberated about driving the LaSalle to Hershey. My father did not feel the car was up to it. I 'exercised' it locally during September and the round trip was successfully made—much to the amazement of my father who had opted to ride in a friend's truck instead.''

The Waters' Series 303 Convertible Coupe has had an interesting six decades of life: six years on the road by original owners George & Ethel Coram (who purchased a LaSalle Seven-Passenger Sedan from Inglis M. Uppercu Cadillac in New York City at the same time as this one), thirteen years powering a sawmill, twenty-seven years garage stored, eight in home restoration and eight to date for Wesley & Mary Ann in shows and driving fun: ''As beautiful as it is functional, the 75 hp LaSalle V-8 runs glass smooth. Exhaust manifolds are glazed black porcelain, while a masterpiece of the casting art houses the carburetor. The Buffalo wheels and hubs are a thesis in functional art. The front end treatment features large headlamps, matching cowl lights and Trippe lights. Between the headlights is the LaS script logo bar. The stance of the LaSalle defines stability. The place to enjoy motoring is the LaSalle's driver's seat. State-of-the-art in 1928, the interior is replete with artistic details challenging the casting process and in the use of organic materials such as the burl walnut dash fascia and leather upholstery.''

1928 LaSalle Series 303 Convertible Coupe (interior on page opposite)
Owners: Wesley A. & Mary Ann Waters of Sterling, Virginia

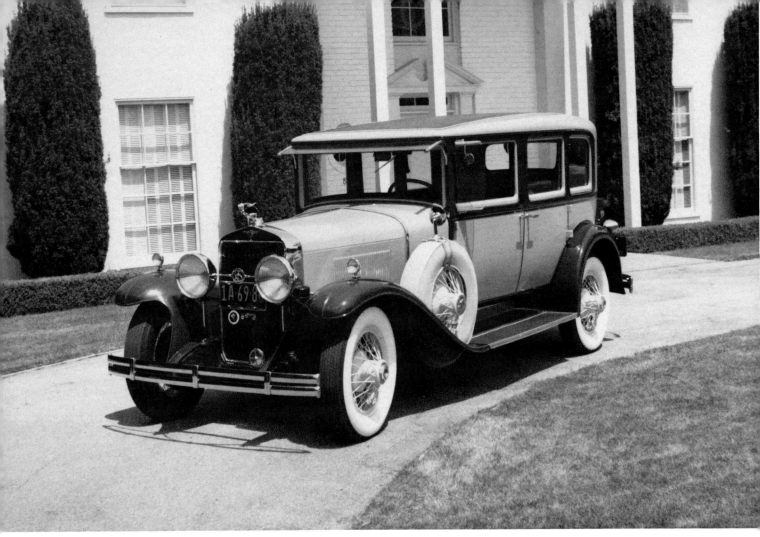

1929 LaSalle Series 328 Five-Passenger Sedan   Owner: H. Fred Bausch of San Carlos, California   Photo: Bud Juneau

Reboring of the LaSalle's V-8 resulted in 328 cubic inches and 16 more horsepower in '29. All Fisher bodies except roadster and phaeton were on a new 134-inch wheelbase chassis. New features included synchromesh transmission, safety glass, chrome plating of all brightwork, and an adjustable front seat on all closed bodies save limousines. Nearly 23,000 1929 LaSalles were sold.

Al Copsetta is the third owner of his Series 328 Phaeton: "The car was originally purchased by a Boston jeweler named Shreve who drove it, mostly during summers, until 1938 when he was too old to do so anymore. His neighbor, a Mr. Nichols, asked to buy it but Mr. Shreve said no. In 1955 Mr. Nichols acquired the car upon the original owner's death. I bought the car from him in 1977. It remains in original condition."

"This car went through a series of brief ownerships before finding a home in my garage," says Fred Bausch of his Series 328 Five-Passenger Sedan. "It's a comfortable and reliable tour car that I'm not afraid to take on long trips."

The Hoelschers' Series 328 Family Sedan was their first Classic and Don's first full restoration: "It was completely apart when we bought it fifteen years ago, so extensive research was necessary—and it took four years to complete. I like the '29 LaSalle so much that I am now working on another, a '29 rumble-seat coupe."

1929 LaSalle Series 328 Phaeton
Owner: Al Copsetta of Lindenwood, New Jersey

1929 LaSalle Series 328 Family Sedan   *Owners: Don & Joan Hoelscher of Bridgeton, Missouri*

1930 LaSalle Series 340 Phaeton, Fleetwood   Owner: Mary K. Rowan of Chatham, New Jersey   Photo: K. Karger

Engine revisions for the 1930 LaSalle resulted in 90 hp from 340 cubic inches, the same displacement as the previous model year's Cadillac V-8. All LaSalles now rode on a 134-inch wheelbase. Fleetwood-bodied models increased to six while Fisher bodies, which previously had represented about 75% of LaSalle production, decreased to seven. But the attention usually accorded the marque was diverted—to Cadillac's new V-16. Sales decreased to less than 15,000 in this first post-Wall Street crash model year.

Nancy Collins has owned her Series 340 Fleetwood Phaeton for four years: "This car was one of five purchased by the Glacier Transport Company in 1930 to transport guests from the railroad depot to the lodge at the Glacier National Park. It is a comfortable and enjoyable Classic to drive."

Agreeing with that is Mary Rowan: "The Series 340 Fleetwood Phaeton is a very dependable tour car capable of cruising all day at 60 mph with its new rear axle ratio. And there's plenty of room for our family of four. The windwings are very effective; this is the only open car we have that does not mess up my hair."

1930 LaSalle Series 340 Phaeton, Fleetwood   Owner: Nancy E. Collins of Gastonia, North Carolina

1931 LaSalle Series 345-A Five-Passenger Coupe
Owner: Lester P. Wax of Sharon, Massachusetts

Cadillac's reaction to the onset of the Depression was to make its eight-cylinder lines as closely identical as possible. The LaSalle's new engine was Cadillac's 353-cubic-inch V-8. Cadillac V-8 models were now fitted on the LaSalle's 134-inch-wheelbase chassis. Interchangeability promoted manufacturing economy, but the LaSalle lost much of its individuality as a result. LaSalle sales—at 10,095 cars—were some 600 less than the Cadillac V-8. Initially, from a distance, only the single-bar bumper differentiated a 1931 LaSalle from a 1930 but mid-model year hood doors replaced the former ventilation louvers. Their presence on the 1931 LaSalles shown here indicate that all three of these cars were produced late in the model run.

Lester Wax has owned his Series 345-A for over two decades: ''It had been delivered new in Boston, to whom I do not know. Since I've owned the LaSalle, it has been in a PBS movie, exhibited at the Museum of Transportation in Brookline, Massachusetts, and circled the Indianapolis Speedway track for a few of the 9,000 miles I've driven it. But, most importantly, the LaSalle was used on my first date with my future wife, Barbara.''

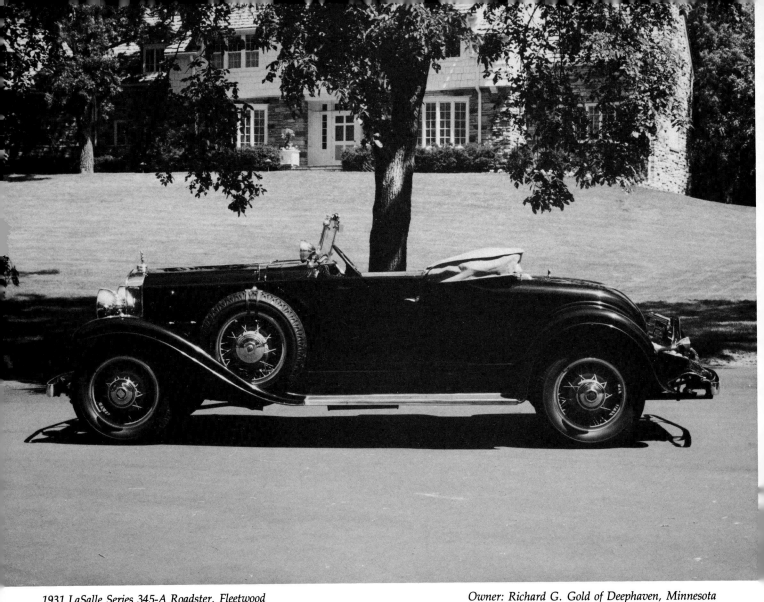

1931 LaSalle Series 345-A Roadster, Fleetwood   Owner: Richard G. Gold of Deephaven, Minnesota

1931 LaSalle Series 345-A Roadster, Fleetwood
Owner: Jack Royston of Scottsdale, Arizona

The romance factor attaches to Jack Royston's Series 345-A as well: "My wife and I dated in a '31 LaSalle in 1936. My father had the Cadillac/LaSalle distributorship in Pittsburgh, Pennsylvania from 1928 to 1932, and I fell in love with these cars. I've driven my LaSalle 21,000 miles since 1973."

"Nineteen thirty-one represented the last of the traditional LaSalle look," says Dick Gold, "and the last LaSalle with a fold-down windshield. We use this car for short tours; with the rumble seat, it's great for kids. Classic LaSalles are rare for a reason. Back in the late twenties and early thirties, as they began to appear on used car lots, the cars were snapped up quickly by young people just able to afford them. LaSalles were fast, sleek and appealed to go-fast kids; indeed, LaSalle gears and transmissions were commonly used in hot rods of that era. Lots of these cars were just plain used up long before collectors began admiring them."

1932 LaSalle Series 345-B Town Coupe   *Owner: George A. Von Essen of Gulf Stream, Florida*

The 3,386 LaSalles sold in 1932 was 700 better than the Cadillac V-8. Engineering refinements brought 115 hp, the synchromesh transmission was refined to ''Triple Silent'' with all three speeds helical, and a mechanical fuel pump eliminated the former vacuum system. Only Fisher bodies were used for LaSalles which were mounted on two wheelbases of 130 and 136 inches, each four inches shorter than the corresponding Cadillac V-8. The overall look of the LaSalle, save for detail differences, was that of the Cadillac.

''I have always felt the Town Coupe or victoria is *the* outstanding closed body style,'' comments George Von Essen. ''Although this body is a Fisher, the interior is Fleetwood. When restored in 1977 my car had experienced only 37,500 miles of service. It continues to drive like a low-mileage car.''

1932 LaSalle Series 345-B Town Coupe   *Owner: Steve Chapman of Waxahachie, Texas*

Steve Chapman's Series 345-B Town Coupe was originally ordered by Don Lee Cadillac in San Francisco, California for the dealership's introductory stock of 1932 models: ''The car was shipped to Don Lee on December 31st, 1931. When next heard from, in 1954, it was in Playa Del Rey, near Los Angeles. Dave Pennington saw the car parked in a driveway and inquired if it might be for sale. The woman who answered the door said yes, that it belonged to her son. Her son then came to the door and, although reluctant, soon revealed that he had lost his driver's license and was under certain pressure to sell. Eighty-five dollars later, Dave owned the car. Still in service, it was perfectly sound and solid with 61,000 miles but had suffered a home repaint and over-heated due to a collapsing radiator hose. Towed back to Dave's home in Corpus Christi, Texas behind a Hudson, the LaSalle was stored with a number of other fine unrestored Classics in a secure garage. It stayed there until 1968 when Maxon Graham, a lifelong friend of mine, bought and restored it. In 1989 the LaSalle was moved a couple of blocks to its new residence in Waxahachie.''

306

1933 LaSalle Series 345-C Convertible Coupe   Owner: James T. Wilson of Richmond, Virginia

A new radiator grille, skirted fenders, no-draft ventilation and vacuum-assisted brakes were shared by both the Cadillac V-8 and the LaSalle for '33. Differentiating the latter were the four-inch-shorter wheelbases, the four hood doors, bumpers front and rear, and the design of the lighting. Sales decreased to 3,482 cars. The handwriting on the wall was legible. With the Depression at its worst, producing a LaSalle that was virtually a Cadillac with five hundred dollars lopped off the price tag didn't make economic sense. Thus in 1934 the LaSalle would be reintroduced as a brand-new car with off-the-shelf parts from other divisions and offered for at least a thousand dollars less. Nineteen thirty-three was the LaSalle's last Classic year.

"As best I can determine, approximately 150 of my body style were made," says Jim Wilson. "I especially like the Convertible Coupe, with the look of the roadster and roll-up windows. I've owned the car for twenty years, and its restoration is 90% complete."

The Series 345-C Coupe in the Raines' garage was Ted's first restoration. Comments Jo: "It came home in boxes in 1970, looking terrible. Never having restored a car before, Ted put the pieces together, and the first time he turned the key, the engine ran beautifully. We named this car Eagle, and have driven it more than any other car Ted has restored. Once on our way to a tour, we were stopped by a highway patrolman who wanted to cite Ted for driving with our daughters in 'an unsafe passenger compartment.' He thought the rumble-seat was a trunk! After a great deal of discussion, we were on our way without a ticket, having assured the officer that both girls had seatbelts buckled and that what was in the back of our LaSalle was a legal passenger area."

1933 LaSalle Series 345-C Coupe
Owners: Ted & Jo Raines of Castro Valley, California

Greyhound mascot on Frank Mulderry's '31 Model K Convertible Coupe, photo by Daniel B. Lyons

The Lincoln Motor Company was named for the first U.S. president for whom its founder had voted. The year was 1917; Henry Martyn Leland was seventy-four years old. He had just left Cadillac, which he had led since its birth, because General Motors wasn't moving into wartime production fast enough to suit him. Leland was a super patriot, and something of a stubborn old man. The Armistice, unfortunately, came too early for the aero-engine-building Lincoln company to realize financial stability. Faced with a mountain of debts, a big factory and 6,000 employees with nothing to do, Leland (by now seventy-seven) decided to build an automobile again. Three hours after being placed on sale in 1920, $6.5 million in stock in the new Lincoln Motor Company was subscribed. Public confidence in the man was high. Leland justified that confidence by half. The Lincoln's 60° V-8 engine with radically new fork-and-blade connecting rods was an engineering triumph. The styling of the new Lincoln was an aesthetic disaster. Many orders placed before the new car was shown were cancelled immediately after. By 1922, much to Leland's chagrin, his board of directors put the Lincoln Motor Company up for sale. The purchaser was Henry Ford. Not surprisingly, Leland soon departed. Moving into Lincoln's presidency was Henry Ford's son, Edsel. Henry Leland had long been known as the master of precision. Edsel Ford would soon demonstrate that he was a master of style. . . .

*1925 Lincoln Model L Five-Passenger Cabriolet, Brunn
Owner: Frank Cassello of Chicago, Illinois*

*1926 Lincoln Model L Club Roadster, Dietrich
Owner: Anthony Pacione of Los Angeles, California*

*1926 Lincoln Model L Four-Passenger Berline, Judkins
Owner: P. H. Cooper of Casper, Wyoming*

With its 357.8 cubic-inch engine delivering close to 90 hp in a chassis of consummate durability, the Leland Lincoln was a favorite of the Detroit Police Department, amongst other progressive law enforcement agencies in the United States. The Ford Lincoln underneath, and wisely, remained pretty much as Leland had built it. What Edsel did immediately was lengthen the wheelbase six inches (to 136) and then he contacted the finest custom body houses in the land. Lincoln catalogues became virtually a Who's Who of the coachbuilding craft. If a particular body style appealed to Edsel, he ordered it in lots of 100 or more. This meant a Lincoln custom could be priced between $5,000 and $6,500, a great deal of money at the time, but far less than a coachbuilder charged for producing a single car specifically to order. All this would not, of course, pass unnoticed by other manufacturers of luxury cars.

Leading the stylish new Lincoln down the road was Edsel's next good idea: the lithe greyhound hood ornament produced for him by Gorham, one of America's most honored silversmiths. Symbolic of fleetness and grace, the greyhound was also part of the family crest of Abraham Lincoln's English ancestors and that association may also have led Edsel to its selection. The mascot was introduced as an option early in 1925 but soon became the finishing touch applied to all Lincolns.

Frank Cassello's Brunn Five-Passenger Cabriolet, believed to be the only one extant, is also thought to have been a special order for show use. Much of its subsequent life was spent on an estate in Pittsburgh. Frank has owned the car since 1985.

That the Lincoln was a "showgoer" during this era is exemplified by Anthony Pacione's 1926 Dietrich Club Roadster. This design won concours d'elegance in Paris, Milano and Monte Carlo—and Ray Dietrich returned to the States with three gold medals plus, as he remembered, "a loving cup big enough to swim in."

Phil Cooper's 1926 Judkins Four-Passenger Berline was acquired a year ago. Delivered new, the car had been priced at $5,400. Phil doesn't know the first owner, but he does the second: Felix Braun of Phila-delphia. The bill of sale from 1929 remains extant. "The car was three years old when Braun purchased it for $1,495," says Phil. "I had to pay more for it."

The Yellowstone Park Transporta-tion Company was the first owner of

1926 Lincoln Model L Seven-Passenger Sport Touring, Brunn

Owner: P. H. Cooper of Casper, Wyoming

Phil Cooper's 1926 Brunn sport Touring: "It was one of fifteen 1926 Yellowstone Lincolns. There was also one each from model years 1923, 1927 and 1928. The cars remained in service until World War II closed the park, then they were sold off. It is believed that six or eight of the Yellowstone Lincolns remain in existence. My car had been sold to a Montana rancher, from whom I bought it thirty-six years ago."

Bullet-shaped headlamps was the styling change that immediately identified Lincolns for 1927. Readily apparent to new owners on the road were the four-wheel brakes which had earlier been fitted to Lincoln police cars and now were made standard equipment.

Robert H. McElroy, a director and vice president of the Standard Oil Company, was the original owner of Ken Pearson's 1927 Lincoln-built

limousine. Following McElroy's death in 1938, the car was stored on his estate for many years. Ken has owned it since 1961: "The Lincoln is a fine machine. It has a distinguished body style, is steady on the road and very comfortable to travel in. The car had a trifle over 20,000 miles on the odometer when I acquired it. The odometer now reads 35,890 miles. My wife Louise has driven this car frequently too."

1927 Lincoln Model L Berline   Owner: Ken Pearson of Crystal Lake, Illinois   Photo: Langdon Studio

*1927 Lincoln Model L Imperial Victoria, Fleetwood
Owners: Jack & Nancy Dunning of Cambridge, Ohio*

Obviously one-of-a-kind is the 1927 Fleetwood Imperial Victoria owned by Jack & Nancy Dunning: "Although soon to be brought wholly into the General Motors fold, Fleetwood was still building on outside chassis at this time. In this case, the chassis was the 150-inch professional car frame, and the car cost its original owner $15,000. Ten inches longer, six inches higher and two inches wider than the average formal Lincoln, the body is a four-door victoria-top touring not dissimilar to the 'park phaetons' fashionable on Locomobile or Peerless chassis of the 1906-1910 period, although the driver is at least protected by full-size doors (all with carriage-type handles) and a two-panel opening windshield on which is mounted a single wiper. A small storage compartment separates the front seats. The folding black leather top is internally lined and incorporates plated external landau irons, dual courtesy lights and an oval rear window. The rear compartment is protected by two separate folding windshields, the first protecting occupants of the two armchair-type jumpseats, the second protecting the rear seat beneath which is housed the hidden microphone of a 'Motor Dictograph' by Dictograph Products of New York. The driver's loudspeaker is mounted over the front seat at the back of which is a robe rail. The rear-mounted trunk rack accommodates two trunks, one behind the other. Bumper and horn equipment is stock Lincoln, though the hood ornament is an unusual French one entitled 'Le Hurleur,' purportedly contemplated (though never adopted) by Lincoln as an alternative to the greyhound. Lamp equipment is very special: head and dual spot lamps by Marchal of France and a pair of German silver electric carriage lamps. It is understood that this car was commissioned by a wealthy Frenchman who enjoyed going to the Paris Opera and had this car built to take him and his friends in grandeur. It appears to have been designed to be operated by a chauffeur and a valet—and could be equipped with an inclement weather top. Carried in the forward trunk, this top does seal the car pretty well, but it is a time-consuming two-man job to install. The jumpseats don't fold up but are removed with wing nuts, with the center windshield then folded and stored behind the front seat. All this tends one to believe that the crew prepared the car for the evening before leaving the garage."

Boring out the Leland V-8 an eighth of an inch boosted displacement to 384.8 cubic inches and provided the Lincoln about ten more horses in 1928. Total Lincoln production that year was 6,363 cars of which 226 were the four-passenger Sport Phaeton by Locke.

James Sullivan has owned his car since 1982: "The original owner was from northeast Connecticut, and the car remains completely original. The Locke Sport Phaeton body is a fine design, close-coupled with an attractive rear quarter and a rakishly slanted windshield. In 1928, this body style was ahead of its time."

1928 Lincoln Model L Sport Phaeton, Locke
Owner: James C. Sullivan of Hudson, North Carolina

1929 Lincoln Model L Town Sedan
Owner: James C. Sullivan of Hudson, North Carolina

Nineteen twenty-nine was the Model L's penultimate year, the cars distinguished by a higher and slimmer radiator shell. The array of coach-built styles in the Lincoln catalogue continued undiminished, although some models were brought in-house. The Town Sedan in James Sullivan's collection is a Willoughby design that had been built by Willoughby in 1928 but in '29 the same car was produced in the Lincoln plant: "My car was bought new by Ben Minturn of Chicago. I have the original invoice. The base price was $4,949 but Minturn also ordered fender wells, sidemounts, trunk rack, six tires, folding armrests front and rear, special paint and upholstery, which added another $690—in a day when you could buy a Ford or Chevy for about $500. Then after he took delivery of the car Minturn added the police-type Lorraine spotlight, the large leather trunk—and had Zenith in Chicago

1929 Lincoln Model L Convertible Victoria, Dietrich   *Owner: Ken Kenewell of Fenton, Michigan*

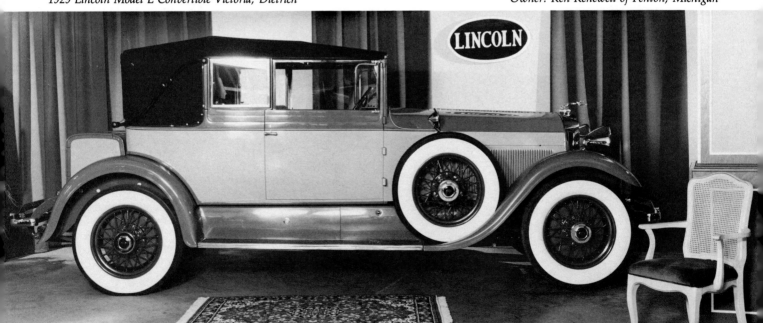

1929 Lincoln Model L Convertible Victoria, Dietrich   Owner: *Henry Ford Museum & Greenfield Village, Dearborn, Michigan*

install a radio later in 1929. I've owned the car since 1972. The radio still operates.''

The Dietrich Convertible Victoria continued to be Dietrich built and is an early example of a two-door

convertible with rear quarter windows. The Henry Ford Museum car was originally owned by Harvey Firestone.

Ken Kenewell's Dietrich Convertible Victoria, which he has

owned since 1970, was discovered in a New York City parking garage in the late fifties.

William Lyon's Locke-bodied Sport Phaeton was one of fifty-eight built and is a four-passenger car.

1929 Lincoln Model L Sport Phaeton, Locke   Owner: *William Lyon of Trabuco Canyon, California*

1929 Lincoln Model L Seven-Passenger Sport Touring, Locke
Owner: Classic Car Club of America Museum, Hickory Corners, Michigan

The Seven-Passenger Sport Touring by Locke in the CCCA Museum was one of eighty-eight built and was formerly owned for nearly three decades by the late Harold Emmons. His father had been Detroit's police commissioner during the Prohibition Era and on weekend visits from college Hal would accompany him on liquor raids. Hal's appreciation for Classic Lincolns was lifelong.

Walter Kahn's Locke Two-Passenger Roadster was one of just seven built in 1929: "The original owner was Ruth Hanna McCormick Simms, the only daughter of Mark Hanna, the power behind the Republican Party. Her first husband was Medill McCormick, brother of the *Chicago Tribune* publisher, and the two of them published a newspaper in Rockford, Illinois. Medill later represented Illinois in the U.S. Senate, and after his death in 1925 Ruth was appointed a U.S. Representative to Congress. Then she married a lawyer from Albuquerque, Albert Simms, who became a Representative from New Mexico. I remember seeing her driving this car when I was going to high school in Albuquerque in the early thirties. Later George Blodgett, a sculptor from Sante Fe, owned the car until his death in 1959. It went through several other hands before I acquired it in 1963. It is the car I had always wanted, and I waited thirty-two years to get it. The Locke Roadster will stay in my family; it is willed to my oldest daughter."

1929 Lincoln Model L Two-Passenger Roadster, Locke
Owner: Walter S. Kahn of Sante Fe, New Mexico

1930 Lincoln Model L Panel Brougham, Willoughby
Owner: Raymond N. Eberenz of St. Louis, Missouri

Because 1930 was the Model L's final year, changes were minimal. A few coach-built styles were deleted from the catalogue, but the array remained impressive.

The Brunn All-Weather Landaulet owned by Ken Kenewell was one of thirty-six produced in '30.

Ray Eberenz's Willoughby razor-edged Panel Brougham was one of five: ''A Ford Motor Company regional manager stated that he shipped three of them, one to New York, one to an Indian chief in Oklahoma and one to California. Mine is the New York car, purportedly destined for Mayor James 'Jimmy' Walker.''

1930 Lincoln Model L All-Weather Landaulet, Brunn
Owner: Ken Kenewell of Fenton, Michigan

For years the Seven-Passenger Touring owned by Greg & Mary Bilpuch had been sorely neglected and abused: ''The car's history is unknown until 1940 when it was sold to a junkyard in the mountains of Upstate New York. The engine was removed and stored in the back seat, and there it remained with the harsh New York winters taking their toll. In 1961 the car was bought to be restored but soon after the new owner died and it was resold in the same sad condition in 1963, was moved to Albany, stored for ten years and never touched. During the next decade the car was sold again two more times and taken to Massachusetts where the body was stripped from the chassis and shipped off to Kentucky. The chassis went to Indiana where it was totally torn down, every nut and bolt, and put in baskets, boxes and bags. In 1981 we found this challenge in a want ad. Being young, inexperienced and with a limited budget, we decided this Lincoln was the Classic for us. Actually what we purchased was a very large pile of parts. When we arrived home, we knew we had a lot of pieces for the Lincoln and some other cars, but had no idea how they went together. The first things we bought were parts and service manuals. Little by little, the parts were identified, restored and assembled. In 1983 the original body was located, purchased, stripped down, and a new wooden ash frame made as well as aluminum body panels where required. Virtually every part of the chassis had been in those bags and boxes. After eight long and determined years, the car was finished in 1989. It was the first time this Lincoln had been a complete running automobile since before 1940. Never again shall it fall into the disarray and neglect so unworthy of such a stunning Classic.

The Lincoln is home again in Michigan, a scant forty miles from where it was made sixty years before.''

1930 Lincoln Model L Seven-Passenger Touring
Owners: Greg & Mary Bilpuch of Lake Orion, Michigan

1931 Lincoln Model K Five-Passenger Sport Phaeton
Owners: Phil & Carol Bray of Grosse Ile, Michigan

1931 Lincoln Model K Seven-Passenger Limousine
Owner: Dick Chapman of Indianapolis, Indiana

1931 Lincoln Model K Town Sedan
Owner: Samuel L. Dibble of Wickenburg, Arizona

Why the Model K followed the L is anyone's guess, although that alphabetical letter had been used on a luxury Ford way back in 1906. The K's engine remained the same, which allowed Leland-like ''precision-built'' references in advertisements. Refinements included a Stromberg downdraft carburetor, more efficient manifolding and a mechanical fuel pump replacing the former vacuum system. The K's styling was longer, lower and more lithe than its predecessors. The radiator was peaked; headlamps were bowl-shaped and beneath them were dual trumpet horns with separate sounds for town and country. The L's torque tube drive and floating rear axle were retained in the K's 145-inch-wheelbase chassis, but double-acting Houdaille shock absorbers front and rear, free wheeling and synchromesh on second and third gears were new.

One of seventy-seven built in 1931, the Brays' Five-Passenger Sport Phaeton was delivered new to a Nebraska town police department and in the 1940's was used as a drag racer: ''The car is very fast from a standing start and at top end. It is an excellent driver. Factory features on this body style include roll-up three-quarter windwings and twin rear wood glove boxes.''

The original owner of Dick Chapman's Seven-Passenger Limousine was Hilda Moller of Leonia, New Jersey: ''Because of a bad arthritic back, she found this Lincoln easier to get in and out of than modern cars. She had the same chauffeur for twenty-six years, and I have his maintenance log of the car's service, as well as its New Jersey registration from 1959, which was the year she died. I am the second owner and have driven this Lincoln over 65,000 miles including eighteen CARavans. This car has never been on a trailer.''

Sam Dibble has owned his Town Sedan (a Brunn design built by Lincoln) since 1958: ''The car's original owner was Dr. L. F. Vielliard of Jamaica, New York. The trade-in on its purchase was a Winton Six, for $700. This Lincoln was used most for vacations in the Catskill Mountains and picnics on Long Island. According to Dr. Vielliard's son, its longest trip was from New York to the Chicago World's Fair in 1933. The car was stored from 1943 to 1957; when I bought it I found the gas ration card from World War II in the glove compartment. The quality and reliability of the '31 Lincoln is remarkable. I've driven my car over 20,000 miles. Among its unique

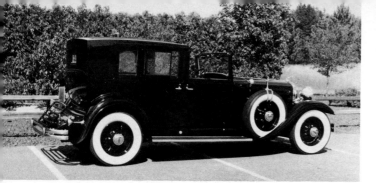

1931 Lincoln Model K Panel Brougham, Willoughby

Owner: James G. Griffin of Minocqua, Wisconsin

1931 Lincoln Model K Convertible Coupe, LeBaron
Owner: James C. Sullivan of Hudson, North Carolina

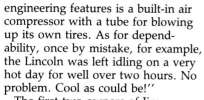

engineering features is a built-in air compressor with a tube for blowing up its own tires. As for dependability, once by mistake, for example, the Lincoln was left idling on a very hot day for well over two hours. No problem. Cool as could be!''

The first two owners of Jim Griffin's Willoughby Panel Brougham were Edward Connelly of Ridgefield, Connecticut and his chauffeur to whom the car was willed. It passed through two more owners before Jim acquired it two years ago: ''This car is an exceptional original with 48,250 miles. One of only fifteen Panel Broughams built by Willoughby in 1931, its base price was $7,400, making it one of the most expensive Lincolns in the catalogue. It's a real pleasure to drive.''

Among the sporty open cars in the Lincoln catalogue, the LeBaron Convertible Coupe was the most popular, with 275 built in '31. Both James Sullivan and Frank Mulderry have owned their cars since 1984. ''The most noticeable feature is quality,'' says Frank, ''no pot metal, everything brass; with the top down, the car is long, low—and gorgeous.''

The original owner of Ken Kenewell's LeBaron Convertible Coupe was Erle Stanley Gardner: ''He had just sold his first book and probably bought the car to celebrate. His hobby was horses, and he often used the Lincoln to pull his horse trailer. Because he liked the car, he kept it almost thirty years before trading it in. Jesse T. Jarrett, the foreman on the Gardner ranch, was the next owner. I acquired the car in 1977.''

1931 Lincoln Model K Convertible Coupe, LeBaron
Owner: Ken Kenewell of Fenton, Michigan

318

1931 Lincoln Model K Convertible Coupe, LeBaron
Owner: Francis P. Mulderry of Albany, New York   Photos: Daniel B. Lyons

If automotive journalists wondered in 1931 why the K's chassis was an overkill construction nine inches deep with six cross members and cruciform bracing, they had their answer in 1932. The chassis had been planned for a new engine: the twelve-cylinder KB. Massive, rugged and weighing an installed half-ton-plus, Lincoln's 60° V-12 displaced 447.9 cubic inches and developed 150 hp at 3400 rpm.

"This is a wow car," says Tom Lester of his Sport Touring. "I have owned most Classic marques and this KB, along with a 1937 Packard Twelve, are the best in my opinion. In 1932 the British *Autocar* tested over eighty automobiles including a KB Town Car which exceeded 95 mph. Only one other car was faster—a blown Alfa!"

Joe Folladori is amazed by the KB's performance too: "The fork-and-blade engine has a tremendous amount of torque, so much that you can start from a dead stop in high gear. This car is a driver, and a wonderful one. The chassis is equipped with an overload type of spring which activates when there are five very large people in the rear compartment. The original owner, G. S. Jephson, supposedly ordered the seven-foot Rollston body specially designed so that he wouldn't have to remove his hat while riding inside. Some years later Gerry Joynt acquired the car from Admiral Byrd's estate in Maine. I purchased the car from Gerry six years ago."

For Marie Graver, the "only clutch in the world that loves me" is among the enchanting features of her KB Dietrich Coupe: "Art and I bought this car in 1971 in Michigan. A '33 Lincoln Dietrich four-door convertible was also purchased on the same trip. When I asked Art how he was going to drive two cars home to California, he said we would worry about that when the time came. The time came as the '33 was being backed out of the driveway, and he casually asked me if I would like to drive the '32 around the block before heading for the West Coast. What an intro-duction to Classic cars! I did drive the '32 around the block and that's when I found the clutch didn't go 'glunk, glunk' like the other clutches I had met; it just squeezed away like soft butter, and it was love at first shift. I got to drive as far as Iowa, when his overheating '33 had to be shipped home and he took the keys away from me. But I stole them back the minute we got home, and the KB Dietrich Coupe was 'Marie's' car ever after."

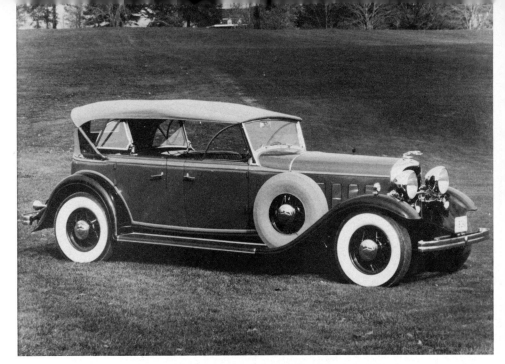

1932 Lincoln Model KB Seven-Passenger Sport Touring
Owner: Thomas J. Lester of Deerfield Beach, Florida

1932 Lincoln Model KB Two/Four-Passenger Coupe, Dietrich
Owner: Marie Graver of Los Altos Hills, California   *Photos: Bobbie'dine Rodda*

1932 Lincoln Model KB Seven-Passenger Limousine, Rollston

Owner: Joe Folladori of Indianapolis, Indiana

From the beginning, Lincoln financial figures were on the debit side of the ledger but, protected by the colossus of the mass-produced Ford, the marque had motored serenely on. KB sales of over 1,600 units for 1932 compared favorably with the somewhat smaller and less expensive Cadillac V-12 at 1,709 units and Packard's twelve at less than 600. But 1933 saw all luxury multi-cylinder cars dwindle in sales—to just 583 for the KB Lincoln, which scarcely pleased Henry Ford. A double-drop frame was new for the chassis, and Edsel Ford's fine aesthetic sense was seen in the elegant sloping chrome mesh grille that was the KB's new face.

"No expense was spared in the design and manufacture of these cars," comments Stephen Brauer. "They were the flagship of the Ford automotive empire. Of the fifteen Dietrich Convertible Sedans built in 1933, only a handful remain."

"The Dietrich Convertible Sedan was the most distinctive and luxurious open car Lincoln ever made," declare Charles Allen & Bill Sloan. "Flowing contours reflect the effortless smoothness of the Lincoln's motion. The car is a unity in graceful appearance as it is a unity in mechanical perfection. The KB's of 1932-1933 represent Lincoln's finest hour in both engineering and style."

1933 Lincoln Model KB Convertible Sedan, Dietrich
Owner: Stephen F. Brauer of Bridgeton, Missouri

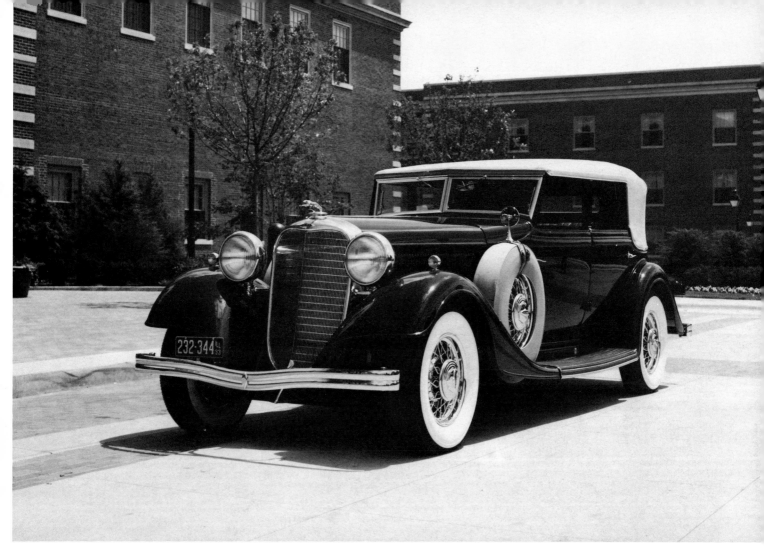

1933 Lincoln Model KB Convertible Sedan, Dietrich   Owners: Charles Allen & Bill Sloan of Kenilworth, Illinois   Photos: Torque

With Lincoln incurring Henry Ford's continuing displeasure, Edsel had to think fast. The solution was the discontinuation of the fork-and-blade V-12 and replacement by a 67° V-12 of 414.2 cubic inches engineered by Frank Johnson and staff. Its compression ratio of 6.3:1, virtually unheard of at the time, was made possible by the newly-available 70 octane Ethyl gasoline. With fewer cubic inches, the new V-12 developed the same 150 hp of its predecessor and made for an easy 95 mph car. Lincoln V-12 sales for 1934 topped 2,400 cars, easily outpointing both Cadillac and Packard models boasting the same number of cylinders. The KA on the 136-inch chassis garnered the lion's share; 740 of the pricier KB on the big 145-inch chassis were sold.

Del Beyer's LeBaron Convertible Roadster, one of forty-five built in '34, was base priced at $4,400 and weighed in at 5,085 pounds. Del has driven the car about 40,000 miles since acquisition in 1964.

1934 Lincoln Model KB Convertible Roadster, LeBaron
Owner: Del Beyer of Hartford, Wisconsin

All Lincolns for '35 were designated simply K once again, offered on both the 136- and 145-inch chassis. A fully-automatic spark control was new, and helical cut gears for second and third were a transmission addition. But the big news was outside. The new models were voluptuous—softer, rounder, with the grille shell and headlamps painted body color, horizontal hood vents that stretched back toward the windshield and dramatic one-piece bumpers.

Gerald Greenfield's Brunn Convertible Victoria was fitted to the 136-inch chassis and, at $5,500, was priced at about a dollar a pound: ''Amazingly, despite the small production run of 1,411 Model K's in 1935, Lincoln's output of V-12's exceeded that of its combined competition—Cadillac, Packard and Pierce-Arrow. Fifteen Convertible Victorias like mine were manufactured; two are known to exist today. This was a new version of the Brunn Convertible Victoria. The updated body was combined with Lincoln's last usage of wire wheels and traditional classic style fenders and running boards.''

1935 Lincoln Model K
Convertible Victoria, Brunn

Owner: Dr. Gerald Greenfield
of Federal Way, Washington

1936 Lincoln Model K Seven-Passenger Touring   *Owner: Del Beyer of Hartford, Wisconsin*

The Lincoln went all-helical in transmission in '36, and its headlights were dropped down for a racier look further enhanced by the more sharply-raked windshield. Again, overall K sales of 1,515 cars was impressive vis-à-vis the competition, and even more so when the figures for the new Lincoln Zephyr were included, Lincoln (like Cadillac and Packard) introducing a popular-priced non-Classic line during this period. Interestingly, all three owners of the top-of-the-line 1936 Lincolns shown here remark on the dependability of the cable-operated mechanical brakes with vacuum booster. Henry Ford abhorred hydraulics and wouldn't allow the Lincoln to have them until several years after they became standard on other luxury cars.

Touring cars were a rarity by '36. Just eight such Lincolns were built, the two shown here enjoying long ownership, since 1956 for William Abbott, since 1967 for Del Beyer.

1936 Lincoln Model K Seven-Passenger Touring   *Owner: William S. Abbott of Jerseyville, Illinois*   *Photo: Jerry Manis*

1936 Lincoln Model K Two/Four-Passenger Coupe, LeBaron   Owner: Robert A. Johnson of Burton, Ohio

The president of Lake Erie College in Painesville, Ohio was the first owner of Robert Johnson's LeBaron Coupe: "The distinctive body style and the few remaining examples, along with the exceptionally high quality, make this car an enjoyable and attention-arresting vehicle to own. Just twenty-five of these Lincolns were produced. I don't know of another one on the road. At 35,384 miles, the car is original except for paint. A great hill climber with power to spare, we would not hesitate to drive it anywhere."

1937 Lincoln Model K Seven-Passenger Limousine
Owner: James G. Milne III of Lucerne, Colorado

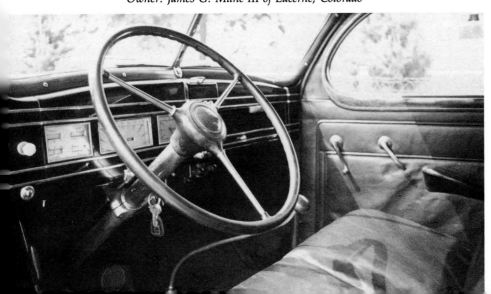

For the first time, in '37, Model K production dipped below 1,000 as the Zephyr cannibalized sales. Model K headlights blended into the front fender à la the revolutionary and popular John Tjaarda-designed car. And the K Lincoln was more zaftig than ever.

Most body styles in the Lincoln catalogue—seventeen in all—were coach-built, Lincoln choosing to concentrate on only sedans and limousines. Admiral Richard Byrd, whose fondness for the marque was well-known, is believed to be the original owner of James Milne's Seven-Passenger Limousine: "One of 248 manufactured, it's the only factory-bodied limousine I've ever seen. Hydraulic valve lifters were new this year. The streamlining given to the body would be the last major change in K styling until its demise. Other than cosmetic painting and some plating, the car is original. Full-leather upholstery is in the chauffeur's compartment. The woodwork trim is beautiful. The car has the privacy divider window between passenger and driver compartments with owner-to-chauffeur intercom as well as privacy shades on all passenger compartment windows."

Amongst the five Brunn offerings in the 1937 Lincoln catalogue was the Touring Cabriolet in the Henry Ford Museum. Priced at a hefty $6,950, just ten were sold.

Another milestone was reached for the 1938 K Lincoln. Sales were just 416 cars, lower than even the worst Depression year. Among the five Willoughby body styles, the Seven-Passenger Limousine was the most popular, with forty-six sold (as compared to the ninety-one of the factory-built version). Bob Doepke has owned his Willoughby K Lincoln since 1969.

Precise production figures for the 1939 Model K are not known, but precious few were built. Dick Haeberle's LeBaron Convertible Roadster is one of two produced: "It may be the only one remaining. This LeBaron body styling had been introduced in 1937. This was its last year."

The Henry Ford Museum's Brunn Convertible Sedan is mounted on a special 160-inch wheelbase and, indeed, is special throughout. The first-line Presidential parade car at the White House from 1939-50, it was also the first car to be specifically built for this function and was known everywhere as the "Sunshine Special." Armoured and updated with a custom front-end in 1942, the Lincoln was used at all world peace conferences at the end of World War II. Its vital statistics: six feet high, twenty-one and one-half feet long, 9,300 pounds. "That car keeps rolling like Old Man River," a Secret Service agent said. The only reason for its retirement in 1950 was because it looked rather out-of-date for a progressive democracy.

The lofty look of the Kughns' LeBaron Formal Convertible Sedan was to make it fit for a king. Built in Dearborn for Ford of Canada, it was one of four parade cars built in 1939 for George VI's and Queen Elizabeth's Royal Tour of North America. The untoward height allowed the couple both to see and to be seen. In 1959 their daughter Queen Elizabeth II and Prince Philip motored in the car during their tour of Canada. In 1989 the LeBaron Convertible Sedan was again pressed into parade service, for the Queen Mother when she toured Toronto to commemorate the 50th anniversary of her visit.

1937 Lincoln Model K Touring Cabriolet, Brunn
Owner: Henry Ford Museum & Greenfield Village, Dearborn, Michigan

1938 Lincoln Model K Seven-Passenger Limousine, Willoughby
Owner: Robert P. Doepke of Cincinnati, Ohio

1939 Lincoln Model K Convertible Roadster, LeBaron
Owner: Dick Haeberle of Summit, New Jersey

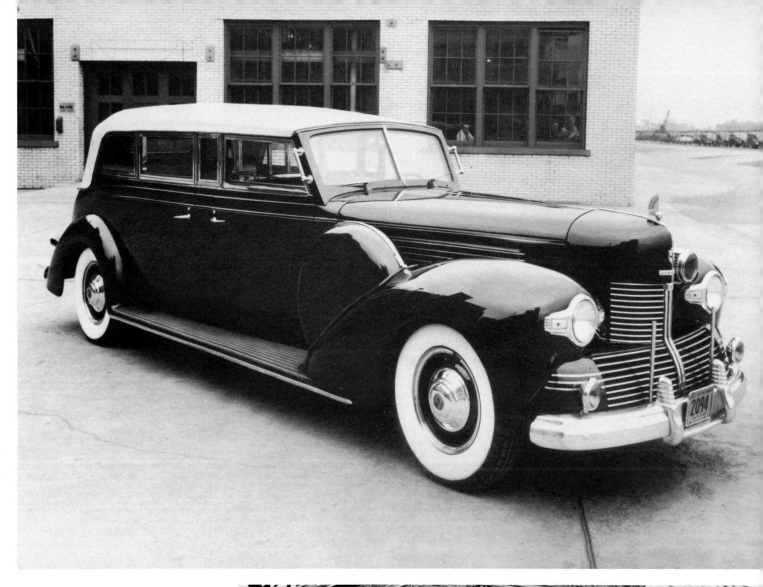

1939 Lincoln Model K
Convertible Sedan, Brunn

Owner: Henry Ford Museum
& Greenfield Village,
Dearborn, Michigan

1939 Lincoln Model K
Formal Convertible Sedan, LeBaron

Owners: Richard & Linda Kughn
of Southfield, Michigan

1940 Lincoln Continental Coupe   Owner: Thomas F. Lerch of North Canton, Ohio Photo: Detroit Institute of Art

The demise of the big Model K in 1940 was accompanied by the arrival of a new Lincoln that arrived rather accidentally. In September of 1938, upon returning from Europe, Edsel Ford asked stylist Bob Gregorie to design a special car for him that would be "strictly Continental." As legend has it, while driving the result around Hobe Sound and Palm Beach in Florida, Edsel received about 200 blank check orders for one just like it. Production was virtually cried for.

The Lincoln Continental was, in essence, a custom-built Zephyr. It shared the latter's 125-inch-wheelbase chassis (with hydraulic brakes) and its 75° V-12 (292 cubic inches, 120 hp). But the Continental was three inches lower, had seven inches more hood, sported a "continental" tire at the back—and continental flair everywhere. A tad under $3,000 (twice the Zephyr's price tag), the Continental was available only as a cabriolet (like

Edsel's original) and a coupe (which followed the open car to market in late May of 1940). Total production for 1940 was 350 cabriolets, 54 coupes.

Tom Lerch's car was the first production Lincoln Continental Coupe built: "After exhibit at the New York World's Fair, it was purchased by Governor Earle of Pennsylvania who was then serving as U.S. ambassador to Yugoslavia. An aide to Ambassador Earle had it next for nearly twenty years. When I acquired the car in 1965, it had been driven 240,000 miles. Except for upholstery, paint and chrome, I restored the car myself. The odometer now reads 384,000 miles. I've driven the car everywhere, on at least one trip a year of a thousand miles or more. My wife and I love this Lincoln Continental. To me, it's the most beautiful closed car ever built; the only flat surface on it is the

glass. It's silent, fast, very comfortable, reliable and smooth. For twenty-five years I had dreamed of owning a 1940 Lincoln Continental Coupe, and in the twenty-five years since, it's been everything I had ever hoped it would be—a dream come true."

Russell & Marie Bjorklund have owned their 1940 Continental Cabriolet for thirteen years: "Edsel Ford's good taste established it as a milestone in automotive styling. Our car had been badly abused and was totally in rags when we got it. Since restoration, we've driven it about 3,000 miles a year. Factory records show this car to be the only 1940 Continental equipped with a vacuum-operated antenna and it was shipped from Dearborn on rims for the owner's tires to be mounted at destination. We don't know who the first owner was, but he lived in Newport Beach, California."

1940 Lincoln Continental Coupe   Owner: Thomas F. Lerch of North Canton, Ohio Photo: Chad Coombs

1940 Lincoln Continental Cabriolet
Owners: Russell & Marie Bjorklund of New Brighton, Minnesota

1941 Lincoln Continental Cabriolet (engine view below)

Owner: Steven W. Hastings of Springfield, Massachusetts

With a full model year for both body styles, the coupe (850 built) passed the cabriolet (400) in production in 1941.

To the Henry Ford Museum, its cabriolet is an "important design-history object originally owned by the person who fathered it." And that, of course, was Edsel Ford.

Steven Hastings' cabriolet was the 41st car completed (on September 17th, 1940) and shipped thereafter to Edgewater, New Jersey: "As an early '41 it has the flat taillight lens, beige color on interior painted items (steering column, brake handle, cowl vent handle, etc.) and voltage regulator on the cowl shelf. The car was sold new in New York City but I don't know to whom. To the base $2,700 price was added $48.00 for radio and antenna, $40.00 for heater-defroster, $17.00 for four-ply whitewall tires, $65.00 for overdrive, for a total $2,870—a far cry from today's luxury cars perhaps, but an amount approximately equal to the cost of three new 1941 Ford convertibles."

Edgewater, site of a Ford assembly plant, was the first destination for Harvey Oberg's cabriolet too: "That a wealthy lady from Morristown was the first purchaser is all that I know to this point. I've owned the car since 1983. It's unusual in having the automatic choke carburetor that was installed on only 5% of the 1941 Lincoln Continentals. I like the push-button door releases and the foot control you use to select radio stations. But mostly I like the styling; the Lincoln Continental has the best looking rear end I've ever seen!"

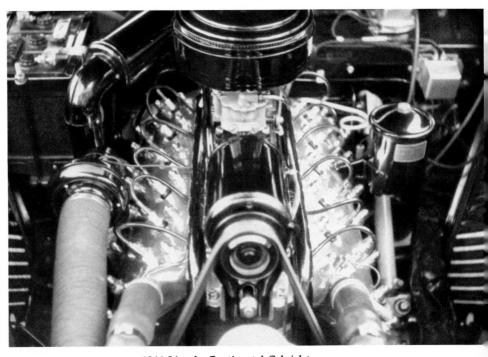

1941 Lincoln Continental Cabriolet
Owner: Henry Ford Museum & Greenfield Village, Dearborn, Michigan

332

1941 Lincoln Continental Cabriolet   Owner: Harvey V. Oberg of Woodbury, Minnesota

The Lincoln Custom Limousine was designed and produced in-house as a replacement for the discontinued Model K. Randy Still has owned his car since 1984: "Edsel Ford loved custom-bodied luxury automobiles and instructed chief stylist Bob Gregorie to design a limousine of approximately the same size as the defunct K, using Zephyr components as much as possible. The wheelbase on this car is thirteen inches longer than the Zephyr. Gregorie oversaw the design development but subrogated most of the work to Henry Crecelius, the master body craftsman Edsel had lured away from Brewster in the late twenties. According to factory records, my Custom was ordered by a Chicago resident who requested that the initials C.G.P. be painted on the rear doors. Continental-style push-button door openers were specified instead of the stock lever-type handles. Radio controls were mounted in the right rear armrest. Further customer requests included center bumper guards and 6-ply tires. Further, in addition to the center-mounted front heater, two under-seat heaters were installed to cope with Chicago winters. From 1964 until my acquisition in 1984, the car was on exhibit at Harrah's Automobile Collection. My fascination with V-12 engines coupled with my preference for limousines made this car irresistible to me. The light gold plating on the dash trim and interior hardware adds to the luxury aura. The car steers and maneuvers well in tight spaces. The lights, heater, wipers and gauges all work well, and I have been pleased with the driveability of my unrestored Custom."

1941 Lincoln Custom Model 168H Limousine
Owner: E. Randy Still of Kingsport, Tennessee

A larger 306-cubic-inch 130 hp V-12 powered Lincoln Continentals for 1942. Vacuum-operated power windows were new, and so was front-end styling. Overall, the cars were lower, longer and wider. A total of 136 cabriolets and 200 coupes were built before the Second World War called a halt to production. Purportedly, the Lincoln Continental commanded the highest prices on the black market during the war years.

Ed Spagnolo has owned his coupe for six years: "Frank Lloyd Wright said the first Lincoln Continental was the most beautiful automobile he had ever seen; he owned several, as did Raymond Loewy. Today a high percentage of architects and designers are Lincoln Continental owners. That says a lot. But in addition to its styling, I like the car's driveability. It's very 'long legged' on

1942 Lincoln Continental Coupe

Owner: Ed Spagnolo of Waterbury, Connecticut

interstates; cruising at 65-75 mph for hours is not a problem. And the car is so quiet that it's almost impossible to detect if it's running without looking at the gauges. Since restoration, I've driven (never trailered) the Lincoln Continental Coupe 8,400 miles with no trouble or oil consumption. In either sub-zero or 90+ temperatures, the car has always started. It made me wonder a couple of times, but *never* failed. That says a lot too.''

1947 Lincoln Continental Cabriolet   *Owners: Den & Jan Fenske of Hidden Hills, California*

   With the coming of peace, America was ready to celebrate by buying new cars. Lincoln Continental sales for 1946 totalled 466 cars (as many as could be built) and 1,569 for 1947 (for the Classic Continental's best year ever).

   "At the age of fourteen, this model was the first new car I saw when World War II was over," says Den Fenske. "I was so impressed that I said to myself, 'someday I have to have one'—thirty-five years later I finally got one! Even today, the Lincoln Continental is never seen as 'just an old car.' Clean uncluttered lines and elegant styling never get old."

   "I've owned this beautiful 'piece of art' for seventeen years," comments Jack Coleman. "However, I've known this 'piece of art' since new, as it was owned by a friend of mine during college years. I really enjoy this car."

   Paul Hem enjoys his '47 cabriolet equally, although that's been for only two years of ownership thus far: "Nineteen forty-seven was the fifth year of the long-hood/short-high-rear-deck look. And that look still looks good!"

   Of the total 1947 Lincoln Conti-

1947 Lincoln Continental Cabriolet   *Owner: Jack Coleman of Berlin, Pennsylvania*

1947 Lincoln Continental Cabriolet   *Owner: Paul Hem of Toledo, Ohio*

nental production, 738 were cabriolets, 831 coupes like that owned for nearly two decades by Wesley & Mary Ann Waters: ''The most attractive engineering feature of the Lincoln Continental is also a purported weakness. Although seeming to always lack horsepower, the V-12 powerplant is one of the most attractive engines of the Classic Era. Included among the unique design and functional features are the twin water pumps, front-engine-mounted twin-point distributor driven directly off the camshaft and the awesome oil bath air cleaner canister and duct assembly. Although ostensibly underpowered, the proper description of the Continental's driving performance is sedate. Looking at it from that perspective, the inner beauty of the automobile encourages the driver to sit back, enjoy and finally savor the nuances of its comfort. These are highway machines. They are annoyed when driven stop-and-start. Preferring second and third gear, the Continental is begging to go! Few words can describe the exhilarating pleasure of cruising in overdrive at fifty miles an hour for a hundred miles or so.''

1947 Lincoln Continental Coupe   *Owners: Wesley A. & Mary Ann Waters of Sterling, Virgina*

1948 Lincoln Continental Cabriolet　　　　　　　　　　　*Owner: Dom Pacitti of Dearborn Heights, Michigan*

Among the 452 Lincoln Continental Cabriolets produced for 1948 was Sylvia & Joseph Sher's car: "Twelve cylinders, leather interior, a limited production convertible with power windows and power top, drives like a dream—what more could one ask?"

Except for vapor lock problems (common to most Classics), Dom Pacitti has enjoyed the "very smooth and quiet ride" of his '48 Lincoln Continental Cabriolet for over twenty years.

Robert Messinger's Lincoln Continental Coupe was one of 847 built in 1948: "The lines of the Continental were exceptional when first introduced and to this day the LC is always included in lists of the top ten best-designed automobiles of all time. This particular Lincoln Continental is special to me because it was the first Classic I purchased. Although many CCCA members prefer convertibles, I enjoy closed automobiles because they rattle much less, are less drafty in cool weather and usually have fewer water leaks. Since restoration in 1971, I've driven this car over 14,000 miles. It rides and handles beautifully on the road. There is a lack of instant power compared to some other cars, but the Lincoln Continental cruises nicely at 55-60 mph. And I enjoy the overdrive."

Nineteen forty-eight was the end of the Classic Era and it was also, coincidentally, the end for the first-generation Lincoln Continental. By now the price had increased to over $4,500 but still Lincoln continued to lose a reported $600 on each

1948 Lincoln Continental Cabriolet
Owners: Sylvia & Joseph Sher of River Forest, Illinois

1948 Lincoln Continental Coupe   Owner: Robert Messinger of Grand Rapids, Michigan   Photos: Dorothy Olsson Messinger

automobile sold. A vast investment would have been necessary both to lower production costs and to make the Continental competitive in the post-war market, and the company was not willing to invest further in what seemed to be a losing proposition. Moreover, Edsel Ford had died in 1943 and, without him, the car lost its most vigorous champion. But, oh, what the man had started when he asked Bob Gregorie for a Lincoln that was "strictly Continental."

M A R M O N

Hubcap from Ben Birbeck's 1931 Big Eight Four-Door Sedan

Of all the fine cars on the American road at the dawn of the Classic Era, perhaps the least appreciated and the least understood was the Marmon. Which is a pity—for, in many ways, it was the most interesting. And that was because of the man who built it. Engineering genius isn't a phrase to be lightly used, but it certainly fits Howard Marmon. The first car he ever built had overhead valves, pressure lubrication, selective transmission and shaft drive—in 1902, when the majority of automobiles in America were little more than motorized buggies. As early as 1904 he recognized the advantages of aluminum in motor construction. That luxury cars had to be big and heavy was a given in the industry when Howard Marmon decided that light and fast was better. A racing variation of his Marmon 32 won the first Indianapolis 500 in 1911. In 1916, when his Model 34 was introduced, Howard Marmon was making his engine almost entirely of aluminum. But he wasn't making many cars. The greatest strength of the Marmon company was also one of its major weaknesses. Howard Marmon was a brilliant engineer but a lackluster manager. And his brother Walter didn't have the tough business savvy necessary for the automobile industry either. According to a *MoToR* survey in 1924, the Marmon 34 was a good 10 mph faster than a Cadillac or Packard. All three marques were priced on a par, but Marmon sales of 2,597 units put the company a distant last from its competitors. In May that year, George M. ''Monty'' Williams, former head of the Wire Wheel Corporation of America, purchased a substantial block of stock in the Indianapolis company and was invited to the Marmon presidency. Howard Marmon knew he had a superior product. Perhaps Monty Williams could turn it into a moneymaker. . . .

The Series E-75 was the final evocation of the Marmon 34. Its pushrod-operated overhead valve six of 339.7 cubic inches developed 84 hp at 2700 rpm. The wheelbase was 136 inches. Curb weight of the Marmon complete was up to a half ton less than its quality competitors, which made even the Seven-Passenger Speedster catalogue custom by Locke a very lively performer with an easy 80 mph top speed. Comments Bill Cameron: "I have been partial to Marmons since boyhood—some sixty-five years. I knew of this car in 1945 in a small museum ten miles from my home. When 'rediscovered' many years later it had been on blocks in a cow barn for nearly a decade and a half. The restoration, most of which I did myself, required over two years."

1927 Marmon Series E-75 Seven-Passenger Speedster, Locke
Owner: William T. Cameron of Minocqua, Wisconsin

1930 Marmon Big Eight Seven-Passenger Touring

Owner: Robert S. Ehinger of Shawnee Mission, Kansas

Monty Williams regarded the E-75 Marmon as an exemplary car with an Achilles heel. Its basic design had been laid down in 1916; the 1927 version was a facelift of a facelift. While the famous Marmon quality remained, the car was badly out of date. And it had six cylinders, at a time when the luxury market was moving to eight.

Moreover, although he had managed to almost double sales in a short time, elevating the company's standing in the industry from 27th to 13th place, Williams was convinced that Marmon couldn't survive exclusively on upscale cars. "A straight-eight General Motors" was his plan; before the last roar of the twenties, new models began to be issued like junk bonds of the

eighties. By 1930 Marmons ranged in price from under $1,000 (the Roosevelt, named for Teddy) to over $5,000 (catalogue customs on the largest chassis). This bold and ambitious plan might have worked save for the Wall Street crash. The expansion couldn't have been more poorly, if inadvertently, timed.

Because a "straight-eight General Motors" violated Howard Marmon's concept of what his company was all about, the man whose name was on the door had retreated in 1926 with a couple of his most trusted engineers to form the Midwest Aviation Company. Consequently, Monty Williams brought in a cadre of new engineers to develop the company's new cars. At the top of the line was the Big Eight.

With 125 hp developed from 315.2 cubic inches, Marmon's largest straight eight was the first to combine dual carburetor with dual downdraft manifold. Wheelbase remained the same 136 inches of the Series E-75. Styling was modish, courtesy of the Hayes Body Company and, most especially, Hayes' new stylist, the Russian emigré Alexis de Sakhnoffsky, for some models. Big Eight bodies were courtesy of LeBaron, furnished in the white by that coachbuilder to the Marmon factory and finished there.

Bob Ehinger has owned his Big Eight Seven-Passenger Touring for over a quarter of a century. Just one other car like this remains extant, owned by a family in Norway since before World War II.

341

1930 Marmon Big Eight Four-Door Sedan

Owner: Steve Wolf of Goulds, Florida

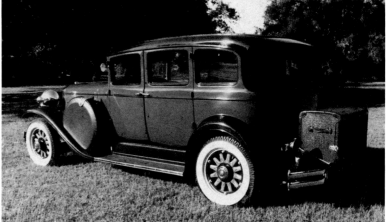

1931 Marmon Big Eight Four-Door Sedan
Owner: Ben Birkbeck of Grand Rapids, Michigan

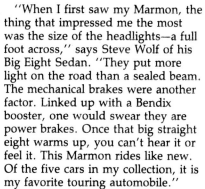

"When I first saw my Marmon, the thing that impressed me the most was the size of the headlights—a full foot across," says Steve Wolf of his Big Eight Sedan. "They put more light on the road than a sealed beam. The mechanical brakes were another factor. Linked up with a Bendix booster, one would swear they are power brakes. Once that big straight eight warms up, you can't hear it or feel it. This Marmon rides like new. Of the five cars in my collection, it is my favorite touring automobile."

Ben Birkbeck's Big Eight Sedan was originally a gift from the president of a Cleveland bank to his wife: "The classy lines and the craftsmanship in the body are outstanding. When I discovered the car, the odometer read 14,000 miles. A cosmetic exterior restoration was done, but inside remains original, complete with genuine down-filled seat cushions. The women in my family love the interior."

Howard Marmon had retreated only from his company. His automobile remained indelibly on his mind. What was needed, he thought, was a brand-new model so unexcelled that America would have to sit up and take notice. For a long time Marmon had been quietly considering this super car—since 1917, in fact, when he travelled to France as a member of the Bolling Commission and saw a sixteen-cylinder Bugatti aircraft engine demonstrated on a test stand. Its smoothness and power mesmerized him. A sixteen in an automobile had to be the ultimate.

Marmon's sixteen was. A superbly crafted unit, it boasted the largest displacement of any engine on the market, yet was lighter than most smaller eights. At 200 hp and only 930 pounds, Marmon's 490.8-cubic-inch V-16 boasted a power-to-weight ratio of 4.65 lb/hp, extraordinary for the era. The overhead-valve aluminum engine bristled with sophisticated features, among them the steel cylinder wall inserts that the New York Chapter of the Society of Automotive Engineers praised mightily in awarding Howard Marmon a gold medal for ''the most notable engineering achievement of 1930.''

Every Marmon Sixteen built was delivered with a certificate attesting that it had exceeded 100 mph for at least five miles on the Indianapolis Speedway. A completely stock car won the Stevens Challenge Trophy in 1931 by averaging 76.43 mph for twenty-four hours, breaking the former Stutz record by nearly eight miles an hour.

The body styling of the Marmon Sixteen verily exuded power and was as much the quintessence of modernity as the car's engine. The wheelbase was a long 145 inches. Walter Dorwin Teague, Jr. was largely responsible for the design. LeBaron built the bodies. Alas, there would not be many of them.

Ray Miller's '31 Convertible Sedan was sold new to Dr. G. H. A. Clowes, who developed the Similac baby formula for the Eli Lilly Company.

Clive Cussler's '31 Town Car was a birthday present to U.S. Supreme Court Justice Louis Brandeis. Because his wife wanted the gift to be very special, she had the original close-couped sedan body modified into a town car and painted in a pink-and-white combination. Said Justice Brandeis, ''I refuse to ride in that courtesan's car''—and he never did. Subsequently converted back to sedan configuration and given to Dr. San Martin, then president of Cuba, the car was found many years later with 1,000 miles on the odometer and every speck of cellulose material eaten out of it by termites. During Clive's restoration many years after that, vestiges of the town car modification were discovered, and he decided to return the car to the style Mrs. Brandeis had selected for the Justice's birthday present.

1931 Marmon Sixteen Convertible Sedan
Owner: S. Ray Miller, Jr. of Elkhart, Indiana

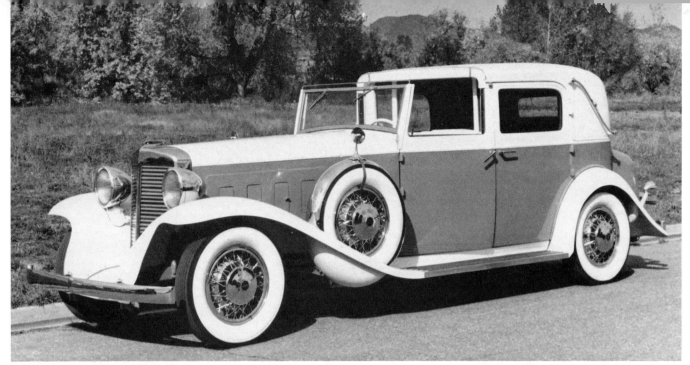

1931 Marmon Sixteen Town Car   Owner: Clive Cussler of Golden, Colorado

1931 Marmon Sixteen Two-Passenger Coupe with Rumble Seat   Owner: M. R. ''Duke'' Marston of Pasadena, California

Lorenz Iverson, president of the Mesta Machining Company of Pittsburgh, was the original owner of the '31 Two-Passenger Coupe that has been in the Marston garage for eighteen years. Duke is an avid enthusiast of the marque: ''We always had Marmons in my family. I drove the Sixteens before they were sold to the public, so I have a deep background. When I got crazy enough to restore a Classic as a hobby, nothing but a Marmon Sixteen would do. The design is superb from radiator to those sweeping curves on the rear of the body (Teague's contribution was from the front bumper to the windshield, incidentally). And the engineering is impeccable. This is the best performing, best riding and best handling of all American Classics. Nothing else drives as well. The engine in my car was restored by the late Alan Bartz of Can-Am racing fame and dyno tested to its full rated 200 hp. This Marmon was seventeen years in restoration which is probably unusual, but it must be remembered that during most of that time I was earning a living! Actually the restoration is not really quite finished. Is it ever?''

346

1931 Marmon Sixteen Convertible Sedan
Owners: Berta & Jay Leon of Hubbard, Texas

It was from the estate of the late Alan Bartz that Berta & Jay Leon acquired their '31 Convertible Sedan. Jay is equally a Marmon enthusiast: "The Sixteen engine provided the highest horsepower to pound of weight in the industry. Mine has pulled 216 hp on the dynamometer, using 12 volt ignition coils. The advanced styling, fine engineering and outstanding performance of the Marmon Sixteen have always been an attraction to me. Fred Moskovics (a colleague of Howard Marmon's who became famous at Stutz) drove a stock Sixteen at the Indianapolis track and achieved 111 mph electrically clocked. The comparative light weight of the cars (a little over 5,000 pounds) enhanced performance. And the Marmon Sixteen changed the silhouette of automobiles, which had been substantially unaltered for many years, introducing basic aerodynamic principles."

1932 Marmon Sixteen Convertible Coupe   *Owner: William Lyon of Trabuco Canyon, California*

Howard Marmon's sixteen was introduced at the Chicago Automobile Show in November of 1930. But production delays at the factory resulted in deliveries not beginning until April of 1931. The clientele able to afford $5,000+ for an automobile didn't tend to be patient. Many purchased Cadillac's V-16 instead, which had already been on the market for over a year.

Of the eight body styles continued

for '32, two were open cars, the convertible sedan like Knox Kershaw's and the convertible coupe like William Lyon's. A full range of thirty-two custom body designs was announced but never realized. Rare indeed is the custom Sixteen.

Bruce Williams' Waterhouse Seven-Passenger Phaeton was one of just two built: "Both cars were ordered by the same person—Ezra Parmalee Prentice, John D. Rockefeller's

personal attorney. They were identical except for the fitting of a non-removable California-style hardtop on my car which belonged to Alta Rockefeller Prentice (John D.'s daughter and Ezra's wife). Both cars were kept on the Prentices' Williamstown, Massachusetts estate where there were 200 employees, 300,000 chickens and 10 great Classics." During the early sixties Mrs. Prentice's Waterhouse Marmon was

1932 Marmon Sixteen Convertible Sedan   *Owner: Knox Kershaw of Montgomery, Alabama*

1932 Marmon Sixteen Seven-Passenger Phaeton, Waterhouse

Owner: Bruce R. Williams of Gates Mills, Ohio

in her brother Winthrop Rockefeller's museum in Arkansas, during the seventies Bill Harrah acquired it for his collection, since the mid-eighties it has been in the Williams' garage.

For the first two years the Sixteen was built alongside the straight-eight Marmons. Late in 1932 the company announced that the following year the Sixteen would be its sole product. Production for 1933 totaled fifty-six cars, one of them Joe Folladori's Five-Passenger Victoria Coupe: "The Sixteen's rubber-mounted spring shackles, anti-shock stabilizer on the steering and ride control make it a superb driving and riding car. And the body styling has a clean, forthright beauty. An estimated 390 Marmon Sixteens were built; sixty-nine remain today. Of Victorias like mine, nine of the approximate thirty-four produced are extant."

On May 1st, 1933 the Marmon Motor Car Company was in receivership. Earlier Howard Marmon had personally financed the development of a V-12 as exemplary as the Sixteen. It cost him $160,000 and brought no return other than a single prototype—and a certain satisfaction. If the Marmon automobile had to fail in the early thirties—and hindsight indicates that inevitability—Howard Marmon succeeded in leaving the Classic scene spectacularly.

1933 Marmon Sixteen Five-Passenger Victoria Coupe

Owner: Joe Folladori of Indianapolis, Indiana

Photo: Dottie Gheen

PACKARD

Pelican hood ornament from Don Sears' 1933 Twelve 1006 Dietrich Convertible Sedan

"Tell him to ask the man who owns one." Legend says that was the response James Ward Packard gave his secretary at the turn of the century when she arrived with a letter from a prospective customer requesting information. The Warren, Ohio company hadn't published a catalogue yet. Thus perhaps was one of motordom's most famous slogans born. It would endure for the life of the marque, though James Ward would not follow his company when it moved to East Grand Boulevard in Detroit a few years later. Socially prominent Detroiters with money to invest had recognized the Packard as an automobile tailormade for upper-echelon marketing. And were they ever right. The marque moved from strength to strength. By early in the Classic Era the company was outselling every other prestige car manufacturer in the world. When the cornerstone of Hampshire House on Central Park South in New York City was laid, a capsule representing the American "creative spirit" was included; included in the capsule was a Benet poem, a Hemingway novel, an O'Neill play, and photographs of a Benton mural and a town car by Packard. Captains of industry adored the marque. Owning one seemed requisite in high government circles: five sitting Supreme Court justices, many Senators and Congressmen, better than one out of five governors of the States. Ambassadors shipped Packards to their embassy posts. University presidents wouldn't be seen on campus without one. The Packard was an old-money car that new money coveted to establish arrival status. And owner loyalty was fierce. It remains so today. Just ask the following people who own one. . . .

1926 Packard Eight 243 Seven-Passenger Touring
Owner: Frank Cassello of Chicago, Illinois

1926 Packard Six 326 Runabout
Owner: Art Kenniff of Southold, New York

Packard model designations of the early Classic Era perplex collectors today, and probably did Packard owners then. This resulted from the introduction of the new six-cylinder Packard in 1922 (the 126/133) followed in 1923 by the eight (136/143); each year thereafter model numbers were raised by a hundred which meant that the six and eight never marched to the marketplace in step. The last two digits of the model designation were easy to understand, however; they represented wheelbase length.

The 126-inch wheelbase of Art Kenniff's Six 326 Runabout makes it among the smallest Packard Classics. April 26th, 1926 was the date that Boston Packard delivered this car, complete with the new chassis lubrication system invented by Joseph Bijur which other manufacturers would soon find worthy as well. "I have a special liking for the Packard Runabout of 1925-1929," says Art. "The styling in my opinion is the best of the early Classics."

Frank Cassello has owned his Eight 243 for almost two decades. Originally purchased from Packard's Michigan Avenue showroom for $3,850, the car was sold by its first owner immediately following the stock market crash. The new owner—for $250.00—was Wilbur Irwin, a back alley mechanic, who drove the car from 1929 until 1941 when rationing forced it onto blocks. "Getting only two gallons of gas a week," as Frank says, "Mr. Irwin could just about warm the engine on that big eight." In 1971, after considerable pestering, Frank was able to purchase the Packard: "When I got to the garage, Mr. Irwin was removing all the junk he had stored in her. It was then that I took a good look and saw what was missing . . . He said he had been in the process of restoration and had misplaced a lot of parts." Three years and one frazzled wife later, Frank had everything together. All the work, except for paint, he did himself.

The Third Series Six and Second Series Eight enjoyed a long model run: February of 1925 through July of 1926. Production figures were: Eight 236, 2,794; Eight 243, 5,118; Six 326, 24,688; Six 333, 15,690. Disc wheels and balloon tires were standard. Bijur was a super new idea, the Skinner Oil Rectifier was not; it would be dropped by 1927, as would the Fuelizer that was a vestige of Twin Six days. Vis-à-vis the former 424-cubic-inch 90 hp twelve which had been discontinued in 1923, the

Six 326/333 displaced 288.6 cubic inches and developed 60 hp; the figures for the Eight 236/243 were 357.8 and 85. And better was to come.

Aluminum pistons, turbo-head combustion chamber and revised manifolding made a phenomenally peppier performer of Packard's six in 1927. With no change in displacement, horsepower shot up to 81. (Boring out and the same refinements made for a horsepower increase to 109 for the 384.8-cubic-inch eight.) The extra power appeals to Warren Hoye, of course, who has owned his Six 426 Roadster for over a decade. But more appealing to him is its Dietrich body. Readily apparent custom features include the three hood louver doors and 23-inch wire wheels. Packard had gone custom in a big way during the spring of 1926 with a new catalogue offering "Original Creations by Master Designers." It was the beginning of a glorious age. Sales for 1927 were salutary: Six 426/433, 14,401 and 10,934; Eight 336/343, 1,245 and 3,241.

1927 Packard Six 426 Roadster, Dietrich

Owner: Warren J. Hoye of New Castle, Pennsylvania

1928 Packard Eight 443 Phaeton   *Owner: William P. Burchett of Brea, California*

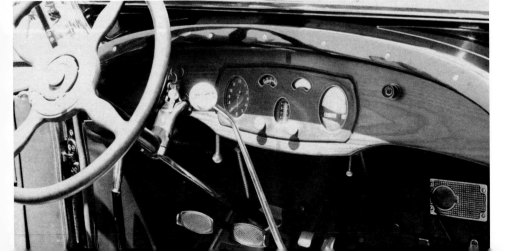

Nineteen twenty-eight was Packard's last year for drum cowl and headlights, the moto-meter and primer cups on the engine. The 443's engine was mounted on rubber shocks and featured a dual coil Delco Remy ignition system. The Fourth Series Eight represented the only instance in which Packard offered frames in color, any paint scheme desired, sidemounts and trunk rack at no additional cost. And it saw the first production use of vent doors replacing louvers on the side of the hood, this feature introduced on the 443 to distinguish it from the smaller Packard Six. At $5000+, the highest priced 443 was nearly twice that of the highest-priced Six. Comparative sales figures were: 7,800 for the 443; 28,336 for the Six 526, 13,414 for the Six 533.

"The 443 is rare, elegant, always looks aristocratic whether in motion or parked and exudes being a car of the 'rich and famous'," says Bill Burchett of his Eight Phaeton. "The seats are very comfortable and the handling characteristics are excellent for a 1928 automobile, making it a pure pleasure to drive." Bill should know. He has put thousands of miles on this Packard.

1928 Packard Eight 443 Phaeton   Owner: Del Beyer of Hartford, Wisconsin

Equally well driven in the nearly quarter of a century that he has owned it is Del Beyer's 443 Phaeton.

Bob Turnquist's 443 was delivered new on March 13th, 1928 to Winfred Woods, an investment banker who used it only in the summertime and in 1942 presented it to fellow stockbroker Skew Smith for use as a station commuter. Bob acquired the car in 1946: "It has shared with me my entire life. During my college days at Rutgers, it went to football games and fraternity parties. Following graduation, I drove the car to work on Saturdays. I took it on dates and later to meets. The only time it would not run was the day I wanted to use it for my wedding. The next day it started and ran fine." And has ever since.

1928 Packard Eight 443 Phaeton   *Owner Robert E. Turnquist of Morristown, New Jersey*

Sam Roosendaal's 443 Convertible Coupe was one of five Dietrich designs in Packard's 1928 custom coachwork catalogue. Dietrich, Inc. would become a design consultant to Packard later that year. Sam purchased the car from the Rollie Hunter estate ten years ago. The polished aluminum crankcase is original to the car, as is the windshield frame, door handles and running board trim of chrome-plated brass. The doors and quarter panels are aluminum; redoing the interior required 10½ hides of leather. "This vehicle loves to run at approximately 55-65 mph," says Sam, "and with the roll-up windows there is no interference from the wind."

1928 Packard Eight 443 Convertible Coupe, Dietrich
Owner: Sam Roosendaal of Vernon, British Columbia

1928 Packard Eight 443 All-Weather Cabriolet, Rollston
Owner: Tom Kerr of Bethlehem, Pennsylvania

"Town cars speak to me," says Tom Kerr. "They breathe history, an aura of elegance, an era that's gone forever." His All-Weather Cabriolet was one of two Rollston town cars offered by Packard in its 1928 custom catalogue. That five were available by Dietrich and two by Holbrook indicates how avidly Packard courted the carriage trade. The original driver of this town car was James Gudmundsen. His boss was Cornelius Kelley, president of the Anaconda Copper Mining Company. Weekdays Gudmundsen chauffeured Con Kelley from his Fifth Avenue apartment to his Wall Street office, weekends to his Long Island estate. The Packard was in the Kelley garage when the Copper King died in 1957. Tom has owned it since 1973. His daughter Karin plans to travel to her wedding in the car, as did several of the Kelley daughters a half-century ago.

1928 Packard Six 526 Five-Passenger Sedan

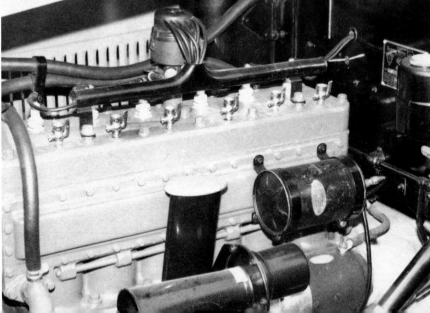

The Woods' 526 Sedan was sold new from the Earle C. Anthony showroom in Oakland, California. Its delivery date of December 22nd, 1927 leads Greg to believe it was someone's Christmas present. A standard 526 sedan was priced at $2,285 that year, but the original purchaser of this car elected to have the extra-cost features of cowl lights and twin sidemounts. The 526 represented the end of a long and successful run for Packard. In 1929 the company would move to eight-cylinder cars throughout its model line-up. This 526 Sedan has been in the Wood family since the early 1960's when it was acquired from a wealthy Mill City, Oregon farmer by Greg's father, Dr. G. B. Wood. In 1975 Greg purchased the car from him. Its restoration required six years because, as Greg says, ''before the car was touched, I read books, looked at photos and cars, talked to people and just plain thought about what I was about to undertake.'' Greg did his homework well.

1928 Packard Six 533 Phaeton, George Sprankle
Owner: Al Copsetta of Lindenwood, New Jersey

Although the coachbuilt body styles in Packard's 1928 custom catalogue were available on the 133-inch Six wheelbase, most Packard customers opted for the eight-cylinder 443. Not George Sprankle, but then he would be designing his own car anyway. Well known for his work in custom boats and for the railroad—he had invented the railway crossing signal in 1909—Sprankle spent two years building this Packard as his answer to European styling which he regarded as superior to American. Most of the car is aluminum, and everything on the car was lowered, with the floor submerged into the frame. The windows in the header bar allowed the driver to see traffic lights easily. The stoneguard preceded Packard's use of this feature by a year. George Sprankle owned and exhibited his Packard for over two decades, then it was sold and dropped from sight. After acquiring the car in the mid-1970's, Al Copsetta traced it back to its designer, then in his late eighties, who was surprised that it remained in existence. ''This car was well ahead of its time,'' comments Al. ''Once I had a 533 Touring and it looked like a covered wagon comparatively.''

1929 Packard Speedster Eight 626 Runabout
Owner: Henry Ford Museum & Greenfield Village, Dearborn, Michigan

All Packards for 1929 carried eight-cylinder engines and Sixth Series designations, the last two digits continuing to indicate wheelbase. The Standard Eight 626 and 633 were built in 26,070 and 17,060 examples respectively. And approximately 70 Speedster 626 versions were produced as well.

The Speedster was Packard's first high-performance car of the Classic Era. Just putting the big eight engine of the 640/645 in the small eight chassis would have resulted in a faster Packard than the norm. But chief engineer Jesse Vincent and crew conjured a lot more: a high-lift camshaft, high compression head, metric plugs, high speed vacuum pump and fine tuning for 130 hp (twenty-five more than the 640/645).

At first glance, the Speedster looks like any other 1929 Packard roadster, but closer examination reveals a longer hood vis-à-vis the rear deck. The weight differential of the car overall was 455 pounds (3830 pounds versus the 640 Runabout's 4285). All this made for a hot automobile.

Emil Fikar, the original owner of the Henry Ford Museum's 626 Speedster, insisted on a speed

1929 Packard Custom Eight 640 Seven-Passenger Touring
Owner: R. S. Daryman of York, Pennsylvania

capability of 100 mph before purchase. Unwilling to take the factory's word for it, he travelled from Chicago to Detroit to test the car for himself. Satisfied, he accepted delivery on October 10th, 1928. Base price of the Speedster Runabout was $5,000, to which Fikar added $250 for chrome-plated wire wheels and $10 for the DeLuxe goddess of speed hood ornament.

Most probably among the reasons Speedster 626 sales were so few was that the company didn't promote this new Packard much. But then this same benign neglect would be given the successor Speedster 734.

―――――――

Packard 640 Custom Eight (9,081 units built) and 645 DeLuxe Eight (2,061 units) production models for 1929 were augmented by the ''Individual Custom Line'' featuring body designs from several coachbuilders and making a misnomer of the ''Custom'' designation for the production 640. No one seemed to mind. The 640/645 engine remained the 348.8-cubic-inch unit. Throughout the Packard line-up, parabolic headlamps replaced the former drum type, a dash-mounted temperature gauge replaced the moto-meter, and all brightwork formerly painted was now chrome-plated.

But for most purchasers the changes didn't matter so much as the simple fact that the car was a Packard. R. S. Daryman has the original bill of sale for his 640 Seven-Passenger Touring whose first owner was Mrs. Minnie Richards of Brooklyn, New York: ''It's interesting to note that people were willing to pay quite a premium for the Packard name. Mrs. Richards was allowed a thousand dollar trade-in on her Packard Sport Phaeton with motor no. 209254, which made it a Second Series Eight 1925 model selling new for $3,750. In four years depreciation amounted to about $687.00 per year or the equivalent of a medium-priced car at the time.'' Although disc wheels remained standard, Mrs. Richards chose to spend an extra $80.00 for wire wheels, plus another $383.50 for such other accessories as step-plates, trunk, tire mirrors, bugle horn and ''giant bumpers,'' bringing the total purchase price of her Packard to nearly $4,000.

The base price for John Paulson's 645 Dietrich Sport Phaeton was $4,935.00. ''A fun car,'' says John who has owned this Packard for twenty-eight years. ''Everybody always has a big smile when I drive by.''

1929 Packard DeLuxe Eight 645 Sport Phaeton, Dietrich
Owner: John R. Paulson of Golden Valley, Minnesota

1929 Packard DeLuxe Eight 645 Phaeton, Dietrich   Owners: Earl & Blanche White of Tucson, Arizona   Photos: Steinberg

Earl White has owned his 645 Dietrich since 1959 and tells a marvelous story of its acquisition: "Two men home on leave from the Air Force; one lived in Wilcox, Arizona, the other in Chicago. The man in Chicago found this car but was broke, so he called his friend in Wilcox to send him $100 to buy a 1929 Packard sitting on blocks with 6,000 miles on it. The guy in Wilcox told him to get out of jail the best way he could. Finally convinced that his friend on the phone hadn't been arrested for drinking, he went to Western Union, sent the hundred dollars and hitched a ride on an Air Force plane to Chicago. After purchasing a new battery and filling up with gasoline, the pair left in the Packard for California. In Tulsa, Oklahoma they ran into a snowstorm and almost froze since the car had no side curtains." What the Packard had continues to fascinate Earl: such nice touches as "the solid German silver arm rest hinges, the brass extrusions on the running board with chrome-plated mitered corners, the chrome-plated brass windshield frames—and no pot metal anywhere."

362

1929 Packard DeLuxe Eight 645 Roadster, Dietrich
Owner: Tom Kerr of Bethlehem, Pennsylvania   Photo: K. Karger

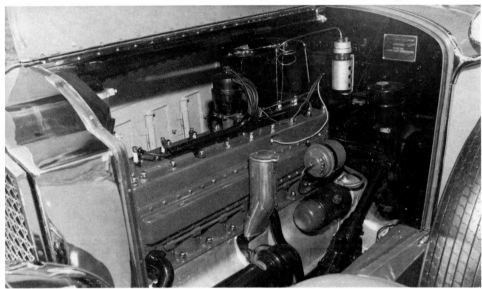

With an original price tag of $4,585 and a shipping weight of 4,785 pounds, the 645 Dietrich Roadster (Packard preferred ''Runabout'' for the same body style) was less than a dollar a pound. What an incredible bargain that would be today. Only a handful of these cars remain in existence. Tom Kerr saw his at Hershey in 1987 and couldn't resist. Bob Fischer has owned his since 1959 when he purchased it from Wes Hartman of Green Bay, Wisconsin. It was not a pretty sight at the time. Says Bob: ''Mr. Hartman owned a lumberyard and the Packard had apparently been used as a pick-up truck. The entire rumble assembly, including the lid, was missing and the fenders were chewed away by chains. Lumps of coal and wood were also found in the rumble area. . . . Since restoration in 1962, we've driven the car about 20,000 miles. Most of the interesting experiences in this vehicle surround the weather, as can well be imagined. The rumble seat and the single windshield wiper are not well suited to heavy rain.'' But such inconvenience scarcely matters to an owner who revels in a Packard that he regards as ''a beautifully proportioned automobile . . . and one of the most pleasing and sporty body styles of that era.''

1929 Packard DeLuxe Eight 645 Roadster, Dietrich (engine above)   *Owner: Robert N. Fischer of Evansville, Indiana*

The original owner of the Indy Museum 645 Packard was famed racing aviator Roscoe Turner. Its Holbrook body has no exterior hardware (door controls are inside), and Turner further personalized the car with a miniature airplane as the radiator mascot. He also returned the Packard in subsequent years for updating of headlights, radiator shell and spring-loaded bumpers as featured on twelve-cylinder models. Following his retirement from air racing, Roscoe Turner made his home in Indianapolis and devoted time to furthering general interest in aviation. Frequently addressing chambers of commerce dinners in small cities to urge establishment of local airports, he would fly to the outskirts of town, having sent his Packard ahead to park at the end of a selected field and land his plane using the illumination from the car's headlights. In 1973 the Indianapolis museum acquired the car from Roscoe Turner's widow.

1929 Packard DeLuxe Eight 645 Sport Phaeton, Holbrook
Owner: Indianapolis Motor Speedway Hall of Fame Museum

Of the 36,363 Packards produced in the Seventh Series, 15,731 or nearly half were the 726 Sedan. At $2,375 the 726 was the least expensive Packard in the line, although many purchasers opted for such extra-cost accessories as the artillery wood wheels, sidemounts, fender lights and trunk rack as seen on both Ben Lalomia's and John Chipurn's cars. "I like sedans and I like wood wheels," comments John.

This was the last year for the vacuum tank and chassis lubricator operated by a handle under the dash. The transmission was a four-speed with an extra low gear. To accommodate the redesigned water pump with dual fan belts, the chassis was lengthened to 127½ inches. John has owned his 726 for twelve years. Ben purchased his in 1955 from its first owner for $80.00. Both remark about what an easy car to drive the 726 is.

1930 Packard Standard Eight 726 Five-Passenger Sedan   *Owner: John Chipurn of East Detroit, Michigan*

1930 Packard Standard Eight 726 Five-Passenger Sedan   *Owner: Ben Lalomia of Williamsville, New York*

The Wheelers have owned their 726 since 1971 and have driven it almost 10,000 miles. The first thousand were the hardest: ''Immediately after the engine was rebuilt, we drove the car to the Grand Classic in Monterey (four hundred miles from our home). Halfway up the hill just north of San Luis Obispo, it overheated. What a place to have to stop, but stop we did and the water really boiled. Since this was my first trip of any distance with an old car, I had neglected to take along water. Not very astute! Within minutes a CCCA member also on his way to the Grand Classic stopped and donated four gallons of H_2O and stayed with me until I was 'over the hill.' Each time I drive that hill I recall this adventure. . . . The next year we were ready for another challenge: Silverado, five hundred miles each way and with four gallons of water in the trunk. However, the water pump started leaking and I had to stop every fifty miles, and each time it took more water. By the time we reached Salinas, the water pump nut was as tight as possible, the water was pouring out and my wife's patience had run out. Behold!

Another CCCA member saw us and came to our rescue: George Vernon Russell with his open Bentley and complete tool chest including water pump packing. We made it to Silverado and back to Claremont with no problem other than a howling generator and exasperated wife. The generator was replaced—still have the same wife, and a second-place trophy for our efforts.'' The many miles driven by the Wheelers since include a dozen trips for the weddings of family and friends—and the Packard has always made it to the church on time.

1930 Packard Standard Eight 726 Five-Passenger Sedan
Owners: Barbara & Don Wheeler of Claremont, California

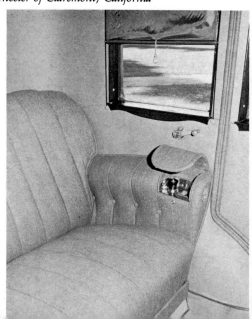

Like the 726, the 733 chassis was longer by an inch-and-a-half (134½ inches). Unlike the 726 which was available only as a five-passenger sedan, the 733 was offered in a variety of body styles. Moreover, as exemplified by the Chipurn and Fitz cars, with options the Standard 733 could be transformed into a DeLuxe model. On Wallace & Mary Lee Fitz's Packard, these accessories included wind-wings, Trippe lights, fender lamps, sidemounts with chrome covers and attached mirrors, and a trunk rack.

1930 Packard Eight DeLuxe 733 Five-Passenger Coupe   *Owners: Wallace & Mary Lee Fitz of Fraser, Michigan*

1930 Packard Eight DeLuxe 733 Five-Passenger Sedan   *Owner: John Chipurn of East Detroit, Michigan*

The original bill of sale which John Chipurn has for his car reveals its purchase from Packard Washington by Morton O. Cooper of the U.S. Department of Agriculture. DeLuxe equipment added $325 to the Standard version's $2,675. ''If I could have only one Classic car,'' says John, ''this would be it.''

The open fenders and sun visor are two styling details which Ray and Kathy Fairfield find especially appealing about their 733.

A former owner added the luggage trunk, stoneguard and ''Daphne at the well'' mascot to the 733 Club Sedan which the Halbauers acquired mainly because of its outstanding

1930 Packard Eight DeLuxe 733 Five-Passenger Coupe   *Owners: Ray & Kathy Fairfield of Morgan Hill, California*

1930 Packard Standard Eight 733 Club Sedan   *Owners: Ronald & Sonja Halbauer of Lawrenceburg, Indiana*   *Photo: John Sutton*

condition as an essentially original car. ''All the instruments work including the lighters,'' says Sonja. ''The car is exercised a few hundred miles each year adding to its present 38,000 miles. The only time the

Packard was trailered it considered that an insult for the engine refused to turn over when unloaded and had to have a quick jump start.''

The 733 Convertible Coupe which W. Robert Vitz acquired in 1974 was

originally sold in Hollywood but its star had lost considerable luster years later when it served as a tow truck near Sacramento. The ''total disaster of its condition,'' as Bob relates, required a virtual resurrection.

1930 Packard Standard Eight 733 Convertible Coupe   *Owner: W. Robert Vitz of Palm Desert, California*   *Photo: Waldon*

The 734 Speedster was Packard's answer to the high-performance sporty automobiles produced by Stutz and Cord Corporation as well as an oblique rebuttal to Cadillac's recently-introduced V-16. Basically, this new car was a highly modified Standard Eight 733 chassis into which had been stuffed an equally modified DeLuxe Eight engine which with high-compression head delivered 145 hp at 3400 rpm and coupled with 3.3 differential provided a Packard capable of better than 100 mph. Lesser states of tune were available so Speedster purchasers had a choice of hot, hotter and hottest.

Choosing the last named was industrialist S. Northrup Castle of Honolulu, the original owner of the Vaccaro Speedster Runabout. "He pursued an engineering career which I think accounts for his interest in high-performance automobiles," comments Bill. "He loved Packards but also kept a Model A Duesenberg. Honoluluans were accustomed to seeing Mr. Castle in his boattail Packard Speedster. He used the 734 until he sold it in 1957." Bill purchased the car six years ago from the Oborne collection. "Driving this 734 is the most rewarding experience," he says. "It handles like a European sports car of the 1930's—steering, braking and acceleration."

"Tremendous performance and handling with a very rare body," enthuses John Mozart whose Speedster has also been driven extensively. "This was probably one of the first introductions of a quasi sports car on a relatively large American chassis with an engine that was modified by the factory."

Argentina was whence the Carroll boattail 734 was recovered years ago. Writing about it for this book prior to his tragic death, Rick said: "The 734 Speedster has the best proportions of any car I have ever owned. Novice or expert alike immediately recognize this is what Classic cars are all about. The body design with its staggered seating was a significant styling venture for Packard." Rick bought the car in pieces: "My son who was with me saw the look of doubt in my eyes. He was barely in his teens but in a manner of wise old Mother Hen, he put his arm around my shoulder and said, 'Don't worry, Dad, you'll get it back together'." And very nicely.

1930 Packard Speedster 734 Runabout
Owners: William & Helen Vaccaro of Bedminster, New Jersey

1930 Packard Speedster 734 Runabout
Owner: John Mozart of Palo Alto, California

1930 Packard Speedster 734 Runabout
Owner: Rick Carroll of Jensen Beach, Florida

1930 Packard Speedster 734 Phaeton

Owner: R. Bruce Grinager of Pittsburgh, Pennsylvania

1930 Packard Speedster 734 Phaeton   Owner: George K. Jepson of Hillsdale, New Jersey

About the Speedster Series, Bruce Grinager comments: ''The most powerful big eight engine Packard had ever used is fed by the rare two-barrel Detroit Lubricator carburetor. The exhaust manifold and the brake drums are finned for heat dissipation, and the wheels have retainers on the lock rings for high speed safety. Probably 118 Speedsters were built in five body styles and likely thirty-two were phaetons of which only five are known to remain. It was sleek to minimize 'head resistance' so the car is four inches narrower than the Packard norm and has probably the smallest windshield the company ever used. The body accent moulding does not extend across the top of the hood side but is about two inches lower than non-734's since the door

tops are that much lower. Because of the overall lowering of the car by at least four inches, parking a 734 next to some of its contemporaries has led people to suspect that the top has been cut down. The long hood—fully six feet from radiator to end of cowl—is further emphasized by the comparatively short 134½-inch wheelbase.'' Bruce has owned his Speedster Phaeton since 1960 and describes it as ''a good combination of looker and driver, great for Pennsylvania since it climbs hills well and competes nicely on turnpikes.''

Agreeing with that is George Jepson who has driven his Speedster Phaeton on at least ten CARavans and acclaims it ''a very happy, very fast road car that has been one of the family for over thirty years.''

Speedster Phaeton owners are rather proud of the fact that not one of the handful remaining extant has changed hands for over a quarter of a century. Witness Guy Slaughter who was in uniform with the Navy Department in Washington when he bought his for $450 on December 18th, 1945. The car was nicknamed Pepalonious: ''We drove him the length and breadth of the land before moving to Hawaii in 1947, the Packard following in the hold of a Navy transport ship. A family and driving-to-work car until the early fifties, Pepalonious became more of a hobby thereafter and was totally restored in the late sixties.'' And the car has become a movie star since, appearing in *Blood & Orchids* and the television series *Magnum P.I.*

1930 Packard Speedster 734 Phaeton   Owner: Guy Slaughter of Aiea, Hawaii   Photo: Brodie Spencer

Wheelbases remained the same on the big Packards for 1930, but fender-mounted parking lamps were new and so was the four-speed transmission which Margaret Dunning reports as "heavenly" in third in her 740 Roadster. Dual-mounted spares were standard on the 745 and an option on the 740 which their presence on both the Harguindeguy and Dunning cars would indicate was a popular choice. "I just love the body style," says Jacques, a sentiment echoed by Margaret: "With its sleek body lines, it's a graceful vehicle. And it's powerful, very quick to accelerate."

1930 Packard Custom Eight 740 Roadster
Owner: Margaret Dunning of Plymouth, Michigan

Like all Packards in the Seventh Series, the 745 featured a Detroit Lubricator updraft carburetor. Mid-year a vacuum booster pump was added on the big eights. All windows were given non-shatter laminated glass, and there were two glove compartments, one on each side of the dash. Both steering wheel and driver's seat were adjustable. Brakes remained mechanical, transmission non-synchro. Disc wheels were still standard, though many owners availed themselves of the optional wire or artillery types.

Bill Lassiter finds that the long 145½-inch wheelbase of his 745 dual cowl Sport Phaeton makes for a smooth riding and good handling car.

The top mechanism of chrome and curved oak on Ken Kost's Seven-Passenger Touring says "majestic" to him and so does the "incredible rear compartment space" even with two folding rear seats. The Kost car is a relatively recent acquisition which at this writing its new owner says he is "not secure in driving anywhere except around home!"

1930 Packard Custom Eight 740 Roadster
Owners: Jacques & Betty Harguindeguy of Walnut Creek, California

1930 Packard DeLuxe Eight 745 Sport Phaeton   *Owner: W. G. Lassiter, Jr. of West Palm Beach, Florida*

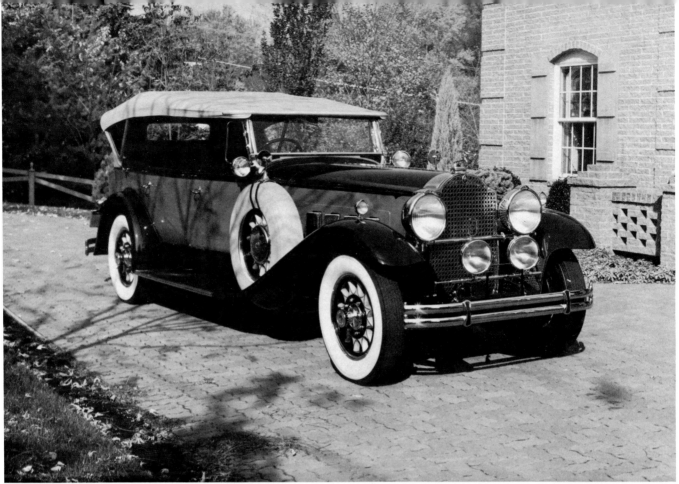

1930 Packard DeLuxe Eight 745 Seven-Passenger Touring　　　　*Owner: Kenneth R. Kost, M.D. of Kittanning, Pennsylvania*

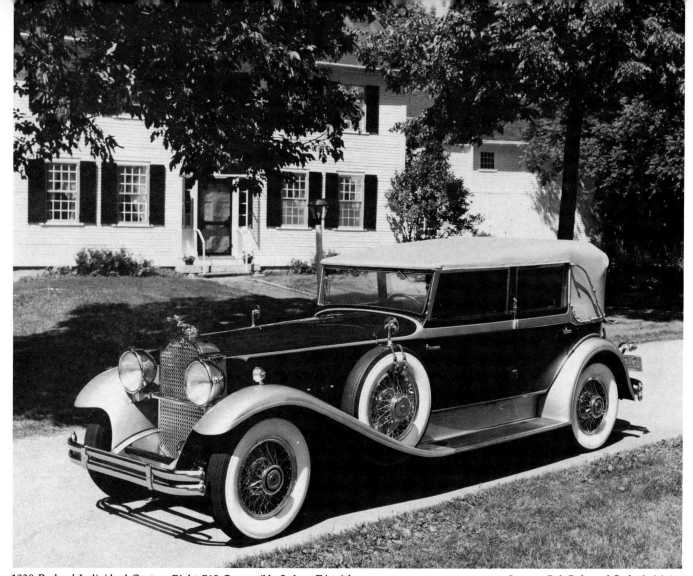

1930 Packard Individual Custom Eight 745 Convertible Sedan, Dietrich

Owner: Bob Bahre of Oxford, Maine

Fifteen coachbuilt cars were offered in Packard's 1930 Individual Custom catalogue: six by LeBaron, five by Brewster, two each by Rollston and Dietrich. Convertible Sedans were available only in the Individual Custom line, exemplified here by Bob Bahre's Dietrich which he has owned for sixteen years, and the Brewsters which have been in the Vaccaro and Darling garages for over two and three decades respectively. The Dietrich had been offered in '29, the Brewster was a brand-new entry for 1930; not until 1932 would a convertible sedan become a Packard production model.

"One of the interesting features of Brewster was its trimming of the interior in a very attractive broadcloth and leather combination," says Bill Vaccaro. "Another interesting fact was that Brewster painted the dashboard to match body color on some or all of its Packard line of cars for 1930, rather than following the Packard practice of woodgraining the dash. I purchased the Brewster in

basket-case form. It took ten years to restore but was well worth the effort." Bill's and Andrew Darling's are the only two 745 Brewster Convertible Sedans known to exist.

Joseph Mollo's LeBaron Town Car is one of perhaps two remaining extant. Unlike Bill who bought a car needing everything, Joe was attracted to his LeBaron because of what it

didn't need: "The car was in excellent original condition with only 32,518 miles, the excellence extending to its paint, interior and mechanics." The original owner of the Mollo Packard was the Lindsay family of the Sibley, Lindsay, Curr Company of Rochester, one of the oldest and largest department stores in Upstate New York.

1930 Packard Individual Custom Eight 745 Convertible Sedan, Brewster
Owner: Andrew D. Darling of Edina, Minnesota

1930 Packard Individual Custom Eight 745 Convertible Sedan, Brewster
Owners: William & Helen Vaccaro of Bedminster, New Jersey

1930 Packard Individual Custom Eight 745 All-Weather Town Car, LeBaron   *Owner: Joseph A. Mollo of Rochester, New York*

"The move was on in 1930 to make driving more comfortable and pleasing to the opposite sex," comments Bob Fischer. "Therefore carpeting, previously only in the rear, was added in the front compartment, the driver's seat and sun visors were now adjustable, and a map light was added to the dash." Bob purchased his 745 Touring in April of 1958 sight unseen because his wife was eight months pregnant and he had to move fast. Subsequently the three Fischer children were practically raised in the back seat: "This Touring is a wonderful handler and loves to go!" Bob has acceded to the car's desire, over 55,000 miles to date: "A book could be written on the experiences we have had in this car, some good, and some not so good. On one occasion the engine caught fire in the hills of North Carolina. A few mountaineers were whittling in front of a little country store watching the whole thing. I don't think they missed a stroke during the ordeal. Fortunately, the only casualties were my shirt and my Bic pen. . . . Overall, this car has been great fun for the family. We have driven to the Atlantic Ocean four times. It is an exhilarating feeling to look over the long majestic hood topping a mountain as the sun is coming up, especially when the car's not vaporlocking. Ahh, this must be heaven! But, we always carry wooden clothespins in the glove compartment just in case. I'm not sure this helps, but it doesn't hurt."

*1930 Packard
DeLuxe Eight
745 Touring*

*Owner:
Robert N. Fischer
of Evansville, Indiana*

378

1931 Packard Standard Eight 833 Roadster

Owner: George E. Staley of Stamford, Connecticut

More power, fewer cars. That in essence was Packard in 1931. With engineering refinements adopted from the 734 Speedster, the Standard Eight now developed 100 hp (from 90), the DeLuxe Eight was up to 120 (from 106). A Stewart Warner fuel pump replaced the former vacuum tank, and the "pull daily" routine for the lubrication system was eliminated as the Bijur became a vacuum-operated automatic. Chassis suspension was greatly improved with wider springs and Delco-Lovejoy shock absorbers. Hubcaps were larger, fenders deeper, running boards thicker. The Packard remained lovely to behold—everywhere.

"The porcelain coated exhaust and intake manifolds contrasted with the aluminum crankcase make for a look under the hood as interesting as the outside," says George Staley of his 833 Roadster. Of the nearly fifty historic cars in the Staley collection, he likes his 1931 Packard best: "The engine has so much low-speed torque it never requires downshifting on today's roads."

The production figures tell their own story; the 6,096 Packard 833's built represented less than half the figure for the 733. Among them was Guy Slaughter's Club Sedan, which was delivered June 10th, 1931 to Honolulu through Packard's Export

Division. Hawaii was then a territory, of course, and regarded as a "foreign country" by Packard. The original owner was the Rev. Seichi Kawamoto, from whom Guy bought the car in 1959. The price was the same $450 that Guy had paid for his Speedster Phaeton; he nicknamed this car Daphne and, like brother 734 Pepalonious, she has since become a movie star in Hawaii. Unlike George Staley, Guy uses his clutch foot frequently when behind Daphne's steering wheel: "She's a heavy car for her Standard Eight motor and really needs her four-speed gearbox on the steep hills in our neighborhood."

1931 Packard Standard Eight 833 Club Sedan   Owner: Guy Slaughter of Aiea, Hawaii   Photo: Brodie Spencer

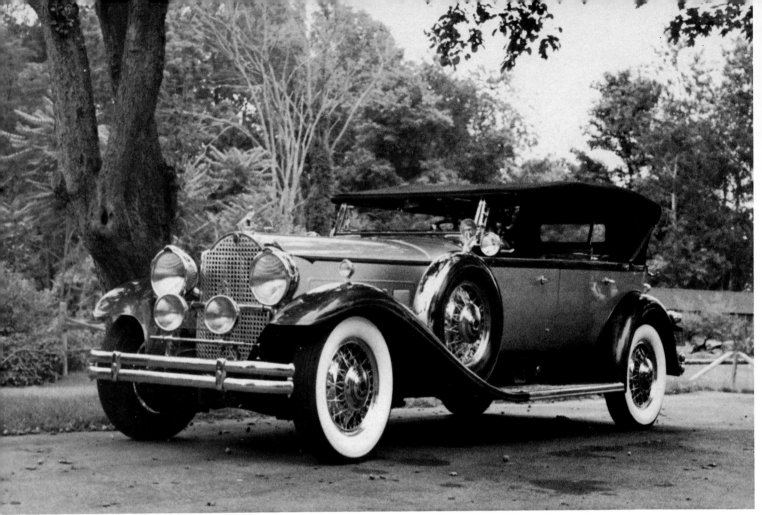

1931 Packard DeLuxe Eight 840 Sport Phaeton
Owner: Joseph Morgan of Lynnfield, Massachusetts

1931 Packard DeLuxe Eight 840 Sport Phaeton
Owners: Phil & Carol Bray of Grosse Ile, Michigan

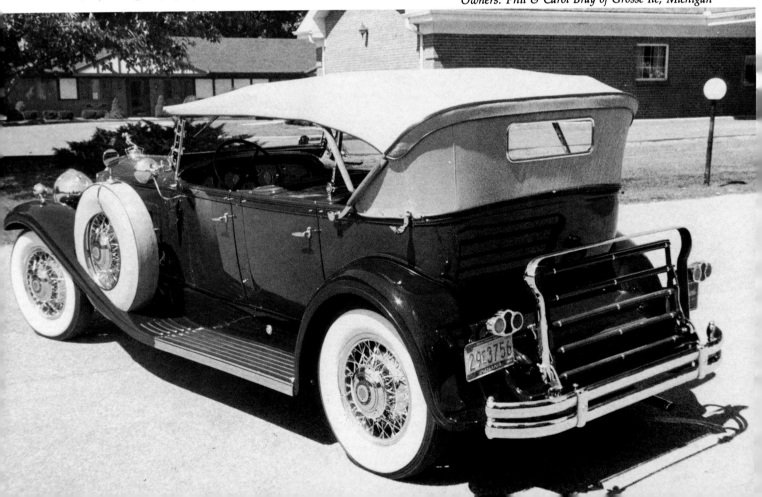

More devastating than the 833's production decrease was the veritable plummeting of the 840: the 2,035 sold was a third that of the 740. The long-misnomered Custom designation was dropped in 1931; the 840, like its larger 845 companion model, was now called DeLuxe. The long sweeping fenders of the 745 were adopted on both 840 and 845 but not the 745's long hood which resulted in the car doors infringing the fender area and creating the possibility of a fender being trod upon, a situation Packard neatly solved with the addition of six chrome strips.

Dual cowl 840 Sport Phaeton production totalled ninety-seven; no more than twenty remain extant. Joseph Morgan's car was originally delivered in Los Angeles; to whom he knows not, but obviously the new owner had suffered little following the stock market crash because the car was fully optioned. "It is a bit 'trucky' around town," he says, "but is great on the highway."

Phil and Carol Bray's dual cowl was barn stored from the early fifties until their acquisition in 1985. "It was totally original," says Phil, "unrusted and undented, the dual cowl hardware in place and only the dual cowl lid missing. The odometer registered 47,000 miles. We totally dismantled the car and lovingly returned every piece to showroom condition."

———

In David Schroeder's fine phrase, America was "standing in the foyer of the Great Depression" as the Eighth Series Packards were introduced. Over the next year luxury car sales would drop from ten percent to two percent of the automobile industry total. For the first time, the long-wheelbase Packard was not part of the Individual Custom line; just two production body styles were offered—sedan and limousine, each a seven-passenger car. The Schroeder 845 Sedan was originally delivered in October of 1930 and possibly to someone in show business since numerous makeup containers were discovered during restoration. At $4,150 the new owner enjoyed a real bargain; the same car the previous year had been priced over a thousand dollars more. David Schroeder regards the Packard 845 as too long overlooked by historians and hobbyists: "The car makes a striking formal presentation with understated but undeniable elegance. The 145½-inch wheelbase provides an equally elegant ride."

The original owner of Joseph

1931 Packard DeLuxe Eight 845 Seven-Passenger Sedan
Owner: Joseph E. Peters of Baltimore, Maryland

Peters' 845 Sedan is most definitely known: "The car was purchased new in 1931 for my father, H. Edwin Peters, upon his graduation from Johns Hopkins University. It has remained in the family since that time. The wood spoke wheels had been specially ordered by my grandfather. My father used the car actively through the late 1950's. His children grew up in the car. We used to refer to it as 'The Queen Mary'."

1931 Packard DeLuxe Eight 845 Seven-Passenger Sedan
Owner: David H. Schroeder of Kankakee, Illinois

1931 Packard Individual Custom Eight 840 Convertible Victoria, Dietrich
Owner: Edward John Blend II of Irwin, Pennsylvania

Nine "Individual Custom Cars" were offered in Packard's 1931 folio, seven of them carrying the "Custom Made by Packard" designation, two with Dietrich plates. Both the Dietrich Convertible Sedan and Convertible Victoria are shown here. Each of them was among the last cars built under Raymond Dietrich's personal supervision before he left his namesake company. And each was a show car.

Bob Turnquist's Convertible Sedan was exhibited at the New York Automobile Salon at the Commodore Hotel in December 1930. Following service by New York Packard, it was delivered to its purchaser on January 2nd, 1931. Ownership history is unknown from that date until 1947 when Bob discovered the car on a used truck lot in Plainfield, New Jersey. Its latterday life had not been felicitous. During World War II the Scranton (Pennsylvania) Packard dealer had sold the Dietrich to a trucking firm that specialized in fabricating tractors out of Classic formal cars by excising the rear

section of the body and adding a fifth wheel. This car was thusly used by a firm hauling coal from the collieries to the Jersey City waterfront. "It was a nightmare to restore," says Bob. Indeed, an 840 Limousine (which with freight-car steel wheels had been working on the railroad of the Pittsburgh & Shawmut) was purchased for parts. Ultimately the nightmare was over. "Convertible sedans were the epitome of styling because their low silhouette couldn't be obtained in a closed body. They were often ordered as formal cars with divider window partitions for privacy and the tops were never lowered," comments Bob. "The convertible sedan is big and roomy with luxurious lounge leather seats and hot air heaters front and rear."

Ed Blend's Convertible Victoria was also shown at the Commodore Hotel salon and a week later was exhibited at the New York Automobile Show at Grand Central Palace. Presumably that's where it was seen by Charles Schwab, the grocery store clerk who had risen to become the first

president of United States Steel, subsequently chairman of Bethlehem Steel and, at the time he bought this Packard, also the majority stockholder of the Stutz Motor Car Company. After minor alterations the car was delivered to him from the Packard showroom on Broadway in April 1931. It would be among the last assets of the Schwab estate to be sold following his death. Ed Blend has owned the car since 1951, and has driven it 60,000 miles to date: "The Convertible Victoria is a car for all seasons. Some called it a roadster, even the company alluded to that; however, it is a semi-formal car because the large blind quarter shields the back seat from staring eyes. The rumble seat had come in out of the cold. The Convertible Victoria is not a hot performer, nor was it ever intended to be, just 50 mph all day long. Charles Schwab had been an acquaintance of my father's and is still a legend in Pennsylvania. It's a privilege owning something of this great man's life and preserving it for posterity."

1931 Packard Individual Custom Eight 840 Convertible Sedan, Dietrich
Owner: Robert E. Turnquist of Morristown, New Jersey

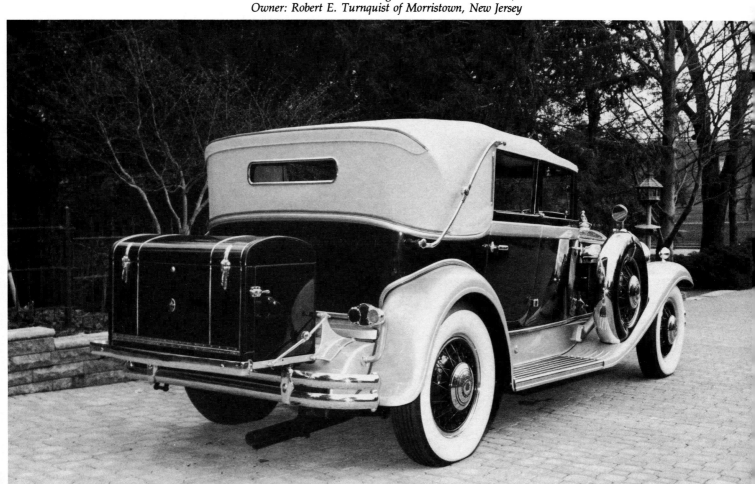

In 1931 Packard's own catalogued customs ranged from $4,000+ (833) to $5,000+ (840). That there was much of a market for cars higher priced than that seemed unlikely, but the factory made available the long-wheelbase 845 chassis to independent coachbuilders whose clients asked for it. Packard had been right. Few were requested. One is shown here. The owner for whom this LeBaron Convertible Coupe was built is not known, but its history since 1940 is—and is wonderfully told by Bob Meyer: ''The car was being used as a tow truck in King City by Walter Paine's Chevrolet garage. My father was a friend of Mr. Paine's and bought it for the same use on our ranch—to tow tractors, trucks, pick-ups, whatever needed a pull or a shove. After much use and abuse, Dad sort of fell in love with the 'Ole Packard.' Meanwhile the garage owner had purchased a truck chassis to convert into a tow truck, so a trade took place. My father gave Mr. Paine the crane that had been installed on the rear of the Packard in exchange for his installation of a trunk lid to make the Packard look like a car again. Then Dad installed a trailer hitch on the rear and had a small trailer built to pull his 1903 Mitchell in local parades or to carry

1931 Packard DeLuxe Eight 845 Convertible Coupe, LeBaron
Owner: Robert L. Meyer of King City, California

the sheriff or mayor or whichever local dignitary needed to be paraded. Nothing ever fazed 'Ole Packard' because it would always run, practically in spite of itself. Upon my return from college I tinkered with the car occasionally but it was really always Dad's. Then in the mid-sixties he gave me the pink slip to 'Ole Packard' as a birthday present. At the time I thought, 'what the hell am I going to do with this old thing?'

Secretly I had hoped that he might have given me something I could have used, like a sweater or jacket. However, Dad thought I should keep the car since it might turn out to be rather rare some day. We always pondered why we could not find a photo of a car just like ours.'' Since discovering the reason, and a full restoration, Bob has retired 'Ole Packard' from the tow circuit to the show circuit, needless to say.

1931 Packard V-12 Front Wheel Drive Prototype   Owner: Bob Bahre of Oxford, Maine

With the Ruxton and the L-29 Cord making news with front wheel drive by mid-1929 and rumors of the impending introduction of automobiles from other manufacturers with cylinders numbering more than eight, Packard launched a project to come up with a car that would offer both. ''Problems, very serious ones, have confronted our distributing organization, dealers and salesmen,'' said Packard president Alvan Macauley in April 1930 as the first sales repercussions were felt in the wake of the stock market crash. Packard registrations had fallen by over thirty percent from the first quarter of 1929. New concepts, it was thought optimistically, might sell more cars. Packard had, of course, built a twelve-cylinder automobile before, but had not previously experimented extensively with front wheel drive. Enter Cornelius Van Ranst. Tommy Milton, the retired racing driver now working as development engineer for

Packard, had suggested him to chief engineer Jesse Vincent. Van Ranst's expertise with front wheel drive had been established by his development of the Detroit Special which Milton had driven in the Indianapolis 500 in 1927—and which in turn had persuaded Errett Lobban Cord to hire Van Ranst for the team that would engineer the L-29. Following the Cord assignment, Van Ranst had left for Chrysler. Following the Packard board of directors' approval on June 25th, 1930 of the front-wheel-drive project, Van Ranst moved over to East Grand Boulevard. The plan was for a twelve-cylinder Packard in the Buick price range which, Van Ranst argued, would be possible because of the manufacturing economy of a front-drive set-up—and which promised to be a world-beater. The prototype was a paragon of ingenuity. Its 138-inch-wheelbase chassis boasted an X center frame brace with H cross section at the dropped rear axle. Hydraulic brakes

were fitted. Likewise ingenious was the Van Ranst-designed V-12 engine with vertical spark plugs. But the prototype's complicated transaxle was its Achilles heel. Its problems demanded a complete redesign; Packard elected instead to scrap the front-wheel-drive idea. With it went the plan for a multi-cylinder Packard in a Buick price-range car. Fortunately not scrapped was the front-wheel-drive prototype itself. Van Ranst recalled seeing the car being driven through the factory gates in 1935 presumably destined for the junkyard and was surprised years later when Greg and Gerry Fauth brought it to a Classic Car Club meet attended by the long-retired engineer. The front-wheel-drive prototype resided awhile in the Thompson Products Museum (forerunner of the Frederick C. Crawford Auto-Aviation Museum) in Cleveland and in Harrah's Automobile Collection in Reno. Bob Bahre acquired the car in 1982.

Packard took its Ninth Series to market early—June of 1931 instead of late summer. Production would continue into early 1933 for a markedly long sales period. The Depression, of course, was the reason. No longer did Packard designations indicate wheelbase length. At 129½ inches, the new Standard Eight 901 (which continued to be available only as a five-passenger sedan) was three inches longer than its predecessor 826. Similarly lengthened to 136½ inches was the new Standard Eight 902 available in twelve body styles. Engineering refinements were many. Horsepower was boosted to 110. The frame was a new double-drop X. Ride control, with shock absorbers adjustable from the dashboard, was standard; a front-bumper harmonic stabilizer was optional. The four-speed transmission with what Jack Hunley describes as its "extra low 'stump puller' gear" was retained until January of 1932 when a three-speed with synchromesh and vacuum clutch was adopted. The Ninth Series was the last for unskirted fenders and the headlight bar, and the first for the vee grille of the radiator and round instruments on the dash. The Standard Eight was provided the hood doors (instead of louvers) and the spear-shaped hood side moulding which had previously been reserved for the larger Packard eights.

1932 Packard Standard Eight 902 Phaeton
Owner: William A. Helling of Faribault, Minnesota

Options available were many. On the Hunley 901 Sedan, these include stoneguard, fender lights, wire wheels, sidemounts and trunk rack, pinstriping and painted window reveals, chrome-plated lock rings on the wheels, monogram, external horns and white wall tires.

Options aplenty also appear on William Helling's 902 Phaeton which he has owned and driven since 1981 and which was used as the wedding car for his daughter Lisa in 1986.

Jackson Brooks' Phaeton has been on the road for 70,000 miles since it was delivered new by the Newark (New Jersey) Packard dealer in May of 1933. Original owner Harry Dunn paid $2,850 for the car which, with its many options, was a bargain doubtless forced on the dealer by the late date of the sale.

1932 Packard Standard Eight 902 Phaeton   *Owner: Jackson Brooks of Estes Park, Colorado*

1932 Packard Standard Eight 901 Five-Passenger Sedan   Owners: Jack & Lupe Hunley of Burlington, North Carolina

1932 Packard Standard Eight 902 Phaeton   *Owner: Roger F. Pratt of New Vernon, New Jersey*   *Photo: K. Karger*

Roger Pratt's Phaeton suffered the ignominy of being gutted and turned into a wrecker by the Wampum Corners Garage in Wrentham, Massachusetts before his acquisition a quarter-century ago. "I learned the hard way that not many sedan body parts can be used on a Phaeton," he says. "Also not too many mechanical parts on 1932 Packards are interchangeable with the year before or the year after."

Fortuitously not faced with that problem was Frank Wemple who became the third owner of his 902 Five-Passenger Coupe eight years ago. Dealer accessories on this car include dual outside horns, fender lights, right-hand taillamp, deluxe radiator mascot, metal tire cover and tire cover protector, to which Frank has added Packard Trippe lights, outside rearview mirror, 7.00x19 tires (vis-à-vis the standard 6.50x19) and chrome-plated lock rings. "The Packard now has over 59,000 miles on it," he says. "In driving it I have come to appreciate that there is nothing like a well-maintained, tight, low-mileage car." The man from whom Frank bought the car informed him that its original home had been an estate in Putnam, Connecticut where it had been used by the staff to run errands for the household. "Usually one reads that a particular Classic was owned and used by a famous actor, politician or business magnate," muses Frank, "but not *servants*!" One wonders what other Classics resided in that Putnam estate garage . . .

1932 Packard Standard Eight 902 Five-Passenger Coupe   *Owner: Frank Wemple of Andover, Connecticut*   *Photo: K. Karger*

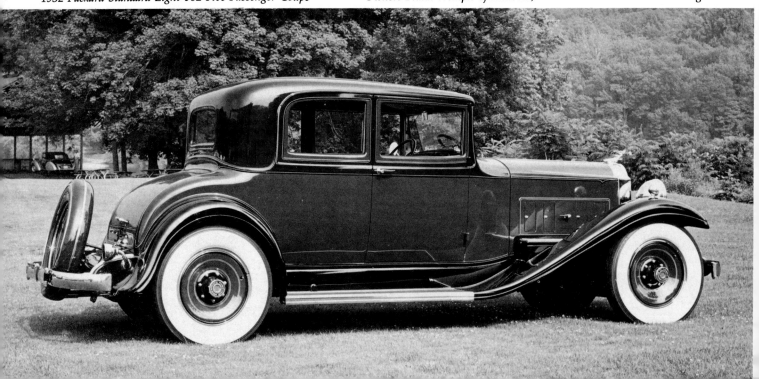

1932 Packard DeLuxe Eight 903 Sport Phaeton
Owner: N. Gene Perkins of Greenwood, Indiana   Photo: Nancy Bailey

For the 384.8-cubic-inch DeLuxe Eight, horsepower was up to 135 for 1932, and wheelbases were two inches longer at 142½ for the 903 and 147½ for the 904. Both ride control and the harmonic stabilizer were standard on the DeLuxe series, as were fender lamps and the dual trumpet horns mounted under the headlights. Like the Standard Eight, these cars were introduced with the four-speed transmission which was changed to a synchro three-speed with vacuum clutch in January of 1932. Standard Eight 901/902 sales were 7,659 cars; 1,655 DeLuxe Eight 903/904 Packards were sold.

Of these about twenty were the dual-cowl Sport Phaeton, of which Don Sears' car which he acquired from the Murdo, South Dakota museum ten years ago is body No. 16.

It was thirty years ago that Gene Perkins found his Sport Phaeton in the basement of a delicatessen in Queens, New York. The car had 20,000 original miles. ''It's the best Packard I own,'' says Gene, who has quite a few.

1932 Packard DeLuxe Eight 903 Sport Phaeton
Owner: Don Sears of Omaha, Nebraska

1932 Packard DeLuxe Eight 903 Coupe-Roadster   Owner: N. Gene Perkins of Greenwood, Indiana   Photo: Nancy Bailey

Another favorite of Gene Perkins is the 903 Coupe-Roadster which he's owned over two decades and which he has driven on three CCCA CARavans: ''There was no true Packard roadster in '32; the Coupe-Roadster with roll-up windows was it. Selling any Packard was difficult for the company at the time, but I believe 1932 was Packard's finest year in design.''

Agreeing with Gene is Frank Mulderry who regards the 1932 long-wheelbase dual cowl Sport Phaeton as ''the ultimate Packard.''

1932 Packard DeLuxe Eight 903 Sport Phaeton   Owner: Francis P. Mulderry of Albany, New York   Photos: Daniel B. Lyons

1932 Packard DeLuxe Eight 903 Convertible Sedan   Owner: *Warren J. Hoye of New Castle, Pennsylvania*

Thirty-two is also the favorite Packard year for William Helling, who drove daughter Julie to her wedding in 1987 in his Coupe.

Warren Hoye's Convertible Sedan has been a ''family affair'' since acquisition in 1962: ''We bought the car sight unseen, then flew to Kansas City with the four little kids and started home. After five days and many, many pit stops, we entered Pennsylvania.'' The Packard has since provided the Hoyes many miles of trouble-free driving, including the Nova Scotia CARavan.

1932 Packard DeLuxe Eight 903 Two/Four-Passenger Coupe   Owner: *William A. Helling of Faribault, Minnesota*

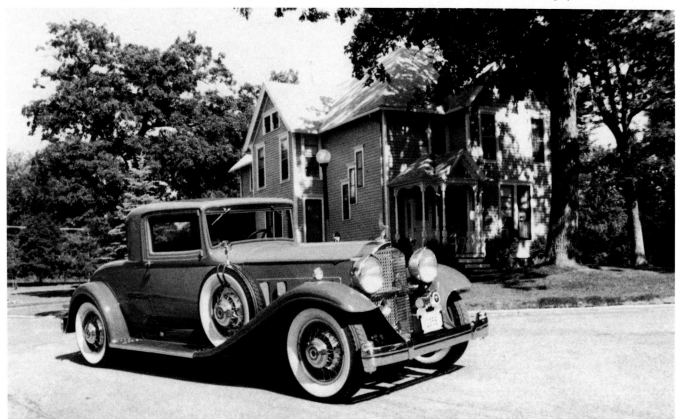

1932 Packard DeLuxe Eight 903 Phaeton   Owner: John M. Wheatley of Tulsa, Oklahoma

1932 Packard DeLuxe Eight 903 Club Sedan   Owner: Robert Marks of Providence, Rhode Island   Photo: K. Karger

The first owners of several Packards in the 903 portfolio are known. Bob Marks acquired his Club Sedan from the estate of Walter C. Nye, president of the Citizens Savings Bank of Providence, Rhode Island. Chauffeur-driven only, the car had been put up on blocks following its owner's death just nineteen months after taking delivery; his grief-stricken widow couldn't bear to see the Packard on the highway. "The car remains completely original with not a scratch on it," says Bob. "1932 was the prettiest Packard made and I think the Club Sedan was the nicest of the closed body styles. This car performs wonderfully. You cannot duplicate originality."

Completely original too, with only 35,000 total miles, is the dual-windshield Phaeton of John Wheatley which is nicknamed Abby for first owner Hattie F. Abercrombie (of the sporting goods house of Abercrombie & Fitch): "When you see the Wheatleys on a Classic car function, you will see Abby." Further, the car is a two-year veteran of the Great American Race.

1932 Packard DeLuxe Eight 903 Coupe-Roadster   *Owner: Morton Bullock of Baltimore, Maryland*   *Photo: K. Karger*

Reputedly the first purchaser of Mort Bullock's Coupe-Roadster in New York City was Admiral Richard Evelyn Byrd, whose nautical background could account for the nautical cord laced on the steering wheel spokes as was done on ships sailing in frigid waters to prevent skin from sticking to cold metal. Comments Mort, "It's a beautiful lacing job obviously done by some boatswain's mate."

The original owner of the Gooding Sport Phaeton was Jean Harlow who bought the car for $3,590 on April 15th, 1933 from the Thompson Motor Company in Beverly Hills. Its odometer read 27,000 miles when the actress died in 1937; two years later the Packard was bought for $350 by Walter & Nancy Bersticker of Whittier who discovered its top in like-new condition since Jean Harlow preferred driving with the wind sensuously breezing through her platinum hair. The top had seldom been raised. The Berstickers added another 90,000 miles to the odometer principally in pulling their house trailer and carrying their canoe on camping trips. Clifford & Joyce Gooding acquired the car in May 1963 and had it restored. The 22,000+ miles they have driven it since includes the 1982 Tournament of Roses Parade when Jean Harlow's Packard was fittingly chosen to chauffeur Grand Marshall Jimmy Stewart and the movie actor's wife Gloria.

1932 Packard DeLuxe Eight 903 Sport Phaeton   *Owner: Clifford & Joyce Gooding of Marina del Rey, California*

As in 1931, production bodies on the longest-wheelbase eights were confined to seven-passenger sedan and limousine. Unlike 1931, this chassis was also utilized for the Individual Custom line; in fact it was the only eight-cylinder chassis so used. Five Dietrich designs together with ten "Custom Made by Packard" styles were included in the custom folio.

Rare indeed are custom-built Packards for 1932. The Brighams' Dietrich Convertible Victoria is one of four known to exist; Gene Perkins' Dietrich Stationary Coupe is one of just two. On the latter the window between the interior and the rumble seat rolls down. Both cars feature the Dietrich vee windshield. The lower cowl necessitated recessing the instrument panel. Gene has owned his Stationary Coupe for over two decades. The Dietrich Convertible Victoria was Ike Brigham's choice in 1953 as the "most beautiful of all Classic Packards of the thirties . . . it took me almost thirty years to get one." Acquired by the Brighams in 1981, this Packard had been owned by artist Melbourne Brindle from 1948 to 1974.

1932 Packard Individual Custom Eight 904 Convertible Victoria, Dietrich
Owners: Ike & Sandy Brigham of Indianapolis, Indiana

1932 Packard Individual Custom Eight 904 Stationary Coupe, Dietrich
Owner: N. Gene Perkins of Greenwood, Indiana   Photos: Nancy Bailey

"Packard Plays for High-Low Markets" headlined *Automotive Industries* in January 1932 when the new Twin Six and Light Eight were introduced. The headline was somewhat misleading because in an era when a new Ford or Chevrolet was available to purchasers for little more than five hundred dollars, the just under $1,800 asked for a Light Eight scarcely made it "low" priced. But for that matter the 4,000 pounds of the Light Eight was nearly double that of a low-priced car, which made it "light" only by Packard standards. Still, the new car was the company's first marketplace attempt to counter the Depression—and it didn't work. Just 6,750 Light Eights had been produced when Packard discontinued the 900 before year's end. Expensive to build, the car was not significantly enough less expensive to buy than the Standard Eight (the 901's price tag was $2,485) to introduce a new clientele for the company. The Light Eight was a remarkable car, nonetheless. Its 110 hp engine was almost identical to the Standard Eight and, with its shorter 128-inch wheelbase and 500 or so less pounds, promised a lively performance. Ride control, angleset differential, automatic clutch and vacuum-powered brakes were featured. The Bijur chassis lubrication was not, replaced by plain grease fittings. The company called the Light Eight "a snappy car," with a top speed of 72 mph and faster acceleration than any 1932 Packard save the Twin Six. "Very peppy," says Bill Kranz of his Coupe-Roadster, "fun to drive." And the Light Eight looked as snappy as it performed with sweeping lines and a chic radiator profile that earned the sobriquet "shovel nose."

1932 Packard Light Eight 900 Coupe-Roadster
Owner: H. William Kranz, Jr. of Bay Village, Ohio

1932 Packard
Twin Six
Individual Custom
906 Sport
Phaeton, Dietrich

Owner: Bob Bahre
of Oxford, Maine

1932 Packard Twin Six 905 Two/Four-Passenger Coupe   *Owner: Howard H. & Violet W. Baker of Pacific Palisades, California*

With the scuttling of the front-wheel-drive project, the logical new home for a Packard V-12 engine was the DeLuxe Eight chassis. Logical too was Packard's decision to call the new car a Twin Six, the same designation the company had used for its World War I era V-12 and a subtle reminder that Packard enjoyed plentiful practice in the multi-cylinder field. Increased to 445 cubic inches (from the 375.7 of the front-wheel-drive V-12), the engine developed 160 hp. Packard clocked a sedan at 101

mph but chose to understate the car's potential in advertising by claiming only 85+, which was going some for a car that in some body styles closed in on three tons. Price tags for the 905 ranged from $3,650 to $4,395.

Stephen Brauer has owned his Sport Phaeton for nearly ten years; the Two/Four-Passenger Coupe that has been in the Baker garage for over three decades was the first of that body style off the line. Total 905 production was just 311 cars.

The longer-wheelbase 906, which included the production seven-passenger sedan and limousine as well as the Individual Custom cars, was produced in only 238 examples. The Bahre Dietrich Sport Phaeton was one of two built on the twelve-cylinder chassis and features a roll-down rear windshield with folding wind-wings. Bob Bahre purchased the car in 1985 from Dick Dewey who had driven it extensively since 1962. The mileage Dick did not know, but he wore out three speedometers.

1932 Packard Twin Six 905 Sport Phaeton   *Owner: Stephen F. Brauer of Bridgeton, Missouri*

The Bodines bought this Packard over four years ago from CCCA member Richard Griffin who had owned the car for fourteen years. Its restoration and sale were for the purpose of a retirement fund. Dick plays the lottery regularly, however; should he win, the Bodines have agreed to return the car to him. That they are gambling on the fact that he won't is indicated by Paul's comments about the Coupe-Roadster: ''All Packards looked the same from the front in the Tenth Series. They were neither as chic nor as modern looking as the Light Eight, though the Packard rationale was logical enough. To have given its successor a similar look for more money might not have settled well in the marketplace. Moreover, a commonality of styling between Eight and Super Eight—the new name for the old DeLuxe—made for upper echelon democracy, for prestige rub-off, which Packard encouraged. The Super Eight nomenclature was advanced on the theory that the old DeLuxe Eight designation went out with high button shoes. The Standard Eight nomenclature was upgraded to the single noun Eight. After all, 'Standard' imparts to the buyer 'ordinary,' and this was a time when most manufacturers had an eight-cylinder engine, including the low-priced Ford. With the 127½-inch

wheelbase, my Eight 1001 is very nimble and easy to drive. The dashboard setting for brake pressure is convenient and a boon for a woman driver. Push-button starting, Bijur lubrication and ride control are all luxury features on a 'Poor Man's' Packard. This is a dashing automobile with the top down and a flush boot—and its diamond-tufted seats are more luxurious than top-of-the-line models. This was the first year for brake pressure adjustable from

the dash, skirted fenders, downdraft carburetor, automatic choke and twin ignition—and horsepower was up to 120 for the Eight. The bold Packard grille on a 'stubby' car is beautiful. The only disadvantage in our 1001 is luggage space. When Nancy and I drive the car any distance, we have to settle for wearing pretty much the same clothes for the duration 'cause there ain't no room, after the tools and clean-up gear, in a Coupe-Roadster.''

1933 Packard Eight 1001 Coupe-Roadster
Owners: Paul & Nancy Bodine of Kildeer, Illinois

1933 Packard Super Eight 1004 Coupe-Roadster
Owner: Frank Champagne of Saginaw, Michigan

The Tenth Series Eight and Super Eight introduced the X-member frame, cooling fins on connecting rod bearing caps, diaphragm-type vacuum pump, three-position (low, high and passing) headlight system, electric-operated oil level gauge on the dash, and wheels pared down to seventeen inches. The Bendix BK vacuum booster brakes of the Twin Six were fitted, with a four-position power selector on the instrument panel. The starter moved from the floorboard to the dashboard. Adopted from the Light Eight was the angle-set hypoid differential. The four body styles of the Light Eight were incorporated into the Eight 1001, which had previously been offered only as a five-passenger sedan. The Eight 1002, on a 136-inch wheelbase, carried thirteen body styles. The 135-inch-wheelbase Super Eight 1003 was a five-passenger sedan only. The Super Eight 1004 offered thirteen body styles on a 142-inch wheelbase. Eliminated was the long 147½-inch wheelbase for the Super Eight, which meant that anyone desiring a catalogued custom Packard in 1933 had to take twelve cylinders to get it. Like every other luxury manufacturer, Packard was struggling to find the key to survival in the depths of the Depression. Its Tenth Series cars were introduced in January 1933, the Eleventh Series that August—for a short eight-month production run that saw just 2,970 Eights and only 1,300 Super Eights built.

The situation in '33 has had concomitant repercussions today. ''The Classic I wanted most was this Packard 1004,'' says Frank Champagne of his Super Eight Coupe-Roadster. ''I waited a long time to get it.'' Finally he did, in 1985.

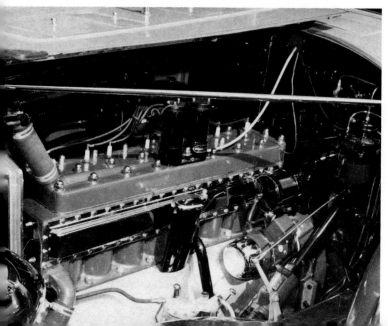

Lonnie Fallin's Victoria-Coupe, which he regards as the most "classic" of Packard body styles of the early thirties, was originally in the garage of Governor Gifford Pinchot of Pennsylvania. Since restoration in 1985, Lonnie has driven this "great road car" over 3,000 miles, averaging 10.5 mpg at highway speeds.

Restoration of Tom Hartz's Seven-Passenger Sedan was a family affair: "While I couldn't stir much interest in the sanding, painting and assembly, I did have some much needed help from my wife with the interior. This car does not have a custom body or a convertible top, but it is certainly a piece of art. And while there's a solid front axle and a tremendous amount of unsprung weight, the Packard nonetheless drives with a style and feel all its own. It truly 'glides' over bumps and is surprisingly smooth for a 1933 automobile. By then most cars had begun to show streamlining while Packard continued to retain a more conservative look. The company's only concession was to add skirts to the fenders and a slight slope to the windshield."

1933 Packard Super Eight 1004 Convertible Victoria
Owner: Lonnie Fallin of Littleton, Colorado

1933 Packard Super Eight 1004 Seven-Passenger Sedan   *Owner: Tom Hartz of Indianapolis, Indiana*

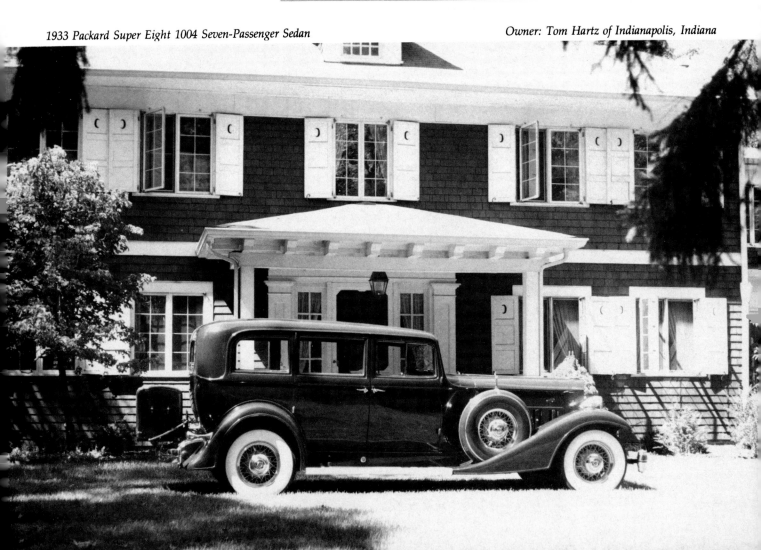

1933 Packard Twelve 1005 Convertible Sedan
Owner: Bob Larivee, Sr. of Rochester, Michigan

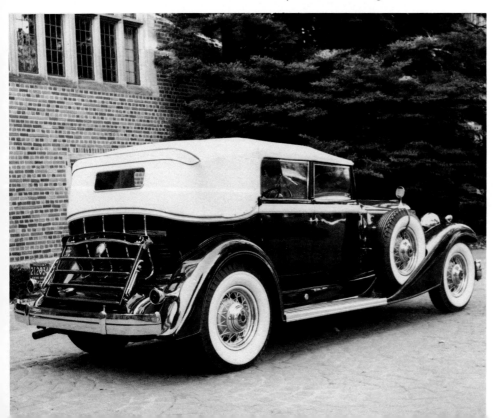

Changing the designation of its multi-cylinder line in 1933 was done for the same reason Packard changed the designation of its eights: marketing. Being nostalgic and subtle wasn't nearly as important as insuring that all potential customers were fully aware of just how many cylinders the Packard had. Hence the Twin Six became the Twelve. Horsepower and wheelbases remained the same, but the former double-drop frame of the Twin Six gave way to the tapered frame of the Twelve. A single dry-plate clutch replaced the two-plate, and the Stromberg carburetor was provided an automatic choke with fast idle. Among the twelve body styles offered in the 1005 was the Convertible Sedan—"a wonderful car to drive"—owned by Bob Larivee. The long-wheelbase 1006 was retained for seven-passenger sedan and limousine and the catalogued customs, although the designation "Individual Custom" was no longer used. Total Twelve production during the eight-month run was 520 cars.

These three Dietrich customs on the Twelve 1006 chassis represent half of that designer's body styles in the Packard custom catalogue for 1933. Don Sears takes pride in his Convertible Sedan being ''the most original Dietrich in the world.'' The car's first owner was Theodosia Hamilton of Santa Barbara, California; when Don acquired the Packard seven years ago, he also acquired the ''Certificate of Approval'' that Theodosia had received in '33 signed by development engineer Tommy Milton and attesting to the car's test run at the Packard Proving Grounds, as well as completed forms for mileage ration and tire inspection required by the Office of Price Administration during World War II. ''The car's style is fantastic, its originality is priceless,'' says Don. ''It's phenomenal that the paint and interior has lasted this long. The original tires remain in the sidemounts; Theodosia Hamilton's name is still on the door.'' Don has driven the Convertible Sedan over 10,000 miles.

''The smoothness and raw power that the V-12 engine provides'' is among the reasons Charlie Worthen enjoys driving the Stationary Coupe that has been his for over two decades.

Among the drives that Mitty Mittermaier has taken in the Convertible Victoria that he has owned for over three-and-a-half decades was on the Packard Proving Grounds track in 1953 when the first CCCA CARavan trekked to Detroit: ''To drive this Packard, 6000 pounds curb weight and 147½-inch wheelbase, was like coming to a bump in the road that the car just pushed out of its way.''

1933 Packard Twelve 1006 Convertible Victoria, Dietrich
Owner: Armin F. Mittermaier of Fort Wayne, Indiana

1933 Packard Twelve 1006 Convertible Sedan, Dietrich (engine and dashboard below)　　　Owner: Don Sears of Omaha, Nebraska

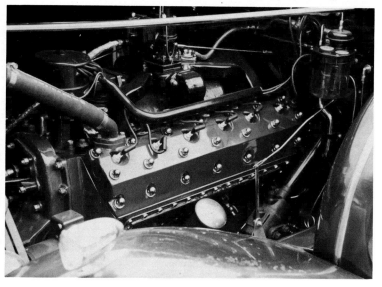

1933 Packard Twelve 1006 Stationary Coupe, Dietrich　　　Owner: Charlie D. Worthen of Houston, Texas

Wheelbases were three, and longer, for the Packard Eights in '34: the 129½-inch 1100 the small sedan, the 141½-inch 1102 the large sedan and limousine, the 136½-inch 1101 with ten body styles. Bumpers were slotted, simulating a double-bar look, the gas tank filler was incorporated into the left rear taillight assembly and an oil cooler was added. "A perfect representation of styling for a sedan of the Classic Era" exemplifies the pride Pam & Ed Rittenhouse have for their 1100 which they acquired five years ago.

The 1101 Phaeton has been the Scheils' pride for two decades and enjoyed an owner restoration requiring nearly nine years: "Nineteen thirty-four was the end of an era for Phaeton styling. Only the fenders had changed from '32. On our car the skirts extend further down in front of the front wheel, creating in our opinion the culmination of the Phaeton design. Our Packard was the 44th built in a year that produced 5,120 Eights. According to Jim Pearsall, who for years has kept a roster of '33 and '34 Packards, ours was most likely the first Phaeton built of no more than a total of forty. In 1989, through a New Jersey antique dealer, Jim found what he believes is its body plate. Incredibly, the plate for our car has been reunited with the body itself after being lost for more than twenty years. Renee and I now have four children and fit snugly into the five-passenger Phaeton. The car never overheats, always runs cool. Its best feature, however, is the sound of that large straight-eight engine going through the gears."

1934 Packard Eight 1101 Phaeton
Owners: Tom & Renee Scheil of Mission Viejo, California

1934 Packard Eight 1100 Five-Passenger Sedan   Owners: Pam & Ed Rittenhouse of Mercer Island, Washington

1934 Packard Eight 1101 Convertible Victoria, Dietrich
Owner: John A. Larch of Lafayette, Indiana

Custom-built cars on the Eight chassis were available only through independent coachbuilders and as such are rare. The Convertible Victoria which John Larch has owned for over a quarter of a century was bought new by a Greek wrestling promoter named Nick Loftis: "I know of only three other such cars that are up and running. The Convertible Victoria was an early attempt to get five people into an open two-door car comfortably and is one of the few convertibles that looks better with the top up than down. The car is comfortable at 45-50 mph, rides well and is very dependable, but it's a bear to back up since rear visibility is so minimal."

A resort on Long Island was the first home for Bill Chorkey's 1102 Station Wagon which was the only one built by Bridgeport in 1934: "This unique body style has more of a passenger car appearance than that of a truck. It does not sit up too high in the rear as most other wagons of the era. It also has a sloping rounded tailgate and sliding windows on the back doors and rear compartment—very advanced for 1934. I purchased this Classic in 1987 and am looking forward to the completion of its restoration. With passenger car comfort and ample room in the rear for luggage and necessities, we will be able to breeze down the highway, with the windows open, in safety, beauty and comfort."

1934 Packard Eight 1102 Station Wagon, Bridgeport
Owner: William J. Chorkey of Farmington Hills, Michigan

Total Super Eight production for 1934 was 1,920 cars. The long 147½-inch wheelbase and catalogued custom bodies were reinstated on the 1105. The 1103 remained the bread-and-butter sedan. Eleven body styles were offered in the 1104 line, including the Showers' Coupe-Roadster: "Oil cooler, full flow oil filter, chassis lubrication system, finned con-rod caps, power brakes, down-draft dual throat carburetor, modern two-shoe brake system, full X-member frame, kingpins mounted in ball bearings top and bottom, ride control—in sum, at least thirty years ahead of the industry in driveability. This Packard's road manners are impeccable. It has probably the best long-term maintenance-free engineering of any fine car." Ken knows whereof he speaks. He's owned the Coupe-Roadster for nearly three decades, has put 57,000 miles on it since restoration, and uses this Packard for everyday transportation.

1934 Packard Super Eight 1104 Coupe-Roadster   *Owners: Ken & Heather Showers of Victoria, British Columbia*

Twelves were offered in three models in 1934 with a total production of 960 cars. All factory bodies save the seven-passenger closed cars were on the 142-inch-wheelbase 1107. The Zamba Phaeton is fascinating because it was delivered from the factory in one body style, then revised at the dealership into another: "One clue is the squareness of the metal section behind the front seat which is characteristic of the dual cowl Sport Phaeton body No. 741. On dual windshield Phaeton body number 731, this section was rounded. There are two notches under that section on my car where hinges may have existed. Further there are the side vent doors between front and rear doors which existed on the dual cowl 741 bodies."

Bill Chorkey has determined that his Five-Passenger Coupe—which has 22,000 original miles—was either a show car or a dealer's promotional vehicle: "It is the only one of the six Victorias known extant that was delivered with a leather interior including headliner. Leather would better withstand various potential purchasers entering and exiting the car. And they certainly would have been impressed by the extra chrome, not to mention the floral surround on the instrumental panel and the dash and gauge bezels trimmed in 24-carat gold. Although often overlooked in favor of open Classics, I believe that the Victoria—or Five-Passenger Coupe, in Packard parlance—carries an overwhelming sensation of personal comfort, both visually and functionally. The styling of the body lends itself perfectly to conversation between front and rear seat passengers; overall, a Victoria creates a cozy atmosphere."

1934 Packard Twelve 1107 Phaeton
Owners: Mary & Al Zamba of Pittsburgh, Pennsylvania

1934 Packard Twelve 1107 Five-Passenger Coupe   *Owner: William Chorkey of Farmington, Michigan*

For Bob Dibble, the Club Sedan reigns supreme: "I admire its dignified 'cathedral-like' appearance. This was the first year for Packard's integral rear trunk, and also the first for the no-draft front vent windows. Overall, the symmetry of the body design is outstanding." The Club Sedan's first owner was John Bromley of the Quaker Lace Mills near Philadelphia. With accessories the purchase price was about $4,500, not a lot by today's standards but, as Bob points out, an eight-room Spanish style stucco house in his native California could have been purchased for about five hundred dollars more at the time. "This car has original paint and upholstery in excellent condition," he comments. "I've driven it 10,500 miles since acquisition in 1972 and it has appeared in the movie *79 Park Avenue* and the television series *City of Angels*. The car is now in full retirement to preserve its fine originality."

1934 Packard Twelve 1107 Club Sedan
Owner: Robert Dibble of Thousand Oaks, California

Ed Blend's 1107 Coupe-Roadster was the thirty-third produced of probably no more than fifty. Its first owner was the general manager of the truck-producing Autocar Company of Ardmore, Pennsylvania. Ed has owned the car since 1955: "When you see an Eleventh Series Packard, you are looking at the end of an era that began almost immediately following World War I. In my mind's eye, it all came together in 1934. This series of Packard was the high-water mark for the straight beltline school of design. New owners of these cars today are always pleased with the tractable manners of a vehicle weighing close to three tons. The trickiest part of a Packard Twelve is having a tight distributor and attaining the one-half degree tolerances between the points properly set up. The car is a pussycat on the road. I've driven mine 40,000 miles. It cruises best at an indicated 60 mph, corrected to 71 mph as various minions of the law will attest. Wife Trudy prefers driving it over any of the Classics I've owned since 1951."

1934 Packard Twelve 1107
Coupe-Roadster

Owner: Edward John Blend II
of Irwin, Pennsylvania

1934 Packard Twelve 1107 Convertible Sedan
Owners: Mr. & Mrs. Jerry W. Jones of Indianapolis, Indiana   *Photos: Tim Turner*

For over three decades, Jerry Jones has been driving his 1107 Convertible Sedan: "Most of all, it has been a family fun car. When first purchased, we had six small children; the Packard still can't go past an ice cream store without turning in. I suppose over the years enough milk shakes have been spilled in the back seat to fill a good-sized bathtub." The Eleventh Series was the first re-engineered by Packard for radio. Jerry's car has one, in both front and rear, with an antenna about three feet square that snaps into the roof. It also has a three-position top with divider window: "Thus the car can be driven as 1) a fully-enclosed sedan, 2) a limousine, 3) a town car, 4) an open touring, 5) a double-windshield touring—and the windows can be moved up or down in each configuration." With options, this car sold new for just under $6,000, about a dollar a pound.

411

1934 Packard Twelve 1106 Sport Coupe by Packard   *Owner: Bob Bahre of Oxford, Maine*

The 1106 was the Packard Twelve on the Super Eight's 135-inch wheelbase offered in just the two body styles shown here from Bob Bahre's collection. These cars, together with most of the Packard customs in the Eleventh Series, reflect the increasingly formidable presence of Edward Macauley (Packard president Alvan Macauley's son) on the Packard styling scene, and the entrance of Count Alexis de Sakhnoffsky. These two men would be largely responsible for the unification of Packard styling. De Sakhnoffsky's principal contribution was the "false hood," or as de

Sakhnoffsky explained, "Though the actual distance from the radiator to the front door remains the same, by extending the hood almost to the windshield, the effect of length is considerably increased." The count abhorred short hoods. On both these Bahre cars, the front end seems to go on forever. The un-LeBaron-like Runabout Speedster reflects de Sakhnoffsky's false hood as well as the pontoon fenders of Ed Macauley's personal and perennially revised speedster that was known as the "Brown Bomber" by Packard Engineering. The Sport Coupe by Packard also reflects the

straightforward Dietrich waistline and the split windshield of Packard's "Car of the Dome" for the World's Fair. The LeBaron was purchased by Carole Lombard as a gift to her husband; Clark Gable had a few styling ideas of his own and had the top, running boards and windshield modified. The original owner of the Sport Coupe is not known. At about $10,000, it was the most expensive catalogued Packard of the Classic Era. Precious few were built, but a good many styling features of subsequent Packards saw their first appearance on this model, as will be seen as this portfolio unfolds.

1934 Packard Twelve 1106 Runabout Speedster, LeBaron   *Owner: Bob Bahre of Oxford, Maine*

1934 Packard Twelve 1108 Convertible Sedan, Dietrich
Owner: William S. Hirsch of Newark, New Jersey

Of the half-dozen Twelve 1108 customs which follow, the original owners of two are known. Both were formidable personalities.

Purchaser of Bill Hirsch's Dietrich Convertible Sedan in 1934 was Louise Boyd, a California heiress who spent much of her life travelling and often to the Arctic, where she led eight expeditions and about which she wrote two books. At $6,555, this car was the most expensive offered on the 1108 chassis, but Miss Boyd's was pricier yet because of her addition of a division window between front and rear compartments and reading lights for the latter so she could work in comfort and privacy. From August to October of '34, Louise Boyd motored 6,300 miles throughout Poland in her new purchase. "My automobile, being a Packard," she recounted, "was frequently found to be too long to permit [garage doors] to be shut."

1934 Packard Twelve 1108 Sport Phaeton, LeBaron   *Owners: Ray & Lou Bowersox of Milton, Pennsylvania*

That the original owner of Ray & Lou Bowersox's LeBaron dual cowl Sport Phaeton experienced similar difficulty is not known, but he wouldn't have cared anyway. Alexis de Sakhnoffsky liked l-o-n-g cars. This particular automobile was Packard's show car for the Paris Salon, and most probably the count accompanied it to Europe since he enjoyed escapes to the Continent generally and sojourns in Paris especially. Following Lenin's arrival de Sakhnoffsky had been smuggled out of his native Russia by an aunt who lived in France; following design work for Van den Plas in Belgium, Alexis had sought the more lucrative styling pastures of America, arriving on these shores in the late twenties to launch a free-lance career which saw him design for a variety of automotive manufacturers, Packard of course among them. Among subsequent owners of this Packard was television talk show host Herb Shriner, who drove the car from coast to coast during the fifties. "Undoubtedly, this is the finest driving and handling Classic I have ever owned," says Ray. And there are a lot of Classics in the Bowersox garage.

414

1934 Packard Twelve 1108 Sport Phaeton, LeBaron
Owner: Bob Bahre of Oxford, Maine

1934 Packard Twelve 1108 Convertible Roadster, Dietrich
Owner: Bob Bahre of Oxford, Maine

1934 Packard Twelve 1108 Convertible Victoria, Dietrich
Owner: N. Gene Perkins of Greenwood, Indiana   Photo: Nancy Bailey

1934 Packard Twelve 1108 Stationary Coupe, Dietrich
Owner: Bob Bahre of Oxford, Maine

1935 Packard Eight 1201 Phaeton
Owners: Robert & LaVerne Bailey of Gig Harbor, Washington

Factory attention was focused on the new non-Classic Junior series introduced in 1935, but Packard did not neglect its big cars. Streamlining debuted in a five-degree rake to the radiator, pontoon rear fenders, chromed side louvers—a careful and typically Packard transition. All production models featured the rear-hinged doors which had previously been seen only on custom models. Horsepower was up to 130 for the 320-cubic-inch Eight, 150 for the 384.4-cubic-inch Super Eight, 175 for the 473.3-cubic-inch Twelve. Wheelbases decreased a couple of inches, and sales declined at about the same ratio: to 4,781, 1,392 and 788, respectively. Nearly 25,000 of the new Junior Packards were sold. The Depression had taken an enormous chunk out of the luxury market.

"Owning a Senior Packard is to realize a fantasy of our childhood when only the rich were so blessed. To drive one is to feel, however belatedly, that Grand Exhilaration evoked by no other machine. This is a precious reminder, thankfully preserved, of an era gone but not yet forgotten by the generation born and reared during the Great Depression." Thus write Robert and LaVerne Bailey of their 1201 Phaeton. The Bailey Packard is unusual in having been marketed in Britain. The car carries a plaque indicating Leonard Williams & Co. of London as "sole concessionaire" and has "USA" in two-inch letters pressed as part of the right-hand fender behind the front bumper. Interestingly, the car is left-hand drive, a mystery the Baileys are working to unravel.

1935 Packard Eight 1201 Convertible Coupe   *Owner: Hans Edwards of Cadiz, Spain*

Writes Hans Edwards of his 1201 Convertible Coupe: "It has always been on top of the list in my mind for open body styling—clean, uncluttered and, with the rear spare, sporting. I just hate sidemounts—not so much the look of them but the weight penalty they impose on an already overweight front end, plus the cramps they give you trying to adjust most anything in the engine department (unless you take them off first, which is a terrible drag). This Packard could have done with a stabilizing rod at the rear, and maybe an anti-roll bar at the front. But it remains a superb driving car even with the 3.54 rear end. The small eight gives away a liter or so to the Super but gains on the scales—and this, plus the absence of the two great lumps of spare wheels at the front, makes the car very light to handle. I've driven it in Spain, 1,000 miles or so, in 100 degree heat, without any bother."

Fifteen thousand miles have been enjoyed by Charlie Kerner in the Eight 1202 Convertible Sedan he has owned since 1972. "Quiet, smooth, powerful," says Ike Brigham of his Twelve 1207 Convertible Victoria: "No squeaks or rattles, an absolute joy to drive." These cars were completed in the Detroit shops of Dietrich, Inc., of course, as indeed were all Senior open Packards for 1935 as the new Junior Packard consumed the company's main body shop.

1935 Packard Eight 1202 Convertible Sedan, Dietrich
Owner: Charles W. Kerner of Center Harbor, New Hampshire

1935 Packard Twelve 1207 Convertible Victoria, Dietrich
Owners: Ike & Sandy Brigham of Indianapolis, Indiana

418

1936 Packard Super Eight 1404 Formal Sedan
Owner: Franklin L. Farnsworth of Wheatland, Wyoming

The Fourteenth Series Senior Packards were virtually a reprise of the Twelfth, the most obvious decision being not to use the unlucky number thirteen. With minimal changes from the year previous, these cars became memorable for providing the final curtain call for a number of Packard traditions: solid front axle, mechanical brakes, wire wheels, Bijur lubrication, adjustable shock absorbers, vibration-dampening front bumper, and the 384-cubic-inch engine of the Super Eight. Again, sales saw a downturn: to 3,973 for the Eight, 1,330 for the Super Eight, 682 for the Twelve.

Franklin Farnsworth has owned his 1404 Formal Sedan since 1953: ''The car had been sold new in Hollywood, California. At the time of my purchase, one of the spare tires was missing, a gift to the war effort when only one spare tire was allowed. The Formal Sedan is truly elegant and unique in that it could be used as a family car with divider window rolled down and everyone joining in the fun of the ride, or it could be chauffeur-driven with the window rolled up and the staff along, the maid in the jump seat, the owner and his wife in the rear seat with the arm rest pulled down, and the butler next to the driver! Apparently my Packard spent much of its life being chauffeur-driven for just one passenger, however. Only the driver's seat and the right-hand rear carpet were worn when I purchased it. The car remains largely original.''

1936 Packard Twelve 1407 Convertible Coupe　　　　　　　　　*Owner: Theodore Fuller of Greenwich, Connecticut*

Ted Fuller bought his first Packard in 1939 and was without one for only two years thereafter, a situation he does not plan to repeat. He's owned his 1407 Convertible Coupe for eighteen years: ''Nineteen thirty-six was one of the better years for Packard, in my opinion. The cars are almost identical to '35 except for the slightly increased rake (about five degrees) to the radiator, which I believe is more aesthetically appealing.''

Club sedan coachwork, to George Dickerson, provides the most elegant and beautiful of all closed bodies. His 1407 was one of fifteen Twelve Club Sedans produced for 1935.

1936 Packard Twelve 1407 Club Sedan　　　　　　　　　*Owner: George W. Dickerson of San Antonio, Texas*

1936 Packard Twelve 1407 Five-Passenger Coupe   Owners: Robert & Donna Neal of Kent, Washington

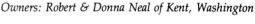

Equally limited in production was the Twelve Five-Passenger Coupe, Bob & Donna Neal's car being one of ten produced and one of only three known extant. ''Even though it is a coupe, there is more room in the back seat than in my current Cadillac,'' says Bob. ''The Twelve's great power combined with power-assisted brakes and clutch and ride control make it a pleasure to drive even on an eight-hour day. We have taken it through the Washington Cascades and as high up Mount Rainier as the roads go, never out of high gear, at whatever was the posted speed limit.'' The Neals, who are the seventh to own this Packard, have traced it back through all six previous owners. The purchaser to whom it was originally delivered in 1935 by Packard Evanston (Illinois) was Mrs. Robert Stockton, who drove the car approximately 55,000 miles before selling it in 1952. The Neals' mileage since 1982 has been nearly 13,000.

1936 Packard Twelve 1408 All-Weather Town Car, LeBaron

Owners: Don & Carol Alexander of Riverside, Illinois

Likewise well traveled today is Don & Carol Alexander's LeBaron All-Weather Town Car, which was originally owned by Colonel Robert McCormick, publisher of the *Chicago Tribune*. "When I purchased the car over thirty years ago, it had only 18,000 miles on it," comments Don. "The odometer now reads 36,000. An interesting fact is that at the time of purchase I also bought new Martin tires for the car and in all the years since I've never had a flat tire. The Martins are still on the road wheels, and the original Goodyears from 1936 remain in the sidemounts."

"Beautiful" is the single word Alvin Hollen uses to describe the driving qualities of the Dietrich Convertible Victoria that he has owned for over a dozen years.

1936 Packard Twelve 1407 Convertible Victoria, Dietrich
Owner: Alvin L. Hollen of Mica, Washington

All eight-cylinder Senior Packards were called Super in 1937 and all carried the former Eight's 320-cubic-inch engine. Independent front suspension arrived, and brakes were hydraulic with centrifuse drums. Rear-hinged front doors—though never as ''suicidal'' as jokingly claimed—were no more. The Packard radiator was given a thirty degree slant, and redesigned bumpers were fitted front and rear. Sales rose a bit—to 5,793 from the combined 5,303 for the Eight and Super Eight of '36.

The Supina 1500 Touring Sedan was built for export to England. Bob tells the story: ''Leonard Williams, the London Packard agent, installed the Weathersfield sliding sun roof with built-in drains, Marchal headlamps and driving lamps, Bosch trafficators (turn signal flippers), Yale 'bonnet locks,' Stephenson jacking system, Lucas back-up light, fender mirrors, dual defroster and painted the bumper guard centers black. When we purchased the car at the closure of a Texas museum in 1980, the mileage read just 8,342. The tires are believed to be original, with red rubber inner tubes; the four road tires are English Dunlop, the spare an unused American Firestone. We noticed the owner's manual was very thumbworn, puzzling for a car with such low mileage. But, after investigation, we surmised why. The car had been purchased in London by Frederick Carmichael for his wife Gladys. Naturally we decided to name the car 'Lady Gladys.' We have since become close friends with the granddaughter of the original owner; Stephanie Nicholson told us that, in addition to the Packard, the Carmichael garage had a Rolls-Royce,

1937 Packard Super Eight 1500 Touring Sedan
Owners: Bob & Joyce Supina of Friendsworth, Texas

Daimler and Rover, all chauffeur driven. Now that thumbworn owner's manual became clear; I can just imagine their English chauffeur Gill studying this 'foreign' car. Several weeks after purchasing Lady Gladys, we gave some English friends a ride. Asked if the radio worked, I turned it on and, after the familiar hum, we heard an announcer comment 'and Scotland Yard says . . . ' We were all flabbergasted that this English automobile was still receiving British radio—and in Texas! Impulsively, I turned the radio off and said, 'See, I told you so.' Actually, as it happened, the Scotland Yard report was because Iranians had just seized an embassy in London.''

Eugene Langkop bought his 1500 Touring Sedan from an estate in San Antonio, Texas in 1954. The odometer read 22,000 miles and the purchase price was $475. ''We have been on five CARavans, driving our Packard all the way from Dallas to wherever and never once had to stop for any repairs,'' Gene says. ''I would have no hesitation to drive the car anywhere in the United States. Its handling is impeccable. Mechanics who've driven this Packard ask if it has power steering, which of course it does not—it just feels that way. The 1500 Touring Sedan is a piece of metal art to my eye. I like the balance of body dimensions on the 127-inch wheelbase as compared to the longer 134-inch wheelbase of the 1501.''

1937 Packard Super Eight 1500 Touring Sedan   *Owner: Eugene Langkop of Dallas, Texas*

1937 Packard Super Eight 1501 Formal Sedan   *Owner: Stanley A. Hamel of Seabrook, New Hampshire*

Most probably Gene would be given a friendly argument on that point by the four 1501 owners whose cars appear here. Stan Hamel's 1501 Formal Sedan, which he's owned since 1962, was purchased new by a New York City family who kept it most of the time at their summer home in Bar Harbor, Maine. The Eckenroths' 1501 Club Sedan was first purchased by a Massachusetts foundry owner who had the car delivered to his winter home in St. Petersburg, Florida. Both these cars are often on the road today, as is the 1501 Dietrich Convertible Victoria that Kay Duffy has owned for over three decades: "I was in college when this one was built. Couldn't have one then, so am thrilled to have one now." In the first six months Dan & Mary Malumphy owned their 1501 Touring Sedan, they drove it about twelve hundred miles, which perhaps matched the mileage for the same period by the original owners, the Roman Catholic Diocese of Newark (New Jersey), back in '37.

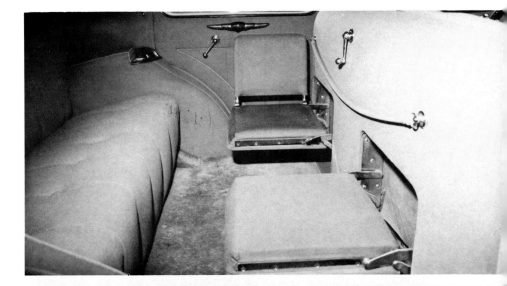

1937 Packard Super Eight 1501 Club Sedan   Owners: Mr. & Mrs. C. Stanley Eckenroth of Terre Hill, Pennsylvania

1937 Packard Super Eight 1501 Convertible Victoria, Dietrich
Owner: Mrs. George Y. Duffy of Port Huron, Michigan

1937 Packard Super Eight 1501 Touring Sedan
Owners: Dan & Mary Malumphy of New Milford, Connecticut

1937 Packard Twelve 1508 Convertible Sedan, Dietrich   *Owner: Courtland J. Cross of Georges Mills, New Hampshire*

The Twelve for '37 enjoyed the same chassis changes as the Super Eight—and the added fillip that, with the elimination of the lengthiest Super Eight, anyone wishing a long-wheelbase catalogued Packard now had to take the twelve-cylinder engine to get it. Twelve production doubled—from 682 in the Fourteenth Series to 1,300 in the Fifteenth.

Fifteenth Series Packard Twelve owners are unanimous about the car's roadability. Neil Torrence: "The incredible power-assisted brakes and the smooth V-12 engine torque make it one of the best Packards I have ever driven." Bud Juneau: "The clutch is so light you can reach in and depress it with one finger with the car idling at curbside. Most on the road today continue to work perfectly without maintenance, adjustment or repair." Milton Miner: "My father owned a Packard when I was at Stanford, but I rarely had the use of it. The big V-12 is an outstanding road car." Kenneth Kamman: "The engineering excellence is very apparent, especially the ride and the 473-cubic-inch engine."

Courtland Cross: "Super is the word for the way the car drives and handles." Dick Haeberle: "That it is a V-12 is info enough to attest to its smoothness and reliability." Hans Edwards: "Setting up the suspension and steering properly (i.e., as it was when new) is the key; I spent weeks setting up the front end on this car, add a shim here, take away a shim there, adjust here, etc., and it was worth every minute of it. Driving enjoyment is manifold. Those twelve pots pull the high-speed rear end for effortless 60-70 mph cruising."

1937 Packard Twelve 1508 Seven-Passenger Limousine   *Kenneth Kamman of Birmingham, Michigan*

1937 Packard Twelve 1507 Coupe-Roadster
Owners: Kathleen N. Miner & Milton A. Miner of Los Angeles, California

1937 Packard Twelve 1507 Convertible Victoria, Dietrich
Owner: Neil Torrence of Arcadia, California   Photo: Vince Mannochi, Collectible Automobile

1937 Packard Twelve 1507 Two/Four-Passenger Coupe   Owner: Hans Edwards of Cadiz, Spain

Ken Wessel's 1507 Coupe-Roadster was delivered to Packard Pittsburgh in 1937 and went on to two more Pennsylvania dealers prior to Ken's acquisition: "Based on the previous dealer-only possession, you might say I am the first owner of this car." Ken has a point.

The first owner of Barbara & Don Wheeler's 1507 Club Sedan was Vernon Kreuter, vice-president of American Laundry Machinery Industries of Rochester, New York: "The styling is very pleasing with the long hood, short body and large trunk, the last named quite a bit bigger than on the regular sedan."

That his 1507 Two/Four-Passenger Coupe provided the "smallest body on the longest chassis" appealed to Hans Edwards: "This is the craziest strictly-Classic-Era combination, none of the maximum-interior-with-minimum-exterior logic." The original owner of Hans' car was Howard Keck, founder of the Superior Oil Company of California.

1937 Packard Twelve 1507 Coupe-Roadster
Owner: Kenneth C. Wessel of Rocky River, Ohio

1937 Packard Twelve 1507 Club Sedan

Owners: Barbara & Don Wheeler of Claremont, California

1937 Packard Twelve 1508 Seven-Passenger Touring Sedan

Owner: Bud Juneau of Brentwood, California

1937 Packard Twelve 1507 Formal Sedan   Owner: Gene Perkins of Greenwood, Indiana   Photo: Nancy Bailey

1937 Packard Twelve 1508 Seven-Passenger Limousine
Owner: Cavitt Caufield of McGregor, Texas

Gene Perkins' 1507 Formal Sedan spent its entire life in California prior to his purchase four years ago: "The leatherette on the top, the microphone from rear to front, the divider and small rear window, the dual vanity cases, the storage area in back of the front seat . . . all fine details on this car. I like the way the sidemounts are held to the body, and also the fact that when you open the hood on a '37 you can still see and get at the engine."

February 1st, 1937 was the date Arrow shirt heiress Beatrice Cluett Black took delivery of the 1508 Seven-Passenger Limousine now owned by Cavitt Caufield. Mrs. Black's father, Sanford Cluett, invented the process to prevent cotton from shrinking, her husband was president of a Fifth Avenue jewelry firm. The Blacks lived palatially in Pelham Manor, a home they allowed to be pictured in the "New York's Westchester prefers Packards" advertisement. Mrs. Black truly did prefer Packards; at the time she owned four of them. The Caufield car, which Cavitt purchased from the Black estate in 1967, was her favorite. It remains totally original.

The 1508 Seven-Passenger Touring Sedan that Bud Juneau has owned since 1972 attended the World's Fair at Treasure Island on San Francisco Bay in 1939 and may have been one of the first cars across the new Golden Gate Bridge.

1937 Packard Twelve 1508 Convertible Victoria, Rollston
Owner: Dick Haeberle of Union, New Jersey   Photo: K. Karger

Whether it was the son or son-in-law of Great Northern Railroad president James J. Hill who was the first owner of Jack Shy's 1508 Berline has not been determined, but his was the only 1937 Twelve custom built by Packard with a "stretched" formal club sedan body on the factory's longest (144-inch) chassis. Jack has owned the car since 1971 and particularly relishes such amenities as "the instrument panel lights that say PARK, CITY, DRIVE, PASS for the four different light beams, the front *and* rear seat heaters, the front and rear dome lights, plus quarter reading lights, smoking sets in each quarter panel and in each rear arm rest, a pocket containing a small mirror (for m'lady) and a notebook with gold pencil (for the master)."

A "one-of-a-kind" as well is the Rollston Formal Sedan that is an original 79,000-mile car that William Gehring has owned for over a quarter of a century.

Yet another one-off is Dick Haeberle's 1508 Rollston Convertible Victoria, originally owned by the Shattuck family of Schrafft's candy.

1937 Packard Twelve 1508 Formal Sedan, Rollston
Owner: William M. Gehring of Cleveland, Ohio

1937 Packard Twelve 1508 Berline

Owner: Jack V. Shy of Dearborn Heights, Michigan

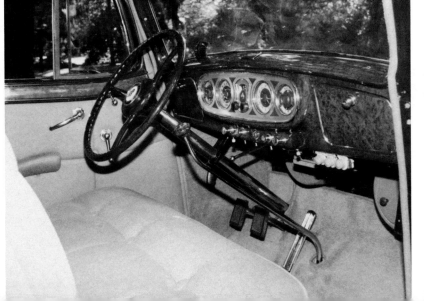

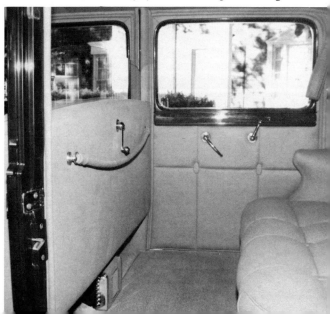

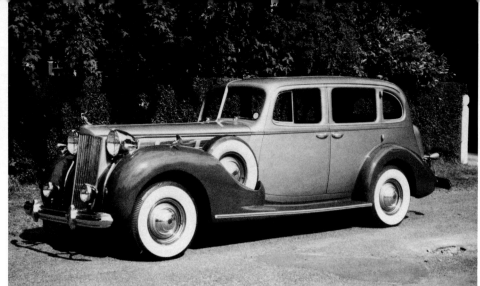

1938 Packard Super Eight 1603 Touring Sedan   *Owner: Martin Coomber of Bromley, Kent, United Kingdom*

Because the Junior Packards were brought into the company's numbering code in '38, the Super Eights moved up several notches. (The 1603 was the five-passenger sedan which had been the 1500 the year previous). Wheelbases remained the same, but the look was new. The radiator was set more upright, the front fenders were pontoons enveloping the sidemount on cars carrying them, and a split vee windshield (previously seen only on customs) with center chrome strip extending into the roof line was added. The '38 Twelves not only shared these changes, but the Super Eight's chassis too. Gone was the wheelbase that stretched 144 inches. All Senior Packards, except the 127-inch-wheelbase sedan, were on the 134- and 139-inch chassis. Production was down by half or more: 566 Twelves, 2,478 Super Eights.

Martin Coomber's 1603 Touring Sedan was first registered to a director of Marks & Spencer, a major department store chain in the United Kingdom. So far as is known, this Packard never left England, except perhaps for visits to the Continent. The huge Marchal headlamps and Lucas spotlights bespeak a Packard that was delivered Over There. Beauty is the name Martin has given her: "With no Twelves manufactured with right-hand drive, this model is the ideal Classic Packard for use in the United Kingdom. Such a car is, of course, a rarer sight on this side of the Pond than in the States, and so she excites enormous and gratifying interest and admiration wherever she goes. And this great pleasure is occasionally spiced by the wicked and wholly regrettable thought that should any member of the lower

1938 Packard Super Eight 1604 Formal Sedan, Brunn
Owners: Larry & Aloma Douroux of Eugene, Oregon

434

1938 Packard Super Eight 1604 Convertible Coupe   Owner: *Jack O'Connor of Cincinnati, Ohio*   Photos: *David Clark Wendt*

orders be careless enough to try to impede the car's majestic progress, they will be appropriately impaled on the razor-sharp wings of that justifiably proud (if pious) pelican mascot. In every respect except that of foot-down power, this Packard surpasses my Phantom III. In some ways the car feels ten years younger than the Rolls-Royce, even though of similar age, and is fully at home in today's very different driving conditions from the time she was built. The silky smooth gearshift is always a delight to operate, though

occasionally and absentmindedly she moves off from traffic lights in reverse gear, to the consternation of drivers behind. Automatic choke and tinted windows seem, on this side of the Atlantic, little short of a miracle for 1938. One appreciates the luxury touches of *two* cigar lighters, rear window blinds and hand mirror and leather-covered notepad for the rear passengers. And she boasts a Philco radio, with the aerial fitted under the nearside running board. The Art Deco styling of the interior trim and door and window hardware is a delight. And the dashboard is simply the most attractive of any car I know. Beauty must be one of the few Packards to have been inside the Palace of Westminster, as a bridal car for a wedding there two years ago.''

An estate in Hartford, Connecticut was home to the Super Eight 1604 Convertible Coupe that Jack O'Connor has owned for four decades: ''When I was fourteen I saw a car identical to mine one night in conservative Cincinnati, where great Classics were almost non-existent. A flamboyant local builder bought it, and his teenage son totaled it. I made up my mind that I would own one someday and did. It took me two years to find. The deceased owner in Hartford had willed the car to his chauffeur. Nineteen thirty-eight started a bulbous design trend some purists don't like, but I think it

works—a great evolution! The convertible top has not been up for thirty years. This wonderful car drives like a dream.''

The first owner's initials (E. C. M.) are still on the rear doors of the 1604 Brunn Formal Sedan owned by Larry & Aloma Douroux: ''This is one of the best original cars I have ever had. The full padded leather top and division window make for a very elegant automobile. The odometer just turned 40,000; being low mileage, it handles as if it were a new car.''

1938 Packard Twelve 1607 Two/Four-Passenger Coupe   *Owner: Warren J. Hoye of New Castle, Pennsylvania*

Of his '38 Packard Twelve, Warren Hoye comments, "A big, powerful and expensive automobile but the passengers travel outside in the rumble seat."

George Arents had his 1607 Formal Sedan restored "not as a show car but for the road, as a 'new' 1938 Packard Twelve to give me the experience of a true time warp. A family association with Packard plus the demonstrable performance of the Twelve against all comers, the reliability and the ever aristocratic styling have always attracted me to the marque. This was the first year the V-12 engine was moved forward in a chassis of reduced wheelbase, which improved handling, yet there was no reduction in interior roominess."

Keith Snyder agrees: "These were the best handling Senior Packards due to the changes in weight distribution and steering geometry. My 1607 Club Sedan was first owned by Philip K. Wrigley of the chewing gum Wrigleys. It represents to me the used Packard Twelve I wanted my father to buy when I was a boy. He didn't because that car only got nine miles to the gallon, which he didn't regard as sensible during the Depression. Nothing has changed . . . this restored beauty gets nine miles to the gallon."

The 1608 Brunn Touring Cabriolet

1938 Packard Twelve 1607 Formal Sedan
Owner: George Arents of Burbank, California

1938 Packard Twelve 1607 Club Sedan
Owner: Keith S. Snyder of Lincoln, Nebraska   Photo: Craig G. Andresen

436

1938 Packard Twelve 1608 Touring Cabriolet, Brunn

Owners: William & Jennifer Walker of Hudson, Florida

owned by Bill and Jennifer Walker debuted in the San Francisco showroom of Packard dealer Earle C. Anthony and was subsequently purchased by Florence Moore as a birthday present for her husband whose Moore Dry Dock was a prime contractor in the building of the Golden Gate Bridge. The $10,500 price tag included the substitution of black tires for the showroom white walls, a specially made set of fixed wind-wings and a sheared beaver rug for the rear passenger compartment.

Subsequently, a second radio was installed there, operating independently of the front unit and with the wire mesh antenna concealed in the roof. Just ten Brunns were produced in 1938; this was number ten. Amusingly, the body plate on the car is misspelled ''costom.'' Some have called the two small smoked-glass windows above the windshield the original ''moon roof.'' The Walkers have owned this Packard over two decades and driven it over 50,000 miles. Says Bill: ''A startling feature

is the silence of its engine. When stopped at a traffic light, one must watch the oil pressure gauge to be sure the engine is running; it cannot be heard. Another interesting feature is its ability to start forward in high gear without bucking. This is accomplished by putting the transmission in high gear, then turning on the ignition switch without touching the clutch or gas pedal. Push the starter button and the engine will start and the Packard will proceed thinking it has an automatic transmission.''

The 1608 Dual Cowl Phaeton owned by Robert Meyer is a one-of-a-kind custom built by Rollston for King Faisal II of Iraq, who was three years old at the time. Atypically, Rollston made little use of original body parts; virtually everything (including window frame castings) was specially made. The specifications supplied the coachbuilder by the royal family included a flag staff. A hand-formed brass filigree with illuminated panels in the colors of the Iraqi flag was made in Baghdad and added as the finishing touch. The ''Boy King'' ascended the throne a year after taking delivery of his new Packard and ruled Iraq until his death in 1958. Bob Meyer has owned the Faisal Packard since 1981.

1938 Packard Twelve 1608 Dual Cowl Phaeton, Rollston
Owner: Robert L. Meyer of King City, California

1939 Packard One Twenty 1701 Convertible Victoria, Darrin   *Owner: Floyd D. Kennedy of Bethlehem, Pennsylvania*

1939 Packard Super Eight 1705 Sedanca de Ville, Franay
Owner: Robert A. Titlow of Indianapolis, Indiana

By 1937 Howard Darrin had ended his Paris coachbuilding days and returned to the States. For the flamboyant "Dutch," there was just one place to settle: Hollywood. Setting up shop in an old bottling plant on Sunset Strip, he designed a sporty Packard for actor Dick Powell which attracted the attention of other filmdom luminaries as well as the Packard company, though there were misgivings on East Grand Boulevard initially. A Packard without running boards was a daring concept and Dutch, always known for building gorgeously, was not so esteemed for building well. Darrin prevailed in ultimately getting his Packard into the company catalogue, though production of these custom cars was always limited—in Hollywood into the summer of '39 and thereafter in Connersville, Indiana (the old Auburn-Cord plant) and Cincinnati (home of hearse-producing Sayers & Scoville). Available production figures indicate three cars for 1938, less than ten in '39, forty-three in '40, fewer than that in '41 and '42. Celebrity purchasers of Darrin Packards included Gary Cooper, Errol Flynn, Clark Gable—and tennis star Helen Wills Moody, who doubtlessly was as enamored of the car then as its current owner Floyd Kennedy is today: "The Darrin Packard developed the innovative closed-fender styling that emerged in 1933 into a sporty style in 1937 that took hold for a half-decade and commanded attention wherever it appeared. I like the 1939 edition in particular because less than ten were produced and therefore each was a little different from its companions, yet enough had already been built so that details were refined, and possible faults corrected. For instance, the cowl was made of cast aluminum to give the front end added stiffness. The Darrin has a large-car comfort feel on the road, and an engine that performs effortlessly. Except for the lack of an automatic transmission, it has all the desirable features of a much newer car, such as overdrive, sensitive brakes and highway hugging security. Most commanding is its styling, with a long hood, majestic front end, clean sweeping lines and enchanting low profile."

Meanwhile, in Paris, another Packard was being designed, the Super Eight 1705 Franay Sedanca de Ville owned by Bob Titlow: "This was the second 1705 built and the first 1939 model chassis received by Etablissements Barbezat, the Packard dealership in Paris. Bodied by Franay for Packard showroom display, it was purchased in February 1939 by a wealthy Frenchman and appeared that June in the Concours d'Elegance. After the surrender of France in 1940, the car was confiscated for the personal use of General Heinrich von Stuelpnagel, military governor-general for Vichy France. Following the liberation, it was taken over by the U.S. military as a headquarters staff car, initially for Paris, then Frankfurt, Germany. Wrecked in 1948, the car was acquired by the Packard dealer in Frankfurt, repaired and sold to U.S. Master Sergeant William Kimmel who brought it to the States. I purchased the car in 1968. Although Franay bodied a few Delahaye and Delage chassis after the war, this Packard to me represents the end of the linear-ally graceful custom body era in France."

1939 Packard Twelve 1707 Club Sedan
Owner: Mary W. Clarke of Fenton, Michigan

Nineteen thirty-nine represented the end for the venerable Packard Twelve as well. Just 446 were produced. Though a steering-column gearshift was standard for the rest of the Packard lineup, it was an option for the Twelves. John & Koko Carlson's 1707 Convertible Victoria was so fitted; their car also sports a Packard radio and a Lalique crystal mascot. With its high rear-end gear ratio, the Carlsons' Twelve is capable of better than 100 mph, which John documented in July of 1986.

The original owner of Mary Clarke's 1707 Club Sedan was ''Fifi'' Dorrance Calcut, an heiress to the Campbell Soup fortune. Before taking delivery, Mrs. Calcut had the car shipped from the dealer to Derham for fitting of a full Burbank tan padded top, curved glass roll-up divider window and grey Persian lamb fur carpet and hassocks. Gently driven by the same family chauffeur until 1972, this Packard transported the Calcut family each year from Bryn Mawr, Pennsylvania to Bar Harbor, Maine. The odometer reading today is 77,000.

1939 Packard Twelve 1707 Convertible Victoria
Owners: John & Koko Carlson of Port Moody, British Columbia

1939 Packard Twelve 1707 Convertible Victoria
Owners: Dee & Don Gerlinger of Mequon, Wisconsin

Dee & Don Gerlinger have owned their 1707 Convertible Victoria since 1984: "Although the car steers rather poorly on freeways that have been rutted by trucks, it is so well balanced and heavy that when we blew a tire I thought it was someone else's car. The Packard just rolled to the shoulder without swerving." The original Packard pushbutton radio in the Gerlinger car works just as well. Neither of these factors, however, was foremost in their desiring this particular car. "My wife and I, both being of the '40s era," says Don, "just couldn't resist a Packard painted yellow with red wheels and red leather seats."

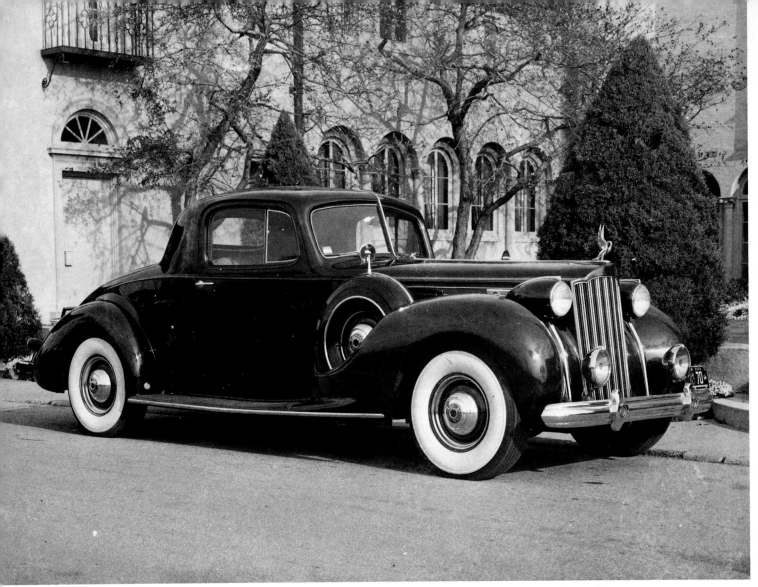

1939 Packard Twelve 1707 Two/Four-Passenger Coupe
Owner: Paul W. Clancy of Huntington Woods, Michigan   Photos: Doug Houston

Equally impressed with his 1707 Coupe is Paul Clancy: ''Every person has his favorite among those cars which he considers truly Classic. This fills all the criteria for me, as it is big, beautiful, elegant and expensive. In 1939 dollars it cost about $4,185. Today's money equivalent would be somewhere around $80,000. The thing was for all practical purposes a custom-built car, for Packard did not build a Twelve unless it had a firm order from the dealer. Hence the cost. I must also say it is a most satisfactory car in the area of performance. For all its weight—which is 6,030 pounds with two passengers, a load of gas and my forty-pound toolbox—this Packard will get up and go. The handling is impeccable. The clutch is as smooth as a schoolmarm's leg. The ride is so majestic as to put you to sleep. The seat is the acme of comfort. When you sit in it, you feel like you are the lord of all you survey. As far as I can determine, it was one of twelve coupes built that year. I am proud to be its caretaker.''

1940 Packard Super-8 One-Sixty 1803 Club Coupe
Owner: Bill Deibel of Seattle, Washington

For 1940 the Senior Packards had one engine (a new 160 hp 356-cubic-inch straight eight) and three wheelbases (127 inches for most body styles, 138 for five-passenger sedan and 148 for limousine and sedan accommodating eight). This was the last Packard year for a trunk rack, running boards as standard equipment and cable-controlled radio with floor speaker. Sealed beam headlights were new but they remained traditionally free-standing. ''Cooled by Mechanical Refrigeration'' was the way Packard announced its brand-new option of air conditioning. Trim and appointments—and higher price tags for same—differentiated the newly-designated One-Sixty and One-Eighty, the latter carrying the company's catalogued custom cars. Respective production figures were 5,662 and 1,900.

Writes Bill Deibel of his 1803 Club Coupe (the opera seats of which would be discontinued the year following): ''The first money I ever earned was 10¢ a week for whisk-brooming out the floor of my Dad's '39 Packard Super Eight Club Coupe and I've always had a desire to own a '40 . . . basically the same car but with the more powerful and brand-new 356 engine. This Packard has the highest torque-to-weight and horsepower-to-weight ratio of all 1940 model U.S.-built cars. It goes like hell.''

1940 Packard Super-8 One-Sixty 1805 Town Car, McNear   Owner: William R. Patton of Newport Beach, California

1940 Packard Super-8 One-Sixty 1803 Convertible Coupe   Owner: Don Sears of Omaha, Nebraska

1940 Packard Custom Super-8 One-Eighty 1807 Touring Sedan
Owner: Charles Nuckols Davidson, Jr.

1940 Packard Custom Super-8 One-Eighty 1808 Seven-Passenger Sedan
Owners: Jim & Myrna Schild of St. Louis, Missouri

1940 Packard Super-8 One-Eighty 1806 Club Sedan
Owners: Bud & Judie Hicks of Marshall, Michigan

Don Sears' 1803 Convertible Coupe drives "like a new car," he says, as well it might being a totally original 33,000-mile Packard.

Conversely, Bill Patton's McNear Packard, with 46,000 miles on the odometer today, became a new car a half-century ago: "Coachbuilder Egerton B. McNear of Brookline, Massachusetts produced this stylish town car on a One-Sixty chassis for Miss Emily Sears, who also resided in Brookline. McNear designed and built quite a few magnificent Classics. This particular body was delivered on a 1924 Locomobile Type 48 chassis, but by 1939 it was becoming difficult for Miss Sears' elderly chauffeur to wrestle through traffic. Because she so loved the coachwork design, McNear widened the body eight inches for her and installed it on the new Super-8 chassis. Thus this town car combines mid-1920's coach styling and elegance with the streamlined features of 1940 Packard fenders, hood, grille, etc.—a truly unique automobile."

"A smooth, powerful, luxury ride," says Charles Davidson, Jr. of his 1807 Touring Sedan, sentiment echoed—"with overdrive, it's like a modern car"—by Bud & Judie Hicks regarding their 1806 Club Sedan. The totally original 1808 Seven-Passenger Sedan owned by Jim & Myrna Schild was purchased from the son of original owner Henry C. Hartenbach: "The quality of the interior is very impressive, with wool broadcloth, fur carpeting and down-filled cushions."

1940 Packard Custom Super-8 One-Eighty 1806 Convertible Victoria, Darrin
Owners: Phil & Carol Bray of Grosse Ile, Michigan

The swoopy good looks of the Packard Darrin Convertible Victoria attracted forty-odd purchasers in 1940—and raves from four owners today. David Holls: "One of the all-time great designs." Gene Perkins: "Low to the ground, cutdown door, looks great with top down." Dick Gold: "My favorite Packard style." Phil & Carol Bray: "Sexiest convertible ever produced—and an excellent road car, especially with the R-9 overdrive transmission." The Bray car was the eighth 1940 Darrin produced, and together with number nine was begun in Dutch's shop on Sunset Strip and completed in Indiana after the Connersville plant was leased for Darrin production.

1940 Packard Custom Super-8 One-Eighty 1806 Convertible Victoria, Darrin
Owner: N. Gene Perkins of Greenwood, Indiana   Photos: Nancy Bailey

1940 Packard Custom Super-8 One-Eighty 1806 Convertible Victoria, Darrin
Owner: David Holls of Bloomfield Hills, Michigan

1940 Packard Custom Super-8 One-Eighty 1806 Convertible Victoria, Darrin
Owner: Richard G. Gold of Deephaven, Minnesota

1941 Packard Super-8 One-Sixty 1903 Convertible Sedan
Owner: Robert L. Meyer of King City, California

Wheelbases remained the same, but the 1941 Senior Packards looked longer and were—by five inches. Radiators were pushed forward and headlamps were integrated into the fenders, with the parking lamps mounted directly above them. If a customer so requested, running boards were eliminated; a black rubber gravel shield was fitted on closed cars, a chrome shield on convertibles, in the One-Sixty line. All One-Eighty models without running boards carried the latter. Introduced on One-Eighty closed cars were hydraulically-operated windows, and wood replaced the wood-grained metal mouldings of the year previous. Catalogued customs were carried in the One-Eighty line as well; in fact, the company noted that all One-Eighty Packards were "custom" cars available on special order only. Company focus that year was on the new non-Classic Clipper. Super-8 production decreased to 3,525 for the One-Sixty, 930 for the One-Eighty.

All One-Sixty Packards in this portfolio are road cars, Bob Meyer's used "primarily for pleasure driving," the Hulls' "a strong performer at both highway speeds and on steep mountain roads," and Marc Ohm's "a good tour car with most available options, including twin sidemounts, accessory bumper guards front and rear, driving lights, radio, heater, defroster, over-

1941 Packard Super-8 One-Sixty 1903 Convertible Coupe
Owners: Jim & Betty Hull of Littleton, Colorado

1941 Packard Super-8 One-Sixty 1904 Touring Sedan   Owner: Marc S. Ohm of St. Louis, Missouri

1941 Packard Super-8 Custom One-Eighty 1907 Formal Sedan   Owners: Lt. Colonel & Mrs. John Blaine of Milford, Michigan

1941 Packard Super-8 One-Sixty 1903 Convertible Sedan
Owner: Robert M. Messinger of Grand Rapids, Michigan   Photo: Dorothy Olsson Messinger

1941 Packard Super-8 Custom One-Eighty 1907 Formal Sedan
Owner: Gene M. Peltier of Lake Elmo, Minnesota

1941 Packard Super-8 Custom One-Eighty 1907 Touring Sedan
Owners: Harry Corson & Sharon Corson of Scottsdale, Arizona

drive—and air-conditioning!''

Bob Messinger's One-Sixty Convertible Sedan was a virtual resurrection, brought back to life from junkyard status—''wrecks to riches'' in Bob's fine phrase—and winner of the CCCA Michigan Region's ''Biggest Challenge Award'' in 1982.

A banker in White Plains, New York was the first owner of the Blaines' One-Eighty Formal Sedan: ''This car can transport seven full-sized adults in complete comfort. There are 'lazy susan' type swiveling, lighted, mirrored vanities built into each of the two rear blind pillars. The electric division window can be operated from either the front or rear passenger compartment. The car holds the road at least as well as our two modern Cadillacs. We especially enjoy the nostalgic reminiscing it evokes. Many senior citizens become misty-eyed when they see it.''

The Corsons have added 26,000 miles to the 50,000 on the odometer of their One-Eighty Touring Sedan when purchased in 1972. They are the third owners; the first was the proprietor of the Spic & Span Cleaners of Altoona, Pennsylvania.

Included among the many miles Gene Peltier has driven his One-Eighty Formal Sedan was a problem-free round trip from Minnesota to Rhode Island in 1984.

1941 Packard Super-8 Custom One-Eighty 1907 Limousine
Owner: Joel Prescott of Huntington Beach, California

Packard limousines in 1941, as previously, were catalogued only on the long 148-inch Super-8 chassis. Specially ordering such a car on the 138-inch chassis was Matilda Frelinghuysen of the brewery, copper mining and politically prominent family of Morristown, New Jersey. The Packard was delivered to her townhouse on Beekman Place in New York City. Joel Prescott owns it today: ''The big Packards just before World War II represent the denouement of true Classic Era styling—running boards, sidemounts, double-opening hoods, tall radiator, etc. The hydraulically-operated division glass in this car works as well as the windows. The single side-facing jumpseat makes it a true seven-passenger body. To all this, I've added one personal and extremely rare accessory: a gray mouton lap robe with the 'Packard Motor Company' label, which was handed down in my family from my great-grandparents who had a 1935 Packard Twelve.''

Among the coachbuilder cars offered on the 1941 Packard One-Eighty chassis was Dutch Darrin's Convertible Victoria, a catalogue entry for the second year. A "zippy" car, says Bill Lester of his example.

1941 Packard Super-8 Custom One-Eighty 1906 Convertible Victoria, Darrin
Owner: William M. Lester of Livingston, New Jersey

New customs included three from LeBaron, two of which appear here. Paul Hem's Seven-Passenger Touring Sedan has been a Toledo (Ohio) car for the whole of its life. One of nineteen such LeBarons produced (one of two believed extant), the car was originally ordered by the president of the Bunting Copper & Brass Company. Its $5,000+ price tag made it, together with the LeBaron Limousine, the most expensive catalogued Packard in '41. Paul purchased the car from the Bunting estate three decades ago: "It has traveled 28,000 flawless miles since. The odometer now registers 67,000 but this Packard must think the gauge is lying because it behaves like a 10,000 mile car. After driving contemporary Cadillacs, Lincolns and Mercedes, it's a real treat to get behind the wheel of the whisper-quiet and powerful Packard LeBaron of 1941. This is true luxury!"

Attracting Gene Perkins to his One-Eighty Sport Brougham were such LeBaron touches as the chrome-trimmed window openings, the sweep of the roofline, the absence of sidemounts, the close-coupled look,

the fender skirts. The radio antenna of this car is under the running boards, and there's a foot rest for the right front passenger. No more than eighty of these cars were produced, fourteen are known to exist.

Bob Bahre's One-Eighty Con-

vertible Victoria, independently built by Bohman & Schwartz, was one of three produced, two of which remain extant. Remarkable on this car is the smooth non-louvered sweep of the hood and the fender line which sweeps back into the front door.

1941 Packard Super-8 Custom One-Eighty 1908 Seven-Passenger Touring Sedan, LeBaron
Owner: Paul Hem of Toledo, Ohio

1941 Packard Super-8 Custom One-Eighty 1907 Sport Brougham, LeBaron
Owner: N. Gene Perkins of Greenwood, Indiana   Photo: Nancy Bailey

1941 Packard Super-8 Custom One-Eighty 1907 Convertible Victoria, Bohman & Schwartz
Owner: Bob Bahre of Oxford, Maine

1942 Packard Super-8 Custom One-Eighty 2006 Convertible Victoria, Darrin
Owner: Andrew D. Darling of Edina, Minnesota

Turn signals, electric windshield wipers, an accelerator pedal starter, dish-shaped hubcaps that no longer said ''Packard'' and a straight-eight engine generating five more horsepower (165) were new to the Senior Packards for 1942. But the main word at the company remained Clipper, with the styling of the new model permeating all Junior Packards (except convertibles) and some of the Seniors. On the 127-inch wheelbase, the Darrin Convertible Victoria was the only non-Clipperized '42 Packard. The traditional Super-8 look remained on the 138- and 148-inch wheelbase cars, though the radiator's flanking grilles were set on a Clipper-like horizontal rather than the vertical of yore. During a model year abbreviated by Pearl Harbor, 2,580 One-Sixty and 672 One-Eighty Packards were produced.

Bob Turnquist's Darrin was not only the first of fifteen Convertible Victorias produced for '42 but also the first chassis off the Twentieth Series production line. The car was purchased new by Arthur McEwan: ''The seven McEwan brothers owned the largest paper mills in the East. They all drove Packards. Whenever a brother bought a new model, the oldest one in the garage would be given to a less wealthy McEwan. At one point, there were forty-two

1942 Packard Super-8 Custom One-Eighty 2006 Convertible Victoria, Darrin
Owner: Robert E. Turnquist of Morristown, New Jersey

1942 Packard Super-8 Custom One-Eighty 2008 Seven-Passenger Limousine
Owner: Warren J. Hoye of New Castle, Pennsylvania

Packards sitting under the McEwan family tree. When this Darrin was bought, Arthur McEwan's stable included a '41 Packard Station Wagon, a '36 Packard Dietrich Victoria and a '34 Standard Eight Club Sedan. The sedan was given to his father-in-law, and the McEwans gave a small New Year's Day party to toast their brand-new acquisition,

suggesting to my parents that I be brought along since they knew I loved cars. The fact that it was a Darrin didn't mean all that much to me; however, the lines of the car, the electric clutch, the overdrive, the directional signals, the speedometer needle that changed colors with speed and a shortwave radio were fascinating. The following day Morristown (New Jersey) Packard put the Darrin in a railroad boxcar and shipped it to Palm Beach where the McEwans wintered.'' Bob Turnquist acquired the car from the McEwan family in 1981.

Andrew Darling's Darrin was sold originally in Palm Beach, where it spent most of its life prior to leaving Florida for the Darling collection in Minnesota a decade ago: ''The narrow door posts, the vee windshield, the cut-down door . . . this is one of the most handsome cars that was produced in 1942 and a great credit to the Packard marque.''

Like the Darrin, the 148-inch-wheelbase Seven-Passenger Limousine owned by Warren Hoye represents the end of an era. It was the swan song for the traditional Super-8 body, at least on a Packard. During the war the company sold the dies for its non-Clipper models to the Soviet Union, where the familiar body lines emerged on the ZIS, which enjoyed Russian state car status for years.

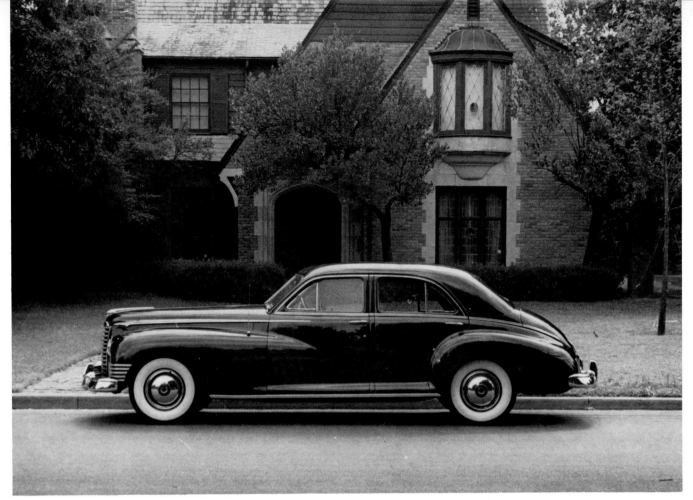

1947 Packard Custom Super Clipper 2106 Touring Sedan   *Owner: Steve Chapman of Waxahachie, Texas*

Clipper. When introduced before the war, the car was a real surprise to Packard loyalists and, as sales indicated, a pleasant one. Lower than any other Packard on the market and wider than virtually every other car in the industry, the Clipper was sleek and streamlined—and a marked departure from traditional Packard styling. Responsible for the design concept was Dutch Darrin, who had been offered a thousand dollars a day and given a ten-day deadline for the assignment. Packard refined the Darrin concept for production. With the sale of its other body dies, the company committed itself wholly to the Clipper postwar. The Twenty-First Series was introduced in 1946 with only detail differences—a new center grille the most prominent—from the prewar Twentieth Series.

Classics in the Packard lineup were two: the 2106 on the 127-inch and the 2126 on the 148-inch wheelbase chassis. Models available likewise were two for both. Steve Chapman's 2106 Touring Sedan has a factory original interior and "the engine has never been apart, but is still as quiet and smooth as you could hope for—quieter, in fact, than most modern cars."

Gene Perkins' 2106 Club Sedan is, as he points out, the "most sporty model offered in the Twenty-First Series because there were *no* convertibles."

1947 Packard Custom Super Clipper 2106 Club Sedan   *Owner: N. Gene Perkins of Greenwood, Indiana*   *Photo: Nancy Bailey*

1947 Packard Custom Super Clipper 2126 Seven-Passenger Sedan, Henney
Owner: Reg Collings of Calgary, Alberta

1947 Packard Custom Super Clipper 2126 Seven-Passenger Sedan, Henney
Owner: Kenneth R. Kost, M.D. of Kittanning, Pennsylvania

Bodies on the long-wheelbase 2126 chassis were a seven-passenger sedan and a limousine built by Henney, the coachbuilder long renowned in the professional car field. Both Reg Collings' and Ken Kost's 2126 Packards are original cars.

Ken has driven his Seven-Passenger Sedan some 52,000 miles in seven years, including seven CARavans during which the car often served as a "First Aid Station" for other Classics in distress.

Reg finds the ride and performance of his similar car superior to that of his two pre-war Rolls-Royce: "But with the amount of driving our son Darcy has done with the car, a little bird tells me it is not mine anymore. Of course, Dad still pays the insurance, storage and all the expenses . . ."

The Packard Motor Car Company introduced new body styling for 1948. The last Packard Classics were the Custom Super Clippers of '47. Production totaled less than 10,000 cars.

459

PIERCE-ARROW

Archer mascot from Steven & Sandra Horowitz's 1929 Model 133 Seven-Passenger Sedan

That one of the proudest and most prestigious marques ever to grace American roads descended from a company that began life building birdcages is among the more delightful anomalies of automobile history. Adding bicycles to the firm's household product line during the Gay Nineties provided the transition. The first cars of the George N. Pierce Company of Buffalo, New York were called simply Pierce. By 1904, with the addition of a $4,000 Great Arrow model, the company found its niche in the luxury market. After winning the famed Glidden Tour an astounding five consecutive years, the corporate and marque name changed to Pierce-Arrow. "Great" was dropped as redundant. Nineteen thirteen brought the fender-mounted headlamps that would be a Pierce-Arrow signature ever after. The company's advertisements were literally works of art—and, at 824.8 cubic inches, Pierce's mighty 66 shared honors with Peerless as America's biggest-ever production engine. Only Packard built more luxury cars during this era. Then progress seemed to shuffle by the venerable Buffalo company. As other prestige car builders moved to eight cylinders, Pierce stayed with six; styling clung tenaciously to the traditional. But America's rum runners had put their stamp of approval on the Pierce-Arrow engine (finding its supreme silence ideal for their boats), and the obduracy in design had a piquant appeal (not until 1920 was the marque switched from right- to left-hand drive). The Upstate New York company whose graceful archer mascot pointed the Pierce-Arrow down the road liked doing things its own way. . . .

1925 Pierce-Arrow Model 80 Four-Passenger Coupe
Owners: Phelps & Joan Chamberlain of Oakland, California

The Model 80 had joined the Pierce-Arrow line in 1924 as a smaller companion car to the T-head Dual Valve Six introduced following the Armistice. At 130 inches, its wheelbase was eight inches shorter and its price range was a couple of thousand dollars less. The Model 80's 288.5-cubic-inch L-head six developed 70 hp, thirty less than its bigger T-head brother.

Phelps & Joan Chamberlain have owned their Model 80 Four-Passenger Coupe for eight years: "The body is aluminum, the framework hardwood, the wheels measure twenty-two inches. Four-wheel brakes were fitted. The temperature gauge is on the dashboard, the gasoline gauge on the fuel tank. The oil filter is Pierce-Arrow's own. We like this body style. It's 190 inches long, 68 inches wide and 76 inches high—and the trunk is built in. The interior has a bucket seat for the driver, the jump seat next to him folds under the dash, and there is a 'parcel box' next to the rear seat.''

At $2,895, Tom Sparks' 1926 Model 80 Roadster was $800 less expensive than the Chamberlains' Coupe (closed cars often carried the premium in those days). For both 1925 and 1926, Pierce-Arrow sales remained comfortably above the 5,000 mark.

1926 Pierce-Arrow Model 80 Roadster
Owner: Tom Sparks of North Hollywood, California

above and page opposite
1927 Pierce-Arrow Model 36
Seven-Passenger Sedan

Owners: Eric & Molly Rosenau
of Ramona, California

1927 Pierce-Arrow Model 36 Runabout
Owner: Alfred Ferrara of Gates Mills, Ohio

Among Pierce-Arrow idiosyncrasies was the preference occasionally to refer to its larger cars by smaller numbers. The Model 36 carried the T-head 414.7-cubic-inch engine. Both cars shown here were priced at close to $6,000.

A previous owner of the Rosenaus' Seven-Passenger Sedan was Richard Byrd, Jr. (Admiral Byrd's son). The car, which they have owned since 1961, remains largely original: "It runs very well and is very reliable, if not very fast. Comfortable cruising is 40-45 mph. The Model 36 was the last T-head dual valve Pierce-Arrow built. It was also one of the first American cars with vacuum power-assisted brakes. Pierce-Arrow workmanship in this period was unexcelled."

"Quality engineering and quality products all around," echoes Al Ferrara, who has owned his Model 36 Runabout since 1974.

1928 Pierce-Arrow Model 81 Roadster   *Owner: Frederick Z. Tycher of Dallas, Texas*

Nineteen twenty-eight was Pierce-Arrow's last six-cylinder year. The Model 36 continued unchanged, the new Model 81 had five more horsepower (for 75) than its predecessor Model 80.

Comments Fred Tycher: ''There were a number of very unique and interesting design features and details on the 1928 Pierce-Arrows. The company had engaged J. Saoutchik, a noted French designer, as styling consultant for this model. Many of his touches have a definite continental flair; from the placement, size and trim of the famous Pierce fender headlamps to the very deco-looking dashboards, the 81's were certainly the most European-looking Pierces ever built. I personally do not regard the mid-twenties as a high point of automotive styling. However, there always seem to be exceptions within each marque, no matter how drab the majority of the line happens to be. If I am to believe all the compliments this 1928 Roadster has received, it is an exception. Today it is a tattered, torn and well-worn little car, needing every phase of the restorer's art, but it still turns heads wherever it goes. From the day I picked up this Pierce-Arrow in Romeo, Michigan for a long weekend trip (1,248 miles) to Dallas, it has been a much-travelled Classic. In ten years, through ten different states, it has logged thousands of miles. Although no match to the later Classics for sustained high-speed motoring, it is a peppy, fun car to drive.''

Nineteen twenty-eight had been a pivotal year in Pierce-Arrow history. Company chairman Colonel Charles Clifton, one of the industry's most revered figures and the man who had guided Pierce's automotive venture from the beginning, died. And company president Myron Forbes, believing the end near for small producers in the industry too, engineered a merger with Studebaker of South Bend, Indiana. In doing so, Forbes engineered himself out of the company, Studebaker's Albert Erskine adding the Pierce-Arrow presidency to the one he already held in South Bend. The two companies continued to operate independently, however, and the honeymoon period was felicitous for Pierce as sales nearly doubled to 9,840 cars for 1929. The new Pierce-Arrow eight, developed in Buffalo prior to the merger, was widely lauded. The new Pierce-Arrow model designations, with uncharacteristic logic, translated to wheelbase length.

Ben Lalomia limns the '29 Pierce-Arrow: "The new L-head straight-eight engine with detachable head and nine main bearings was cast en bloc, displaced 366 cubic inches and developed 125 hp at 3200 rpm (maximum was 3800 rpm). This was the first year for non-shatter glass throughout, the driver's seat was adjustable and the all-steel body panels were sound-proofed by an anti-rumble compound. My car sold for $4,250 when new. It is very comfortable to drive and has very good low-speed pulling power."

1929 Pierce-Arrow Model 143 Seven-Passenger Enclosed Drive Limousine   *Owner: Ben Lalomia of Williamsville, New York*

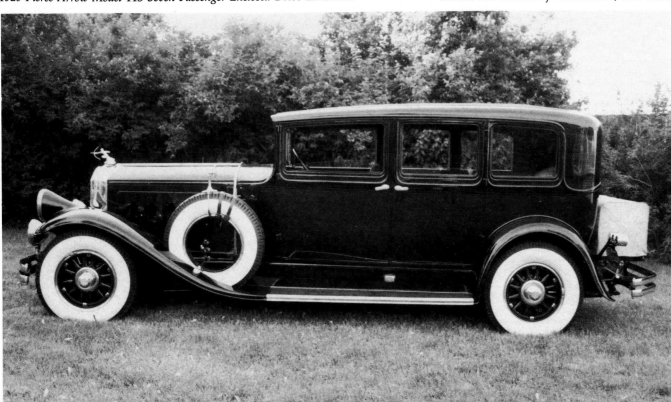

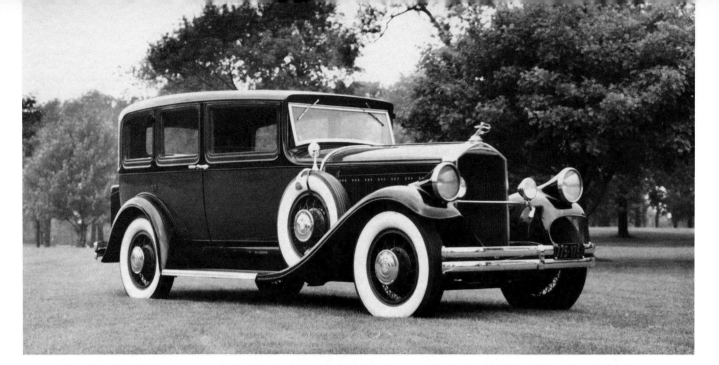

1929 Pierce-Arrow Model 133 Seven-Passenger Sedan
Owners: Steven & Sandra Horowitz of Flossmoor, Illinois   Photos: Sheila O'Donnell

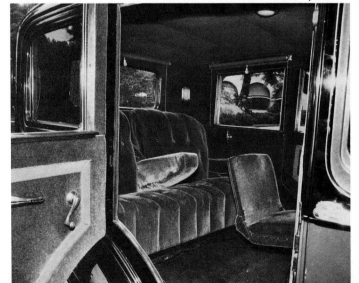

1929 Pierce-Arrow Model 133 Sport Coupe,　　　　　　　　　*Owner: Frank Aksamit of Wichita, Kansas*

A funeral director in Colorado was the first owner of Steven & Sandra Horowitz's Seven-Passenger Sedan: "Sleeker in styling than previous Pierce-Arrows, our car is roomy inside, the kids love the jump-seats—and it handles well, is reliable and cruises the highway at 55 mph. In an 'economy run' competition sponsored by the Greater Illinois Region CCCA through 175 miles of rustic countryside, our car did *not* get the worst mileage. A Packard Twelve and Chrysler Airflow beat us."

Frank Aksamit has owned his 1929 Sport Coupe for nearly two decades: "My wife Becky and I were 'depression kids.' We both grew up on Kansas farms riding in and driving boneshaking Ford T's and A's so we especially enjoy the wonderful smooth ride and power of this Classic. The Sport Coupe had been purchased new from a Wichita dealer by the second husband of a wealthy lady rancher, who drove it until he was fatally shot during a family dispute. Stored for years by a Flint Hills rancher until we bought it, the car had only 18,000 miles. We've added another 10,000. This Pierce-Arrow still has the original inner tubes in its new tires, including some of the old air in the tubes!"

1929 Pierce-Arrow Model 133 Club Sedan
Owner: Frank Aksamit of Wichita, Kansas

In 1984 Frank Askamit added the 1929 Club Sedan to his collection: "Being priced at the top end of the standard series, this body style has several of the features of Pierce-Arrow's custom models such as louvered hood doors, deluxe interior and the same dashboard layout. Unlike the Sport Coupe which I just painted and provided a new interior, the Club Sedan has been given a frame-up restoration. The car had been so well kept, however, that no new wood replacement was necessary."

In 1990, just as this book was in final preparation, Roy Judd completed the three-year restoration of his Convertible Coupe: "To my view, Pierce-Arrow was the premier car in '29. Quality was the highest, few cars were more powerful, the styling with those signature headlights was tops. I've always liked the Pierce-Arrow emphasis on details, the white back-up light, the stop light with 'S' showing when the brake is applied. Before installation in the chassis, every Pierce-Arrow engine was tested in a sound-proof room for twenty-four hours."

1929 Pierce-Arrow Model 133 Convertible Coupe
Owner: Roy A. Judd of Hermosa Beach, California

1930 Pierce-Arrow Model A Seven-Passenger Touring Owner: Theodore Fuller of Greenwich, Connecticut

Pierce-Arrow returned to its fetchingly inscrutable designations for 1930—the Model B with the '29 engine on 134- and 139-inch wheel-base chassis, the Model A fitted with a slightly larger (385 cubic inches, 132 hp) straight eight in a 144-inch chassis.

Since the mid-Twenties the Broad-moor Hotel in Colorado Springs had been a stalwart customer of Pierce-Arrow with fully sixty of the Buffalo cars in its fleet. Because climbing Pikes Peak without radiators boiling dry or engines burning out was a requirement, these cars had been

mechanically modified at the factory. Ted Fuller's Seven-Passenger Touring was one of the new fleet of Pierce-Arrows dispatched to the Broadmoor in 1930: "Basically, the car is standard Pierce with dual coils and points and an updraft carburetor. Geared low for Pikes Peak, it is not a

speedy car but it is the most reliable of all my automobiles. No mechanical repairs have been made since those I performed when I bought it in 1952. This is a great car for taking a group of friends someplace. It can hold seven comfortably, and of course the kids love it. It is also a good car for parades because of the extra-low gear which permits it to creep along at marching speeds. Local politicians have called this Pierce-Arrow into play on many occasions.''

Mort Bullock's Sport Phaeton is on the shorter of the two Model B chassis: ''I have always admired the styling of the 1929-31 Pierce-Arrows, a vast improvement over the boxy '28 cars. The phaeton is one of the most desirable models with its body moulding swooping over the rear fender to form the entire rear end of the car and lending itself to a striking two-tone paint scheme. Interesting engineering details are the ignition lock which also locks the steering column and the recycling of breather fumes from the crankcase back into the carburetor, features reintroduced a few years ago as new developments. I consider myself lucky to own this car. When Seth Pancoast died, his widow Elsa wanted the Pierce-Arrow to go to a good home and made inquiries to many of Seth's friends in the hobby as to who would take the best care of the car. I was flattered she offered it to me over other prospective purchasers, subject to two conditions—first, I would never reveal the purchase price and, second, I would not resell it unless I was in dire financial straits. I have honored both of those requests for the past seventeen years.''

Driver's compartment and open doors showing seven-passenger seating
—from Theodore Fuller's 1930 Pierce-Arrow Model A Touring

1930 Pierce-Arrow Model B Sport Phaeton   *Owner: Morton Bullock of Baltimore, Maryland*   *Photo: K. Karger*

1931 Pierce-Arrow Model 43 Roadster   *Owner: David C. Engel of Greenland, New Hampshire*

From 7,000 cars in 1930, Pierce-Arrow sales fell to less than 3,000 in 1931. Designations hearkened back to the smaller-figure/larger-car formula. The Model 43 carried Pierce's small eight on 134- and 137-inch chassis. The large eight was fitted to the 142-inch-wheelbase Model 42 and the 147-inch wheelbase Model 41.

David Engel's car, which he has owned since 1964, is one of seven 1931 Model 43 Roadsters known to exist: "It has been driven all over the northeastern U.S. and into Canada. An excellent road car, it is easy to handle and steer and has superior mechanical brakes. Six 19-inch wire wheels were fitted; the back-up light and the double baffle exhaust manifold were standard equipment. This car is often referred to as a 'five-door' roadster. The two front doors and those to the rumble seat and golf compartment are readily seen, but behind the front seat (and hidden with the top down) is a padded compartment with a lock. The car was built during Prohibition, of course, and legend says this fifth door was for a 'fifth'—and padded so the glass bottle wouldn't break if the car went over a severe bump."

1931 Pierce-Arrow Model 43 Tourer   *Owner: Thomas J. Lester of Deerfield Beach, Florida*

''An excellent driver with light steering,'' says Tom Lester of his Model 43 Tourer. ''It's a Pierce and just looks great.''

Dick Gold's Model 42 dual cowl Sport Phaeton is one of five extant: ''I bought this Pierce as a low-mileage (17,500) used car in 1948, and it's been part of our family ever since. It's been driven coast to coast twice. Our two children grew up with the car, and now we're raising five grandchildren in it. The bracket headlights, which were a Pierce option, are unusual. Interestingly, for a time New York State, where the

cars were produced, didn't allow the traditional Pierce-Arrow fender-mounted lamps. I'm the third owner of this Sport Phaeton. The original owner was a U.S. Navy officer who traded it even up for a 1930 Essex Coupe because the Pierce was such a gas hog. During World War II fuel economy overrode all!''

Originally delivered in Connecticut, the Zappones' Model 42 Convertible Coupe has a documented 49,000 miles. Comments Tony: ''The long 142-inch wheelbase accentuates the small top (copied from the Derham customs of 1930) and passenger com-

partment. The car features the smooth top lines of a roadster with the convenience of roll-up windows. There is no outside handle for the rumble seat; an inside pull sends the lid literally catapulting up. An excellent original vehicle, the car needed only cosmetic enhancement. All glass is original, including the beveled rear window. Pierce-Arrow trim shop tags are still stapled on the bottom of the seats. The car was fitted with the optional four-speed transmission without freewheeling. Shifting isn't necessary in city driving except for complete stops.''

1931 Pierce-Arrow Model 42 Sport Phaeton   *Owner: Richard G. Gold of Deephaven, Minnesota*

1931 Pierce-Arrow Model 42 Convertible Coupe

Owners: Tony & Claire Zappone of Brockport, New York

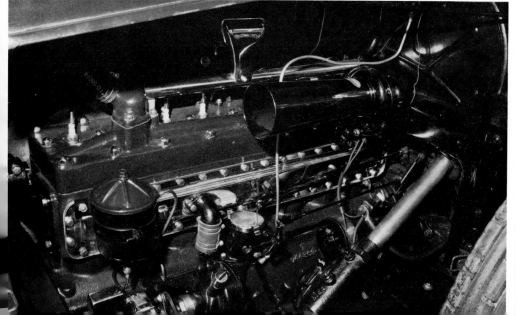

1931 Pierce-Arrow Model 41 Salon Group Seven-Passenger Tourer   *Owners: Jon & Sandra Lee of Brunswick, Maine*

Since November of 1988, the Model 41 Seven-Passenger Tourer has been in Jon & Sandra Lee's garage: "We haven't driven this car much yet but we have followed it a lot. On two CARavans it passed us often so the only way we could get past it was buy it. One previous owner had traded a Duesenberg for this Pierce and claimed he delivered a truck and drove home in a real nice car. The Pierce is surprisingly easy to handle and does not exhibit the lumbering feel of some of the similar vintage Packards and Cadillacs we have driven. In Pierce advertising, the Model 41 Salon Group was compared to the Cadillac V-16, although the Pierce was closer in size, performance and price to the V-12 Cadillac. Despite the base price of our car being promoted as $4,275, a hand-written notation in the salesman's fact book gives the figure as $5,200. Prices were padded then too."

LeBaron provided the only catalogued custom Pierce-Arrows for 1931. The advertised price tag of the Brownings' Model 41 Club Sedan was $5,375. "Our car is number 17 of 25 produced," says Matt. "In my opinion, this is one of the most beautiful and comfortable American

sport sedans of its day. On the long 147-inch wheelbase, the car is low and superbly stable on the road. Its power and speed with overdrive make it a great pleasure to drive on the highway. What appears to be a pistol holder, made of the original upholstery material, is underneath the dash and just forward of the front door in plain sight on the passenger side. This might be explained by the car's original owner,

Dennis Cooney, a Chicago notable reputed to be the number one competitor of Jim Colosimo (who was employed by Al Capone). Cooney sold the Pierce to Montana Conklin, a commission merchant dealing with sheep in the Union Stockyards of Chicago. His wife used the Pierce, always chauffeur-driven, until her death soon after. It passed through several other owners before my acquisition in 1973."

1931 Pierce-Arrow Model 41 Salon Group Club Sedan, LeBaron   Owners: Mr. & Mrs. Matt S. Browning of Ogden, Utah

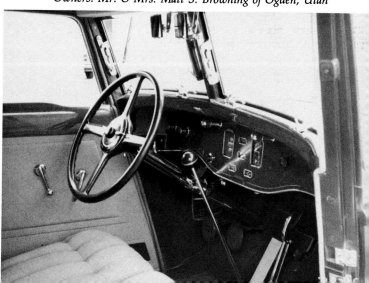

1932 Pierce-Arrow Model 54 Convertible Sedan
Owners: Berta & Jay Leon of Hubbard, Texas

With sales continuing to fall, Pierce-Arrow straight-eight models, save for the vee grille, were not significantly changed for 1932. The Urlik Model 54 Convertible Sedan, which Len & Nancy drive frequently, is unusual again for the bracket headlamps, which have enabled the Urliks to trace the car's prewar ownership to Florence Colwell of Patchogue, New York.

The artillery wood wheels were an option on the Leons' Model 54 Convertible Sedan which was Jay's present to Berta in 1981: "I had asked her what she wanted to do for her 50th birthday, and she said she was going to cry all day but something special to ease the pain would help. When I located this car and asked if it would do, she replied, 'what pain?' The front of this Pierce-Arrow is an astonishing sight: those famous headlights on the fenders, the two matching park lights in between, the pair of driving lights on the bumper, the chrome-plated horns, etc. Convertible sedans are always elegant bodies. This car is particularly so.''

1932 Pierce-Arrow Model 54 Convertible Sedan
Owners: Leonard & Nancy Urlik of Beverly Hills, California

476

By 1933 the Studebaker/Pierce-Arrow marriage had fallen apart. The South Bend company was in receivership; Albert Erskine committed suicide. A group of Buffalo bankers purchased Pierce-Arrow, retaining as president Arthur J. Chanter, a former Studebaker man who had assumed that post during the final few desperate months of Erskine's life. Desperation was writ everywhere in Buffalo, if belied by the introduction of the new 365.6-cubic-inch 135 hp straight-eight models.

"This was rare engineering for 1933," says Glenn Shaffer, "hydraulic valve lifters, low-silhouette worm drive, unusual power servo-type mechanical brakes, Bendix Startix. In my opinion, this was the best ever Pierce-Arrow in both styling and performance, produced at a time when nobody could afford to buy one. This straight-eight Pierce outperforms our Packard Twelves; indeed, it is the best driver of the nine Classics we own. It's not a V-12, it's not a custom-bodied car, it isn't even an open model. But, wherever this car goes, it draws many admirers. I guess the proper word is charm. It has that intangible quality usually reserved for the more exotic Classics."

1933 Pierce-Arrow Model 836 Club Brougham   *Owners: Glenn E. & Margaret Shaffer, Jr. of El Dorado, California*

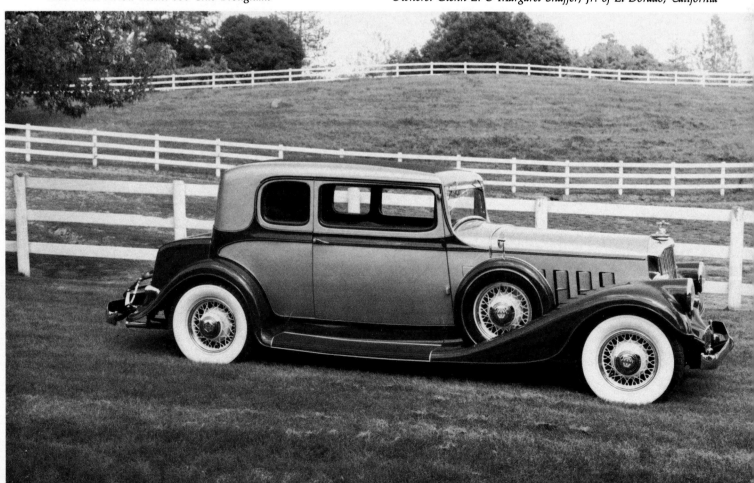

The competition had forced Pierce-Arrow to a twelve-cylinder line introduced in November 1931. The company promoted it vigorously with a 24-hour record-breaking run on the salt flats of Bonneville in 1932. Behind the wheel was D. Absolom Jenkins, a teetotaling and tough Mormon who knew not the meaning of the word fatigue. Driving unassisted, Ab both averaged more than 125 mph during the last hour and shaved so that he could be photographed without stubble as he alighted from the car.

Al Zamba has owned his 1933 LeBaron Convertible Sedan since 1978: "The engine is smooth, quiet and with 461.8 cubic inches and 175 hp, very powerful. The graceful elegance of the body design is perfectly expressed on the 147-inch wheelbase: the long hood covering all those cylinders, the massive five-inch-thick doors with real wood trim all around the sills and dash, the impressive grille and flowing headlights . . . the car is meticulous."

1933 Pierce-Arrow Twelve Model 1247 Convertible Sedan, LeBaron
Owner: Alvin Zamba of Pittsburgh, Pennsylvania   Photos: Carl Lindquest

1933 Pierce-Arrow Twelve Silver Arrow Show Car
Owner: Blackhawk Classic Auto Collection of Danville, California

One of the most talked-about cars in America in 1933 was the Silver Arrow from Pierce. It was a dream car with a $10,000 price tag. Pierce-Arrow spokesmen insisted their intention had not been "to be 'smart' or to develop a freakish automobile." The Silver Arrow was revolutionary but not otherworldly. Pierce-Arrow fully planned to make its dream car come true in a new line of production automobiles.

Ironically, the Silver Arrow concept had originally been sketched by Phillip Wright for one of the "car of the future" contests Harley Earl promoted among stylists in the Art and Colour Section. General Motors wasn't interested in Wright's idea, but Pierce-Arrow (where the young designer had friends) was. Five V-12 chassis were pulled from the assembly line in Buffalo and shipped

to South Bend for the building of the bodies. Three months was the deadline. Behind locked doors, work continued around the clock. The deadline was made.

By 1933 streamlining was being given a cursory nod by U.S. luxury car makers. The Silver Arrow was a full and glorious curtsy. From the split rear window in its gracefully tapered back to the spare wheels concealed behind the fenders up front, the car was breathtakingly sleek. No wooden structural parts intruded. The roof had been hammered from a single sheet of steel. All body panels had been welded into a smooth envelope. Door handles were recessed; wind resistant and removable full skirts were added to the rear fenders. The only place on the Silver Arrow where aerodynamics was not considered was the top of

the radiator, where Pierce's archer mascot rode proudly.

At the New York Automobile Show, where the car debuted in January, Pierce-Arrow executives were exultant—"a number of people of national prominence" had asked when they could get one. At the Century of Progress Exposition in Chicago, others posed the same question. But turmoil soon followed in South Bend, chaos in Buffalo, as Studebaker moved into receivership and Pierce-Arrow ownership changed hands. The project was lost in the rush of events. January 26th had been the day the Silver Arrow now in the Blackhawk collection was shipped from Buffalo to the Chicago World's Fair. Its next home was that of an artist from Lake Forest, Illinois. The other four Silver Arrows were sold off as well.

1934 Pierce-Arrow Twelve Model 1240 Silver Arrow Coupe-Brougham
Owner: N. Gene Perkins of Greenwood, Indiana   Photos: Nancy Bailey

Listing losses of $1,027,000 for the first seven months of the year, the Pierce-Arrow Motor Car Company filed for reorganization in 1934. But if dealing with that exigency meant the show car would not see production reality, a production Pierce-Arrow could be given those styling concepts which might logistically be rendered into a model with a less-dream-like $3,295 price tag. As Gene Perkins' 1934 production Silver Arrow indicates, the result was not revolutionary but it was most certainly radical for 1934, and beautifully so.

1934 Pierce-Arrow Model 840A Enclosed Drive Limousine
Owner: Reggie N. Nash of Richmond, Virginia

In 1934 Pierce-Arrow built less than 1,500 vehicles on four different wheelbases with two different engines, eleven factory body styles and two different levels of body trim. It was an embarrassment of production riches which showroom sales proved the company could ill afford.

Reggie Nash's Model 840A Enclosed Drive Limousine carries the 385-cubic-inch straight eight (now producing 140 hp) in the 144-inch chassis: ''The base price for this model was $3,350 but original owner Harry Frazier ordered a lot of options—six demountable artillery wheels, trunk rack and two spare wheels with tires in fender wells for $150.00, a pair of tire covers for $32.00 plus tire cover mirrors for $17.50, chrome-plated radiator shutters for $25.00, special color combination for $90.00, hassocks in lieu of a footrest for $25.00 and $50.00 for leather upholstery in front. This was Pierce-Arrow's first year for cross-beam dimming of the headlights, an adjustable rear seat for lounging or regular position, tinted safety glass and complete body insulation against noise and heat. The car floats down the road smooth as an arrow. Sitting in the back seat and gazing through the division window, it looks a block long. Standing outside, looking at its 'maroon light' and 'maroon dark' paint scheme striped in 'fireglow' I say to myself, 'What a beautiful car! I would buy it, but I already own it!'''

1934 Pierce-Arrow Twelve Model 1240A Enclosed Drive Limousine
Owner: Pat & John C. Meyer III of Canoga Park, California   Photos: Jason Meyer

For a quarter of a century John Meyer has owned his 1240A Enclosed Drive Limousine on the 144-inch chassis: ''Yes, it's true extant Pierce-Arrow V-12's are about one-third the Duesenbergs surviving, and the engine is a fantastic achievement —and, yes, the styling is truly elegant but it's the support of my family that makes this car worth having. Restoring this Classic was a family affair of sanding and rubbing that stretched out for fourteen years. The biggest compliment we receive each time this Classic is driven is the frequent comment from people that it seems to be an all-original car to them—not a brand-new automobile, but one that is like the factory meant it to be.''

Bob Reeve's Model 1248A Enclosed Drive Limousine on the 147-inch chassis is an all-original car including paint and interior. Originally delivered to H. H. Tammen, the owner of the *Denver Post*, the car was displayed in several museums prior to Bob's acquisition in 1986.

''My car has body number one and was probably the only one built in 1934 with this styling,'' says Bob Sands of his 1248A Brunn Town Brougham. ''Few cars were as powerful as the 462-cubic-inch V-12 Pierce-Arrow. Neither Packard's nor Cadillac's twelve could match it. The transmission is synchromesh free-wheeling type with silent helical second gear. Since 1933 Pierce advertising had stated that 'full automatic power brakes are available for the first time on any American passenger car in the present Pierce-Arrow'.''

1934 Pierce-Arrow Twelve Model 1248A Town Brougham, Brunn   Owner: Robert Sands of Buffalo, New York

1934 Pierce-Arrow Twelve Model 1248A Enclosed Drive Limousine   Owner: Bob Reeve of Golden, California

1935 Pierce-Arrow Model 845 Convertible Coupe   Owner: Morton Bullock of Baltimore, Maryland   Photo: K. Karger

In 1935 Arthur Chanter noted with pride that, alone among American automakers, Pierce-Arrow was committed to luxury cars exclusively. Popularly-priced models might be introduced by others in the field but in Buffalo the accent remained resolutely upper echelon. Sales dropped to less than one thousand.

"I like Pierce-Arrow styling, especially the convertible coupes with their sculptured semi-boattail appearance," says Mort Bullock of his Model 845 Convertible Coupe. "This is an easy car to drive, encompassing fully synchronized transmission and servo power brakes. The brake pedal looks like a second accelerator pedal, and the braking is very good after you get used to the split second delay in its taking effect. Ironically, when I purchased this car in Dallas recently, I was given papers showing that it had originally been owned by a man who resided in the same apartment house in Baltimore where I rent garage space. I have since found the mechanic who serviced the car here in Baltimore. After more than three decades, this Pierce-Arrow has returned to its original home."

Marshall Tycher has owned his Model 1245 Convertible Coupe since 1978. Negotiations for its acquisition were very friendly since the car had previously belonged to his father Fred: "It is most significant that the Pierce twelve-cylinder engine, which later became the main powerplant for Seagrave fire engines, can boast the

longest continuous usage of any American V-12 (1932 to 1981). This is a testimonial to the design skills of Karl Wise, the company's chief engineer. I think the styling of the 1935 Pierce-Arrow Convertible Coupe individually epitomizes some of the finest elements of the Art Deco period. The black lacquer body color with accents of red serves as the perfect background for the finely-fashioned chrome trim. An interesting aspect of this car's appearance is that it takes both a step forward and one backwards in its

design. The front fenders of this 1935 Pierce are from the previous year, while the car's bumpers are 1936. Early photographs of the car show it in this manner so the changes hardly seem to be whimsical additions made by a collector. Story has it that the car was frequently seen in the Buffalo area in the middle and late thirties and was thought to be an executive or factory car. This might be an explanation for the design variations. In any case, the car will remain this way with me since I think the overall effect is beautiful."

1935 Pierce-Arrow Twelve Model 1245 Convertible Coupe
Owner: Marshall Tycher of Short Hills, New Jersey

*1936 Pierce-Arrow DeLuxe Eight
Model 1601 Five-Passenger Sedan*

*Owner: Robert Sands
of Buffalo, New York*

Pierce-Arrow's straight eight was delivering 150 hp for 1936, and the V-12 185 hp, but alas deliveries of all Pierces fell to less than 800.

"The company was on very shaky ground, yet introduced completely new body styling for 1936," comments Bob Sands. "My 1601 Five-Passenger Sedan was purchased new by Earl Snell who at the time was serving as Oregon's secretary of state. Subsequently Mr. Snell, who was a Republican, was twice elected governor of Oregon and served until October 28th, 1947 when he was killed along with Robert Farrell who had succeeded him as secretary of state. The car remained in the Pacific Northwest until my acquisition three years ago. Following a complete mechanical rebuild, it runs, drives and acts like a 'new' 1936 automobile. I've driven this Pierce approximately 1,500 miles to date."

Driven a lot as well in the three years he has owned it is Ray Hunter's 1601 Sedan: "I bought this Pierce sight unseen in Salem, Oregon and drove it the 1,211 miles home to Los Angeles with no problems at all. I really like the free-wheeling and overdrive. After first gear, you can shift without depressing the clutch and can coast at speeds below 40 mph. The car is smooth driving, easy handling and, best of all, quiet inside. On trips the Pierce gives me about 11 mpg in normal drive and 14.8 in overdrive at speeds from 45-70 mph. No matter whether the weather is hot or cold, the engine always starts immediately. Crossing the California desert in the summertime, heating was no problem. As with any side-mounted Classic, a tire change on the highway really isn't my favorite thing."

*1936 Pierce-Arrow DeLuxe Eight Model 1601 Five-Passenger Sedan
Owner: Ray Hunter of Covina, California   Photos: Jason Meyer*

1936 Pierce-Arrow DeLuxe Eight Model 1601 Convertible Sedan

Owners: Tony & Claire Zappone of Brockport, New York

The Zappones' 1601 Convertible Sedan was body number five: "The only other known vehicle is number six, so we assume that no more than six or seven were built. The 1936 Pierce-Arrow catalogue does not show this car (the 1937 catalogue does). In contrast to the closed sedans Pierce made in '36, this car, with its low roofline, 144-inch wheelbase and massive size, is very impressive. It weighs slightly over 6,000 pounds and is equipped with a formal division. The inboard lights on the front of 1936-1938 Pierces, in conjunction with the fender headlights, present the most complicated lighting system we have ever encountered—three headlight switches, four toggle switch positions and a floor button combine for a mind-boggling array of possible permutations, impossible to memorize."

The 1603 Derham Town Car that has been in Bob Sands' collection for seventeen years has an intriguing history. It was commissioned by Pierce in 1936 as a possible catalogue custom offering for the following year, either to join or replace the Brunn Metropolitan Town Brougham which had been offered since 1934.

For whatever reason, the project did not proceed beyond the single prototype, which Pierce subsequently sold to Charles Walker of Manchester, Massachusetts, an enthusiast of the company's cars who had as many Pierces in his garage then as Bob Sands does now. "Since restoration I've driven the 1603 Derham

approximately 2,500 miles," says Bob. "It drives and rides like a Pullman car. Its looks, appointments, styling and quality can be best summed up as the closest an automobile can get to a palace on wheels. The ease of steering is unbelievable, and the engine is whisper silent at any speed."

486

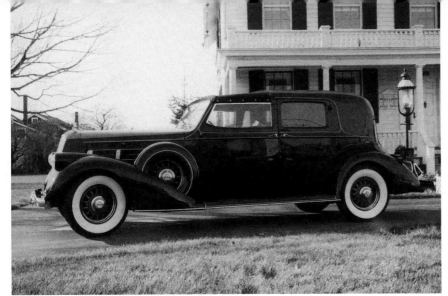 

1936 Pierce-Arrow Custom Twelve Model 1603 Town Car, Derham   Owner: Robert Sands of Buffalo, New York

1937 Pierce-Arrow Eight Model 1701 Metropolitan Town Brougham, Brunn   *Owner: Frederick Z. Tycher of Dallas, Texas*

The 1937 Pierce-Arrows were almost exact copies of the 1936 models. The biggest change was a lamentable one: sales of just 167 cars in 1937.

Fred Tycher has owned his 1701 Metropolitan Town Brougham for seven years: "The custom coachwork by Brunn is exceptional. For a huge car, the 'sweep panel' concept of its design is not only elegant but its carefully-formed indentation of sheet metal creates the perfect change of planes for a two-toned color combination. The Pierce-Arrow and Brunn companies were the 'only games in town' when it came to manufacturing automobiles in Buffalo during this era. As a result of their close proximity, some very fine examples of Classics were created. This 1937 Pierce-Arrow Metropolitan Town Brougham by Brunn is the only example believed extant."

Likewise the 1703 Town Car owned by Jim & Ruth Dougherty: "This factory body is pictured in the 1937 catalogue. Ours is body number one. There is a 1938 town car with an identical body, also carrying the same number. Likely as not, these two factory town cars were the only ones produced."

1937 Pierce-Arrow Twelve Model 1703 Town Car
Owners: James & Ruth Dougherty of Indianapolis, Indiana

From the fragments of what we know about Pierce-Arrow's final days, both a frenzied and a fatalistic aura prevailed at the factory—the wild hope that somehow something might reverse the inevitable, the crushing realization that most probably nothing would. In October of 1937 the company had stalwartly sent publicity releases and photos to the automotive trade press announcing the new line for '38. But the pictures sent were often of 1936 or 1937 models. Meanwhile, the factory machines, tools and equipment—everything, even a six-foot sailfish mounted on a plaque—were being quietly inventoried.

"How many 1938 Pierce-Arrows were built is not known," comment Eric & Molly Rosenau. "Our car was the fifth long-wheelbase V-12 that year. Total production is estimated at no more than twenty vehicles, of which over 50% still exist." That in itself is a fine tribute to the marque, to which the Rosenaus add: "The late model Pierce-Arrows (1936-1938) are great driving cars for modern road conditions. The factory overdrive makes speeds of 70-80 mph easy cruising. We know of no other American car of this period that will perform as well. Our '38 Pierce has been driven 23,000 miles since 1979 and is often used as a family car when we need to transport more than three or four people."

1938 Pierce-Arrow Twelve Model 1803 Enclosed Drive Limousine   *Owners: Eric & Molly Rosenau of Ramona, California*

1938 Pierce-Arrow Twelve Model 1803 Formal Limousine   Owner: Peter Lambert of Los Angeles, California   Photos: Rick Lenz

It was after the assembly line had been shut down and the workforce laid off that Peter Lambert's 1803 Formal Limousine was built: "It is unusual in its sloping rear end and rear quarter windows. The amber lenses in the front auxiliary lights and the reverse colors on the hubcaps indicate the total 1938 changes from the previous year's model. This car is the only formal limousine listed in 1938, the first of its type built and one of the very last cars turned out by the factory after it was in receivership. Several chassis remained that were to have been used for the 1938 automobile shows, but since the company was effectively defunct before that, the cars were left at the plant unfinished. A Mr. Ryan, who had been foreman of the Heavy Repair Shop, was still there and had one of the old-time upholsterers come in to finish the interior of my car. During the assembly, odd parts were used from what was available before the junk men began tearing the factory apart."

Soon there was a silence in the great Pierce-Arrow assembly rooms—a haunting quiet that could only be compared to that of a Pierce-Arrow engine.

490

S T U T Z

The Egyptian god Ra hood ornament from W. J. Ridout's 1931 SV-16 LeBaron Speedster.

"The Car That Made Good in a Day" was built in just five weeks. Harry Clayton Stutz was in Indianapolis in early 1911 when he heard that a big race was planned for the newly-bricked speedway in town. His career thus far had been spent bouncing among various automobile companies in the Midwest. Stutz wanted to be his own boss. He had enough money saved to produce one car; the race would be his "advertising department." Stutz did not win the first Indianapolis 500. Incessant tire changes relegated his car to 11th, but every finisher ahead of it had considerably more cubic inches than the Stutz's 390, and its 68.25 mph average was something to crow about. Harry Stutz did his crowing with that famous slogan. Stutz began winning races regularly in 1912 with cars that were little different than the ones sold in the showroom. Most memorable was the model that was described matter-of-factly in the catalogue as "a speedy car of the semi-racing type." The Bearcat roared onto the scene even before the twenties—and would ever after be identified with that raucous decade. Ironically by the early twenties, the biggest roar from Stutz was heard on Wall Street. With racing success increasing the demand for his cars, Stutz had decided to take his company public in order to expand. A speculator named Alan A. Ryan bought controlling interest; by 1919 a heartbroken Harry C. Stutz left to begin another automotive venture (H.C.S.); in 1921 Ryan engineered the infamous corner on Stutz stock; by 1922 he was broke. "Schwab Takes the Wheel at Stutz" was the next big headline. For $2.7 million the steel magnate bought control of the Indianapolis company. Now the question was what would "Genial Charlie" do next. . . .

1925 Stutz Speedway Six Model 695 Sportster

Owner: Joe Folladori of Indianapolis, Indiana

Charlie Schwab, it was widely acknowledged, didn't know what a mechanical drawing was, much less what it meant. But the livery owner's son hadn't risen to the top of the Carnegie hierarchy, become U.S. Steel's first president and spun off on his own into Bethlehem Steel without knowing a few things about business. Stutz's venerable 360-cubic-inch T-head four, introduced in 1917, was still the mainstay of production when Schwab took over. The marque's sporting image, nurtured over years of its racing rivalry with Mercer, remained indelible. Just a couple more cylinders would do the trick, the Schwab group thought.

The most sporting new Stutz was the Speedway Six, an overhead valve 288.6-cubic-inch 80 hp machine. Joe Folladori has owned his for three years: "It is the only five-passenger touring Sportster in existence, to my knowledge. The model was built only in 1924 and 1925. Following restoration, I discovered this Speedway Six to be a really fine driver with plenty of power and good brakes. Stutz engineered a good car."

True, to be sure. The Speedway Six had more horses than most prestige cars with two more cylinders. It was, in the Harry Stutz idiom, a magnificent masculine brute of a car. But

buyers in the Stutz price class wanted more than performance by now. Refinement and sophistication were demanded. Stutz needed an image change.

492

In 1925 Charlie Schwab hired a new president for Stutz, gave him a million dollars in development money and a clean sheet of paper. Among the first things Fred Moskovics did upon arriving in Indianapolis was to phone across town to Marmon, where he had previously worked, and convince Edgar S. Gorrell to join him at Stutz. Already there was veteran engine designer Charles R. "Pop" Greuter. The team got to work. The "Stutz Vertical Eight, Safety Chassis" arrived for the 1926 model year.

The designation had been carefully chosen. Vertical was the Stutz word to rhetorically differentiate its straight eight from the competition. And it *was* different: a nine-main-bearing single-overhead-camshaft 287-cubic-inch unit developing 92 hp at 3200 rpm. Safety glass with imbedded wiring was featured. The safety engineered into the chassis included hydraulic brakes and an underslung worm drive that significantly lowered the car's center of gravity from the usual bevel gear rear axle—and allowed for coachwork sensuously lower than the norm. Stutz sales in '26 neared the 5,000 mark, nearly doubling the annual figure of earlier in the decade.

Jean Gorjat is the second owner of the '26 Stutz Victoria Coupe which he acquired from the estate of S. O. Curry of Camp Hill, Pennsylvania in 1986. The odometer read 22,000 miles and the Indianapolis-to-Harrisburg railway shipping manifest was inside the car which, except for a repaint, remains original: "I already owned a '28 Stutz BB so getting this AA was terrific. So is the car, especially from a mechanical point of view. It was so advanced that it remained up-to-date for decades. The car is kind of like a Bugatti, but even better with hydraulic brakes and shocks."

The Bugatti reference is well taken. The Hungarian-born Moskovics had apprenticed in Europe and returned there frequently. Late in 1926, at the Paris Automobile Salon, he met Ettore Bugatti. The two men became good friends and talked awhile about a reciprocal alliance which would see Stutz represent Bugatti in the U.S., Bugatti to do the same for Stutz in France. Nothing came of that, but an offhand comment of Bugatti's about how he water-cooled his exhaust valves was mentally noted by Moskovics in Paris and adopted on the revised BB Stutz engine back in Indianapolis. Horsepower of the 298-cubic-inch BB was 115 at 3600 rpm.

1926 Stutz Vertical Eight Series AA Victoria Coupe   *Owner: Jean Gorjat of Harrisburg, Pennsylvania*

1928 Stutz Vertical Eight Series BB Custom Coupe
Owner: Bruce A. Harlow, Rear Admiral U.S.N. (retired) of Poulsbo, Washington

1928 Stutz Vertical Eight Series BB Four-Door Sedan   *Owner: Jean Gorjat of Harrisburg, Pennsylvania*

1928 Stutz Vertical Eight Series BB Dual Cowl Phaeton
Owner: Edward Rowan of Chatham, New Jersey

The Series BB Stutz was offered in no fewer than twenty-five different body styles. ''The Type 3-C was the first announced on June 9th, 1928,'' says Bruce Harlow of his Custom Coupe. ''This strikingly beautiful close-coupled body is somewhat similar to the five-passenger LeBaron except it is a two-door type on a 131-inch wheelbase. This is an excellent original car with just 47,000 actual miles since new.''

Edward Rowan's Series BB Dual Cowl Phaeton spent much of its life in South America. Ed acquired the car two years ago. It is currently undergoing engine and mechanical restoration.

Jean Gorjat's BB Sedan remains mechanically original: ''I was living in Brazil in 1985 when I learned about the car, sent a friend to have a look and bought it over the telephone. The wife of a Stutz dealer in Florida was the original owner; it had been put on blocks with only 18,000 miles following her death in 1934. Repainting and reupholstery only have been done. As a European, I consider the Stutz and the Duesenberg the two best cars ever produced in the United States.''

1928 Stutz Vertical Eight Series BB Roadster   Owner: Ernest J. Toth, Sr. of Chagrin Falls, Ohio   Photo: Torque

Both BB Roadsters shown here have enjoyed long residence in their respective garages. Philip Reed purchased his from its original owner sixteen years ago.

Ernie Toth acquired his in 1967 at the Latham, New York auction of the estate of Earl Pfannebecker: "I took a set of 1928 plates and held them up as I bid. I was so excited I even jumped my own bid at one point. When the Stutz was mine, I surveyed my acquisition and noticed the Egyptian sun god Ra hood ornament was not on the car. I asked Mrs. Pfannebecker and she said, 'You'll have to give me something extra for it. What will you give?' I replied, 'How about a big hug and kiss?' She said, 'I'll take that,' so in front of this huge crowd, I hugged and kissed her and she gave me the Ra. She must have been a flapper in 1928. This Stutz exemplifies the spirit of the roaring twenties, when cars were cars, men were men, and women were women. We were constantly invited to gala Gatsby parties after we got it. The car has been an absolute joy to drive—except once, back in 1976 when we decided it was roadworthy enough for the Bi-Centennial CARavan. On the way to the departure point in Williamsburg, the Stutz developed a ticking noise which I assured my dear wife was a noisy speedometer cable. When the noise persisted, I said I would look into the matter in depth when we got to Alexandria that night. No sooner had I made that decision when, with a horrendous explosion, the engine disemboweled itself and the roadway was covered with wristpins, miscellaneous engine parts and twelve quarts of oil. I hated to lose the fresh oil I had just put in. But the bright spot was that I met Dick Gold who loaned me his 454 Chevy with new trailer to transport the car to my friend Bill Johnson's in Camden, New Jersey. I still would not admit the situation was hopeless and planned to make repairs on the road. This proved impossible. Fourteen years later my Stutz received a brand-new engine for Christmas. And it will be back on the road for the New England CARavan in 1990."

1928 Stutz Vertical Eight Series BB Roadster
Owner: Philip Reed of Whittier, California

The Black Hawk Speedster was Fred Moskovics' answer to Harry Stutz's fabled Bearcat. That Stutz would relinquish its sporting image was unthinkable. Racing had been on the agenda since the Vertical Eight's inception. Set on the shorter of the two (131- and 135-inch) Series BB chassis, the Black Hawk was a whopping 1,377 pounds lighter than the sedan and, with a higher 6.25:1 compression ratio, delivered 125 hp. All this combined with impressive torque and the Stutz's superb handling and braking made the Black Hawk the car to beat in 1927. No one managed it. Stutz won every major stock car event that year except one, and only because the factory chose to sit that race out.

Early in 1928, following a two-way average of 106.53 for the flying mile at Daytona, the Black Hawk was proclaimed America's fastest production car. True, that April a Black Hawk did lose the match race against an H6b Hispano-Suiza at Indy. The mitigating circumstances included nearly eight liters of Hispano versus not quite five of the Stutz, which Moskovics had confidently believed would be surmounted by the superior long-run capability of the

Black Hawk over the twenty-four hours of the race. What he did not count on was his driver—aware of the $25,000 wager his boss had riding on the outcome—attempting to win the race in the opening laps. Over-revved to a fare-thee-well, the Stutz swallowed an inlet valve. Moskovics found his pride easier to swallow, however, when his match race adversary, Charles Weymann, chose a Stutz and not an Hispano for the Twenty-Four Hours of Le Mans that June. There the lone Black Hawk relentlessly battled the vaunted three-car Bentley team, led for a while, dogged two of the Bentleys into retirement and finished a splendid second to the third. Even W. O. Bentley admitted that the Black Hawk was a better handling car than those of his own team. And the Stutz which finished second had to run the last four hours (nearly 200 miles) without top gear; in second the car had a 7.01:1 ratio limiting speed to 68 mph at 5000 rpm. Now that is amazing!

These were the glory years for Stutz. With three million dollars in orders arriving at the factory during the first week of the Vertical Eight's introduction, the Indianapolis

company had launched a program that made Stutzes available in every conceivable guise. For about $5,000 the sporting driver could purchase a Black Hawk Speedster like Miles Collier's from the showroom floor. The bank president might select the Biarritz Sedan, his wife the Monaco Coupe. Stutz designations were posh; so were the cars. Many carried Weymann fabric bodies, Stutz contracting to take Charles Weymann's entire American output during the spring of '28.

But then things went awry. The Stutz legal department became a busy place as the company was sued for breach of confidence by James Scripps-Booth who had shown Charlie Schwab an underslung worm-drive design of his own prior to Moskovics' appearance on the scene. The drawings were meaningless to Charlie, and Howard Marmon would testify on Fred Moskovics' behalf that he and Fred had worked on the low-slung chassis idea together when the latter was with Marmon years before. But the situation was very unpleasant. Schwab pulled out of Stutz, followed soon by Moskovics. Edgar Gorrell became the new Stutz president.

1929 Stutz Vertical Eight Series BB Black Hawk Speedster   *Owner: Miles C. Collier of Naples, Florida*

1930 Stutz Vertical Eight M-46 Convertible Coupe, LeBaron (engine and instrument panel facing page opposite)
Owners: Bill & Barb Phillion of Grand Blanc, Michigan   Photos: Cars & Parts

1930 Stutz Vertical Eight Model M-27 Cabriolet Coupe   Owner: Louis M. Groen of Cincinnati, Ohio   Photo: Milton Gene Kieft

Bad to worse. The stock market crashed that October. Stutz sales dropped to half the '29 figure. Edgar Gorrell found himself at odds with the new regime at Stutz. The new regime wanted to bail out already. The only good news in Indianapolis remained the Stutz cars themselves.

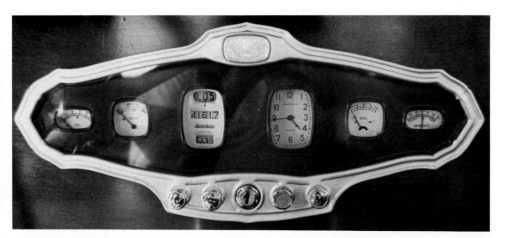

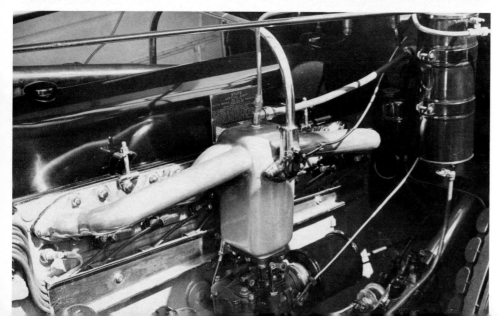

"The quiet, understated elegance of the styling speaks to me," says Louis Groen of his '30 M-27 rumble-seat convertible. "And a very positive statement is made in the 5,100 pounds of solid protection that gives the driver the feeling of assurance. Broadway and Ziegfeld Follies star Maddah Bowman bought my car for $3,395 in 1930 and drove it for eleven years. It remained in storage until three years ago, when I acquired it from the second owner."

Bill & Barb Phillion have owned their '30 M-46 LeBaron Convertible Coupe since 1954. Comments Bill: "The price was $650 which my wife of a little over a year and I had previously earmarked for household furnishings. I drove the car home from Upstate New York to Michigan in February through rain, sleet and snow with no problems. I have an understanding wife. Our Stutz is very special to us because, first, it's fun to drive and, second, we've owned it for so long it's part of the family. A lot of standard features on the 1930 Stutz did not appear on most makes until years later— vacuum-boosted power-assist hydraulic brakes, overhead cam engine, side marker running lights, all engine accessories driven by the timing chain (no fan belt). Most 1930 Stutzes extant are on the 134½-inch wheelbase. Our LeBaron is on the 145-inch chassis. All those extra inches are in the forward portion of the rumble-seat compartment, making the leg room back there more than ample."

1930 Stutz Vertical Eight Model M-36 Versailles Sedan, Weymann
Owners: Roger S. & Frances M. Chase of Broadalbin, New York   Photos: Daniel B. Lyons

The history behind the 1930 Weymann Versailles owned by the Chases is captivating, as related by Roger: "This car was purchased off the floor of the New York Automobile Show by William Menge. The person who ordered it had lost a bundle in the stock market crash and couldn't take delivery. Fifty years later I acquired the car from the Menge family. It had been driven 50,000 miles and then put on blocks in 1937. What Stutz called its 'Chateau series' of Weymann fabric coachwork was introduced in August of 1929 at the Saratoga Racetrack. A Versailles-bodied Stutz like this one was featured there. In 1930 Cannon Ball Baker drove a car identical to mine from New York to San Francisco in three days, averaging 50 mph and breaking the transcontinental record. During the five-year 5,000-hour frame-up restoration of this Stutz, my admiration for it grew immeasurably. Stutz was a name that had fascinated me since childhood. The Weymann body gives the car an international distinction; it would look good in New York, London or Paris. And it provides an almost silent ride. Those heavy-duty running boards act as safety bumpers among

the numerous features in the remarkable Stutz 'safety' chassis. And unique features abound in the car: an ignition/transmission anti-theft lock, a directional compass in the headliner directly over the driver's head, a pull-out cigarette lighter on a long retractable cord that converts to a trouble light by exchanging the lighter head with a small spot light

that is stored conveniently behind the dash, a rear window curtain that can be driver-operated by a silk cord through an intricate series of miniature pulleys, a back-up light that is automatically actuated when the car is shifted into reverse. So many features separate this Stutz from most of the Classics of that era."

1931 Stutz Series SV-16 Model MB Seven-Passenger Sedan
Owner: Dale K. Wells of Kalamazoo, Michigan

In 1929 the Stutz Vertical Eight engine had been bored out to 322 cubic inches. Curiously, horsepower was advertised as 113 at 3300 rpm. All this remained the same through 1931. The differences are explained nicely by Dale Wells, who has owned his '31 Seven-Passenger Sedan for over two decades: ''Nineteen thirty-one was the last major body restyling for Stutz, mainly through the use of longer flowing front fender lines and hood doors replacing louvers. Chassis changes were few since Stutz, like most independent Classic manufacturers, was barely surviving the Depression years. The MB Stutz featured the long 145-inch wheelbase as opposed to the MA on the shorter 134½-inch chassis. Mechanically, the cars were the same with the over-head camshaft, dual ignition system, Bijur chassis lubrication, header-style exhaust manifolds, nine main bearings and hydraulic brakes. With the introduction in 1931 of the DV-32 (the number translating to valves), the M series cars were redesignated SV-16 since they only had sixteen valves as commonly used on straight-eight engines. If you like to talk to spectators about your car, you should have an SV-16 emblem on your Stutz. Someone will invariably comment about sixteen cylinders and ask to see the engine. You can then launch into historical commentary about Stutz model designations. Purportedly, my car was originally owned by a staff member at Notre

Dame. When I acquired it, 47,000 miles showed on the odometer and the physical condition and completeness suggested it was not the second time around. Although one sees more open models at shows today, this 'gangster' type sedan is more typical of the great masses of Classics seen on the highway in their own era. With mine, I just over-hauled the motor, repainted the body, did a few cosmetics and proceeded to drive it. That is the way to really enjoy a Classic car.''

Ray Miller has been enjoying his '31 Cabriolet Coupe since 1979: ''I like the car for its distinctive lines and its all-around road performance. This 'Twentieth Anniversary' Model MA Stutz is a refinement of the advanced engineering and safety features which made the Stutz one of the finest performance and luxury cars of the era.''

''The Classic Era provided us with many quality automobiles. The SV-16 Stutz stands up to all of them in every way,'' comments W. J. Ridout, Jr. ''My LeBaron Four-Passenger Speedster drives like a dream, is very powerful and extremely rare. I like the extra low gear and the device which prevents the car from backing up if the motor stalls. The driving lights turn with the front wheels, and the Bijur chassis lubricating system works perfectly.''

1931 Stutz Series SV-16 Model MA Four-Passenger Speedster, LeBaron
Owner: W. J. Ridout, Jr. of Bracey, Virginia

502

1931 Stutz Series SV-16 Model MA Cabriolet Coupe
Owner: S. Ray Miller, Jr. of Elkhart, Indiana

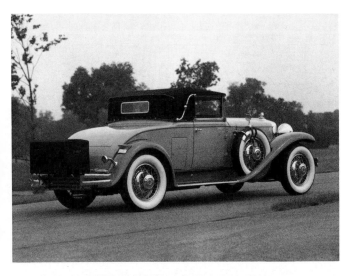

In 1931 why did Stutz not join the multi-cylinder race? Lack of development money is the logical answer but, if anything, only partly true. Twelve or more cylinders virtually decreed a vee configuration, and Stutz had no experience with vee-type engines. The company was justly proud of the Vertical Eight. Better to carry its concept of high efficiency from small displacement to an ultimate conclusion. To "Pop" Greuter, the conclusion was double overhead camshafts, four valves per cylinder and a single spark plug in a polished hemispherical combustion chamber. The DV-32 developed a potent 156 hp from 322 cubic inches and torque by the gobs (300 lb/ft at 2400 rpm). Stutz commented casually that 100 mph was possible.

Quite possibly, this fabulous new Stutz might not have been produced save for Edgar Gorrell's s.o.s. to Charlie Schwab. Stutz had survived the involuntary bankruptcy brought by decidedly unfriendly creditors in 1930, but the post-Schwab regime desperately wanted to be rid of the Indianapolis company. Gorrell asked "Genial Charlie" to help and, with several associates, Schwab repurchased control. "Nothing short of marvelous" was his phrase for the new DV-32 Stutz. The trade press was equally enthusiastic.

"I love the body style and the double overhead cam engine, which is much like the Duesenberg, only smaller," comments William Abbott of the DV-32 Bearcat Speedster he has owned for forty years.

If that longevity of ownership is impressive, heed now the wonderful story of Bruce McBroom's DV-32 Cabriolet Coupe: "My grandfather, Arthur N. Powers, saw this car at the Chicago Automobile Show in the winter of 1931 and arranged to buy it when the tour of auto shows concluded. In June of 1932 he took delivery and gave the car to my mother Gwen as a high school

graduation gift. She drove it awhile at Northwestern University. Later in the forties my grandfather bought her a new car and kept the Stutz himself for trips to the golf course as it had a convenient golf bag door. I received the car in 1977 and did a paint and upholstery restoration to original. The car now has 29,000 miles on it. This Stutz is a very fast automobile. My grandfather used to race the streamliner *City of New Orleans* from Chicago to his home in Kankakee, Illinois along the straight track bordering the highway. I once raced a Stearman bi-plane on the runway at Santa Paula, California airport."

1932 Stutz Series DV-32 Bearcat Two-Passenger Speedster
Owner: William S. Abbott of Jerseyville, Illinois   Photos: Jerry Manis

1932 Stutz Series DV-32 Cabriolet Coupe

Owner: Bruce McBroom of Los Angeles, California

To the production DV-32 body styles and the Weymann Chateau Series, Stutz added a flurry of designs by LeBaron (eight), Rollston (three), Brunn, Waterhouse and Fleetwood (one each), all save the Waterhouse on the long 145-inch wheelbase. All of the body styles were available on both the SV-16 and the DV-32 chassis, the increment an even $1,000 for the latter. Bill Lassiter's DV-32 Rollston Convertible Victoria was priced at a hefty $7,400. His Rollston Sport Phaeton—the famous ''Dragon Phaeton''—was a one-off built especially for the New York show.

In the checkered career of Clive Cussler's DV-32 LeBaron Town Car was work awhile as a pick-up and tow car at NHRA events for the drag racer Eddie Hill of Texas. Clive acquired the car five years ago: ''Little is known of the history. Rumor put it in a junkyard in 1941 somewhere in Mohawk Valley, New York. The car is thought to have been originally bodied as a coupe but was restyled before it went to the junkyard. The design is unusual in that the slant on the divider window is at the same angle as the windshield. The rear passenger's compartment has a liquor bar.''

1932 Stutz Series DV-32
Convertible Victoria, Rollston

*Owner: W. G. Lassiter, Jr.
of West Palm Beach, Florida*

1932 Stutz Series DV-32
Sport Phaeton, Rollston

*Owner: W. G. Lassiter, Jr.
of West Palm Beach, Florida*

506

1932 Stutz Series DV-32 Town Car, LeBaron   *Owner: Clive Cussler of Golden, Colorado*

The Bearcat name had not been used at Stutz since the mid-twenties when Fred Moskovics decided that car's hairy image wasn't in keeping with the refined Vertical Eight. But Moskovics was by now long gone—and in the depths of the Great Depression, Stutz concluded that reviving the legendary name might help sales. It was in the Series DV-32 that the Bearcat returned—as a speedster model on the 134½-inch chassis, as William Abbott's car shown earlier. And as the Super Bearcat on a truncated 116-inch wheelbase, as Bob Bahre's car seen here. The factory guaranteed that each Bearcat had been driven 100 mph before delivery. The performance of the lighter and smaller Super Bearcat was even more super!

1933 Stutz Series DV-32 Super Bearcat Convertible Coupe
Owner: Bob Bahre of Oxford, Maine

1933 Stutz Series DV-32 Monte Carlo Sedan, Weymann   *Owner: William S. Abbott of Jerseyville, Illinois*   *Photos: Jerry Manis*

No one agrees about precisely how many Stutzes were sold during this period, but consensus puts the figure very low—for 1932 few more than 100. This makes all the more remarkable the number of refinements to the 1933 Stutz line—downdraft carburetion, automatic clutch, thermostatically-controlled hood doors, automatic choke, new instrument and dash layout, new lights and hood line. But it was not enough. Sales for '33 continued to hover around the 100 unit mark.

Rare is any '33 Stutz DV-32. William Abbott's Monte Carlo, which he has owned for thirty-four years, is rarer yet as an aluminum Weymann which, at $6,895, was priced a full thousand dollars more than the fabric body in the same body style. But prices for Stutz by then were negotiable. The company was desperate.

1934 Stutz Series SV-16 Cabriolet Coupe
Owner: Dale K. Wells of Kalamazoo, Michigan

"The Car Which is Safest Has the Right to be Fastest." Given Stutz's remarkable racing record of the late twenties, this declaration from an independent Classic manufacturer was more than justified. By the mid-thirties, it had become a plaintive cry. Six is the usual figure cited for the number of Stutzes sold in 1934; if there were more, they were precious few.

"Mine is the only open 1934 model I know of," comments Dale Wells who has owned his SV-16 Cabriolet Coupe for nearly three decades. "The embossed hood sides with four side doors were used only on the later cars of 1933-1934. The teardrop parking lights are really quite incongruous with the Ryan headlights but are more typical of the advanced styling going into the middle thirties. This was my first antique car—my introduction to the hobby. It's a driver, never trailered, and is an excellent touring car, handling very well on the highway at freeway speeds, doing the Stutz nameplate and image proud witness. I wonder sometimes if the Stutz sales department liked that cross-bar SV-16 emblem, figuring most people would not appreciate the difference between sixteen valves and sixteen cylinders and this way the Stutz owner would not have to feel embarrassed in the country club parking lot. Everything about the car is luxurious, the Carpathian elm solid wood dashboard with full range of new airplane-type full-sweep gauges, for example. But at $3,495 in 1934, my SV-16 Cabriolet Coupe was about twice the price of many other similarly-sized eight-cylinder cars. The end of production was near at hand."

In January of 1935 the company announced that "it is not a part of the present program to continue manufacture and sale of the Stutz car." Survival was tried awhile with production of a light delivery van called Pak-Age-Car. In 1937 the Stutz Motor Car Company admitted its insolvency. In 1939 the firm was liquidated. The Stutz memory will ever linger on.

CLASSIC ART PORTFOLIO

It follows that the companies producing the automobiles which are the focus of this book also generated sales catalogues and magazine advertisements that were "Classics" in their own right. The same clientele that demanded and purchased automobiles which stood far above the ordinary in design and quality could only be encouraged to consider these automobiles by the use of promotional materials of equal design and quality. Sumptuous catalogues and portfolios were given to well-heeled visitors to the showrooms and to the Automobile Salons, and were mailed to other prospects. Magazines read by the affluent, such as *Vanity Fair* and *Fortune,* contained advertisements for most of the Classic marques. What stands out today is the *artwork* in these catalogues and advertisements. As in all of the applied and commercial arts of the Classic Era, the Art Deco or Art Moderne style predominates (although less so in conservative England than in America or on the Continent). Pert and lively, the illustrations of the 1920's mirror the carefree lifestyle of that period. In the early 1930's the art remains "moderne" yet becomes somewhat more elegant and restrained, which of course was true of the automobiles and the lifestyles then as well. By the late 1930's, and on through the early postwar period, much of the glamour and artistic license had been replaced by a more sedate, realistic and heavier style, often with stronger hues, again in keeping with the times. The following pages provide a sampling of this wonderful artwork, a truly appropriate complement to the Classic cars themselves.

—*Matt Sonfield*

sales & automobile salon catalogues from the collection of Matthew C. Sonfield

magazine advertisements from the collection of Henry Austin Clark, Jr.

Left: Cover illustration from circa 1931 catalogue of the Weymann American Body Company.

Locomobile advertisement from the December 1925 issue of Vanity Fair.

RENAULT

●

MOTOR OF EUROPE'S
SOPHISTICATES

●

719 FIFTH AVENUE NEW YORK

Renault advertisement from the December 1928 New York Automobile Salon catalogue.

Lincoln advertisement from the December 1925 issue of Vanity Fair.

THE way the Chrysler Imperial "80" delivers, at long continued high speeds, its 92 horsepower in a quiet, soft, smooth steadiness hitherto unknown, has evoked an enthusiasm that has contributed not a little to the phenomenal advance of Chrysler from twenty-seventh to fourth place—*in three years*.

The superlative ease of the Imperial "80"—the way its power *flows* in a twinkling from a snail's pace to sixty, seventy, eighty or more miles per hour—the way it flashes in and out of traffic, nimbly outdistancing the fastest and finest—these are the symbols of the supreme motoring luxury into which Chrysler has translated 92 horsepower in the Imperial "80".

CHRYSLER SALES CORPORATION, DETROIT, MICHIGAN
CHRYSLER CORPORATION OF CANADA, LIMITED, WINDSOR, ONTARIO

CHRYSLER IMPERIAL "80"

Eight body styles, priced from $2495 to $3595, f. o. b. Detroit, subject to current Federal excise tax.

CHRYSLER   MODEL   NUMBERS   MEAN   MILES   PER   HOUR

Chrysler advertisement from the April 1927 issue of House & Garden.

"The supreme combination of all that is fine in motor cars."

Beauty ·· It has been said that "beauty is in the eye of the beholder." And yet, while tastes differ, there are some things the beauty of which is agreed upon the world around.

The graceful proportions and distinguished simplicity of Packard design seem to command universal admiration. At home they long ago established a style which other manufacturers sincerely flattered by imitation. Abroad, both the Packard Six and the Packard Eight have time after time won first award in International Car Beauty Contests—being acclaimed by foreign judges as superior in grace and beauty

to the finest custom designs of their own countrymen!

The improved Packard retains the famous lines which have been characteristically Packard for a decade—with refinements of detail which provide still more alluring appearance and luxurious comfort. Its aristocratic beauty is in keeping with the improved Packard's unrivaled mechanical performance.

PACKARD
ASK THE MAN WHO OWNS ONE

Packard advertisement from the January 1927 issue of House & Garden.

CADILLAC

Sport Phaeton

Illustration from the 1928 Cadillac catalogue, ''The New Cadillac.''

Above: LeBaron Five-Passenger Sedan from the 1929 Stutz catalogue, "The Low-Weighted Stutz."
Below: Fleetwood Five-Passenger Transformable Town Car from the same Stutz catalogue.

*Daimler " Double-Six " 50
supplied to
H.M. The King
by
Stratton-Instone Ltd.*

Illustration from 1928 Daimler catalogue, title page reading in part ''The Car of Kings.''

Illustrations of Regent Convertible Coupe, Brewster coachwork, from the 1929 Rolls-Royce of America catalogue for the Springfield Phantom I. (Artistic license taken in adapting horizontal format to this vertical page.)

Le Sport à St. Moritz

THE LaSalle is distinguished by a delightful ease of handling, a quickness and a smoothness far beyond anything else in motoring experience. In fact, of all the factors that form the basis of LaSalle's popularity, perhaps the greatest is its performance. This is due to the remarkable 90-degree, V-type, eight-cylinder engine—the type of engine that has made Cadillac the greatest success in motoring history. Thus the LaSalle, in performance, as well as in richness, luxury, and modishness, is truly born to the Cadillac purple.

LaSalle
PRODUCT OF GENERAL MOTORS

Illustration from the 1928 catalogue, "LaSalle: Creator of Today's Vogue in Motor Car Design."

Au Printemps

Sur La Route

LaSalles in springtime (the French is not nearly as worthy as the art) and on the road, from the 1927 catalogue, "The LaSalle: A Companion Car to Cadillac."

CADILLAC-FLEETDOWNS
Two-Passenger Roadster
BY FLEETWOOD

DEVOTEES of the Roadster will acclaim this spirited Fleetwood model for its dash and smartness which are fully on a par with its brilliant performance. Finely styled throughout, it includes such items as arm rests and foot rail for deck seat passengers, tailored top mounted on chromium-plated slats and ebony bows with concealed folding mechanism, wide-vision windshield, driver's seat individually adjustable.

Above: Two-page spread from the 1930 catalogue, "The Picture Book of the Cadillac."

CONDUITE INTÉRIEURE TRANSFORMABLE HIBBARD ET DARRIN

Below, left and right: French coachwork from the 1929 catalogue, "Les Voitures Renault."

TORPEDO SCAPHANDRIER KELLNER

custom built
vehicle interiors

fine
fabrics

Major Fellen

wm wiese & co inc
234 west 56th street
new york

Wiese advertisement from the ''Illustrated Souvenir Catalogue,'' Automobile Salon, Hotel Drake, Chicago, November 1929.

LeBaron advertisement from the "Illustrated Souvenir Catalogue," Automobile Salon, Hotel Commodore, New York, December 1928.

MINERVA AUTOMOBILES

247 PARK AVENUE
NEW YORK, N. Y.

REPRESENTATION AND SERVICE ALSO IN BOSTON, CHICAGO AND LOS ANGELES

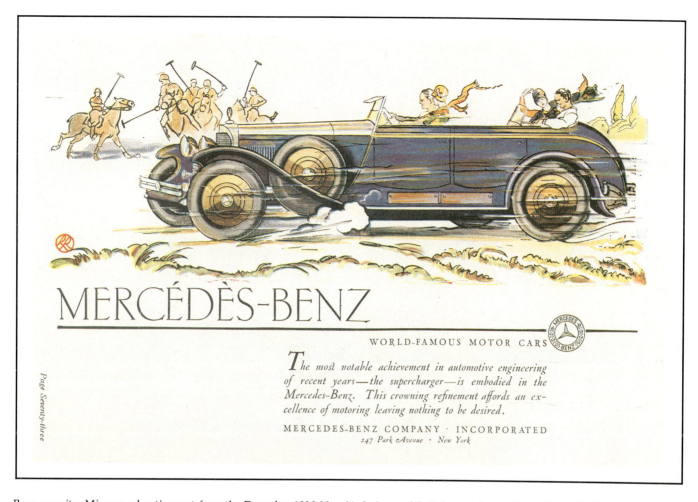

MERCÉDÈS-BENZ

WORLD-FAMOUS MOTOR CARS

The most notable achievement in automotive engineering of recent years—the supercharger—is embodied in the Mercedes-Benz. This crowning refinement affords an excellence of motoring leaving nothing to be desired.

MERCEDES-BENZ COMPANY · INCORPORATED
247 Park Avenue · New York

Page opposite: Minerva advertisement from the December 1928 New York Automobile Salon catalogue. Above: Mercedes-Benz advertisement from the same catalogue. Below: Isotta Fraschini advertisement from the November 1929 Automobile Salon catalogue.

Isotta Fraschini straight eight

ISOTTA MOTORS INC.
U.S. DISTRIBUTORS
119 West 57th Street, New York.
846 Rush Street, Chicago.

MURPHY   PASADENA

EXHIBITING ON CORD CHASSIS

FRANKLIN
Custom Coach Work

Franklin Custom Cars have gained an enviable reputation among discriminating people — a world-wide reputation that places Franklin in a position of distinguished leadership. Through the Franklin Custom Body Division famed American and European custom designers are available. The original designs of Franklin Custom Cars, together with the exceptional facilities, quality materials, masterful coachwork and excellent chassis construction assure distinction and entire personal satisfaction. Details and designs will be gladly submitted to you upon request. Consultations with Franklin custom designers can be arranged by Franklin Representatives at any time convenient to you.

FRANKLIN AUTOMOBILE COMPANY . . . . SYRACUSE, NEW YORK

Page opposite: Murphy advertisement from the "Illustrated Souvenir Catalogue," Automobile Salon, Hotel Commodore, New York, December 1930. Above and below: Franklin and Judkins advertisements from the November 1929 Chicago Automobile Salon catalogue.

Coachbuilders to
Duesenberg Inc.
Lincoln Motor Company
Pierce Arrow Motor Car Company

J. B. JUDKINS COMPANY

MERRIMAC MASS.   DETROIT MICH.

Above: All-Weather Convertible Roadster from the catalogue for the 1932 Studebaker President Eight.
Below: Four-Seater Sports illustration from the Stearns-Knight advertisement, House & Garden, *August 1928.*
Page opposite: Reo Royale advertisement from the June 1931 issue of Fortune.

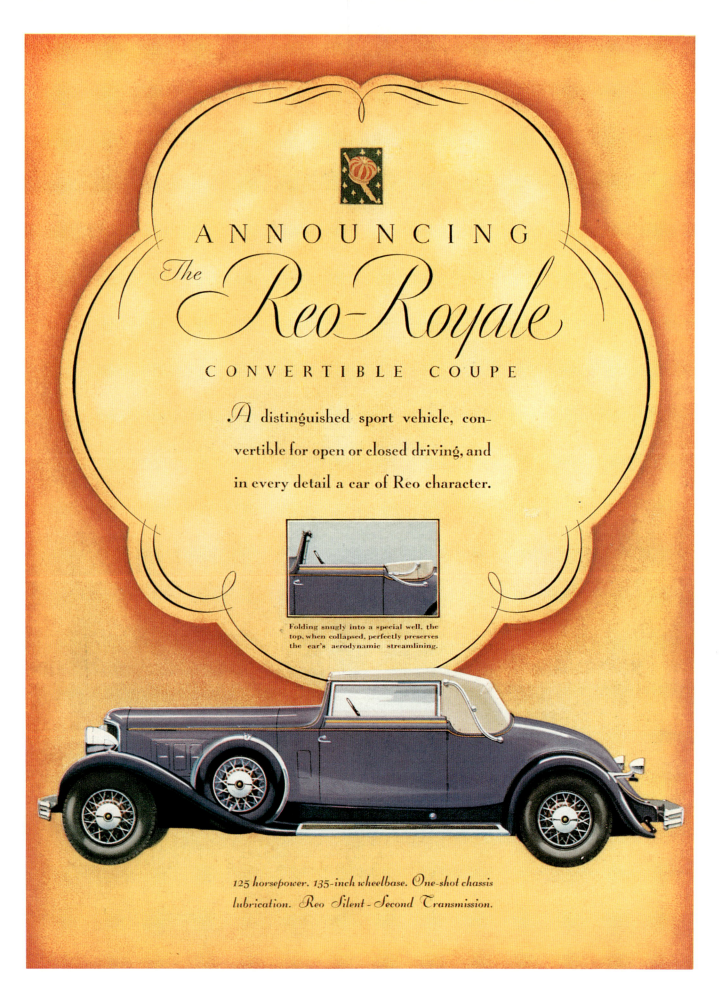

ANNOUNCING

The Reo-Royale

CONVERTIBLE COUPE

A distinguished sport vehicle, convertible for open or closed driving, and in every detail a car of Reo character.

Folding snugly into a special well, the top, when collapsed, perfectly preserves the car's aerodynamic streamlining.

125 horsepower. 135-inch wheelbase. One-shot chassis lubrication. Reo Silent-Second Transmission.

CHRYSLER
IMPERIAL EIGHT

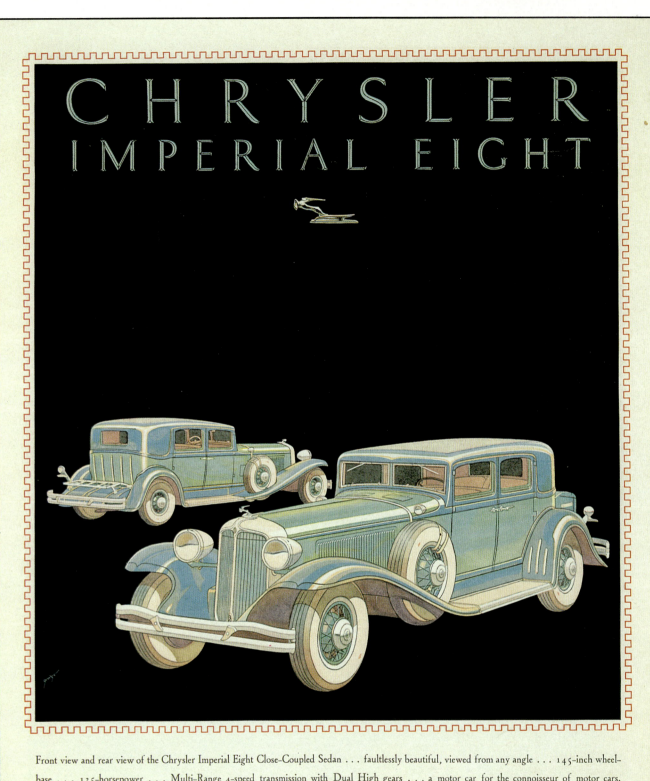

Front view and rear view of the Chrysler Imperial Eight Close-Coupled Sedan . . . faultlessly beautiful, viewed from any angle . . . 145-inch wheelbase . . . 125-horsepower . . . Multi-Range 4-speed transmission with Dual High gears . . . a motor car for the connoisseur of motor cars.

5-Passenger Sedan $2745; Close-Coupled Sedan $2845; 7-Passenger Sedan $2945; Sedan-Limousine $3145.
Custom Body Styles: Coupe $3150; Roadster $3220; Convertible Coupe $3320; Phaeton $3575. F. O. B. Factory.

532

DUPONT MOTORS, Inc.　　SPEEDSTER　　WILMINGTON, DEL.

DUPONT MOTORS, Inc.　　CONVERTIBLE SEDAN　　WILMINGTON, DEL.

*Page opposite:
Chrysler Imperial
advertisement from the
April 1931 issue of* Fortune.
*Above and right:
duPont illustrations
from the 1931 catalogue
portfolio for the Model G.*

LeBaron

GENTLEMAN'S »
SPORT SEDAN »
ON   »   »   »
STUTZ CHASSIS

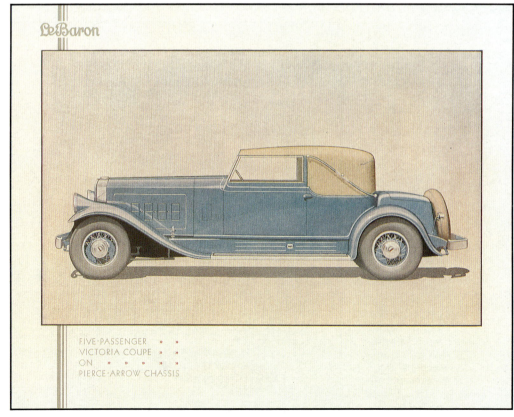

LeBaron

FIVE-PASSENGER   »   »
VICTORIA COUPE   »   »
ON   »   »   »   »   »
PIERCE-ARROW CHASSIS

*This page:
LeBaron illustrations from
the catalogue, ''LeBaron
Custom Coach Work for the
1930-1931 Automobile Salons.''
Page opposite:
Illustrations from the
1931 Pierce-Arrow catalogue,
''America's Finest Motor Car.''*

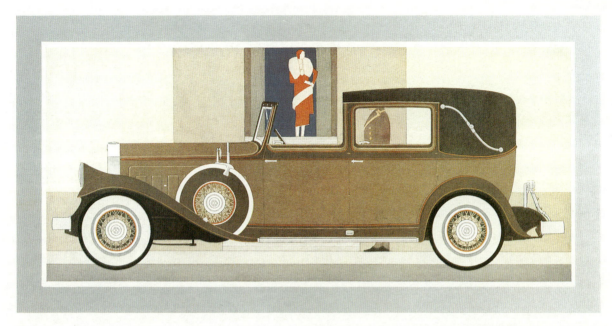

TOWN BROUGHAM (FORMAL) · SEVEN PASSENGERS   MODEL 41 · 132 HORSEPOWER · 147-INCH WHEELBASE

For purely formal occasions, this car meets every requirement.
A convenient canopy for the driver's seat rolls into the top when
not used. In addition a permanent front top section is supplied.

SALON
GROUP

TOURER · SEVEN PASSENGERS   MODEL 41 · 132 HORSEPOWER · 147-INCH WHEELBASE

Ample carrying capacity for seven passengers is provided in this
attractive open model. Upholstery is in genuine leather, including
extra seats. Both top and windshield may be folded down if desired.

SALON
GROUP

Cover and inside illustration (for the Four-Seater Sports) from the 1936 Alvis Speed Twenty-Five catalogue.

MERCEDES-BENZ TYPE 500 SUPERCHARGED · "AUTOBAHN-COURIER" · 2-3 SEATS

*Right:
Illustration from
the catalogue,
''Mercedes-Benz
Model 500 Supercharged''
dated May 1935.
Below: Horch
Model 850 from the
catalogue, ''Horch
100 PS Acht-Zylinder''
dated 1936.*

PULLMAN=CABRIOLET · SONDERAUSFÜHRUNG

Illustrations of the "Cabourg conduite interieure 5 places" and the "Hossegor roadster 2 places" from the Hotchkiss catalogue, c. 1934.

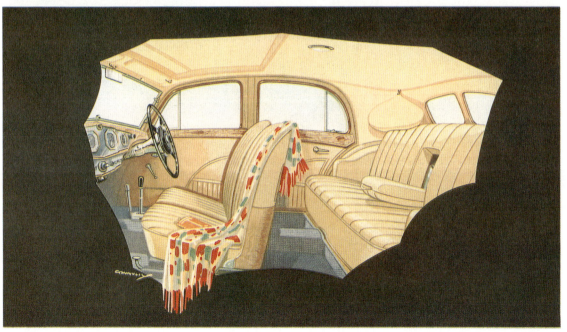

Illustrations from the M.G. 2.6 Litre catalogue carrying the date June 1939.

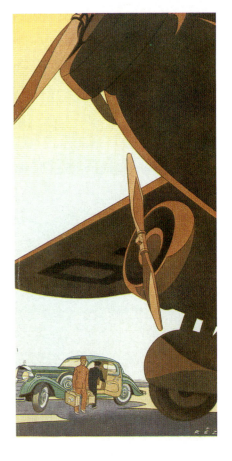

*Illustrations from the catalogue,
"Mercedes-Benz Type 540K," with
publication date of March 1937.*

540

Cover from the 1939 Bugatti catalogue for the Type 57.

WITH a willing nag and well-sprung gig, these rustic lovers set a spanking space : but—brave show though they made—their turn-out could not match in elegance the thoroughbred trotter and the graceful chaise of a Brummell or a d'Orsay. And so it is with cars to-day. The most "slap-up" of mass-produced bodies can never compare, in grace of line and beauty of colour, with craftsman-built coachwork by

OWEN of Berkeley Street

London's Leading Retailer of Rolls Royce and Bentley cars.

4½-LITRE BENTLEY "AEROFOIL," PILLARLESS SALOON, BY H. R. OWEN LTD., 17, BERKELEY STREET, W.1. . . MAYFAIR 2933.

Above: Bentley from "Coachwork of Tomorrow for Cars of Today" catalogue for H. R. Owen Ltd. (a London Rolls-Royce and Bentley retailer) dated October 1937. Although not cited as such, the coachwork for the Bentley was by Gurney Nutting.
Below: Rolls-Royce from the same catalogue. Again, the coachwork for this Phantom III was by Gurney Nutting.
Page opposite, above: Cover from the 1937 catalogue, "The Lincoln V-12 Designs for 1937."
Page opposite, below: Cover from the catalogue, "Lincoln Continental for 1941."

542

THE LINCOLN V·12
DESIGNS FOR 1937

Lincoln Continental For 1941

DELAHAYE
VITESSE

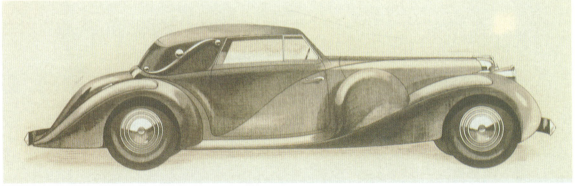

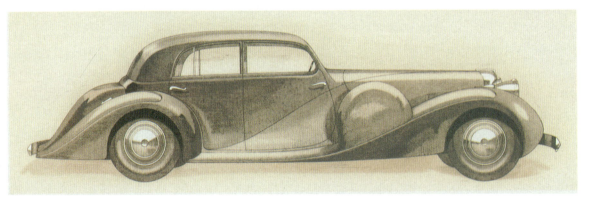

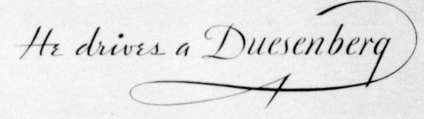

Duesenberg advertisement from the May 1934 issue of Fortune.

EUROPEAN MARQUES

Driver's compartment of Jack & Shiela Rabell's 1938 SS 100 Roadster

In Europe, more than America, automobiles remained the province of the privileged for much of the Classic Era. Such a generalization is perhaps risky but class distinctions were more pronounced abroad, and manufacturers producing for the multitudes were fewer. Ownership was not the norm on the other side of the Atlantic. There was not "a car in every garage"—far from it. On the top rung of the ownership ladder, luxury could be dearer as well; Classics produced in Great Britain and on the Continent were sometimes twice the price of American luxury marques. And they were often more sporting, as the portfolios that follow indicate. In addition to the glamorous concours d'elegance held annually in the glittering capitals of Europe, there was glamour galore in such competitive events as Le Mans, the Mille Miglia, the Targa Florio, the Tourist Trophy, the Grand Prix—and the widely varied races held on that marvelous circuit known as Brooklands. In a way, the European Classic car reflected the social order of the between-the-wars era—and the denouement of the Classic Era clearly showed how that order was changing. As in the American section of this book, European Classics are presented alphabetically, with individual sections for the more prolific marques in the club. . . .

The initials remained the same—for AutoCarriers, the little three-wheeled commercial vehicles the company had begun producing prior to the First World War. And the factory remained in Thames Ditton, outside London in Surrey. But, with the Armistice, A.C. history took a memorable turn because company founder John Weller was ready with a new two-liter wet-liner single-overhead-cam engine. The A.C. Six was introduced in 1919. Production began in 1920. In 1921 the legendary Selwyn Francis Edge (of Napier fame) joined the firm, changing its name to A.C. Cars Ltd. and irritating Weller sufficiently to cause him to leave. Edge himself took leave in 1929 as A.C. went into voluntary liquidation. In 1930 the Hurlock brothers —Charles and William—acquired the company, initially to use its factory for other purposes but, upon examining the product, decided they'd rather be carmakers after all. For the A.C. that John Weller had engineered and S. F. Edge had taken racing and record-breaking with considerable success was a very worthy automobile. Just a few chassis changes (the prickly Edge didn't accept criticism well) would make it exemplary. And so it was. By the mid-thirties, the four-speed crash box had been replaced by an E.N.V. synchromesh (with a Wilson pre-selector available optionally) and three carburetors were fitted to the engine which was available in three stages of tune, the 16/60 standard with 70 hp and 80 hp for those desiring more performance. All this from a mere 1991 cc.

"The grandfather of the famous A. C. Cobra and one of the best British sporting cars of the period," says Jean Gorjat of his 1936 Type 16/80. "The roadability is excellent, and the A.C. is comfortable, which cannot be said of similarly-configured cars like the SS 100."

David Hill is similarly enthusiastic about his Type 16/60: "I purchased this car in London in 1976 and learned from previous owner Alan L. Peer that it had been found under a pile of lumber where it had been hidden away during the Second World War to avoid its being pressed into service or condemned as scrap for the war effort. The car was draped in canvas and the junk carefully piled around it. Thus entombed it slept until 1973. Most of

1936 A.C. Type 16/80 Sports Two-Seater
Owner: Jean Gorjat of Harrisburg, Pennsylvania

1937 A.C. Type 16/60 Greyhound Drophead Coupe   *Owner: David L. Hill of Fenton, Michigan*

the leather upholstery survived intact. Mr. Peer was responsible for a new top, carpeting and paint. He also overhauled the engine. I toured Great Britain for three weeks after purchasing the car. It likes to cruise along at 50 to 60 mph, with a characteristic hum at those speeds that seems to say 'all is well, thank you.' Other than its personality, I am fondest of the car's styling. The fenders retain the classic sweep, and yet the body is channeled over the frame, giving it a low, road-hugging appearance. Everything seems to be in proper proportion, with the hood length being about half the total of the car. A.C. has remained a small marque throughout its nearly ninety-year history. The company has resisted being absorbed by larger automotive manufacturers. Like the more prestigious Rolls-Royce, the Thames Ditton factory has a large service facility where owners' cars can be serviced routinely or even rebuilt. Also, cars are made to individual order, with each being handwritten into a large leather-bound ledger. The engine of my car was produced with little change from 1919 until 1962. A production run of forty-three years has to be an industry record.'' Indeed.

A L F A   R O M E O

"Every time I see an Alfa Romeo pass by," Henry Ford is supposed to have said, "I take my hat off." The remark is not unlikely. The man who had given the world the Model T began his automotive career on the race track. He could but be impressed with an Alfa Romeo. In its first four decades of motor sport, this *grande marque Italiane* won more competitive events than any other automobile. Comparatively, Alfa's 560 checkered flags represented about 100 more than Bugatti, well over twice the figure for Mercedes. The man responsible for this success during the Classic Era was the brilliant engineer Vittorio Jano. Hired away from Fiat in 1923 by Nicola Romeo, the industrialist who had acquired A.L.F.A. (the acronym for Società Anonima Lombarda Fabbrica Automobili), Jano was instructed, as he remembered, "to accumulate a respectable competition record." His first Grand Prix car, the legendary P2, won the first race it entered in 1924 and was still winning in 1930 when it was superseded. Meanwhile,

Jano had developed his first production car for the Milanese company—the equally legendary 6C (six-cylinder) series which commenced with the 1500.

"A Classic among Classics," comments Jack Becronis of his 6C 1500 Zagato Spyder. "Everything about an Alfa Romeo is significant, but most of all the double-overhead-cam layout of its engine. The 1500 demonstrated the value of twin cams

for high-performance street engines and showed that a small efficient powerplant in a lightweight car is an ideal combination for sporting drivers. With modification and enlargement, this engine continued in production until 1950 and established a great road race reputation. Alfas of this period are famed for their wonderful handling and driveability. Annual production was only in the hundreds. My car, which I've owned for a dozen years, was one of just three made in this '3-posti' body style by Zagato to be sold exclusively by Thomson & Taylor, Ltd., the London Alfa Romeo dealer."

1928 Alfa Romeo Tipo 6C 1500 Sport Spyder, Zagato
Owner: Jack Becronis of San Marino, California   Photo: Roy Query, Automobile Quarterly

Few more than a thousand 6C 1500 Alfas had been built by 1929 when the car was enlarged from a liter-and-a-half into the 1750, available with or without supercharging. Blown 1750's for the marketplace produced as much as 95 mph from 85 hp. In competition trim, 102 hp was on tap for a 105 mph top—and victories in the Mille Miglia and Tourist Trophy, amongst many others, followed. Total 1750 production was 2,579 cars from 1930 through 1933.

Edsel Pfabe's supercharged 1750 was a one-of-a-kind built by the British coachbuilding house of Freestone & Webb: "The original owner was a pilot and the radiator mascot is a model of the Supermarine seaplane which won the Schneider Trophy. When I acquired the car in 1971, the original registration and manual came with it. Total mileage to date is 20,804."

1932 Alfa Romeo Tipo 6C 1750 Gran Turismo, Freestone & Webb
Owner: Edsel H. Pfabe of Ft. Pierce, Florida

1934 Alfa Romeo Tipo 8C 2300 Corto, Touring
Owner: John Mozart of Palo Alto, California

1934 Alfa Romeo Tipo 8C 2300 Corto, Touring (engine above)
Owner: Miles C. Collier of Naples, Florida

The record says it all. The 8C 2300 Alfa Romeo won Le Mans for four successive years and wouldn't allow another car in the top four at the Mille Miglia (unless it was a more powerful Alfa). While similar in basic dimensions and layout to the 1750, the eight-cylinder 2300 engine was unusual in having the camshaft and supercharger drives between the fourth and fifth cylinders, taken from two spur gears in the center of the crankshaft. The engine had ten main bearings and dry sump lubrication—and, in production form, 142 hp at 5000 rpm. The 8C 2300 was designed as a road racer that could also be made available for fast touring in 122-inch lungo (long) and 108-inch corto (short) chassis versions. The price was about $10,000 and bought astonishing acceleration (zero to sixty in under ten seconds) as well as flabbergasting flexibility (the 2300 was as docile in traffic as it was feral on the open road).

Historians today relish finding fault with the 8C 2300, if only to demonstrate the thoroughness of their research. Vittorio Jano himself insisted the design was no masterpiece because the ''chassis was simply too heavy.'' With the car's total weight a comely 2200 pounds, Alfa's engineer was taking himself too severely to task. A genuine failing was the sequestering of the dashboard instruments under the cowl which made them difficult to check for anyone reasonably tall. But, given the remarkable automobile the 8C 2300 was, that is truly nitpicking. From 1931 through 1934, just 188 of these cars were produced, most of them two-seaters, many of those with Touring coachwork like the Collier and Mozart cars seen here.

1937 Alfa Romeo Tipo 8C 2900 B Corto, Touring
Owner: John Mozart of Palo Alto, California

Again, evolution with a dual purpose. Alfa Romeo wanted to continue dominating the Mille Miglia and needed a prestige model to succeed the 2.3-liter production car. Ergo the immortal "Two-Nine" which magnificently achieved both aims. The 2900 A made its debut in the 1936 Mille Miglia, easily finishing one-two-three. In '37 the 2900 B followed, detuned from 220 to 180 hp for road use. It bears mention that the engine of the 2900 A had itself simply been detuned from the 255 hp of Alfa's P3 Grand Prix car.

Just twenty-six 8C 2900 B Alfa Romeos were built. Many of them had *superleggera* (super light) coachwork by Touring. John Mozart's car, the first Touring 2900 B produced, was delivered new in New York City to MacClure Halley. "One of the greatest cars of all time," comments John, "matching great performance with great style."

"Probably the most famed sports car of the late thirties," says Bob Bahre of his Touring 2900 B.

No proud owner exaggeration is present here. Many impartial observers likewise view the 2.9-liter Alfa Romeo as the ultimate evocation of a sports car which arguably had been the ultimate to begin with.

1938 Alfa Romeo Tipo 8C 2900 B Corto, Touring *Owner: Bob Bahre of Oxford, Maine*

1948 Alfa Romeo Tipo 6C 2500 SS Drophead Coupe, Ghia

Owner: Jean Gorjat of Harrisburg, Pennsylvania

Evolution once more. Vittorio Jano had always provided elegant transport for those discriminating motorists for whom supercharging was too much of a good thing. In the mid-thirties his unblown d.o.h.c. 2.3-liter six had replaced the 1750 and 8C 2300. This car was developed by Bruno Treviso into the Tipo 6C 2500 of 1939, available in both Sport and Super Sport as well as Turismo and Coloniale guise. Interestingly, these cars remained in production, in very limited numbers, throughout World War II and were continued when peace came.

Production of the 6C 2500 totaled 451 cars in 1948 when Jean Gorjat's Super Sport Ghia Coupe was built: "This is one of the few Alfas with a Ghia body in aluminum and, I'm told, was a gift from Prince Aly Khan to Rita Hayworth. It behaves like a modern car and, on mountain roads, equals the performance of a VW GTI. To my mind, the 6C 2500 represents the last of the real Alfas."

Jean's point is well taken in the historical sense—for in 1950 Alfa Romeo moved into unitary construction and production that would ultimately reach six figures annually. The Alfa Romeo that was solely a luxury car handbuilt in small numbers could not survive in the postwar era.

553

A L V I S

Shortly after the First World War, Thomas George John made two decisions: first, he preferred becoming an automobile manufacturer rather than remaining merely an automobile engineer and, second, naming his new car after himself was not a good idea. Though the word did not carry the same slang definition as in America, driving a John in England still didn't have exactly the right ring. Chosen instead was the name of an obscure metal foundry in South London; then T. G. John came up with a radiator emblem which brought objection and threatened litigation from one of Britain's top airplane manufacturers, a situation he maneuvered around by the expedient of turning the Alvis triangular badge upside down. Such pragmatism became the hallmark of the marque. The cars, all of them coachbuilt, were noteworthy for their high quality, their rugged longevity and their fine performance. Models proliferated as T. G. John Ltd. metamorphosed into Alvis Car & Engineering Co. Ltd. (in 1927) and ultimately Alvis Ltd. (a decade later).

Most sporting of the Alvis range in the early thirties was the Speed 20, which in 1934 was provided two major changes: independent front suspension and an all-synchromesh transmission. Quite possibly, the changes may have been partly prompted by Alvis owners since the company often asked their advice. Customers were regarded as friends. The Coventry factory organized rallies and races, even dinner dances, for its clientele. Alvis was, in a way, its own intimate club. Alvis owners were fiercely loyal to and wildly enthusiastic about their cars then. Alvis collectors are equally so today.

"It is a sports car and a Classic," declares Walter Fuelberth of his Speed 20. "It looks sporty, sounds sporty, drives sporty—and is Classic in style (Vanden Plas coachwork) and features (one-shot lubrication, P-100 headlamps, etc.)—and singularly so with a transmission synchronized in all four forward speeds. U.S. practice was usually a three-speed synchronized in second and third only; we didn't have a synchronized 'four on the floor' until the 1957 Corvette. This car is fun to drive and interesting for an American driver because of the right-hand steering, of course, but also because the throttle is located between the clutch and brake pedals. I've owned this Alvis since 1974. Wherever we go, it attracts much attention."

1934 Alvis Speed 20 Tourer, Vanden Plas   *Owner: Walter Fuelberth of Mesa, Arizona*

1935 Alvis Speed 20 Drophead Coupe, Charlesworth   *Owners: Kay & Milton A. Miner of Los Angeles, California*

The Speed 20 in the Miner garage has been there for a quarter of a century. ''The styling first caught my fancy,'' comments Milton, ''then when I found it to be an excellent driving car, I had to have a Speed 20. Alvis enjoyed the use of the GM synchromesh transmission under license. Left-hand shifting is no trick at all. Nor is tire changing, with built-in mechanical jacks front and rear and the jack crank mounted on the firewall. The body of this car was one of four specially built by Charlesworth, and the car was originally owned by one of the four directors of Charlesworth Ltd.''

1935 Alvis 3½ Litre Pillarless Saloon, Vanden Plas
Owner: Colonel Daniel G. Barney of HQ USAREUR

The Speed 20 was a 2511 cc six from 1932-'34, 2762 cc from 1935-'36. The 3½ Litre exemplifies Alvis pragmatism, as explained by Col. Barney: ''In the fall of 1935, Alvis had completed development of a new six-cylinder 3.5-liter engine which would later power the Speed 25 model. Anxious to get the engine in a production automobile, the factory modified a Speed 20 chassis to accept the new power train and the 3½ Litre model was born. Sixty-two chassis were produced in 1935 and 1936 until the Speed 25 replaced this short-lived stopgap. My particular car has the first production model or, some say, the last test model of the 3.5 engine. Displayed on the Vanden Plas stand at the 1935 London Motor Show, it was one of only two four-door pillar-less saloons made. The coachwork, with the sharply-curved cycle front fenders favored by dealer Charles Follett, is impressive. The car is low, less than five-and-a-half feet high with only seven inches ground clearance, yet is roomy inside and has considerably more headroom than modern cars. The rear passengers gain leg/foot room by having the foot wells drop well below the top of the driveshaft tunnel and under the front bucket seats, which is possible due to the almost nine-inch frame depth at that point. The windshield opens to allow fresh air, and special spring-loaded plungers are in the base of the windshield wiper arms so they can be moved out of the way from the inside when the window is opened. A unique touch is the side window on the driver's side which is raised and lowered by a one-push/pull lever rather than a crank as on the other three doors. Follett had purchased the car as a chassis. The car's succession of owners cannot be fully documented, although there have been quite a few, at one point including a Scottish policemen. This is the only Classic I have ever owned and I bought it in 1986 because I fell in love with its looks. Since then I've found it to be a solidly engineered car which is fun to drive and a real attention-getter on the road. European drivers—even those with 500 Mercedes—yield to you. The Alvis is stopped by cable-operated fourteen-inch drum brakes, no mean task for a two-ton automobile. Despite its weight, it is still lively, responsive and fully capable of the published 90 mph speeds of the thirties. Except for one test run at the Hockenheim Track in Germany, the car has been driven at more sedate speeds in a very gentlemanly manner the past few years.''

"A very special car with a lot of unusual features," comment the Erds about their Speed 20. "There's the four-speed all-synchro transmission and independent front suspension, of course, but consider also the triple S.U. carburetors, dual electric fuel pumps, dual ignition (coil and magneto), built-in jacks, cast aluminum firewall, one-shot lubrication, André Telecontrol shocks adjustable front and rear from the dashboard, three-Imperial-gallon oil sump with built-in filter (and float sight oil level gauge). Each valve has nine springs for a total of 108. The four-wheel brakes (14-inch ribbed drums) can be adjusted while driving by a knob on the floor. The body is low slung and, with 87 hp, the top speed is 90 mph."

1936 Alvis Speed 20 Drophead Coupe, Charlesworth
Owners: Larry & Sally Erd of Toledo, Ohio

1936 Alvis Crested Eagle Limousine, Mayfair
Owner: Art Kenniff of Southold, New York

The Crested Eagle was an Alvis designed for the luxury rather than the sporting buyer. Introduced in 1933, and itself introducing i.f.s. to the marque, the new model was seen principally with formal coachwork. By 1936 it carried the Speed 20's 2762 cc engine and was available in two chassis lengths, a Speed 20ish 123 inches and 132 inches. Art Kenniff's Mayfair Limousine is on the longer chassis: "This Crested Eagle is a rare bird. The best information I have is that the price was around $5,000. Not many were built. In 1979 I became the fourth owner of this car. It is my understanding that of the four Crested Eagles in the U.S., mine is the only limousine. It is a very smooth car on the road and will travel at highway speed all day. The gearbox is a joy and the independent front suspension makes the steering positive and easy."

1939 Alvis 4.3 Litre Drophead Coupe, Charlesworth   *Owners: Kay & Milton A. Miner of Los Angeles, California*

The 4.3 Litre Alvis was the final flowering of the Speed 25, its engine bored out to 4387 cc providing 125 hp. "One of the most modern British cars of the late thirties and a genuine 100 mph car," comments Jean Gorjat. "I bought mine in 1986 in Volo, Illinois and drove it the 850 miles home to Harrisburg in one day. Easy trip."

"Our Alvis, chassis no. 14871, was the last unit produced before Hitler's Lüftwaffe destroyed Coventry and the Alvis complex," note the Miners of their 4.3 Litre. "There is no record as to when Charlesworth completed the body as the coachbuilding plant was also in Coventry and was badly damaged. It is believed that the car was finished and in a London showroom at the time of the Blitz. As did all British automakers, Alvis converted completely to war work by 1940."

With peace came austerity in Great Britain. The production policy Alvis inaugurated after the war did not include any of the Classic Era models.

1938 Alvis 4.3 Litre Drophead Coupe, Charlesworth
Owner: Jean Gorjat of Harrisburg, Pennsylvania

From the beginning, Aston Martin had more ups and downs than an elevator. ("Lift" is perhaps the better operative word.) In 1914 the first example of this renowned British car won a hill climb at Aston Clinton, Lionel Martin deciding to commemorate the event by adding Aston to the vehicle's name. The second car had to await the end of the First World War. When production finally began in 1921, Martin and partner Robert Bamford didn't have the money to carry on—and sold out to the Hon. John Benson who produced about fifty cars in four years and then went into receivership. From that downer, Aston Martin went up again as an ex-patriate Italian, Augustus Cesare Bertelli, and a sporting Englishman, W. S. Renwick, took over and produced 130 cars in four years, not enough to turn a profit, however. More upbeat was the arrival of Sir Arthur Sutherland, who took financial control of the company at the end of 1932. The Bertelli-designed single-cam 1.5-liter engine

from the late twenties was improved, the cars which had never stopped racing now gave promise for victories, production of 105 cars in 1933 came close to the hoped for, and the good-looking Mark II arrived in 1934.

"It has often been said that the last phase of an established type is always more successful than earlier examples of an improved principle, and there is no better example of this than the Aston Martin Mark II," comments Chris Salyer. "At 1495 cc, the engine remained the same as from 1927 and, at first glance, the cars looked alike, but there were differences. The First Series International had a flat radiator, 21-inch wheels and an underslung worm drive rear. The Second Series Standard gave up the worm drive and lengthened the wheelbase from 103 to 112 inches. The Le Mans variation offered both wheelbases, reduced the wheels to 18 inches and increased the compression ratio from 6.0:1 to 7.5:1. The Third Series Mark II had the 7.5 compression, 73 hp

and mechanical cable brakes (rather than rods) operated by 14-inch drums. 'The Sportsman's Car' and 'Gentleman's Fast Motoring' were among the advertising slogans. The Mark II was one of the greatest sports cars of the thirties. Mine was one of 166 produced, one of only 61 short-chassis (103-inch) versions. The Ulster was basically a Mark II tuned and bodied for racing. Aston Martins were individually produced and modifications were relatively inexpensive. For example, silver replaced chrome on one car, padlocks could be had on the hood, and four Mark II short chassis bodies were fitted to Ulster engine-chassis. For about $250 over the $3,500 of a Mark II, Aston Martin was happy to 'hot-rod' the car for you. In the first half-decade of the thirties, Aston Martin exemplified the twilight of the stark, spartan school of sports car design. Racing successes at Le Mans and in the Tourist Trophy were many, the weight of the car (a little more than a ton) being more suited to endurance

1934 Aston Martin Mark II 2/4 Seater   *Owner: Christopher M. Salyer of Oklahoma City, Oklahoma*

1934 Aston Martin Mark II 2/4 Seater
Owner: Christopher M. Salyer of Oklahoma City, Oklahoma

racing. As an outstanding example, Aston Martin finished the Twenty-Four Hours of Le Mans in 1935 in 3rd, 8th, 10th, 11th, 12th and 15th out of a field of 28 finishers. The 3rd place car was beaten by a Lagonda and Alfa Romeo of much larger engine capacities.''

John Mozart's Two-Seater would have raced at Le Mans in 1936 save for the cancellation of the event in strike-torn France. ''Extremely fast for a relatively small cc engine,'' comments John of this car, one of two built for the Sarthe circuit which subsequently became the basis for a new production sports car. Aston Martin continued racing until the war. With peace, the company did not seriously return to production until after the arrival of David Brown at the close of the Classic Era.

1936 Aston Martin Le Mans Two-Seater   *Owner: John Mozart of Palo Alto, California*

1930 Austro-Daimler Type ADR Alpine Tourer   *Owner: Bernard Berman of Allentown, Pennsylvania*

A U S T R O - D A I M L E R

Austro-Daimler's reputation was made in 1910 with the Prince Henry model, named for the punishing 1206-mile reliability trial it had won, that event in turn named for H.R.H. Prince Henry of Prussia, brother to Wilhelm, the emperor of Germany. Though its origins dated back to the turn of the century, the Viennese firm's first cars had been—as the name suggests—merely copies of the Daimlers (soon to be renamed Mercedes) that were built in Germany. Independence from the parent company arrived in 1906, together with the chief engineer services of one Ferdinand Porsche. Austro-Daimler fortunes soared. The

Prince Henry model, one of the finest sporting cars of the period, was built up to World War I. Following the Armistice, Professor Porsche developed a series of advanced and elegant Austro-Daimlers until, in a fit of pique, he abruptly resigned from the Viennese firm and entrained for Stuttgart to design a few memorable Mercedes.

Porsche's successor, Karl Rabe, produced an even more advanced Austro-Daimler, the Type ADR with tubular backbone chassis and independent rear suspension. The car was fitted initially with the predecessor 3-liter 100 hp 100 mph ADMIII six-cylinder engine, subse-

quently with a new 3.6-liter Bergmeister six good for 120 hp and ideal for Alpine touring. A combination of events conspired to mortally wound the Austro-Daimler company. First, the ADR's chassis design was too Tatra-like for the Czechoslovakian firm not to notice. Litigation followed. Then, in the depths of the Depression, to survive, three Austrian firms merged—Steyr, Puch and Austro-Daimler. The marque ceased to exist soon thereafter. Any Classic Era Austro-Daimler is rare. Bernard Berman is lucky to own two: the ADR Victoria Convertible for over a decade, the Alpine Tourer since 1966.

1930 Austro-Daimler Type ADR Victoria Convertible   *Owner: Bernard Berman of Allentown, Pennsylvania*

B M W

Although ultimately its victories would be so numerous that recitation of them all might produce ennui, the BMW 328 looked anything but a winner when it first showed up at a starting line in June of 1936. In an era when most racing sports cars were stark or stripped, the new model of the Bayerische Motoren Werke was sleek and stylish—too civilized surely for competition. Then the 328 won the Eifelrennen on Germany's Nürburgring in a romp.

An all-new idea of what a competition car could be, the BMW 328 was powered by a 1971 cc 80 hp six-cylinder engine—supercharging not necessary, thank you. Over a 94.5-inch twin-tube chassis with independent front suspension, a streamlined body was fitted, neither its headlamps nor fenders easily removable (which was *de rigueur* in some racing circles).

Miles Collier's BMW 328 was one of just 459 built. The influence of the car far transcended that small number and the few years of the 328's career. Well beyond the Classic Era, its engine was adapted to other sports cars, and this Bavarian bombshell's look was widely imitated.

1938 BMW Type 328 Sports Roadster   *Owner: Miles C. Collier of Naples, Florida*

1935 Brough Superior 8 Drophead Coupe, Atcherley
Owner: Joseph N. Moreland, Jr. of Orlando, Florida

B R O U G H
S U P E R I O R

An American engine and a British coachbuilt body were crossbred to result in the Brough Superior, which was built in the fabled town of Nottingham, England from 1935 to 1939. Joe Moreland has owned his car for over a quarter of a century: ''The British term for it is Anglo-American

Sports Bastard. I tend to prefer Quality Hybrid. The Brough Superior was conceived and marketed by George Brough of motorcycle fame. He was a perfectionist who demanded a high standard of quality. Attesting to this is the fact that his two-wheelers were referred to as 'the Rolls-Royce of motorcycles.'

''My particular car bears British number plate BSM-390, supposedly translating to Brough Superior Motors, three speeds, 90 miles per hour. The special number obtained due to this very early machine's status as the factory test car. Utter reliability coupled with sparkling performance seems common experience for a Brough Superior. Mated to the British chassis is the 125 hp Hudson 8 engine which provides a high power-to-weight ratio that will outperform my (admittedly weightier) 1938 Lagonda LG6 pumping out 145 lusty horses. The handsome aluminum coachwork was executed by a talented, if perhaps obscure, coachbuilder: Atcherley of Birmingham.

''The Brough Superior boasted such refinements as automatic lubrication, hydraulic jacking, semi-independent front suspension, quick release caps, and an instantly operated top which lent credence to its designation as a dual-purpose car. In some models, a bit of window dressing surfaced in a polished cover to dress up or disguise the flathead non-exotic engine. Old George must have purloined this one from the Americans: duPont did it first. Sadly, my car is minus this goodie.

''The Brough Superior was available for the modest sum of £695 ex-works. Total production for the marque was some eighty units, with less than half the output being the eight-cylinder variety like mine. The balance of the cars were powered by the Hudson six of less gusto, though some of these were delivered with an optional blower. The smaller displacement cars were also available in attractive saloon form. Today, thirty-six Brough Superiors are extant worldwide, not a bad survival rate.

''That the creator was the essence of his car was brought home to me a number of years ago at a concours in Virginia. There I was fortunate enough to meet an English lady who had dated George Brough in the thirties. An interesting conversation ensued. It seems the old boy had a weakness for the flesh as well as fast motorcars, and was perhaps something of a free spirit in his own time. In any case, he was certainly not the stiff-upper-lip Britisher that was the stereotype of the period.''

1930 Bucciali TAV Roadster, Saoutchik   Owner: Blackhawk Classic Auto Collection, Danville, California

B U C C I A L I

Few things can be said about the Bucciali without inviting controversy. That Bucciali Frères, as the company styled itself, had a factory at 8 rue Gambetta in Courbevoie and a showroom on the Champs-Elysées is one of them. That the *frères* involved were two is another—one was Angelo, the other Paul-Albert, though he preferred Albert-Paul or just Paul or Albert on occasion—and friends (perhaps for that reason) usually referred to him as Buc. Angelo Bucciali was business manager for their automotive venture, Buc was designer and engineer.

An aerial acrobat awhile, the multi-named Bucciali built his own monoplane before he turned twenty-one, flew with the Groupe des Cigognes during World War I and later adopted that squadron's stork mascot for Bucciali automobiles. (Marc Birkigt did likewise, and earlier, for his Hispano-Suiza.) With brother Angelo, Buc capitalized Bucciali Frères in 1922 at 200,000 francs (less than $20,000), indicating the Buccialis had no intention of becoming another Henry Ford. Indeed, selling their cars seems to have been almost an afterthought.

Competition absorbed the brothers' time for awhile. Early efforts included race cars powered by a two-stroke

twin and a V-4. Victories were few, but that seems not to have bothered the Buccialis either. Such production cars as were built were conventional —at first. The unorthodox arrived at the Paris Salon in October 1926, but this new Bucciali was tucked under a stairway leading to the buffet and was overlooked by hungry reporters. For the 1927 Salon the brothers were awarded a more strategic location, and journalists had considerably more food for thought. "The most unconventional of all the unusual cars exhibited," wrote one. Front wheel drive, independent steering, independent suspension on all four wheels and a Sensaud de Lavaud infinitely variable automatic transmission were startlingly progressive.

How many TAV (for *Traction AVant*) Buccialis were produced is a mystery. Buc claimed thirty-six, at a cost of $20,000 each. Some historians

put the figure as low as fourteen. A press release claim that the cars were fitted with "Mercedes SS supercharged" engines was glorious nonsense. Most were powered by American-built Continental straight eights. Nonsense aside, the TAV Bucciali was glorious.

The only complete Bucciali in existence is the Blackhawk Classic Auto Collection's TAV Roadster by Saoutchik. In the Blackhawk collection as well is the show chassis of the Double Huit, the Bucciali brothers' bombshell for the 1930 Paris Salon—a cubist sculpture with a U-16 engine, except that, upon examination years later, old French newspapers were discovered stuffed in sheet aluminum boxes under the rocker arms. That Bucciali was going nowhere.

Separating fact from fantasy in the Bucciali saga shall probably ever remain dicey. The Bucciali brothers gambled that a sophisticated motoring public would be astounded by what they wrought. On that score, they clearly won.

D A I M L E R

In May of 1896 the Prince of Wales had his first ride in a horseless carriage—a Daimler built in Cannstatt, Germany. Queen Victoria's son found the experience exhilarating though, as an enthusiastic equestrian, he hoped the motor vehicle would not entirely supersede the horse. And he did not rush out to buy one. Soon after the turn of the century, however, the Prince of Wales was Edward VII, and there was a Daimler in the Royal garage. A tradition had been established.

Though the Daimler Motor Syndicate Ltd. (later Daimler Co. Ltd.) of Coventry began life as a licensee of the Cannstatt company, the two firms pursued independent courses virtually from the beginning. By 1902 the German company had relocated to Stuttgart and renamed its product Mercedes. And the Coventry Daimler became as British as crumpets and tea.

Genteel motoring was the mark of the Daimler and the company's adoption of the Knight engine in 1909 was in keeping with that policy. The quiet running of a sleeve valve provided a worthy alternative to the sometimes audible valve gear of the firm's principal rival, Rolls-Royce. The fleet of Coventry Daimlers ordered by King George V in 1910 remained in the Royal garage until 1923. The year following, when Rolls-Royce replaced its venerable Silver

Ghost with the New Phantom, Coventry replied with the Double-Six, sporting twelve sleeve-valve cylinders.

By the mid-thirties, however, Daimler decided sufficient progress had been made with poppet-valve engines to render them preferable to

the Knight, even for Royal equipage. By the late thirties, the Coventry firm's rejoinder to its foe in Derby was the 4 Litre, an overhead valve 90 hp straight eight capable of 80+ mph motoring in traditional Daimler splendor. A fluid flywheel preselector transmission was fitted, and individual jacks were built in each wheel.

The Gilmore Car Museum's 4 Litre, purchased nearly a quarter-century ago by Donald Gilmore, is unique in its body styling. Though the

1939 Daimler 4 Litre Sedanca Coupe, Gurney Nutting
Owner: Gilmore Car Museum, Hickory Corners, Michigan

1939 Daimler 4 Litre Sedanca Coupe, Gurney Nutting (interior below)
Owner: Gilmore Car Museum, Hickory Corners, Michigan

1937 Daimler EL 24 Limousine, Charlesworth
Owner: Farrell C. Gay of Springfield, Illinois

characteristic and distinctive radiator shell remains, the Gurney Nutting Sedanca Coupe coachwork is, by conservative Daimler standards, almost voluptuous. But one thing didn't change. As curator Norm Knight comments, ''Purportedly, license plates FLN 1-5 were issued to Windsor Castle. Our plate number is FLN-2.''

All of the foregoing is not to suggest that Daimler produced only for clients whose blood was very blue. So far as Farrell Gay knows, the Limousine he has owned for nearly two decades was not a Royal mews car, but remains memorable for other reasons: ''It is the only one of its kind in the United States. The six-cylinder engine develops 75 hp, and the 121-inch wheelbase is only a couple of inches less than the 4 Litre. Its early type of automatic transmission has gear selection on the steering column. There's a divider window between the chauffeur and passenger areas, with a microphone from one to the other. The back seat has a crank adjustment to change the seat configuration for the comfort of the passengers. And the passenger compartment also has a small (eight-inch square) 'sun roof' for ventilation.''

D E L A G E

The originator of the aphorism that one drives an Alfa Romeo, is driven in a Rolls-Royce, but gives only a Delage to his favorite mistress is unknown. Undoubtedly it was no one from Automobiles Delage. "The Car with a Reputation" was among the firm's slogans, though it had nothing to do with romantic liaisons and was generally followed with "Gained by Performance."

In 1905 Louis Delage began his automobile company in Courbevoie on the Seine. In 1906 he began racing. Victories were many and the Delage reputation was made. In the twenties Louis Delage continued racing not so much to promote his product as to indulge himself. Winning the European Grand Prix Championship had become an obsession.

The Delage obsession resulted in a milestone in race car design. The engine was a double-overhead-cam straight eight with two valves per cylinder, a Roots-type supercharger, a jewel-like look and 170 puissant horses at 8000 rpm. The radiator was raked and the engine offset to provide for a startlingly slim profile

and one of the lowest frontal areas of any Grand Prix car for years. In 1927 Delage was all-conquering. Every race entered was won, the European Championship belonged to Louis Delage.

The Grand Prix Delage shown here is the only original 1927 team racer which remains in existence. Brought to this country in 1929 for the Indianapolis 500—where Louis Chiron finished 7th—the car was subsequently purchased by Briggs Cunningham, whose collection was acquired several years ago by Miles C. Collier for his museum in Naples, Florida.

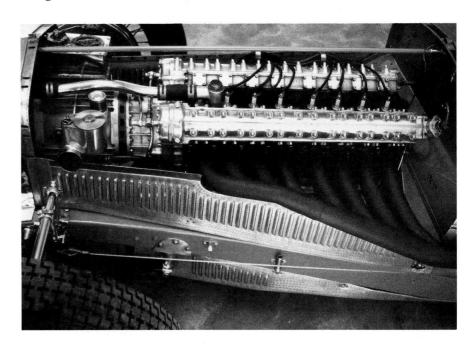

1927 Delage 1.5 Liter Grand Prix Car   *Owner: Miles C. Collier of Naples, Florida*

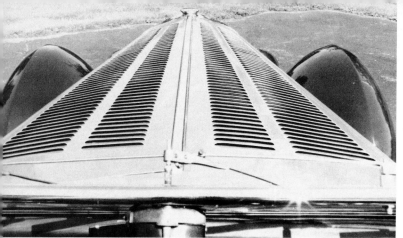

In 1928, his obsession realized, Louis Delage had closed his race department, sold off the race cars and returned wholeheartedly to manufacture. The most glamorous of the Delage line was the straight-eight D8 series introduced in 1929. Whether this car won more awards at major concours d'elegance than any other marque of the era, as Louis Delage claimed, is moot. Conceivably only the Hispano-Suiza won more. And comparatively, the Delage was a bargain: $3,125 for the chassis, half that of an Hispano. Competitors wondered how Louis Delage could sell such a superb motorcar so inexpensively. In 1935 they had their answer, as a financially devastated Delage was forced to sell out to archrival Delahaye. Changes were many under the new ownership but Delahaye continued the magnificent D8 series. The Delages which follow are D8-120 models from 1938. Their Delahaye-built ohv straight-eight engines displace 4744 cc and develop 115 hp. Their coachbuilt bodies are on 133-inch chassis. The chassis price was $5,220. Unchanged was the Delage clientele.

A French count and the curator of the national museum in Paris were early owners of Alberta Berndt's D8-120 Torpedo by de Villars: "This is a one-off body and a huge two-seat car. Seldom seen on a Classic of this period is the extremely raked windshield which is effectively kept clear in rain by three wiper blades. Since 1971 my husband and I have driven this car over 14,000 miles. The Cotal electro-magnetic gearbox is completely smooth and has never faltered. Independent front suspension makes for great handling and ride; the hydraulic brakes are superb. The long-stroke straight-eight engine will go on forever. The car cruises effortlessly at 65 to 75 mph with reserve power. Although I am five feet one inch and 107 pounds, I can handle this Delage as well in city traffic as on the highway."

1938 Delage D8-120 Torpedo, de Villars
Owner: Alberta Berndt of Milwaukee, Wisconsin

1938 Delage D8-120 Delta Sport Convertible, Letourneur & Marchand
Owner: Henry Uihlein II of Lake Placid, New York   Photos: Cindy Lewis

The two D8-120 Delages in the Uihlein collection were commissioned by the French government for display at the 1939 World's Fair in New York City. Each a one-of-a-kind with body by Letourneur & Marchand, these Delages were designed to epitomize the French flair in automotive art, which undoubtedly they did very well for the duration of the exposition. Meanwhile France fell to the Germans. Because of the war, the cars were not returned home.

Henry Uihlein tells their subsequent story: ''The Delta Sport was purchased for $7,430 by Robert S. Grier, who took delivery at the World's Fair and actually drove it out of the French Pavillion at the close of the exposition. The Aero Coupe was purchased by Bruce Crarey. This was the first Delage I acquired, in 1963 at the estate sale of the Crarey collection. I attended merely as a curious onlooker with no intention of becoming a purchaser. Nevertheless, when I saw this car, my eyes melted and a sudden inherent urge seized me and said I should try to buy it. I had no one to advise me so I phoned my cousin Brooks Stevens, the automobile designer and builder of Excaliburs, for advice. He was utterly surprised that such an outstanding and famous French car was for sale in my isolated neck of the woods. He advised me without hesitation to acquire it.

''Then in 1985 I learned that the Delta Sport in the Harrah collection would be selling at auction. I had to have it too. To own the pair was really a ten-strike as far as I was concerned. For the first time since the conclusion of the 1939 World's Fair, these two sister cars were brought back together. Each, in its own way, brings together the quintessence of French design of the Classic Era. The Aero Coupe features the *Vutotal* pillarless window concept pioneered by Henri Labourdette; the Delta Sport the grand sweep of line characterized by Henri Chapron. Both cars were state-of-the-art.

''Experts may differ on the precise ranking of many of the fabulous French cars of the past, but any list of the truly eminent that omits the Delage is incomplete. So often you hear spoken, particularly in Paris, 'Delage is French for elegance.' How true.''

1938 Delage D8-120 Aero-Coupe, Letourneur & Marchand
Owner: Henry Uihlein II of Lake Placid, New York   Photos: Cindy Lewis

DELAHAYE

His last name was Weiffenbach, but everyone called him Monsieur Charles. From the late 1890's when he joined the company as chief engineer to its last days in the 1950's, Monsieur Charles *was* Delahaye. For years this French company prospered in the manufacture of commercial and passenger vehicles of no especial excitement. By the mid-thirties, however, Monsieur Charles thought Automobiles Delahaye needed a change of image. Purportedly, Ettore Bugatti gave him a nudge in that direction by commenting that there was not much difference between a Delahaye truck and a Delahaye car: they were both heavy and slow. *Le Patron* may later have rued that remark.

Monsieur Charles's venture into a new automotive arena was a three-pronged assault. First, his new six-cylinder 3237 cc 130 hp Type 135 was a glamorous *boulevardier*, destined to be cloaked with seductive coachwork by the *crème* of French carrosseries. Second, with the optional 160 hp competition engine, the Type 135 was a sporting car that would give Bugattis a run for the money in French racing events. Third, Monsieur Charles made sure there would be enough customers for his fast and elegant new car by purchasing the troubled but prestigious Delage company in 1935 which, among other plums, gave him a great new mailing list.

Matters proceeded splendidly, with a V-12 introduced to the lineup just prior to World War II when—at the behest of the Germans—the Delahaye factory was turned over solely to truck production. With peace, Monsieur Charles picked up where he had left off. Not surprisingly, he did not focus on the grand Delages of the prewar era. Instead, he revived his beloved top-of-the-line Delahayes, the sixes updated as the 135M and 135MS (sport), the six in the V-12 chassis as the 175. The market in postwar France was small. The cars were spectacular.

The 1946 Figoni & Falaschi Drophead Coupe that has been in the Windfelder garage for the past two decades was originally owned by the Marquis Bernard-Alexis Poisson de Menars. Comments Ed: "This car's pontooned fenders, skirted wheels and fins are hallmarks of Figoni & Falaschi and represent the peak of Art Deco automotive styling. A four-speed Cotal electro-magnetic gearbox is fitted to the Delahaye, and it also has two built-in jacks for changing tires. The steering wheel and dash knobs are clear lucite."

Among the stars of the 1947 Paris Salon was the Delahaye Cabriolet by Figoni & Falaschi, the coachbuilder most often identified with the marque today. Noel Thompson's car was originally commissioned by Aly Khan and was later raced by King Farouk II in Tripolitania (now Libya). Behind the seat in Bob Bahre's car is a bar. Its original owner is unknown.

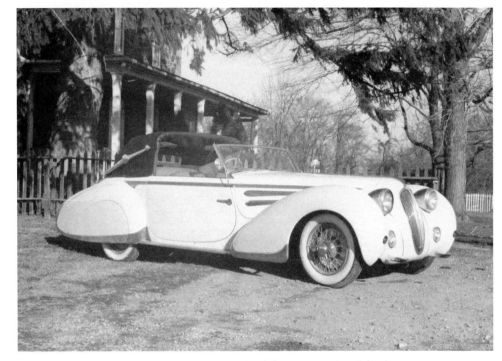

1946 Delahaye 135M Drophead Coupe, Figoni & Falaschi
Owners: Mr. & Mrs. Edward A. Windfelder of Baltimore, Maryland

1947 Delahaye 135M Cabriolet, Figoni & Falaschi
Owner: Bob Bahre of Oxford, Maine

1947 Delahaye 135MS Cabriolet, Figoni & Falaschi
Owner: Noel Thompson of New Vernon, New Jersey   Photo: K. Karger

Guilloré of Courbevoie bodied this 135M Cabriolet, one of two such cars built, owned by Walter Appel: "The sheer elegance of this body style was way ahead of its time, and its rumble seat is a usable feature. With its sturdy six-cylinder engine with three carburetors, these Delahayes were very powerful and dependable. The handbook quotes 0-60 in 13 seconds, with a 105 mph top speed. I don't know the original owner of my car, but the letters 'CH' on the rear deck indicate it probably spent some of its life in Switzerland (Canton Helvetia). In the fifteen years I have owned this 135M, I have driven it over the highest roads in the Rocky Mountains. It has never overheated. The car is still suitable for everyday use, except in the dead of winter."

1947 Delahaye 135M Cabriolet, Guilloré   *Owner: Walter M. Appel of Denver, Colorado*

1948 Delahaye 135M Drophead Coupe, Figoni & Falaschi
Owner: Dana L. Reed, Jr. of Bergenfield, New Jersey   Photo: K. Karger

1948 Delahaye 135M Drophead Coupe, Figoni & Falaschi
Owner: William Adamson, Jr. of Marion, Massachusetts

Dana Reed has owned his Figoni & Falaschi Drophead Coupe since 1957: ''The previous owner was a personal friend. Until the mid-sixties, I drove this car on a daily basis. Its performance was flawless—quick shifting Cotal gearbox, excellent cornering ability, easy to drive. Mileage to date is 30,669—after more than four decades. The car has a three-position top—and an absolutely beautiful body.''

Some of the unusual features in the Adamson 135M Drophead Coupe are explained by Bill: ''The lack of external landau arms is a rarity which I like because the landaus stick out so far and the car's body width in the rear is quite great anyway. Also the parking lights fore and aft are recessed into the fenders and are attractively shaped. I have both a manual shift and a Cotal preselector gearbox available for this car since the original Cotal was replaced in England in the early 1960's. The car is faster with the manual box so, for the present, I'm keeping it that way. This is a fast car even though a 135M as compared to the 135MS with the more highly tuned engine.''

"The 135MS was the road version of the Delahaye which won the 24 Hours of Le Mans in 1938 and the Monte Carlo Rally in '39," comments Jean Gorjat. "My car is the only 135MS with a Pinin Farina coupe body."

The '48 Figoni & Falaschi 135M Cabriolet was restored by Craig Jackson and is commented upon by Russ: "This car can still go down the highway at over 100 mph and handles great. And the styling is sensational. Six similar bodies were produced, no two alike. To me, this car synthesizes the Figoni & Falaschi approach to coachwork and carries it to a zenith: the flamboyant chrome, the disappearing top, the fold-down windshield, the extra-long rear section which is due to the rumble seat. The fins on the rear fender and trunk are the highest of all the 'C' (concave) fendered Figoni & Falaschi cars. And it has the longest nose of all the 'nasal' cars, as they were called. This design won the 1948 Paris Auto Salon, and was the last year of victory there for Figoni & Falaschi."

Nineteen forty-eight was the last Classic year for the marque as well, of course. Automobiles Delahaye soldiered on awhile, but time was against its survival. In 1953 the company merged with Hotchkiss. The few car chassis remaining were bodied for sale through '55 but the only new Delahayes thereafter were trucks, and in a few years they bore the name Hotchkiss too.

1948 Delahaye 135MS Coupe, Pinin Farina
Owner: Jean Gorjat of Harrisburg, Pennsylvania

1948 Delahaye 135M Cabriolet, Figoni & Falaschi   *Owners: Russ & Craig Jackson of Phoenix, Arizona*

H O R C H

The Horch was a celebrated German Classic with a very checkered career. Its saga is confusing, mainly because so much quarreling was going on. Founder August Horch had worked with Carl Benz in Mannheim before a disagreement sent him to Cologne to begin his own company in 1899. But by 1909, following an earlier move of his firm to Zwickau, Horch had argued with his board of directors there and departed to start yet another automobile company elsewhere in town. Denied use of his own name, he chose the Latin translation of *horch* (imperative of the German verb "to listen") and thus his new car was the Audi, which began to routinely beat the Horch in competition. After a falling out with his new backers in 1920, August Horch went to work for the Ministry of Economics in Berlin.

Meanwhile, Paul Daimler was feuding with his directors at Daimler-Motoren-Gesellschaft in Stuttgart, principally because of their reluctance to build the straight-eight Mercedes he had designed, so he left the company his father had founded and joined Horch in 1923. Ferdinand Porsche took his place, and a few years later Daimler merged with Benz.

Under Paul Daimler's tutelage, August Horch's old company moved into prestige ranks. The new straight-eight put the marque squarely in the German luxury class then dominated by Mercedes and Maybach (the latter car built by the son of Gottlieb Daimler's oldest collaborator who had left Mercedes in a huff years before). But by 1930 Paul Daimler tiffed with Horch, which brought in Dr. Fritz Fiedler. Fiedler would later desert to BMW, but not before he developed the V-12 (plans for which Paul Daimler had begun) which was introduced at the 1931 Paris Automobile Salon. A super car priced attractively less than the Mercedes or Maybach, the new Horch was powered by a 5990 cc 120 hp engine capable of moving these big (135- or 147-inch wheelbase, weight approaching three tons) automobiles about 90 mph.

Noel Thompson's 1932 V-12 Sport Cabriolet by Gläser of Dresden stretches nearly eighteen feet from bumper to bumper and was custom-built, at a price of $10,045, for Joachim von Ribbentrop, the German ambassador to England. The car

remained his until commandeered by the British following the outbreak of the war. Gläser touches include the dual rear-mounted spares, individual luggage compartments fitted into the back of the front seat, and a convertible top padded with horse-hair. Apparently, Ambassador von Ribbentrop liked to travel in comfort because the front seats recline. Just 73 V-12 Horchs were produced in little more than two years, when the model was discontinued. The Thompson car is one of just three known to survive.

In 1932 the raging depression forced a merger among four German automobile companies: DKW, Wanderer, Horch and Audi. The combine was called Auto Union. That summer August Horch returned to his old factory for the first time in twenty-three years. He was officially reinstated as the head of the

Horchwerke the following year.

With the V-12 discontinued, A. Horch & Company proceeded to the end of the decade producing V-8 and straight-eight cars. The Riddells' 830 Cabriolet is one of the former, as explained by Dick: "This was the first German V-8 and not without its problems, carburetor and fuel pump mainly. After a six-month run, the 830B followed. Our car is one of only two Type 830's with Gläser bodies to have the spare wheels in the fenders; all the others have them at the rear. This was my first Classic, purchased in 1967 in pieces for $350. The car is still not fully restored but close."

The flurry of Horch models during these years was perplexing but the marque remained high on the German prestige ladder, the cars second in favor only to Mercedes among high-ranking Third Reich staff officers. And the famous Auto Union race cars were built in the Horch factory.

Nineteen thirty-nine was the last year of Horch production. At the top of the marque's straight-eight line

1932 Horch Type 670 V-12 Sport Cabriolet, Gläser
Owner: Noel Thompson of New Vernon, New Jersey

1939 Horch Type 853A Straight-Eight Sport Cabriolet
Owner: Barbara D. Hughes of Essexville, Michigan

1933 Horch Type 830
V-8 Cabriolet, Gläser

Owners: Bobbie & Dick Riddell
of San Clemente, California

was the 4944 cc 120 hp Type 853A.
Very few Sport Cabriolets were built
like the car Barbara Hughes has
owned since 1965: ''What do I like
about this car? First, its beauty of
design and body style. Then
engineering; the car's behavior on
the road is fabulous, especially after
it is up to speed. Lastly (which could
justifiably be exchanged with the first
mentioned) is the Horch's dependability and integrity. Cars, you know,
can be compared to people. Every
warm clear day from June through
October's bright blue weather, time
and other critical appointments per-
mitting, the Horch will be seen on
some of the kinder, gentler highways
and byways of beautiful Michigan.''

In Germany fate did not deal
gently with the Horch. The Third
Reich had other plans for the
company by the fall of 1939. V-E Day
found the plant in disarray—and in
East Germany. The factory was
nationalized later in 1945.

Hotchkiss et Cie. of Saint Denis on the Seine was a French company organized in 1867 by an American ordnance manufacturer whose sales back home had fallen lamentably following the end of the Civil War. Benjamin Berkley Hotchkiss' timing couldn't have been better. Scarcely had he arrived in Paris than the Franco-Prussian War erupted. By the time of his death in the mid-1880's his business was flourishing.

Shortly after the turn of the century, however, Hotchkiss' successors were faced with the same problem: no big wars, no lucrative government contracts for munitions. So the company turned to automobile manufacture—and quickly became famous for the development of the system in which power is transmitted via an open propeller shaft through the rear springs, a concept ever after known as Hotchkiss drive.

All this has tended to obscure the noteworthiness of the Hotchkiss cars themselves. They were always fine, and became even finer during the twenties. A company slogan was ''Qualité Totale,'' but perhaps the company managing director privately preferred ''bloody good.'' He was Englishman Harry M. Ainsworth, who had begun in the Hotchkiss drawing office in 1904 and had taught himself to be a first-rate engineer. By the late twenties, Ainsworth enjoyed the estimable services of first-rate engineer Vincenzo Bertarione—yet another non-Gallic entry in Hotchkiss ranks.

The 3½-liter Hotchkiss sixes of the thirties were exciting cars. In Grand Sport (GS) guise from 1936 onward, they could take on virtually any other car on the road. The company never laid claim to more than 125-130 hp but with a short 110-inch wheelbase and weight held down to little more than 3,000 pounds, the performance was electric. A zero to 60 acceleration time of 9.5 seconds put to shame the Bentley that Rolls-Royce was building, as well as the V-12 Lagondas and eight-cylinder Delages. Bendix brakes stopped the cars efficiently. Compared to the five thousand dollars for a Delahaye or the six for a Talbot-Lago, the Hotchkiss asking price of $3,375 was a real bargain.

If Hotchkiss erred, it was mainly in the matter of conservatism. Sales of 4,213 cars in '36, 2,500 annually from 1937 through 1939 sufficed. The

company promotional budget was minimal, tradition was ever served and, though his car was, Harry Ainsworth was not much of an adventurous sport. And possibly he didn't brag enough.

Jean Gorjat, whose two Classic Hotchkisses appear on these pages, is happy to boast: ''My 1936 686 GS—with a one-off body by Park Ward—was the wedding present of Lady Curzon, daughter of Earl Howe, cousin of King George VI, and driver for Bugatti, Alfa Romeo and Maserati. That says something about the sporting nature of this Hotchkiss all by itself. With a top speed of about 110 miles an hour, what production car was quicker in 1936? It's faster than a standard Bugatti Type 57 or Mercedes 500K. I drive this car quite often at 90 miles an hour; once a policeman did not believe his radar reading! The road

holding is excellent. In addition to other competition, the Hotchkiss 686 GS won the Monte Carlo Rally five times, despite the fact that the factory never participated in nor supported any competition event.

''An identical car to my 686 GS3 won the 1939 Monte Carlo Rally, driven by Jean Trevoux. My particular car was shipped to Argentina at the end of 1939 and participated in much road competition there in the forties and fifties, competing against the vaunted Italian *monoposti* and winning quite a few bets for its owner. The car is fitted with twin Solex carburetors, Cotal electro-magnetic gearbox and, with the light Chapron body, is very quick. The windshield folds down as on British sporting tourers. And, again, the road holding is incredible.''

Postwar, Hotchkiss found the going tough. The market for luxury sporting cars was virtually nil in France. Merger with Delahaye in 1953 was followed by truck manufacture only.

1936 Hotchkiss 686 GS Drophead Coupe, Park Ward
Owner: Jean Gorjat of Harrisburg, Pennsylvania

1939 Hotchkiss 686 GS3 Drophead Coupe, Henri Chapron
Owner: Jean Gorjat of Harrisburg, Pennsylvania

J A G U A R

1946 Jaguar 2½ Litre Saloon
Owner: Auburn-Cord-Duesenberg Museum, Auburn, Indiana

In March of 1945 an "Extraordinary General Meeting" was held at SS Cars Ltd. in Coventry, England. Allied victory in the war was inevitable; V-E Day was less than two months away. Because of its now sinister connotation, SS was no longer deemed suitable as the marque name for the sensational automobile William Lyons had created over a decade earlier. The decision for its replacement was easily made. In 1936, aware that a distinctive car should have a distinctive name, Lyons had settled upon a breed of cat. Jaguar designated some of the SS models thereafter. Now the company would be called Jaguar Cars Ltd. And all of its cars would be called Jaguar too.

Aside from the wording on the radiator badge, a monogrammed "J" where "SS" had been and other minor changes, the new cars, which began rolling off the assembly line that fall, were much the same as their predecessors. Merely converting from wartime production had been a chore. Though the sportier models were shown in the catalogue, only saloons—like the Auburn-Cord-Duesenberg Museum car—were built in 1946.

1947 Jaguar 3½ Litre Drophead Coupe
Owners: Ronald & Sonja Halbauer of Lawrenceburg, Indiana   Photo: John Sutton

Most early postwar Jaguars were produced for the foreign market. Britons who placed orders in 1946 sometimes had to wait six years for delivery. And they paid more dearly for a Jaguar than they had for an SS, inflation and purchase taxation in the austerity of postwar England raising the price of the 3½ Litre to £991. In 1947 the six-cylinder drophead coupes were reinstated, exclusively for export, though some natives cleverly latched on to one by ordering overseas and taking delivery in the UK.

Egypt was the first home of the '47 3½ Litre Ronald & Sonja Halbauer have owned for seven years: "When cleaning the front fender wells after buying the car, considerable sand was found. We immediately thought it must have been from sandblasting during refurbishing by a former owner. Later it was discovered to be dry desert sand never cleaned from this area on the car. The original owner was a C. Saloma of Cairo. The car's days in Egypt may account for its lack of rust. We have put an Egyptian license plate on it, in addition to the requisite Indiana tag; this Jaguar would never have had an English license plate. The English instruction book provided some amusing moments. 'How to change

the lights on the doors,' it read; at first we thought our car was not correct since it did not have any lights on the doors, but then we found that 'lights' in England at that time translated to 'windows' in America. The instruction book also showed the second position of the three-position top rolled above the height of the car but we preferred to roll it under. Since then we have seen photographs of Clark Gable, Errol Flynn and Walter Pidgeon, each having had their Jaguar drophead

coupe with the second-position top rolled under. Must be an American taste. Our car was the thirteenth drophead coupe built by Jaguar after the war. With 125 hp (two S.U. carbs plus 'starting' carb), it has plenty of zip. This is a car to use for many fun trips. It is always faithful in every way."

"I love the lines of the 3½ Litre Saloon," comments John Ryon. "I've added trumpet horns and FT 58 Lucas lights which I feel add to its attractiveness."

1948 Jaguar 3½ Litre Saloon
Owner: John L. Ryon, Jr. of Clarks Summit, Pennsylvania

1948 Jaguar 3½ Litre Drophead Coupe   Owner: Albert R. Pincus of Huntington, New York   Photos: Dennis Blachut

"My car is restored as it was originally," says Al Pincus, "but the shift ball was replaced by me with a bronze Jaguar head (the only one in the world) which I found in England. This car had been purchased new from Hoffman Motors in New York City in August of 1948. The original owner was Mrs. William Paley. Her husband was well known as the president of CBS, but Babe Paley was just as famous in social circles for her exquisite style. She's in the Fashion Hall of Fame. This car certainly suited her. Recently I had a visit from the largest Jag dealer in the world. When he saw the car, he informed me that his dealership in Hempstead, Long Island had serviced it for many years. He gave me the final missing tool for my tool kit as a gift. Only 375 of these cars were made with left-hand drive; I think only 70 are still alive. The timeless styling and beauty of this car appeals to me. The nostalgia of days gone by, of driving for the sheer pleasure of it, is wonderful—a remembrance of calmer times and a simpler lifestyle."

With the arrival of the Mark V in '49, the postwar 3½ Litre was designated Mark IV by the press. These cars were the last Jaguars in the SS idiom. William Lyons was about to turn his car into another very smashing breed of cat.

1939 Lancia Astura Ministeriale Convertible Sedan, Pinin Farina   *Owner: Behring Museum, Danville, California*

L A N C I A

Lancia the unlucky he was frequently called, but that was only during his racing days—and, in truth, it was not so much that Vincenzo Lancia was unlucky but that the cars he was racing were not up to the strain he inflicted upon them. When he turned to making cars of his own, which even he couldn't break, Lancia's luck changed. As a race driver, Vincenzo Lancia was spectacular; as an automobile manufacturer, he was magnificent. In 1906 he set up Fabbrica Automobili Lancia e Cia in Turin; in 1910 he hung up his driving gloves to devote the rest of his life to automobile engineering. And what an engineer he was.

It was while cruising on the high seas shortly after the Armistice that Vincenzo Lancia first got the idea that would make his name immortal in automobile annals. Noting how a ship's hull so effectively handled buffeting by the ocean's prodigious forces set him to thinking about the comparative archaism of motorcar construction, based as it was still on principles set down during the horse-

drawn carriage era. Naval design made eminently more sense. Lancia patented his stressed-hull concept in 1919—and pioneered unitary construction. The same car carried independent front suspension. The first prototype was road tested in September 1921, officially unveiled at the Paris and London automobile shows in the fall of 1922, in full production by early 1923. Lancia called the model the Lambda, carrying on the tradition of Greek letter names he had begun with his first Alpha of 1907. There tradition ended. The Lambda was both revolutionary and prophetic, one of the landmark automobiles in world history. Through 1931, in nine series, 12,530 Lambdas were produced.

Its successors were two, one of them seen here: the Astura (Latin place-names having replaced Greek letters in Lancia designations by now). Vincenzo Lancia introduced this model in November 1931 and thereafter turned his engineering acumen to smaller light automobiles which he believed, sooner than most

European manufacturers, would allow his company to better withstand the buffeting of the Great Depression. The Astura was an unabashed luxury car. That this model became a favorite of Benito Mussolini probably didn't appeal to Vincenzo Lancia much. He didn't suffer buffoonish poseurs gladly. That the Astura proved a favorite of the Italian coachbuilding industry —and particularly to the inventive Battista Farina, who had been nick-named the diminutive "Pinin" as a child—was more to his liking.

Sadly, Vincenzo Lancia was dead—at fifty-six, at the height of his creative powers—by the time the Behring Museum Astura Ministeriale was delivered to *Il Duce*. Its compact V-8 engine, with cylinders set at 17.5 degrees, developed 82 hp, sufficient to propel this lengthy parade car 75+ mph. The roof was heavily padded, the rear seat upholstered in deep rolls of leather. In supreme comfort, Mussolini traveled in this car until . . . Fortunately, this Astura didn't suffer the same ignoble fate. It was barn stored for awhile, then saw service as a taxi on Capri. Today it rests in the Behring Museum as an enduring monument to the genius that was Lancia.

1932 Maserati 8C 3000 Grand Prix Car
Owner: Henry W. Uhle of New York City, New York

There were six Maserati brothers. Mario became an artist, Carlo built motorcycles. The remaining four —Bindo, Alfieri, Ettore and Ernesto— were responsible for one of Italy's most celebrated competition cars of the Classic Era.

It all started in a tiny garage near the Ponte Vecchio in Bologna where the brothers began making spark plugs during World War I. Producing race cars for Diatto followed and, when that Turinese firm got out of competition in the mid-twenties, the brothers Maserati plunged in. Their speed shop became a factory. Unlike most manufacturers, the Maseratis weren't much interested in the marketplace. Probably no more than 130 road cars were produced through the end of the Classic Era and, although a competition license wasn't required for purchase, it helped. Maseratis were not for the meek.

The brothers' principal interest was the manufacture of thoroughbred race cars. Henry Uhle explains: "This Maserati has a twin-cam straight-eight engine with Roots super-charger. Maximum rpm's are 5500, each thousand equal to 28 mph. The engine develops 230 hp. There's a twenty-five gallon fuel tank in the tapered tail with twin filler caps; an eight-gallon oil tank is in the cowl ahead of the cockpit. The brakes are fifteen inches in diameter—and powerful. The wheels are nineteen. The 'fishtail' exhaust is Brooklands type; the steering wheel has 1¼ turns lock to lock. The accelerator is between brake and clutch.

"This car was built for Sir Henry 'Tim' Birkin, the English driver who had earlier become famous as one of the 'Bentley Boys.' He finished third in the 1933 Tripoli Grand Prix and probably would have won except for a slow pit stop and the severe arm burn he suffered from the exhaust pipe. Sadly, the burn turned septic and he died three weeks later. The Maserati was subsequently, and extensively, raced by various owners until its 'retirement' in 1946. At that time it was road equipped with fenders, lights, starter, horn, battery box and portable luggage rack. It was in that form that I acquired the car in the mid-fifties. I've always loved racing cars (full Grand Prix, pre-1940); this one I could use on the road. Never any trouble with police! This Maserati was the most potent machine I ever drove—tremendous acceleration, fantastic handling and performance. All of the Maserati brothers' engineering knowledge went into this car which was an expression of their talent and also a most beautiful one to look at."

M A Y B A C H

1931 Maybach Zeppelin Convertible Coach, Spohn
Owners: Truman A. & Ruth S. Stockton of Lakewood, Colorado

In 1912 Wilhelm Maybach and his son Karl founded Maybach-Motoren-Gesellschaft in Friedrichshafen for the production of engines to power Ferdinand Graf von Zeppelin's airships. In 1921, because of Versailles Treaty restrictions, the Maybachs switched to the automotive field. That the Maybach would be a top-market luxury car was virtually preordained. At the turn of the century Wilhelm Maybach had created the first Mercedes; Karl was determined to put the family name on a vehicle that would compete with the three-pointed star. The son would be responsible for engineering the Maybach as his aging father

looked on with pride. In two decades, no more than 2,300 Maybachs were produced, each hand assembled and with coachwork generally by Hermann Spohn of Ravensburg.

In 1930 the Maybach Zeppelin was introduced. Promotion emphasized its airship-derived engine and the round-the-world voyage ("no better proof of reliability") of the *Graf Zeppelin* the year before. Landship is the best single word to describe the car, as explained by Truman Stockton: "The wheelbase of my two-door convertible coach is 147 inches. The weight is close to three tons. The engine is a 7999 cc V-12 developing 200 hp at 3200 rpm. There's an oil radiator as well as one for water. And there are eight main bearings, No. 8 behind the timing gears at the rear of the engine. Each bank of cylinders has its own coil, distributor and carburetor; heads are interchangeable and, with the plugs removed from one bank, the car can be run as a six. The *Doppelschnellgang* (double fast gear) dual-range transmission was a Karl Maybach invention: three-on-the-floor with standard shift plus an over-and-under vacuum-controlled box behind it providing six forward speeds and two in reverse. Mechanics who've worked on this car have told me it's the finest piece of automotive machinery they've ever seen. This Zeppelin was one of three purchased by Carlos Gustavo Zingg, the German consul in Venezuela. A large limousine was for himself, a four-door convertible for the son of then-dictator Juan Vicente Gomez, the 'Tyrant of the Andes.' My car was for Zingg's daughter, a small girl for whom the front seat was raised two inches so she could see over the wheel. Zingg was an ardent Nazi and was confined to his estate outside Caracas during the war. During the mid-fifties, the Maybach was purchased by an American engineer with the Venezuela-Atlantic Refining Company. He sold the car to me in 1957 because he was home so seldom he couldn't play with it much. Its luggage arrangement is most interesting; the top strap-on trunk—with an inside tray for linens, etc.—was designed to be taken into the hotel each night, the lower trunk being bolted on. Unusual too are the double-drum tire covers. The odometer shows less than 90,000 kilometers. The car remains as I purchased it except for the paint which I changed back to the original ivory, blue and gold of the Hohenzollern family."

1936 Maybach Type SW38 Convertible Sedan, Spohn   *Owner: William R. Patton of Irvine, California*

Maybach's Type SW38 was introduced in 1936. It carried the *Doppelschnellgang* transmission and was fitted with a six-cylinder 3790 cc 140 hp engine. The traditional Maybach mechanical brake system with vacuum servo assist was utilized. "SW" translated to *Schwingachswagen* or, literally, "swing-axle car." (Chevrolet would later imitate the Maybach's rear-end geometry in its early Corvettes.) Although not as expensive as the Zeppelin ($8,000 for chassis alone), the $10,000 required to buy an SW series Maybach was twice that of its rival 3.4-liter Mercedes or 3.5-liter Horch V-8.

William Patton has owned his '36 SW38 Convertible Sedan since 1965:

"General Field Marshall Werner von Blomberg was the first owner. The highest ranking officer in German history, he had been appointed Minister of War in 1933 by President Hindenburg, Hitler promoting him to Commander-in-Chief of the Armed Forces. Never before or since were all three branches of the service in the command of one man. As a Prussian member of the elite German officer corps, von Blomberg was never fully trusted by Hitler, who used a scandal involving von Blomberg's wife to force him into retirement. He and his Maybach spent the war years in Bavaria, remote from the fierce Allied bombing. Von Blomberg died of a heart attack during the Nuremburg

trials. His car, confiscated by the Allies, was given to the City of Vienna and used for diplomatic events. I purchased it in Vienna."

The SW Convertible Sedan in the Blackhawk Classic Auto Collection was delivered new in 1939 to Total KG Forstner & Co. of Berlin-Charlottenburg. It is estimated that no more than 100 Maybachs of all types survive.

Following the war, Karl Maybach rebuilt his heavily-bombed Friedrichshafen factory. In 1960 the Maybach and Daimler-Benz companies joined forces to produce heavy-duty diesel engines, after a half century linking once again the Maybach and Mercedes names.

1939 Maybach Type SW38 Convertible Sedan, Spohn   *Owner: Blackhawk Classic Auto Collection, Danville, California*

M. G.

In 1929 the M.G. Car Company evolved from Morris Garages, Ltd. The move was perhaps overdue. For a half-dozen years Cecil Kimber had been souping-up the standard product of William Morris' automotive empire and selling the result as the M.G. In 1928 Morris introduced his Minor, and Kimber decided to create a sporting M.G. in a minor key too. The M.G. Midget was England's first inexpensive and practical sports car. And it begat a worthy series of successors, most memorably in the supercharged K3 Magnette which was sold ready to race and enjoyed more competition victories than most people care to count.

In March of 1936 the SA was introduced with a pushrod ohv 78½ hp six-cylinder engine, hydraulic brakes (which Kimber distrusted so much he wouldn't allow them on his race cars) and a 123-inch wheelbase (the first time an M.G. chassis stretched more than two digits since the Midget). This new M.G. was obviously aimed at the carriage trade and was priced attractively less than an Alvis or Lagonda. The only problem was that traditional M.G. enthusiasts had always thought small and ignored the car. And an all-new clientele couldn't be persuaded to equate touring luxury with the M.G. image.

''Just 2,745 Type SA's were built, less than 700 of those the Tickford,'' says Curgie Pratt. ''The SA was aimed to compete with, and resembles, a Jaguar. All my cars have

1938 M.G. Type SA Two-Litre Saloon
Owner: Barry M. Briskman of Scottsdale, Arizona

names. This one is 'Bella Donna,' a lovely lady.''

Comments Barry Briskman: ''A very rare and handsome car. I have other unusual non-Classic M.G.'s, both pre- and post-war, but this SA really stands out among them. In addition to hydraulic brakes, the car features a wet clutch, four-speed gearbox, sun roof and built-in hydraulic jacking system. Apparently, the company was proud of this car; the M.G. logo appears eleven times in the interior, fifteen times on the exterior and four times in the engine compartment.''

Pride did not overcome practicality, however. Production of the luxury M.G. was not resumed after the war.

1938 M.G. Type SA Two-Litre Tickford Drophead Coupe, Salmons & Sons
Owner: Curgie Pratt of Phoenix, Arizona

R A I L T O N

The Railton was a Great Depression baby. In 1933, after eight years of producing the Classic Invicta, Noel Macklin and associates were forced to move operations to the firm's service garage in London, which was more than ample to continue Invicta's drastically reduced program. This left an empty factory in Cobham—until Macklin had an idea and juggled some figures. An American chassis and British coachwork could be combined in a sporting car to sell for under $3,000, he concluded, which compared favorably with the $3,500 asking price for native products of three liters or so, particularly since the straight eight from Hudson he was planning to use provided upwards of four. Next Macklin talked to Reid Railton of land speed record fame who agreed to lend both his expertise and his name to the project. Fewer than 1,500 Railtons would be produced, but the venture proved a money-maker until after the war when the car's necessarily inflated price and the ban on dollar imports combined to halt manufacture of the car that Reid Railton called "the poor

man's Bentley" and most historians since have regarded as the best of the Anglo-American hybrids of the Classic Era.

"I have driven this car all over the country and from coast to coast," says Ken Kenewell of the Ranalah Sunroof Saloon he has owned since 1973. "I drive it a lot not only because it drives well, but the air-bag cushions in the individual front bucket seats make it a very comfortable vehicle for extended motoring. These cars were significant because they incorporated ride control (Andre Telecontrol) which enabled the English driving enthusiast of the thirties to race around the hay bales on weekends with the same vehicle that he drove to the office during the week."

That the Berkeley Sports Roadster owned by the McManuses was raced has been well documented, as detailed by Pete: "This was a one-off short-wheelbase (105 versus the usual 116 inches) trials car. Its 254-cubic-inch engine features a Vertex magneto, racing camshaft, two-barrel carburetor and larger exhaust

manifold as it could have had for racing purposes in the late 1930's. The car was used in England during that period for off-road competition events by its various owners, including Donald Maclean who drove it in the 1938 Cambridge University trials. Maclean was one of the spies in the Philby-Burgess-Maclean group whose defection to Russia in 1951 provoked a major security crisis in the U.K. I've owned this Railton since 1982. The notoriety of one of its former owners is intriguing, needless to say; so is the Macklin/Invicta and Reid Railton association. The Railton grille was designed by famed *Autocar* artist F. Gordon Crosby, incidentally, who also designed the original Bentley radiator shell for W. O. Bentley. Brute American horsepower and minimum English coachwork were a potent combination. Hudson's very smooth wet clutch and high torque engine enabled a driver to start effortlessly and smoothly from a dead stop in third (top) gear. The slogan 'Quickest by Railton' reflected zero to sixty road test times of less than ten seconds, phenomenal acceleration that wouldn't be matched by many other sports cars until well after the war."

1934 Railton Sports Roadster, Berkeley   Owners: Pete & Joanne McManus of Thornton, Pennsylvania

1935 Railton Sunroof Saloon, Ranalah   Owner: Ken Kenewell of Fenton, Michigan   Photos: CCCA

R Ö H R

Like the Maybachs, Hans Gustav Röhr was constrained from returning to his usual work by the Versailles Treaty. And like the Maybachs, this former aero engine builder and World War I pilot chose the automobile field. After designing cars for Priamus of Cologne, Röhr was able to secure financial backing to start his own company—Röhr Auto-mobilwerke AG near Darmstadt-Hessen. The first Röhr created a sensation in 1928. A specification that

included a platform chassis, swing axles in the rear and parallelogram front suspension, plus Lockheed hydraulic brakes guaranteed that. But, alas, it did not guarantee commercial success.

By 1930 Gustav Röhr had left to work for Adler and subsequently Daimler-Benz where he was responsible for engineering the Mercedes-Benz 500K into the 540K. Meanwhile, his former factory manager found fresh financial backing to carry on. The Type F was introduced in 1932. Ironically, the engineer responsible for modifying the Röhr design was former Mercedes-Benz alumnus Ferdinand Porsche. The Type F engine was the

Röhr's biggest ever—an ohv 3.3 liter straight eight generating 75 hp and offering 70 mph motoring. The striking coachwork on the car seen here is by Autenrieth of Darmstadt.

It was, understandably, the similarity in name which initially attracted the late Edgar E. Rohr to this car, which had been brought to this country by a U.S. Army officer after the war. There was no family connection. Through research, Ed was able to learn that this Type F had been specifically built for the 1933 Automobile Exposition in Berlin. Its "step-down" design and lack of running boards were remarkably progressive for the period. With the window open, the central door posts

fold down to provide an early example of what later would be called hardtop styling. Overall, the car presents a fascinating amalgam—Teutonic massiveness with a touch of teardrop streamlining more commonly associated with the French school of design.

Unfortunately, the Neue Röhrwerke AG did not long survive this show car. By 1935 the factory was turned over to the manufacture of agricultural implements. In 1937 Hans Gustav Röhr died of a lung infection at the age of forty-two; at the time he was at work on a front-wheel-drive project for Mercedes (which died with him). Only a handful of Röhr automobiles are known to exist.

1933 Röhr Type F Special Sedan, Autenrieth
Owner: Mrs. Edgar E. Rohr, Rohr's Museum, Manassas, Virginia

S. S.

The teaser ad began appearing during the summer of 1931. "S.S. is the name of a new car that's going to thrill the hearts of the motoring public, and the trade alike," it read. The trade press obliged with provocative reports of a "marvelously low-built" automobile still in the 'unrevealed secret' stage."

Big build-ups frequently lead to even bigger let-downs. This one didn't. When the S.S. appeared at the Olympia Motor Show in October 1931, the reaction was a collective gasp. It had a "£1000 look," everyone agreed, but its price was just £310. It was unique, one reporter commented, in being "the first car to be designed around a body." It was a smash hit.

William Lyons was the reason. The man always had class. An early picture shows him sitting astride a Harley Davidson, his body erect, his sweater and racing leggings spotless, his helmet no-nonsense, his look one of supreme confidence. In short, he cut a very dashing figure. There wasn't a car William Lyons ever built of which the same could not be said.

Since the twenties, when his Swallow Sidecar and Coachbuilding Company had begun providing prettier coachwork on plebian British chassis, the Lyons touch had become increasingly more deft. The S.S. was built on a special Standard chassis, Lyonized to a fare-thee-well. Its wheelbase was longer by three

1935 S.S. I Drophead Coupe
Owner: Albert J. Gayson of Alhambra, California

inches, its 2054 cc side-valve six-cylinder engine was moved back six, the frame was double dropped with long semi-elliptic springs mounted outside (not beneath) the main members, amongst other modifications so Lyons could realize a car as long and low as humanly possible.

The resulting S.S. was a full thirteen inches closer to the ground than the Standard. And, with a top speed of 71 mph, over ten miles an hour faster. Perhaps it overheated and the roof leaked—problems soon rectified—but what did that matter when the car you were driving redefined ''rakish'' and made any graced with the term previously seem staid and old-fashioned.

''I purchased my S.S. I in 1949 and apparently we enjoy it as we have driven it every summer since,'' says William Abbott.

Comments Albert Gayson about his S.S. I from 1935: ''This was the first and last year for production of the drophead coupe. I have traced only four others like mine in the world.''

1934 S.S. I Open 4 Seater Tourer
Owner: William S. Abbott of Jerseyville, Illinois   Photos: Jerry Manis

1936 SS I Open 4 Seater Tourer   Owners: Ronald & Sonja Halbauer of Lawrenceburg, Indiana   Photos: John Sutton

By the end of 1932 William Lyons had sold 776 of his S.S. cars, the larger designated I retrospectively with the arrival of the smaller non-Classic S.S. II. S.S. Cars Ltd. was organized in 1934. By the autumn of 1935 the side-valve engine was superseded by an overhead valve and Lyons, anxious that a stronger statement be made for his 2½- and 3½-liter cars, asked publicity department head E. W. Rankin to come up with a good model name. From the list Rankin submitted, Lyons chose Jaguar. At the same time, S.S. became incontrovertibly SS. Actually, company advertising had vacillated about using periods or not from the beginning. Lyons meanwhile was looking to buy the rights and complete presses needed to produce his engines in-house. This would be realized by the late thirties. Subsequently chassis would also be built in the Coventry works. Lyons was a whirlwind. By 1935 his long-time partner William Walmsley had retired, preferring a life of leisure to the accelerated pace at which Lyons was moving.

Sonja Halbauer provides an inkling: ''In 1935 SS I production totaled 98 cars. About ten of them still exist. Ours is one of 17 tourers built late that year which were fitted with '36 grilles because there were no more 1935's left. Therefore, these last 17 cars of '35 were called 1936 models but should not be confused with the 1936 SS I which had the new overhead valve engine. The company used the slogan, 'The World's Most Beautiful Sports Cars.' And the press didn't disagree. Autocar said that the SS 'has been paid that sincerest form

of flattery, imitation.' And Motor bought a tourer and put 10,000 miles on it in four months, with a broken fan belt the car's only failing for the duration. Although not initially conceived as a competition car, the SS I was competitive. In the 1934 Alpine Trial, the factory team of four tourers won its class and received the second-place team award. At the

Monte Carlo Rally Concours de Confort, first place in the unlimited open class was won, as well as the premier award in the M.C.C. Speed Trials at Brooklands. These cars have exceptional acceleration and fine cruising speed in comfort. Somehow William Lyons managed to produce a performance and luxury vehicle at half the price of other marques.''

1938 SS 100 Roadster   *Owners: Jack & Shiela Rabell of Alpine, California*

With the SS 100, introduced in 1936, William Lyons began his inexorable climb to immortality. Like the predecessor SS 90, the new car was on a wheelbase truncated to 104 inches from the SS I's 119. A single glance suffices: the perfect proportions, the sweep of the fenders, the gloriously enormous headlights, the snug cockpit. The SS 100 was a virtual definition of a Classic Era sports car. Behind its wheel, one looked like a million dollars for less than five hundred pounds sterling —and with 60 miles an hour about twelve seconds away and an easy 100 mph available from there. A super car.

The Rabells have owned their SS 100 for over fifteen years, Jack restoring the car himself over a period of a half-decade: "The body is all aluminum except for the gas tank. The overhead valve engine has twin carburetors and exhaust. From 1936 to 1940, 309 were produced in 2½- and 3½-liter form. Just sixty-five 2½-liter SS 100's were built in 1938; forty-six remain extant. In 1988 I participated in the Great American Race in a similar car—4,200 miles across the U.S.A., a great ride and top down all the way!"

Coventry was heavily bombed during the war. When the rubble was cleared in 1945, the SS marque was reborn under the model name that had designated the larger cars since 1936.

599

S U N B E A M

"Too fast for its chassis." Perhaps the praise is more than faint, but the Twin-Cam Sunbeam has forever been damned by the notion that it was not structurally sound enough for its performance. Somehow it doesn't seem fair. Consider the Twin-Cam's debut in the 1925 Twenty-Four Hours of Le Mans. Granted, of the two cars entered, one retired early, although not before winning the Gustave Baehr Award for covering the greatest distance in the first hour. The second car motored on, driven by veteran Jean Chassagne and S.C.H. Davis, who was a rookie to international road racing on the Continent. "Finish the race. Keep the revs down to 3200. Do not skid on the corners. Be gentle with the brakes," Sammy was told. He did so. Over twelve hours into the race, about 6:00 a.m., with Chassagne at the wheel, the Sunbeam was forced off the road by a competitor and emerged from a gully with its rear axle bent. Still, it motored on. During Sammy Davis' next stint, pot holes in the road jarred the dashboard loose and, to keep the gauges from breaking, he had to hold the dash up with one hand. Not a great way to race. Chassagne was behind the wheel when the Twin-Cam crossed the finish line several hours later, placing a remarkable second to a 3.5-liter Lorraine-Dietrich. It bears mentioning that neither of the two Bentleys in the same race went the distance. So far as robust chassis are concerned, the Bentley was built like a tank. "Personally I walked with the gods for weeks after that race," Sammy Davis said, "and no calamity had power to touch me."

Meanwhile, calamity befell the Sunbeam Motor Car Company Ltd. in Wolverhampton. Early in 1926 came word that racing was over. The reason was largely financial; the sprawling Anglo-French Sunbeam-Talbot-Darracq empire was in disarray. Louis Coatalen, the French-born engineer responsible for the English company's competition success since before the First World War, was distressed—until he hit upon the idea of building a single car in which Henry Segrave would attempt to break the land speed record. That plan—as students of L.S.R. history know—worked very well. Sammy Davis' Sunbeam racing days were over. He would become one of the "Bentley Boys." The Sunbeam that raced at Le Mans in '25 was put on the market.

Double overhead camshafts in a production car was rare in the mid-Twenties. So was a 90 mph performance. One had to pay dearly for it, more so as time went on. During the Twin-Cam's penultimate production year of 1929, the U.S.-delivered price was $6,750, higher than any American luxury marque save the Locomobile and the brand-new J Duesenberg.

Fewer than twenty Three-Litre Twin-Cams remain extant. Figures vary on the total number built. An indication of the pace at which production and sales moved is illustrated by the car in Miles Collier's collection. Its engine was completed in 1926, the chassis in 1927, the car itself was assembled in 1928, a customer was found in 1929. The Collier car also illustrates the production quagmire of the S-T-D empire. Its French-built engine uses the metric system; the English-built chassis/body is to British Whitworth standard. Price and perplexity kept customers away in droves.

In 1949 this Sunbeam was raced against a three-liter Bentley team in the Vintage Sports Car Club races at Silverstone. The result was the same as at Le Mans in '25. Sunbeam enthusiasts regarded this as nicely significant. It has long been thought that Louis Coatalen built the Twin-Cam in the first place to go W. O. Bentley one better.

1929 Sunbeam Three-Litre Twin-Cam Super Sports   *Owner: Miles C. Collier of Naples, Florida*

1934 Triumph Dolomite Roadster   Owner: *John Mozart of Palo Alto, California*

T R I U M P H

Had not the Coventry company suffered one of its periodic financial crises at the time, the collecting world might enjoy the availability of more Triumph Dolomites like John Mozart's today. Its rarity appeals to John, of course, and Triumph history is all the richer for the cloak-and-dagger saga that saw this car born.

To lend perspective, it should be noted that Siegfried Bettmann of Nuremberg was Mr. Triumph for over a half century. He had settled in England in 1885, initially as a cycle exporter in London. Bicycle manufacture was begun in Coventry a few years later, leading Bettmann, perhaps with some inevitability, to the motorcycles which made the Triumph name famous. In 1923 the first Triumph automobile arrived. By 1930 Bettmann was confident enough of its future to change his firm's name from Triumph Cycle Co. Ltd. to Triumph Motor Co. Ltd. Nearing seventy, he retired a few years later, assured that all was well. Supervision of Triumph automobiles now fell to Lieutenant-Colonel Claude Vivian Holbrook. In September of 1933, Holbrook hired Donald Healey as technical manager.

Ostensibly, Healey's job was to carry on the Triumph tradition of producing fours and sixes of a liter or a liter-and-a-half in sedan and sporting styles. But that wasn't much of a challenge for a man who was already internationally famous as a trials driver and winner of the Monte Carlo Rally for Invicta. Somehow Healey was able to convince Holbrook that what Britain, ergo Triumph, needed was a world-beater of a sports car. What that meant was a car akin to the Alfa Romeo which had staked out the Mille Miglia as its private territory.

Healey was given a budget of purportedly less than £5,000 at first, part of which he used to travel to Italy and talk with Vittorio Jano at Alfa Romeo. If an Alfa-like car was the aim, why not a version of the Alfa itself? A verbal agreement was reached. Healey was given copy privileges of the 8C 2300 in exchange for permission for Alfa to use the Triumph twin-cylinder motorcycle. From Jano's viewpoint, he wasn't abetting a potential competitor since the 2300 was being phased out and he was absorbed by now trying to engineer a Grand Prix car that would beat the Mercedes and Auto-Union. The deal was bizarre. No money changed hands, but neither did blueprints for the Alfa.

Instead, back home, Donald Healey bought one and tore it apart. Chassis details of the Alfa didn't interest him; the Dolomite would differ in gearbox (Wilson preselector), axle (spiral bevel) and suspension (half-elliptic leaf springs all-round). The Alfa's straight-eight twin-cam engine was his prime concern. "I got one of my engineers to copy and draw up every last detail, down to the nuts and bolts," Healey said. "Our engine *was* a bit different, of course. I wanted a two-liter, which meant that we used a smaller cylinder bore, and because we kept the supercharger like the Alfa that automatically meant that our boost was higher. Compression was a bit higher, too." As for the Dolomite styling, obviously the Alfa had been given another careful look.

None of this happened in the Triumph factory, but instead in super secret at a nearby private house. And quickly. By the summer of '34, the first Dolomite was being tested, the second and third being built. That October the new car was the star of the Olympia Motor Show. The British press went wild. The Alfa resemblance went unmentioned. Once the hoopla died down, so did further mention of the Dolomite itself.

What happened? The aforementioned financial crisis. The straight-eight Dolomite project was written off as effectively as Healey did a prototype in the 1935 Monte Carlo Rally when he lost an argument with a locomotive at a railway crossing in Denmark. Healey himself sold off the remaining prototypes. The Dolomite name would be revived on a Triumph in '36, which was another car altogether. The Healey name would become renowned in sports car circles after the war, on another car altogether. The Triumph Dolomite by Healey courtesy of Alfa Romeo has Hollywood written all over it. What a movie it would make.

601

1939 Talbot-Lago Type T23 Teardrop Coupe, Figoni & Falaschi
Owner: Sam Mann of Englewood, New Jersey

In the mid-thirties the Anglo-French conglomerate of Sunbeam-Talbot-Darracq fell with a mighty thud. The man who picked up the pieces in France was an Italian named Antony Lago who had spent much of his career in England.

Lago's resumé read well. His experience in the automobile industry had been widely varied: selling Isotta-Fraschinis in London, assisting Wilson in the perfection of the preselector gearbox, driving with the Armstrong-Siddeley factory race team, serving on the management team at Sunbeam in Wolverhampton. It has been said that during the S-T-D era, with the exception of yearly financial statements, the British hand never knew what the French hand was doing. That the situation at Suresnes was more critical than Wolverhampton had become apparent by 1933, however, when Lago was dispatched to France to help. Following the collapse, he fell natural heir to Société Anonyme Darracq cum Automobiles Talbot. What he had inherited was almost a corpse.

A luxury car with a performance image was Lago's prescription for revival. Another Italian living in France had been using the same formula successfully for years. It was at Ettore Bugatti that Tony Lago took aim. In 1936 he enticed René Dreyfus, the former Bugatti factory driver then competing in Alfas for Scuderia Ferrari, to become his team captain. "Your job will be to stay ahead of the Bugattis for as long as you can," Lago told Dreyfus. "That's all I want." In race after race René had the fastest lap but failed to finish. That point made, Talbot-Lago reliability became the priority of the engineering department. Victories would follow.

The heart of Tony Lago's car was

its engine, redesigned from the Talbot-Darracq K78 into a brilliant four-liter 140 hp six with seven-main-bearing crankshaft, hemispherical combustion chamber and overhead valves operated by cross-over pushrods. This same engine was installed in touring cars capable of better than 120 mph and competition machines good for more than 130. "It is essential to maintain a close and constant tie between the *bolide* and the customer's car," Tony Lago declared, ". . . high performance has no true worth unless its results can be passed on to the average driver." A contemporary put it more succinctly: "Bugatti builds what he

races, Lago races what he builds."

The coachwork which surrounded the Talbot-Lago engine and its formidable cross-braced chassis (which featured independent front suspension and, of course, the Wilson preselector gearbox) was memorable. Like Bugatti, Tony Lago was perpetually broke. Production of prosaic and lesser-powered sedans helped the exchequer. The cars Lago himself preferred were the cabriolets and coupes which lent themselves more facilely to the coachbuilding art.

"A piece of sculpture on wheels," says Lindley Locke of his Figoni & Falaschi Lago SS Coupe. "This car has the most gorgeous, voluptuous,

sexiest styling imaginable. Someone once remarked that its lines are positively indecent."

"Very fast, terrific performing," comments Sam Mann about his T23 Teardrop Coupe. "And, with all that, an incredibly elegant car too."

Tony Lago's Italian nationality prevented the Third Reich from seizing his factory during World War II. Afterwards, production was resumed. The Talbot-Lago formula didn't change, but the times had. Talbot-Lago held on longer than most exclusive French manufacturers, but by 1959 the company had been quietly absorbed by Simca. One year later Tony Lago was dead.

1939 Talbot-Lago Type T150C Lago SS Coupe, Figoni & Falaschi   *Owner: Lindley T. Locke of Fallbrook, California*

1927 Vauxhall Type OE 30/98 Velox   *Owner: Miles C. Collier of Naples, Florida*

V A U X H A L L

Among the characters in *Those Barren Leaves,* Aldous Huxley's popular novel of the mid-twenties, was Lord Hovenden. He was a wimp, except when he was behind the wheel of his Vauxhall 30/98. It was only while doing seventy-five on the Great North Road that His Lordship was able to tell Mrs. Terebinth, seventeen years his senior, who had four children and adored her husband, that she was the most beautiful woman he had ever seen. At eighty miles an hour he told her he loved her. With the 30/98 to give him courage, His Lordship could make all sorts of promises he couldn't keep when his car was in the garage. If only, he wished, one could spend all one's life in a Vauxhall.

Social satire, yes, but still a stirring testimonial for the car. Whether the 30/98 was the last of the Edwardians (as it was affectionately known) or the first British sports car worthy of the name (as its maker implied) is moot. Some cars defy logic. Other cars ooze character. The Vauxhall 30/98 did both.

In the 19th century, Scottish engineer Alexander Wilson had founded his iron works on the Thames near London. Interested in

heraldry, he chose the crest of Fawkes de Breauté, a vassal of William the Conqueror, to adorn his products and a variation of Fawkes Hall, as legend said de Breauté's estate was called, as the name for his company. Shortly after the turn of the century, Vauxhall moved into automobile manufacture and to Luton which, fortunately, didn't lessen the pertinence of the crest or name since de Breauté had also had a place there. Vauxhall's place in history followed the arrival of the estimable Laurence Pomeroy, Sr. as chief engineer.

Pomeroy's Prince Henry model of 1910 was named (like Porsche's Austro-Daimler) after the German trials in which it excelled. The Type 30/98 followed in 1914 and was a habitual winner at Brooklands for almost a generation. Beginning its career as the side-valve Type E, the 30/98 was revised to a 4224 cc overhead-valve four-cylinder OE for 1923. And front brakes were fitted, though Vauxhall was leery of them, advising owners "to check the car's progress" with the hand brake, reserving the foot "for emergency." The hydraulic brakes, added to the front wheels and transmission in late 1926, leaked copiously. This

apparently bothered owner enthusiasts not at all.

Many owners raced their cars. The 30/98 in Miles Collier's collection is typical. Its natural aluminum Velox body is standard except for the competition windscreen. The hydraulic brakes were competition modified, and the engine fitted with non-standard S.U. carburetors by an American owner shortly after World War II. Mention of just one of its races tells all. In the first U.S. Grand Prix, at Watkins Glen in 1948, this venerable 1927 Vauxhall finished fourth, behind a '38 supercharged 2.9-liter Alfa, Briggs Cunningham's '39 racing Bu-Merc and a brand-new supercharged M.G.—a singular performance.

Singular coachwork distinguishes the 30/98 owned by Charles Mallory: "This Derham is a one-off, the only 30/98 chassis exported to America to be bodied. I've owned the car since 1985 and drive it about 500 miles a year. Totally reliable, this Vauxhall is a better handling vintage Bentley with a booming exhaust note and comfortable 75 mph cruising speed. Back in the twenties, race tuned, the factory guaranteed a lap at Brooklands at 100 mph."

Alas for the 30/98, General Motors acquired Vauxhall Motors Ltd. in 1926 and replaced the low-production OE (310 were built in all) with models that would sell in greater numbers. Lord Hovenden wouldn't have been pleased.

1927 Vauxhall Type OE 30/98 Roadster, Derham   Owner: Charles Mallory of Stamford, Connecticut

V O I S I N

Fewer than 20,000 Voisins were produced. Only about 90 survive. Their high aluminum content made them attractive as scrap, and confiscation of the cars by the Germans during the Occupation was widespread. For nearly two decades before, the singular character of the Voisin itself had made the car attractive to owners for whom the usual was not quite enough. "One man's meat is another man's poison," the ditty went, "My favorite car is an Avions Voisin."

Gabriel Voisin was, as the French say, "*un type*," a character, a one-of-a-kind. He went to his deathbed—at age ninety-three, a longevity he proudly claimed had nothing to do with clean living—still insisting that the Wright brothers had been given credit for an achievement he had realized earlier. His factory for building aircraft at Issy-les-Moulineaux was the world's first. Converting to automobile production following the First World War, Voisin went his own way from the beginning. What made his cars unusual was not their component parts—other manufacturers used the Knight sleeve-valve engine, were as devoted as he to finding the answer to easy gear-changing and regarded scientific light weight as gospel.

Voisin was simply more passionate on these subjects, forever railing about the "technological imbecility" rampant in the industry. He broke rules whenever he could. Luxury cars were supposed to be big, he made some of his small. Luxury cars were not for racing, he raced some of his. He chose "*La Cocotte*" ("chick") for his car's emblem, but the word could also mean a woman of easy virtue, a floozy, a tart. Most luxury car manufacturers would have thought twice about that. Most luxury car manufacturers sought the services of coachbuilders too but, with rare exception, Gabriel Voisin preferred his car to be his alone and provided the coachwork himself. A few of his styling ideas are seen on these pages.

The Browns have owned their 2.3-liter C-14 Wicker Roadster since 1984. Dick tells the story: "Some skeptics have questioned the authenticity of the body because they have never seen another one just like it. Well, that's the way it is with one-of-kinds. My fianceé and I purchased this car on Labor Day, were married three weeks later and drove the car on the Glidden Tour which started the same day. On the second day of our honeymoon, we suffered a minor breakdown—of the car, not the marriage. The moral is: Never start a honeymoon with an untried car and an untried bride. Something always seems to go wrong. Everything's been right since. On the Michigan CARavan, ours was the smallest car but just 'took a licking and kept on ticking.' It is my understanding that the Avions-Voisin has now been declared a 'national treasure' in France and can no longer be exported. I hate that. This delectable little French bon-bon is delightful to look at and a true joy to drive. Also the smoke from the sleeve-valve engine helps keep the mosquito population under control. The Cotal electro-magnetic gearbox giving six speeds forward and Dewandre vacuum-power brakes make the C-14 Voisin very advanced for 1929. Gabriel Voisin built many different models and not one of them was mundane or normal. Nobody really owns a Classic but instead merely takes care of it and worships it until the next generation takes over. We are the temporary caretakers of 'Wee Willie Wicker,' basket case extraordinaire.'

The Blackhawk Classic Auto Collection C-20 Simoun Demi-Berline has twice the cylinders (twelve, 4860 cc) as the other Voisins in this portfolio. Fewer than sixty were sold. Typically, Gabriel Voisin said the reason was that the cars were "too scientific," but the $7,800 price tag in a Depression year probably contributed. The Blackhawk car is a Cubist fantasy, and startling, even for a Voisin.

1929 Voisin C-14 Wicker Roadster

Owner: Richard & Monia Brown of Corydon, Indiana

1931 Voisin C-20 Simoun Demi-Berline

Owner: Blackhawk Classic Auto Collection, Danville, California

1936 Voisin C-28 Ambassade Berline

Owner: Clive Cussler of Golden, Colorado

1935 Voisin C-25 Cimier Demi-Berline   *Owner: Roger P. Smith of Thousand Palms, California*

"The most unusual car in my collection," comments Clive Cussler about his 3318 cc C-28 Ambassade Berline. Clive's entire collection comprises unusual cars.

Roger Smith has owned his C-25 Cimier Demi-Berline since 1987: "A hardtop coupe de ville, its open driver's compartment and windshield unsupported across the top give a sense of openness. The car is a structural tour de force, light in weight, carefully machined and bristling with innovation. Its styling breathes integrity and panache and imparts a rare mixture of substance and flair that speaks eloquently of the genius of its creator. Add to that a low center of gravity, nearly fifty-fifty weight distribution, electric gearbox, electric sunroof, bucket seats, pull-to-open door handles, raked windscreen, two carburetors, eight to one compression, variable shock absorption front and rear—all in 1935! Voisin owners included Rudolph Valentino (who had four), Josephine Baker, H. G. Wells, Maurice Chevalier, Anatole France, Le Corbusier, the President of France and others with independence of spirit and ample pocketbooks. Gabriel Voisin met with customers to match their needs to his own fierce convictions about what the very best possible automobile could be. Each car was essentially custom-made.

Siding, for example, was seen in wicker, wood, stretched and lacquered canvas, varnished leather and clan tartan. Each Voisin automobile was an original, produced in a factory that was more an atelier in the mode of Peter Paul Rubens than a rationalized, bureaucratized industry—which perhaps explains the high rank of the Voisin in the field of automotive sculpture. It's a pity it all had to end."

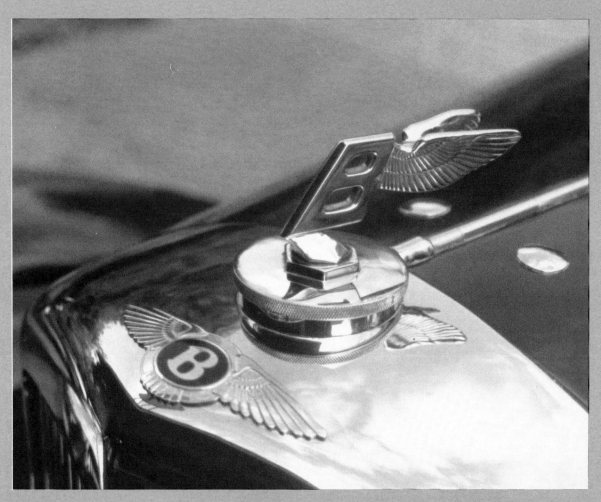

"Winged B" and logo from Lee Zuker's 1939 4¼ Litre James Young Sedanca Coupe

In 1912, bored with his job at the National Motor Cab Company, W. O. Bentley talked a brother into acquiring the British agency for the French D.F.P. Selling didn't interest W.O. so much as racing. Largely via use of aluminum pistons, he could extract more power from the D.F.P.'s two liters than its makers initially deemed either wise or possible. An astonishing performance in the 1914 Tourist Trophy convinced them otherwise. Less than three weeks later Sarajevo ignited World War I, and W.O. went to work for king and country in the aero industry. By the Armistice, much to D.F.P.'s discomfiture, Bentley decided to produce his own car. He started, he said, with "nothing but a few bits of paper and some ideas." Hyperbole, perhaps. But W.O.'s Bentley would virtually redefine the word. Everything about it was overstated, but in a heroic not an exaggerated sense. This was one epic automobile. "It has been the lot of very few firms to achieve fame with their first cars," *Autocar* noted in 1923. Fortune was another matter. The 3 Litre Bentley was introduced at the Olympia Motor Show in 1919. Not until 1921 did Bentley Motors Ltd. have the wherewithal to move into manufacture. There wasn't much wherewithal left for promotion. Naturally, W.O. decided to advertise by going racing. . . .

In 1924 a Bentley won Le Mans. In 1925 the 3 Litre owned by Don Weber might have. The fastest car on the course—100 mph down Mulsanne straight—Bentley No. 10 was in the lead until a pit stop to adjust the oil filler cap dropped it back—and then a quirk relegated it a d.n.f. Practice fuel consumption calculations hadn't considered the sustained hard driving of the race, and Bentley No. 10 ran out of gas a lap and a half short of its next permitted stop. Behind its wheel at that time was H. ''Bertie'' Kensington Moir. His co-driver was a bacteriologist, Dr. J. D. Benjafield. ''Bertie'' and ''Benjy'' would become members of that spirited fraternity known as ''The Bentley Boys,'' probably the largest group of men ever to drive to stardom under the banner of a single marque.

Don Weber has owned Bentley No. 10 for fourteen years and in that time has become something of a latterday Bentley boy himself: ''In 1979 I drove this 3 Litre from Texas to Monterey, California, racing at Laguna Seca and finishing second to Phil Hill in his 4.5 Blower Bentley. After Monterey, I left the car with Briggs Cunningham at his museum in Costa Mesa. The year following Tom Danaher and I left Briggs' house in Newport Beach on a scheduled non-stop run to René Dreyfus' Le Chanteclair restaurant in New York City. It may sound a little

strange, but we simply wanted to see how we would fare on modern freeways running against Cannon Ball Baker's 1925 cross-country record of 41 mph, which had been an astounding feat when you consider that only a portion of the roads were paved. Unfortunately, our light cotton clothing was of little protection against the last of that winter's arctic cold fronts that roared down out of the Rockies with temperatures in the thirties and a six-inch snowfall in El Paso! Needless to

say, the brutal cold made it impossible for us to stay in the open Bentley, and we abandoned the run in Amarillo at two in the morning. We managed to average over 70 mph from Newport Beach to Amarillo, with the judicious assistance of a good radar detector. A few years earlier, Bentley No. 10 had been driven on a 'thousand miles in a day' run from San Antonio to El Paso and return, 4:30 a.m. to 9:35 p.m., cruising at a steady 80 mph all the way. The car is truly a delight to

1925 Bentley 3 Litre Sports Tourer, Vanden Plas   *Owner: Donald E. Weber of San Antonio, Texas*

drive on the open road—a real thoroughbred. Frankly, I can think of very few American cars, essentially stock, that would do what the Bentley did that day. Its engine is an early predecessor of what is called a 'Quad Four'—four cylinders, overhead cam, four valves per cylinder, dual carburetors, dual magneto ignition (eight plugs); aluminum crankcase, sump, valve cover, firewall and pistons. The transmission is a four speed, and the large aluminum brake drums provide superb stopping power, as good as discs.''

Richard Morrison has owned his 3 Litre Tourer for over a decade: ''I think the vintage Bentley (pre-1931) is the ultimate British sporting car of its era. W. O. Bentley pioneered the aluminum piston before World War I and with that knowledge greatly improved WWI aircraft engines. The reliability required concurrently with performance carried over to his motor cars. I am intrigued by W. O. Bentley's engineering. Overhead cam, four valves per cylinder and twin magnetos are features only recently being utilized

on high-performance sports cars. I am also amazed that the Le Mans race-winning cars were so little modified from the production chassis. I like the similarity in style of my 3 Litre to the Le Mans team cars.''

The 3 Litre Bentley won Le Mans again in 1927. World records held by the car included 1000 kilometers at 97.11 mph, 1000 miles at 97.40, twenty-four hours at 95.03—all set in 1925 at Montlhéry. The year following a long-tailed streamlined version took 2000 kilometers at 100.23 mph and twelve hours at 100.96 at that same track.

1925 Bentley 3 Litre Tourer, Vanden Plas

Owner: Richard Morrison of Salina, Kansas

1926 Bentley 3 Litre Speed Model, Vanden Plas

Owner: Miles C. Collier of Naples, Florida

So massively built and doggedly reliable was the 3 Litre that W. O. Bentley guaranteed its mechanicals for five years. Ninety miles an hour straight from the showroom floor was the guarantee for the Speed Model. From 1924 into early 1929, a total of 507 Speed Models left the Bentley works at Cricklewood, most of them carrying Vanden Plas coachwork. A deft combination of nickel and brass brightwork distinguish the boattail speedster owned by Miles Collier.

1928 Bentley 6½ Litre Weymann Saloon, Gurney Nutting   Owner: Richard Morrison of Salina, Kansas

The 3 Litre was developed into the 4½ Litre four which won Le Mans in 1928. The six-cylinder 6½ Litre, introduced in 1926, was W. O. Bentley's first bid for the carriage trade market. Comments Richard Morrison: ''The overhead cam engine with four valves per cylinder is smooth and powerful, the hand-scraped aluminum castings are beautiful and the 'three-throw' camshaft drive system is an engineering marvel. This is a wonderful touring car that stays cool in 100+ degree weather, climbs Rocky Mountain passes with ease, and has powerful brakes. Being in the structural fabrics business, I am also attracted to its 'Weymann Patent' fabric body which is strong, lightweight and very quiet. Mine is one of the few 6½ Litres to retain its original closed body and is probably one of the most 'original' ones existing. Most closed cars have been converted to tourers or Le Mans replicas. W. O. Bentley introduced the 6½ Litre chassis to carry the large closed bodies previously fitted to the 3 Litre chassis which had been designed for light open bodies. That this luxury chassis could also win Le Mans two times is truly amazing.''

The Speed Six was the 6½ Litre that won Le Mans in 1929 and 1930. And practically every other race it entered. Once it finished second, but only after putting up the fastest lap. And only once did a Speed Six fail to finish a race because of a mechanical failure. Just 171 were built.

The light fabric-covered Le Mans-type body was among the factors attracting Bill Lassiter to his car.

Miles Collier, whose Speed Six is fitted with the three-carburetor competition set-up and is known to have raced, is fascinated by its engineering: ''the unique method of driving the camshafts by cranks instead of gears or chains, reminiscent of locomotive practice.'' Well put. Early in his career W. O. Bentley had apprenticed in a locomotive works.

1929 Bentley 6½ Litre Speed Six, Vanden Plas
Owner: W. G. Lassiter, Jr. of West Palm Beach, Florida

1930 Bentley 6½ Litre Speed Six, Vanden Plas
Owner: Miles C. Collier of Naples, Florida

1931 Bentley 4½ Litre "Blower Bentley" Tourer, Vanden Plas   *Owner: Miles C. Collier of Naples, Florida*

The Blower Bentley never won a single race and the man whose name it carried didn't like it. Still, the car has mythic status. Sheer audacity has undeniable appeal.

The audacity initially belonged to "Bentley Boy" Sir Henry Birkin. To continue winning Le Mans, W.O. had created the Speed Six. Birkin thought the same result could be achieved by supercharging the four, and he convinced fellow "Bentley Boy" Woolf Barnato that it was worth a try. W.O. was aghast but since Barnato's money was largely keeping Bentley Motors Ltd. afloat as the depression raged, he had no choice but to reluctantly give his okay and find room in his factory for the manufacture of the fifty cars necessary for homologation at Le Mans. Fortunately, the Hon. Dorothy Paget had been persuaded by Birkin to finance premises at Welwyn for race preparation of the cars, so W.O. did not have to witness the final desecration which, in his words, would "pervert" his engine and "corrupt its performance."

Its engine bench-tested at 240 hp (vis-á-vis the 130 of the unsuper-charged 4½ Litre), the Blower Bentley was blindingly fast. At Le Mans in 1930, it set a new lap record, then retired—typically. The Blower was the antithesis of the Speed Six. Finishing a race was the rarity. In the 1930 French Grand Prix the car did place second to a Bugatti that weighed half its 4395 pounds. This was a noteworthy achievement, but didn't impress W. O. Bentley much. By 1931 the Blower had gained in reliability but lost in efficiency. Reportedly, it swallowed a gallon of gasoline every fifty-nine seconds. But in short spurts, the car remained spectacular. In the spring of 1932,

Birkin broke the Outer Circuit record at Brooklands at 137.96 mph.

At $7,375, about two thousand dollars more than an unsupercharged 4½ Litre, the Blower Bentley chassis was put on sale to the public. The original purchaser of Miles Collier's car is not known, but it was brought to this country in 1932 and was for a time owned by the Packard Motor Car Company.

The magnificence of its failure perhaps destined the Blower Bentley to immortality. A healthy assist was given by Ian Fleming when, in his early novels, he chose it as James Bond's transportation. That 007 was a "secret" agent in such a conspicuous car remains one of the tantalizing contradictions that was the essence of the Blower Bentley itself.

Le Mans in 1930 had brought the expected Bentley victory and, shortly thereafter, the unexpected announcement that Bentley Motors Ltd. was closing its competition department. Again, W.O. was without choice, and agreed reluctantly. His company was in deep financial trouble. Among the reasons, his board of directors had concluded, was the Bentley image. As a carriage trade automobile, the 6½ Litre had not fared well in the marketplace—it was thought—because of the Speed Six association. The marque's sensational racing career had left in the public mind a lingering notion that only one of the "Bentley Boys" could drive the car properly. Ergo, the next Bentley would be a production automobile solely.

1931 Bentley 8 Litre Sports Touring, Corsica
Owner: Miles C. Collier of Naples, Florida

The 8 Litre was an unabashed luxury car. The chassis price was $9,000. Its specification: six cylinders, single overhead cam, four valves per cylinder, three S.U. carburetors, 7983 cc (several hundred more than Rolls-Royce's Phantom II), 250 hp. Wheel-bases were two, 144 and 156 inches, most of the 100 8 Litres that were produced carrying formal coachwork on the longer chassis.

The sporting Corsica body on the short chassis makes Miles Collier's car a rarity. Even more noteworthy, it was one of just two 8 Litres to enjoy speed-enhancing modifications by L. C. McKenzie, the high priest of Bentley tuners.

The Hooper/McEwan car was the fifth to the last of the 8 Litres, delivered to H. R. G. Colclough in August of 1932. Comments Al McEwan: ''The 8 Litre marks the epitome of W. O. Bentley's work, a chassis designed to carry formal coachwork at high speeds (up to 100 mph) on the Continent. While a very high percentage of these cars survive, many have had the original formal and/or closed coachwork replaced with later, more sporting bodies. This car retains its original H. J. Mulliner sports saloon body on the longer wheelbase chassis. Heavy to drive in slower city-type environments today, the car is particularly light and responsive at speed. The 8 Litre Bentley was one of the most powerful of all Classic automobiles.''

1931 Bentley 8 Litre Sports Saloon, H. J. Mulliner
Owners: R. B. Hooper & A. W. McEwan of Bellevue, Washington

1933 Bentley 4¼ Litre Roadster, Offord

Owner: Miles C. Collier of Naples, Florida

"Bentley Motors—Purchase Surprise" was the headline. "The expected absorption of Bentley Motors Ltd. by D. Napier and Sons Ltd., the aero-engine makers, will not take place," the story read. "An unexpected and last-minute bid yesterday afternoon secured the Bentley assets for a rival buyer, a syndicate known as the 'British Central Equitable Trust.' Nothing is known of the syndicate's intentions." W. O. Bentley didn't know either, nor was he aware who the syndicate represented. During the summer of 1931, when the receiver put his company up for sale, it was Bentley's fervent wish that Napier be the buyer, as it was Napier's. Indeed, preliminary plans had already been made for the first Napier-Bentley. It was several days before W.O.—and the world—found out that the Cricklewood company now belonged to Rolls-Royce. As "hostile takeovers" go, this one was a beaut. W.O. was engaged as an employee though he would find that working

for Derby was not his cup of tea.

Rolls-Royce had lusted for Bentley Motors for the strategic advantage of owning a rival, of course; now for a purchase price of £125,000 (a bit over $600,000), Derby could produce a sporting model carrying the name which for a decade had virtually defined a sports car. Introduced at the Olympia Motor Show in 1933, the first Bentley by Rolls-Royce was based on Derby's pushrod 20/25 with four-speed synchromesh transmission and servo brakes. The slogan was "The Silent Sports Car," a scarcely subtle refutation of the rumbleguts image when the marque belonged to W.O. Still, even in saloon form, the new Bentley 3½ Litre could reach 90 mph—which was marvelously sporting no matter how little noise was made.

Among the earliest purchasers was E. R. "Eddie" Hall, a Yorkshire industrialist who took the car now in Miles Collier's collection to learn the Mille Miglia circuit prior to his racing there in an M.G. K3 Magnette. After

4,000 practice miles, Hall concluded that this Bentley deserved to be raced as well. Surprisingly, Derby didn't blanche. Factory sponsorship was out of the question, of course, but Rolls-Royce agreed to modify the car for Hall to race in the Tourist Trophy. The factory updated the engine to the 4¼ Litre in '36, the same year Hall had Offord & Sons, Ltd. build a new windcheating roadster body. Hall and his Bentley competed three times in the TT, with the result always the same. Easily the fastest in the field, the car finished a heartbreakingly close second each time on handicap. But Hall's 78 mph average in '34 was 9 mph faster than ever recorded in the Tourist Trophy by any of W.O.'s Bentleys, and his 80.81 mph average in '36 was the fastest that would ever be recorded in the TT by any car. Nowhere did Eddie Hall and this Bentley ever lose its class. One wonders what the record would have been had Rolls-Royce let down its dignity and gone racing seriously during the thirties.

To the properly conservative gentlemen at Rolls-Royce, motor sport was anathema. Their sporting Bentley was its own *raison d'être*, and was refined through the years with the same lavish attention to detail that had long been the hallmark of Rolls-Royce. From 1933 to 1936, 1,177 Bentley 3½ Litre chassis were produced. All carried custom coachwork.

Miss E. E. S. Mathieson of Ayr, Scotland was the original owner of the James Young Drophead Coupe that has been Matt Sonfield's for a decade and a half: ''I corresponded with Miss Mathieson who wrote, 'I would drive all over the Highlands of Scotland . . . on roads where many people would not take a Bentley, but it was so reliable I would take it anywhere.' The 3½ Litre has Rolls-Royce quality and silence combined with sporting performance, speed, agility, etc. And this car is an unusual design for an English drophead body of the period with its 'sweep-panel' mouldings and rear quarter windows.''

1935 Bentley 3½ Litre Drophead Coupe, James Young
Owner: Matthew Sonfield of Syosset, New York
Photo above: M. Karger

"Very nice lines for a four-door saloon," comments Jerry Sokol of the Barker body on the 3½ Litre he has owned since 1980. The Marquis of Bath was the original purchaser of this car.

Roger Morrison has owned his Barker Drophead Coupe for two decades: "The car was purchased new by H. H. Prince Aly Khan and delivered to him at Chateau Lafitte in Paris. Quoting a *Life* magazine article,

'In 1935, when he was 24, Aly was named as co-respondent in a divorce suit by Thomas Loel E. B. Guinness . . . heir to a brewing fortune. Mrs. Guinness and Aly were married in Paris a week after the divorce.' Was

1934 Bentley 3½ Litre Saloon, Barker   *Owner: Jerry L. Sokol of Squaw Valley, California*

1935 Bentley 3½ Litre Drophead Coupe, Barker   *Owner: Roger Morrison of Salina, Kansas*

it the Prince or his Bentley that turned Mrs. Guinness' head? Idle speculation, but this car is a head-turner. The one-off body by Barker has a dickey (rumble) seat, most unusual for an English car of the period. Design features include the bonnet louvers which extend onto the cowl sloped at 20 degrees. The dashboard is covered in leather. Among the special requests were instruments with white faces and black numerals, and the steering column to be moved two-and-a-half inches further back from the dash. Did the prince have short arms or just prefer the steering close to the vest? Whichever, this was a great car for him to motor in. The lightweight aluminum body, the overhead valve engine with twin carburetors and the adjustable shock absorbers make it one of the better driving and performing automobiles produced by Rolls-Royce in the thirties. When I bought this car, I was an absolute rookie who was just plain lucky to find it in a small Nebraska town. This was my first Classic—a big change from a 1967 427 Corvette! Both this Bentley's body style and its road-ability appealed to me. Only after acquisition did I discover its interesting history.''

1937 Bentley 4¼ Litre Sports Saloon, Vanden Plas   *Owner: Jean Gorjat of Harrisburg, Pennsylvania*

In 1936 the Rolls-Bentley grew from 3669 to 4257 cc; the chassis remained at 126 inches. The additional displacement was necessary because of the rising avoirdupois of the Bentley's bespoke coachwork.

Like Roger Morrison, Jean Gorjat entered Classic ranks with his 4¼ Litre Vanden Plas Sports Saloon: "This was my first Classic car. In six years of driving, it has failed me only once. On my birthday, on the way to the restaurant for dinner, at a busy intersection downtown, all four brakes locked due to a faulty servo. So I went the rest of the way by taxi and, after champagne and a gourmet dinner, returned to disassemble the servo—at 2:00 a.m. This is a wonderful automobile—the silent sports car with handsome sedan body and sun roof."

The Freestone & Webb Top Hat Coupe was a Christmas present to Bege Remlinger from her husband Jerry: "The reason for the body designation is obvious when you look at the car. But its first owner never wore a top hat, to the best of my knowledge. This Bentley was commissioned by a lady who wanted a two-passenger car for herself that could carry another person, if necessary and if small enough. Personally, I wouldn't care to ride in that third seat any further than around the corner to the store."

1937 Bentley 4¼ Litre Top Hat Coupe, Freestone & Webb
Owner: Bege Remlinger of Massillon, Ohio

1938 Bentley 4¼ Litre Sports Saloon, Mann Egerton   *Owners: Mr. & Mrs. Gordon J. Fairbanks of Indianapolis, Indiana*

"The razor-edge styling plus the general overall sporting look make this Mann Egerton very pleasing to the eye," comment the Fairbanks about the 4¼ Litre they have owned for fourteen years. "The car has P-100 headlights which have the interesting operation of dipping one light and extinguishing the other when the dimmer switch is activated. The dipping is accomplished by a solenoid built into the lamp which tilts the reflector. This Bentley is a great tour car able to maintain highway speeds with ease."

Bentley 4¼ Litre production totaled about 1,250 cars. Because of the high-speed motoring afforded by new super highways on the Continent, refinements were made to the final 200 Bentley 4¼ Litres produced from late 1938. Lee Zuker explains: "Ours is one of the 200 'M' series, with several features not found in earlier cars. The most significant is the change of the gearbox, so that third gear is direct drive and fourth is an 85% overdrive, giving a final gear ratio of 3.65 and an engine speed of about 2000 rpm at 60 mph. Top speed is over 100 mph. Also introduced in this series was Marles recirculating ball steering, and the tire size was reduced from seventeen to sixteen inches to improve road handling. The car includes all of the features standard in Bentleys of the late prewar era: centralized chassis lubrication activated by a lever under the dash; four-wheel servo-operated brakes (in fact, anti-skid brakes since the servo action is proportional to the rear wheel speed); variable rate suspension adjustable with a lever on the steering wheel; and dual S.U. carburetors. Although Rolls-Royce did not publish horsepower developed, stating only that it was 'adequate,' a magazine of the period reported 125 hp at 3500 rpm.

1939 Bentley 4¼ Litre Sedanca Coupe, James Young
Owners: Lee & Marlene Zuker of Bellevue, Washington

"Our particular 4¼ Litre was designed by A. F. McNeil who was hired in 1938 as chief designer by James Young, having previously held the same position at Gurney Nutting. The coachwork is unique, a one-off, although similar to the Owen-Gurney Nutting design used previously for several Rolls-Royce and Bentley automobiles. It is all aluminum and features a very large trunk containing a complete set of tools on the underside of the lid. The ease with which the front top opens and closes further enhances this car's utility, while its ability to cruise comfortably and quietly at thruway speeds makes it a car of pure pleasure and outstanding for CARavanning.

"The original owner was Mrs. E. V. Young who lived on Basil Street, near Harrods, in London. The purchase price was £1,780; Mrs. Young traded in her '28 Rolls-Royce 20 H.P., for which she received a credit of £230. During the war the car was purchased by a company in the Midlands for use by its managing director, and after the war it was owned briefly by Humphrey Cook, the financial backer of E.R.A. race cars. This Bentley arrived in the United States in 1960. We have owned it since 1984. The first trip the car made thereafter was at night, in the pouring rain, to Centralia, Washington, about seventy-five miles away. The purpose of this run was to deliver the Bentley Drivers Club signature book, on its way around the world, to the driver on the next leg of the trip. Mileage to date on this car is 125,000."

1939 Bentley 4¼ Litre All-Weather Convertible Sedan, Vanden Plas
Owner: Joseph L. Carman III of Tacoma, Washington

Joe Carman has owned his Bentley 4¼ Litre since 1966: "The original owner was Ben Jacobson of London. Much of the car's life after World War II was spent on the Continent, Bermuda and England. It arrived in the United States in the mid-fifties. Excluding five interim dealers, I am the eleventh owner. This Bentley has a particularly attractive and rare body by Vanden Plas which, combined with outstanding performance characteristics, makes it one of the most delightful prewar touring automobiles. The odometer now reads 173,000 and tells me that this Bentley has provided us with 20,000 miles of delightful motoring experiences over the past twenty-four years."

Coincidentally, Robert G. Lawrence has owned his 4¼ Litre Bentley twenty-four years as well: "The car was purchased on June 9th, 1939 by Major Jack Kay of London. A long series of owners followed, including Viscount Althorp (Lord Spencer, father of the current Princess of Wales) in the mid-fifties. Between 1936 and 1939, H. J. Mulliner & Company produced approximately twenty-five aluminum drophead bodies with disappearing hoods on Derby Bentleys. My car was among the last, one of two built in mid-1939 with an enlarged boot and other small changes. Since I have been unable to trace the sister car, it may be the only one extant. But this Bentley is special to me simply because it is a pleasure to look at and very pleasurable to drive, cruising nicely at 65-70 mph. Present mileage is 85,000, and we look forward in a few years to seeing five zeros."

1939 Bentley 4¼ Litre Drophead Coupe, H. J. Mulliner
Owner: Robert G. Lawrence of Victoria, British Columbia

1946 Bentley Mark VI Drophead Coupe, Freestone & Webb
Owner: Akin T. Davis of Washington, D.C.   Photo: K. Karger

Shortly after Hitler's army moved into Poland, Bentley production ceased in Derby. On June 11th, 1946 Lillie Hall accepted delivery of the Freestone & Webb Drophead Coupe which, following a succession of further owners, was acquired by Akin Davis precisely thirty years later: "I have driven the car over 70,000 miles since 1976. The body style is a one-off, and probably the second oldest postwar convertible Bentley in existence. The road performance is marvelous."

The Mark VI was, with detail modification, the successor to the Mark V introduced shortly before the war, which added coil-spring and wishbone independent front suspension to the M series' 4¼ Litre specification. Most impartial observers have since agreed that Rolls-Royce did not do at all badly by W.O.'s Bentley.

B U G A T T I

Radiator cap and logo from William Cook's 1939 Type 57C Gangloff Cabriolet

The stories told about Ettore Bugatti are wonderful. When a customer complained that his Type 55 was hard starting on cold mornings, *Le Patron* replied that anyone who could afford the car could surely also afford a heated garage. To another who complained about the brakes on his Bugatti, the man who long preferred cables over hydraulics, pooh-poohed, ''I make my cars to go, not to stop.'' Another customer brought his Type 46 back to the factory three times for adjustment. ''Do not,'' Bugatti deadpanned on the third occasion, ''let it happen again.'' Obviously there was a giant ego at work here, and the foregoing might suggest Ettore Bugatti was insufferable. But such was not the case. Imperious to a fault, he cloaked his ego with a sly, sardonic wit and an almost impish delight in oneupmanship. He wore his arrogance like a banner. ''Loud in voice, high in colour, overflowing with life, a brown bowler sitting on the back of his head,'' journalist W. F. Bradley wrote of him, ''he looked . . . like a horseman strayed among motor cars.'' The description is apt. Ettore Bugatti was a devoted equestrian. He never built an automobile that was not a thoroughbred. The 7,500 cars he produced in approximately 50 different variations ranged from an exquisitely wrought jewel of a Grand Prix car that was among the world's most successful to the most uncompromisingly opulent production automobile the world had ever seen. That there were better cars than the Bugatti can be debated pragmatically; that there was ever one more fascinating reduces discussion to the equivalent of arguing the number of angels that can sit on the head of a pin. And that is, singularly, because of the man who built it. ''There is no figure more amazing or captivating,'' said Charles Faroux, ''Bugatti is Bugatti which says everything. . . .''

Ettore Bugatti was an Italian who produced his automobiles in Alsace-Lorraine, the picturesque land separating France and Germany which for centuries had been a political pawn between the two nations. When Bugatti arrived there in 1909 to set up shop in a former dyeworks in Molsheim, the area belonged to Germany. Following the First World War, and the Versailles Treaty, Alsace was French once again. Already Bugatti's name, if not made, was well known. In 1911 his diminutive 1.4-liter Type 13 had placed second in the French Grand Prix to a Fiat with an engine five times as big. Now he went racing with a 16-valve derivation of the 8-valve Type 13, the design for which had been completed prior to the war, and won the Voiturette Grand Prix at Le Mans in 1920. In 1921 in the Italian Grand Prix at Brescia, the Bugatti victory was overwhelming, a neat 1-2-3-4 finish after which the Type 13 was rechristened the Brescia. The Brescia continued its winning ways until the arrival of the Type 35 which would overwhelm the competition to the end of the decade.

As initially designed, the Type 35 represented a new chassis with a developed version of the production Type 30's two-liter eight-cylinder engine. *Le Patron* abhorred supercharging at first, but as blown Italian and German cars threatened his marque's prominence, Bugatti relented. The supercharged 1493 cc Type 39A was first, and then in 1927 the 35 was supercharged into the 2262 cc Type 35B, like the car in the collection of William Lyon.

The Riddells' Grand Prix Bugatti was delivered new in 1925 to the Juneks in Czechoslovakia. Čenek Junek was a banker in Prague; his wife Elisabeth was the most celebrated and successful woman race driver of the era. Keenly competitive, she returned the car to the factory in 1926 for installation of the supercharged Type 35C version of the two-liter engine. The Riddells have owned the Junek car for eighteen years. "It is an unbelievable machine," says Dick. "The handling is fantastic. The top speed, clocked in 1985, was 136 mph. Although street legal and licensed, the car is too loud for road use. The Type 35 needs a wide-open circuit."

Although Ettore Bugatti reserved the most up-to-date race cars for his factory team, the others were available for outside purchase. In 1930, for example, a race-ready Type 35B was priced at 165,000 francs (about $6,500) f.o.b. the Molsheim factory. Among the purchasers was René Dreyfus, a young amateur driver, whose victory in the Monaco Grand Prix that year over the entire Bugatti works team did not please *Le Patron* much. Molsheim was Bugatti's fiefdom, his rule was absolute, his word was law. He did not like being upstaged. During these years of incredible competition success, money flowed into Molsheim but it left just as quickly. Bugatti's pursuit of perfection at all costs was one reason. His expensive lifestyle was another. "He was always broke," remembers René Dreyfus, whom *Le Patron* forgave by hiring him in 1933. "A few times during the two years I drove for the factory, I accepted a Bugatti chassis instead of cash for my monthly salary and prize money. I then drove the chassis to the Paris showroom, where it was sold for me. It was a roundabout way of being paid, but paid we always were, one way or another."

1927 Bugatti Type 35B Grand Prix Car   *Owner: William Lyon of Trabuco Canyon, California*

1925 Bugatti Type 35 Grand Prix Car
Owners: Bobbie & Dick Riddell of San Clemente, California   Photos: D. M. Woodhouse

With his rise in the world of motor sport, Ettore Bugatti began listing the victories his cars had enjoyed in the previous season in the new edition of his catalogue. Often as many pages were devoted to the Bugatti laurels as were expended in descriptions of the Bugatti production cars for sale. From 1926 to 1930 the Type 40 was a marketplace Bugatti. A 1.5-liter four, it had replaced the touring Brescia.

Gerald Willburn has owned his Type 40 for seven years: ''It was one of the first built and is the oldest 'complete' Type 40 in the United States. Shipped as a chassis only to Paris in 1926, it was bodied by one of the many obscure coachbuilders in the city at the time. There is no body plate to identify which. The rumble seat makes for great open air touring for four people. The car is driven about 1,500 miles a year.''

''This is a fun car on which to learn vintage racing,'' comments Dick Riddell of the Type 40 he and Bobbie have owned for fourteen years. ''It's reliable, dependable and easy to work on. There's not much power, but there is the classic Bugatti handling. Probably the cheapest Bugatti made (the price in London in 1929 was £365), it's a great driver.''

*1929 Bugatti
Type 40
Torpedo Roadster*

*Owners:
Bobbie & Dick Riddell
of San Clemente,
California*

1926 Bugatti Type 40 Roadster

Owner: Gerald Willburn of Cypress, California

1927 Bugatti Type 43A Roadster   *Owner: Gilmore Car Museum, Hickory Corners, Michigan*

The Type 43 was a 100 mph car for the sporting driver. Its chassis derived from the production Type 38; its 2.3-liter supercharged engine was from the Grand Prix Type 35B. Gentleman racers adored the car, as did professionals for hill climb and Brooklands activity. Ettore Bugatti himself demonstrated the 43's flexibility; during a trial run in Alsace, he stopped the engine, engaged top gear, pressed the starter button and accelerated away without gear change to a speed of 90 mph. The editor of *Motor Sport* described driving the car as ''sheer joy''—light steering with adequate caster, almost unconscious cornering and terrific acceleration in the gears. The standard Type 43 had a boattail body and disc wheels. The Gilmore car—with its dickey (or rumble seat), golf bag door and wire wheels—is unusual. Most likely its first owner spoke English rather than French.

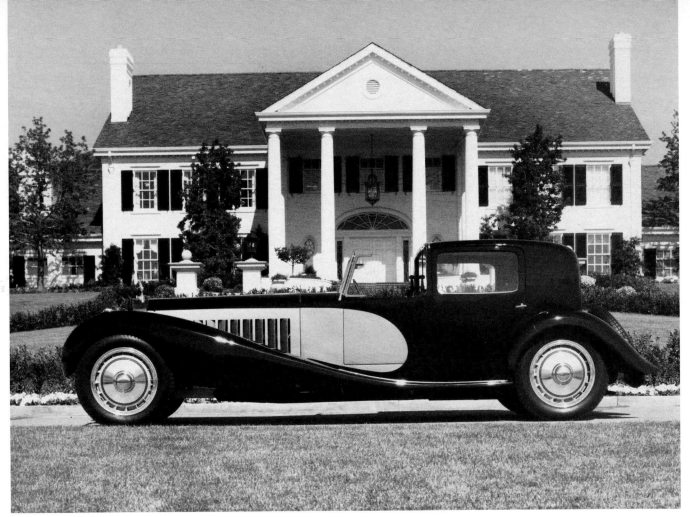

1931 Bugatti Royale Type 41 Coupe de Ville, Henri Binder   *Owner: William Lyon of Trabuco Canyon, California*

Like many of the outlandishly grand Classics of the early thirties, the Bugatti Royale had been developed during the halcyon years of the twenties. A limited production of perhaps twenty-five was the aim. Just a half-dozen would be realized. The onset of the Great Depression contributed to this, of course, but so did Ettore Bugatti. As its name suggests, the Type 41 was envisioned as an automobile for royalty. But the royals had to measure up to *Le Patron*'s standards of what a monarch should be. It is said that he refused to sell a Royale to King Zog of Albania. "Never!" he told an assistant after the Balkan ruler visited Molsheim: "The man's table manners are beyond belief!"

The idea for producing the Royale had been born at the dinner table too, so the story goes. Over wine a British dowager had turned to the man of Molsheim and, after allowing that he built the finest sports and competition cars in the world, added that for elegant touring one had the world's finest in a Rolls-Royce or Daimler. Perhaps Bugatti regarded the remark as a personal challenge and was spurred into action. He had

been thinking about a super car since before the First World War. As he wrote a friend in 1913, this ultimate Bugatti would have eight cylinders, be "made with irreproachable care . . . be extremely expensive . . . [and] beyond any criticism."

By any measure, the Royale was fantastic. Its straight-eight engine displaced 12,760 cc (784 cubic inches) and developed from 275-300 hp. That many horses were needed to propel a 170-inch chassis which with coachwork could weigh up to four tons. They did their job well. A Royale could surpass 100 mph. The chassis price was $30,000, a king's ransom.

Ironically, the unfortunate Zog excepted, Carol of Romania is the only king believed to have ordered a Royale. This is the car now in the collection of William Lyon. It had begun life as a roadster for another owner: Armand Esders of Paris who had requested that Henri Binder eliminate headlights since he never drove after dark. Apparently Esders' daylight motoring in the Royale was of short duration because the car was returned to Binder for revamping into a coupe de ville for King Carol. That delivery was made is uncertain.

The Royale Cabriolet by Weinberger of Munich that is now in the Henry Ford Museum was commissioned by a German physician, Joseph Fuchs. Dr. Fuchs brought the car to the United States in 1937, where it remained following the outbreak of the war and was rescued from a New York scrapyard in 1943 by Charles A. Chayne of General Motors. "While in some ways the Bugatti does not fit our collecting agenda," comments curator Randy Mason, "it has become a museum 'icon' and is emblematic of the depth of our auto collection. We use it to represent 'style' in automobiles carried to the extreme. In size, expense and glamour, the Royale defines the superlative. It is today perhaps the most valuable car, monetarily, on our planet."

For this, among other reasons, the belief that there was a seventh Type 41 persists. All six known cars remain extant. And the historical census is they represent the total. Still, the legend will not die. Who wouldn't, after all, like to discover another Bugatti Royale under decades of dust somewhere, sometime.

632

1931 Bugatti Royale Type 41 Cabriolet, Ludwig Weinberger
Owner: Henry Ford Museum & Greenfield Village, Dearborn, Michigan

1931 Bugatti Type 50T Coupe Profilé   *Owner: John Mozart of Palo Alto, California*

Allowing that the Type 41 was in a class all by itself, the 5.3-liter Type 46 was Bugatti's large luxury model of the early thirties. About 400 were built. Production of the 46's companion on the shorter chassis, the Type 50, totaled about 60 cars. Displacement of the latter's straight-eight engine was 4972 cc, and the crankshaft was carried in nine plain bearings as earlier touring Bugattis. There was a big difference, however, in cylinder head layout. *Le Patron* abandoned vertical valves for 90° inclined valves operated by twin overhead camshafts. It is known that Bugatti had acquired two Miller race cars following Monza in '29 and apparently he studied them carefully. Thermodynamics was not a subject Ettore Bugatti knew well. Why not simply adopt what had proven successful for others? After all, others had profited from what had proven successful on Bugattis.

"Tremendous horsepower, 200 or more, for the period," comments John Mozart of his Type 50T (for

tourisme). "This supercharged car handles and brakes nicely. It epitomizes the perfect packaging of performance and style. Jean Bugatti designed the profile body. Just one of only two such cars that exist, the Coupe Profilé is significant because of its rarity and radical design. Note the extreme slant to the windshield." Indeed, note every line of this exquisite automobile. Ettore Bugatti was an aesthete; his unerring sense of style had been inherited by his son Jean, who was responsible for the look of many Bugattis of this period.

The Type 55 Super Sport Roadster owned by Miles Collier is yet another Jean Bugatti coachwork design. Some people, not necessarily all confirmed Bugattistes, regard the Type 55 as the most beautiful sports car ever built. And its engine, like all powerplants produced by Ettore Bugatti, was no less gorgeous.

The Type 55 was, in essence, the double-overhead-cam supercharged 2.3-liter straight eight of the Grand Prix Bugatti Type 51 fitted into the

foot-longer 108-inch frame of the GP Type 54. Its performance was astounding. Road tests from the period quote zero to sixty times of less than thirteen seconds. At 98.9 mph at the quarter mile, one tester was still accelerating; another didn't lift his foot from the accelerator until he reached 115.

Just thirty-eight Type 55 Bugattis were produced. Fourteen survive. The price for the car was approximately $7,500. For all it says about the prowess of Bugatti sports cars of the period, the Collier Type 55 also comments effectively upon another aspect of the character of its maker. Dictatorial though he was, Ettore Bugatti was a benevolent monarch. From lathe worker to race driver, his employees loved him. He could be a very generous man. There is evidence that the engine in the Collier Type 55 originally belonged to a Type 51 Grand Prix car which *Le Patron* had given as a present to the Bugatti Owners Club in England during the thirties.

1933 Bugatti Type 55 Super Sport Roadster   *Owner: Miles C. Collier of Naples, Florida*

The most celebrated non-competition car that Bugatti ever produced—again excepting the Royale—was the Type 57. Introduced in 1934, it remained in production until World War II. A few were assembled even afterward. By Bugatti standards, the car saw big-scale manufacture—about 700 units. Production began with the normally-aspirated Type 57 fitted with a variety of factory and coachbuilt body styles. Nearby Gangloff was often used. The Type 57S, introduced in 1935, was on a lower and shorter (117.3 versus 130-inch) sport chassis. The 57C, introduced in 1937, added a compressor to the 57's twin-cam 3.3-liter straight-eight engine, and the 57SC, which debuted that same year, was the supercharged model on the short chassis. By late 1938, Ettore Bugatti had foregone his allegiance to cable-actuated brakes and switched to hydraulics. By then, his son Jean, whose influence on Bugatti styling came to full flower with this model, had created some very memorable motorcars.

The Ventoux in the Riddell collection is a Jean Bugatti concept car. Comments Dick: "This was probably the last of a style begun in 1932, the final custom-built refinement, so to speak. It's much more elegant than the earlier cars, with dual sunroof, skirts and a luxurious interior."

Of the Riddell Graber Cabriolet, Dick says: "This body was the first on a Type 57 for Graber. The chassis was delivered to the Swiss coach-works in October of 1934, then returned to the factory for the soft-mounted engine (the first 57 so equipped). Graber installed its own hydraulic brakes, which are awful, incidentally. The car was finished in May 1935, in time for the Geneva Automobile Show. A Dr. Kalbern of Zurich bought it. This Bugatti is unusual in being a Swiss car with a high rear-end gear ratio. The styling is rare too. Later Grabers were more streamlined with greater rear over-hang."

Noel Thompson's Atalante Coupe shows Jean Bugatti thinking very avantgarde: "This is one of the very few cars on the lowered 'S' frame. It is an exceptionally fine original automobile."

"Tremendous performance and a great styling exercise," comments John Mozart about his Type 57SC. "The body is a one-off by Corsica of England. The car handles extremely well and is very fast, with a top speed easily surpassing 120 miles an hour."

1937 Bugatti Type 57 Ventoux Coupe, Gangloff
Owners: Bobbie & Dick Riddell of San Clemente, California

1937 Bugatti Type 57 Atalante Coupe, Gangloff
Owner: Noel Thompson of New Vernon, New Jersey

1935 Bugatti Type 57 Cabriolet, Graber   *Owners: Bobbie & Dick Riddell of San Clemente, California*

1938 Bugatti Type 57SC Roadster, Corsica   *Owner: John Mozart of Palo Alto, California*

1938 Bugatti Type 57C Cabriolet, Gangloff
Owner: Gary Tiscornia of Milford, Michigan

Gary Tiscornia's Type 57C Gangloff Cabriolet was the 1978 realization of a Bugatti dream that began for him at age nineteen and was first effected in his early sixties acquisition of a Type 37 Grand Prix car.

The 57C with Gangloff coupe coachwork in the Cussler garage is, Clive says, "an unusual body style as it is the only known Bugatti with the radiator extending to the front fenders."

Paul Pazery's 57C Gangloff Cabriolet was delivered to a M. Teilhac in Paris in 1939, hidden during the war in a barn in unoccupied France until 1946, and owned by two Parisians thereafter, until Paul's purchase of the car in 1959: "In the thirties, while a student in France, I used to race on a Bugatti Type 35B. This car is a most exciting one to drive today. Its roadability is unsurpassed. The car has been completely restored. It took ten years!"

1939 Bugatti Type 57C Coupe, Gangloff   Owner: Clive Cussler of Golden, Colorado

1939 Bugatti Type 57C Cabriolet, Gangloff   Owner: Paul H. Pazery of Sante Fe, New Mexico

The '39 Type 57 Gangloff Cabriolet has been in the Cook family since 1960 when Hubert bought it for $2,650. His son Bill has owned the car since 1982: ''This Bug's most memorable Grand Classic was its first, in Indianapolis in 1965, the memorable part being the distance and the weather. The round trip was 1,900 miles, the temperature was 100+ and in those days the CCCA didn't allow trailering. That same year, my father drove the Bug in a hill climb in Arkansas for a second-place finish, the winner being a Bentley driven by a girl. Wish I had been the driver; I wouldn't have let a girl beat me. In 1980 I raced this Bugatti at Laguna Seca in California and, out of twenty entries, finished 7th, not bad for a passenger car among ten all-out racing machines. The Bugatti is a remarkable auto-mobile. Gaskets were deemed unnecessary because of the phenomenally close tolerances between surfaces. The steering is light and precise and doesn't become unsteady when the roads are bad. And the car's looks? Photographs answer that question. The Bugatti can be summed up easily: the fusion of function with form. Auto meets art.''

And so it did throughout the Classic Era. Tragically, Jean Bugatti was killed in an automobile accident while test driving a factory car in August of 1939. In August of 1947 Ettore Bugatti died in Paris after an illness of three months. The marque, in essence, died with him. Without *Le Patron*, there couldn't really be a Bugatti.

1939 Bugatti Type 57C Cabriolet, Gangloff
Owner: William R. Cook of Dallas, Texas

640

Flying stork from Noel Thompson's 1937 J-12 Cabriolet de Ville, photo by K. Karger

That he was one of the greatest engineers in the history of the automobile has been acknowledged so often and by so many that it is a virtual commonplace. For more than three decades every example of one of the world's most admirable motorcars bore his signature, his imprint, his genius. The name Hispano-Suiza itself—though students of Spanish might cavil at the mixing of genders in its spelling—recognized both the birthplace of the car in Spain and the nationality of its creator. Marc Birkigt was Swiss. Ironically, the Hispano-Suiza is most often thought of today as a French car, this because the grandest versions arrived from the Barcelona company's branch plant in Paris. The H6 series, introduced at the Paris Automobile Salon in October of 1919, was widely heralded at the time as the most advanced automobile in the world. Its 6597 cc all-aluminum overhead camshaft six-cylinder engine derived from the Birkigt-designed aero unit which had powered over half the planes flown during World War I, a fact the company poignantly noted in the car's radiator ornament—the flying stork mascot of French ace Georges Guynemer's fighter squadron. The chassis was innovatively exemplary, as Rolls-Royce would attest, and the styling was sensational, as Harley Earl cheerfully admitted when the time came for him to design the LaSalle. The Hispano-Suiza was in a class by itself. . . .

1925 Hispano-Suiza H6b Dual Cowl Phaeton, LeBaron
Owner: William J. Ingler, Jr. of Columbus, Ohio

1926 Hispano-Suiza H6b Cabriolet, Million-Guiet
Owner: Truman A. Stockton, Jr. of Lakewood, Colorado

Several thousand dollars more highly priced than a Rolls-Royce, the Hispano-Suiza was Europe's most expensive car. The company sold only the chassis. Coachwork was the purchaser's prerogative.

Million-Guiet of Paris was the coachbuilder of choice for the original owner of the H6b Cabriolet which has been Truman Stockton's since 1957. D'Ieteren Fréres of Brussels bodied the H6b Cabriolet which Clive Cussler has owned for a decade.

The LeBaron Dual Cowl Phaeton has been in the Ingler family for over forty years. Comments Bill: "The original owner was Peggy Guggenheim, the noted art collector, who gave the car to her husband Laurence Vail as a divorce settlement in 1928. During the thirties it was acquired by American race car driver Ray Gilhooley. During the forties the car was in the D. Cameron Peck collection, sold by Peck to Ed Greiner in 1947 who in turn sold it to my father—W. J. Ingler, Sr.—in 1949. With its aluminum body, this Hispano-Suiza weighs less than 4,000 pounds. It is quick, handles beautifully and will cruise comfortably at 55-60 mph at 1800 rpm. One of the most interesting features of the car is the servo-brake system which utilizes the torque of the driveshaft to apply tension to the brake cables with a very light pressure on the brake pedal."

1926 Hispano-Suiza H6b Cabriolet, d'Ieteren Frères   Owner: Clive Cussler of Golden, Colorado

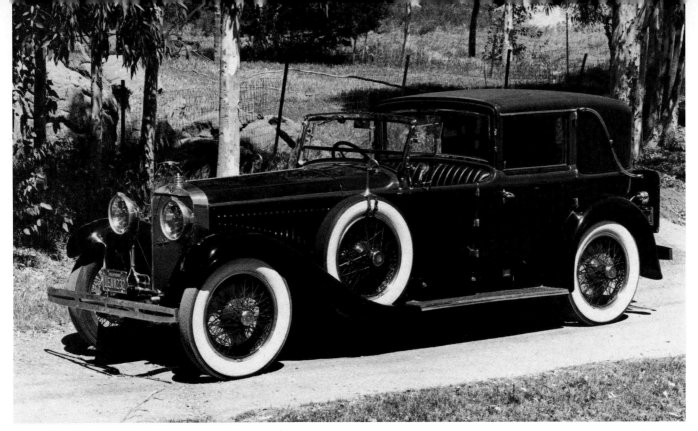

1927 Hispano-Suiza H6b Coupe-Chauffeur, d'Ieteren Frères   *Owners: Eric & Molly Rosenau of Ramona, California*

Hibbard & Darrin designed the Coupe-Chauffeur built by d'Ieteren Frères which Eric & Molly Rosenau have owned since 1982: ''The car was delivered in June of 1927 by the Clarke D. Pease dealership in New York City to a Miss Skinner, possibly Cornelia Otis. While many town cars of this era had stodgy styling, this one is different. It is about the best looking town car we have ever seen. The design of the Hispano-Suiza overall is so well integrated that its accomplishment by one person is strongly implied. The workmanship is incredible. Aircraft heritage shows throughout the car. For example, all studs and bolts in the chassis and engine bear a Brinell hardness test mark. They tested every one!''

1928 Hispano-Suiza H6c Speedster, Kellner   Owner: Miles C. Collier of Naples, Florida

In 1927, on a visit to Paris, Seymour Knox stopped by two showrooms on the Champs-Elysées: Hispano-Suiza's and Hibbard & Darrin's. The year following, in East Aurora (New York), he took delivery of the H6b Cabriolet de Ville that has been in Mort Bullock's collection for the last quarter century: "When I purchased the car, it was on consignment at Inskip's in New York City. The salesman was Charles Willmore, who sold the first two Rolls-Royce cars delivered to the U.S. around 1906. I later contacted original owner

Seymour Knox. The Hispano-Suiza has always had a fascination for me for reasons of its rarity, workmanship, engineering genius and stylish coachwork. It is not the easiest car to drive with square-cut transmission gears and stiff steering, but it performs well on the highway with ample power and exceptionally good brakes. Hispano pioneered a number of unique engineering features such as the servo brake system and spring-loaded serrated interlocking wheel hubs. Both these items were adopted by Rolls-Royce under a

licensing agreement."

Among the most gloriously schizophrenic cars of the period, the Hispano was favored by women for its style and by gentlemen racers for its performance. The latter was enhanced in the H6c model. With an enlarged engine (7982 cc, 194 hp at 3000 rpm) and a short chassis (133 inches versus the usual 145-inch wheelbase), the car was capable of 110 mph. Miles Collier's boattail speedster by Kellner of Paris was one of only a handful of short chassis H6c's produced.

1928 Hispano-Suiza H6b Cabriolet de Ville, Hibbard & Darrin   Owner: Morton Bullock of Baltimore, Maryland   Photo: K. Karger

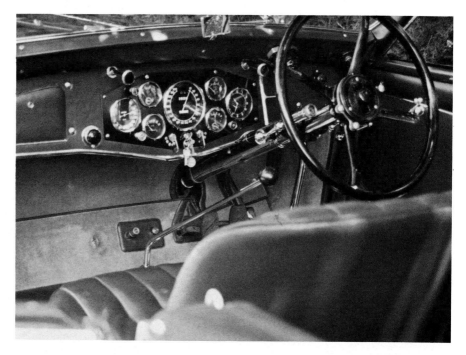

1933 Hispano-Suiza J-12 Cabriolet, Van Vooren
Owners: Jacques & Betty Harguindeguy of Walnut Creek, California

Soon after the new J-12 was introduced in 1931, Charles Faroux drove one from Paris to the Riviera, then headed straight back to the company's Champs-Elysées showroom where he parked over a clean white sheet. Not a single drop of oil spilled from the car's chassis, a fine tribute to the precision engineering of Marc Birkigt.

Birkigt's V-12 was the biggest, most complex and most expensive Hispano-Suiza in history. A 60° vee, the engine was introduced with 9424 cc and horsepower approaching 200 at 3000 rpm. The car's top speed was a genuine 100+ mph, 80 was "almost ambling," in one road tester's phrase, and reachable in second gear. But most awesome was the acceleration: 0 to 60 in just twelve seconds—over a half-century ago. Among all V-12 engines in the world, only Maybach's Zeppelin approached the Hispano's power. And very soon Birkigt settled any argument by offering an alternate crankshaft, increasing the engine to 11,310 cc and 250 hp.

Only two or three of the total 100 J-12's (or Type 68) were originally provided the larger engine, among them the Van Vooren Cabriolet which Jacques & Betty Harguindeguy have owned for nine years: "A

French airplane manufacturer ordered the car originally. In 1937 the artist Pablo Picasso became its second owner. He kept the car until 1952 when he traded it plus some money for a brand-new Buick convertible. In

addition to the extraordinary engine, this Hispano-Suiza is distinguished by the Van Vooren coachwork with its unique body moulding panels and rear fenders which point inward at the ends."

646

1934 Hispano-Suiza J-12 Coupe de Ville, Fernandez & Darrin   *Owner: Blackhawk Classic Auto Collection, Danville, California*

The two Hispano-Suizas shown here were his and hers cars. Following exhibition at the Olympia Motor Show in London during the fall of 1934, they were delivered to the Rothschild estate. His—Anthony de Rothschild's—was the 9.4-liter J-12 Coupe de Ville. Hers—Yvonne d'Anvers de Rothschild's—was the 5.2-liter K-6 (six-cylinder) Coupe Chauffeur. The chassis price was $13,200 and $6,600 respectively; the total price went discreetly unmentioned in the press. This matched pair of Hispano-Suizas for Britain's preeminent banking family provides a sublime study in contrasts. The husband's car, now in the Blackhawk collection, is masculine, conservative yet intimidating. The wife's car, now in Noel Thompson's collection, is feminine, stylishly intimate and with that chic Parisian flair which a lady who had been born in France would wish. In later years Dutch Darrin commented about how much he enjoyed designing for the Rothschilds. There was never any haggling over price. Indeed, the question of money never came up.

1934 Hispano-Suiza K-6 Coupe Chauffeur, Fernandez & Darrin
Owner: Noel Thompson of New Vernon, New Jersey   Photo: K. Karger

Wheelbase lengths for the J-12 chassis were four, designated as follows: 134½ inches (short), 146 inches (light), 150 inches (normal), 157¾ inches (long).

The light chassis was used for the Fernandez & Darrin Sedanca in Bob Bahre's collection: "The J-12 is powerful and smooth, a very easy car to drive. This example, with its three-position top, vee windshield, long hood/cowl and polished brass belt moulding, has a very Continental look."

Knox Kershaw's Saoutchik Cabriolet is likewise on the 146-inch chassis: "According to research performed by a French automotive historian, this car was delivered originally to a Czechoslovakian film star. It has the larger of the two J-12 engines."

1934 Hispano-Suiza J-12 Sedanca Cabriolet, Fernandez & Darrin

Owner: Bob Bahre of Oxford, Maine

1934 Hispano-Suiza J-12 Cabriolet, Saoutchik   *Owner: Knox Kershaw of Montgomery, Alabama*

1936 Hispano-Suiza K-6 Limousine, Van Vooren *Owners: Berta & Jay Leon of Hubbard, Texas*

Wheelbases for the K-6 were two: 134½ and 146½ inches. The Leons' Van Vooren Limousine is on the longer. Comments Jay: ''Since I was born in Spain, the Hispano-Suiza has a special meaning to me. As a limousine, this car is conservative but with flowing lines. The interior has leather in front, broadcloth in back and lovely rosewood everywhere. There is a divider window, of course, and a sun roof over the driver's seat.''

Total production of the K-6 Hispano-Suiza was 204 cars. Henri Chapron bodied the three-position Cabriolet owned by Jacques & Betty Harguindeguy: ''This is a very rare two-seater body with rumble seat. It's the only Chapron Hispano-Suiza two-seater in existence today.''

1936 Hispano-Suiza K-6 Cabriolet, Chapron *Owners: Jacques & Betty Harguindeguy of Walnut Creek, California*

1937 Hispano-Suiza J-12 Cabriolet de Ville, de Villars (rear door monogram above)
Owner: Noel Thompson of New Vernon, New Jersey   Photos: K. Karger

The original owner of Noel Thompson's three-position Cabriolet de Ville by de Villars was His Royal Highness, the Maharajah of Rajkot, Sardeja who specified that the parking lights be in two different colors in order that his loyal subjects might know at all times just who was in the car (right lens red for the Maharajah, left lens green for the Maharanee). "Extremely elegant," comments Noel, "and a fantastic road car."

That nicely sums up the Hispano-Suiza. Cavilling seems petty in the presence of such a magnificent motorcar as the J-12, though one might point to the multi-plate clutch and the choice of gear ratios as not up to the perfection par of the rest of the chassis. Too, at some point Marc Birkigt might have chosen to update the chassis with independent front suspension. Possibly he never felt the need to do so. By the mid-thirties, in any case, Birkigt had turned his genius to the aviation field. From parts on hand the last few Hispano-Suiza chassis were assembled in 1938 in Paris. In Barcelona, Hispano-Suiza automobile production did not survive World War II.

ISOTTA FRASCHINI

Running board with toolbox from the Hooper/McEwan 1929 Type 8A Castagna Limousine.

Italy's most aristocratic motorcar was the result of the partnership of Cesare Isotta and three brothers named Fraschini—Vincenzo, Antonio and Oreste. Shared interest was a trait of this partnership, Cesare, Vincenzo and Antonio marrying one each of the three daughters of Bianchi Anderloni. Oreste remained resolutely a bachelor and, the most mechanically inclined of the quartet, worked closely with technical director Giustino Cattaneo on development of the Isotta Fraschini product. In 1909, at the Paris Salon, the Milanese company introduced four-wheel brakes, practically a generation before same would enjoy general adoption in the industry. In 1919 Isotta Fraschini introduced the Tipo 8 with the first straight-eight engine put into series production anywhere in the world. The Tipo 8 also introduced a new policy for the company: one model only with an emphasis on unabashed luxury. Oreste Fraschini reasoned that because of the devastation of World War I only the rich on the Continent would be able to afford cars, and in the United States there was only room at the top as well since Henry Ford had the mass market sewn up and middle-class automobiles were legion. Oreste's death in 1921 changed the Milanese firm dramatically, his brothers and brother-in-law bowing out soon after. Count Lodovico Mazzotti acquired Isotta Fraschini. Fortunately, Giustino Cattaneo stayed on, the one-model policy continued and export remained a priority. . . .

1925 Isotta Fraschini Tipo 8 Torpedo, Sala
Owner: Clive Cussler of Golden, Colorado

Retrospectively, historians have liked to have fun at the Isotta's expense, critically reviewing its straight-eight engine as showing ''little evidence of a desperate search for efficiency'' and the car as ''almost as big as a hotel.'' Granted, the 360 cubic inches (5901 cc) of the Tipo 8 developed just 80 hp at a langorous 2200 rpm, the wheelbase was a long 145 inches, and the car weighed in at over two tons. With light coachwork, 80 mph was possible; more formal bodies sacrificed about ten miles an hour. Blistering performance wasn't the car's reason for being, however, elite grandeur for the motoring pleasure of the grandly elite was. By the mid-twenties the roster of Isotta Fraschini owners included the Kings of Italy and Iraq, the Queen of Romania, the Empress of Abyssinia, Prince Louis of Monaco, two Maharajahs, the Aga Khan and the Gaekwar of Baroda, amidst a galaxy of untitled folk with plenty of money.

An Argentine rancher was the original owner of the Tipo 8 Torpedo by Sala that has been Clive Cussler's for a decade. ''Steers like hell,'' says Clive, ''but rolls along like a super-charged tank.''

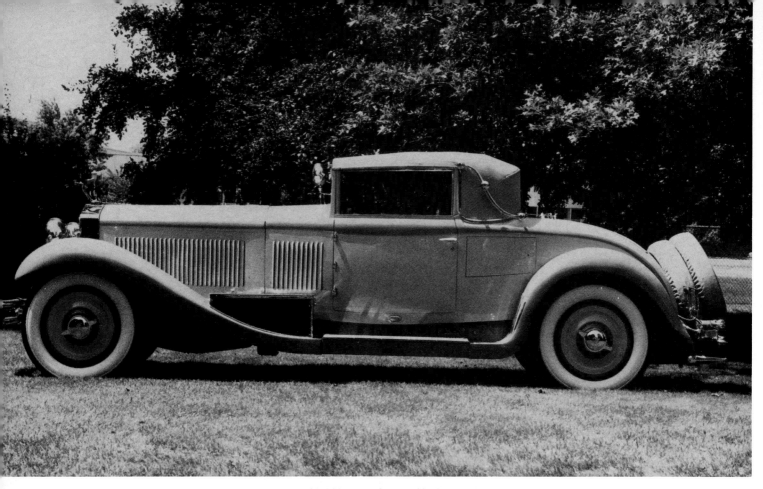

1929 Isotta Fraschini Tipo 8A Convertible Coupe, Castagna
Owner: Francesca Ferrara of Gates Mills, Ohio   Photos: Torque

Nearly a third of the Classic Era Isottas were imported into the United States. The renowned Italian poet Gabriele D'Annunzio was an enthusiastic supporter of the marque and had encouraged his son Ugo to set himself up in New York City as the U.S. distributor. Despite a $9,750 chassis price that was twice the cost of a complete American luxury car, Ugo's business was brisk. Clara Bow, Jack Dempsey and William Randolph Hearst joined Rudolph Valentino in adding Isottas to their star-studded garages. The car became America's darling among luxury imports.

The D'Annunzio agency delivered Francesca Ferrara's Tipo 8A Castagna Convertible Coupe new to Cleveland, Ohio in 1930. Comments Al Ferrara: "The car had been ordered by Mrs. Sterling of the Sterling, Linder, Davis Department Store in Cleveland. There can be no doubt that the store was a roaring success! The very high price of an Isotta Fraschini bought excellent engineering and a body that is perfection in workmanship. This car has resided in Cleveland all these years, same as myself. Subsequently the Sterling family lived on Old Mill Road where we have lived for the last thirty years."

With its long straight-eight engine dictating an equally long expanse of hood, the Isotta Fraschini was the darling of coachbuilders as well. An ungainly Classic Isotta seems almost a contradiction in terms. Fleetwood and LeBaron bodied some of the cars on this side of the Atlantic, but the vast preponderance of Isottas carried coachwork by such Italian houses as Sala, Farina, Touring—and most especially Castagna, as witness the

Hooper/McEwan Tipo 8A Limousine: "Castagna coachwork is particularly appealing due to the high level of interesting detail. This particular car is unique in being significantly lower than other formal Castagna bodies of the period. Among its interesting details are the two-tone paint scheme which is highly unusual and the one-foot-square-opening glass roof vent that is in the rear compartment."

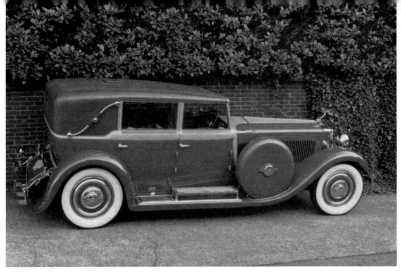

1929 Isotta Fraschini Tipo 8A Limousine, Castagna

Owners: R. B. Hooper & A. W. McEwan of Bellevue, Washington

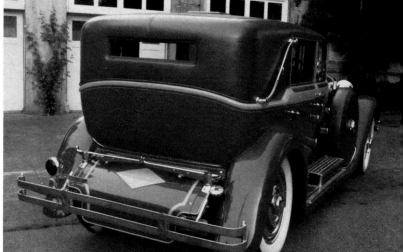

1929 Isotta Fraschini Tipo 8A S Roadster Cabriolet, Castagna   Owner: Bob Bahre of Oxford, Maine

1929 Isotta Fraschini Tipo 8A SS Roadster Cabriolet, Castagna   Owner: W. G. Lassiter, Jr. of West Palm Beach, Florida

The mid-twenties had seen the original post-Armistice Tipo 8 evolve into the 8A. Refinements to the overhead valve straight-eight engine brought cubic inches numbering 449.5 (7.4 liters) available *normale* delivering 110 hp at 2400 rpm or in a *spinto* (sports) version known as the Tipo 8A S which produced 135 hp at 2600 rpm. In the 8A SS (or Super Spinto), like Bill Lassiter's car, the horsepower claimed was a rousing 155/160—and 100 mph was guaranteed. This nicely quieted any critics who suggested an Isotta Fraschini was all show and no go.

Still, beauty could have remained an Isotta's sole *raison d'être*, as indicated by Bob Bahre's Castagna Roadster Cabriolet: ''The long hood, vertical windshield, short convertible top with landau irons and dual rear spares give this car a truly Classic look. The full set of Stephen Grebel lights and the Cobra hood ornament complement the design, and both the driver's compartment and rumble seat are finished in beautiful decorative woodwork.''

656

1930 Isotta Fraschini Tipo 8A SS Dual Cowl Phaeton, Castagna   *Owner: William Lyon of Trabuco Canyon, California*

It might be said that Isotta Fraschini was a teacher in the l-o-n-g hood school of design with apt pupils on both sides of the Atlantic. William Lyon's car exemplifies how an unusual two-door dual-cowl style dramatically accented the concept.

Noel Thompson's Castagna 8A SS, which enjoyed a loving twenty-year restoration by John Nagel, accents the attention to detail that was an Isotta hallmark.

1930 Isotta Fraschini Tipo 8A SS Convertible Coupe, Castagna   *Owner: Noel Thompson of New Vernon, New Jersey*

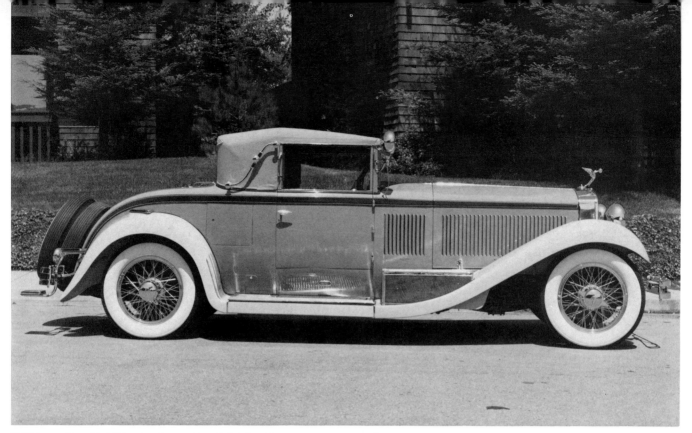

1930 Isotta Fraschini Tipo 8A Commodore Cabriolet, Castagna   *Owner: Blackhawk Classic Auto Collection, Danville, California*

The Castagna Commodore Cabriolet in the Blackhawk Classic Auto Collection made its sensational debut at the New York Automobile Salon in December 1929. Named for the luxurious Manhattan hotel in which the salon was staged each year, the Commodore Cabriolet spanned 17½ feet and was priced at $12,000. The Blackhawk car was originally purchased in February 1930 by Connecticut sportsman Eugene Maxwell Moore, who died five weeks later. When rediscovered decades after that, the odometer showed only 8,000 miles. Probably less than a dozen Commodore Cabriolets, no two of them identical, were produced.

But the numbers for Isotta, with its one-model/all-out-luxury policy, were small throughout the Classic Era. And they tell their own story of what happened to the company when the Great Depression set in. Tipo 8A production (in all versions) was 950 cars from 1925 to 1931; just 20 examples of the Tipo 8B (a refinement of its predecessor) would be built from 1931 until the mid-thirties when the big factory in the Via Monterosa began producing only aero engines. By then Count Mazzotti and Giustino Cattaneo had left the company. But glorious legends never fade. Years later an Isotta Fraschini would be as much a star—certainly to Cecil B. DeMille—as Gloria Swanson in *Sunset Boulevard*.

L A G O N D A

*Hydraulic jacking system, tire hammer, spark plugs and auxiliary light nestled in the
tire cover of Berta & Jay Leon's 1937 LG45 Drophead Coupe—photos by Ray King*

The Lagonda was a quintessentially English sporting car produced by an American who wanted
to be an opera singer. His musical ambition thwarted in his native Springfield, Ohio, Wilbur
Gunn had left for Victorian England. Actually, scandal was as much the reason for his move
across the Atlantic. He had walked out on his wife and family as well, unthinkable in Middle
America in that era. Apparently the closest Wilbur came to realizing his dream now was
marrying an English widow who was a singer and well-to-do and settling in at her pleasant
home in Staines, Middlesex. Apparently, too, his creativity in the mechanical field far
overshadowed his musical talent. In the potting shed of his backyard, Gunn began building
motorcycles, then automobiles, which he called Lagonda, the name of a creek back home in
Ohio. The ''motorcyclist's Mercedes'' his two-wheeler was dubbed; his automobile was
favorably greeted among the sporting set too. Wilbur Gunn's death in 1920, largely from
overwork, left the company in turmoil. In the enthusiast market, the Lagonda remained
popular; the sobriquet ''poor man's Bentley'' was a compliment, given its price tag of half that
of W.O.'s product. But money wasn't being made, and by the early thirties, it was being lost at
an alarming rate. By 1935 Lagonda was in receivership. But there was a bright side. In 1935
Lagonda also won Le Mans. . . .

1934 Lagonda M45R Tourer

Owner: Frederick L. Berndt
of Milwaukee, Wisconsin

Among the Lagonda company's problems in the mid-thirties was the bewildering proliferation of models offered which strained a factory that had essentially been jerrybuilt out of a potting shed. Still, some very fine cars were being built. Chief among them was the 4½ Litre—or M45—which used the 4453 cc pushrod ohv Meadows six-cylinder engine and which was an unabashed copy of the fabled 4½ Bentley. Perhaps hopeful re-creation is a better term, since W.O.'s rumbleguts 4½ was now history and he was now, none too happily, in the employ of Rolls-Royce. The subsequent M45R—for Rapide—boasted 100 hp and 100 mph.

Fred Berndt's car was the factory prototype for that model: "Lagonda sold the car in 1935, it remained in England until about 1967, I've been its owner since 1971. The car was restored at home by me, and has been driven nearly 33,000 miles since. This is truly a superb touring machine with tons of torque and all-day high-speed driving capability. On 2,000-mile cross country runs in both 94° heat and 25°-30° temperatures, it has performed without fault. This car has a truly documented 336,000 miles since new."

Given Fred's experience, the 1935 victory of the 4½ Litre at Le Mans perhaps doesn't surprise. All England was overjoyed. Not since the Bentley's last victory in 1930 had a British car won the twenty-four-hour classic. For Lagonda, the timing couldn't have been more fortuitous. The firm was for sale. A company in receivership is not necessarily a bad proposition, but a company that had just won Le Mans was a far better one. Two parties were very interested.

A little pre-history is in order. In 1931 when his bankruptcy-bound Bentley works went to the auction block, W.O. had hoped Napier would be the successful bidder. Instead, Rolls-Royce was. Now Rolls-Royce hoped to bring Lagonda into the Derby fold as well. Instead, a wealthy solicitor named Alan Good won out this time. Almost immediately there came the announcement that W. O. Bentley was on his way to Staines to take over Lagonda's technical directorship. There had been certain discussions about this beforehand, of course.

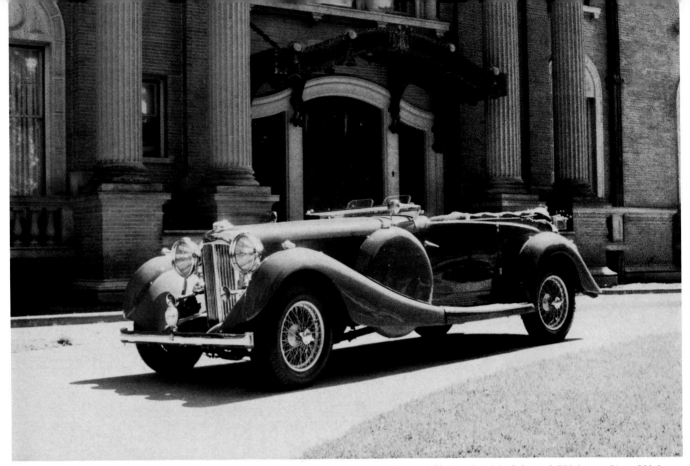

1937 Lagonda LG45 Tourer   *Owner: Christopher M. Salyer of Oklahoma City, Oklahoma*

L.G. Motors, Ltd. (combining the initials of Lagonda and Good) was the designation for the reorganized company. The LG45 was its first new model, conjured by W. O. Bentley of M45 Rapide engine in a revised version of the M45 chassis.

Chris Salyer has owned his LG45 Tourer since 1987: ''Three body styles were offered in the LG45—saloon, tourer and drophead coupe. Approximately 278 cars were built from 1935 through 1937. Improvements—or 'sanctions,' as the factory called them—were engineered in periodically. My car is a Sanction III with Weslake cylinder head; G10 gearbox with synchromesh on second, third and top gears; optional center or right-hand change; revamped gauges and new induction manifolding since W. O. Bentley had detested the original engine's 'quite outrageous crankshaft roar.' Other features of the LG45 include automatic chassis lubrication (the 'Tecalemit One-Shot System'), hydraulic 'Jackall' system by Smiths, twin magneto and twin plug head. The wheelbase is 129 inches and the brakes mechanical cable. Further, for the first time on a Lagonda, a bumper was added as standard equipment, to the front only. It was of the harmonic stabilizing type and fitted to improve handling rather than to protect the car from shocks.''

661

Jay & Berta Leon's LG45 was the Lagonda which Alan Good co-drove with Charles Brackenbury in the 1938 Monte Carlo Rally—2,369 miles from Athens through Yugoslavia, Hungary, Austria, Germany and France to the finish line in Monaco. L. G. Motors' chairman was naturally anxious to keep Lagonda in the news, and this venture did that nicely. Amongst the special light cars tailormade for the Monte, this car finished twenty-ninth of the 94 finishers (125 cars had started) and second in its luxury class. That this was Alan Good's car was just one of the surprises that greeted Jay Leon following acquisition in 1975: ''Initially, I thought the car had two spare tires. But only the right-hand cover had a spare; the left contained the hydraulic system to lift the car for ease of tire changing.'' Following the Monte Carlo Rally, most probably Alan Good did not continue to drive the LG45 long because by now there was a brand-new Lagonda for him to use.

1937 Lagonda LG45
Drophead Coupe

Owners: Berta & Jay Leon
of Hubbard, Texas
Photos: Ray King

Shortly after acquiring the company, Alan Good had announced that Lagonda was now going to build the best car in the world. That phrase had been carefully chosen. Since the name Bentley was magic, probably no one outside of Derby thought it excessive hyperbole. The new V-12 Phantom III had just been introduced. Following W. O. Bentley from Derby to Staines were a few Rolls-Royce engineers with P-III blueprints tucked under their arms. It's always helpful to have a definitive picture of the competition.

"I would have given my right arm to have had another two years to develop the car before it was placed on the market," W. O. Bentley would later lament. But Alan Good's money could flow in one direction for only so long. The new Lagonda V-12 barely made it to the Olympia Motor Show in the fall of '37. Alan Good had hoped to drive a V-12 in the Monte Carlo Rally but building the thirty cars necessary for homologation prior to the Monte's starting date was impossible, which was the reason Jay Leon's car had been pressed into service.

Still, if not all hopes were realized, the new Lagonda had arrived. Historians since have called it W. O. Bentley's *pièce-de résistance.* The 60° vee ohv overhead-cam engine displaced 4480 cc (273 cubic inches) and developed approximately 180 hp. Featured were dual carburetors, distributors, fuel pumps (electric) and a twelve-quart sump. In many respects, this V-12 was years ahead of its time: complex, to be sure ("fully equal to Bugatti's worst," in one critic's jibe), but positively masterful in engineering nuance. The chassis W.O. engineered for it was no less: enormous (17½-inch) Lockheed hydraulic brakes with dual master cylinders, a finely tuned suspension system with an independent torsion-bar front and long half elliptics at the rear, adjustable shock absorbers—plus the automatic chassis lubricator and built-in jacking system adapted from earlier Lagonda practice. Wheelbases were three: 124, 132 and 138 inches. Bodies were hand-made and all aluminum.

Lagonda V-12 production would total 185 cars. John Larch has owned his for seven years: "Most of the cars were dropheads. The Sport Saloon is exceedingly rare. Its lines are unique and, though 'very British,' the car has a fleet and flowing appearance and is quite streamlined for 1938. It sits low and corners well, drives and handles like a sports car. The power curve is rather flat up to 60, but from then on you can fly. The car is particularly comfortable at 70-80 and acts as if there is no top end. The brakes are very powerful. Unfortunately, although a revered name in England, Lagonda is not well known in the U.S. The V-12 was priced at about $9,000 when new so it's no wonder few were sold. In engineering and design, the car was way ahead of the pack in 1938. It runs circles around a P-III Rolls."

1938 Lagonda V-12 Sport Saloon
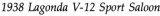

Owner: John A. Larch of Lafayette, Indiana

663

The LG6 was directly descended from the V-12 and looked almost exactly like it. The chassis was essentially the same save for being three-and-a-half inches longer—at 127½ and 135½—in the two wheelbases available. The reason for the difference, surprisingly, was that the V-12 engine was shorter than this car's straight six. The LG6's unit was the well-proven Meadows 4½ Litre in Sanction IV spec (modified camshaft and valve timing).

The price tag for a Sport Saloon like Joseph Moreland's was £1195. ''A magnificent carriage, the one large car I enjoy driving,'' comments Joe. ''Reportedly, Gary Cooper drove his 1938 Lagonda coast to coast yearly for a tune-up at Zumbach's, the famous foreign car garage in New York City.''

1938 Lagonda LG6 Sport Saloon
Owner: Joseph N. Moreland, Jr. of Orlando, Florida

1939 Lagonda V-12
Drophead Coupe

Owner: Jean Gorjat
of Harrisburg, Pennsylvania

1939 Lagonda V-12 Saloon,
Freestone & Webb

Owner: Gordon Strauss
of Kelvin, South Africa

''Some 60,000 miles from new by an American actor in Hollywood, an oil company chairman and me,'' declares Jean Gorjat of his Lagonda V-12, while at the same time revealing some of its foibles: ''The rods, made of aluminum, run on the crankshaft without bearings, but on high pressure oil, like some aircraft engines; if pressure decreases or the pump breaks, it's five seconds and it costs you $10,000 and 3,000 miles to run in again, steaming like a locomotive even in freezing weather.''

''This is presumed to be the only razor-edge Freestone & Webb V-12 Lagonda Saloon,'' comments Gordon Strauss of his car. ''It was repainted shortly after arrival from the U.K. but the panel shop went bankrupt during the job. The stripped car was offered for sale (illegally) and rescued in the nick of time. Left in the open in England for about a year with the sliding roof open, much work remains to be done on the interior as a result. Because the body is aluminum, rust is not a problem. The Lagonda V-12 is an exceptionally well-engineered car with excellent performance—100+ mph.''

The Stocktons' V-12 Lagonda is rare in being a Rapide. Earlier cars with that designation had been ''breathed on'' to improve performance, but this wasn't the case (nor need it have been) with the V-12. Here Rapide meant a lighter body and a more sporting appearance. The sidemounted spare moved to the rear of the car and, inside, the seating arrangement was revised to a single seat set sideways behind and theoretically three abreast in the front, although they would have to be close friends. Probably no

1939 Lagonda V-12 Rapide
Owners: Truman A., Jr. & Ruth S. Stockton of Lakewood, Colorado

more than twenty V-12 Rapides were produced. "We bought this car in 1957," says Truman. "One of its early owners was nightclub star Phil 'The Singing Cop' Regan. At least two new car dealers, a radio talk show and newspaper reporter and a machinist also owned it before I did. The car seems to have arrived in this country around 1945. The top is a three-position, and the body style is most unusual."

In 1939 two special versions of the V-12 finished third and fourth overall at Le Mans. Given Lagonda's earlier victory there, this was not the all-conquering debut desired. W. O. Bentley commented that the Le Mans assault was too rushed. In 1938 Lord Howe had put up an hour at Brooklands in a standard saloon at 101.5 mph, which included a tire change along the way. The prowess of the Lagonda V-12 was unquestionable. Its minor failings would no doubt have been ameliorated but time was not on the big car's side. The onset of World War II ended production. In the austerity of postwar Europe, the car was not revived. Alan Good's interest waned By late 1947 Lagonda belonged to tractor man David Brown, whose other recent acquisition was Aston Martin. Another interesting saga was beginning.

MERCEDES BENZ

Three-pointed star from Gary Gallup's '27 Type K Sport Cabriolet—photo by Dennis Adler

In Germany, in workshops just sixty miles apart, two inventors worked feverishly on the same idea at the same time. In early 1886 Carl Benz patented the three-wheeler he had completed a few months before. Later that year, Gottlieb Daimler tested the four-wheeler of his design. These were the first successful gasoline automobiles the world had ever seen. The two men were profoundly different. Daimler was a visionary; gripped with the universality of his engine, he was forever experimenting. Carl Benz's vision was solidly focused on his vehicle, and at the turn of the century, he was the world's largest automobile manufacturer. By then Daimler was dead at the age of sixty-six. A few years later, at the age of sixty, Benz became little more than an adviser in his company, and his advice wasn't asked much. Rather like Henry Ford a generation later, he had thought his simple little car could be built forever. His retirement was effectively forced when his board of directors began producing more progressive versions. The rival companies, famous the world over, prospered awhile. The Daimler-Motoren-Gesellschaft model engineered by Gottlieb Daimler's long-time associate Wilhelm Maybach and named for the daughter of dealer Emil Jellinek who ordered it, had taken the world by storm. In concept, the Mercedes was the first modern automobile. It won races everywhere. DMG soon adopted the name and, in 1909, added the three-pointed star hood ornament (to memorialize Gottlieb Daimler's pioneering of motorization on land, on sea and in the air). In 1911 the gargantuan 1312-cubic-inch Blitzen Benz stormed the sands at Daytona at 141+ mph, a world speed record not to be broken until after the First World War. But by then Daimler and Benz were only famous. Prosperity was gone. In the chaos of postwar Germany, the two rival companies, with some initial reluctance, concluded that merger was the only way to stay alive. . . .

666

1926 Mercedes-Benz Type K Convertible Sedan, Saoutchik
Owner: Blackhawk Classic Auto Collection, Danville, California

On June 28th, 1926 Daimler-Motoren-Gesellschaft and Benz & Cie. became Daimler-Benz AG. The managing director of the new firm was Wilhelm Kissel, the Benz man whose quiet diplomacy made the difficult transition easier. Making the new cars of the new company memorable was a DMG man, former Austro-Daimler engineer Ferdinand Porsche who had joined the Stuttgart factory in 1923. Porsche brought with him colleague Alfred Neubauer, a man of epic proportion who would find that he was better at managing a race team than being a race driver. Motor sport, long a tradition for both firms, was now pursued with increasing fervor. Rudi Caracciola was the Mercedes-Benz racing star. In 1926 he was winning races with the new Type K.

Derived from the 24/100/140 (triple-barreled designations were a company practice which will not be followed here in the interest of readability), the K was powered by a single-overhead-cam six-cylinder engine of 6240 cc (381 cubic inches). The alphabetical letter represented *kurz* (or short, for the 134-inch wheelbase, over a foot less lengthy than its predecessor) but it could also have appropriately translated to *kompressor*. Unsupercharged, the K developed 110 hp; with Roots-Gebläse blower engaged, the hp figure shot up to 160. The flexible exhaust pipes boldly jutting from the right side of the hood were a Mercedes feature subsequently adopted by a number of other factories building supercharged cars, Duesenberg among them.

The K chassis was heavy in both weight and price—3,417 pounds and $11,000. But with a factory-guaranteed 90 mph, the car could be honestly advertised as the fastest standard touring model in the world. It could go. Stopping was another matter. In one road test, 145 feet were required before the K came to a halt from 40 mph.

Still, the sporting thrill of the K appealed to well over 200 buyers during the five years of its production. In addition to factory-bodied versions, the K was dressed by the *crème* of European coach-builders. Jacques Saoutchik, the Russian-born cabinetmaker who had established his carrosserie in Paris in 1906, created the Type K Convertible Sedan in the Blackhawk Classic Auto Collection.

1927 Mercedes-Benz Type K Sport Cabriolet, Hibbard & Darrin
Owner: Gary C. Gallup of Santa Barbara, California   Photos: Dave Gooley

And those Americans in Paris—Tom Hibbard and Howard Darrin—were responsible for Gary Gallup's Type K Sport Cabriolet: ''We were able to talk with both Mr. Hibbard and Mr. Darrin about this car before their deaths. Dutch Darrin thought they made only three of these bodies for Mercedes-Benz. One was sold to the King of Sweden. This one was originally sold in New York to an opera star (name so far unknown). I've owned the Type K for thirteen years. It's a very fast car. Admittedly, it is also something of a handful to drive. The brakes are inadequate which makes for a real fun challenge.''

1927 Mercedes-Benz Type SS Convertible Coupe, Corsica
Owner: Paul Dauer of Chicago, Illinois

1927 Mercedes-Benz Type S Roadster
Owner: Edward H. Wachs of Long Grove, Illinois

Introduced in 1927, the 6.8-liter (415-cubic-inch) Type S was lower (by several inches), lighter (by over 500 pounds) and more powerful (180 hp) than the K. "The acme of motor car perfection," the U.S. distributor's catalogue read, "the car of cars for the great sport." In 1927 the S won twenty-seven races and captured ten speed records. A few less than 150 sportsmen would buy one, among them the first (and unknown) owner of Edward Wachs' car: "With its factory roadster body, my S is similar to the one driven so successfully by Rudi Caracciola. In the thirty years I've owned it, I've raced the car too in vintage events and hill climbs." And without stopping problems. The inadequacy of the K's brakes was a matter Ferdinand Porsche remedied in the S.

In 1928 the SS, or Super Sport—with 7.1 liters and 200 (later 225) supercharged horsepower—followed, and found about 111 buyers. Among other modifications was a slightly higher radiator which was much appreciated by coach-builders who had found it difficult to design graceful and commodious bodies on the S with its hood line barely clearing the engine. Corsica of London created the coachwork for the SS which Paul Dauer has owned since 1971: "The chassis was shipped to England in 1930. Reportedly, Corsica bodied only seven S series Mercedes. In a sense, this series represented the last of the big-bore, long-stroke, slow-revving Mercedes engines. In the SS, handling was improved via an undersprung rear axle."

1929 Mercedes-Benz Type SSK Roadster   *Owner: Miles C. Collier of Naples, Florida*

''K'' designated *kurz* again in a chassis shortened a foot-and-a-half to 116.1 inches. The radiator was from the S, the engine from the SS. The aptly-named ''elephant blower'' was the SSK's own. In competition form, the engine developed over 300 hp. In competition, the car was indomitable. It had been developed by Ferdinand Porsche at the behest of his friend Alfred Neubauer. The S and SS won races routinely whenever the road was straight, a limitation that had distressed Mercedes' race manager. A less wieldy car for hill climbs was his

desire—and he got it. The sound of the SSK—a Valkyrie's cry to some ears, a banshee's scream to others—became a metaphor for victory. With the SSK, all hills belonged to Rudi Caracciola.

Just thirty-one SSK's were produced in three years. Miles Collier's car was built for English sportswoman Dorothy Paget, sponsor of the Blower Bentley team.

Among the last SSK's produced, Bob Bahre's car was raced by Baron Michl Tüssling on behalf of the factory during those years of

galloping inflation in Germany when Daimler-Benz could no longer afford an official race team.

Reluctantly, Wilhelm Kissel had discontinued competition after 1931 and the triumphal year of the SSK's successor—the *leicht,* or light, SSKL. Of the handful built, strictly for competition, none survives. Gone by now, too, was the brilliant and tempestuous Ferdinand Porsche, his departure as cacophonous as the towering cars he had created for Mercedes. The automotive world would hear of him again, of course.

1931 Mercedes-Benz Type SSK Roadster   *Owner: Bob Bahre of Oxford, Maine*

1930 Mercedes-Benz Type 770 "Grosser" Cabriolet Limousine, Voll & Ruhrbeck
Owner: Indianapolis Motor Speedway Hall of Fame Museum

According to the sales literature, the model was designed for those "who always view a maximum achievement as just sufficient for their needs." A massive 7.7-liter supercharged pushrod straight-eight engine developing 150 hp was required to keep this tremendous three-ton-plus car moving on the road. The "Grosser" was well named. Performance wasn't the aim. Like the low-production S series which carried Mercedes colors in the sporting arena, the Type 770 was carefully targeted for the ultra prestige market. Just 117 examples of the first series (1930-1937) Grosser were built, many of them destined for heads of state.

Faisal I, King of Iraq, was the first owner of the Indy Museum Cabriolet Limousine. The multi-position top permitted use of the car in a variety of configurations: full touring, cabriolet, town car, limousine or sedan. Following Faisal's death, the car passed to his successor, King Ghazi I. The Crown Prince, Faisal II, was a child when King Ghazi died in 1938, this car of state subsequently being stored until Faisal II took power in 1954. Completely over-hauled at the Daimler-Benz factory in 1957, it was used only twice before Faisal II's death in 1958. Ten years later Tony Hulman imported the car for the Hall of Fame Museum.

The head of state most often identified with the 770 Mercedes today, of course, is Adolph Hitler—though the number of his Grossers has been as exaggerated as the number of places George Washington slept.

1935 Mercedes-Benz Type 500K Sedanca Drophead, Corsica   *Owner: Larry Nicklin of Leo, Indiana   Photo: Nicky Wright*

The coming to power of Adolph Hitler produced dramatic changes at Daimler-Benz. Neither the sporting nor prestige cars had ever filled the treasury significantly; the bread-and-butter models accomplished that. The low-production Mercedes did enhance the renown of the three-pointed star but in the threadbare years of the early thirties such cars were a luxury for the company as well. With the economic turnaround which followed the establishment of the Third Reich, the Stuttgart factory flourished once more. A racing program was launched the likes of which the world had never seen. Soon the only competition a Mercedes had was Auto Union, another German company which enjoyed state blessing. Little did these factories know how double-edged was the supportive sword which *Der Führer* had offered them.

For the moment, Alfred Neubauer revelled in a competition team that was a virtual armada. And Porsche successor Hans Nibel and crew enjoyed engineering development unencumbered by stringent budgeting which produced the world's first diesel production car and the world's first production use of independent front suspension in the Type 380.

Introduced at the Berlin Auto-mobile Show in 1934, the 500K was the 380's successor and the spiritual descendant of the fabled S series. Lighter by half a ton than the 3.8-liter 120 hp Type 380, and with forty more horses, the 500K was priced in the $5,000 range, which bought two cars: a fast, docile tourer with super-charger disengaged and a stupendous

performer when the blower was cut in. Zero to sixty in 16.5 seconds was amazing acceleration for such a big car in the mid-thirties.

The 500K Cabriolet C which Paul Dauer has owned since 1965 represents one of several standard-ized bodies built by Daimler-Benz's in-house coachbuilding operation at Sindelfingen: ''The four-wheel independent suspension utilizing coil springs was remarkable, but the pushrod straight-eight engine was not progressive, given the overhead camshaft of the earlier S series. And, although lighter than the 380, the 500K was undeniably weighty at 5,000 pounds.''

But it was also undeniably beautiful, most especially in some coachbuilt examples. Witness Larry

Nicklin's Corsica-bodied Sedanca which he has owned for fifteen years: ''Certain styling features on the 500K-540K series are universally accepted yet this one-off, to me, is like a special song. The car got to me emotionally, humbling any experience I myself may have had in the business of car styling. It still does. This was Corsica's only effort on a Mercedes chassis of the thirties; one-of-a-kind cars on a variety of chassis was this London coachmaker's stock in trade. Sir Max Aitken commissioned Corsica to build the car in February 1935. Subse-quently, it was used, fittingly, by the German embassy in London, but during World War II the car was shipped to Chicago. I am its seventh owner.''

1935 Mercedes-Benz Type 500K Cabriolet C   *Owner: Paul Dauer of Chicago, Illinois*

1937 Mercedes-Benz Type 540K Special Roadster
Owner: Noel Thompson of New Vernon, New Jersey

Total Type 500K production was 354 cars; just over 400 Type 540K's would be produced. With a displacement increase contributing to the 180 hp on tap, a maximum speed of well over 100 mph and the ability to cruise an autobahn indefinitely at 85, the 540K was advertised as the world's fastest standard production automobile. There were few arguments. Massive, solid and overengineered in the Mercedes tradition, this new car was most memorable for its styling. With sensuous curves and bold lines, the Mercedes design team produced a 540K that was sporting as well as elegant, flashy without being gaudy. Not easy to do.

The Special Roadster exemplified Sindelfingen's jaunty flair. Noel Thompson's car, which he has owned since 1987, was originally purchased by Sir John Chabb of England. The purchase price was 28,000 reichsmarks, more than $12,000.

The King of Afghanistan was the original owner of Bob Bahre's Special Roadster; Mohammed Zahir Shah was just twenty-three when it was delivered to him in Kabul. At the outbreak of World War II, the car was shipped to the Afghanistan embassy in Paris. It was brought to this country by Vernon Jarvis in the early fifties. Special Roadsters are rare; this one is rarer yet with its covered spare tire and low fin, only three such cars being so designed.

''Aside from being fun to drive, it is also a work of art,'' comments Alfred Hassinger of the 540K Saloon he has owned for over two decades. ''When I first became interested in Classics, I wanted an open car but when I saw this rare body style with right-hand drive, thoughts of convertibles soon left me. The car was originally purchased by Heinrich Behrens, a German who was living in Paris at the time. It was hidden for most of the war. When I purchased the car from Mr. Behrens' niece, it had the carburetor he had hand-made for it. The original had been taken off to forestall use of the car during its time in hiding, and had

1937 Mercedes-Benz Type 540K Special Roadster   *Owner: Bob Bahre of Oxford, Maine*

1937 Mercedes-Benz Type 540K Saloon   *Owner: Alfred Hassinger of Rumson, New Jersey*

been misplaced. The Behrens'
carburetor worked fine for me, except
when using the supercharger, until I
was able to acquire the correct one.
Except for paint, tires and chrome
plating, the car remains original.''

For over three-and-a-half decades
the 540K Vanden Plas (as the Belgian
coachbuilder spelled its British
branch) Convertible Victoria has been
in the garage of Andrew D. Darling:
''I purchased this car from Randolph
Hearst of the newspaper publishing

1938 Mercedes-Benz Type 540K Convertible Victoria, Vanden Plas   *Owner: Andrew D. Darling of Edina, Minnesota*

1939 Mercedes-Benz Type 540K Cabriolet B   *Owner: William Lyon of Trabuco Canyon, California*

family. Although the body is English, it's a left-hand drive. The convertible top recesses level into its well and the spare tire is recessed into the body, making very smooth flowing lines. This is a very exciting car to drive and, with the supercharger

engaged, howls like a German Messerschmitt diving from the clouds. I'm also proud of the fact that it starts and runs with the original fuel pump and oil pressure system. No electric pump is necessary on this car."

The panache of Sindelfingen stylists is deftly seen in the Cabriolet owned by William Lyon and the Coupe owned by William R. Patton, the latter car having originally been purchased by Frau Ida Herzberg of Essen, Germany.

1939 Mercedes-Benz Type 540K Coupe   *Owner: William R. Patton of Irvine, California*

1939 Mercedes-Benz Type 540K Saloon, Freestone & Webb   Owner: Clive Cussler of Golden, Colorado

Freestone and Webb produced the saloon coachwork for the 540K that Clive Cussler has owned for over a decade: ''It's the only known example of British razor-edge styling on this Mercedes chassis, and one of only two known to exist with a sedan body. As for the 540K, it speaks for itself.''

And so it did. But for little longer. Just sixty-nine 540K's left the Stuttgart factory in 1939. On September 1st, Hitler ordered his army into Poland. The Classic Era was over for Daimler-Benz. *Der Führer* had other plans for the company.

MINERVA

"Minerva" from the Graver 1932 Type AL Town Car by Ostruk

Sylvain de Jong had a fondness for mythology. A native of Holland, he emigrated from Amsterdam to Antwerp in 1883 at the age of fifteen, manufactured bicycles called Mercury beginning in 1895, traveled to America the year following to learn about machine tools and machining, returned home to Belgium in 1897 to begin building a better bicycle called Minerva, and followed with his first automobile in 1899. De Jong must have had second thoughts about an immediate plunge into the automotive field because only prototypes ensued for several years as his bicycles were motorized, and motorcycles and trikes were produced. Not until 1904 did serious automobile manufacture begin. In 1909 de Jong made a pivotal decision which would endure for as long as the Minerva did: the adoption of Charles Yale Knight's sleeve-valve engine. Quiet, efficient, trouble-free and durable, the Knight was the perfect powerplant for a *grand luxe* carriage. That it was expensive to build didn't bother de Jong because the top-of-the-line Minerva's healthy price tag would take care of that. That it was expensive to repair didn't either since a Knight rarely required attention before 120,000 miles, which was impressive. Less impressive was the Knight's thirst for oil which combined with the big Minerva's thirst for gasoline to make driving one pricey. But that scarcely mattered to the clientele of the Belgian marque. As the twenties roared, the Minerva motored silently into a position of renown. . . .

1925 Minerva Type AC Town Sedan, Ostruk/LeBaron
Owner: Robert C. Rooke of Morristown, New Jersey

The largest Minerva in 1925 was the 5.3-liter 82 hp Type AC or 30 CV (*chevaux-vapeau*, for taxable horsepower). A multi-disc clutch and four-wheel brakes were new this year, as was the longer 146-inch wheelbase. Paul Ostruk was the importer and agent for Minerva in New York City. The chassis price was approximately $10,000. Coachwork Ostruk designed was usually built for him by LeBaron. The Minerva was a favorite of America's moneyed elite: Clifford V. Brokaw owned two of the cars, Flo Ziegfeld three, Harold Vanderbilt four. The garages of the various members of the duPont family housed no fewer than fourteen.

John Huntington Hartford, founder of the A&P supermarket chain, was the original owner of the one-off Ostruk/LeBaron Town Sedan which Bob Rooke acquired a dozen years ago: "This is a huge, elegant, regal Classic. The wheels measure almost two feet. With a twelve-volt electrical system, the car starts easily. The fourth speed ratio is 3.61:1. This Minerva is fast. It uses fuel quickly too; at six miles per gallon, it tends to run rich. On the Garden State CARavan in 1981, I ran out of gas—twice."

Like Rolls-Royce which introduced its 20 H.P. during the reign of the Silver Ghost, Minerva had its smaller companion car as well. Smaller is the operative word, though only relatively speaking. The 3.3-liter 55 hp Type AB (or 20/24 CV) was on a 142-inch-wheelbase chassis and rode on the same size wheels as the Type AC.

In 1983, after a blowout during a 150-mile trip, Ray Katzell decided to replace the four road tires on his Minerva and, as he says, "experienced the joy of demounting and mounting 895x135 mm clinchers." But his enthusiasm for the Minerva remains undiminished: "I have long been attracted to marques that are relatively rare, in addition to having the choice features that qualify a car as Classic. As a Belgian product, the Minerva has for me the further virtue of having ties to my paternal family. The market for high-priced cars in a small country like Belgium was necessarily limited, so Minervas were manufactured largely for export, especially throughout the British Empire. The chassis of my car was exported to Australia, where it was bodied by a local coachbuilder. At the time, Australia levied high importation taxes on complete automobiles. Since a majority of Minervas imported to the U.S. had formal coachwork on the largest chassis, this car is especially attractive because of its open body on the shorter wheelbase. The polished aluminum hood and dual sidemounts are additional sporting touches. The Knight sleeve valve provides the quietest and smoothest performance of any gasoline-engined Classic that I have experienced. Handling is easy and precise, and the four-wheel brakes make for sure stops."

1925 Minerva Type AB Phaeton, Hooper & Jackson
Owner: Raymond A. Katzell of Medford, New Jersey

1925 Minerva Type AB Cabriolet, Woodall & Nicholson   *Owner: Reginald P. Ghys of Antwerp, Belgium*

"Minervas were as trouble-free as any car I have known before or since," wrote Tom Hibbard in the CCCA magazine *The Classic Car* in the mid-sixties, ". . . the big six-cylinder Knight engines seemed to go forever even when driven continually at top speeds." Tom spoke from first-hand experience, for in addition to the coachbuilding house he had established in partnership with the inimitable Dutch, Hibbard & Darrin served as the Minerva agency for France. Naturally the marque was often graced with coachwork by these two Americans in Paris, as exemplified by the elegant Hibbard & Darrin Town Car Landaulette which Clive Cussler has owned for over a decade.

The Type AB Cabriolet by Woodall & Nicholson has been owned by Belgian member Reginald Ghys since 1975 and is a veteran of such rallies as the Paris-Deauville (1980 and 1983) and Paris-Bordeaux (1985): "This Minerva motors in silence and comfort. It's a massive five-seater cabriolet with very large windows and an unusual door arrangement. On the passenger side, the door is set at the front; the driver's side door is set to the rear."

1925 Minerva Type AB Town Car Landaulette, Hibbard & Darrin   Owner: Clive Cussler of Golden, Colorado

1928 Minerva Type AF Town Car, Ostruk/Hibbard & Darrin   *Owner: Thomas J. Lester of Deerfield Beach, Florida*

The Type AF succeeded the AC in 1926. The wheelbase was increased to 149½ inches and Dewandre servo-assisted brakes were fitted. The big Minerva was even bigger.

Tom Lester's Type AF Town Car was ordered by a New Yorker, designed by the American agent and built by the Minerva agency in France. The coachbuilder's plate includes the names of both Paul Ostruk and Hibbard & Darrin. "I have never seen nor do I know of another like this," says Tom. "Fully collapsible, it can be used as a formal town car, in semi-formal or in open touring guise. The styling, workmanship, appointments and other details on this car are simply superb and most elegant. Even moreso than a Bugatti Royale, I think."

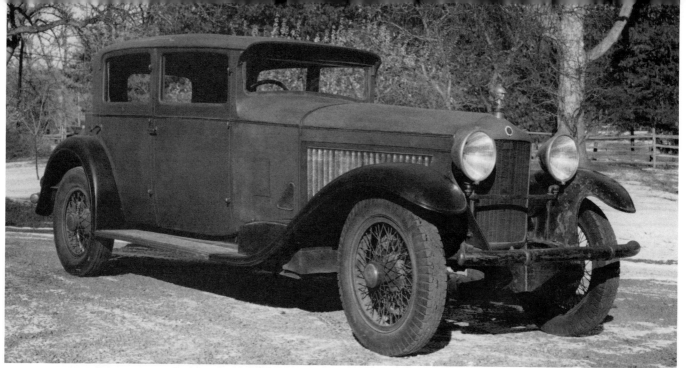

1928 Minerva Type AK Weymann Club Sedan, d'Ieteren Frères
Owner: J. Stephen Babinsky of Bernardsville, New Jersey

Introduced in 1928, the Type AK was the last of the big six-cylinder Minervas, its Knight engine bored out to six liters and designated the 32 CV. "No matter where I go, I will never see another one like it," comments Steve Babinsky of the Type AK he acquired three years ago. "Totally original, it is very interesting to examine. The car was purchased overseas, shipped to this country and has only 7,000 original miles. Its first home was an estate which is now part of the University of Bridgeport. I am in the process of tracing its original Connecticut owner. I like the long hood, the long wheelbase and the proportions of this car. And the body construction fascinates me. Built by d'Ieteren under the Weymann patent, it is all wood covered with Zapon fabric. Even the hood is covered."

1928 Minerva Type AKS Cabriolet, d'Ieteren Frères   *Owner: Reginald P. Ghys of Antwerp, Belgium*

The AKS was the sporting version —shorter wheelbase, smaller wheels, higher gearing, etc.—of the AK. Reginald Ghys has owned his d'Ieteren Cabriolet since 1985: "The 32 CV was the best Minerva ever built, in my opinion—the usual silence and comfort but with a four-speed transmission and braking servo by Dewandre. My car is a rare sporty cabriolet built by d'Ieteren probably with Hibbard & Darrin influence. Many Minerva cars sold by Hibbard & Darrin in Paris were built in Brussels at the d'Ieteren coachworks."

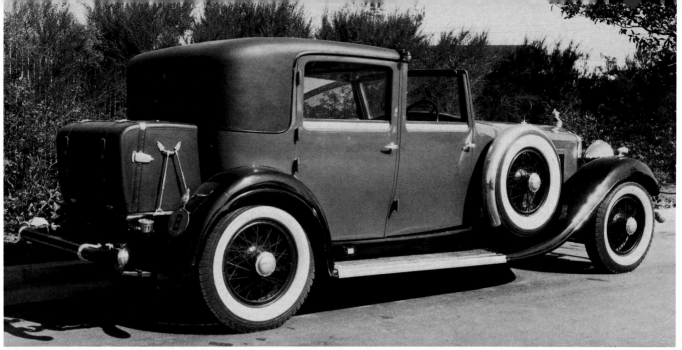

1932 Minerva Type AL Town Car, Ostruk

Owners: Art & Marie Graver of Los Altos Hills, California

Introduced at the 1929 European automobile shows, the Type AL was the Minerva concept carried to its zenith. A 6616 cc (403.7-cubic-inch) straight eight, it had nine main bearings and two of almost everything else: oil pump (the second tending to the oil radiator), dual ignition and dual-choke carburetor with electric hotspot. There was a thermostat in the cooling system, and a mechanical pump instead of the usual vacuum. The engine mated with a multi-disc clutch and four-speed non-synchronized transmission, this ensemble alone weighing 1,400 pounds. The wheelbase stretched 153½ inches for a total chassis weight close to two tons. Still, the top speed—achieved in sybaritic silence—was 90 mph.

"I have two basic impressions of Minerva," wrote the late Art Graver in *The Classic Car* regarding the Type AL he and Marie acquired in 1971. "First, it is constructed like a tank, big and massive in all areas. Second, it requires only gentle handling to achieve a desired response. For example, one is pleasantly surprised that the vacuum-assisted brake is equal to a modern-day power brake, only light foot pressure being required to bring this 6,000+-pound machine to a quick and safe stop."

"The one-shot chassis lubrication system keeps the ride squeak-free," adds Marie. "The sleeve-valve engine looks neat and uncluttered under the hood. And our car is so sumptuous inside, with beautiful silver-plated hand-made lead crystal decanters in the gorgeous burled wood bar in the back seat. Further, I like the rarity of the AL. Of the approximately fifty built, only seven plus one chassis remain in existence, maybe eight plus one chassis. Anyway, not many!"

The Type AL Minerva was a luxury in which few could indulge as the Great Depression took hold on the Continent. In a desperate struggle to survive, the company introduced more modest models. Desperation was also the reason for the merger in 1934 with Imperia, the only other Belgian factory still manufacturing production cars. Thankfully, Sylvain de Jong did not live to see his company diminished. He had died in 1928 at age sixty. By 1938 the Minerva had seemingly breathed its last too. Two comebacks were attempted following World War II, the last one in 1956 fitting the emblem to a four-cylinder Continental-engined Jeep lookalike. Fortunately for the glory that had been Minerva, it did not succeed.

685

ROLLS·ROYCE

*The Flying Lady—on the left, with smaller wings and cylindrical base on Roger Morrison's
1927 Springfield Silver Ghost; on the right, on Bill Lester's 1937 Phantom III*

Some purists refer to the car only as a Royce. Others, less vociferously, suggest that the words surrounding the hyphen should be the other way around. Still, just how successfully Frederick Henry Royce, the miller's son, would have proceeded into the automobile industry without the collaboration of Charles Stewart Rolls, third son of Lord Langattock, is debatable. Probably any objective forum on the subject would conclude not far. Most certainly history was made that May day in 1904 when the two men met. Royce was a consummate engineer; Rolls, a prominent automobilist in England since his days at Cambridge, had the social clout to guarantee the new marque entrée to a distinguished clientele. By 1910, when Rolls was killed in a plane crash at Bournemouth at the age of thirty-three, Rolls-Royce Ltd. was settled, solidly and comfortably, into the one-model policy that had given birth to the immortal Silver Ghost. It was for this Rolls-Royce that the ''Spirit of Ecstasy''—the famous flying lady mascot—was introduced . . . and the slogan ''the best car in the world'' adopted. Horsepower figures were never quoted, the chassis cost figure was only whispered. ''The quality will remain,'' said Rolls-Royce, ''when the price is forgotten.'' By 1921 forgetting the price in $ was as convenient as forgetting it in £—for the Rolls-Royce was being manufactured in the United States. . . .

The two-to-three year backlog of orders in England following World War I was the reason the British company decided to open a factory in Springfield, Massachusetts. Rolls-Royce business genius Claude Johnson had no intention of neglecting the lucrative American market. The first product of Rolls-Royce of America, Inc. was an exact duplicate of the Silver Ghost as built in Derby. The price of the 143½-inch Springfield chassis was $11,750, a tad less than in England. Displacement of the venerable Silver Ghost six-cylinder engine was given in both liters (7.5) and cubic inches (453). Inevitably, certain American vestiges were allowed to intrude: soon virtually the entire electrical system was U.S.-made (American Bosch twin ignition with two spark plugs per cylinder) as were the Buffalo wheels. This, together with the later conversion to six volts, made service easier an ocean away from the parent factory. And a further bow was made to the American market. In England, Derby delivered only chassis; in Springfield, the Silver Ghost was also offered as a complete car in eleven different body designs (albeit often with fetchingly English designations) and constructed for Rolls-Royce by a variety of Eastern coachbuilding houses. So salutary was the Rolls-Royce business in America—320 cars in 1924—that the company established its own Rolls-Royce Custom Coach Work shop on Waltham Avenue in Springfield. But some traditions died hard. It was not until 1925 that Rolls-Royce of America was allowed to change to left-hand drive.

Roger Morrison's Silver Ghost, serialed S128MK, was one of the first left-hand drive chassis built in Springfield: "The Salamanca body, which is a convertible town car, is highly unusual and very complicated. The body portion of this car's $15,560 price tag was three times that of a standard tourer. The window frames on the doors and behind the driver are hinged and fold so that the car can be fully open as a tourer when the top is folded. All brightwork is either nickel plate or solid German silver. Factory specs called for a top gear speed range of 3 mph minimum to 70 mph maximum. The original owners of this car were silent movie stars Rod LaRocque and Vilma Banky. They purchased a Silver Ghost Tourer the same day. In 1935 the car was acquired by Warner

1925 Rolls-Royce (Springfield) Silver Ghost Salamanca Collapsible Town Car
Owner: Roger Morrison of Salina, Kansas   Photos: K. Karger
(start and run engine control levers below)

1925 Rolls-Royce (Springfield) Silver Ghost Roadster   *Owners: Berta & Jay Leon of Hubbard, Texas*

Brothers Studio and appeared in the John Wayne movie *Blood Alley*. In 1970, with approximately 50,000 actual miles, it was sold together with other studio cars. I've owned the Salamanca for over a decade and have met Miss Banky who recalled experiences she and her husband had with the car. For me, the best experience is the feeling when I drive it. I think about the heyday of Hollywood and an era that will never be repeated: the Roaring Twenties. The Salamanca's elegant proportions are indicative of the birth of the Classic period of automotive design.''

"Our Silver Ghost is special because it was Number One for us," comments Jay Leon. "In 1964, after acquiring the car in New York, Berta and I drove it home to Texas, taking a leisurely eleven days and doing a great deal of tourism along the way—and without a bit of trouble, even though the car still had the original tires. Must have been 'beginner's luck,' as it was the first Classic of many we would buy. After exhaustive investigation, we discovered that our car's original body was a Brewster Pall Mall which had been removed to another Springfield chassis and that this roadster body was from a Cole Aero-8. The car drives very well with enough power for high speeds but the gear ratios are such that the huge engine throbs at higher rpm.''

S370PL, the Fleetwood Silver Ghost owned by J. Carey Thomas, is noteworthy both for its coachwork and its previous owners: ''Fleetwood built only seven bodies for Springfield Ghosts, and this was the only open-body style produced. The car was originally ordered by T. F. (Tommy) Manville, the gentleman of fame for thirteen wives and heir to the Manville asbestos business. The

second owner was Dr. Allyn Roberts, who sold the car while in medical school and later repurchased it when he began his practice. It is believed that the car initially was a gift from the doctor's father, Montague Roberts, mechanic and co-pilot of the Thomas Flyer which won the New York to Paris 'round-the-world race of 1908. A plaque on the dash is in memory of Montague Roberts.''

1926 Rolls-Royce (Springfield) Silver Ghost Dual Cowl Tourer, Fleetwood
Owner: J. Carey Thomas of Pompano Beach, Florida

1926 Rolls-Royce Phantom I Torpedo Phaeton, Van den Plas   Owner: Blackhawk Classic Auto Collection, Danville, California

Revisionist historians enjoy decrying the Silver Ghost as merely modern when introduced and decidedly démodé when discontinued. This neatly overlooks the requisite excellence of any car that can remain in production for two decades. "Above rubies" was T. E. Lawrence's assessment of the Silver Ghost's value in the desert during World War I. Asked later what he desired most in the world, Lawrence of Arabia replied, "a Rolls-Royce with enough tyres and petrol to last me all my life."

By 1926 the Rolls-Royce would have been the New Phantom, which retrospectively became the Phantom I when the P-II was introduced a few years later. Overhead valves and refinement throughout distinguished the P-I's six-cylinder engine which, at 7668 cc and 467.9 cubic inches, was marginally larger than the Silver Ghost's. The New Phantom's chassis was essentially that of the old Ghost, though braking had been enhanced by adoption of a mechanical servo,

and a long 150½-inch wheelbase was added.

The Blackhawk Collection's Derby-built P-I carries coachwork by Van den Plas and the distinctive touch of the Belgian coachbuilder's premiere stylist, Alexis de Sakhnoffsky.

The Ford Museum's Springfield-built P-I Brewster Limousine was originally owned by J. P. Morgan, Jr. Comments curator Randy Mason, "This car is a great example of unrestrained opulence in one of America's wealthiest families."

1926 Rolls-Royce (Springfield) Phantom I Limousine, Brewster
Owner: Henry Ford Museum & Greenfield Village, Dearborn, Michigan

Of 1,241 Springfield Phantom I's produced in fifty-two body styles, just twenty were the Piccadilly which in turn was one of only two roadsters available. The Randells have owned their car a bit over a year, more than enough time to become thoroughly enamoured, as Alexandra explains: ''This quintessential roadster is a sports enthusiast's delight, having quick-detachable wire spoke wheels, rumble seat with side-opening door, collapsible windshield, wind wings, side curtains and rear-mounted luggage trunk. The chassis features drum headlights (the lenses of which, with age, have turned a beautiful rose color), servo-operated four-wheel brakes, enclosed driveshaft, crankshaft vibration damper, low-angle 'D' type steering, separate starting carburetor, twin ignition, centralized lubrication, vacuum fuel feed and driver-controlled adjustments for throttle, spark and fuel mixture. The car drives like a dream and has already provided us with experiences both numerous and bizarre. For instance, pulling up to a red light, a woman in the next car asked, 'It that a *real* Rolls-Royce?' Indeed it is! More than this particular Phantom I's rarity, we appreciate the rarity of its age because the car is a 'living' testament to an extinguished era. It lets us experience a time when there was an understanding that glitz is not glamour, when people dressed beautifully, when music was romantic with melody and lyrics of love. Our purchase was unique. The car wasn't found for us. We were found for the car. The gentleman who owned it wished to sell to a younger couple, but only if they understood and valued what he loved about the car. Only one friend of his was informed that the car was for sale, and he in turn was told to inform only potential buyers who met the requirements. The owner's friend and my husband had lunch one day. I have known Barry for eighteen years. Never before had I seen the look on his face that he wore when he walked in the door of our home that evening. He hadn't even yet *see* the car! The next day, when we did, we committed to buy it on the spot. We are slow-to-act, careful people. Love-at-first-sight had never happened to us before. This car made it happen, and the love affair continues.''

1927 Rolls-Royce (Springfield) Phantom I Piccadilly Roadster, Merrimac

Owners: Alexandra & Barry Randell of New York City, New York

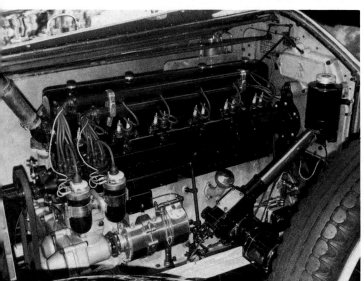

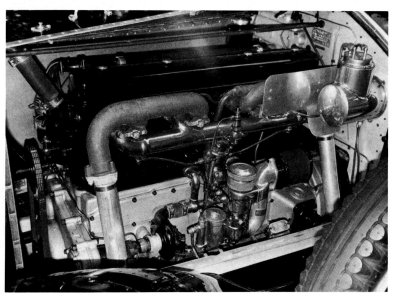

Joseph Carman's love affair with his Piccadilly Roadster is over three-and-a-half decades old: "As far as I can tell, there were six owners before me. The first was an M. Pratt of Rochester, New York and subsequently the car was owned awhile by Joe Sinel, an artist who did work on the 1928 Springfield catalogue. S268RM started life as a four-passenger Brewster Tourer but in 1929 became a Piccadilly Roadster. Body changing was a common practice in those days with new or old owners thinking little of requesting such work. After the many years of my ownership, this Phantom is truly a member of our family, having helped raise four children in addition to teaching them how to drive. The odometer now reads 112,000, telling me this wonderful machine has given us 25,000 miles of wonderful fun."

1927 Rolls-Royce (Springfield) Phantom I Piccadilly Roadster, Merrimac
Owner: Joseph L. Carman III of Tacoma, Washington

1927 Rolls-Royce (Springfield) Phantom I Trouville Town Car, Brewster   Owner: Walter E. Gosden of Floral Park, New York

In December of 1925 Rolls-Royce of America had acquired Brewster & Company, William Brewster remaining as its president and becoming a vice president of the Springfield company. The interesting history of Walt Gosden's P-I Brewster is this: "The first owner was Mildred F. Devereux of Nutwood Farm, Wickliffe, Ohio. The body at that time was a Paddington limousine, which Rolls-Royce junked for scrap in 1933 since it was an archaic style even when first fitted. The fenders, bumpers and lamps were updated when the new town car body was fitted. The German silver radiator shell and shutters remained, while other brightwork was chrome plated to be in vogue with cars of 1933. The car still has its original upholstery and finish on decorative woodwork. Brewster 'borrowed' the style and name of this body type from one shipped to the

firm from Hibbard & Darrin of Paris. It was carefully copied before mounting on the Springfield chassis. Rolls-Royce of America described the Trouville as a 'false cabriolet . . . a car of soothing graciousness.' The wheels remained their original twenty-one-inch size from the 1927 manufacture; the usual practice was to cut them down to make the up-dated car 'look modern' with the smaller wheel/tire size of the thirties. Following the Trouville rebody, the car was sold to Gustave Myers, a prominent author and historian of that era. I became its owner in 1987. Despite its 5,750 pounds, the car has lots of power and can run at low speeds in traffic in humid warm weather with not a trace of vapor-lock! It handles quite well if given adequate room in which to maneuver; the steering is light at higher speeds, quite ponderous at low speed. Interestingly, the original book of instruction quotes fuel consumption as one gallon per eleven to thirteen miles. This was most optimistic, since the car is a very thirsty beggar preferring a gallon every six miles. To me, the town car body style is the epitome of elegance from the Classic Era. Although a formal design, it has a fairly low roof line, particularly in the rear quarter section. As an open car or an almost 'sporty' closed car with roof enclosed over the front compartment, this P-I has panache."

The trend in Europe following World War I was toward smaller cars for a wider market. The Twenty or 20 H.P. was introduced in Derby in 1922 to answer that demand. Since a similar desire did not exist in the United States, the car was seldom seen here. The first small R-R Henry Royce had designed since 1906, the 20 H.P. was a splendid 3127 cc overhead valve six in a 129-inch chassis. Production through 1929 totaled 2,940 cars.

Tim Sharon has owned his 20 H.P. with coachwork by Hooper & Company Ltd. since 1985: "This was a special-ordered one-of-a-kind car built to look like an 1890's horse-drawn carriage with leather fenders and covered step-plates to keep the inside clean. The man who ordered it at the Paris Rolls-Royce office was Juan Pedro Baro of Cuba, but he never took delivery. Instead, Hooper sold the car to Mrs. E. Hutton of New York. It was shipped from London on December 13th, 1928 on the *S.S. Caronia*. Some time in the early thirties, Doris Duke acquired the car. But the American Tobacco heiress and Duke University patroness used it little. From the late thirties, the 20 H.P. was successively in the collections of James Melton, Winthrop Rockefeller and William Harrah. Because most of its life had been spent in museums, the car had only 10,932 miles when I bought it at a Harrah auction. The car is nick-named 'Miss D' for Doris Duke."

1927 Rolls-Royce 20 H.P. Sedanca de Ville, Hooper
Owner: Tim Sharon of La Crescenta, California

1928 Rolls-Royce (Springfield) Phantom I St. Stephen Landaulette, Brewster
Owners: Berta & Jay Leon of Hubbard, Texas

''This early Phantom I has an iron cylinder head, later ones had an aluminum head,'' comments Jay Leon of the P-I he and Berta have owned since 1975. ''Records indicate that this Brewster body was referred to as a St. Stephen Formal Landaulette and that the car was first sold to a Mrs. Lena Dolmetsch of New York City. We purchased this Rolls-Royce in Kalamazoo, Michigan and drove it home to Texas with no problems. Despite its bulk, the car is easy to manage, once you get it out of tight spots. It can hold seven people easily, so we drive it for special visitors. Anyone who comes to Hubbard from the outside is a special visitor.''

The Zukers' P-I was the second of thirty Ascots produced and its body one of four that was put on the ''iron-head engine'' chassis. Explains Lee: ''At some time early in the car's life, it was modified to the configuration of the later post-1928 Ascots. Changes included replacing the cylindrically-shaped lights by conical ones and the round tubular bumpers by flat ones. Also, the dash was replaced by the later version which contained glove boxes, and the top frame changed to the shape of the Derby model, that is, sloped forward to the back rather than being vertical. S307KP was originally sold to film director Roy Del Ruth who sold it two years later to Hamilton Garland of Beverly Hills. The list price was $17,800. In 1936 the car was shipped back to the Boston sales office of Rolls-Royce and was purchased by W. E. Edel of Boston. The afore-mentioned changes were made either before delivery to the first owner or when the car returned to the East Coast, since at that time new Brewster Ascot bodies were still being put on older chassis.''

1928 Rolls-Royce (Springfield) Phantom I Ascot Tourer, Brewster   *Owners: Lee & Marlene Zuker of Bellevue, Washington*

1928 Rolls-Royce (Springfield) Phantom I Speedster Phaeton, Brewster   Owner: Rick Carroll of Jensen Beach, Florida

The unique rear fenders set the Speedster apart from the Derby phaeton. Just three of these cars survive. This one was originally owned by Herbert Farrell, son-in-law of Colonel J. O. Cheek, founder of Maxwell House Coffee. The late Rick Carroll told a wonderful story about the first owner for this book: ''Mr. Farrell was informed the Speedster would do better than 85 mph but he could not get over 76. Rolls-Royce dispatched Art Soutter and Tom Colvin to Nashville to find the missing 9 mph. Following valve adjustments and such, and two trial runs, the desired speed was achieved. Mr. Farrell was asked to get in for a demonstration ride. 'Have you done it?,' he asked Art Soutter. Assured that he had, the now delighted owner said, 'That's all I wanted to know. I'll take your word for it'.''

1928 Rolls-Royce (Springfield) Phantom I Convertible Touring, Locke
Owners: Jeff Davis & Jim Stickley of Cedar Rapids, Iowa

In 1988 Jeff Davis & Jim Stickley became the third owners of the Locke P-I: ''The first owner was Jeremiah Milbank, a famous barrister of New York and Greenwich, Connecticut. The second owner was James F. Bragg, president of U.S. Steel in its heyday. The car spent its entire life in a heated garage and showed 34,342 miles when we bought it, which is accurate as the original pedal pads were only somewhat worn. It gives one a sense of history to replace the radiator hose for the first time in a car that is over fifty years old. Then there was the joy of discovering the original jack, tools and owner's handbook in its protective cover in the toolbox. How many times do you get two sets of original keys with a newly-purchased Classic? Nowadays you are lucky to get a title. S177RP came with its original registration slip from 1928, the current registration, two letters from the Connecticut Department of Transportation explaining why no title was necessary and a letter from the probate judge! In the rear compartment are his and hers vanities with the items still inside plus the original Locke clock. The instruments work beautifully. The car was painted in the fifties and retrimmed in the seventies. Shortly after our purchase we took it to a concours and placed third without sweaty preparation of any kind. A truly happy car! Factory records describe the unique one-off coachwork as a convertible touring car. The uniqueness derives from the fact that the coach does not have roll-up windows but can be enclosed in glass in inclement weather. Basically, there are four panels of glass that, when folded, form a division window. The rear panels can be folded out and attached to the rear doors to enclose the rear compartment. In like manner, the front panels can be rotated forward to enclose the front compartment when the adjustable wind wings are closed. This arrangement makes for a very versatile, comfortable and sporty vehicle. In addition to the handsome styling, which seems to be fetching from any angle, the car's major attraction is its unspoiled and well-cared-for demeanor. It literally drives and steers like new, with a pleasing ride and no eccentricities. The car starts instantly even at 30° ambient and breaks into a smooth quiet idle. The original exhaust system is still fitted.''

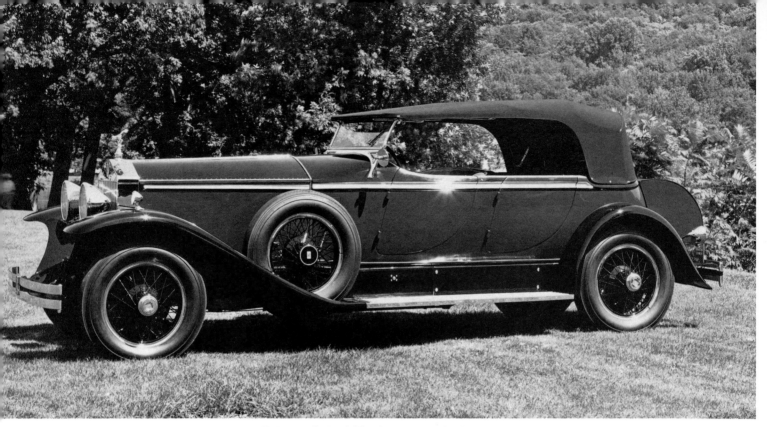

1929 Rolls-Royce (Springfield) Phantom I Derby Phaeton, Brewster
Owner: Virgil Millett of Huntington, New York   Photo: K. Karger

"The Derby style to me is the most beautiful and appealing of all Rolls-Royce designs," comments Virgil Millett of his P-I. "It captured the sleek look not found in many British and American coachbuilt bodies. I believe this car introduced 'style' to Rolls-Royce coachwork."

The first owner of the P-I York Roadster was Tommy Manville, who perhaps changed cars more often than he did wives. He kept this Rolls-Royce less than a year. Bill Davis acquired the car in 1962: "Put very simply, I think it is the most handsome open body built by Brewster for Rolls-Royce. It is the roadster variant of the Derby phaeton body. One of my English friends refers to the car as 'that smashing two-seater.' I confess. I agree."

1929 Rolls-Royce (Springfield) Phantom I York Roadster, Brewster
Owner: William M. Davis of Charleston, West Virginia   Photo: K. Karger

Stephen Brauer's Rolls-Royce was one of about thirty Ascot Tourers built on the Phantom I chassis: "The car was delivered new to C. M. Rice, Jr. of Worcester, Massachusetts in August of 1929. I've owned S226KR for ten years. The price new for the Ascot was $17,250. By comparison, a 1929 Chevrolet phaeton was $495, a '29 Cadillac sport phaeton $3,950. After minor restoration, I participated in the 1987 CCCA CARavan through the Rocky Mountains. The P-I serenely cruised up and over the 12,183-foot-high Trail Ridge Road pass, while a lot of other Classics coughed, sputtered and frequently died."

1929 Rolls-Royce (Springfield) Phantom I Ascot Tourer, Brewster   *Owner: Stephen F. Brauer of Bridgeton, Missouri*

1929 Rolls-Royce (Springfield) Phantom I Riviera Town Car, Brewster   Owner: Robert E. McVoy of Poland, New York

That New York State Governor Nelson Rockefeller chauffeured Bob McVoy in his P-I is a nice reversal of the usual, among other unusual facets of the Rolls-Royce Bob has owned since 1965: "The speedometer had 50,000 miles when I bought it. There was no rust or rot, and all the original wood. Of the six Riviera Town Cars built, this is the only one with gold-plated interior and exterior trim. The windshield has a real rake to it and folds forward like a roadster. The canework, upholstery and inlay on the rear section are original. It has a snap-on roof and the original side curtains. The buffed aluminum hood really sets it off. It is believed the car was originally purchased by beer baron (and Yankee baseball team owner) Jacob Ruppert for a New York showgirl. She must have been some gal."

Steve Hiltebrant's P-I has had nearly as many lives as the proverbial cat: "This was one of the last cars ever rebodied by Rolls-Royce's Massachusetts division. The first owner was a Mrs. C. Rosenbloom. Repossessed in 1933, the chassis remained in Springfield after the decision was made to close the plant. The Newmarket body was added to improve appearance and, with its tilted windshield, it did that. The car overall is a real eye-catcher. But it had to be to sell during the

Depression. Sold again, it was repossessed in 1949 by J. S. Inskip, the former Rolls-Royce of America president and then Rolls-Royce dealer in New York City. In all, it appears that the chassis has had six owners, the body five. I've owned the car since 1972."

The P-I Regent that Jack Trefney has owned since 1951 was originally ordered by Wesson Seyburn, described in Detroit newspaper obituaries as a "financier and socialite." His widow Winifred was the daughter of John Dodge, one of the two automotive Dodge Brothers.

1929 Rolls-Royce (Springfield) Phantom I Newmarket Convertible Sedan, Brewster
Owner: Steve Hiltebrant of Sagamore Hills, Ohio

*1929 Rolls-Royce (Springfield) Phantom I Regent Convertible Coupe, Brewster
Owner: Jack Trefney of Bedford Heights, Ohio*

When purchased by Jack, the car had 49,000 miles. Now mileage is up to 92,000, among the car's extended trips being the very first CCCA CARavan to Detroit in 1953. "S137FR was the first Regent-bodied Phantom I with the up-to-date slant windshield," comments Jack. "There are earlier chassis numbers with Regent convertible coupe bodies; however, these are rebodied chassis which J. S. Inskip/Rolls-Royce did in the early thirties in order to sell the glut of town cars. Twenty-one Regents were built in all. One of the interesting features of this body is the entrance door to the rumble seat; most convertible coupes of that era had step-plates which made for a very awkward entry. Another outstanding feature is the Jaeger Chronograph, an eight-day stop watch, on the dashboard, surrounded by the other instruments. This chronograph is the same one used in the Duesenberg automobiles. Brewster used an extensive amount of aluminum in the construction of bodies for Rolls-Royce. The body is a wooden framework with aluminum skin, the hood and firewall also aluminum. In the chassis, the cylinder head, crankcase, oil pan and transmission case are aluminum. The fenders are steel. Still, even with the extensive use of aluminum, my Rolls-Royce tips the scales at 5,400 pounds. But it was a very fast, comfortable, reliable and trouble-free automobile which accounts for the rather high survival rate today."

1930 Rolls-Royce (Springfield) Phantom I Huntington Sedan, Brewster
(sidemount wheel and instrument board on page opposite)
Owner: Jon P. Leimkuehler of Pittsburgh, Pennsylvania

"This is an exceptionally large seven-passenger sedan and so was just what I was looking for to accommodate my wife and five children," reports Jon Leimkuehler regarding his P-I Huntington. "The man I bought it from had won it in a raffle. His comment was, 'Everybody else wins a new car or a boat, but I was unlucky enough to win this old one.' His dislike for the car worked to my benefit. I enjoy this Rolls-Royce so much and have put so much time and effort into it that I plan never to sell it. Records indicate that the first person to whom the P-I was sold was Mrs. A. L. Purcell on October 8th, 1932. On July 2nd, 1935 Rolls-Royce received information that the car was owned by Frederick Coyne of Long Island, with the notation that it had been sold to him by the Duesenberg company. Thereafter, until 1958, the car was in storage in a Brooklyn warehouse, wearing its 1937 license plates. Several other people owned it from that date until 1981 when the Rolls-Royce was donated to the Cleveland Heights Athletic League and won for a $1.00 ticket by somebody who thought himself unlucky. Now I'm the lucky one."

1930 Rolls-Royce (Springfield) Phantom I Regent Convertible Coupe, Brewster
Owner: Robert S. Daryman of York, Pennsylvania

Although Bob Daryman has owned his P-I Regent Convertible Coupe for only two years, he has already been able to find out a good deal about it which, with the help of his son, he relates: ''I purchased the car at an auction held by an old gentleman who had acquired the car from a scrapyard in Scranton, Pennsylvania in 1951. It had sat in his shed until June of 1988. After acquisition came research and I learned that the car had been sold new to Robert McCormick of Chicago in April of 1933. McCormick was, of course, the publisher of the *Chicago Tribune*. I thought the car to be a coupe but when I began dismantling it for restoration, something very interesting transpired. The car actually was a Regent convertible with a fixed top. I wondered why Col. McCormick (1) bought this type car and (2) had it altered this way. The answer came from the First Division Museum in Wheaton, Illinois. This museum was founded as a memorial to the McCormick family. It seems Col. McCormick was at odds with Al Capone and was waging his own war with the famous gangster via his newspaper. Early in 1933 Capone had one of the *Tribune*'s reporters gunned down in broad daylight. At the time the Colonel was being chauffeur-driven around Chicago in a Rolls-Royce town car. As his battle with Capone intensified, those close to McCormick felt his motoring style made him too easy a target for Capone's henchmen. Because time was a factor, a new car was needed in a hurry, hence the purchase of the Regent convertible. The vehicle was altered with a fixed top to allow McCormick to inconspicuously ride in the front with his body guard and to accommodate his six-feet-six-inch body. That is as far as I've been able to get thus far with this car's history. I do not know when the car left McCormick's estate or how it ended up scrapped in Scranton, Pennsylvania. But I hope to find out.''

The Phantom II, introduced in 1929, was the first new car from Henry Royce's drawing board in four years. Its predecessor P-I's 100 horses from 7.7 liters had not been a figure to shout about and though Rolls-Royce never published horsepower figures, extra oomph was clearly needed to stay abreast of the competition. With a cross-flow cylinder head, separate inlet ports, better manifolding and higher compression, another 20 hp or more was realized in the P-II. The clutch housing and gearbox were now built in unit with the engine; new to the chassis was Hotchkiss drive to a hypoid rear axle, which allowed a lower floor line.

The new Phantom II was good news in England but rocked Rolls-Royce of America to its foundation. As the reader may have inferred from the narrative thus far, Springfield had been hit hard by the stock market crash. The company simply

couldn't afford to tool up for production of the P-II. Considerable parts for P-I's remained, however, and Springfield continued to put these cars together and sell them as new for the next several years at prices greatly reduced from pre-Depression levels. Derby supplied Springfield approximately 125 left-hand-drive P-II chassis as well which would be cloaked with Brewster coachwork. But the Rolls-Royce manufacturing days in America would soon be history. Jack Inskip designed a new Brewster on a Ford V-8 chassis, which horrified Rolls-Royce but not enough to banish Inskip from Rolls-Roycedom. He remained a dealer thereafter, and very successfully once America recovered from the Great Depression.

Bill Greer's P-II Barker Sedancalette is fascinating because its owner lived on one side of the Atlantic and the car on the other: "Andrew N. Jergens, whose business was Jergens

1930 Rolls-Royce Phantom II Sedancalette, Barker

Owner: William Greer of Indianapolis, Indiana

Lotion, ordered the Phantom II for touring Britain and Europe. Special Brooks touring trunks were specified as well as D.S.M. spares and tool-boxes under the running boards. There are five large hinged louvers on each side of the hood to vent the engine plus double lower louvers and a large upper one on the cowl for passenger comfort. All the bright-work is silver plate except the radiator shell, louvers and running board trim which are of 'Staybrite,' a type of stainless steel. Perhaps the most interesting detail is the adjustable rear seat. Mounted on a track, it can be positioned in the blind quarter or cranked forward so that the rear passengers can enjoy the window and footrests. Another detail is the backward rake of the division window at half mast. The speedometer is in both mph and kph. The car was kept in England from 1930 to 1961, and was occasionally flown to France for touring. I think it somewhat unusual for an owner to maintain a car with driver ready to go for over three decades, particularly when the car resided in London and the owner in Cincinnati, Ohio. In 1972 I purchased this car from its second owner, Ray Sadler of Indianapolis. I appreciate the versatility of the elegant body style which includes a stylish padded top, convertible front with adjustable windshield, crankdown division,

facing jump seats and the aforementioned adjustable rear seat. The long 150-inch wheelbase easily accommodates seven passengers, and the Sedancalette can be used as a town car, formal or touring sedan, or as a limousine. This Rolls-Royce remains essentially original and has been much driven. Total mileage is unknown. The minimum is 125,000+; 225,000 is very possible.''

In 1928 the 20 H.P. had metamorphosed into the 20/25. The engine was bored out to 224 cubic inches; the wheelbase was increased from 129 to 132 inches. This small Rolls-Royce continued in production with refinements into 1936.

Susan Partington has owned her 20/25 Thrupp & Maberly Convertible Saloon for a decade and a half: ''This is an owner-driver car, a 'country car' needing no bumpers. It has a Tickford top (state of the art at that time) which rolls back with a crank (kept under the driver's seat) inserted at the left rear of the car. It is characteristic of Rolls-Royce that each tool rests in a specially formed place in the tool carrier beneath the driver's seat. Purportedly, the original owner was Winston Churchill, which was the reason for the continuation book being missing when we purchased the car (because of the value of Churchill's signature). The car has had many owners. We heard that once it changed hands in a very high-stakes poker game! Total mileage is about 600,000. Following our purchase from a man in Milwaukee who had it in a barn, the car was completely restored. The true charm of a Classic is not just in 'viewing' it but in 'experiencing' it. To sit on the down-filled real leather cushion seats of this Rolls-Royce is like sitting in a big, comfortable overstuffed chair in your own den.''

1932 Rolls-Royce 20/25 H.P. Convertible Saloon, Thrupp & Maberly   *Owner: Susan T. Partington of Palm Beach, Florida*

1932 Rolls-Royce Phantom II Continental Roadster, James Young

Owner: W. G. Lassiter, Jr. of West Palm Beach, Florida

With all due reverence, the Continental model might be described as the hot Rolls-Royce of its era. Probably the Schneider Trophy was the impetus for its production. In 1929 the famous air race had been won by a Rolls-Royce-engined Supermarine S6, returning the prestigious cup to Britain and earning a baronetcy for Henry Royce from George V. In the ensuing festivities, Sir Henry was introduced to aviators and other sportsmen who preferred driving to being chauffeured, and driving fast to merely motoring. The P-II Continental was a genuine 90 mph car—all two-and-a-half fully equipped tons of it. The chassis was the short 144-inch wheelbase. Initially, Rolls-Royce had balked at introducing this model, so Sir Henry said he would just build one for himself. Thereafter, entreaties from sporting Britons anxious to have one like it changed the company's mind.

An English sportswoman was the first owner of Bill Lassiter's P-II Continental. She was Betty Carstairs, a noted racing boat pilot and sometimes Brooklands competitor of that era. She named the car ''Atalanta II,'' after one of her favorite racing boats. This Rolls-Royce resided for many years in the Briggs Cunningham Collection.

Andrew D. Darling has owned his P-II Brewster Sports Sedan for nearly four decades: ''289AJS is one of two of this style originally purchased from J. S. Inskip. Both cars were ordered by the same family, one for the owner's use, mine as a wedding present to his daughter. This is an original car and one I've driven around 30,000 exciting miles, including many 300-500 mile trips. The coachwork was very advanced for its time, the chrome-framed windows being a forerunner of the four-door hardtop. The hood extends all the way to the vee windshield. And I love the beautiful mahogany running boards. The car uses no striping but is trimmed in burnished aluminum. The original equipment side mirror was delivered new with the car. The sloped rear deck provides this Phantom II exquisite proportions.''

1933 Rolls-Royce Phantom II Sports Sedan, Brewster
Owner: Andrew D. Darling of Edina, Minnesota

1933 Rolls-Royce Phantom II Trouville Sedanca de Ville, Brewster
Owner: James H. M. Partington of Palm Beach, Florida

Also owned for nearly four decades is James Partington's P-II Brewster Trouville: "I am the second owner, having purchased 214AMS from a friend, Harold F. LeBaron. I have forgotten the name of the man who ordered the car but I recall that he paid Inskip $23,000 for it in 1933 and that he was president of the New York Central Railway System. Mr. LeBaron married his widow. Originally, the first owner's Silver Ghost body was installed on this P-II but then he changed his mind and had the Brewster people build a new body in 1935. Mr. and Mrs. LeBaron laid the car up in Long Island City after their chauffeur left. He was asked to clean the venetian blinds in their River House apartment, which offended him. 'Rolls-Royce chauffeurs do not clean venetian blinds,' he said upon departing. This Phantom II is one of twenty-two in Rolls-Royce's AMS chassis series. Original mileage is 98,000. The car is in active use. This P-II has taken many brides to the church (always on time!). In forty years, it has never let me down."

1933 Rolls-Royce Phantom II Continental Sedanca Coupe, H. J. Mulliner
Owner: Mark Tuttle of Shadow Hills, California

H.H. the Prince of Nepal was the first owner of Jeff Davis' P-II Continental: "His Highness and his family lived in London after he was deposed as ruler of the mountain kingdom. He loved France and was frequently seen in Paris at the Hotel Georges V. This car originally had a Windovers saloon body. By 1936 His Highness was contemplating trading in the P-II for a new P-III but changed his mind. The reason: Figoni & Falaschi whose coachwork on Delahaye chassis he had admired during his visits to Paris. The P-II's long bonnet and positioning of the radiator over the front axle was a better basis for the execution of the Figoni design philosophy than the P-III with its radiator ahead of the axle. Besides, the P-II Continental provided the Prince of Nepal all he required in a fast touring car. So in August 1936 the new coachwork was installed. This Figoni & Falaschi body is the only one ever fitted to a P-II Rolls. By tipping all vertical lines to a ten-degree rearward slope, the body gives the impression of surging power, that the car is being pulled forward and stretched out like a straining and flexing muscle. This is the largest automobile bodied by Figoni & Falaschi and demonstrates how sports car design philosophy can still apply to a large sedan. Figoni succeeded in creating a visibly dynamic form. Precisely when the Prince of Nepal relinquished the car is not known. I can find no record of its whereabouts from 1939 to 1945. From that point it passed through a half-dozen owners—including Capt. Frederick Henry who traded his Binder-bodied Bugatti Royale for it in 1951. I acquired the car in 1985 following ten years of neglect. It is now in the last stages of a complete renaissance. This sole example of the design genius of Figoni & Falaschi on the P-II chassis will soon be on the road again."

"Just 281 P-II Continentals were produced," comments Mark Tuttle of the Rolls-Royce he has owned for over a quarter-century. "Mine is believed to be the only example of the half-dozen or so Mulliner bodies of this design extant with a rear-mounted spare. The others have side-mounts. The three-position drophead coupe styling is among the most striking English coachwork from this era of Classic design."

1933 Rolls-Royce Phantom II Continental Pillarless Saloon, Figoni & Falaschi
Owner: Jeff K. Davis of Bombay, India

1933 Rolls-Royce Phantom II Sedanca de Ville, Gurney Nutting
Owner: Philip Reed of Whittier, California

Philip Reed has owned his P-II Gurney Nutting Sedanca de Ville since 1977.

The Windovers P-II Sedanca de Ville joined the other Classics in the Leon collection in 1986. "This is an excellent example of Rolls-Royce understated elegance," comments Jay. "With a wheelbase of 150 inches, the car has an excellent ride. The driver compartment opens up, there is a divider window and a phone connecting the passenger with the chauffeur. Rolls-Royce records indicate this car was owned originally by G. E. Philcox of London."

1933 Rolls-Royce Phantom II Sedanca de Ville, Windovers   *Owners: Berta & Jay Leon of Hubbard, Texas*

1933 Rolls-Royce 20/25 H.P. Sedanca Coupe, Freestone & Webb　　　　　　*Owner: Dr. James J. Stickley of Cedar Rapids, Iowa*

''The beauty of this car is its 'one-off' sedanca coachwork by Freestone & Webb,'' says James Stickley about his 20/25. ''The sculptured contours of the wings and the sweep of the fender line are very graceful. There are special compartments under the seats for the top irons. This 20/25 represents the intention by the factory and coachbuilder to produce a very special and expensive car that the owner was expected to drive himself, an extraordinary social statement for the era. I prefer this Freestone & Webb design to that of the popular Owen-Gurney Nutting sedanca coupe because the trunk is not as massive and boxy; moreover, the treatment of the rear wings as they sweep down and mold into the valance between trunk and wings shows an unusual attention to detail. It must have taken a world-class panel beater to accomplish this.''

1933 Rolls-Royce Phantom II Henley Roadster, Brewster   *Owner: Rick Carroll of Jensen Beach, Florida*

The P-II Henley Roadster became part of the Carroll collection five years ago. Prior to his death, Rick wrote about it for this book: "The AJS series Phantom II was imported from England during the Depression under strict trade agreements. Only the chassis was sent, no mascot, tools, spark plugs, bumpers or coachwork. Brewster did the body. The result was an American-Anglican combination with the best of both countries. This particular car was originally owned by E. L. King, banker and owner of the Watkins Company. Eight P-II Henley Roadsters were produced and are considered by many collectors as the most beautiful Classic Rolls-Royce built. The Henley drives like a dream and, with the 150-inch wheelbase, feels like it is floating on water. It is a delightfully roomy Classic meant to be driven and enjoyed."

1933 Rolls-Royce Phantom II Continental Sedanca Coupe, Owen-Gurney Nutting
Owner: Dr. Gerard E. Schultz of Clarence, New York

"Absolutely gorgeous styling," enthuses Gerard Schultz regarding his Gurney Nutting P-II Continental which was originally owned by Anthony de Rothschild of London.

Bill Davis' Barker P-II Continental was ordered new by a gentleman from Paris who apparently was unable to complete the purchase. The car was retained by Rolls-Royce and sold two years later to Lord Farington. Bill has owned it since 1984: "The car's great moment in the sun came in 1935 when it was used by H. M. King George V to review the Royal Air Force at Mindenhall. In today's parlance, this was a 'photo opportunity' and is well documented photographically. I like this car's looks, especially the long hood which extends beyond the firewall into the scuttle and the low windscreen. And mechanically it is very strong—to the top of Trail Ridge (12,000 feet plus) on the vacuum tank without incident, for example. The car is a joy to drive on the open road. I have loved every moment of my ownership and look forward to more pleasant times in the future."

1933 Rolls-Royce Phantom II Continental Tourer, Barker
Owner: William M. Davis of Charleston, West Virginia   Photo: K. Karger

1934 Rolls-Royce 20/25 H.P. Sedanca de Ville, Hooper   *Owner: Dennis Somerville of Arlington, Washington*

"This car has a boot like a sports saloon; however, it is a sedanca de ville with formal division glass," comments Dennis Somerville of his 20/25. "Opera lamps are nice for the mid-thirties. The first owner was P. H. Bushell, Esq. of England. This car has a special long bonnet that extends all the way to the windscreen—rare for a British Rolls-Royce and pretty for a Hooper."

1934 Rolls-Royce Phantom II Continental Sedanca Coupe, Owen-Gurney Nutting

Owner: Duncan H. Bull of Fairport, New York

"My car is one of about fifteen sedanca coupes, or three-position dropheads, built by J. Gurney Nutting on a P-II Continental chassis," comments Duncan H. Bull. "This was the first year for a synchromesh gearbox on the Phantom II. The six-cylinder 7.5-liter engine powers this Classic smoothly and aggressively down the road as it turns many heads."

1934 Rolls-Royce Phantom II Continental Sedanca Coupe, Owen-Gurney Nutting   *Owner: Matthew Sonfield of Syosset, New York*

Of the 1,767 Phantom II's produced from 1929 through 1935, 281 were the Continental model. T. J. Hughes of Liverpool and London was the first owner of Matt Sonfield's Continental. Matt explains the reason for its hyphenated coachbuilder reference: ''This car was the product of an unusual business arrangement in which the body style was built (and probably designed) by Gurney Nutting, but the design was registered and promoted by H. R. Owen, a London Rolls-Royce retailer. 'The prize winner at nearly every important Concours d'Elegance both in England and on the Continent,' the Owen catalogue said. And noted English automotive writer Lawrence Dalton, publisher of many books on Rolls-Royce, has commented that 'the combination of this Gurney Nutting body and the Phantom II Continental chassis is considered by many to produce the finest and most elegant grand touring motor car of its day.' I agree!''

1934 Rolls-Royce 20/25 H.P.
Sedanca Coupe, Owen-Gurney Nutting

Owner: Charles B. Gillet
of Baltimore, Maryland

Lady Castlerosse of London and Tony Curtis of Hollywood were among the previous owners of Charles Gillet's 20/25 Sedanca Coupe: "The charm of this car is that it combines elegance and sportiveness in a *small* Rolls-Royce. During this period many coachbuilders were creating a variety of body styles for Rolls-Royce. Some were less successful than others, especially when viewed today. But Gurney Nutting always got it 'right.' His designs today look as fresh and clean as they did over a half-century ago."

1934 Rolls-Royce Phantom II All Weather Tourer, Gurney Nutting
Owner: Jean Gorjat of Harrisburg, Pennsylvania

"Phantom II's incorporated many technical improvements over P-I's," comments Mort Bullock, "and they are far less complicated to maintain than P-III's. Notable features include the power-assist servo braking system, locking wheel hubs and synchromesh on third and fourth gears. Phantom II's are my favorite of all Rolls-Royce cars. They perform well on the road, are extremely reliable and have superb styling. In my opinion, 55RY is one of the most desirable of all the P-II's."

The Gorjat P-II is a low-mileage (54,000) original car, and Jean explains why: "The first owner was a Scotsman and only used it when required for important functions! The all-aluminum body provides closed car comfort with the windows in or sporty touring with the dual cowl and *sans* windows. The car drives like new, with hydraulic correction of damping according to speed. I bought it in '84 and drove it on the Paris-Deauville Rally in '85."

1934 Rolls-Royce Phantom II Continental Drophead Coupe, H. J. Mulliner
Owner: Morton Bullock of Baltimore, Maryland   Photo: K. Karger

1934 Rolls-Royce Phantom II Sedanca de Ville, Thrupp & Maberly
Owner: Tyrnn M. Long of Issaquah, Washington

Thrupp & Maberly built three sedanca de ville bodies for the Phantom II chassis. The car that Tyrnn Long has owned for a decade is the only one believed to exist: "The original owner was Lady Mendl, the former Elsie de Wolfe, noted for her successive careers as a Broadway stage star, interior decorator and international hostess. She lived near Versailles, France which is the reason this car sports Marchal headlamps rather than the usual Lucas P-100 units. Her biography was subtitled 'A Life in the High Style.' And that was certainly true. When the Germans invaded France, Lady Mendl left and stayed just ahead of the advancing Third Reich army. Her fifty-four pieces of luggage followed, closely, in a Ford station wagon. She used this Rolls to escape to Spain and then to America."

Jeff Broderick's P-II by Barker is one of just two produced in this body style: "This magnificent automobile is the essence of the Classic Era. It is a chauffeur-driven design with division window complete with 'Halls' Flap' for instructions to the driver. The chauffeur's compartment is black leather and can be totally enclosed or opened to the elements. The whims of the wealthy were many and varied. The windshield opens out completely and is covered for its entire length by a tinted sunscreen of glass. The passenger compartment is opulence extended. The upholstery is hand-done needlepoint and the woodwork (as in the driver's compartment) is the rare tiger maple and Art Deco styled. Twin vanities are in the solid rear quarters. The interior also carries two center-facing additional seats on each side of a complete Waterford crystal-stocked bar. There are two trunks: the standard-sized enclosed variety and one equipped with extending arms to hold a touring trunk with matched luggage for Continental touring. Details on this car abound. The sterling silver carriage lamps have a lapis lens on the outermost side which matches the dark blue paint of the exterior. On the scuttle is a second mascot of German silver, a Hart deer, placed there by Barker at the request of the first owner. He was Charles Jeffery Hart and it was for his family that this species of red deer was named. Hart was killed during World War II; his widow stored the car until the fifties. It passed through four more owners prior to my acquisition. Since buying the car in 1987, I have driven it extensively. With a 150-inch wheelbase, this P-II is enormous but is an absolute pleasure to drive. One would think a car of this size would

require constant shifting but just the opposite is true. Once in fourth gear, the driver rarely has to downshift except in traffic, and turnpike speeds are an easy lope for an engine that is

one of the largest and quietest sixes ever produced. Whether in the chauffeur's or passenger's compartment, the feeling of absolute elegance is overpowering."

1934 Rolls-Royce Phantom II Sedanca de Ville, Barker
Owner: Jeffery P. Broderick of Gap, Pennsylvania

1934 Rolls-Royce Phantom II Continental Close-Coupled Saloon, Barker

Owners: Berta & Jay Leon of Hubbard, Texas

Details abound as well in the Leons' P-II by Barker, as Jay explains: ''The car is graced with two huge Marchal headlamps. The instruments were specially ordered to include a large Bentley-type speedometer, tachometer and clock, with navy blue dials on all instruments. Also specified was an unusual blueish green shade on the windshield and silk window screens hidden in the wood window sills. The trunk is an integral part of the body. 83RY was originally ordered by Hugh Tevis of Wynberg, who requested all these special features for traveling in South Africa. However, he never took possession of the car. Three years later it was acquired by Douglas Fairbanks, Jr. for use as his London transport. The movie actor brought the car to the U.S. at the beginning of World War II. It reappeared in England in 1947 and went through various owners, ending up in Zimbabwe whence it was taken back to the U.S. to coincide with the independence of that country. When I purchased the car in 1978, it had Zimbabwe license plates.''

The original owner of this Phantom II Limousine de Ville was Gracie Fields, the famous English singer who became a star as well in American films. Gordon Dysart has owned it for nearly two decades: ''This was the last year for the Phantom II and its 7.6-liter (468-cubic-inch) engine, the largest built by Rolls-Royce for automobiles. I like the dual ignition (spark plugs on both sides of the engine, one side using coil and distributor, the other magneto) which can be switched one to the other or both used. The twelve-volt system is very good, as are the servo brakes, adjustable shock absorbers, electric wipers, built-in wheel balancers and jacks, extra oil to cylinders when started, four-speed gearbox and detailed workmanship throughout. The coachwork was handmade from thick aluminum sheets, an art that almost terminated at the beginning of World War II. Most English cars of this period were black, or had black fenders, but Miss Fields had this one painted two-tone blue. The car was well known in London as she used it for theatre, shopping and parties—chauffeur-driven only, of course. It survived the bombing of London and was not driven for the six years of the war. The car arrived in Texas in 1969. In 1975 Miss Fields wrote me from Capri, saying 'So you've got the very, very old Rolls-Royce . . . like Johnny Walker and me, still going strong!' She called it 'the Posh Car'—I agree.''

1935 Rolls-Royce Phantom II Limousine de Ville, Gurney Nutting
Owner: Gordon R. Dysart of Dallas, Texas

720

"Excellent body lines and a great road car" is Ted Warner's capsule summary of the 20/25 by Mann-Egerton that he and Helen have owned for six years: "In full parlance, the car is a Continental touring close-coupled sport saloon. Production records from Mann-Egerton indicate that 500 cars were bodied by this coachbuilding company during its tenure from 1901 to 1938. Mann-Egerton was noted for excellent finish, good workmanship, durability and soundness. Today the firm serves the motor industry as engineers and distributors of refrigerated commercial vehicles. Previous owners of my car included the Cavalry Club of London, Rupert Patrick Kilkelly of Norfolk and David Aston Kyle of Middlesex, these names taken from the records of the Motor Taxation Department of the Isle of Wight County Council. The car is equipped with a large sun roof—and with a trailer hitch which shows no evidence of ever having been used. I understand that during World War II vehicles in England were required to have hitches installed in order to move materiél if needed. The hitch is installed inside the boot and cannot be seen unless the lid is opened."

1935 Rolls-Royce 20/25 H.P. Sport Saloon, Mann-Egerton
Owners: Theodore M. & Helen G. Warner of Indianapolis, Indiana

The original owner of the 20/25 by Hooper was William Morrison of Renfrewshire, Scotland. Seven years ago, Scoop Collins became the third owner of this car: "The original works shop order describes the body as an 'open touring with windows in the doors' and includes a notation that the car was for use in 'the United Kingdom—town and touring.' Rolls-Royce was very particular about knowing just where its cars were going to be used and how. Even the weight of the rear bumper (thirty-five pounds) was considered. The front bumper was not original equipment. Legend has it that the engine compartment was sealed at the factory. This is true to the extent that both sides of the bonnet (hood) had locks, and the chauffeur had custody of the keys. He was the only person who was supposed to perform routine maintenance. A complete set of tools was supplied in a drawer extending the full width under the front seat. The Hooper body on my car is very comfortable with the windows up, and the convertible top is easy to put down. GPG70 is a good driver on the road. The rear axle is full floating of the spiral bevel type, and the road wheels are carried on axle tubes. The final drive ratio is 4.55:1. The complete chassis is lubricated from a manual (foot-operated) one-shot lubricating system. The four-wheel brakes are mechanically assisted by a servo device driven through the gearbox and operated by the foot brake lever. A fuel cut-off valve is provided, has three positions ('R' for reserve, 'O' for off, 'M' for main tank) and is operated from the inside on the firewall. The valve itself is on the engine side under the Auto-Vac."

1935 Rolls-Royce 20/25 H.P. All Weather Tourer, Hooper
Owner: J. Edward (Scoop) Collins, Sr. of Ocean City, Maryland

1935 Rolls-Royce 20/25 H.P. Sedanca de Ville, H. J. Mulliner   Owner: Richard Halprin of North Haven, Connecticut

Richard Halprin has owned his 20/25 by Mulliner for a decade: "The bill of sale indicates the car was purchased new by a G. L. Ricketts in England late in 1935. From there the list bounces from one owner to another with little continuity. The next real bit of information I can use to trace the car arrived from George Valassis who purchased it from a Mr. Ogenczry of Chicago who, as the story goes, found the car in a barn in Budapest. Apparently, at the time, it belonged to an official of the government (possibly a G. F. Charvat, Esq. whose name also appears on the title) and was in danger of being confiscated by the Third Reich and destroyed—hence it was hidden in the barn. This 20/25 remains in good original condition. As with all Classics, its rarity and quality are the main attractions. A sedanca de ville has the most regal and elegant lines of all body styles, I think. Convertibles may be fun and sedans may be practical, but town cars always have a formal shine about them."

In 1932 Derby engineers began work on a replacement for the Phantom II. Company executive W. A. Robotham had visited Detroit earlier that year and been cordially welcomed at General Motors. Impressed by the multiplicity of cylinders in the new Cadillac and other American luxury cars, Robotham was effectively wowed by GM's new independent front suspension system designed by Maurice Olley, former supervising engineer of Rolls-Royce of America. Returning home and learning that Hispano-Suiza was going to a V-12, Robotham concluded Rolls-Royce could do no less to keep up with its traditional rival on the Continent—and that i.f.s. might put Derby one step ahead.

The basic outline of the Phantom III engine was ready prior to Sir Henry Royce's death in April 1933. But most of the design and engineering work remained to be completed by others, A. G. Elliott among them. The 60° 447.7-cubic-inch V-12 his team developed was remarkably advanced with light alloy castings and wet liners drawing on Rolls' estimable aero engine experience. The use of i.f.s.—the GM system licensed and adapted by Rolls to the new car—allowed elimination of the traditional dumb irons and the pushing forward of the engine in a chassis which retained the traditional Rolls-Royce stiffness. The Phantom III would be widely regarded as the best handling large car in the world. It was also among the most complex. Without Sir Henry to lecture on the virtues of simplicity and practicality, Elliott and his crew had overlooked two things: cost of manufacture and ease of maintenance. The company had estimated the P-III would be £100 less expensive to build than the P-II; instead it was £400 more. And owners discovered that a complete engine overhaul could cost as much as £700. How much all this perturbed purchasers then is moot; owners today accept it in stride.

"Engineering-wise, there is nothing like the feeling of power the twelve-cylinder motor produces," says Andy Johnson. "My car was originally owned by Sir Adrian Baillis of London. Custom-built by Mulliner, it is a close-coupled limousine with beaded fenders and unique razor-edged styling. The fittings include rear-seat picnic tables, rear compartment speedometer and a quick-release-control driver's window. I love my Rolls most for its beauty. The roof line is so rakishly low that from the front it looks like someone chopped the top."

1936 Rolls-Royce Phantom III Sport Saloon, H. J. Mulliner
Owner: Andrew W. Johnson of Roslyn Heights, New York

1936 Rolls-Royce Phantom III Enclosed Drive Imperial Limousine de Ville, Van den Plas
Owner: Martin Coomber of Kent, United Kingdom

Martin Coomber has owned his P-III by Van den Plas since 1978: "At the time of my purchase in August that year, the odometer read 80,000 kilometers or 50,000 miles (just nicely run in!). In the family the car quickly acquired the nickname of Fanny. Since 1978 she has covered a further 11,000 kilometers to date in regular use most weekends throughout the year. The car has an interesting history. She was ordered in 1936 by the Rolls-Royce agent in Brussels for display at the 1937 Brussels Motor Show. There seems to have been some confusion over who was to build the body and what type it would be. In the end, the order was given to Carrosserie Van den Plas to create a four-light Imperial limousine. The result was apparently disappointing visually and in very short order the body was converted to a six-light limousine with a de ville front. Most likely the car was intended to be a demonstration model, but Mme. Fernand Pisart, the agent's mother, evidently appropriated it for her own use in preference to her Grosser Mercedes. Either way, the car was ideally placed to be maintained in tip-top order until the outbreak of World War II, as a constant flow of parts

from Rolls-Royce demonstrates. She may well also have benefited from various minor modifications introduced by the factory in order to keep her up-to-date as a demonstrator. A number of Phantom III's were sold in Belgium but, surprisingly to me, no repeat orders were received for Van den Plas coachwork. Fanny's next unusual experience was to find herself requisitioned in 1940 by the occupying German forces for the use initially of Field Marshal Kesselring while he planned the invasion of Britain. Following the failure of that enterprise, the car was passed on to General von Falkenhausen, who was the military governor of Belgium and who therefore enjoyed appropriate transport until implicated in a plot to kill Hitler. Finally, the car was allocated to the head of the S.S. in Brussels, who evidently decided that 10 mph petrol consumption was excessive for his ultimate flight from Belgium. So she was then returned to her owner, having been—unlike most Phantom III's—meticulously maintained and kept running during the course of the war. Following Mme. Pisart's death in 1952, the car was bought by Sir Geoffrey Allchin, ambassador to Luxembourg who

brought her back to the United Kingdom upon his retirement from the diplomatic service. Upon Sir Geoffrey's death in 1968, the car was acquired by Roy Woollett. Ten years later she passed into the hands of her present fortunate owner whose contributions to her well-being have been regular exercise and continuing refurbishment by others' expert hands. Most recently, the driver's compartment was put in the care of the craftsman who trims the carriages of H. M. the Queen. Nothing is too good for this wonderful car! Driving Fanny has always been an experience and mostly a pleasure. She has misbehaved twice: a flat tire at Duxford Aerodrome (which proved the value of the built-in jacking system) and once she 'failed to proceed' due to an electrical fault. Even then her record of 'getting us home' remains unblemished. She runs very cool for a Phantom III but does not much like being stuck in lengthy traffic jams. It has recently been discovered that on the high octane petrol which of late she has been obliged to consume here she travels better at a steady 70 mph than a sedate 50 mph. On the odd occasion I have had her up to 90 mph.''

1937 Rolls-Royce Phantom III Sedanca Coupe, Barker
Owner: William M. Davis of Charleston, West Virginia   Photo: K. Karger

This Phantom III Barker Sedanca Coupe was ordered new by T. J. Hughes, conceivably as successor to his P-II Continental as seen earlier in this portfolio. Bill Davis has owned the car since 1967: ''Despite general bad press, a Phantom III is a marvelous automobile and in proper running order is superb. A two-door version is a rarity (probably about twenty built), and this example is strictly a one-off car built to the purchaser's special requirements. It has been a joy to own, show and drive. The car was restored by Rolls-Royce in 1962, incidentally, and the colors (donkey brown and Farina grey) were chosen by Count Alexis de Sakhnoffsky—an interesting link with the past.''

Special features on the P-III Sports Torpedo Cabriolet by Barker include a tiger hunting light on the left front fender, a police siren under the bonnet, an umbrella stand behind the rear seat and a detachable folding seat on the luggage platform for a servant. Some readers may have surmised already that this car was built for a maharajah. ''It was shipped to Bombay in September of 1937,'' comments Stephen Brauer, ''and was destined for His Highness the ruling chief of Keonjhar state, Orissa, India. I've owned the car for seventeen years. The mileage shown is 9,200. Expert examination revealed the engine had been virtually untouched since leaving the factory over fifty years ago.''

1937 Rolls-Royce Phantom III Sports Torpedo Cabriolet, Barker
Owner: Stephen F. Brauer of Bridgeton, Missouri

Records indicate that this P-III chassis was delivered February 10th, 1936 to Gurney Nutting, the Sedanca de Ville was completed in 1937 and sold to a Mr. Thorton, the owner of a chocolate company who has been described as the "Milton Hershey of England." The Heaths have owned the car for nearly a quarter of a century, eventfully at first, as explained by Erle: "From England we had it shipped directly to Cleveland rather than through New York, this to try to avoid damage by New York stevedores. I followed the course of the car through the Welland canal and notified the shipping company not to unload it until our driver was present. He arrived at 7:00 a.m. on the appropriate Monday and found the car already on the dock with all four fenders caved in by the cables from the sling and a drunken seaman in the back seat among empty beer cans. The first trip after restoration was equally calamitous. Bonnie was being driven to the airport to meet her parents arriving from Florida. At a right angle turn, a woman driving an Avanti at high speed smashed the entire front of the car—back to the shop for re-restoration. I thought we would have difficulty obtaining suitable used parts. However, on a visit to Rolls-Royce on Conduit Street in London, I mentioned the accident to a company executive who replied, 'Would you like new parts? Let's call Mr. Trimings at Crewe.' Sure enough, Mr. Trimings could supply everything—brand-new—from stock. I requested the parts be shipped air freight. When they did not arrive in two weeks, I sent a cable to Rolls-Royce and received a reply, 'Dreadfully sorry—Mr. Trimings is on sick holiday.' One month later, another cable brought the reply, 'Horribly sorry, Mr. Trimings is still on holiday with bronchitis.' Three weeks later a message on my answering machine advised, 'Mr. Trimings has returned from sick holiday.' In two days, all of the parts were in Pittsburgh."

1937 Rolls-Royce Phantom III Sedanca de Ville, Gurney Nutting
Owners: Erle & Bonnie Heath of Pittsburgh, Pennsylvania
Below, the double-door trunk, the tool tray inside the half upper door, the inside of the outer door for luggage or picnic baskets.

The 25/30 H.P. succeeded the 20/25 in 1936. Wheelbase remained at 132 inches, but the six-cylinder engine was increased in displacement to 4.24 liters (260 cubic inches). Total production of this smaller Rolls-Royce model through 1938 was 1,201 chassis.

The 25/30 Gurney Nutting Sports Sedanca de Ville in Jack Nethercutt's collection was a one-off created for Lady Sainsbury. With French-inspired curvilinear styling, pontoon rear fenders and a diminutive rear-passenger compartment sized for two persons only, this Rolls-Royce is considerably more sporty than most town cars.

1937 Rolls-Royce 25/30 H.P. Sports Sedanca de Ville, Gurney Nutting
Owner: Jack B. Nethercutt of Sylmar, California

1937 Rolls-Royce Phantom III Sport Saloon, Henri Binder   *Owner: Jean Gorjat of Harrisburg, Pennsylvania*

Two sport saloons on the Phantom III chassis appear here, one with an English body, one with a French, each owner equally enthusiastic about his car.

"The body style is beautiful; the engine runs cool, is quiet and perfect" is the testimonial of Bill Lester regarding the Mulliner P-III he has owned for a decade and a half.

"The car performs and rides as a Rolls-Royce should and its rakish flowing lines represent the most attractive styling of all Phantom III's in my opinion."

Jean Gorjat's opinion regarding his P-III is the same: "To me, the French body by Henri Binder of Paris is not so bulky as most other P-III's. And the car provides trouble-free driving,

including 900 miles to the 1989 Rolls-Royce Owners Club Meet in Newport, Rhode Island. The first owner of my car was Herr Cron of Germany who sent it off to Switzerland for the duration of World War II. Then it was off to Great Britain, then to the U.S. and the Baldwin family of the steam locomotive works—then, in 1987, to me!"

1937 Rolls-Royce Phantom III Sport Saloon, H. J. Mulliner   *Owner: William M. Lester of Livingston, New Jersey*

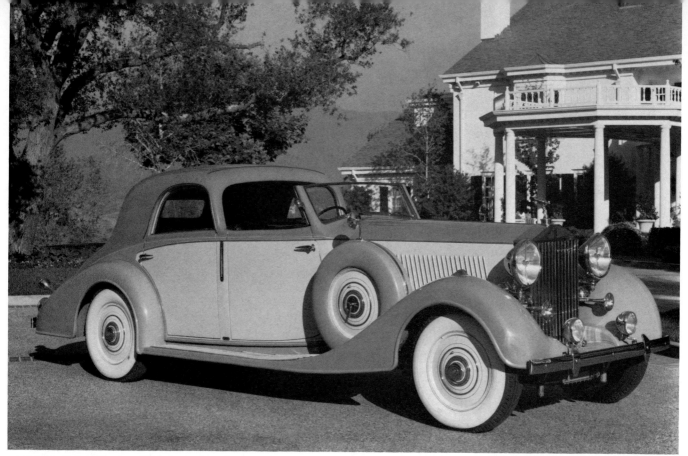

1938 Rolls-Royce Phantom III Sedanca de Ville, Franay   *Owner: William Lyon of Trabuco Canyon, California*

Parisian flair is evident in the P-III Sedanca de Ville from the French coachbuilding house of Franay that is in the collection of William Lyon.

And Andrew Darling's P-III surely exhibits the Brewster touch: "This is the only Henley P-III ever produced and it's truly a great car. In the thirty years of my ownership, I've driven it 20,000 miles. It cruises at highway speeds with quick acceleration and whisper-quiet movement. I have an almost new Rolls convertible and it can't compare in smoothness and power features with this '38 P-III."

Bob Rostecki's Rolls-Royce was the only 25/30 produced with coachwork by Kellow-Falkiner of Australia: "This car was built in December 1937 in Derby with cowl, front fenders, lighting equipment, bumpers, hood and radiator—and it arrived in Melbourne the following March. Kellow-Falkiner completed the body in about three months for a General Motors executive named Carter. The GM styling influence of that era is readily seen. After much use in Australia, the car ended up in England in late 1946. Since then it

has been owned by a dentist, a retired English admiral, a lady breeder of thoroughbred dogs and, since 1969, by me. Nineteen thirty-seven was the last year for the 'big' nineteen-inch wheels and straight front axle; 1938 introduced the Wraith with seventeen-inch wheels and independent front suspension, a 'modernized' 25/30. This car is very attractive and nice to look at—and is an excellent tour car with comfort, reliability, good handling and Rolls-Royce quality. It cruises wonderfully at 60 mph."

1938 Rolls-Royce Phantom III Henley Roadster, Brewster   *Owner: Andrew D. Darling of Edina, Minnesota*

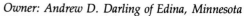

1937 Rolls-Royce 25/30 H.P. Sports Coupe, Kellow-Falkiner   Owner: Robert K. Rostecki of Winnipeg, Manitoba

1939 Rolls-Royce Phantom III Saloon, Gurney Nutting

Owner: Ken Karger of Exton, Pennsylvania

The Karger P-III is a twice-told tale, as Ken explains: "The Rolls-Royce you see here is actually the result of combining two Phantom III's. It happened this way. The chassis (3DL122) was sold new in October 1940 to tractor magnate Harry Ferguson, the Ferguson in Massey-Ferguson. Its original body was a Barker swept-tail limousine. The coachwork fitted now is a Gurney Nutting owner-driver saloon and was originally mounted on a slightly earlier chassis (December 1937), 3CP142. The latter's first owner was Hubert Scott-Paine, the inventor of the PT boat. During his entire life, Scott-Paine only owned four cars, all Rolls-Royce. The first three he purchased as used cars. The Phantom III he bought new and brought to the U.S. in 1939. Unfortunately, it turned out to be a bad car and could not be made right even by Jack Inskip. Accordingly, it was sent back to England in 1952 where it was bought by the London retailer Jack Barclay. In 1953, the Earl of Shrewsbury, wishing a fine car for the coronation of Queen Elizabeth II and not caring for the then-current Silver Wraith, went into Barclay's, selected the Phantom III with the handsome coachwork, and bought it. But it proved still to be a bad car, so the Earl took it back to Barclay's, part-exchanged it for 3DL122, retaining the Gurney Nutting body from 3CP142 (for only £100!), had 3DL122 overhauled at the factory car repair depot with only 28,000 miles from new, then had his chauffeur-handyman remove the Barker body and fit the Gurney Nutting. Mermie and I have owned the car since 1968 when we drove it across the country from California (where we acquired it) to Pennsylvania. The forty-gallon (U.S.) fuel tank has led to a number of interesting adventures. When we bought the car, we took advantage of truck rates for fuel, so traveled at .29^9 per gallon, modest even then. Phantom III performance is staggering even with the weight (nearly three tons) carried. New, zero to 60 figures were under seventeen seconds. The gear change lever is well back, so does not intrude at all. Of course, it is on the right on this right-hand-drive car. Brakes, steering, suspension are all a delight, light and easy. Sometimes we feel that taking this car on an old car tour is cheating because everything it does is so effortless. Because of the metamorphosis of this Rolls-Royce, we have named it Ovid."

1939 Rolls-Royce Phantom III
Touring Limousine, James Young
(tool set page opposite)

Owner: Charles W. Curtin
of New London, Connecticut

Charles Curtin is the second owner of his P-III Touring Limousine by the British coachbuilding house of James Young. The first was Dr. R. J. Campbell of New York City from whom he purchased the car in 1962.

Mort Bullock's Phantom III is a much traveled car, although only in the destination sense, as he explains: "Three cars in this body style were to be built by Hooper. One went as a display car to the New York World's Fair. Mine went to the Amsterdam and Geneva international automobile shows. The fate of the third car is unknown; possibly it was never completed because of the war. The history of my car is obscure following the Geneva show. It ended up in the Philippines, where it belonged to a Manila sugar plantation owner. He gave the car to the Catholic church to be used by the Cardinal. A vice president of the American President Line brought the car to the West Coast. It was then sold to Herb Schoenfeld; I bought it from him twelve years ago with only 44,000 original miles. It represents an interesting body style for a formal car—big, luxurious, yet streamlined. As one of the last P-III's, it has some unique features such as solid lifters (replacing the former hydraulic tappets) and overdrive, making it an excellent road car. There is a disappearing steel sliding roof over the driver's compartment; the rear roof lifts up and the front roof slips underneath it, as the accompanying photograph indicates. The rear compartment has indirect lighting in the ceiling and a bar with crystal decanter and four crystal wine glasses. An electric division window and pull-out swivel jump seats were also fitted."

1939 Rolls-Royce Phantom III Limousine de Ville, Hooper
Owner: Morton Bullock of Baltimore, Maryland   Photos: K. Karger

1939 Rolls-Royce Wraith Sports Saloon, Park Ward
Owners: Barbara & Stanley Evans of Rochester Hills, Michigan

The Wraith was one of the lowest production cars ever built by Rolls-Royce: just 491 had left the factory when World War II brought a halt to manufacture. Engineering refinements over the predecessor 25/30 included a welded rather than riveted frame and independent front suspension. The engine remained the 4257 cc six; the wheelbase was a bit longer at 136 inches.

''Our Rolls was built for what the English call 'town work','' comment Barbara & Stan Evans. ''It therefore is not very fast as far as top speed is concerned. For what it was designed (elegant travel), it is unsurpassed. Four months were required to build our Wraith. The chassis was completed in March of 1939; the car was delivered to first owner F. P. Williams that July. Rolls-Royce keeps very meticulous records, and we are very fortunate to have photocopies of all the 'build cards' involving this Wraith. These are the handwritten record of the details of construction including such gems as 'owner must try seats' and 'owner to provide his own Phillips radio.' There is also a reference to the owner not desiring a Flying Lady mascot when the car was originally ordered and specifying only a radiator cap. He later changed his mind and requested a 'kneeling Flying Lady.' Rolls-Royce used spectre-like designations in naming its cars from the Ghost through the Phantoms. Interestingly, according to Webster's, a wraith is 'the supposed ghost of a person in his exact likeness seen immediately before or after his death'.''

The Silver Wraith was the first Rolls-Royce to appear after the Second World War and the only Rolls-Royce model through the end of the Classic Era. The Phantom III was too expensive to return to production in this austere period. The engine shared the former Wraith's 4257 cc but was a new inlet-over-exhaust design allowing the use of larger valves. Two chassis lengths (127 and 133 inches) were offered, and it was only as a chassis that the car was available from Rolls-Royce.

"One of the most impressive Rolls ever in appearance and performance," says Jack Royston of his Hooper Touring Limousine. "The engine is excellent and smooth and, with only 76,000 original miles, everything works as new, even the radio and lighters."

1948 Rolls-Royce Silver Wraith Touring Limousine, Hooper
Owner: Jack Royston of Scottsdale, Arizona

"The graceful flowing lines of the coachwork can best be described as sheer elegance," comments Gordon Fairbanks. "There are many interesting details on our Hooper Touring Saloon. Each door opening has its own running board, for example, which is exposed when the door is open and covered when the door is closed. The sun visors are curtains that pull down, and there is also a curtain at the rear window operated electrically by a switch on the dash. A drawer in the dashboard contains a compartmented tool tray. The tools are the originals and look as if they have never been used. The window opener (on the driver's side only) is a larger lever which with one motion can raise or lower the window. The rear compartment contains such luxuries as a small bar and foot rests that fold out of the

1948 Rolls-Royce Silver Wraith Touring Saloon, Hooper
Owners: Mr. & Mrs. Gordon J. Fairbanks of Indianapolis, Indiana   Photos: Cordy Purdy

1948 Rolls-Royce Silver Wraith Sport Convertible, J. S. Inskip
Owner: Andrew D. Darling of Edina, Minnesota

back of the front seats. The Hooper body sill plates contain the following inscription—'Motor Body Builders and Coach Builders to His Majesty the King, Her Majesty Queen Mary, H.R.H. the Princess Royal'.''

Jack Inskip built just two sport convertibles on the Silver Wraith chassis. The second was modernized several decades ago, so Andrew Darling's remains the only original. He is its second owner. ''The body style is very distinctive and shows that Inskip must have been an admirer of Saoutchik,'' comments Andy. ''The cut-down door is very rakish for a Rolls-Royce. This car is absolutely a show stopper. In the nearly four decades of my ownership, it's been driven around 20,000 miles, including four trips from Minneapolis to Fort Lauderdale, and three years ago a trek to Toronto. The car has 100% reliability. You can tune it once every two or three years, and it will run like a charm. That's a Rolls-Royce!''

DIVERS CLASSICS

Coachwork by Franay on the Type RH straight-eight Ballot chassis, the car seen on exhibit at the Paris Salon in the autumn of 1929. Photograph from the collection of David R. Holls.

The marques which follow do not appear in either the American or European Classic sections of this book. The reason: no examples were submitted by members. This is not to suggest that all of these marques are unrepresented in the Club. Some cars were undergoing restoration as this project unfolded, others were unavailable for reasons as divers as the gallery that follows. But it is true as well that Classic Era examples of a few of the marques in this portfolio are not believed to exist. Hopefully, this might mean only that none have been found yet. One of the ongoing delights in our hobby is the frequent emergence from decades of dust of vehicles enthusiasts had long assumed were irrevocably lost. Perhaps there are still a few automotive equivalents of King Tut's tomb out there waiting to be discovered. The CCCA would very much like to have within its midst examples of all Classics. Until then, we present this portfolio of photographs or illustrations from the Classic Era itself which brings to 100% in this book the roster of Classic marques designated by the CCCA.

ADLER

Manufactured by Adlerwerke vorm. Heinrich Kleyer A.G., Frankfurt am Main, Germany. The word "Adler" translates to "eagle." This majestic automobile was well named. Photograph of the eight-cylinder 80 CV Seven-Passenger Pullman Limousine accompanied the Adler announcement for the 1930 Salon International de l'Automobile in Paris. From the collection of Henry Austin Clark, Jr.

AMILCAR

Manufactured by Ste. Nouvelle pour l'Automobile Amilcar, St. Denis, France. The name was an anagram for its makers, Emil Akar and Joseph Lamy. The Amilcar was the most famous, the most sophisticated and the most successful of all the French sporting voiturettes. Illustration of the supercharged Super Sport appeared in a 1925 Amilcar brochure. From the collection of Henry Austin Clark, Jr.

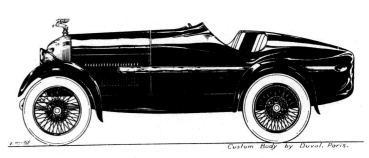

THE "SUPER SPORT"
(SUPERCHARGED)

ARMSTRONG SIDDELEY

Manufactured by Armstrong Siddeley Motors Ltd., Coventry, England. Cars were produced alongside aero engines and planes. The Wilson gearbox was introduced by Armstrong Siddeley. This factory photo, dated 10/10/33, is of the six-cylinder five-liter Siddeley Special Limousine. From the collection of Henry Austin Clark, Jr.

BENZ

Manufactured by Benz & Cie., Rheinische Automobile & Motorenfabrik A.G., Mannheim, Germany. The photograph, of engineer Fritz Nallinger in the 16/50 PS Sport Tourer following victory in an Alpine hill climb, appeared in the 1925 catalogue for Benz. This was among the last Benz models on the marketplace prior to the firm's merger with Daimler Motoren Gesellschaft. From the collection of Henry Austin Clark, Jr.

BALLOT

Manufactured by Etablissements Ballot, Paris. Style and advanced engineering distinguished this French marque. The company, in financial difficulty, was taken over by Hispano-Suiza in 1932. Advertisement is from the October 1924 edition of L'Illustration. From the collection of Henry Austin Clark, Jr.

CHENARD & WALCKER

Manufactured by S.A. des Anciens Etablissements Chenard & Walcker, Gennevilliers. Victory in the inaugural twenty-four-hour race at Le Mans brought new renown to this traditional French company. Advertisement is from the October 1924 edition of L'Illustration. From the collection of Henry Austin Clark, Jr.

DAGMAR

Manufactured by the M.P. Möller Motor Car Company, Hagerstown, Maryland. Named for Matthias P. Möller's daughter, the Dagmar offered—its makers said—"the most stylish custom body as a standard proposition." The marque did not survive 1927. Photograph is of the Model 8-80 Close-Coupled Sport Sedan from 1925. From the collection of Keith Marvin.

DARRACQ

Manufactured by S.A. des Automobiles Talbot, Suresnes. In 1912 Alexandre Darracq left the company he founded to rest on his laurels and enjoy his millions. The subsequent Darracq story became a tangled web as the firm moved into the S-T-D (Sunbeam-Talbot-Darracq) empire. Antony Lago was in charge by the mid-Thirties. This brochure extolled the 1939 line. From the collection of Henry Austin Clark, Jr.

DELAUNAY BELLEVILLE

Manufactured by S.A. des Automobiles Delaunay Belleville, St. Denis, Seine. The most expensive and luxurious automobile in France—and some said the best car in the world—prior to the First World War, Delaunay Belleville saw its elite territory invaded by others following the Armistice. But a carriage-trade car it remained. The round radiator remained the Delaunay Belleville signature into the early Classic Era. The 1925 advertisement is from the collection of Henry Austin Clark, Jr. By the late twenties, the Delaunay Belleville look changed, as indicated by the Paris Salon photo from the collection of Walter E. Gosden.

DORRIS

Manufactured by the Dorris Motor Car Company, St. Louis, Missouri. Approximately 3,100 cars were produced during the twenty years of this company's existence. George Preston Dorris liked to advertise that his cars were "practically hand-built." By the Classic Era, the cars were actually hand-built to custom order as the firm died a slow death in bankruptcy court. The illustration shows the 6-80 Sedan as produced to the very end. From the collection of Karl S. Zahm.

EXCELSIOR

*Manufactured by S.A. des Automobiles Excelsior, Saventhem.
Excelsior shared premier status in Belgium with Minerva
until taken over by Imperia in 1929. This photograph, taken
that year, shows New York socialite Mrs. Jonathan Starr with
her car. From the collection of Henry Austin Clark, Jr.*

FARMAN

*Manufactured by Automobiles Farman, Billancourt, Seine.
The Farman brothers, Henry and Maurice, were famous as
race drivers and aero engineers before becoming car
manufacturers in 1920. Rival to Hispano-Suiza in luxury,
the Farman survived to 1931. Approximately 120 were
produced. The illustration appeared in a 1925 ad.
From the collection of Henry Austin Clark, Jr.*

F.N.

*Manufactured by Fabrique Nationale d'Armes de Guerre,
Herstal-lez-Liége. Belgium's most prolific marque, the F.N.
distinguished itself with rally and luxury touring models
until its death in the mid-thirties. Ad is from a 1926
issue of the German magazine* Motor. *From the collection of
Walter E. Gosden.*

FRAZER-NASH

Manufactured by A.F.N. Ltd., Isleworth, Middlesex, England. Fewer than 350 were produced from 1924 through 1939, but the ''chain gang'' sports car developed by Captain Archie Frazer-Nash won fame far beyond numbers. Photograph is c. 1930. From the collection of Walter E. Gosden.

HUMBER

Manufactured by Humber Ltd., Coventry, England. Beginning with bicycles in 1868, Thomas Humber added automobiles to his company's line in 1898. A solid upper-middle-class English family car, the marque was characterized by conservatism and craftsmanship during the Classic Era. Illustration is from the frontispiece of a 1934 brochure. From the collection of Henry Austin Clark, Jr.

FIAT

Manufactured by Fiat SpA, Turin, Italy. In 1899 the firm was founded as Fabbrica Italiana Automobili Torino. By the Classic Era it was already an industrial colossus commanding over ninety percent of the Italian market. Fiats came in all shapes and sizes, including luxury models like this big sedan photographed in 1929. From the collection of John A. Conde.

INVICTA

Manufactured by Invicta Cars, Cobham, Surrey. The Invicta began life in 1925 as the idea of sportsman Noel Macklin and sugar king Oliver Lyle. Although other types were produced, the name is best remembered for the low-chassis 4½-liter models with the mean and hunkered-down look. No sporting car of the thirties hugged British roads better than the Invicta. Photograph is of a 4½ Litre Tourer of 1931. From the collection of Walter E. Gosden.

JENSEN

Manufactured by Jensen Motors Ltd., West Bromwich, England. Richard and Alan Jensen were brothers with a talent for creating coachwork that demanded to be noticed. In 1934 Clark Gable sent the Jensens a chassis from Detroit to be bodied. A little later Edsel Ford gave the brothers permission to use the Dagenham V-8 in a car of their own. This photo is from the '36 Paris Salon. From the collection of Walter E. Gosden.

LOCOMOBILE

Manufactured by the Locomobile Company of America, Bridgeport, Connecticut. The Locomobile star had begun to wane by the dawn of the Classic Era. But still produced was the magnificent Model 48 Sportif, a $10,000 car. It died only when the Locomobile did following the stock market crash. Illustration is from 1927. From the collection of Henry Austin Clark, Jr.

LANCHESTER

Manufactured by the Lanchester Motor Company, Birmingham, England. The ultimate gentleman's carriage was a sobriquet enjoyed by the Lanchester during the early Classic Era. Its beginnings in 1895 paralleled the British industry itself. By the 1920's Lanchesters were revered for exemplary engineering and wonderful workmanship—and were priced accordingly. Ad appeared in the 1929 London Motor Show program. From the collection of Walter E. Gosden.

JORDAN

Manufactured by the Jordan Motor Car Company, Cleveland, Ohio. Ned Jordan is best remembered as a wordsmith and adman. The advertisements he created for his car were pacesetting for their lyrical romanticism, which occasionally proved a bit too sexy for the censors. Sexy cat's-eye Woodlites were standard on the sport Model Z Speedway Ace in 1930. The photograph was taken at the New York Automobile Show. From the collection of John A. Conde.

ITALA

Manufactured by Fabbrica Automobili Itala S.A., Turin, Italy. The big Italas of the mid-twenties were reminders of the marque's glory years of the decade previous. The memory lingered until the mid-thirties. These illustrations appeared in a catalogue of 1925. From the collection of Henry Austin Clark, Jr.

CARROCERÍA TORPEDO
SOBRE CHASSIS ITALA MOD. 61

CARROCERÍA CONDUCIÓN INTERIOR
SOBRE CHASSIS ITALA MOD. 61

RAYMOND MAYS

Manufactured by Shelsley Motors Ltd., Bourne, England. The company was named for the hill that race driver Raymond Mays made famous while making himself legendary. His car was introduced in 1938, this photograph taken that year. Just five examples were produced before World War II called a halt to the project. From the collection of Henry Austin Clark, Jr.

REVERE

Manufactured by the ReVere Motor Company, Logansport, Indiana. Grand larceny was charged but was never proved. Still, the scandal was death for this fine sporting luxury car. The photograph shows the final model, in 1926, with a stylish new hardtop and offering dual-ratio steering. From the collection of Keith Marvin.

ROAMER

Manufactured by the Roamer Motor Car Company, Kalamazoo, Michigan. The company had originally carried Albert Barley's name and was born in Streator, Illinois. By the start of the Classic Era, however, Barley had sold out to a largely Canadian consortium, although the firm's factory remained in Kalamazoo, as it had been since the year 1917. Mary Pickford and Buster Keaton were Roamer owners, but there were not enough others like them to allow the marque to survive. The end came in 1930. The illustration is of the 1926 Model 8-88 Sport Tourer. From the collection of Henry Austin Clark, Jr.

ROCHET SCHNEIDER

Manufactured by S. A. des Etablissements Rochet Schneider, Lyons, France. The company was begun well before the turn of the century by Edouard Rochet, a mechanic's son, and Théophile Schneider, a silk manufacturer. For nearly four decades Rochet Schneiders were known for their excellent mechanics and silken performance. "Typique exemple de la construction française de luxe" read the caption to this photograph from 1931. From the collection of Henry Austin Clark, Jr.

NAG

Manufactured by the Nationale Automobil-Gesellschaft A.G., Berline-Oberschöneweide, Germany. An electrical company was the basis for NAG at the turn of the century. The Protos company of Berlin was acquired in 1926. Automobile production ended in 1934. The striking illustrations are from "Das Golden Buch des NAG Protos," c. 1929. From the collection of Robert N. Tuthill.

RILEY

Manufactured by Riley (Coventry) Ltd., Warwickshire. "Sausage making"—that's what Victor Riley called automobile manufacture, adding, "I can only continue in business as long as it holds some promise of romance." Racing did, and Riley did very well at it. This photo is of one of the 1934 Alpine Trial team cars. From the collection of Henry Austin Clark, Jr.

PEUGEOT

Manufactured by S.A. des Automobiles Peugeot, Sochaux, France. Corset stays and coffee mills were among the firm's successful products before Armand Peugeot took his family's company automotive in 1889. The marque became known for innovation, as indicated by this Paris show car of 1936 with retractable hardtop. From the collection of David R. Holls.

SQUIRE

Manufactured by Squire Car Manufacturing Company Ltd., Henley-on-Thames, England. At the age of sixteen, Adrian Morgan Squire produced a six-page brochure for a 1½-liter two-seater sports car he wanted to produce. At the age of twenty-four, he built it. Two years of epic striving later, he admitted commercial defeat. Total Squire production had been just seven cars. A few more were assembled from parts on hand following liquidation in 1936. "A Squire deal is a Square deal," Adrian had punned. And it was. But £1,220 for the 1½-liter Squire put it in the 3½-liter Bentley league. Slashing the price below £1,000, which was done in 1935, had meant no profit at all. The end was inevitable. But the Squire was a jewel of a sports car, as shown in the chassis photograph. From the collection of Henry Austin Clark, Jr.

STEYR

Manufactured by Steyr-Werke A.G., Steyr, Austria. Challenging Mercedes in the luxury market was Steyr's aim in the twenties. By the mid-thirties, merger with Austro-Daimler and Puch was the road taken for survival. The advertisement from the glory years appeared in a 1925 issue of the German Motor. From the collection of Walter E. Gosden.

TATRA

Manufactured by Tatra-Werke A.G., Koprivnice, Czechoslovakia. Named for the largest mountain range in the land, the Tatra was always remarkable and often revolutionary. Chief engineer Hans Ledwinka's answer to the question of how Czech dignitaries should be driven was the 5.9-liter V-12 Type 80, this photo from 1935. From the collection of Keith Marvin.

STEVENS-DURYEA

Manufactured by Stevens-Duryea Motors Inc., Chicopee Falls, Massachusetts. At $10,175, the 1925 Model G Town Cabriolet was pricey for an American luxury car even during the Roaring Twenties—one reason this exemplary New England marque went under even before the stock market crash. "There Is No Better Motor Car" had been a slogan—and no exaggeration. From the collection of Keith Marvin.

This index is divided into three sections: Cars, Coachbuilders and People. The last named comprises the owners of the Classics today (including museums) and other persons mentioned in the text (original owners and the designers, engineers, entrepreneurs, etc. who were responsible for the cars being built). It is fitting, we think, to juxtapose the principal players and participants of the Classic Era with the people who are the caretakers of the Classic legacy today.

Hibbard, Tom, 104, 668, 680
Hicks, Bud & Judie, 94, 99, 445
Hill, David, 547-8
Hill, Eddie, 506
Hill, James J., 432
Hiltebrant, Steve, 700
Hindall, Brad & Jane, 274
Hirsch, William S., 413
Hitler, Adolph, 671, 672
Hodgman, W. H., 34
Hoelscher, Don & Joan, 296, 300-1
Holbrook, Lt.-Col. Claude Vivian, 601
Hollen, Alvin L., 422
Holls, David, 96, 133, 447
Hooper, R. B., 617, 652, 654-5
Horch, August, 580
Horowitz, Steven & Sandra, 460, 466
Hotchkiss, Benjamin Berkley, 582
Houston, C. Douglas, 153, 155, 157, 161, 174, 176
Howe, Lord, 665
Howe, W. Deering, 180
Hoye, Warren J., 352, 391, 436, 457
Hoyt, Gaylord, 291
Hubbard, Tom, 284-5, 290-1, 292
Hudson, Joseph L., 41
Hughes, Barbara D., 580-1
Hughes, Glenn, 258
Hughes, Howard, 30
Hughes, T. J., 726
Hull, Jim & Betty, 273, 448
Humber, Thomas, 743
Hummel, George, 152
Hunley, Jack & Lupe, 386-7
Hunt, George, 72, 75
Hunter, Ray, 485
Hurlock, Charles & William, 547
Hutton, Barbara, 266
Huxley, Aldous, 604

Imbasciani, Onofrio, 102
Indianapolis Motor Speedway Hall of Fame Museum, 137, 218, 231, 364, 671
Ingler, William J., Jr., 642
Inskip, John S., 23, 700, 704, 706, 733, 737
Irwin, Wilbur, 351
Isotta, Cesare, 652
Iverson, Lorenz, 346

Jackson, Charles, 236
Jackson, Russ & Craig, 103, 579
Jacobson, Ben, 625
Jahant, William F., 143
Jano, Vittorio, 549, 553, 601
Jarrett, Jesse T., 318
Jarvis, Vernon, 673
Jellinek, Emil, 666
Jenkins, Ab, 72, 97, 264, 478
Jensen, Carl, 105
Jensen, Richard & Alan, 744
Jephson, G. S., 320
Jepson, George K., 373
Jergens, Andrew N., 704
John, Thomas George, 554
Johnson, Andrew W., 173, 724
Johnson, Claude, 687
Johnson, Frank, 324
Johnson, Kenneth R., 282-3
Johnson, Robert A., 326
Jolson, Al, 23
Jones, Allan E., 156
Jones, Jerry W., 411
Jordan, Ned, 744
Joynt, Bob, 204-5, 211
Joynt, Gerry, 320
Judd, Roy A., 129, 468
Juneau, Bud, 426, 430-1
Junek, Elisabeth, 628

Kahn, Walter S., 314
Kaiser, Henry, 40
Kamman, Kenneth, 426
Karger, Ken, 732
Karr, Craig, 47-8
Kaskel, Murray, 146
Katzell, Raymond A., 679
Kausal, John Robert, 152
Kavenagh, Ted, 8
Kawamoto, Rev. Seichi, 379
Kay, Major Jack, 626
Keaton, Buster, 746
Keck, Howard, 428
Kelley, Cornelius, 357
Kelley, Stillman F., 291
Kelso, Robert, 268
Kenewell, Ken, 85, 312-3, 315, 318, 592-3
Kennedy, Floyd D., 438-9

Kenniff, Art, 279, 351, 559
Kensington Moir, H. (Bertie), 610
Keonjhar, Orissas, Maharajah of, 726
Kerner, Charles W., 160, 172, 418
Kerr, Tom, 357, 363
Kerr, Whitney E., 73-5
Kerr, Whitney M., 70-1
Kersh, Phil, 68
Kershaw, Knox, 92, 102, 264, 348, 648-9
Kesselring, Field Marshal, 725
Ketteman, Donald F., 182
Khan, Prince Aly, 553, 574, 620-1
Kilkelly, Rupert Patrick, 721
Kimber, Cecil, 590
Kimmel, William, 439
King, Admiral Ernest Joseph, 149
King, E. L., 711
Kirkoff, L. G., 164
Kissel, George & Will, 46, 65, 67
Kissel, Wilhelm, 667, 670
Kleba, Mike, 12
Knapp, Robert, 275
Knight, Charles Yale, 68, 677
Knight, Norm, 13, 15, 568
Knox, Seymour, 645
Kost, Kenneth R., 375, 459
Kranz, H. William, Jr., 396
Kreuter, Vernon, 428
Kroll, Raymond F. & Carol T., 88
Kughn, Richard & Linda, 149, 192, 232-3, 276, 328-9
Kulas, E. J., 169
Kyle, David Aston, 721

Labourdette, Henri, 572
Lago, Antony, 602-3, 741
LaGuardia, Fiorello, 166
Lalomia, Ben, 365, 465
Lambert, Peter, 490
Lamy, Joseph, 739
Lancia, Vincenzo, 586
Langkop, Eugene, 423
Larch, John A., 406, 663
Larivee, Bob, Sr., 401
LaRocque, Rod, 687
Larrabee, Robert D., 295
Lassiter, W. G., Jr., 33, 35, 65, 67, 132, 202, 251, 374, 506, 615, 656, 706
Lawrence, Gertrude, 23
Lawrence, Robert G., 626
Lawrence, T. E., 690
Leamy, Al, 82, 87-8, 216, 218
LeBaron, Harold F., 707
Ledwinka, Hans, 748
Lee, Don, 143, 164, 296, 306
Lee, Jon & Sandra, 474
Leich, Robert A., 137
Leimkuehler, Jon P., 702-3
Leland, Henry Martyn, 110, 308-9
Leon, Berta & Jay, 136, 347, 476, 650, 659, 662-3, 688-9, 695, 709, 719
Lerch, Thomas F., 330
Leslie, C. A., Jr., 41-2
Lester, Thomas J., 51, 53, 59, 75, 83, 192, 320, 472, 682
Lester, William M., 453, 686, 728-9
Lewis, Earl, 186
Lewis, Henry H., 110, 113-4
Liebhardt, Harry G., 258
Light, Allen E., 223
Lindbergh, Charles, 14, 276, 280, 288
Locke, Lindley T., 603
Locke, William S., 19, 49, 50, 221
Loewy, Raymond, 334
Loftis, Nick, 406
Lombard, Carole, 262, 412
Long, Edward, 202
Long, Tyrnn M., 717
Loree, Paul J., 44
Løve, James, 105
Loy, Myrna, 194
Ludington, C. T., 240
Luna, Maurio, 131
Lyle, Oliver, 744
Lyon, William, 23, 193, 232, 242, 261, 313, 348, 583, 585, 596, 598-9, 628, 632, 657, 675, 730
Lyons, Mary Byers, 172

Macauley, Alvan, 385, 412
Macauley, Edward, 412
Mack, Gilbert A., 150
Macklin, Noel, 592, 744
Maclean, Donald, 592
MacManus, Theodore, 110
Malaney, Joseph R., 179
Mallais, Sir Ralph, 240
Mallory, Charles, 604-5

Malumphy, Don & Mary, 424-5
Mann, Sam, 602-3
Manning, Lucius B., 242
Mano, George F., 116
Manville, Tommy, 689, 698
Marketti, Skip, 90
Markey, Rear Admiral Gene, 245
Marks, Robert, 392
Marmon, Howard, 340-1, 344, 347, 348-9, 497
Maross, August G., 77
Marsh, Fred Dana, 34
Marston, M. R. (Duke), 346
Martin, J. W., 253
Martin, Lionel, 561
Marx, Zeppo, 251
Maserati, Alfieri, Bindo, Ernesto & Ettore, 587
Mason, Edward R., 229
Mason, Randy, 83, 153, 196, 210, 297, 632, 690
Mathieson, E. E. S., 619
Maybach, Karl, 588-9
Maybach, Wilhelm, 588, 666
Mays, Raymond, 746
Mazzotti, Lodovico, 652, 658
McBroom, Bruce, 504-5
McCormick, Col. Robert, 422, 703
McCormick, Medill, 314
McElroy, Robert H., 310
McEwan, Al, 617, 652, 654-5
McEwan, Arthur, 456-7
McFarlan, Harry, 47
McKenzie, L. C., 616
McManus, Pete & Joanne, 24-5, 592-3
McNear, Egerton B., 445
McNeil, A. F., 625
McQuerry, George, 244
McVoy, Robert E., 700
Melchior, Lauritz, 183
Melton, James, 694
Mendl, Lady, 717
Menge, William, 500
Merle, Henry J., 255
Messinger, Robert M., 182-3, 339, 451
Meyer, John C., III & Pat, 482
Meyer, Robert L., 384, 437, 448
Milbank, Jeremiah, 697
Miller, Frank, 144
Miller, Harry, 213, 218
Miller, S. Ray, Jr., 52-3, 60-1, 64, 67, 73, 344, 502-3
Miller, W. Everett, 30, 262
Millett, Virgil, 698
Milne, James G., III, 327
Milton, Tommy, 385, 402
Minden Automotive Museum, 68
Miner, Milton & Kathleen, 426-7, 556, 560
Miranda, A. J., Jr., 32
Mitchell, William, 153
Mittermaier, Armin F., 402
Moller, Hilda, 317
Möller, Mathias R., 740
Mollo, Joseph A., 376-7
Montano, Charles, 190, 201
Montgomery, Robert, 143
Moody, Helen Mills, 439
Moore, Eugene Maxwell, 658
Moore, Steve, 227
Moran, Charles, Jr., 32, 38
Moran, John, 126
Moreland, Joseph N., Jr., 565, 664
Morgan, John E., 20, 40, 74-5
Morgan, Joseph, 192, 196-7, 380-1
Morgan, J. P., Jr., 690
Morris, William, 590
Morrison, Richard, 612, 614
Morrison, Roger, 620-1, 686-7, 689
Morrison, William, 722
Morton, Wade, 82
Moskovics, Fred, 347, 493, 497, 508
Mott, Mary, 286
Mozart, John, 119, 122, 234-5, 242-3, 266-7, 370-1, 551-2, 562, 601, 634, 636-7
Mueller, Donald V., 159
Mulderry, Francis P., 308, 318-9, 390
Muller, William J., 64-5
Murray, Bill, 253
Murray, Max Davis, 147-8
Mussolini, Benito, 586
Myers, Gustave, 693

Nagel, John, 657
Nallinger, Fritz, 739
Nash, Charles W., 51
Nash, Reggie N., 481
Neal, Robert & Donna, 421
Neubauer, Alfred, 667, 670, 672

Nepal, H. H. Prince of, 708
Nessor, Pete, 85
Nethercutt, J. B., 728
Newhall, George A., 46
Newport, J. Herbert, 262
Nibel, Hans, 672
Nicholson, Stephanie, 423
Nicklin, Larry, 667
Nienaltowski, Walter, 146
Nippert, Albert D., 198-9, 270, 288-9, 294-5
Northup, Amos, 60, 79
Nye, Walter C., 392

Oberg, Harvey V., 332-3
Oberhaus, Alyce R., 278
O'Connor, Jack, 435
O'Hara, John, 253
Ohm, Marc S., 117, 449
Olds, Ransom Eli, 60
Olley, Maurice, 725
Olson, Richard & Ruth, 276
Opp, Alfred & Helgard, 186-7
Osborne, Bruce & Norma, 95
Ostruk, Paul, 678, 682
O'Sullivan, John Patrick, 131
Oswald, John, 218
Otis, Whitney B., 168
Owen, H. R., 714

Pacione, Anthony, 309
Pacitti, Dom, 338
Packard, James Ward, 350
Paddock, Alice, 233
Paget, Hon. Dorothy, 616, 670
Paine, Walter, 384
Palaska, Countess Max de, 104
Paley, Babe, 585
Palmer, Honore, 246
Pancoast, Seth, 470
Partington, James H. M., 707
Partington, Susan T., 705
Patton, William R., 444-5, 589, 675
Paulson, John R., 172, 361
Pazery, Paul H., 638-9
Pearsall, Jim, 404
Pearson, Ken, 310
Peck, D. Cameron, 642
Peer, Alan L., 547
Peksyk, Henry, 12
Peltier, Gene M., 162, 451
Pennington, Col. Dave, 239, 306
Perkins, Ed, 255
Perkins, N. Gene, 256-7, 389-90, 394-5, 416, 431, 446, 455, 458, 480
Perry, Theodore Lincoln, 198
Peters, H. Edwin, 381
Peters, Joseph E., 381
Pettit, Bill, 212, 269
Pfabe, Edsel H., 550
Pfannebecker, Earl, 496
Philcox, G. E., 709
Phillion, Bill & Barb, 498-9
Phillips, C. S., 240
Picasso, Pablo, 646
Pickford, Mary, 34, 746
Pidgeon, Walter, 584
Pierson, Bob, 97
Pincus, Albert R., 585
Pisart, Mme. Fernand, 725
Plankinton, Sandra, 104
Pomeroy, Lawrence, 191, 604
Porsche, Ferdinand, 563, 594, 667, 669, 670
Porter, Cole, 23
Post, Marjorie Merriweather, 212
Powell, Dick, 439
Power, Tyrone, 245
Powers, Arthur N., 504
Powers, Charles, 260
Pratt, Curgie, 590-1
Pratt, Roger F., 388
Prentice, Alta Rockefeller, 348
Prescott, Joel, 452
Presson, Don, 22, 271
Pulitzer, Ralph, 251
Purcell, A. L., 702
Putnam, Edward, 135

Rabe, Karl, 563
Rabell, Jack & Shiela, 546, 599
Railton, Reid, 592
Raines, Ted & Jo, 138, 307
Raisbeck, Jim, 154
Rajkot, Sardeja, Maharajah of, 651
Rand, Sally, 161
Randell, Alexandra & Barry, 691
Rankin, E. W., 598
Ranney, Gil & Diane, 125, 186
Reddaway, Donald A., 280

The Classic Car Club of America cordially invites you to join us in celebrating the grand automobiles that were the subject of this book. An interest in Classic cars is the sole requirement for membership. For information, please write CCCA Headquarters, O'Hare Lake Office Plaza, 2300 East Devon Avenue, Suite 126, Des Plaines, IL 60018.